Italian Lives

Cape Breton Memories

Sam Migliore and A. Evo DiPierro

Editors

CAPE BRETON
UNIVERSITY
·P·R·E·S·S·

CBUP recognizes the support of the Province of Nova Scotia, through Film and Creative Industries Nova Scotia, and the support received for its publishing program from the Canada Council for the Arts Block Grants Program. We are pleased to work in partnership with these bodies to develop and promote our cultural resources.

FILM & CREATIVE INDUSTRIES

Canada Council   Conseil des Arts
for the Arts   du Canada

Original cover design by Goose Lane Editions
Book design by Gail Jones, Sydney, NS

Library and Archives Canada Cataloguing in Publication
    Italian lives, Cape Breton memories / Sam Migliore and A. Evo DiPierro, editors. -- New edition.

Includes bibliographical references.
Issued in print and electronic formats.
ISBN 978-1-77206-070-6 (softcover).--ISBN 978-1-77206-071-3 (PDF).--
ISBN 978-1-77206-072-0 (EPUB).--ISBN 978-1-77206-073-7 (Kindle)

    1. Italians--Nova Scotia--Cape Breton Island--History. 2. Italian Canadians--Nova Scotia--Cape Breton Island--History. I. Migliore, Sam, editor II. DiPierro, A. Evo, 1966-, editor

FC2343.8.I8I83 2017   971.6'900451   C2017-900913-3
                                                   C2017-900914-1

Cape Breton University Press
Box 5300
Sydney, Nova Scotia
CANADA B1P 6L2

Quando un popolo, un paese, una collettività grande o piccola che sia, non è disposta a perdere la memoria, vuol dire che non è disposta nemmeno a perdere la libertà.

Leonardo Sciascia

When a people, a nation, a social community (whether large or small) is unwilling to lose its collective memory, it means that it is unwilling to lose its liberty.

Preface

By Sam Migliore (2017)

When Evo DiPierro and I first published *Italian Lives* back in 1999, we had high hopes that the book would be successful, in both representing the richness and diversity of the Italian experience in Cape Breton, and providing members of the various Italian communities of the island with a document they would be proud to share with their children. We hope that the demand for the re-release of the book indicates we have succeeded. One thing is for certain. The book would not have been possible, let alone successful, without the support and assistance of the many people from Dominion, Glace Bay, Sydney and elsewhere who contributed articles, recipes, life histories and the various stories that appear in the book. We thank you all; without you this book would not have been possible.

A great deal has changed since 1999. Evo is now a Roman Catholic Priest with the Diocese of Antigonish, Nova Scotia. And, in 2000, to be closer to family, I moved to British Columbia where I have a position with the Department of Anthropology at Kwantlen Polytechnic University. Although Evo has been in a better position to maintain his links with Cape Breton, I still feel a closeness to the island and its people. We made many good friends, particularly in the Italian communities, and we continue to cherish those friendships.

My wife, Margaret Dorazio-Migliore, and I first arrived in Cape Breton in the late summer of 1990. As we drove towards Sydney, we missed the turn and ended up at the North Sydney ferry terminal (almost bound for Newfoundland). The man in the vehicle in front of us kindly guided us all the way back to our location in Sydney. It was our first experience with Cape Breton hospitality. We were fortunate to experience this type of hospitality on many occasions during our stay on the island. Connie and John deRoche made us feel welcome at UCCB (now Cape Breton University), and Lino Polegato was instrumental in helping us make contact with other Italians in the area. His tragic death a few years later was the saddest moment many of us experienced at the time. He remains my inspiration for this book. Although Lino and I started to develop ideas for research among Italians in Cape Breton, the actual idea to prepare an entire book on the Italian experience came from Rose DeLorenzo of Sydney. The final version of Italian Lives was probably not what she originally envisioned, but she has always been kind with her comments about the book. My prize memento from this period is the small plaque the Italian Cultural Association presented to me in 2000, just as I was preparing to leave the island, as their token of appreciation for my contributions to the publication.

I may no longer live in Cape Breton, but my mind still wanders there at times to share a day-dream glass of wine with the many friends I hope to see again in the near future. I am proud to call you all my friends. At the same time, Evo and I want to acknowledge that a number of the people we worked with, and who contributed to the book in various ways, are sadly no longer with us—including Evo's own parents, Vito and Gina (DiRito) DiPierro. Evo and I have deliberately chosen to not update certain chapters or sections of the book so these dear friends (family members) can live on through the book, and our memories of past celebrations together. We do, however, send our sincere condolences to their families and friends.

Table Contents

Acknowledgments

Evo DiPierro thanks the following individuals for their assistance and/or support during this project: Meaghan Beaton, Sister Peggy Butts, Bonnie Campbell (Library of Parliament), Victor and Olive Dawson, Heather Hayes, the late Anne Marie MacEachern, Russell MacLellan, Sandy McNabb, Dolores Moore, Ron Pearson, the late Frank Rudderham, Susan Sims, Peggy MacAdam, Wes Stewart (*Cape Breton Post*), and Angelo Zorzi.

Sam Migliore acknowledges the assistance of the late Lino Polegato for his support in getting the project started in the early 1990s. He also thanks the following people for their various contributions, suggestions, and encouragements throughout the production of this book: Frank DiVito, Margaret Dorazio-Migliore, Anne MacDougall (University College of Cape Breton [now Cape Breton University, CBU]), Elaine and Bill Merrell, the late Robert Morgan (Beaton Institute, CBU), Carol Ann Shephard (CBU), the members of the Department of Social Science and Practice (both past and current) at Cape Breton University, and Kwantlen Polytechnic University for the time necessary to review and make the necessary changes to this new edition.

Together, we express our appreciation for the help we received from: various research and transcription assistants; all those who contributed photos and articles for the book; John Campbell (*Cape Breton Post*), Kate Currie (Beaton Institute, CBU), Theresa Della Vella, Rose DeLorenzo, Fred Jackson (*Cape Breton Post*), Livio Nicoletti, Penelope Marshall, Gail Jones and staff at the University College of Cape Breton Press (now Cape Breton University Press), Laura Syms (CBU Library), and all the members of the Italian communities of Cape Breton. The research project was made possible, in part, from REC funding, University College of Cape Breton (CBU), and a 1993 Helen Creighton Foundation, Grant-in-Aid. Finally, we express our thanks to Mike Hunter and the current staff at the Cape Breton University Press for their dedicated work with this new edition.

I also acknowledge the contribution of Kwantlen Polytechnic University in providing time to complete some of the changes to this edition of the book

Introduction

By Sam Migliore

Italian Lives, Cape Breton Memories, is a community-oriented project that attempts both to cross certain boundaries and to dissolve a number of stereotypes. Cape Breton Island, for example, often is presented to tourists (and people in general) as a Scottish haven within Canada. It is the place to go to experience a downhome ceilidh, to hear Scottish fiddle music that has a more "traditional" flavour than anything found in Scotland, and to learn or become acquainted with the Gaelic language. Although there is a great deal of truth in this depiction of the island, the tartanization of Cape Breton's (and Nova Scotia's) heritage is a cultural and political construction—a construction that appears to have been set in motion during Angus L. Macdonald's premiership of Nova Scotia from 1933 to 1954.[1] The image of Cape Breton this representation creates tends to mask and devalue the contributions of the Mi'kmaq (Cape Breton's First Nation people) and that of later arrivals (such as the Acadian, Afro-Caribbean, Irish, Italian, Lebanese, South Asian, Ukrainian and many other people) to the social and cultural fabric of the island. Cape Breton's cultural heritage is much more complex than the tourist packages could ever reveal. One of the aims of this book is to make a step toward addressing the diversity and complexity characteristic of the island's culture(s) by focusing explicitly on the lives, experiences and memories of Cape Bretoners of Italian ancestry.

Italians in Cape Breton: The Numbers

Italian settlement in Cape Breton began in the second half of the 19th century. The first documented evidence of this process can be found in the Nova Scotia census of 1871. The census indicates that forty Italians resided in Nova Scotia at the time and that five of these individuals made their home in Cape Breton: Anthony Cecconi (a merchant) and Leivio Bordanordini (a clerk) in Cow Bay, Division #1; the Giovannetti family—Lawrance (Lorenzo, a trader), John (a shopkeeper), and Nikodemus (a shopkeeper)—in Cow Bay, Division #2; and, Franco Cecconi (a peddler) in Louisburg, Division #1.[2] The oral tradition, however, at least as far as I have been able to piece it together, makes no reference to Bordanordini and the Cecconis; it begins with the exploits of Lorenzo Giovannetti. According to the Giovannetti family, Lorenzo travelled from his home in Northern Italy to St. John's, Newfoundland, sometime in the mid 1800s. A short time later, he and brother, Nicodemus, settled in the vicinity of Port Morien, Cape Breton.[3] Information contained in the census records for 1901 tends to support this version of the story. It confirms that Lorenzo immigrated to Canada in 1855 and became a naturalized Canadian in 1872.[4]

By 1901, the Italian population of Cape Breton had increased to 130 people. The vast majority of these individuals were male labourers who had been recruited to work either in the coal industry or the construction of the steel plant. Eighty-five Italians, for example, resided in the Glace Bay-Bridgeport area, while twenty-three lived in Sydney.[5] Forty years later, as Table 1 indicates, the number of Italians on the island had increased to well over 1,700 people. This increase in population occurred in conjunction with a gradual balancing of the ratio of women to men within the different communities. The census records, for instance, show that the population ratio among Italians changed from a low of one woman to every five men in 1911, to a ratio of four women to every five men by 1941. This change occurred, at least in part, as new recruits for the industrial labour pool arrived from Italy with their wives and families, and some of the men already established in Cape Breton married Italian women who, within a relatively short period of time, joined their husbands in Canada.

As the number of Italians in Cape Breton increased and people were able to settle and raise families in the area, cultural "enclaves" began to spring up in places such as Whitney Pier (Sydney), Dominion, Sydney Mines, and the No. 14 Yard of New Waterford. These communities, located near the industrial work sites, became virtually self-sufficient. Families planted gardens, raised animals, and relied on Italian bakeries, corner stores and shoemakers to supply various services and products for their other needs. From a very early period, we also see the rise of Italian social, religious and mutual-aid societies. The Santa Rita mutual-aid society, for example, was formed in 1908, the original St. Nicholas Italian Church was built in Whitney Pier in 1911, and the Italian Hall in

Table 1
Italians in Cape Breton: 1901 to 1941[6]

Community	1901	1911	1921	1931	1941
Bridgeport	005	----	----	----	----
Dominion	----	152	130	295	304
Dominion No. 6	----	069	081	077	083
Glace Bay	080	092	060	106	145
Inverness	----	----	004	008	008
New Waterford	----	----	204	339	355
North Sydney	007	----	017	009	017
Port Morien	012	----	017	023	025
Reserve	----	021	015	021	043
Sydney	023	341	365	417	515
Sydney Mines	----	091	172	134	157
Trout Brook	----	----	----	----	025
Other	003	046	023	052	085
Totals	**130**	**812**	**1088**	**1481**	**1762**

Dominion was constructed in 1936.[7]

A comparison of census figures for 1941 and 1951 indicates that there was no significant change in the number of Italians residing in Cape Breton. The 1951 census lists a total of 1,771 individuals of Italian ethnic origin for the island, an increase of only nine people over a ten-year span.[8] These figures can be explained, in part, by the fact that Italian immigration to Canada was discontinued during the war years. The oral tradition, however, identifies "out-migration" as having a major influence on the population figures. The Second World War was a particularly difficult period

A farewell to Guglielmo Marconi, Sydney, ca. 1907. Madeline DiPenta (later O'Dell) centre, Mr. Frank Gentile fifth from left, Father Viola seventh from left, Antonio DiPistone (Italian Consul) to his left in top hat, and Michele Martinello flagbearer. Photo by C. W. Kelly. Courtesy of Rusty and Betty Gentile.

for Italians in Cape Breton.[9] A number of men were arrested and interned (without charge), while those left behind were exposed to various forms of prejudice and discrimination. In order to avoid the negative effects of this hostility, some families moved to rural areas such as Trout Brook, while others left the province altogether.[10] Later, a large number of both Italians and non-Italians left the area as the steel and coal industries began to experience problems, and the Cape Breton economy on the whole went into a prolonged slump.[11]

A major wave of Italian immigration to Canada occurred during the 1950s. The number of Italians in centres such as Montreal, Toronto, Hamilton and Vancouver increased dramatically.[12] Cape Breton, however, did not share in this process to any great extent. Although some Italians entered Cape Breton after 1951 (from other parts of Canada, Italy and South America), their numbers were relatively small. Yet, by 1991, the number of Cape Bretoners who identified themselves as having at least some link to "Italian" ethnic origin had risen to a total of 3,850 (see Table 2). Most of these individuals reside in Cape Breton County, with the highest concentrations of Italians in Dominion and Sydney.

It is difficult, however, to compare the population figures from the 1991 and the 1951 (and earlier) censuses, because "ethnic origin" was calculated differently. In the early records, "ethnic origin" was traced through the father only. These figures, then, represent an underestimation of the number of people who could have traced their ancestry to Italy. In contrast, the 1991 census encouraged people to identify

Table 2
The 1991 Census:
Individuals of Italian Ethnic
Origin in Cape Breton[13]

(1) County	Population
Cape Breton	3460
Inverness	0260
Richmond	0060
Victoria	0070
Total	3850

(2) Population figures for
specific communities:

Dominion	635
Glace Bay	370
New Waterford	385
Sydney	685
Sydney Mines	170

their "ethnic origin" in terms of multiple entries. The apparent doubling of Cape Breton's Italian population between 1951 and 1991 probably is due to both an increase in the number of Italians on the island, and the change in how "ethnic origin" was calculated in the census records.

Complexity and Diversity: An Alternative Image of Italians in Cape Breton

Evo DiPierro and I have attempted to prepare and organize the book to cross boundaries and appeal to both the general public and an academic audience. The preceding section is useful in establishing the Italian presence on the island—a presence that dates back approximately 150 years. Our aim, however, is to move beyond "numbers" and "generalities" to provide readers with an opportunity to learn more about the Italian communities of the island and to meet some of the people who have made a contribution, in their own unique way, to the colour and substance of life in Cape Breton. With this in mind, much of the book is devoted to including people's "voices" (sometimes with more or less editorial assistance) in the presentation of various details of their personal lives and family histories. In addition, we have focused on topics that show the rich and varied experiences of Italians living in different parts of Cape Breton. Some of the themes addressed in the book include: the early immigration period, work experience, the treatment and internment of Italians during Second World War, the maintenance of both a sense of cultural identity and certain cultural traditions in Canada and the sorrow of seeing family and friends leave the island for employment elsewhere.

These themes give the book a semblance of structure. Our goal, however, is not to isolate themes, patterns or generalizations that will somehow capture the essence of Italianness in Cape Breton. These types of "generalizations" tend to simplify, distort and misrepresent the meanings people give to their lives in specific contexts. I see my role, as an anthropologist, as one of moving away from "generalizations" to address the complex, multiple and variable life experiences of the people with whom I work. This, in my view, is the best way to break down stereotypes that people may have of Italians (or any other group).

Taken together, the articles collected make a contribution to our understanding of community, ethnicity, cultural identity, intra-ethnic diversity and inter-ethnic relations. They demonstrate, for example, that it is difficult to speak in terms of a *single* Italian community for Cape Breton. There are several distinct groupings of people of Italian ethnic origin on the island—groupings that have occurred for a number of reasons, including the location of original settlement, the type of employment initial immigrants were recruited to participate in (e.g., work in the mines, as opposed to work in the steel plant), the number of Italian immigrants who joined the group after the Second World War, and the connections individuals have to specific regions of Italy. The Italians of Dominion, for instance, trace their ancestry primarily to the Treviso area of northern Italy, while people in Sydney are predominantly from the Abruzzi and Molise regions of central Italy. Although there has been, and continues to be, contact and cooperation between these two groups for various activities, they tend to maintain their own organizations and their own sense of "identity." In addition, there are many people who, for one reason or another, have lost contact with other Italians in the area.

Intra-ethnic diversity also is discernable in the types of positions Italians have occupied in Cape Breton society. Although many of the early immigrants were recruited to work in the coal and steel industries, Italians, right from the very beginning, have been engaged in a variety of occupations. These occupations have ranged from homemaking, coalmining and steelmaking to active participation in professional sports, music and entertainment, politics, the fisheries, business ventures, education, farming and medicine. This range of activity makes it difficult to speak of the "Italian experience" in terms of simple generalities.

A number of articles also call into question the depiction of Italian women in terms of the hardworking mamma (mother) who stays at home to care for her family's needs. Although there may be some truth in this depiction, it fails to recognize the full extent of the ambition, determination, hard work and success characteristic of the lives of many women. Italian women have made important contributions to Cape Breton society, and the social and economic life of their families, through both their labours within the home and their paid employment outside of the home.[14] In some cases, the articles also reveal the types of struggles women have had to deal with in order to juggle the demands of both career and family.

In terms of inter-ethnic relations, the treatment Italians received during the Second World War is significant. The Italians of Cape Breton (and Canada in general) *did not* represent a Fifth Column that posed a threat to the Canadian war effort. None of the people forced to register as enemy aliens, submit to interviews and, in some cases, experience arrest and internment were ever charged with any type of offense. They were humiliated and mistreated for being Italian, not for being disloyal to Canada. In fact, Canadian Government policy created a paradoxical situation. A number of young men and women served with the Canadian Armed Forces, sometimes overseas, at the very same time as family members and friends were being denied various rights at home. The book, however, does not focus solely on the negative aspects of inter-ethnic relations. John deRoche's article, "In Other's Eyes: Pit Talk About Italians," for example, provides an interesting account of how non-Italian miners perceived their Italian co-workers. Although not all of the statements in this account are positive, it does show how non-Italian miners recognized and respected the hard work of Italians in the pit. For the more recent period, the articles on "La Sala Italiana in Dominion" and the "Cape Breton Italian Cultural Association" address the ways in which these organizations are trying to include, and/or participate with, non-Italians in various celebrations and activities. Don Fraser's reflection on "What it is Like to Marry into an Italian Family" and Lina Mleczko's "A New Life in Canada" provide very personal accounts of inter-ethnic harmony.

Finally, although the book concentrates on "Italian lives in Cape Breton," these lives have been touched by experiences and migrations beyond the island's shores. Several articles address the movement of people to other parts of Canada and the United States, while others explore how individuals have attempted to rediscover their ancestral "homeland."

The Anthropologist as Community Member: Home Away From Home

My family and I arrived in Cape Breton in August of 1990. We knew that we could count on several individuals at Cape Breton University (where I was employed) to help us get settled in the area, but we had no "people" here. Our families were far away in Ontario, British Columbia and Italy. We were apprehensive; we didn't know what to expect from life on the island.

Yet, we were not entirely new to Nova Scotia. Margaret, my wife, had lived for a period of time in the Halifax area, and I had visited Halifax as a young boy. My parents and I emigrated to Canada from Italy. We set sail from Palermo, on the island of Sicily, and travelled first to Barcelona, Spain, and then through the strait of Gibraltar to Lisbon, Portugal. From there, we made our way across the Atlantic. We arrived in Halifax in January of 1957. The entire trip took about three weeks. My mother was seasick from the moment we departed Lisbon. I enjoyed the trip. The sailors used to put aside buns and oranges as treats for me. But, by the time we arrived in Halifax, I too was seasick.

I was five-years old at the time, and I don't remember much about Nova Scotia. I recall getting a smallpox vaccination, and I remember travelling to Ontario by train. One of the things that stands out in my mind is my first taste of Canadian bread. I had never eaten white, sliced bread. I knew it was bread, but it looked so different from the dark, thick-crust bread of home. I found eating white bread similar to chewing gum. Another thing that stands out in my mind is my mother dressing me in my best clothes for meeting relatives at the Hamilton train station. I wore a white shirt and a dark pair of shorts. Hamilton can be so cold in late January. I may have looked "cool," but I was very cold.

Years later, when many Italians were leaving Cape Breton to seek employment opportunities in Ontario, Alberta and British Columbia, we were on our way to

Cape Breton. We were introduced to the warm hospitality of Cape Bretoners on the very day we arrived on the island. We were on our way to Sydney but took a wrong turn. The next thing we knew, we were approaching the North Sydney ferry terminal. The man in the car ahead of us worked on the ferry. He was parking his car, and we must have looked lost. When he saw our out-of-province license plate, he hopped back into his car to guide us all the way to Sydney. I didn't catch his name, but I remember him calling me "Bud." Since then, we have experienced many good times with friends of both Italian and non-Italian background in Cape Breton.

During my first week at Cape Breton University, I was introduced to the late Lino Polegato who became a good friend and colleague. Through him, we met new friends at the Cape Breton Italian Cultural Association. Margaret and I became part of the Italian community of Sydney and, through my work on this book, we have made good friends with people in other parts of the island. One of my main reasons for working on this book has been to return something to the many people who have done so much for my family and me in Cape Breton. I hope you enjoy meeting these people and come to appreciate them as much as I do.

All Our Fathers: The North Italian Colony in Industrial Cape Breton

By Esperanza Maria Razzolini Crook[1]

Prior to Canadian Confederation (1867), Italian immigration to Canada had consisted largely of scattered individuals. In 18th-century Nova Scotia, Italians from Genoa had founded a settlement, complete with church, at Ketch Harbour, but this remained a rarity until significant migration commenced following Italy's unification.[2] The first Italians to settle in the Dominion-New Waterford area were the Giovannetti brothers—Lorenzo, Nicodemo and Antonio—who immigrated to Port Morien in the 1870s.

The Giovannettis became involved in business activities, which included the shipping of freight to and from Halifax in their own vessels. Nicodemo's two sons, both medical doctors, moved to Newfoundland shortly after 1900, thus creating the base for an Italian community there. He died at Port Morien in 1882 and Lorenzo in 1907. Antonio died sometime afterward in Sydney. In the 1890s, the original Giovannetti brothers were followed by their nephews, William and Lewis, with Angelo and Roddie arriving in 1899. All four were trained as barbers, and they owned and ran various barber shops in Dominion, Bridgeport and Reserve Mines, plus a livery stable behind the Dominion establishment. In addition, Louis operated the Red Onion Hotel in Dominion until 1906, while Angelo owned and operated a modest summer hotel midway on the Dominion-Lingan Beach until 1909. Angelo remained in Dominion (with his wife, Mame Petrie) until his death in 1957, at the age of eighty. His brothers and their wives, less satisfied with their lives in the new land, returned to Italy upon retirement and died there. This, then, was the basis of the Italian presence in industrial Cape Breton at the time of the large influx of immigrants into the area at the turn of the 20th century.

By 1900, almost 200,000 people were leaving Italy every year. The United States responded to the situation with restrictions which pushed more Italians into Canada. By 1901, 10,000 had entered Canada, a figure which rose to 50,000 by 1909, and over 100,000 by 1916, making Italians the second largest group of non-English immigrants in the nation. This rush of immigrants during the years 1880 to 1914 coincided with the economic take-off of Canada. The Canadian Pacific Railway and other construction projects gave impetus to serious Italian immigration.

Giovannetti's Barber Shop and Livery Stable, Mitchell Avenue, Dominion, ca. 1906. Courtesy of Len Stephenson.

In industrial Cape Breton, the general state of affairs paralleled that of the rest of the nation. In 1830, the General Mining Association (GMA) had established itself on the south side of Lingan, at a spot later to become, at first, Bridgeport, and then Dominion. Mr. Henry Mitchell, a pioneer in the Cape Breton mining industry, re-opened the GMA mine in the old Bridgeport area in 1883 and ran it until 1893, when it was purchased, along with most of the then operating mines in the area, by the newly formed Dominion Coal Company. The Dominion No. 1 mine, from which the town of Dominion drew its name, had been in operation for about seven years when the company started importing Italian workers from Italy and the Boston labour market.[3]

Most of the recruits for the coal mines were north Italians, while south Italy provided the majority of labourers for the steel mills, which had been established in 1900. Their tendency to settle near their employment created a natural segregation of the two groups, with south Italians congregating in and near Sydney and those from north Italy residing in and near Dominion and New Waterford. Immigration to Cape Breton, at the time, was a simple process, despite the Canadian government's unofficial attempts to discourage the "importing" of Italian workers in favour of settling the country with farmers from northern Europe. Citizenship cost one dollar and could be granted in hours. The fare was paid by the employer on the understanding that the worker would remain for at least one year. To aid this recruitment, the coal company sent agents-cum-interpreters to Italy to actively promote their offer. Such an agent in the early years was Max Passerini, who, together with several of his brothers, played a prominent role in the early history of both the north and the south Italian communities on the island. Passerini not only held the position of Italian Consul for the area but also owned, or was involved in, such business activities as the operation of a store, a bakery and a meat processing establishment. Max is remembered by a marble statue in Dominion's Ocean Avenue Cemetery.[4]

The north Italian colony did not exist in total isolation from the south Italians in Sydney, as some interactions did occur, especially through the church. In 1908, Father Johnston, a priest helpful and sympathetic to the immigrants, was replaced by Father Domenico Viola of Bari, Italy. Using St. Anne's Glebe House as a base, Father Viola set about consolidating the Italian colony, beginning with the formation of an Italian fraternal society, the "Santa Rita Society," at Glace Bay on Sunday, June 14, 1908. In 1911-1912, he built an Italian church, St. Nicholas, at Whitney Pier. From there, he administered to the Italians in the districts of Glace Bay, Dominion, New Waterford and the Sydneys. The church worked toward the improvement of the immigrants' lot against difficult odds. Integration of the new "foreign" element with the native-born was largely resisted, occasionally violently, especially by the English-Canadians. Immigrants were beaten and robbed of their pay by local toughs sufficiently often for Italians to begin to travel in groups. Finally, the Italians rose in mass protest in Sydney one Saturday morning. They marched in front of the church carrying guns, pitchforks and anything else suitable to serve as a weapon. The priest defused the situation by calling everyone into the church then preaching to the local inhabitants concerning the hardships that the immigrants faced every day. The general situation improved somewhat thereafter, but not necessarily the opinions some Canadians held concerning Italians. Newspaper articles dealing with the colony dwelt upon murders and criminal activities, although modest coverage was given to the achievements of the Italian mutual aid organizations and Italian declarations of loyalty and celebration of victories during the First World War. All in all, intermixing remained limited and superficial and tension endured.[5]

In 1901, the Canadian census listed five Italians in the Dominion-New Waterford area (probably the Giovannettis). By 1911, the Dominion population of 2,589 included 154 Italians. Angelo Cechetto's father was in the town in 1903 when No. 1-A mine burned, an event which required six hundred million gallons of water to quench the flames as the whole area was afire. This fire closed the mine from March 19 to July 27, 1903, and with no work, Cechetto returned to Italy. "Pop" Patsy Peori went to Boston in 1902, at the age of twelve, accompanied by his thirteen-year-old brother. Pop came to Cape Breton, while his brother travelled south— they never saw one another again. Louie Bresson was thirteen years old when he was recruited for the mine. Leo Vaninetti's father arrived to work in No. 3 mine around 1903, returned

Miners of Dominion Coal Co., No. 6 Colliery, Donkin. Phonse Morelatto and other Italians in front rake box. Courtesy of Len Stephenson.

to Italy to marry in 1905, and then came back to work in No. 2 mine in 1909. Both Bresson and Vaninetti became completely bilingual and served as interpreters for new recruits from Italy. My grandfather, Rudolfo Razzolini, a shoemaker, emigrated from Asolo, Treviso, to New Waterford in 1913, the year of the greatest influx. Following the classic pattern, he had gone first to Basel, Switzerland, before coming to Canada. He was the first of nine brothers and sisters to immigrate to Argentina, the United States and Canada—only the eldest son remained in Italy.[6]

Providing housing for the new workers proved to be a considerable problem for coal company authorities. In response to the need, the company built long rows of buildings such as those erected on Henry and Station Streets in Dominion in 1910—on Henry Street, they came to be called the "Shacks" and on Station Street "Bug Row." In addition, many newcomers boarded at such establishments as the Red Onion Hotel in Dominion. While owned largely by English-Canadians, it was operated for years by such Italians as the Ravanellos, Zaniols, Bartilones, Pivas and DiPistones (Antonio DiPistone also served as Italian Consul and unofficial interpreter and spokesperson for the colony). In its heyday, the Red Onion offered room and board for nine dollars a week, while supplying large rooms on the first floor for receptions and weekly Saturday night dances. As most of the immigrants were male labourers, these housing provisions proved sufficient. Slowly, as the number of Italians in the area increased and men brought their families over, the colony took on a more direct form. An Italian Co-operative Store was started on Henry Street, and Passerini purchased a local bakery. Yet, while a great many beginnings occurred in the early years, it was not until the Italian community received its second wave of newcomers during the 1920s that it possessed sufficient numbers to attain a proper organization and nature.[7]

Following the First World War, the male transitory character of Italian life in Canada began to change. Increasing numbers of women arrived to join husbands and start families. Labourers in agriculture and construction were accompanied by more artisans and professionals. Men saved funds and established small business enterprises. Adhering to the dominant goal of "earn, live, save," many adopted a pattern where the man worked and the woman dealt with the public. Despite the constant problem of irregular employment, the founding of homes gave stability, as the children provided roots. The immigrants formed communities with highly organized social and cultural lines. These continued to increase in size as the 1920s boom brought considerable numbers of Italian labourers who found ready employment in construction and heavy industry. Yet, contrary to this movement, the United States contagion of racism and xenophobia began to creep into the Canadian government. It became increasingly difficult for southern Europeans to immigrate to North America, and legislation in 1924 and 1929, plus the Depression, cut the flow of Italian emigrants drastically. Between 1920 and 1930, 15,113 entered (8,725 of them male), while only 2,609 were permitted entry between 1930 and 1936. As with the first wave, this second influx consisted mainly of male labourers, many of whom were seventeen years old, as the Italian military draft became applicable at eighteen years of age.[8]

Giovanni Antonello emigrated from San Martino di Lupari, Padova, in December 1919, at the age of seventeen. Caught in post-First World War's particularly high unemployment rate, he wrote to his sister, then residing in Donkin near No. 6 mine, expressing his desire to leave Italy. Upon acquiring the proper papers from her, he came from Genoa to New York by ship, and hence to Sydney by train. According to the Italian Consul at the time, Antonello and his travelling companion were the first Italians to come to Cape Breton after the First World War. He lived in Donkin with his sister until the mine was closed in 1925 and then moved to Dominion to work in No. 1-A and No. 1-B. His wife came to Cape Breton in 1931. Antonello was a miner for forty-two years, retiring in 1962.

Condo Baggio left his birthplace of Castafranca in September 1920, also seventeen years old and in search of work. He travelled by train to La Havre, France; from there he sailed to Quebec on the *Milita*, arriving on September 23; and then by train again to Sydney, ending his journey on September 25. Three days later, he began his career with the coal company at No. 1-A mine in Dominion, where he worked eight hours a day, three days a week and earning $3.25 a shift. He lived at the Red Onion Hotel, then run by Mrs. Ravanello. My maternal grandfather, Federico Sanvido, came to Dominion in 1920 and worked in the mine or for the town of Dominion until his death in 1955. Romano Scattolon arrived in Dominion in 1921.

Ralph Gatto was born in 1905, the year his older brother, Antonio, emigrated. In 1922, encouraged by company agents and his brother's presence in the area, Ralph and another brother, Giuseppe, came to Cape Breton in search of work. With assistance from Antonio, Ralph acquired work and mined coal in Donkin until the 1925 strike, at which time he went to Quebec to work until the disruption ended. He then returned. His wife (then fiancé) came to Nova Scotia in 1927 at the age of twenty, while the rest of her family (mother, sister and brother) travelled to Argentina to join a brother already there. Fred Gaetan also emigrated in 1927, and worked in No. 12, No. 16 and No. 18 mines in New Waterford and New Victoria until his retirement in 1965. Encouraged by brother Romano, Luigi Scattolon left Salvaroso, Treviso, on March 3, 1927. He travelled to Le Havre, France, by train, and then by ship to Halifax, arriving on March 17, 1927. He lived with his brother in Dominion and worked for the coal company in Reserve Mines. His career as a miner was followed by involvement first in the taxi business and then in the operation of a tavern. He retired in 1975. Mrs. Elia Vaninetti's father emigrated to Dominion in 1927 as well. When he had accumulated enough money, he sent for his family. They left Belluno on March 14, 1927, went by train to Cherbourg, and then sailed to America, arriving in Dominion on March 27, 1927. Mrs. Vaninetti was thirteen years old. As the family was very poor, she worked as a maid in the homes of more prosperous Italian and English-Canadians until her marriage.

During the miners' strike of 1925, the Donkin mine was allowed to flood and was abandoned. At that time, many Italians transferred to Dominion. In the midst of all this movement, Dominion, like other municipalities, requested the government to stop all immigration due to the high rate of unemployment. The last Italian immigrant of that era was Elia (Leo) Vaninetti, who was permitted entry only because he had been born in Dominion in June 1911. He had been taken back to Sondrio in 1912, and raised by his grandparents. Leo left for Dominion on May 5, 1931, arriving after a few stops, on May 27, 1931. He began work at No. 1-B mine three months later and continued to mine coal for thirty-eight years. In 1930, the Dominion Italian colony reached a peak of about 200 people, with New Waterford and Glace Bay and the surrounding area well able to produce at least as many more.

Due to difficulties arising from differences in language and customs, early immigrants tended to settle in separate groups. The Italians were no exception. The main north Italian communities were located in Dominion and New Waterford (No. 14 yard), although there were scattered individuals as close as Glace Bay and Donkin and as far away as Mira and Inverness. While the majority worked in the mines, a number opted for a rural life on the banks of the Mira River. The members of this small farm community supported themselves and supplied food stuffs to the nearby north Italian colonies. Hard manual labour remained the basis of existence, sometimes augmented in the manner of their English-Canadian neighbours, by such pursuits as rum-running and bootleg coal mining. Even artisans, such as my paternal grandfather, first worked in the mines before resuming their trade; few escaped the physical presence of the mines—none their influence. Living conditions had improved from the early days in the "Shacks" but were still difficult. The number of small businesses (some quite imaginative) grew, making the Italian colony almost self-sufficient. In New Waterford, Manello built and ran a merry-go-round for about three years until, like so many other Italians, the 1925 strike forced him to leave. Other ventures started by Italians included cooperatives, grocery stores, service stations, shoe repair shops, tailor shops, taverns and bakeries.

While the Italians mixed socially with other groups, they steadfastly insisted upon marrying among themselves. In this, my family did not follow the norm; both my Italian grandfathers married non-Italians—my paternal grandmother being Annabelle Marsh from Lingan and my maternal grandmother, Renelle Thomas, from Chatelineau, Hainaut, Belgium. While the shortage of women did mean that a small minority married outside, most men married Italian wives—some sought wives from among those women who immigrated to Cape Breton, while others travelled to Italy to find wives through family connections. As part of their

A double wedding in Dominion. Courtesy of Maria Razzolini.

way of life, immigrants brought vegetable and fruit seeds with them to provide their accustomed foods. Most maintained private gardens and kept some livestock (especially pigs). This practice became extremely important during depressed times. Although their early dislike of Canada, with its cold weather and strange ways, had abated largely, the Italians continued to preserve their old ways. They gathered at those private houses large enough to accommodate sufficient numbers in order to socialize and exchange news. In New Waterford, Italian language classes were held at Central School for two or three years. And, the colony was represented by such early consuls as Tony DiPistone and E. J. Julian through the Italian Consular Agency in Sydney.

In 1932, an outdoor rink was erected on the present site of the Italian Hall in Dominion. Named the "Winter Garden," it was operated by Ralph Gatto, Sisto Piva, Mario Morellato and some friends. On September 27, 1936, the Italian Community Club was formed with over eighty members and the following officers: Giovanni Antonello, President; Antonio Amadio, Vice-President; Francesco DeVenz, Secretary; and Bortolo Centa, Treasurer. The following year, the Italian Community Hall was built, providing a focus for social and recreational activities. The Club grew to have more than 100 members at its peak. Annual banquets in the hall were popular, drawing Italians from the surrounding area. My maternal grandfather, Federico Sanvido, one of the original members of the club, served as caretaker for some time, living with my grandmother in the back of the hall itself, as did my parents and myself briefly. One of the most popular of the associated activities was the annual Italian picnic, usually held in Gabarus, the Meadows, or Mira, often in areas where relatives owned farms. Italians from other communities were invited. *Bocce* (similar to lawn bowling) courts occupied numerous backyards (at least nine in Dominion and two in New Waterford), and time was spent cycling or playing card games such as *scopa* (sweep) and *tre sette* (three sevens). In the midst of all this, the majority and minority cultures began to come together as the children of both Italo- and English-Canadians met on the common territory of their home town. The year 1939 was to change all this.[9]

The Second World War brought trouble and ironic contrasts. In industrial Cape Breton, English-Canadian miners refused to work beside Italians who had been their fellow workers for years, while all over the nation, Italian leaders were interned under the *War Measures Act*. Yet, many second generation Italo-Canadians fought in the Canadian Armed Forces. The situation was sadly ironic—John Antonello's sister had two sons in the Canadian Army when her husband was put out of work. The reaction of English-Canadians to Italy's declaration of war against Britain in 1940 shocked Italian immigrants in the industrial area. In June of that year, a number of Italians were arrested and jailed under the *Act*, while some locals indulged their violent tendencies by smashing the tombstones of Italians in area cemeteries. The apolitical but patriotic Italians had been proud of Mussolini and the new, modern era he had brought to Italy, some even wearing black shirts in parades. With the beginning of hostilities, however, everyone began to assume very low profiles, and all such paraphernalia disappeared. Nevertheless, the situation worsened. Starting in Dominion, a number of English-Canadian miners began touring the union locals for the purpose of having the Italians laid-off. This action resulted in a number of skirmishes followed by a general decision that non-Italians would cease working until all the Italians were suspended. The coal company succumbed to the pressure, and all the Italians were put out of work for a total of nine months. For this entire period, Italians had to live off their gardens and livestock and whatever rare odd jobs made themselves available—there was no regular work. The government assistance of $1.50 per adult and 65 cents per child per week did little to help.[10]

Things got tighter. As "enemy aliens" all Italians were compelled by government order to surrender firearms and to register and make weekly reports on their activities to the authorities (the RCMP). Irony abounded—when everyone's guns were turned in, my father's were returned as he had been born in Canada, while a friend who had been brought from Italy at less than a year of age, did not see his again until after the war. Eventually, time eroded these restrictions and work resumed, guns were returned and the reports were phased out completely. The tension and mutual suspicion, however, remained. For some families, the situation proved infinitely worse. In June 1940, the RCMP arrested and jailed about twenty Italian men from the industrial area under the *War Measures Act*. Within twenty-four hours, they were transported to Montreal and, hence, to Petawawa, Ontario. The families were not informed of their whereabouts for some time. All prominent men in the Italian communities, their seizure served as an example to other Italo-Canadians, thus preventing any possible trouble, at least in the minds of the authorities. After the initial internment, many Italians very carefully maintained a low profile. My family bridged both experiences—my paternal grandfather, Rudolfo Razzolini, was taken away while my maternal grandfather removed himself to a lumber camp, out of sight and mind. The men were interned in Petawawa with about 700 other Italians from across the nation. They were held for two-to-four years and finally released. Although conditions in the camp were good, the English-Canadian hatred which had put them there was a reaction that the Italians, most of them naturalized residents of Canada for more than twenty years, would never really understand.[11]

Between 1951 and 1961, Nova Scotia received an influx of new Italian immigrants, most of whom settled in the peninsular area of Halifax. This new ethnic community formed a strong contrast with the older communities in industrial Cape Breton. By 1961, the Italo-Canadian population of the Atlantic region had reached 5,278 in number, with nearly 4,000 in Nova Scotia, most in industrial Cape Breton or the Halifax-Dartmouth Metro area. Assimilation in Cape Breton, however, progressed rapidly. In Dominion, while the Italian Community Hall with its Club and Ladies Auxiliary, endured, interest in Italian culture and heritage declined. As the Cape Breton colony matured into the third and fourth generations, ethnicity decreased, especially in relation to the increasing ethnicity of the Halifax-Dartmouth Metro area community. Many Cape Breton Italians moved to Ontario. As the colony declined in numbers, the physical landmarks of the old community began to disappear. With the first generation either dying or retiring, business hallmarks of the Cape Breton Italian settlement—such as Cosimo Corsano's corner store in Glace Bay—closed, and the links of the past were broken. While the second generation still fluctuated between segregation and acculturation, the third generation migrated out into the majority society, physically and socially. Intermarriage with English-Canadians became common, and the industrious, law-abiding, well integrated and respected Italo-Canadians began to merge with the Canadian mainstream, and a way of life began to die. While a number of individuals more cognizant of the value of ethnic heritage did strive to preserve their unique traditions and identity, the general movement toward assimilation advanced steadily.

Then, in the 1960s, multiculturalism came into vogue in the nation, and Canadians sought their heritage. People returned to Cape Breton and the Italian colony—old and young—and new interest was vested in the Cape Breton Italo-Canadian experience. Ethnicity became the fashion, and examples of Italian culture flowed into the Canadian mainstream. In Dominion, the Italian Community Club boasted forty members as of the 1980s and reasserted its role as a leader of the north-Italian community. Once again, Italian picnics, banquets, parades, cultural activities and reunions abounded, and moves were made to establish lines of communication and cooperation with the colonies in Sydney and the Halifax-Dartmouth Metro area.[12]

Against this backdrop was formed a new culture—a combination of elements both Italian and Canadian. While the physical manifestation of the colony had shrunk with time, its influence had grown more widespread through third, fourth and even fifth generations. While this article hardly constitutes a comprehensive history, it does, I hope, shed light upon some little-known facts, as well as allow others to share in the vivid complexity of Italo-Canadian culture and experience within this country. Purists believe that to legitimately exist an ethnic minority must preserve unchanged the lifestyle carried to this nation by the first immigrants. This approach ignores the chief characteristics of culture—that it is fluid and adaptive—the very qualities which ensure its essential survival. Identity is an intangible element—it is not necessary that we preserve those physical indicators, such as the language, in order to be a legitimate minority. The only completely essential factor is that we interpret part of our individuality in that manner. It is a distinct internal way of looking at ourselves and the world which sets us apart from the majority as different. Thus the world of our forefathers imparts to those of us of the third and subsequent generations a rich diversity of culture and an important, if intangible, definition of self which is both our inheritance from our grandparents and our legacy to our children.

Angela Giacomantonio:
Memories of Whitney Pier

Edited by Sam Migliore

In November of 1996, I had the opportunity to speak with Mrs. Angela (Tortola) Giacomantonio, a long time resident of Whitney Pier in Sydney, Nova Scotia. In addition to the many treats (homemade pizza, cake and drinks) she served that day, she shared with me some personal memories of growing up in "The Pier." This is her story.

Well, I was born in Sydney, down on Tupper Street, in 1922. It was a very nice spot. At that time, Tupper, Laurier and Hankard Streets were part of the Italian community. Our church was in the centre. The night I was born the church burned down; I used to say to my mother, "I guess I was burning hot, so I burned the church down" [laughs]. But, all that area was Italian. Across Lingan Road were the Hungarians and then, up on the other side, there were a few Polish people with some Italians mixed in towards the subway (the "overpass" today). Except for about two or three families living in the Italian area, the Black community was on Currys Lane. There were about eight Italian stores on Tupper Street. And, we were always together.

Now the reason that my father was here was on account of the steel plant. The plant started in the early 1900s. My father got married in 1905, and he travelled to Boston [from Italy] in 1906. He would have stayed there, but it so happened that he and my uncle got mixed up with an underworld gang. They were issued a pearl-handled gun (my mother buried it because she didn't want anyone to have anything to do with it). They didn't know this was an underworld gang until, about three weeks later, a man who knew that my father and uncle were very green told them. He said, "Do you know who you're working for?" They said, "No, but what's the difference as long as we can get money and send it back home." But then, the man said: "You received a gun? What do you think you got the gun for?" They didn't know. But when they heard a certain name mentioned, they got scared. See, it was *la mano nera* (the "Black Hand"), and when they heard this, well, they got out of Boston. They literally walked here. They walked at night and slept all day. They were afraid. So, they came to Sydney, and they got work in the steel plant the next day. They worked twelve-hour shifts, and their wages were 75 cents a day.

Papa was alone. He made two or three trips to Italy to try to convince my mother to come to Canada. She didn't want to leave home. She lived in Miranda, in the province of Campobasso. He finally said to her: "I'm not coming back; there's nothing there for us." Later, one of my mother's uncles persuaded her to come here. He said to her: "Men go astray when they don't have their families with them. You are going to lose your husband." My mother came to Canada, but she had no

St. Nicholas Italian Church in Whitney Pier, 1911. 81-237-5307. Beaton Institute, Cape Breton University.

intentions of staying. My father got cross with her and said: "If you're going, go, but I'm not going back; you'll never see me again." Anyway, that cured her, and she stayed in Sydney.

My mother arrived here on February 20, 1920. She told me that when they arrived in Sydney, there was snow. There was snow in Italy but nothing like here. My brothers were wearing short pants, no coats. They walked from the railroad station to Tupper Street. The snow was waist high, and it was hard to walk with their suitcases. That was the first time she had seen so much snow, and she hated it with a passion. Then she got used to it and, of course, she didn't want to go back. Many times my father wanted her to go back for a trip, but she had no intention of returning to Italy. See, at Tupper Street, they were all Italians. She wasn't lonely. The women would work all day—get the meals ready, wash clothes, whatever had to be done—and then sit outside together exchanging stories. They would laugh and carry on. So they weren't lonely; they had friends to talk to. It's not like today. Everybody talked, told stories, and they would break into song. They would sing, and they would have a merry ole time. And, like I said before, the church was right in our vicinity. We just walked up to church. It was just very, very nice.

They would have picnics in the churchyard. They'd sell crafts and spaghetti and meatballs to make money for the church. And the women would scrub the church every time a bishop or a new priest came to visit. The men carried the water because there was no water in the building, and the kids scrubbed the pews. And we got along very well. The picnic would go for three days. It would start at six in the evening and go right through 'til one o'clock in the morning. Even though they worked so hard, and they were so tired, they would sit and sing. That's what they did every night. Our first priest was Father Viola; he was an Italian Priest. Then we had Father MacLean. He was a Scottish fellow who spoke Italian very well; he studied in Rome. Father MacLean would sit among the people, and they would sing all the Italian songs. The women had very good voices. And, let me tell you, it was beautiful. The men were together; they were all friends. If there was a wedding, everybody was there. It was just one big happy family.

Of course, Whitney Pier was never liked by other people. We were known as "the other side of the track." They looked down on us, and there was verbal abuse. But, we had it all. There was an Italian community, and then there were Polish people, Blacks, Ukrainians and Hungarians. They had funny names for each one of us. When I was going to school, the English-speaking people were very cruel. Now I say cruel, but, at that time, my mother would always say: "Never mind what they said; they didn't hit you, don't bother with them." And you would accept it. But, it was hard to accept. We all were abused verbally. When we went to town, the other side of the subway, they would pelt us with eggs, potatoes.... It was a rough time. It was the English-speaking people. There were very few of them in the Pier; they were way down by Holy Redeemer Church. It used to make me mad when people talked about the Pier as "oh, what a place." We may have been *hunks or dagos*, but the kids were smart, and the families were together. We didn't harm anybody.

[One of the things Mrs. Giacomantonio stressed was that, although many of the Italian families in the Pier were poor, they were able to manage by working hard, helping one another, and by being resourceful.] On Sundays, the men would play cards for a pitcher of beer. They would make their own beer or wine. We would pick choke cherries, blackberries and blueberries. The men would make wine from these while the women would bake cakes. You had to bake your own; nobody could afford to buy anything. We were all poor, and I mean poor. Dolly Parton sings about a "coat of many colours;" well, I had one. My mother used to make my clothes from whatever cloth was available, and I was happy. It was a new garment, whether it was a dress, a slip or a coat. We didn't have anything extraordinary to play with, no playgrounds. It may be dull by today's standards, but there were a lot of children, and we made our own fun.

I was taught to embroider when I was about eight years old and to crochet at fifteen, just to keep me busy. I learned to knit and to cook. I used to make macaroni when I was five. I couldn't reach the table, so my mother would put the bake board on two chairs. Every Friday we would have pasta and beans. You couldn't eat meat, so I would make the macaroni. And of course, my girlfriend would come to play, and I'd say: "I can't come out now, but I will as soon as I'm finished." And I'd hurry up. I was taught to knit, to cook and to bake. Sometimes my cakes went bad, but my father would eat it. He would say, "make another one, it's very good." [laughs] Poor Papa, he ate all my mistakes. He was really good to me.

I worked from the time I was five-years-old. Scrubbing chairs, scrubbing the floor, I did everything. We had a big kitchen, softwood, and many times I got splinters in my hands from scrubbing the floor. I grew, I didn't die from it. We always worked, worked, worked.

Then, on "steelworkers road" [by Prince Street], everybody had a lot of land to make a garden. The older people used to say that it was just like in Italy, where each family would travel from their town or village to the farm. We would go there every evening at about four o'clock. The men would dig it up, the women would plant, and the kids would pick the weeds. There was always something for the kids to do. That's how we got our tomatoes, beans and potatoes. We didn't grow much lettuce. There was a Hungarian lady who lived on this side of Lingan Road; she used to have the most beautiful lettuce. She would give you a great big bag of lettuce, with flowers all around it, for a nickel. She was a lovely lady.

The Pier was not a horrible place to live; it was a beautiful place. We were born and brought up here, and my children were born and brought up here. Nobody harmed us. We never used to close our doors; our doors were never locked. Now you have to lock your doors at four o'clock. I loved those days; I wish they would come back. There were always visitors. Every night there was a place to go. If a person was ill, all the women in that area would cook and bake, and then visit. They would take the clothes, wash and iron them, and bring them back. They didn't wait to be asked for help. No one had to say, "Oh, the mother is sick, who is going to feed the children?" There was always someone in the neighbourhood that would feed them. And that's what I miss today. There is a big difference from the time I was growing up.

[At the same time, Mrs. Giacomantonio pointed out that not all families in the Pier were necessarily poor. There were a number of Italian businesses in Whitney Pier, and these businesses provided a special flavour to the community.] We had four Italian stores. Mr. DeLorenzo had a store that sold Italian cheese, olives and all the groceries. He had a beautiful business. He had groceries on one side and a meat market on the other. We also had two big bakeries—DiPenta's bakery and Del Vecchio's bakery. The one that survived was Del Vecchio's Bakery; it is now Bernie's Bakery.

The Pier had its own stores; you didn't have to go to town for anything. We had grocery stores, a pastry shop, a liquor store and a post office. At night, the street was lit up like a Christmas tree. There were also two movie houses—the Casino and the Star. Movies were only a nickel per show. I used to go to the Casino on Mondays and Wednesdays and to the Star on Tuesdays and Thursdays. After the movies, we would go to Toby's; he had a hamburger joint. Hamburgers were only a dime. And, I was called Coca Cola because I drank nothing but Coke. It was only a nickel a bottle.

Carnival and Easter Celebrations

There was no such thing as Halloween for the Italians when I was growing up in Whitney Pier. We had *carnevale* (Carnival) in February. It was pot luck, and everybody would bring a dish around nine or ten o'clock in the evening, and we would eat together. At that time, nine or ten o'clock was very late. You were usually in bed by eight o'clock. But, we would go to a particular house for the celebration. It could be the Martinello house, the Del Vecchio house, or elsewhere. It was really nice because you could talk to them. There were stories and more stories about different parts of Italy, what they did, and what took place in their homeland. There were games, firecrackers.... It was a party, a big party.

Carnevale was always a day that you ate meat, ate any animal products. And, you knew, that you weren't going to eat anymore of that stuff for forty days. See, our religion, at that time, was very strict. My mother, of course, was number one; I mean, she was strict. We weren't allowed to eat anything from an animal—meat, milk, cheese, eggs—during Lent. You would have a lot of potatoes, a lot of macaroni. And, the macaroni was not made with eggs. But, for *carnevale*, you could have everything. People used to bring spaghetti and meatballs, ravioli or gnocchi with meat sauce, and lots of meat and eggs. Come midnight, though, it was taboo; you wouldn't eat any meat. I mean, you really prayed for Easter to come, believe me.

Come Holy Saturday, the priest would come around to each house to bless our food. The table would be full of all the food you were preparing for Easter Sunday. The first thing we had on Easter Sunday morning was a *frittata* with meat, eggs, onions, whatever you wanted. That's when you broke your fast.

I remember one time, on the Saturday at nine o'clock, we finished singing with the choir, and the bells rang. I said: "Oh good, we're through fasting." I wanted to have a boiled egg. Don't ask me why; the devil was in me at the time. So I went home from church and said: "Mom, Lent is over." She said: "No it isn't; where did you come from?" I said: "I came from church. The bells rang and all the statues are now visible again." She said: "No, no, Christ arose on Easter Sunday morning. You can eat a boiled egg at four o'clock tomorrow morning but not now." That was the end of that. I mean, the food was all there tempting, but you weren't allowed to eat it. Then on Sunday you would break your fast and spend most of the day in church.

[For *carnevale*, people] would dress up like in the old days, the days of kings. Some men dressed as women because it was something funny. But, they were never allowed to wear masks, because the masks would frighten the children. It was really nice. I wish those days were here again. I'm seventy-four, and I would still like those days.

The War Years

During the 1930s and 1940s, the Italian community in Whitney Pier (and elsewhere) experienced a particularly traumatic period in its history. Anti-Italian sentiments increased, people were abused verbally and, in some cases, individuals were interned. The "war years" initiated a major upheaval that had dramatic effects on individual lives and changed the complexion of the community forever.

We moved from Tupper Street during the early 1930s, the Depression years. We lived at Mr. Tucker's place for three years, and then this house was built in 1935. I was thirteen years old. Believe me; it wasn't easy to live here. This area was made up mostly of English people from St. Alban's Anglican Church. And of course, at that time, religion was an important issue. You were either a Protestant or a Catholic. If you were of a different religion, people didn't want to talk to you; they didn't want their children to talk to you. You weren't allowed in their homes. Number one, I was Italian and, number two, I was Catholic. I was sort of isolated. And, at that time, Mussolini went to war in Ethiopia. The kids around here, I guess they heard it at home, would call us "Mussolini," "fascists" and all kinds of names. Then at school, there was more name calling. Today, they would fight over it but, at that time, we didn't fight, because our parents wouldn't allow it. We didn't fight, but we were hurt.

I remember one girl, we were walking together, looked at my clothes and said: "Oh, you're clean; I thought you were going to be right dirty." See, it must have been something she heard at home. I didn't know what she meant at that time; but remembering these things, it hurts, it still hurts. Things are a little better now. But, when we first moved here it wasn't an easy place to live.

[Can you say something about the actual war period?] That's when some of the Italians were taken to the concentration camp. A group of men—Mike LaPenna, Mike Rannie, and others—used to meet at my cousin's (Dominic Nardocchio) shop. Mike LaPenna would always buy the Italian paper, and they would discuss what was happening in Italy. On account of all that, they were arrested and taken to the concentration camp. When war broke out, the police went to their place of work and just took them out. They were brought to the jail, where they were beaten. Then they were sent to the concentration camp in Petawawa, Ontario. Some of the men were not allowed to return to Sydney. Felice Martinello was one; he went to Hamilton, Ontario. Another one went to Montreal. There was a number of them. A lot, though, did come back to Sydney.

My brother Mike was not taken, but he had to report to the Mounties every second week. He was an "alien;" he was not a Canadian citizen. See, this was on account of people saying: "they're Italians, they're aliens, they're sending our secrets back to their country." You couldn't even speak your own language in front of a bunch of English people. But those poor men, they really suffered in the concentration camp. They were gone for years. Now, my husband was in the Canadian army; he went into the army in 1939 and came out in 1945. But no, it wasn't easy. After the war, my brothers got their citizenship papers, and they were okay. Mike worked in Halifax; he made uniforms for the sailors during the war. He was watched everywhere he went.

[What did this do to the community?] Well, those that remained were scared more than anything else. They didn't know what was going to take place—whether they were going to be arrested or not. Mike LaPenna was a lovely, lovely man. He never bothered a soul. Oh God, there were a lot of them. They minded their own business. They weren't "aliens" who took secrets out of here. So, it was a rough go.

Language

I didn't know any English when I first went to school. My mother taught me my prayers in Italian. When I went to school, I knew they were praying, because they blessed themselves, but I didn't know what they were saying. Well, they prayed in English, and I prayed in my own way. Then, I got used to the English, and I started to say different English words at home. But, my mother told me, "we speak nothing but Italian in this house." So I spoke English outside.

See, when we were growing up, we were verbally abused. You were scared to use your own language outside. So, you get used to using the other language, and it's true, if you don't use your language, you forget it. I had forgotten a lot of things. But, more recently, after an Italian friend moved to Lingan Road, I started to pick up different words again.

St. Nicholas Parish

Well, it was a nice little parish. The men built the church, and it was always full on Sundays. We had a beautiful choir. There were spaghetti suppers and picnics every year to make a few dollars for the parish, and we donated money to our Catholic schools—otherwise we wouldn't have had a school. The government didn't put up a school for us; we had to put up our own school. We had Villa Nova School and Holy Redeemer.

I don't know when St. Nicholas, our Italian church, was first built, but it burned down in 1922. I was born on July 15th at five o'clock in the evening, and the church burned down at one o'clock that morning. They say the fire was set, but I don't know. We built another church but,

Rev. E.J. D'Intino,
1943

Rev. D. Viola, P.P.
1911-25

Rev. R. MacLean, P.P.
1926-43

in 1972, that burned down too. On Halloween, I think. The St. Nicholas Hall that we have now was built that same year, and it opened in January of 1973.

We had three priests. Father Viola, Father MacLean, and then Father D'Intino. Father D'Intino was here the longest. He was the parish priest when the church burned down in 1972. He retired after that, and he went to the States.

Father D'Intino was from the Pier. His family was poor. But, when he was a student, he worked hard at the steel plant and helped his family. He was good to them.

Interior of St. Nicholas Church, early 1950s. Photo by Pamela Dawson.

May Parade, 1945, Hankard Street. Courtesy of Maurice Antonello.

And, he wasn't the only student to do that, there were a number of them. So, when he was ordained a priest, we had a big banquet for him. We sold tickets, gave him the money, and he gave it to his family. He was very good to his parents, and he was very good as a priest. He knew every prayer in the prayer book; he knew who the saint was for every day of the year, and he would pray sincerely. As a person, though, he could be cranky.

Now we are part of Holy Redeemer Parish. Holy Redeemer is the caretaker of St. Nicholas Hall. And, I think, it's going to stay like that. The Polish, Ukrainian, and Italian churches are small; there are not enough priests to go around. Holy Redeemer always used to have three priests, but now there is only one—Father MacDonald. So, he says Mass at St. Nicholas Hall at nine o'clock and then the twelve o'clock Mass at Holy Redeemer. The Italians always had their own priest, but now you can't get a priest. No one is going into the priesthood.

[Were the Italians in the Pier from any particular place in Italy?] No. There was a mixture. Mike LaPenna used to call it "*na minestra*" [a mixed vegetable soup]. We were all there together, but we weren't from any particular place. They all had their own little identity. It was lovely. They were very friendly people. I know, I grew up with them.

Section I

The Early Period:
Coal, Steel
and the
Italian Experience

Early Settlement:
The Giovannetti Family in Port Morien

By Lynn Billard and John Giovannetti
Edited by Sam Migliore

On February 2, 1997, Evo DiPierro and I visited John Giovannetti and his daughter, Lynn Billard, in Port Morien. The Giovannettis, as far as can be determined from both census records and oral tradition, are the Italian family with the longest roots in Cape Breton. Census records for Cape Breton County indicate that Lorenzo Giovannetti (1834-1907) arrived in Canada in 1855 and settled in the Port Morien area some time before 1871.[1] During our conversation, John and Lynn shared with us some details about their family history. Lorenzo is John Giovannetti's grandfather and Lynn Billard's great grandfather. What appears below are two versions of the story of how Lorenzo came to settle in Port Morien.

[John]: Lou, one of my uncles, sent up a letter from Newfoundland [for my mother] the time Dad died [in 1962]. The letter talks about how my grandfather landed in St. John's, Newfoundland. He had stowed away aboard a salt ship. That's how he got to Canada.

[Lynn]: Well, that's the story we were always taught. But, when we went over to Italy in the spring of 1996, we heard a different story.[2] It's actually quite interesting. [Guglielmina Giovannetti Fiori] says that my great grandfather, Lorenzo, left Tereglio because there was no work, and there was famine in the area. He walked to France with some gypsum statues on his back. I guess that was all he had, and he planned to use them to pay for his passage on the boat. When he got to France, though, someone broke the statues. The Captain took him anyway, and he travelled from France, not from Genoa, [to Newfoundland]. There was an interesting little [part to the story]; I'll read it to you as she wrote it:

During this travel, a big storm just rolled the ship, and the sailors were tired, but Lorenzo was very on the ball with the hoist, the ship's sails, because he was never tired. And the Captain was astonished. When the ship arrived, the Captain called Lorenzo and told him that if he could not find work that he should come back to the ship and there would be work for him for sure, as a seaman.

So, on the way [to Newfoundland], they got into a storm, and Lorenzo ended up saving the crew.

The story we always had was that he stowed away from Genoa, on a salt ship. They were in the Mediterranean when they found out that he was there, and the Captain was going to throw him overboard. But, they let him work his passage. He landed in St. John's and came from Newfoundland to Port Morien. He and his brother, Nicodemus (1841-1882), settled here in Morien. So, those are the stories; he didn't yield to his fate, he just kept going. I prefer to believe in the "stow away" story myself. [laughs] It sounds more [romantic].

[John]: Yeah, they are buried down here at the bottom of the lane. I never knew him. I don't know if he drowned or fell overboard down at the wharf one winter. He died shortly after. Never saw either one of them—grandfather or grandmother. All I know is hearsay, from listening to people talking. [Lynn]: Oral tradition. [John]: He was a rum-runner, a clockmaker, and he had a store down there. He had his own vessel.

A Letter From Newfoundland, 1962
St. John's, NFLD

Dear Mary,

Today I read a letter ... informing me that Joe had passed away. I am very sorry to know of his demise and my wife and daughter join me extending to you and your children our sincere sympathy....

Uncle Larry [Lorenzo] was the oldest of the family of five brothers and was the first to come to the New World. He knowing of the exploits of Columbus and Caboto, both of Genoa, went there from Tereglio, a beautiful hill top village where his father had a beautiful stone home built in 1745, as the stone by the front door has engraved on it....

Uncle Larry didn't intend to live his lifetime eating grapes and chestnuts, admiring the beauty of Tereglio, so he strolled off to Genoa. At Genoa, he found a vessel loaded with salt coming to Newfoundland. He asked the captain for a job, but there was nothing for him, a land man.... He asked the sailors to stow him away. So they put him in the salt, where he remained until they got far from land in the Mediterranean and came on deck. After much palaver, the captain threatening to throw him overboard, the captain told him ok, but he had to work his passage. That, he was happy to do. Thus the ship reached this city, the oldest in North America. Then only a fishing settlement. After that uncle Larry never lost his love for the sea, which in the end was the cause of his death. Uncle was a handy man, a sailor, a carpenter, a watch repairer and could turn his hand to most anything. But he was the most stubborn man I ever knew. He was a good Christian and attended Mass daily....

With love and kindest wishes,

I am, Your cousin,
Lou Giovannetti

Guglielmo Marconi and His Cape Breton Wireless Telegraphy (Radio) Station (1901-1904)

By Mary K. MacLeod

Born in Bologna, Italy, Guglielmo Marconi, in 1902, astounded the world with a wireless telegraph system that transmitted signals and messages between Europe and North America. Later, Marconi was to develop an international wireless system and a network of companies that would transform the state of world communications. The use of radio waves and antennas to carry signals through space is known today as "radio," but the systems in use in the early 20th century were referred to as "wireless telegraphy."

Marconi's experiments with wireless telegraphy were preceded by his experiments with electricity. He began his experiments as a boy on his parents' estate, Villa Grifone, a vineyard near Bologna. Marconi became so obsessed with his experiments that he lost interest in school and did not pursue any academic qualifications beyond graduation from the Leghorn Academy.

While Marconi received much encouragement from his Anglo-Irish mother, Annie Ross, his father, Giuseppe Marconi, was far more skeptical. By 1894 Marconi had become fascinated with electromagnetic, or Hertzian, waves and wondered if the waves could be used to transmit signals through space and across long distances. After several successful attempts at transmitting and receiving the waves, the father became convinced of the worth of Marconi pursuing his ideas and gave Guglielmo the resources to carry out more demonstrations. Marconi soon devised an apparatus which transmitted and received signals over several kilometres. Delighted with his results and convinced of their importance to world communication, Marconi appealed to the Italian government for assistance to develop his apparatus, but his plan was rejected.

Too late the family realized that Marconi should have approached the Italian navy and not the Ministry of Post and Telegraph which was responsible for communication. Overland communication was already serviced by the telegraph and telephone. The Ministry was "understandably indifferent to a technique that for their purposes, offered no advantages over the well-established technology of conventional telegraphy."[1] Marconi should have directed his proposal and invention at marine communication, specifically at service to shipping. Marine men might have been more aware of the possible applications of wireless communication at sea.[2]

Because of the Italian government's rejection and because of his mother's connections in the United Kingdom, Marconi and his mother decided to move to England to pursue his dreams. Because marine application would obviously be important, it made sense to develop and promote wireless telegraphy in the world's leading maritime nation.[3] In February 1896, Marconi and his mother arrived in London where Guglielmo (with the assistance of the Jameson Family—his mother's relatives, who had made their fortune in Irish whiskey and other ventures) immediately drew up a patent specification to protect his invention. In June, he filed his application in what was to be the world's first radio patent. It was granted in July 1897.

With the assistance of the Jameson family, Marconi established contacts with the British post office which had the monopoly on all postal and telegraphic communication in the United Kingdom. At the post office, Marconi was befriended by Sir William Preece who was responsible for all major forms of communication—mail, telegraph and cable. Preece was also experimenting with wireless telegraphy, although he was not using Hertzian waves, as was Marconi. Preece allowed Marconi the use of his laboratory.

For a year Marconi worked with Preece and other members of the post office conducting experiments, many of which were successful. Meanwhile, rival systems appeared on the scene, and Marconi was forced to establish his own system on a sound business footing. The post office had not offered any financial remuneration or any long-term commitment to assist in the development and promotion of his invention. The Royal Navy, which had paid for any demonstrations Marconi had done for it, had placed no orders, nor had it given him any encouragement to expect future work. Most of Marconi's expenses had been borne by the Jamesons, and "as the pit was not bottomless, it was essential to offset expenditures to some degree with at least a token income."[4]

Marconi's cousin and friend, Henry Jameson Davis, secured the necessary financial backing for the company and, on July 20, 1897, The Wireless Telegraph and Signal Company Limited was registered.[5] (The name was later changed to Marconi's Wireless Telegraph Company Limited.) The company gave Marconi the financial freedom he so desperately needed. He could now operate independently of government. The post office, however, viewed his company as a potential competitor that would eventually challenge its monopoly over British telegraph services. As a result, Marconi and the Post Office severed their relationship.

Marconi set out to publicize his apparatus and company to attract new investors and, more importantly, secure badly needed orders. In 1899 his apparatus spanned the English Channel for the first time. By spanning the Channel (which, in itself, evoked feelings of awe and greatness because of the role it had played in international commerce and British naval history), Marconi captured the imagination of the British public and the world's press. Marconi had inaugurated international wireless telegraphy. Subsequent tests disproved the long-held theory that radio waves could not reach beyond the horizon. Despite this success, however, orders were slow. Nevertheless, Marconi persevered and, within three years, was operating a small number of coastal stations in Britain and had equipped a few commercial vessels with his apparatus.

While the young company was struggling to maintain solvency and attract new orders, Marconi announced his intention to link the continents of Europe and North America with his apparatus. This linkage would be the first step in his dream to unite the British Empire and then the world via wireless telegraphy. Poldhu, England, would serve as the European terminus, and Cape Breton would house the North American station.

Cape Breton was not Marconi's first choice as the location for the western (North American) terminus of his trans-Atlantic service. Newfoundland and Cape Cod were earlier preferences but circumstances dictated otherwise. For instance, his first selection was South Wellfleet near Cape Cod, but the station he had erected there was smashed by a severe storm. Newfoundland was his second choice. In Newfoundland in 1901, via the use of kites and balloons (no station had been established), Marconi had received the first wireless transmission—the Morse Code signal for the letter "s"—from Poldhu. The transmission, while astounding the world, had caused the Anglo-American Telegraph (cable) Company to threaten court action over Marconi's infringement on all telegraphic business within Newfoundland.

Marconi would probably have relocated in Cape Cod had it not been for the intervention of William Smith, Secretary to the Canadian post office, who had been in Newfoundland during Marconi's experiments. Smith alerted Canadian authorities to Marconi's need for a new site. Negotiations brought Marconi to Canada and Cape Breton. The negotiations between Marconi, the Canadian government and Cape Breton authorities lasted from December 1901, through March 17, 1902, and culminated in an agreement including an $80,000 grant, which permitted the establishment of the station in Cape Breton.[6] In addition, the Nova Scotia government and Cape Breton business and municipal leaders offered concessions to Marconi including a provincial monopoly on wireless telegraphy, municipal tax incentives and the offer of free land by the Dominion Coal Company.

Marconi was delighted. The Canadian government's willingness to cooperate was contrary to his experience with the Italian, British and American governments—"governments as a rule do not display very keen interest in new inventions."[7] Marconi's delight was heightened by the financial security which it brought to his enterprise. His transatlantic venture was a tremendous drain on his company's resources—a company which was desperately trying to keep afloat. The Board of Directors had been shocked by Marconi's entrance into the transatlantic venture and was using every means at its disposal to garner new funds and stabilize expenses.

While negotiations were taking place, Marconi tried to decide which of four locations in Cape Breton—Burying Ground Point, Louisbourg; Main-a-Dieu, Port Morien and Table Head, Glace Bay—to select as the site for the station. There was ardent competition among the communities. The *Glace Bay Gazette* urged the town to do everything possible to facilitate Table Head's selection. Because Marconi would need electric power to operate his plant, the *Gazette* urged the town council to offer him "a service sufficient to cover the actual cost of the service" and give him a ten-year exemption from taxes.[8] The *Gazette* stressed that these concessions would be offset by the tremendous commercial advantages the town would gain from the location of a Marconi station at Glace Bay. The $60,000 plant would employ 100 men in the construction phase and a number of men in the operational phase; in addition, "the show qualities of such an enterprise ... would attract thousands of visitors yearly."[9] Prominent members of the Glace Bay community lobbied Marconi on behalf of the Table Head site.

The Nova Scotian press could not believe its good fortune in having the Marconi story to report. Reporters were astounded that one of the most famous inventors in the world might establish a station in their midst.[10] Praise was lavished on the federal and provincial governments for their efforts to attract Marconi to Cape Breton. Toward the end of March, Marconi announced that Table Head had been selected as the site for the new station. Work began almost immediately, and Marconi departed for England.

Marconi assigned the construction of the station to Richard Vyvyan, whom he had appointed managing engineer of The Marconi Wireless Telegraph Company of Canada Limited, a subsidiary of the parent English company.[11] Vyvyan remained in Glace Bay for eight years.

Marconi was due to return to Cape Breton in May 1902, but he was stricken with a severe case of influenza which prohibited a trip across the Atlantic. Rumour mongers attributed the postponement to mental collapse. Meanwhile the engineers and contractors were busy solving "last minute" problems, and by mid-June, most of the difficulties had been overcome. Toward the end of the month, testing began without Marconi and in great secrecy.

Marconi arrived in Glace Bay via the *Carlo Alberto* on October 31 and was greeted by a flotilla of small boats and hundreds of spectators. Marconi was accompanied by a group of experienced, wireless telegraphers to assist with the experiments. His intention was to stay in Glace Bay for about two weeks to install the new apparatus, which he had been working on in England and then to conduct a series of tests with Poldhu. Marconi seriously underestimated the amount of time required—the testing would take three months.

Marconi began testing in November at the onset of a harsh Cape Breton winter. The bitterly cold and stormy weather added to the frustrations when, throughout the following three months, failure followed upon failure. November was especially depressing; from November 1 through November 29, every test failed.

By now Marconi was under intense and increased pressure when news arrived that the delays had caused his company's shares to tumble, thus endangering the financial arrangements required to enable the transatlantic venture to continue. Only a proven success could entice stock market players to invest or increase their investment in his company. This pressure tried the patience and ingenuity of Marconi and his colleagues. And, after one failed test too many, he concluded that either Poldhu had an insufficient supply of power or the arrangement of the plant was unsatisfactory. Marconi decided the fault lay with the former and reversed the experiments. Table Head, with the larger power capacity, would now transmit and Poldhu would receive. Many experiments followed with many different arrangements of plant and aerials, but the results were so inconsistent that it was difficult to know whether progress had been made. The trouble lay with the wavelengths, but at the time, this was unknown:

> We knew nothing then about the effort of the length of the wave transmitted governing the distance over which communication could be affected. We did not even have means or instruments for measuring wavelengths, in fact we did not know what wavelength we were using.[12]

They were using an aerial and circuit to transmit a 2,000-metre wavelength when one of 6,000 to 8,000 was required. Many tests and frustrations lay ahead before they discovered this error.[13]

The first attempt at transmitting from Table Head occurred on November 19th with Poldhu failing to receive the signals. Day-by-day, various changes were made without success. Then, on December 5th, after further adjustments to the apparatus, some readable signals were received over a two-hour period. "Weak, readable signals for the first half-hour; nothing doing during the next three-quarters; last three-quarters readable and recordable on tape."[14]

During the following two nights, using exactly the same aerial arrangements, no signals were received. The inconsistencies made it very difficult to determine whether one transmitting arrangement was better than another, and even Marconi, known for his self-restraint, lost his composure, swore and smashed his fists on the table. Marconi persisted and changed the aerial arrangement every day until December 14, when Poldhu reported "readable signals through the two-hour programme."[15]

Guglielmo Marconi, 1896. Collection: MG 12. 214 E1. Beaton Institute, Cape Breton University.

The first matter to handle was protocol. To whom should the first messages be sent? No one must feel slighted. Financial pressures and the need to silence press criticism dictated the decision: the first message would be sent from a representative of the press to dispel any negative reaction similar to that which greeted his announcement in Newfoundland. Marconi decided the first message would be sent from Dr. Parkin, correspondent for *The Times* of London.

The message was sent the following night, December 15, 1902, using the same aerial arrangement as on the 14. Although the weather did not look promising during the day, with heavy winds lashing the station and swaying the huge aerials, conditions were near perfect as night fell. The air was cold and clear and the moon shone brightly on the snow-covered ground. On the third attempt between 10 p.m. and midnight, the message was transmitted and received. The first message despatched across the Atlantic via wireless read:

> Times, London: Being present at transmission in Marconi's Canadian station, have the honour to send through Times inventor's first transatlantic message of greetings to England and Italy.[16]

Despite the historic nature of the transmission, little celebrating was done at Table Head. Marconi's only concession to the occasion was to gather his men at the foot of one of the towers in the cold Cape Breton dawn and raise the British and Italian flags, which were soon destroyed by a fierce gale and rainstorm which swept the coast. By late morning there was no sign of them to indicate the historic achievement of the previous night.

In reality, Marconi had little to celebrate. Although Parkin's message had been transmitted and received at Poldhu, it could not be delivered to its destination, the *London Times*, until the demands of protocol were met. Protocol demanded that messages first be sent to the kings of Britain and Italy, but Marconi failed to get the messages through. Six frustrating days passed before he overcame the obstacles, including a broken generator that forced him to temporarily discontinue attempts at transmission. Even when this was repaired, difficulties continued. Only through sheer persistence, determination and desperation were the royal messages transmitted, received and delivered on the sixth day, December 21. Only then could Parkin's message be released to the *Times* and the world.[17]

Marconi, Vyvyan and colleagues were almost totally disheartened by the inconsistencies prevalent even when conditions were ideal at both stations. The signals would vary from good, readable signals to absolutely nothing within a two-to-three minute time span. Marconi and his men worked at a frantic pace trying to find the causes of the inconsistencies. They spent their days readjusting the apparatus and their evenings trying to transmit, but they continually failed.

From a technical point of view, Marconi should have closed the station and used his energy to identify and isolate the problem, but he could not afford to. Parkin's message and the messages to royalty had had the desired effect. World interest had been awakened, and hundreds of messages were awaiting transmission. Anyone who was anyone, including reporters, wanted to be part of history and have their messages sent. If they were not transmitted, Marconi would not be able to secure the investments required to keep his company solvent. The more favourable the publicity received, the more shares he could sell. But the inconsistencies could not be overcome, and he was forced to transmit and receive at a painfully slow pace. From December 15th through January 20th, only thirty-eight messages were sent with varying results. According to Vyvyan: "Some were repeated twenty-four times before they were received, whereas others were repeated six times and received correctly on each occasion."[18]

Marconi gave no hint to the outside world that the difficulties confronting efficient and accurate transmissions were of major importance. In remarks to the press, he implied that a regular commercial service would begin shortly. But Marconi soon decided that the testing could not go on as matters stood. He decided to close both Poldhu and Table Head for a period of re-evaluation and readjustment. The three-month closure extending from January 22 to March 20, 1903, brought the Marconi enterprise to the brink of financial disaster, but Marconi had little choice. He could not run the risk of declaring the transatlantic service open for business when it was neither ready nor perfected. Any sign of imperfections would give his powerful competitors, including the cable operators, ammunition to launch a negative publicity campaign that would drive his already financially weakened company into insolvency. It was far better to endure self-imposed financial constraints rather than ones imposed upon the company from outside. If the closure was successful, the company would be able to recover its losses, he hoped.

Marconi spent most of the three-month closure in Britain, where he personally supervised and conducted many of the experiments and adjustments at Poldhu. As he had feared, his critics used the delay to attack the credibility of his apparatus and his vision of a transatlantic network.

On March 20, the stations were reactivated and experiments resumed. With Poldhu's successful receipt of messages during four nights of transmissions, hopes rose, and Marconi succumbed to requests from the *London Times* to initiate a news service from Canada. A limited service was introduced on March 28, 1903, but it came to an abrupt end on April 6, when the Table Head antenna collapsed under the weight of a silver thaw. Although short in duration, this effort constituted the first transatlantic news service.[19] The summer was a difficult one. Inconsistencies continued. It seemed that no experiment could produce any consistent result.

Still more testing was undertaken. Marconi and his men worked throughout the fall with still no hint to the solution. Marconi was becoming quite desperate because of the financial position the failed tests were placing his companies in. He was forced to scramble to save his companies. Although great progress had been made in equipping ships with wireless apparatus and establishing shore stations, the financial returns were too small to cover the huge investments the company had been making. During 1903 and 1904, respectively, the Canadian company lost $33,125 and $36,199. Both losses resulted from expenses incurred at Table Head and the company headquarters at Montreal.[20] In 1903 no revenue at all had been earned at Table Head.

The only way money could be earned was by releasing Table Head and Poldhu from transatlantic experimentation and developing a new transatlantic service to shipping. The Cunard Company agreed to pay ten cents per one hundred words received per day. The service was an outstanding success. By 1905, ship-to-shore communication had become an indispensable way of communicating with ocean-going vessels.[21] The demand for the service was so great that several new shore stations were constructed on both sides of the Atlantic. The revenues were appreciable and helped the companies gain a degree of solvency.

Large as the revenues were, Marconi hated having to orient the stations toward profit-making. The discontinuance of the transatlantic testing was an admission of failure that Marconi was not used to making, especially in public. His critics rejoiced in the setback, while he could only "grit his teeth" and hope their joy would be short-lived. In public he betrayed no emotion and talked as if the setback were only a temporary aberration: difficulties such as these were to be expected when attempting a revolutionary change.

During the closure, Marconi's mind wrestled with the causes that might have generated such inconsistent results throughout the past two years of testing. He finally concluded that the wavelengths generated were far too short. He would have either to erect a mammoth, super power station at Table Head or to relocate to a larger site that could accommodate an antenna capable of radiating a much longer wavelength than Table Head. Either decision invoked staggering financial consequences. He decided to relocate, believing the better chance of success probably rested with the larger site. He could not risk the possibility of another failure at Table Head. It was better to invest the money on a new station.

Marconi relocated his station about six miles from Table Head and three and a half miles inland (which locals quickly nicknamed "Marconi Towers") toward the community of Port Morien. It was from this much larger complex, operating in conjunction with a new European terminus in Clifden, Ireland, that, in 1907, Marconi achieved his dream of establishing a successful, commercial wireless telegraph system which helped to revolutionize forever our communication with each other.

Thomas Cozzolino:
An Introduction

By Elizabeth Beaton

Thomas Cozzolino was born in 1866 in Caiazzo, near Napoli, Italy. He arrived in North America in 1880. At the age of twenty-four, he married Emily Lynch of Madawaska, New Brunswick. By the time he was twenty-six years of age, he had been a contractor in charge of hundreds of construction and excavation workers. He had travelled and worked in many parts of Canada and the United States on railway, pier, bridge, dam and industrial construction. While Cape Bretoners may know of Thomas Cozzolino because of his association with the building of the Dominion Steel (DISCO) plant in Sydney, his role as leader of large numbers of working men had a wider significance within the context of important developments in transportation, industry and immigration policies and attitudes in both Canada and the United States. Cozzolino's story also represents, in a particular way, the experience of the Italians who came to Sydney and have remained.

When Thomas Cozzolino left his home for America at the age of fourteen, he was simply one of thousands of young men who were leaving Italy at that time in search of work. That Cozzolino was involved in the construction and excavation trades was also part of a larger context of the Italian/North American experience. Indeed, of the Italian migrants to North America, some 30 to 50 per cent were found in the construction and excavation trades.[1] While excavation obviously required "pick and shovel" work, it also demanded heavy machinery operators, "shooters" (dynamite blasters) and other highly specialized skills, such as bricklaying and masonry.[2]

Cozzolino's work accounts allow us a chance to see how the internationalization of labour was to become synonymous with industrialization and expansionist policies all over North America. As a teenager, Cozzolino was a water boy on the West

Shore Railway in the Catskill Mountains in New York State. A surprisingly short time later, in 1887, he was a foreman with the building of the CPR line between Smith Falls, Ontario, and Montreal. In the Maritimes, where the Intercolonial Railway was the key to unity in Eastern Canada, linking up the regional economy with that of the new dominion, Cozzolino worked on the section near Boisdale in (1887) and later near Mulgrave and Fort Laurence on mainland, Nova Scotia. Cozzolino and his men were responsible for a significant portion of the sixteen million cubic yards of excavated materials in the Intercolonial's railbed and the two hundred thousand tons of masonry in the railway's bridges.[3] He was foreman over much of the excavation for major parts of the DISCO plant, and he laid water-lines to Sydney from Sydney River. Later, as CEO of the Nova Scotia Construction Company, he was responsible for the building of the subway separating Whitney Pier from Sydney and also the construction of piers in Halifax and St. John's, Newfoundland.

Cozzolino started his life of work in construction jobs as a sojourner. As such, he shared the same transitory, and sometimes brutal, existence experienced by so many young Italian men in North America at the time. He recounts being short of money and food, being poorly dressed for cold weather, being a "greenhorn" in terms of the work itself, and being involved in legal action against an unjust "middleman." The Italian sojourners' comings and goings were haphazard and frequent, depending on available employment. Winter restricted their work, and there was often a stressful waiting period between one project and the next.[4] During those periods, the sojourners were considered to be "indigent" and were in danger of being deported.

Cozzolino's ambition and ability are clearly evident in his decision not to stay in the position of labourer. He found himself a job in a business and was learning accounting and, even more important; he was learning English. It was his capacity for languages, including Russian, that enabled him to become an interpreter, a recruiter and to finally be recognized as an agent and subcontractor. Over his career, Cozzolino had charge of several thousand working men. Most of these men came via New York and Montreal through a very effective network among workers (kinsfolk and people of the same village) in common support of the pursuit of jobs. The passage of Italian workers to Canada was also facilitated by Canadian authorities, even though the *Alien Labour Act* forbade the importation of foreign labour.[5] Many Italians entered Canada before and after the *Act* was passed, mainly because of the need created by Canadian development; indeed, some 50,000 entered Canada between 1890 and 1914. Even at that, the Immigration Branch allowed their admission only as sojourners.[6] However, the normal rules for entry into Canada—continuous journey, sufficient money, literacy—were, at certain times, foregone in order to allow Italians to enter. The "continuous journey" requirement was of particular importance to the Italians, since almost all had worked in the United States for a period of time before attempting to enter Canada. During periods when there was a particularly great demand for Italian navvies, all that was needed was a letter from the contractor guaranteeing work and assurance that they would be allowed back into the United States on completion of their work.[7]

The construction of the Dominion Steel plant brought large numbers of these workers to Sydney, usually through arrangements made by "employment agents" who were either hired by the steel company or who worked privately. Thomas Cozzolino was one of these, as was a Mr. Marazza, who had come to Nova Scotia in 1894, and who had "handled thousands of Italians for local contractors."[8] It was normal practice for these agents to look after the living accommodations for the men they had hired; if the company provided sleeping quarters, then the agent was responsible for providing food. In his descriptions of the work camps which held several hundred single men, Cozzolino recalled that he arranged for food for his men and for an oven to bake bread. Some of the earliest Italian workers in Sydney occupied "Shackville," a cluster of about twenty buildings located across the Sydney & Louisburg Railway tracks just inside gate number five at Railroad Street during the construction of the plant about 1900.[9] They also occupied shacks in rural areas: at gravel and limestone quarries at Crawley's Creek and George's River[10] and at the origin of the water lines at Sydney River. The agent, Marazza, provided privately-owned shacks.[11] A correspondent for the *Halifax Herald* reported on the conditions of this housing:

> The Italian quarter at the coke ovens is squalid, but not tough dives ...
> Mr. Marazza ... maintains a number of dwellings for the men which are
> orderly and in good condition. The men do their own cooking and are
> frugal livers trying to save every cent they can to send away.[12]

As time passed, lodging for Italians was found in tenements or "hotels" which were operated by the employment agents. For instance, Cozzolino maintained several "tenement" houses located on Tupper Street midway between Victoria Road and Lingan Road. Owned by a landlord who resided in Italy, the tenements were occupied by fifty Italian labourers employed at the steel works. Photographic evidence indicates that there were few services for the lodgers: the men had to cook in their rooms and hang their laundry from their windows; their bathrooms and privies were primitive and unsanitary, if they existed at all.[13] To the elite in Sydney, these places represented "low living" in terms of both architectural aesthetics and behaviour. In 1901, a journalist made the connection between worker housing and primitive living:

> "Little Italy" and the Italian hotels are a unique feature of Cokovia. These
> are four oblong, dull red, one storied structures, with windows few and
> small, small doors, and altogether of a most cheerless and depressing
> appearance. Their aspect on a dull rainy day would give an indigo tinge
> to the mind of the most optimistic and robust mortals. Here are lodged

the Italian labourers, who live their sociable, contented if squalid lives, in the way they like best.[14]

In fact, this housing was typical for almost all single, male, wage labourers in Sydney and other boom towns in North America at the time. Living was not luxurious; it was rough and barely adequate, and the workers did with what they had. That the newspapers made special mention of the Italians and their "liking" for the situation simply underlines the generally negative opinions about them in a city that was predominately Anglo-Celtic.

Across North America, nativist attitudes toward Italians were strong wherever they went to work: they were called "Dagos" and were consistently singled out as an undesirable group. We see that Cozzolino felt that his men were under constant threat of violent attack when he worked in the United States, hence they often carried guns. In Sydney, newspapers strove to back the view that Italians were inclined to be violent, immoral or stupid. Long-standing Sydney residents felt so threatened by the Italian presence that two Italians were appointed to the local police force to ensure the "prompt arrest and conviction of their countrymen."[15] Some of the incidents would be considered very trivial in most contexts; yet local authorities appear to have sought harsh penalties, such as the case where a Cokovia Italian was caught robbing a hencoop: "Stole Six Hens, Got Six Months...."[16] Common accidents were often given a particular slant that reflected badly on the workers: "some Italians, while fooling with an explosive at their shack near the light station came near to setting fire to the building."[17] Italian workers were also blamed for smallpox cases[18] in a crowded town which had notoriously bad sewage and drainage systems and where smallpox was endemic because of these conditions. When serious crimes were committed, newspapers made certain that the ethnic origin of the accused Italians was front and centre.[19] The agent, Marazza, defended the Italian workers, declaring that they were law abiding people:

> "...they come out here to labour for the sake of feeding their dear ones; they never give any trouble or ask for anything but work, and, in this way, are not afraid however hard or difficult it may be, so long as they can make money to send to their families."[20]

Nevertheless, these reports fed the strong prejudice against the Italians and, like the attitudes connecting housing with immorality and squalid living, they became incorporated into the ethnocentric lifeview of Sydney residents.[21]

Contrary to some historical interpretations suggesting that Italian sojourners undercut the native-born wage earners, there is evidence that fair wages and reasonable working conditions were an important factor in their work.[22] Cozzolino relates several instances in which he insisted on $1.50 per day or more for his men, wages that were higher than the going rate to other workers, whether native or foreign. In one case, in order to avoid a strike, Cozzolino agreed not to tell other workers what the Italians were getting. If the wages were not considered adequate or if they felt cheated by the contractor, the agent or *padrone* and his men might take the contractor to court or they might refuse all wages until the proper amount was offered. Or, if the dissatisfaction occurred early in the job, the workers might simply walk off the job and go elsewhere. The latter occurred in 1902 when DISCO failed to provide adequate living accommodations for Italian workers under Cozzolino at Marble Mountain: the men packed up and returned to the United States.

The Italian workers' strong expectation of justice and their worker solidarity was demonstrated by their participation in direct "job action" at the steel plant in Sydney. Italian workers, who had come with Cozzolino and Marazza, were "blacklisted" and forced to leave town as a result of "illegal" strikes at the coke ovens in 1900, 1901 and 1903.[23] They also took an active part in the official 1904 strike at the steel plant, suffering the inevitable "black-listing."[24] When the Italians exerted collective resistance to unacceptable conditions, they were branded by the local media as "uncivilized rabble" or "wild and hot," and their struggles were not supported by the mainstream labour organizations.[25] Yet, through these strikes, it was Italians and other immigrants who helped to set standards for working conditions in Cape Breton and other parts of the country. It is also significant that Italians continued to be sought as workers even as their countrymen were being moved out because of strikes.

It is impossible to get any idea of the real numbers of Italians in Sydney during the early years of the steel plant's history. As sojourners and tenants (rather than property owners), they were not included in the 1901 census; their exclusion may also have been a signal of the local feeling toward them. It would appear that Italians migrated in and out of Sydney all during the construction period and into the operational period of the steel plant's history spokesperson, and that many came to Sydney on their own after the initial construction. Italians worked at the George's River dolomite mine and for the Town of Sydney, but the majority found work in the coke ovens, possibly because of their knowledge of brickworks, although any real status as bricklayers was closed to them for many years.

Today's Italian community in Sydney is evidence that several hundred of the workers stayed, that they eventually brought their families and established a vibrant Italian community in Cape Breton. Several factors supported the Italians' community development. The Italian Consular Agency, of which Tony Di Pistone was a spokesperson as early as 1900, helped to maintain ties between the immigrants and the Old Country. But, other, locally based institutions played a more primary role in enhancing ethnic solidarity. St. Nicholas Catholic Church was constructed in 1911-1912, and an Italian priest, Father Viola, was brought in to serve the spiritual needs of the Italian community. At about the same time, an Italian Methodist Mission was established on Lingan Road. Part of the Social Gospel Movement, the Mission offered practical assistance to the Italians (and other immigrants)—such as language training and social services. An Italian mutual benefit society resulted from a meeting at Thomas Cozzolino's residence on Pitt Street in February 1902. The officers of the organization, called "Sabastrano Caboto" were, president, Thomas Cozzolino; 1st vice-president, A. Del Vecchio; corresponding secretary, G. Castellano; financial secretary, T. D. Pistone (*sic*); Treasurer, W. T. Lynch; council, Leopold Di Filipo; J. Caesar, D. Mastroiami, A. Nitto, A. Riccio, D. Gaglirdo, A. Nazzucco (*sic*); book revisors, J. Giovanetti, A. Riccio; flag holders, (British) G. Carazzo, (Italian) E. Artobano.[26] A circular, "Appelio Alia Colonia Italiana," drew attention to the formation of the society to approximately 150 Italians in the area at the time.[27] The extent of the society's activities is uncertain, perhaps because its leadership was middle-class, and its membership was made up of sojourning workers living in Whitney Pier. Another mutual society, St. Rita's, was formed at the construction of St. Nicholas Church on William Street in Whitney Pier in 1912; the society's hall was built behind the church on Hankard St. In the 1920s, the Giovinezza Italia benefit society was formed, which lasted until the 1930s.

On reading this account of Thomas Cozzolino's life, one may be struck by his incredible achievement and obvious leadership qualities. At the same time, Cozzolino showed a deep caring for family and religious values, for the quality and efficiency of the work he provided, and for the well-being of those who worked for him. In keeping with Italian tradition, he also appears to have appreciated the value of good and sufficient food for himself and his workers. Thomas Cozzolino is important to our understanding of both Canadian and Cape Breton history. As an Italian immigrant, he experienced success as well as hardship in his extraordinary work life; his life characterized many of the national and global events and situations of the late 19th and early 20th centuries; and, he exemplified a standard of self-worth and progressiveness that has sustained the Cape Breton Italian community throughout the 20th century.

Memoirs of Thomas Cozzolino[1]

Born in Italy, December, 1866
Died in Sydney, NS, September, 1949

Edited by Sam Migliore

My mother[2] died when I was thirteen years old. She was the last of four to die. My brother died first, at twenty-three years of age, then my sisters—one was seventeen and the other eighteen. They all died of cholera within a three month period in 1879. Many people died of cholera that year. Mother was only fifty-five years old. Father[3] and I were left alone. I was lonely.

I often heard people speaking of America and what a wonderful country it was. At thirteen and one half, I began telling father that I wanted to go there. He laughed at the idea of one so young wanting to leave home to go so far alone. I however spoke of it every day. Finally, to be rid of me, he said: "Well, if you can get the money for your passage, you may go." He felt sure that would be the end of it; there was no one who could or would give me the money for such a trip.

Father, however, had a friend, named Salvatore, who would do anything for him. I knew Salvatore would not give me the money to go away against my father's wishes. But, one day, I took the opportunity to ask. My father was a Contractor of Highways, and he paid the men every Saturday evening. I said to Salvatore, "My father is eighty dollars short and wants to know if you would help." He said yes. The next day, I went to Piedimond, twelve miles from our place, for my papers.

Once the arrangements were made, I told father I was going and asked for his consent. He did not believe me at first, but then said: "If you are so determined to go, I will give you my consent." I told him, "I will earn and will take care of you when you are old." He wanted to know where I got the money, but I would not tell him. He then said, "You'll be sorry when, in the middle of the ocean, you see only sky and sea." I then went to see my godmother. She too tried her best to dissuade me. But when she heard that my father had given his consent, she said "May God bless you in all your undertakings and help you in all your need," and then gave me twenty dollars in gold.

Because of my age, father had to go before a notary to sign my travel papers. He signed them with tears in his eyes. He said, "Boy you are leaving me all alone." I felt sorry for him, but I repeated: "I'll earn lots of money, and I will send it to you." Although delighted that my papers were now signed, I left my father broken hearted, weeping over me, still trying to dissuade me, saying he feared something might happen to me. But I was full of courage and looked forward to my new adventure.

I went to Naples with ten other men from my area. There I called to see an old Auntie of mine and told her of my plans. She thought it was foolish and could not understand why my father had signed the papers. When she realized I was telling the truth, she said: "Son, may God bless and protect you on your long journey and keep you pure in mind and heart; don't forget your religion wherever you are." She then kissed me and gave me eighty dollars in gold.

We left Naples by steamer that evening, the first of December 1880. We went to Genoa, then to Nice, and on to Marseilles in France. Our steamer was a freighter so we went to every port to load and unload merchandise. We remained in Marseilles for two days, then travelled by train to Bordeaux where we stayed for another two days. From there we caught a small steamer, which was to take us to New York in six days time, but it took us all of sixteen days to make it. The sea was rough, and we had engine trouble. For three days, we drifted anywhere the wind would take us. I began to fear that I would never see land again, and I remembered my father's words: "When you see only sky and water you will be sorry." It was true; every porthole had to be closed, and we were all locked downstairs for four days.

I, however, put my trust in God and at once felt better. I asked the cook if he could use some help in the kitchen. I was willing to do anything—wash dishes, peel potatoes. I had a difficult time to make him understand me, but he understood and kept me in the kitchen with three others to help with the work. I was glad not to be locked downstairs. But believe me, the sea was very rough. After getting our engine going again, we encountered a heavy fog for three days. We could not see anything; the whistle was going day and night.

On December 26, 1880, at night, we arrived in New York. The first thing I did was thank God for my safe passage. I was glad to be near land again. I was thrilled at the sight of all the electric lights; the harbour was beautiful.

The next morning, we landed at Castle Garden. As we had no friends to meet us, we remained there and slept on the floor for over twenty days. I still had about eighty dollars, but I helped others to get something to eat, and the money went fast. After ten days, I was broke. To get something to eat, I had to sell some of my gold rings for hardly anything. I began to miss my home; I was afraid of starving, especially when it started to snow. The winter was setting in. It was very cold, and I was not used to such cold weather. I had never seen snow before. I had a pair of light shoes, and they soon got wet. I had a very light overcoat. This is the way I was accustomed to dress for school in Italy. We were in Castle Garden for twenty days, but I thought it was more like two months.

One day a man came and said he wanted 300 men to work on the West Shore Railway, at a place called the Catskill Mountains, New York. We told him we were willing to work, but we did not have the money to travel there. He said, "I will pay your fare, and you can pay me back so much per month from your wages." So early next morning, it was the sixteenth day of January, 1881, we started out. It was awful cold. We arrived at the Catskill Mountains at about ten in the morning and had to walk about ten miles through the snow. None of us were accustomed to such cold and snow. We all had light shoes, no rubbers; in no time my feet got all wet. I had no woolen socks, but I kept on with the crowd. We arrived at the construction camp toward the evening of the same day. We were pretty tired.

The next morning, we went to work. As I had never done any work before, I was made water boy. After a few weeks, they placed me in a "big rock cut;" the weather was so cold I could not stand it. I had a pair of mitts a woman had made for me out of some old pieces of clothes. My fingers were freezing. As an excuse to get home, I took a stone and cut my finger; I told the boss I was hurt and I was going back to the camp. In those days, no one was allowed to remain in the camp. The "walking boss" would come in every morning and get everyone out unless you were very sick. On my way back, I met the "walking boss." He stopped me and wanted to know where I was going. I showed him my finger. He gave me a new job. Even though I had no experience, he sent me back to work as a mule driver. Since they were going to pay me the same wages as the labourers, I thought I would try it.

On my first trip with the mule, we reached the dumping area without a problem. But when I tried to back the mule to the edge of the cliff, I could not hold him. He went over the embankment, cart and all, about thirty-five feet. I was afraid; the cart was all broken up, but the mule was alright. I looked around and saw the "walking boss" coming towards me with a stick. I was afraid he was going to hit me; instead, he went for the mule, then gave me the stick saying "use this stick on him, and he will be alright." I did use the stick and found that the work went well.

That night, however, I began to think about all I had been through. I was getting discouraged, so I wrote my father asking him to send me enough money to return to Italy. But, before I received a reply—it took six weeks—I was doing pretty well. I had a new job in a grocery store selling provisions to the men and making entries into the books when they bought things on credit. When I received my father's letter, there was a ticket for passage from New York to Naples enclosed. I immediately returned the ticket to him and thanked him for being so kind. Later, I sent Salvatore the eighty dollars I had borrowed from him, and thanked him for his kindness as well. I finally let my father know where I had gotten the money to come to America. Salvatore had never mentioned the eighty dollars to him; he thought father was still short of cash and knew that he would be repaid at some point.

I worked in the store for about four months. In all, I stayed in the Catskills for about five months. From there we all went to a place called Amsterdam, New York, where they were building the West Shore Railway and a canal from Buffalo to Albany. I worked on the canal project as a labourer. As they were paying more for men who could drill, two other boys and I would go in the evening after our days work to try to learn to use the hammer. The three of us got so we could use the hammer pretty well. We got on the drilling gang and received 50 cents more per day. I kept that up for several months. From there we went to Little Falls, New York, to do the same type of work.

By the spring of 1882, I had learned a little English and got a position as interpreter for the Italians. I had also learned a bit of Russian, so the contractor sent me to New York to hire more men.

That fall a man came from Indiana looking for labourers to work at a quarry. He offered good pay. Someone sent him to me, and he offered me $75 per month if I would go with forty men to work there for the winter. He promised to pay the men $1.75 per day for ten hours work. The work was at Okalla, Indiana. I got the men, and we went. We liked the place very much; it was warm all winter. We worked there for seven months. During that time, I tried to learn all the English I could. The contractor had a fine family; they were all kind to me and tried to teach me English.

When the work was completed, we went to Summerset, Pennsylvania, where they were building a railway. We worked on the approach to the Laura Hill Tunnel in the mountains, twelve miles from Summerset. After a while, I was made foreman of the "big rock cut." I did not have much experience in rock cuts. Although I had worked at many of them, I had never had charge of one before, and I did not know how to use dynamite, but I had good rock men in my gang. They said, "Go ahead, we will help you, and do good work for you." So, with their encouragement, I took the job. We worked there all winter and did good work. The contractor was well pleased.

The next spring, the contractor, needing someone who could speak both English and Italian, asked me to work in his store. Since he offered to pay me well, I took the job. At the end of the second month, however, the contractor charged the men twice as much as I had recorded. As soon as the men got their pay, they blamed me; they thought I had done this. I told them, "Boys I don't know anything about it, but if the contractor did that he is not honest, for I recorded only what you had purchased." I felt awful bad, so I went to see the contractor. He said, "You mind your own business." The men got together and went to see a lawyer in Summerset. They took legal action against the contractor.

When the case came up, I was called upon to act as an interpreter. I took my books to court. I was not going to tell any lies for anyone. At the end of the hearing, the judge fined the contractor, asked him to pay the court costs, plus return all the money that had been taken from the men. The contractor did not like the decision. Thinking that I had put the men up to suing him, he came to me and said: "I don't need your services any longer." So I lost my job. I did not care; I wanted the men to get what was rightfully theirs. They had worked hard.

The next month, to make up their losses, the contractors tried to cheat each man out of two or three days pay. The contractors did not know that the man kept a written record of the dates and hours they had worked. When the men saw that they had not been given their full wages, they refused to accept the money. They came and told their story to me. After making sure that they were right, I went to Summerset to consult a lawyer. The lawyer thought the men had a good case and proceeded to sue the contractors. I was asked to be the interpreter again, but this time, they paid me five dollars per day. It took several days, because there were over sixty men to be examined. Each man had his book with him, and they were all produced in court. When the judge saw all their books, he said to the contractors: "What are you trying to do to these poor working men." He told the contractors that he was going to use this case to give them a lesson; he ordered them to pay the men in full, plus cover their travel costs to attend the court hearing.

The next spring we all went to Gallizen, Pennsylvania, where a branch line was being built for the railway. I was foreman of a gang of twenty-five men. While there I made many friends. They were all kind to me, especially the Curney family. I happened to meet them in church. I, unknowingly, sat in their pew, but they did not reproach me. We became acquainted, and they would take me to their home. Every Saturday I would spend the night with them. We had a lot of fun. Boys and girls. I played the accordion while they played the piano. I visited them until our work was completed, then I had to look for work elsewhere.

I noticed in the newspaper that a contractor was looking for men to work in Wisconsin. I wired him a note saying I had seventy men ready and willing to work. He replied that there would be work for all of us. Before deciding to accept the offer, however, four of us travelled to Lennoxville to view the work site. We travelled to Wisconsin by train, but it did not stop at Lennoxville. The closest stop was eighty miles from the site. The only way to get there was by horse and wagon. The people at the livery stable, however, wanted eighty dollars to take us there. We found this too high, so we decided to walk. It was fall and the roads were very bad; in fact, there were no roads—we had to travel through the woods.

We started out in the afternoon and had to spend the night in the woods. We made a fire to keep warm as we rested. There were all kinds of wild animals, but we did not mind. After a while we moved on, and toward morning we came to a log house in the middle of a small clearing. We were glad to see it, thinking that we would be able to get something to eat. We found there one man living in one room with a horse and a cow. The three of them slept in the same room. It smelled terrible. We asked this man if there was any place nearby where we could get something to eat. He told us that there was a construction company store about seven miles from there. We started out again, but we came to the Mississippi river; there was no way to get across. We noticed, however, that about a mile lower there was someone crossing with a row boat. He took us across the river for twenty-five cents each. Tired and hungry, we finally reached the construction camp, where we were able to rest and have something to eat.

We were still fifty miles from Lennoxville, however. A farmer we met offered to take us there in his buckboard for fifty dollars. We agreed. He went home and came back with an old wagon; it had a wobbly wheel. The roads were rough and full of boulders and holes. The wheel broke within the first ten miles. We were lucky; no one was hurt.

Half a mile from there, we met another farmer. He offered to take us the rest of the way for thirty dollars. He had a good horse and a new rig, so we agreed. The next morning we started out early. We arrived in Lennoxville that night at nine o'clock. We were very tired because the roads were terrible, so we spent the night in a hotel.

The next morning, I spoke with the superintendent and made all of the necessary arrangements for my men and for myself. The men were to get $1.75 per day for ten hours of work, and I was to get $75 per month as the interpreter. At that time labour was scarce; contractors were obliged to hire foreign labourers, so they needed someone who could speak other languages. As someone who spoke three languages, I fit right in. I made all of the arrangements for sleeping quarters for the men, and then I asked the superintendent if there was an easier way to get to the train station. He told me that there was a steamboat that went out twice a week and that there was one leaving that night. We caught the boat that same night. The next morning, I wired the men from the train station.

For eighty dollars, I made arrangements with the steamboat captain to take us all to Lennoxville. Half way there the boat stopped. The captain told us that we had run out of wood to fire the engine. I went off with ten men in a row boat to cut some hardwood. We also picked up pieces just laying on the ground. We worked for about three hours until the Captain said we had enough wood for the rest of the trip. The boat arrived in Lennoxville at ten o'clock at night. It was so late that we ended up staying in a large cellar for the night.

The next day I got the men to the camp. All seventy men boarded together. We gathered straw for their beds, put up a stove, and bought provisions. By morning, we were ready for work. There was a woman in our gang who did the cooking; her husband helped her. Each man was to pay them two dollars per month. This came out to a total of $140 per month, so they were well paid. The men were pleased as well because it saved them the trouble of cooking after work, and it saved them money besides. The woman was very clean and hard working.

I stayed at the hotel. I paid $25 a month for room and board, and I was comfortable. Since I did not have much to do that winter, I took the chance to go to school to learn more English. My teacher's name was Mr. Alder. He was one of the finest men I ever met, a gentleman in every way. With his help, I learned as much in one term as other boys learned in three. I made the most of my opportunity because I knew I might never get another chance.

Some time in September, 1885, I left Lennoxville, Wisconsin. Mr. Alder travelled to the train station, forty miles on horseback, to see me off. He made me promise to write to him. He said, "You will be surprised to see how much you will learn by correspondence." He was right. I kept writing to him for years. He wrote me such beautiful letters with good advice. After I was married, I sent him our photograph. During the time we corresponded, he became a member of government in Washington.

From Lennoxville I travelled to Girard, Ohio. I worked there for a few months as a foreman in the construction of a new steel plant. I then moved on to Pittsburgh, Pennsylvania, to work as a foreman on the city sewer and water works. It was in May that I came to Canada. The CPR (Canadian Pacific Railway) was building a branch from Montreal to Smith Falls, Ontario. I first landed in Toronto by rail, then took a boat to Cornwall where they were building a canal. I had a gang of men with me, and I asked the superintendent for work. We started work the next day. When noon came I stopped work, and we went for dinner. The superintendent came over to let us know that we had to keep working until the flag came up. In the evening, they kept the men working until six-thirty, instead of six. The men were working ten and three-quarters an hour per day but paid for ten hours. The next day, I left there with my gang, and we went to Apple Hill, Ontario, to work on the new CPR railway.

I worked there for the summer as a foreman, then moved on to St. Anne de Bellevue, and later Sherbrooke to work on different road projects. That winter, we had over eight feet of snow. Every morning we had to shovel snow before we could begin work. In the spring of 1887, the same contractor asked me to work on the next section of road running through Maine to Saint John, New Brunswick. More than half the road ran through the woods and the mosquitoes were terrible, so we decided to go to Ottawa instead.

While in Ottawa, we met someone hiring men to go to Cape Breton where the government was building a railway from Port Hawkesbury to North Sydney. I spoke to the contractor and agreed to take a gang of men to Cape Breton on condition that the company pays our travel fare. He agreed. The men were to be paid $1.25 for each ten-hour day they worked. Our arrangement was for a six-month work period.

We travelled from Ottawa to Mulgrave, Nova Scotia, by rail. From there we were to take a boat to St. Peter's Canal, but the canal was blocked with ice. The railway manager told us to go to West Bay Road, about ten miles away, to wait for a boat. We hired a few teams to carry our baggage, and we started off on foot. We arrived at West Bay Road in late afternoon. The weather was cold along the seashore. We spent the entire night on the wharf waiting for the boat; we nearly froze. There was no accommodation in the little town for such a big crowd of men. The people were afraid of us and would not allow us near their places.

By the next night, the boat still had not come. We decided that we could not spend another night outside; so we broke into the schoolhouse and lit the stove. The people of the place thought we were awful to have done this, but we did no damage. We just kept ourselves warm for the night. It is very cold at night along the seashore.

In the morning, at about nine o'clock, the boat finally arrived, and we were able to continue our journey. We arrived in Grand Narrows that evening and spent the night in a large barn. The next day, we walked the remaining twenty miles to Boisdale. There we rented a large house for the men and got the straw to make the beds. The men were comfortable there, so we made it our headquarters. I boarded at a place called MacIntyre's near the post office. They were nice people. The townspeople, however, were not aware that such a large group was coming to Boisdale. No one had made preparations to supply our food. We could not get any bread, so we lived on potatoes and eggs for a few days. Eggs were very cheap at that time—eight cents per dozen.

I went to Sydney on horseback (no saddle) to try to get some provisions, especially bread, for the men, but I could not get any that day. So, I bought lots of goods, a few barrels of hard crackers and enough bricks to build an oven. In three days, time we baked our own bread.

I was in charge of a gang of men for over a month, then the contractor gave me full charge of a five-mile section of the line. I was pretty young to have that charge, but I managed well. The local people were being paid ninety cents a day, while my men, being under contract for six months, were getting $1.25. The local men were good workers. When they found out that they were being paid less, they all went on strike. But, all along the line, the contractors were paying ninety cents per day; they did not get an increase. I was sorry for them. After our six months were up, the contractor told us that the men would have to accept ninety cents per day if they wanted to stay on the job. The men would not stay. The contractor wanted me to remain to finish the section, but I would not leave my men. So we all left at the end of October 1887.

At this point, Thomas Cozzolino and his men took the train to Riviere du Loup and walked another seventy miles toward Edmundston, New Brunswick. They worked at various jobs in the general Edmundston area from November 1887 to the spring of 1889. While working in New Brunswick, Cozzolino met Emily Lynch, the woman he eventually married.

In the spring of 1889, I went back to Cape Breton again to work on the section of line from Mulgrave to Grand Narrows. I worked there until the completion of the grading that fall. From there, I went to work at Chignecto Bay where an English company was building a seventeen-mile railway from Fort Laurence to Antigonish, Nova Scotia....

I had promised my wife-to-be that I would return to New Brunswick for Christmas. We were to marry in the first week of January. I explained all this to the contractor, but he said I could not go. He needed me there to finish the job. He finally agreed to let me go when I promised to find a good man to continue the work and to return as soon as possible. I left for New Brunswick around the December 22 and arrived there the next day. On January 7, 1890, I was married to Emily Lynch, a farmer's daughter. Ten days later, I left my wife with her parents and went back to work. Once settled at the job, I sent for my wife. I rented a nice little house near the work site, and we were very happy together.

A few months later, the contractor asked me and my crew to help work on the wharf. It was not deep enough to handle the vessels. One crew was already working there, but they were not making much headway. The wharf had to be worked after each tide, and it was slippery wheeling mud with wheel barrows. No one liked the job. The contractor said each gang would take a turn digging, so I agreed to help.

We worked there two or more weeks without relief from another crew. My men began to complain, so I spoke with the contractor. He said: "You are doing pretty well; you better keep working there." I replied: "You promised to relieve my men after a week; they will not work there any more for the same money. It is hard work." He said: "If they don't want to work there, they can go." When I told the men what the contractor had said, they were upset and decided to go elsewhere. I related this to the contractor. His reply was, "Alright, they can go." So that afternoon we all went to get our pay. In the meantime, I wired another contractor in Belleville, Ontario. He replied immediately saying "come at once with your gang;" he was prepared to pay $1.25 per day.

When our first contractor saw that we were leaving, he offered the men 10 cents more per day to stay. The men refused. Later, he offered 25 cents extra per day, but I told him: "No money will keep us here now; I have made arrangements with another firm, and I will not go back on my word." He was sorry, but it was too late; he had not treated us right. We arrived in Belleville at the end of July 1890. We worked for the MacArthur Brothers who had a section of the Grand Trunk Railway to build from Nap to Gannanoque, Ontario. The company gave me the charge of a gravel pit at Foxboro, three miles from Belleville.

After about a week, I sent for my wife. The contractors, in the meantime, built us a camp where we could live near the pit. This camp was an ideal little place for the summer. The summers are lovely in Ontario, and we both loved it. We were the envy of all the ladies who came from Belleville to visit us.

Thomas and Emily (Lynch) Cozzolino, ca. 1910. Courtesy of Dr. John Burke.

We were very happy that summer. In the fall, however, the work closed down. I had a little store near the work site to supply my men with groceries and dry goods. I made a little money that way.

At the time, I was receiving the *Engineering News* from New York and the *Railways Age* from Chicago. These magazines kept me posted on all the construction that was going on. There was a big job in West Virginia building the Norfolk and Western Railway, so I wrote to one of the contractors asking for work for myself and my gang of men. We got a positive response, so around December 27, we started out for the mountains of West Virginia.

We took the train to Peach Orchard, Virginia. The contractor's representative directed us to the work site. He said the site was fifty miles away, and that we would have to walk the last thirty-five miles. The company would supply us with a team to carry our luggage. I had my wife with me, and I knew that she could not walk such a distance. I asked her to return home to her folks for the winter, but she insisted on coming with us. I was lucky, however, to find a lady's saddle. My wife rode a mule to the site; it was something she had never done before. One of my men led the mule, as the roads were all hills, mountains and little river paths.

The first day we spent the night at a construction camp. After supper, I asked the woman there if she had a place for my wife and me to sleep. She said, "We all sleep in the same camp." So I walked out of the camp and met an Italian who had a little camp of his own that he shared with his wife. I asked him if we could camp with them for the night. The two women slept together, while he and I slept on the floor. We were very comfortable, but I again told my wife that she had better go home for the winter. She refused. So, the next morning we thanked those good people for their hospitality, and we left for our destination.

We arrived at the contractor's camp, had supper, and were shown the little log cabin set aside for my wife and me. They had promised me a nice place to stay; instead, the cabin was about 8 by 108 feet. The fireplace blackened everything, and the board at the commissary was very poor. So after three or four days, when our trunks had come in, my wife decided to go home. She could not stay. She was the only white woman there. I did not blame her, for it was a wild place.

I gave her the money for the long trip, and I sent two of my most trustworthy men with her to Peach Orchard where she would take the train. I wrote to her sister in New Brunswick asking them to meet her in eight days time. She was only twenty, so it was quite an experience for her. She said God was good to her and all the people and officials so kind and polite. At the Warsaw Hotel in Ashland, however, she lost a beautiful, large gold filigree pin with diamonds in its centre. My father had sent her the pin as a wedding present. When she finally arrived, she was tired but glad to be home again with her folks.

I kept working in Virginia. In the month of January 1891, it rained for four weeks without ceasing. All the small brooks we had used as a roadbed when we first came, now filled with water fifteen to twenty feet high. We had no cold weather during the winter, but I'd rather have cold weather than rain all the time. None of us liked the place or the people there. The Blacks were better than the Whites. The Whites thought nothing of shooting you; they all carried revolvers, both young and old. Perhaps they thought they had to.

After my wife left, I could not stand the food in the contractor's camp, so I joined the camp my men were staying in. The contractor had built a fine place for them, and they had good food and nice beds to sleep on. The camp was near a river. One night at about eleven twenty, while we were all asleep, someone fired two shots through the keyhole of the door. We all got up and went out. It was a very dark night, but we fired over fifty shots into the air. From that night on, we had peace. They were even afraid to pass by our camp in the daytime, preferring to lengthen their way by a mile rather than come our way. However, none of us went out alone. We went out in crowds of seven or eight and armed.

There was a family of eleven brothers who were regular brigands. They fought all the time, killing Negroes for nothing. One Sunday, after Sunday School, one of them called a Negro to him. The brigand took a bottle out of his pocket, hit the Negro on the head, and nearly killed him for no reason. The other Negroes just watched and said nothing. Had he done that to any of our men, he would never have come off his horse alive.[4] We finally got fed up with the place and left in April 1891.

From West Virginia, Cozzolino and his crew travelled back to Canada to work on the railway project near Belleville, Ontario.

My wife was not very well. She stayed home with her mother all summer. A nice little baby girl was born to us on the 8th day of June 1891. She was named Teresa after my sister who died so young.[5] Needless to say, I was lonesome that summer. When I completed my work in December, I went home for the winter. I stayed with my father-in-law, with my wife and baby.

In April of 1892, the Cozzolinos moved to the Ottawa-Hull area. Thomas worked on projects for the Gatineau Valley Railway and the Canada Atlantic Railway. When work stopped for the winter, he attended night school classes for bookkeeping. He was twenty-six years old. Then, in the spring of 1893, while Mrs. Cozzolino and her daughter remained in Ottawa, Thomas worked on railway projects in Quebec and later in Maine (with contractors Malcolm and Ross).

Meanwhile, my wife became lonely in Ottawa. She returned home to her folks in New Brunswick. I was glad for her sake. By that time, there were two baby girls; Gertrude was born in Ottawa, in March of 1893. My wife's father had two large farms, so she moved into one of the farmhouses. I went home some time in December. I had done well that summer, but I had been away from my family for nearly eight months. I was glad to see them again. We settled down in our farmhouse, and we were happy all winter. As I had nothing to do, I decided to cut all the wood we would need to keep ourselves warm and for cooking. My father-in-law gave me a horse and a sled. I went to the woods every day to cut down trees. After hauling about forty loads of wood, I started to saw and split them into stove length pieces. I had enough wood for the winter and summer. I kept myself pretty busy all that winter of 1894. My wife was handy at sewing and knitting, so we got along fine together, busy and happy.

From spring to late fall of 1895, Cozzolino worked for the Montfort Colonization Railway near Montfort, Quebec. He then returned home for the winter.

In the spring, I went to work for Malcolm and Ross again—on the Ashland branch of the Bangor and Aroostook Railway in Maine. I was foreman for a few weeks when my men urged me to take a subcontract. I said, "Boys the prices are too low, we cannot do it for the price they are offering," but they insisted that I take three miles of the swamp where we were working. I told them that the contractors were offering only fourteen cents per cubic yard. They replied, "Take it and we will work harder for you; you will make some money." So I took the three miles.

We started some time in August. I had fifty good men; they shovelled more material than any other men I had ever seen, and they were very faithful to me. We had no boss on the job. Every man was doing his best. When my estimate came in September, it looked like I would make over $1,500 in profit. When I saw that, I said: "Boys, I am going to pay you $1.50 per day instead of $1.25." Mr. Malcolm, however, said: "You cannot pay your men $1.50 per day; we would have a strike on the job at once. The other 500 men are getting only $1.25." I understood at once. He said, "You can pay your men $1.50 per day, as it is your money, but you will have to rate them at 12½ cents per hour. Give them extra hours to make up the difference." I thanked him and returned to camp to make out a new payroll. I got one of the men to help me, and we made it up during the night. I told my men what I had to do and asked them not to tell anyone how much they were being paid. We completed my three miles by the end of November.

[That winter, Thomas Cozzolino (with the help of his crew) began work on a house for his family in New Brunswick. They also worked for the Montfort Railway Company during the 1896 and 1897 work seasons.] In the spring of 1898, I returned to Montreal as I had spent over $7,000 on my new home. The house was thirty-six by thirty feet, had two stories and a high cellar. The plans were made by an Italian architect. I had all the modern conveniences: water, two toilets, bathtub, furnace, hot and cold water. It was the only house in the country that was equipped that way. By then we had four little girls—Teresa, Gertrude, Dorothy and Regina. I had to work hard to support the family. I was anxious to find work during my stay in Montreal.

In 1898 and 1899, Cozzolino worked on railway construction projects in both Quebec and northwestern Ontario. In addition, he and Alberto Dini, the owner of a grocery store in Montreal, supplied Italian workers at various work sites with Italian bread and other provisions.

I went to Sydney, Nova Scotia, in December of 1889. The chief engineer for the Steel Plant, Mr. Waterman, asked me to get a few hundred men to work on the construction project. In exchange, he agreed to put me in charge of some of the excavation work, pay me well, allow me to supply my men, and provide free camps for the men and room for my store of provisions. He also offered me a good salary and all my expenses paid—including hotel, laundry and a rig to drive me from the hotel to the work site every morning and return me home at night. I decided that I would do well to take the position, especially for the winter months.

After Christmas, I went to New York where I hired 200 men. The company was to pay the men's fare to Sydney if they agreed to remain on the job for six months. I got more men from Montreal under the same conditions. The company built me a large oven, free of charge, to bake bread; between the selling of bread and my pay, I was doing pretty well that winter.

After settling everything in the camps, the company put me in charge of some excavation at the coke ovens to prepare for a small branch of railway. This was in January of 1900. The entire excavation project for the plant was being handled badly. The ground was frozen, and the men were being asked to dig with picks. It was very hard work for them. The superintendent was a bricklayer; he did not know anything about excavation. I spoke to him several times, but he said: "Mind your business, the company is not paying you to teach them anything." I was getting fed up with the way the job was being handled.

One day a young man came to the work site and asked me how I was getting along. I said: "I'm not getting along at all; the work is costing four or five times more than it should. I can't do the work the way I want to do it. I am going to leave this place." Unknowingly, I was talking with the general manager's son. I explained that, if a trestle was put up, eight men and a steam shovel could do at least three times as much work as the eighty men now working on the job. The steam shovel would not remain idle because the cars could dump the material quickly and return for another load. Instead of using picks on frozen ground, we could use dynamite to make it easier for the men to complete the work in less time. The young man told his father all I had said.

The next day the general manager sent for me to discuss my ideas about cutting work expenses. At the end of our discussion, he said: "From now on you will have full charge of the excavation at the Coke Ovens; do the work as you see fit." I went back to work and made many changes to suit myself. I first changed the position of the steam shovel; I placed it on the short side of the loading bank and moved the track to the upper side so that we could take up the cut without having to shovel by hand. At the same time, I ordered wood for my trestle. As soon as the 100-foot trestle was built, I started on the fill using only eight men. Now the train could be unloaded in a few minutes, instead of taking half an hour. In the first week, I had taken out about four times more material than previously. I used dynamite to blast the frozen ground at the site and this brought the cost down by over half.

After finishing the excavation at the Coke Ovens, I asked the manager if he would give me a contract for the excavation at the Open Hearth and the Blooming Mills. He said this was not possible because it was under a six month contract to a company from Boston. When I heard how much they were charging for the work, I said: "Mr. Moxham, that is a pretty high cost for construction excavation." He agreed, but added: "I cannot do anything; they still have another three and half months on their contract." I said: "It would pay you to give them even $50,000[6] and let them go; we can make it up in less than two months." Two days later Mr.

Moxham called me into his office. He had spoken to the head of the construction company, and they had agreed to accept the offer to cancel their contract with the Dominion Iron and Steel Company.

I took full charge of the excavation for the Blooming Mills and the Open Hearth, plus a spur of railway connecting the Blast Furnace to the Coke Oven plant. When I took the work, I had every worker and foreman against me; they thought that I was going to discharge them. That, however, was not my way of doing work; anyone who did his duty was my friend. It was not very long before they changed their minds and did everything for me. Of course, I did fire a few of the leaders and foremen for not doing their duty. After that everything went well. By the end of the first month, the costs were 45 per cent lower than they had been the previous month. Before I took charge of the work, the excavation at the Blooming Mills and Open Hearth cost the company $1.00 per cubic yard; in my first month it cost 55 cents per cubic yard. The spur line to the Coke Ovens, which was costing them 80 cents per cubic yard, now cost about 40 cents. I, however, still found the cost too high. By the end of the job, the cost of work at the Blooming Mills and Open Hearth was down to 42 cents, and the work on the railway spur was down to 20 cents per cubic yard. The general manager was well pleased with both the work and the cost.

By the fall of 1900, the construction work was nearly completed. We also had a baby boy in our family; he was named James after my father-in-law, James Lynch.[7]

The general manager sent me to Buffalo, New York, to find out how they broke the Pig Iron at the Lacawana steel plant. I wired my wife, and we both went to Buffalo. At the time, the Panama American Exposition was going on, and we took it all in. The Exposition made it a nice trip for my wife. Meanwhile, I had a hard time getting into the steel plant. Eventually, being there for about ten days, I did get to see how they broke the Pig Iron.

On my arrival in Sydney, I reported the information to the general manager. The Lacawana plant had a trestle, that was about seven feet high, with a railway track along its side. Every six feet there was a steel deadman with a sharp edge like an axe; the men would lift the Pig Iron and throw it onto the sharp edge, causing the ingot to split in two. In Sydney, they were using the hammer to break the Pig Iron, so it took much longer to split the ingots. The Sydney plant, however, had no yard room to place the trestle, so they kept working as they had. My trip cost the Company $400 for nothing. But, they wanted to give me the trip, seeing that I had worked hard all summer and saved them lots of money.

I went home to New Brunswick in December and returned to Sydney in the new year. I did more work for the company that year and, in the fall, I took a subcontract for the filling of the round house in Sydney and the tracks in the yard. As there was no gravel in the area, I had to go to Sydney River, three miles away, and haul the material by train. I completed the fills by January, 1901.[8] Meanwhile, I had moved my family to Sydney, and we were happy together.

In the spring of 1902, I took a contract for five miles of grading on the Bay of Quinty Railway that ran from Napanee west. My section was near Toronto at Bannockburn, Ontario. While working there, the Dominion Iron and Steel Company wired me to ask if I could send them a few hundred men for their Marble Mountain stone quarry. I replied that if the company would pay for all of the men's expenses, I might be able to get the men for them through some of my New York friends. As for myself, I could not go as I had all I could do to look after my current work. The company agreed, so I wired my friend in New York. He got 100 men and started out for Marble Mountain. When the men arrived there, the company had no camps for them to sleep in. The men, of course, would not stay there. They all left, and the company lost the fare money. But, it was the company's fault, they should have had everything ready when the men arrived.

Once Cozzolino and his crew had completed their work in Ontario, he returned to Nova Scotia to work on a ten-mile railway construction project near Liverpool. He worked there from August 1903 to October 1904. In 1904, the Cozzolinos had another addition to their family; a daughter named Nora after Emily's sister.

In January of 1905, an English company was starting to develop a mine at Broughton, eighteen miles from Sydney, Nova Scotia. Although the pay was low, I took two sections for grading. At the time I signed the contract, there was no snow on the ground. On January 26, however, it started to snow, and it continued to snow for three weeks. I could not make much headway. Meanwhile, I had wired a friend in Liverpool, Nova Scotia, to load all of my equipment and ship it to Sydney. He loaded three cars consisting of dump carts, wheelbarrows, picks, shovels, etc. But, as there had been a big storm, the railway had put my cars in a siding near Halifax, and evidently forgot them as they were snowed under. When my cars finally arrived on February 26, I began to work in earnest.

My contract was for grading earth; it did not give a price for "rock." I had told the general manager that there were rocks in my cuts at the time I signed the contract. He had said: "Go ahead, and I will pay you for the rock." Every day we found more and more boulders, some as large as forty-five cubic feet. So I told my foreman to keep track of all the boulders. When we had finished the cuts, I put in a claim for around 800 cubic yards of rock. The general manager would not pay for this work. I told him that I would not accept a final settlement until he had paid me for the rock.

A few days after the President of the company arrived from England, I went to see him at the hotel. I explained my case to him. He was very nice about it and sent for the general manager to discuss the matter. The general manager got angry and came to see me at my home. He said that I had no right to go see the President, and that I would never get another day's work from the company. I replied: "I lived a good many years before I started working for this company; I guess I can live without it." He then said: "Your contract reads so much per cubic yard for everything, including the rock." He showed me his copy of the contract. Above the word earth, he had written "rock and everything else included." I told him that I could have him put in jail for adding those words to the contract. My copy, which he and two witnesses had signed, did not include those additional words. He cooled down and offered me more work at the Broughton site in exchange for calling off the claim on the rock. Since I would be getting a pretty good price, I agreed. I built about ten long streets and excavated a large foundation for a warehouse.

While working at the Broughton site, Cozzolino took a subcontract, with Rhodes, Curry and Company for work on the Intercolonial Railway construction project in the Truro area. He then took on a partnership with O'Brian and Martin for a construction project with the Transcontinental Railway near La Tuque, Quebec.

I returned to Nova Scotia in the fall of 1908. Once home, I formed the Nova Scotia Construction Company, Limited. We accepted a job that winter to build three cribs at Annapolis, Nova Scotia, but we sublet this work to another contractor. In the spring of 1909, we took a job at St. Timothee, Quebec, from the Canadian Light and Power Company. We worked at this job until 1911. During that period, we purchased a great deal of new equipment; our plant there now was worth over $150,000. At the same time, we had another job in Sydney with the Dominion Iron and Steel Company. We built a four-mile spur line, about two miles of highways, and, inside the plant, we built a blast furnace, a nail mill, as well as work on other construction. We also did some sewer work for them and built a subway near the Coke Ovens.

If my memory serves me right, the Federal Government asked for tenders for work on Pier No. 2 in Halifax in August of 1911. We obtained the contracts. The construction is 800 feet in length by 230 feet in width, and it carries a two-storey freight shed. It is built of reinforced concrete piles. At that time, no pile driver in existence could drive them. A floating pile driver was designed especially for the job. It was built at a cost of over $100,000. We built the scow ourselves at Liverpool, Nova Scotia. The machinery was suspended in leads which could be moved forward, backward, sideways or canted as required, allowing for very accurate placing of the piles and for driving or bracing the piles at a slope. There were over 1,800 concrete piles, many of which weighed twenty tons or more. We made these piles at a special plant we built on two farms at the sand beaches, South Eastern passage, eight miles from Halifax.

For shipping purposes, it was necessary to build a timber pier and to construct over 1,000 feet of trestle. This was necessary to allow for sufficient water depth to take in our boats and scows. We also had to build several cars to convey the heavy piles to the wharf. All this special work took considerable time to plan and to carry out. We had to buy forty tons of brown hoisting and an eight foot boom to move the piles, place them according to their length, and load them on to the cars. To ensure that they did not break, we tied them in three places. We placed a thirty-five ton steel derrick at the end of the wharf, in order to load the piles on to the scows. We had eight scows and four tug boats to carry the piles to Halifax.

We made our own concrete piles and left them in the yard to season for three months. At the same time, we began excavation at Pier 2. By the spring of 1913, we had driven in nearly all of the piles and completed work on the concrete floor. The pier was ready for use when the first regiment sailed from Halifax to the Great War—September 10, 1914. In fact, it was used throughout the war to ship both troops and munitions. Hundreds of thousands of soldiers passed over it during the war period.

In that same year, 1914, our company built two bridges for the Canadian Pacific Railway, one at Windsor and one at Gasparow (*sic*) on the Avon River. It was difficult to work on the Bay of Fundy because there was thirty-five feet of tide and a current of eight miles per hour. I also had a hard time to keep the men from fighting; they were of mixed nationalities, and some would take up for Germany and others for England. I had to build different camps to separate them. We managed, however, to complete the work.

In the spring of 1915, we designed a wooden wharf for the Furness Withy Company in St. John's, Newfoundland. We then sublet and financed two of our foremen to build the wharf. The company was pleased with the work and hired us to design and build a reinforced concrete pier in Halifax. We worked on this job in 1916 and 1917. Wages for labour made a big jump during this period. They went from 17 cents to as high as 50 cents an hour. The cost for materials went up as well. But, lucky for us, we already had purchased the cement and the steel. The steel went up over 100 per cent. We completed the job but made no money. The company knew we had not made any money, so they gave us some work building a few sheds of reinforced concrete. At the same time, we built some concrete structures for the Halifax tram company and did some work filling trestles from Annapolis Valley to Yarmouth for the Canadian Pacific Railway.

We later received a contract from the Saint John Valley Railway to work on a forty-five mile construction project. We were to get the stretch into running order by grading, blasting, laying the track and furnishing everything but the steel rails. The wages, however, were going higher and higher, and the government was taking all of our best men [for the war effort]. We had expected to do well, but we did not make any money there.

It was difficult to find good men; as soon as I brought in a gang from New York, the government would take them away. I had a good man on the steam shovel while we were blasting. The government tried to take him away, but he came back. He was the only man I could get to run the steam shovel; so, to keep him, I went out, bought him long, grey whiskers and changed his name. Every time someone came along, he would put on his whiskers and work very slow. He looked as if he was over sixty years old. I said to the inspector one day: "The young man you took away from here would do as much work in a day as this old man does in a week." The inspector replied, "We cannot help that," and went away. We were able to complete the project.

In December of 1917, the explosion of the French ammunition boat rocked Halifax to its foundations. December 6th began with a perfect morning, then, suddenly, at 9:10 am, three thousand tons of T.N.T. exploded. The explosion was caused by a fire which had broken out on board the munitions vessel after a collision with an out-bound Belgian relief ship. The explosion was so great that it was distinctly heard, and windows were broken, at Truro, 62 miles away. Its vibrations were felt in places as much as 100 miles from Halifax.[9] So many houses were destroyed in Halifax and the district. In addition to those killed and wounded, thousands were left homeless.

At this point in the narrative, Thomas Cozzolino goes on to write about the role he and his company played in the reconstruction of the city. His daughter's narrative, in contrast, provides details not included in the original Memoirs. The following paragraph appears in her version of Cozzolino's story.

I was eating breakfast in the Halifax Hotel when the windows near me crashed down. Pieces of glass filled my pockets. Everyone was running and screaming, wondering what had happened. I thanked God for my safety and immediately threw our organization into the work of repairing and rebuilding—hundreds of temporary dwellings were erected in a short time. Schools, convents, and institutions had to be repaired and converted into temporary hospitals. It was getting late and, since my daughter, Nora, was at the Sacred Heart Convent, I was worried about her. Knowing how my wife would be anxious about us, I paid a truck driver to take me to the convent. When I finally found Nora, she had glass in her ears but was otherwise okay. I put her in the truck, and we drove down to the station where a freight train was getting ready to pull out. We sat on boxes. The train landed in Sydney at three o'clock in the morning. My wife and children were so worried that they had left the lights on at the house. Not having a key, I rang the bell and called to Emily. She thought I was a ghost. I had a hard time convincing her I was real. What a reunion we had! We called the parents of other children at the school to reassure them of their safety. As soon as possible I returned to help with the permanent reconstruction of the city of Halifax—rebuilding convents and schools where many pupils and teachers had met their death.

In the early 1920s, Cozzolino and his company did some work at the Victoria General Hospital in Halifax and then accepted two contracts for work in Quebec: one to build fifty miles of highway and the other to construct several storage dams near Chicoutimi for the Quebec Streams Commission.

As a result of the storage dam project, our company experienced a major financial loss. The commission engineer did not take the proper soundings of the lakes. They showed us where we would find solid rock at a depth of five feet, and, of course, we calculated our prices based on this information. Everywhere we worked, however, we had to dig from fifteen to forty-three feet below water level to reach the rock. If we had known this, our prices would have been different. At the big dam at Portage de Roche, fifteen miles from Chicoutimi, we had to dig nearly forty-four feet under water. The deeper we went, the more it cost; but we received payment for only the first five feet. So our company lost over $440,000 on the work.

In November of 1924, I wrote the Streams Commission asking them for payment of the extra work we had done on the project. They said they would look into things but, two years later, seeing that nothing had come of this, I took legal action. The first judge awarded us $11,000. He said this was what we legally were entitled to, but that morally we were entitled to the full amount of $444,000. The work was done well. Due to the extraordinary conditions at the work site, the Government should pay the full amount, plus 5 per cent interest for three years. The Quebec Government, however, would not give us anything. We applied to a higher court in Quebec, but the judges there said that we should have stopped the work and arranged a new contract because the chief engineer had no power to pay us for anything more without the written consent of the Lieutenant Governor. The case, including witnesses and legal fees, cost us another $5,000. This sum, when added to our losses, crippled the company. I personally lost $305,000.

Thomas Cozzolino and his family moved to Montreal in 1928. He continued to work on several smaller projects in Quebec but, by the early 1930s, economic conditions were not good. It was at this point that he retired and began work on his Memoirs.

I am staying home with my wife and two of my grandchildren—a boy of seventeen, and a girl of twelve. They are both going to school and doing well. I hope that in a few years time they will be a help to me. I find it lonesome doing nothing. It kills me. Of course, I could not stand any hard work, as I will soon be sixty-nine years old. At that age a man cannot do very much. I have taken my time in writing my life story, but I am sure that I have left out many things that I did not remember. I thank God with all my life for having spared me such a long life, without sickness.

Sequel

At the end of the Memoirs' main text, Thomas Cozzolino's daughter (Regina Cozzolino Keating) provides a "Sequel." The following is an excerpt from that piece.

This wonderful, strong man, my father, lived to the age of 82. He was loved by everyone. He was an unpretentious man who fought for his rights, and those of the people with whom he was associated. His integrity sustained him. His father, who worried so much about his son losing his faith, must have been proud of his accomplishments in the new world. It is sad that he never returned to see his father, though they wrote frequently. A monument bearing this inscription is on his father's tomb in Italy—"Erected by his son, Thomas Cozzolino in America."

My father gave his children every educational and social advantage, denying them nothing, although he worked so hard all his life to attain this end. His success reads like an impossible feat. A thirteen-year-old lad leaving his native land and coming to a strange country where he couldn't even understand the language spoken. The obstacles he encountered, his tenacity and strength, made him the man he was. He did not seek fame or fortune for himself, only for his wife and family. He gave two daughters to the religious life, Gertrude who joined the congregation of the Notre Dame Order, and Nora, the youngest, who became a Good Shepherd Nun. His memory is cherished by those he left behind—they could never hope to accomplish in a thousand years what he did during his life time.

There is so much more that can be added, but it would take pages. Our home in Sydney was equipped with a chapel where we often assisted at Mass. Many visiting priests slept in what we designated the priest's room, a room otherwise unoccupied. As a matter of fact, a dear friend who visited us yearly died in that room. Bishop Power, whom we all loved, developed "pneumonia," and the doctor could not save him. He was waked for one day in our front room. My father must have felt bad when he had to sell our lovely home—the place where we had experienced so much happiness. I hear the house has been torn down, but if the stones could speak, how many wonderful incidents they would relate.

The Early Years:
A Talk with Tony Bruno (1902-1979)[1]

Edited by Sam Migliore

My father [Pasquale] came to the United States in 1892. He came from a little village situated between the cities of Rome and Naples. He landed in New York, and from there he went to New Jersey. My mother [Maria Giuseppina] was not with him. He came to the United States just before their first child [Angelina] was born. My mother came three years after that.

My father came looking for work. He had several brothers involved in masonry, stonecutting, in Italy. He learned and followed that line of work, until he decided when my mother was going to have a baby, that there was no chance of making a living in a small village. His father was just a poor man, uneducated. He was a tinker by trade, going along fixing pots and pans with a horse and wagon. My father's opportunity came when the immigration laws [for entry to the United States] were dropped. They took advantage of that and landed in the United States.

He found it hard to get a job in the States. My father was handicapped; he did not know the language. But, he met some older Italians who had come to the States before him. They helped him make connections and get a job. He carried on like that until my mother and sister came. My father didn't know Angelina; she was born in Italy. She was three years old when she was brought over here.

They stayed in New Haven, Connecticut, for several years and then moved to Canada.[2] My father went to Montreal and worked with the CPR (Canadian Pacific Railway)—in railway construction. He worked in Quebec for a while and moved on right through the Prairies to Moose Jaw. My mother following, living in a box car that was made up as a home for her and two kids.... That was still before the 1900s....

The Bruno family. Helen and Tony Bruno, top row, second and third from left. Pasquale and Mary Josephine Bruno, front row, centre. Photo by Ray Martheleur, ca. 1949. Courtesy of Helen Bruno.

Then, my father was given a permanent job in charge of a section of railroad in Sudbury, Ontario, with the CPR. My mother didn't like it there. There were no Italian people, and she couldn't speak English. So they decided to go back to Montreal. She was pregnant, and I was about to be born. [laughs] In Montreal, my father hooked up with Tom Cozzolino and the Nova Scotia Construction Company. He was organizing and hiring men to come down to Sydney to build Number Seven Blast Furnace. Cozzolino brought a whole bunch of Italians, most of the construction crew—Alex Martinello, the Gentiles ... so my father came to Nova Scotia....

When they finished ... Cozzolino got a job up in Chester building a railroad from Chester to Liverpool and Brooklyn. He took my father with him and put him in charge of construction for that job. We lived in Chester, and we lived in Brooklyn and Liverpool, Nova Scotia, right up until 1902. Then my father came back to Sydney ... and went on with the Steel Company ... as a construction boss.... He was a foreman in the steel plant for $1.50 a day....

When I went on at the plant in 1918, I was getting eight cents an hour. Eight cents! I went on as an errand boy and apprentice in the machine shop. I came along from there right up to my retirement. I only had one job in my life after leaving school. I got a job with the Steel Company for eight cents an hour, and I worked [there] for fifty years.[3] When I retired, I wasn't getting ... too much more. [laughs] I don't think I brought home $500 a month after fifty years service.

Strikes in the 1920s

They had two or three strikes in the 1920s. The troubles really started in 1923, during the May Day celebrations. The militia came down during the first big strike when they destroyed the Power Plant at New Waterford. They brought the militia ... in 1925, I believe.... The Power Plant had already been destroyed. The government ... organized the provincial police corps in Halifax. They came down, and they got battered all to pieces, so the government sent the troops in. They declared Marshal Law here and ... read the *Riot Act*. Matter of fact, the night the *Riot Act* was read ... old magistrate Hill was officiating at Number Four Gate. He was standing on the back seat of my car when the car was stoned. [I was the chauffeur at that time.] He was knocked unconscious while reading the *Riot Act*. I ran away; left the car there and ran away. The Steel Company Police took a beating. They had a few troops ... near the mechanical office, and they had a machine gun full of blank bullets. They fired on this gang that broke through the gate. The steelworkers were desperate.

These were strike days before the union, before organized labour came into being here at the steel plant in the early 1920s. They went out on strike; they were looking, at that time, not for money but for recognition for their union and bargaining rights. It took years to get what they wanted, and to get where they are today. They had all kinds of strikes. You see, the Coal Company was looking for the same thing, at the same time. The Coal Company went out on strike, and the Steel Company would come out in sympathy. And it would be vice versa if the Steel Company went out on strike. [When the Coal Company went on strike the steel plant] had no coal to operate their boilers. The plant was all operated by coal; they needed steam, so if they had no coal, they might as well shut her down.

But, the steel plant wasn't 100 per cent unionized, half would go on strike and the other half would stay on the job, that's where the conflict came between the two groups. One was in the union and the other wasn't in the union. Therefore, he would be classed as a scab. He would have to stay in the plant because if he went outside that fence ... he'd get beat up and probably wouldn't be allowed in anymore. So, the Steel Company put up cook sheds, tents ... mattresses ... and fed them and kept them on the job. Cost them a lot of money.

The Coal Company went out on strike in 1925. [That's when the Water Plant was destroyed] down on the lake in New Waterford with millions of dollars of damage. That was the reason that the Reserve mine closed up; they flooded her. Damaged so bad, they couldn't operate her any more. I wouldn't hesitate to say that half the mines in Cape Breton were closed due to strikes. Every time they went on strike there was something damaged down in the mine—the dampness ... floods, gas accumulations. Strikes contributed to a lot of these shut downs.

As far as my father is concerned, I couldn't tell you any more than what I told you right now. After they immigrated to Canada and [worked at various places], he stayed on with the steel plant. He stayed there until they retired him, and he died here. He was always a construction man, always a builder.

The Coal Miner's Strike of 1925
Ron Mazzocca

A typical story depicting the severity of the situation for many young Italian men was told to me by my grandfather, "Beecho" Mazzocca. He arrived in Dominion in 1923 at the age of seventeen and immediately obtained employment in the local mine. He boarded with his cousin and, for the first time in his life, managed to save money. After working ten hours a day, six shifts a week with no vacation for two years, he managed to save the princely sum of approximately $200. Sure that employment prospects where unlimited, he bought a gold-plated razor and sent the remainder of his savings to Italy to help pay for the family farm. Two days later, the miners went out on strike for six months. The mines were closed.

My grandfather was forced to leave the boarding house. His cousin also was out of work and another mouth to feed was a hardship that he and his family could not endure. My grandfather moved into the "shacks"—a row of dilapidated houses constructed in the late 1890s as temporary lodging for young, single immigrant workers. These buildings were poorly heated and without electricity and running water. My grandfather was forced to sell his $20 razor for $2 in order to buy food. The period may be referred to as the roaring twenties because of the post-World War I economic growth in North America, but in Cape Breton, the 1920s were a time of hardship and severe economic decline. Many Italian families left the area for greener pastures.

Learning "English" at Barachois Mountain: A Talk with Romeo Sylvester

Edited by Sam Migliore

My parents were born in Italy—my father (Joseph "Pippino" Sylvester) in 1889, and my mother (Aurora Laura Sylvester) in 1898. Dad's people were merchants, while my mother's family had their own *campagna* (farmland). It was all olive trees. Other people actually worked the *campagna*, and at harvest time, they would give my mother's family a percentage of the profits. The property remained in the family until my grandmother died in 1950. She was ninety-three years old.

Dad came to Sydney with his father (Joseph Sylvester) when he was about ten years old. My grandfather must have had some contact with Cape Breton before that time, but I don't know much of the background on my father's side of the family. Anyway, shortly after they arrived, my father started work at the steel plant. He worked as a water boy at the limestone quarry at Barachois Mountain. While at the quarry, he lived with a Scottish family, the MacDougalls. Of course, he couldn't speak English, but he was determined to learn. They spoke to him continuously to help him learn the language. And, he learned well, or so he thought. One day, he and Hector MacDougall came to Sydney to do some shopping. He probably had a whole month's worth of six dollars in his pocket. They went into a store, and my father asked for something. The guy in the store just looked at him; he didn't know what my father was talking about. Dad checked with some Italian people, his father's cousins, and they said: "You can't speak English! What kind of language are you talking?" See, he was speaking Gaelic all this time, and he didn't even know it. He had learned Gaelic before he learned to speak English. [laughs] Gaelic was all the Scots up that way spoke in the early 1900s.

So there he was, my father could speak Italian and Gaelic, but he couldn't speak English. [laughs] He didn't become fluent in English until after he joined the Canadian Army in 1915. He got his education through the military. He was with the 185th Battalion of the Cape Breton Highlanders, and he saw action overseas with the 185th Battalion RCRs (Royal Canadian Regiment). He was wounded badly at Vimy Ridge.

After the war, Dad went back to Italy and married my mother. But, he didn't stay long; he returned to Cape Breton while my mother remained in Italy. My brother (Frank Dominic Sylvester) was born there. In 1924, Dad went back to Italy for another short period. This is where they came up with me. He then returned to Cape Breton on December 11, 1925, to work in the steel plant. I was born on September 27, 1926. My father didn't meet me until I was four years old. The three of us—my mother, my brother and myself—came to Canada in 1931.

My brother and I couldn't speak a word of English [laughs]; he was nine, and I was four. My brother could write [in Italian]; he went to school in Italy, but I was too young. We learned English at the Mission on Lingan Road [in Whitney Pier].[1] The Mission taught mostly foreign kids—Polish, Italian, Ukrainian—because the steel plant had a lot of foreign workers. Once we knew some English, we started to go to the local school. In terms of customs in the house, Italian was all we knew. Surprisingly, though, my mother learned English quickly. She learned the language from trying to help teach me to read. And, after a while, she could both read and write.

Hector MacDougall and my father ended up working together as security officers at the steel plant. Hector visited us often. He and Dad (and sometimes Andy MacDougall) would sit at the table joking, drinking a glass of wine and then start speaking in Gaelic. [laughs] You ought to have heard them driving 'er in Gaelic back and forth without a stop. They would speak Gaelic all evening. I never picked up more than a few words here and there, but I used to get a kick out of listening to them. Dad spoke Gaelic fluently. He could also speak French; he picked that up in France during the First World War.

Hector is dead now. Dad is dead. They are all gone. All fine people too. Dad died in 1960; the war wounds finally did him in, and my mother passed away in 1963. They all died young. My brother passed away in his sixties. I'm the only one who made it past seventy, and I'm stilling going strong. I've picked up a different style of living. I went back to the old Italian customs. My wife found my mother's Italian recipes, and she uses them to make us various Italian dishes—lasagna, gnocchi, ravioli. The way she cooks, you would think my mother was still here.

[Have you ever been back to Italy?] I never went back, no. I don't think I will ever go back now. I was too small to miss anything, and what I do remember is very vague. Now and then, if they gave me a picture to look at, I might remember something.

[On the ship to Canada] I remember the bunks and being on deck once, but that's about all. Dad picked us up at the Sydney Train Station in 1931. He came in an old car that had wheels with wooden spokes. I didn't know where I was going. I didn't even know who he was. I was only four years old.... But, we all got our education here. I worked in the steel plant and kept going to school. We did alright. I was at the plant for forty-five years and eight months. I did it all. I was with the safety department, machine shop, electric welding. I taught first aid. And, in the end, I wound up in the same job my Dad used to do—security.

Dominic and James Nemis of New Waterford

Edited by John deRoche

Giuseppe (Joe) Nemis and Enrica (Rica) Maccossi Nemis were among the many Italians who immigrated to Cape Breton in the earliest years of the industrial boom. They came from a town named Nimis, near the provincial capital of Udine in north-eastern Italy and close to the border of Slovenia (then part of Austria). Accompanied by an infant son, Johnny, and Joe's father, and having left behind their small daughter, Rena, in the care of her grandmother, Joe and Rica arrived at Glace Bay just after the turn of the century. They settled on Highland Street in the No. 4 (Caledonia) colliery district. Son, Dominic, was born there in April 1908. The family soon transferred to the booming new colliery town of New Waterford, moving into company housing on Arthur Street in No. 14 Yard. Besides his mining, Joe doubled as an interpreter for his fellow Italians at No. 15 pit. Another of the sons, James or "Cookie," was born at the new home in July of 1914. Altogether, apart from triplets who died in infancy, there would be eight children, including Louis, Edith, Anna and Joe Jr.

In 1934, James wed Catherine MacDonald, daughter of Gaelic-speaking Catholics from Inverness County. Dominic married Margaret Finlayson, daughter of Presbyterian Scots immigrants, in 1938. Both couples raised their families in New Waterford.

In 1977, as a young sociology professor, I ran a summer grant project through which university students interviewed retired miners and their wives about their work lives. James, Catherine, Dominic and Margaret Nemis were among the many people who welcomed us and who tape-recorded fascinating accounts of their experiences, struggles, and insights over the years at the pit and in the home. Connie McPherson spoke with Jim Nemis on July 8 and Kathleen Rudderham interviewed him further on August 18, 1977. On July 15, Bev MacLean recorded her talk with Dominic Nemis.

From James and Dominic's own words, I have selected glimpses of the ordinary—yet, to many of us today, quite extraordinary—experiences of making one's way as a miner here in the 1920s through the 1960s. I have also chosen certain stories that speak to us all, even more intensely, of special challenges and courageous responses.[1]

Worklife Sketches from James Nemis

The First Job

Cookie (James) Nemis's story, about first becoming a miner, is typical of the time. It's a one-industry town, with a labour-hungry, mining company. A family needs money. A too-young man has a little talk with the mine manager, and the deed is done. Mother and father accede. The boy starts as a driver, collecting full boxes from the pairs of men who tunnel "rooms" and "crosscuts" through the coal, then guiding the pit pony with the full "trip" of boxes along the rails to the "landing" at the main "haulage deep." Mr. Nemis also echoes what most old-time miners have said about their hard and dirty jobs: "I enjoyed it!"

I was fifteen years old [in 1929 when I started in the mine]. The first thing I done was drove a little pony, in 14 colliery. I made $2.80 a day; that was a boy's pay. [laughs] I got that for three years. A new man, but a boy's pay. At that time, that was good. You take if I worked five days a week, maybe when I went home, give eight or ten dollars to my parents. It was pretty tough at that time, eh. There wasn't much work. A Depression was on, and we didn't have much money. My father didn't tell me [to], I went myself one day to the mine. Sneaked over there and asked the manager. "Oh," he says, "I know your father; come on over this afternoon ... and I'll hire you on."

So I come home and had the job. And my father didn't know. He was *wild*. But he says, "Ok, do what you want. We need the money." We had eight children, and we were young, and it was tough. He was the only fella working. [My mother] jumped to the roof that I had to go in the coal mine, a little boy fifteen years old. But I was big, strong. I didn't mind it. I enjoyed work in the coal mine. People think I was crazy, eh, but I enjoyed meeting the people, laughing, talking, telling jokes. I enjoyed it all my life. Worked with the men that I knew—all the boys I went to school with, starting grade one. That was my living.... I used to go down every day with the intention of coming up. Be careful. That's what I had in my mind all my life, see. So I enjoyed it!

The Pit Pony

Them poor little ponies used to work two shifts [in a row]. We walked me and him, maybe half a mile [with each trip]. I used to walk alongside, show him the light any time he'd want, and he used to enjoy that. I used to like the little pony. His name was Bimbo. First I'd have to go to the stables and take the pony where I'd have to go to work. I had to look after him like a baby to see he wouldn't get hurt. We'd have to walk along dangerous places sometimes—a rake'd pass along. [The "rake" was a string of open railcars that transported workers]. Sometimes we'd have to cross over where the trips were going too. Well, I'd take him to the job. I'd have the little shafts there, harness him up. There'd be a pair of men working in the rooms— "rooms and pillars," you called that the workings, eh. And there'd be another [pair of] fellas up this way, and there'd be another pair up that way, extracting all the coal out. Well, I'd have my pair of men to take care of. I'd take one empty box to them and get a full, take it back to this place, put the full one there, take another one back, maybe do that twenty-five and sometimes thirty times a day. Then in the evening, when the time was up, they'd never go home early. They'd work 'til the last, make as much money as they could. And I wouldn't go home because they *needed* the money. I'd stay there with them. I'd take the pony back to the stables ... and there'd be a stableman [to] give him something to eat and drink. And they'd have an hour's or two rest; go back on night shift.... So that's when I felt sorry for the poor little pony. They were great little workers them ponies. They were all heart. Small but strong. Faithful little ponies. [When] I went to [No.] 12 [in 1962], they had one left, that's all. The place was so low they couldn't use a diesel. They made a little tram, and they had this little pony taking material [timber, etc.] into the walls. They had him for about three years 'til they closed that place, called 19 West. That was the last pony I saw in the mine.

The Work Life
When first I went to [No.] 16 [in 1932], they gave me another job driving another pony. I done that for about three years and then after awhile, see, they want you to advance in other jobs. They want you to go loading coal. So I went loading and brushing [extracting stone to enlarge the haulage tunnel] and things like that. More money. So I worked for quite a few years at that, contract work [paid by output rather than by a fixed daily wage]. No. 16 colliery closed down in 1962. So I was in 12 colliery for the remainder of time. I done all kind of jobs: back brushing, construction work, any jobs they had around, I could pretty well do them. I had the experience, you know, from the mine. They put me here or there but mostly construction after I was a little bit older. They treated me fair, anyway.

I'd work an extra two hours if they'd ask me. Many's a time ... they were stuck for certain jobs and they'd ask me, "Will you stay down, Cookie?" I said, "Of course." They'd pay you well for it. I needed the money, and they needed the work, so I'd stay down. I'd never say no.

I slept in a couple of times, and I was cross at myself the whole day. Slept in, I think, two or three times in my whole [work] life of forty years. Woman said, "I hope you don't sleep in; you're so cranky." I needed the money, do you see, because a shift is a shift, eh. When you have four days instead of five, at that time I'd lose $12 to $13. That was a lot to lose on account of nothing. But I was lucky. I wasn't sick too often; I wasn't hurt too often. I think I worked a year, pretty near two years, not losing an hour. And working hard. I was, well, in pretty good shape. You got to be in good shape to be in a coal mine. It is a tough, rugged job.

I went on longwall to draw chucks for quite awhile [that is, removing temporary supports, to allow the roof to cave in where coal had been extracted, after the "longwall" system replaced "room-and-pillar" mining]. I was a mechanic in the mine for a good many years after. I just learned myself around as a mechanic, fixing on the longwall ... putting the unit in every day. The coal comes down the longwall. There's a big machine goes in ... right underneath where the coal is spilled down. Then when the shift is over, I'd take it out and then put it back in for ... the next shift. I worked on that for about six or seven years. You change to different jobs. If you could do it. Some people couldn't do that job. I could do pretty well every job. I watched people doing jobs. I was very careful.... Say they'd take me for a job. They'd ... make you go with a fella maybe for a day or two. He had that job. You watch him, then you're on your own....

I didn't have to do this, but every time there'd be a young fella come down, they'd give him to me. I used to break him in.... I'd take him with me for three months. I had a responsibility for that young fella all the time, to take him down to work ... show him what to do and then at the end of a shift, make sure he'd get in the wash house. And then I got another fella, then I got another fella, continuous. So I asked the boss one time, "How about giving them to somebody else now. Not that I don't like the young fellas, but," I said, "I got a big responsibility. I'm making no extra money and if they ... get hurt, they'd hold me responsible." I was good at a job. I worked hard, and I was careful at the job. And I know the fellas today, [who say] "I remember when you took me down in the coal mine. Well, I done what you told me. I got along pretty good." Well, that was: be careful. Don't show off in a coal mine. Be careful what you do.

I was brushing, working at the stone for years, too, making the big roadways for the trip to go in, [and for] the people to walk in. That was a hard job. Full of stone, you know—boring that stone, that stone coming in your lungs. It's a dangerous job too. But still, everything is dangerous if you don't watch. Once you go down in the coal mine, you got to be alert all the time. You'll be all right. That's the way I found it.

Looking Back

I retired in 1969, had the pre-retirement. Only for that, I'd still be working. I was only fifty-five years old, and I worked forty years. I was so happy to get the pension, although I was feeling good. My woman was continuous after me: "Cookie, the first day you get your pension, get out of it." The coal mine life, it's a hard, difficult—you got to be in very, very good condition. Now, I'm telling you: a miner, he's stronger than a horse. In my opinion he can take more punishment than a horse—because it gets cold, it's wet, it's hot and it's dusty and everything else. We had a hard, tough grind, the poor miners. Every cent we worked. The last time I worked, I think I was getting about seventeen dollars a day and that was good money. It's all push-buttons today; it's all automatic. We had to push and pull and scrape. Always bull work, we called it. And the wash house we had at that time, I'd come up and I'd get in the wash, and I'd freeze to death washing. Honest to God, there'd be big goose pimples. When I got home, I'd be froze.

[A miner], he'd give you an honest day's work. I'd do a good day's work and the boss never said anything to me in any way because they'd tell me what to do and I done it. I knew how to do it. They're boss and I'm just an employee. I had to do what I was told. But I got along good. I made big money at mining. I worked steady. I was very lucky in the coal mine. I wasn't serious hurt—a little nick in the finger or a nip in the toe but nothing serious. I was well pleased.

We were pretty careful with our dollar. We weren't squandering. I never drank, she never drank, I never smoked, she didn't smoke. That was a big help, you know. I didn't taste any liquor 'til I was fifty-five years old, me and her. That's why I got along pretty good. I educated my family through a pan shovel—with a pan shovel alone.

Stories from Dominic Nemis

Pit Fire

Dominic Nemis uses some mining terms that might confuse an outsider. A "level" was a major coal-transportation tunnel running from the coal-extraction area to the main haulage slope. Usually the level had to be "brushed" to make it higher and more secure: that is, stone was blasted from the roof or floor, and strong roof supports were installed. Brushing was a highly prized job, difficult, skilled and highly paid. "Shotfirers" were highly experienced and specially certified people who discharged explosives. A key responsibility was first to inspect the place for explosive gases using a specifically designed flame lamp.

We were brushing on level. I always made big money in the pit by brushing [in No.] 16 for years, making seventy-five dollars a week. I never worked a day's pay [fixed rate, rather than "contract" piecework]. So a shotfirer come along there. I got shotfirer's papers myself. So I was down below on the gob [stone-waste]. I had another job that day, I was shovelling the stone. There's two people on the level putting up the booms and blasting the rock. I heard the shotfirer, "Fire." And the first thing you know, all the top of the wall went afire. And we were down there trapped. So there's no need of running away. Pretty near everybody run away but only seven of us. They never stopped 'til they hit the surface. So we fought the fire for four hours. I wasn't deaf like I am now. There was a crack in the roof, and the gas was coming down that crack, and it was roaring like a forest fire. You could hear it all over the place. So we all lined up and ... started throwing stone dust. And it kept on out the level where the air was travelling, and it burnt a few of the booms. And we stayed there 'til four o'clock. The manager sent men down to supply us with stone dust, and they were going to hook the water on the air line, so we'd put water on it. But anyway, we stayed there for four hours, we put out the fire, seven or eight of us.

A week later we had an investigation. The superintendent was there.... So I spoke, I said to Mr. Morrison, "You know that you owe the people that fought that fire some money for the job they done." "Well," he says, "Dominic, I'll tell you what I'll do. I'll pay yez a half a shift each." Give us four hours, just what we worked. Isn't that a big deal? We saved the colliery.

Averting a Crisis During the 1947 Strike

Dominic Nemis was president of the UMW local at No. 16 colliery from the mid-1940s 'til the mid-1950s, including the long strike of 1947. "Bootleg" coal was produced clandestinely outside the purview of the company's monopoly. Typically, one man or a small group would access a shallow area of old workings, extracting "pillars" abandoned after "room" and "crosscut" tunnels had been driven through the coal seam. During strikes, in order to dry up the coal market, the union strictly opposed bootleg production for sale.

We were having a [union] meeting. There was about 300 at the meeting. So, I'm kind of easy to get along with. A fella runs down into the meeting and he says, "A point of order." He says, "There's a man selling coal." You know, there were bootleg pillar—working in the mines, getting coal. They were selling it.

"Well," I says, "listen, what are we going to do about that? What are you worried about?"

He says, "You know, Mr. President, that's the way you are. You never worry about nothing."

"Look," I says, "I got just as much guts as anybody in this hall. I'm not worried about little things like that."

He said, "That man said if anybody come in his yard, he'd shoot him. And he's got a rifle in his hand."

I said, "Is that right? Well, that's different. Now, if that's the case now, we'll just do something about it."

Somebody made a motion we adjourn the meeting. He said he'd shoot the first man to go in the yard. There was 500 of us, paraded up to his house. The [union] Board Member was there too. It was his job to go in. So the fella told me that I had no guts, and I was easygoing and everything. So I never said nothing. I opened the gate and I walked right into his house. Now, I say, "Look, we got a report at the meeting that you were going to shoot the first man that come into your gate. Now, I'm in here. I'm not worrying. I want you to look out the window. You know what? They'll carry your house away." He didn't know what to say, and as white as a ghost. So I come out and I told them, "Well, there's nothing happening." He told me where the coal was. They went up, put the coal in a truck, and took it down to the hospital—then we sold it. But I walked into that fella's house, not anybody else.

Three Men of Dominion

Compiled by John deRoche[1]

Just north of Venice lies the city of Treviso, capital of Treviso Province, within the region called Veneto. Most Italians who settled in Dominion were from that vicinity. At the Italian Hall in 1978, I recorded a talk with three senior "Trevisani" who came here as miners in the 1920s.

Condo Baggio

I'm going to tell my story. I'm Condo Baggio. My city where I come from, it's as big as Sydney. But I was from about a mile outside, the first farmland [*campagna*] outside the city. My father was a peasant [*contadino*].

I come here in 1920, seventeen years of age, with a bunch of fellas. The coal company paid the fare. I was supposed to go to Ontario. I have a cousin there, you see. But when we were over in Quebec, a fella who was head of this bunch ... said, "Why don't you come where the mine is? We all go." This guy was here before. And I say, "By jeez, I think I come. Maybe I stay there for a while, and then I go to Ontario." We arrive in Sydney on Sunday. The coal company put on a special train because most of the people went in Waterford. Me and another fella—friends, from the same town—we went to New Waterford too. And a fella over there brings us to some Italians' house. We got our dinner there. And then, who walks in? My cousin. "Jeez, sure nice to see you." You know you got somebody. You're lonesome; you're young and you don't know nobody. I only have eighty-five cents in my pocket, and the other fella had less than me. He said, "You come in Dominion ... I'll look after you." He took me to [a boarding house run by Italians].

Three days after, I got work. The first day I went to work as helper on the punching machine [machine-runner's helper].[2] The second day, I went loading coal [*carricare carbone*]. We loaded sixty tons of coal with three men. I was a boarder at the hotel.... I went into the kitchen, put away the lunch can and water can, and I went right upstairs, and I slept 'til four in the morning. No supper, no nothing. That's how tired I was. I get up, go down in the pit again, go help at the punching machine again. Thursday, Friday, and Saturday, I did three days and I took home eleven dollars. So I was a big-shot [*un signore*]! You know, when we come here from the old country, we want to make a dollar. I was only seventeen years old loading coal. When you were over eighteen, then you got the right rate ["man's pay" instead of "boy's pay"]. After you worked on day's pay a little while, a month or two ... you advance to contract.[3]

I started in 1A [colliery] here in Dominion. And when they started opening 1B,[4] after 1921, I was working under the 1B shaft. I used to walk from here in Dominion all the way to 1B. Going and coming back, on foot. I worked two, three years where the shaft of 1B and 26 are now. And after 1924, I started down in 1B. In 1925 we were [on strike] six months. Me and Paddy McMahon used to work together. He used to work in the winter, and then, in the spring, he went to work his farm. When the strike came, I went there with him. I worked on the farm, boarded.

When they start the longwall[5] in 1B, used to be eight men brushing, one day's pay, $5.25 a shift. Then the company got sick and tired of that because they never used to do the work right. They took four men—me, a Hungarian fella, and two English fellas—and we used to do that work of eight. We used to be on contract, see. And we used to make around ten dollars, twelve dollars a day.

I worked right in the first wall. And I got buried in the stone. She used to take a bump,[6] you know, and everything shifts. All at once, she just starts a loud roar, and she come down, about six or seven inch of stone [from the roof]. It take over an hour to get me out. Got a broken hip, a couple rib broke. But the worst scare I got in my life in the pit, [was] in 1944: 1B rake going by the run.[7] I was on it, just ready to jump off, and one of my friends hold me back. That's the only [reason] I'm here today. Three men killed; about forty, fifty hurt....

In forty-eight years in the mine, I worked at everything. I always worked on contract—with the stone, or loading the coal, or machine-running. I worked twenty years in the coal face, and twenty-eight years in the stone—maintaining the tunnel [*mantenere la galleria*]—it's called "brusher." Forty-eight years and three weeks of work in the mine. But the last five years before going on pension, after I passed age sixty, I went on day's pay. I think it was in 1968 when I went on pension, and the pay was $17.15 a day. I was working in the stone just the same. The highest the company was giving for day's pay was $17.15 or $17.25—because there's a different rate, according to what job you have. When you were brushing on contract, you could make $30-35 in a day, uh?

Every three years I have to go to Halifax, for a check-up [for silicosis]. A little pension, you know. Ah, we get along, you know. We had our hard times, we had our good times. There used to be an electric car bridge over the track, and every evening we'd all sit outside, under the bridge. There'd be maybe fifteen, twenty Italian fellas. Sometimes we'd sing like hell! I used to like the pit, I'll tell you the truth. Didn't want to work no place else, only the pit.

Riccardo Polegato

[J. deRoche: Why did you leave Italy?] Because you couldn't find work. When I was discharged from the army in 1922, I went to France.... I did four and a half years there, until 1927, and I came here. From my home in France, I went to LaHavre. At LaHavre in France, I embarked on this steamship and sailed to Halifax. From Halifax I came by train to Dominion. Then there was work in the mines, and I did what I could. I was twenty-six years old.

I came on October 18, 1927. I worked in No. 12 mine [in New Waterford] a year-and-a-half, and then I came to No. 26 [1B at the time]. I did twenty-seven years there. And then, for the rest of my life, I worked in No. 20 [Glace Bay]—nine years. At first we were treated badly because it was thought that we were coming to steal their jobs. But after, it started to get better. [I made] $3.15 a day in 1927 when I started. When I left the mine in 1962, October 16, [it was] $6.90, I think. Thirty-five years I worked for this company.

Raffaele Gatto

When I came I was going on seventeen. I left Italy in 1922. I arrived in New York, and from New York, I came here.... In Italy I couldn't make a living. My father's land [*campagna*] was small, and we were so many brothers. We needed to look for work.

There was a lot of people here, years and years ago, that came from the same part of the country. And we had an Italian consul ... Tony DiPistone. He was an agent for the coal company. The coal company paid him a trip to recruit the men, and he brings them over here. The company paid the fare, but then you'd pay back through your check-off, two dollars a week.... Before I come over here ... my brother was here. In 1909-1911, 1912, my brother used to tell me, if the Italians stayed home from work, the mine was idle because the Italian people was the people that was loading the coal ... producing the coal. You see, one time, everything was loaded by hand. They call it the "pan shovel." Now there there's all machines, but are all machines, but at that time you needed manpower.

When we arrived here ... I found work the second day.... I worked as helper to my brother. He was machine-runner. He was here nine years ahead of me. I worked from that day 'til 1925. And then there was pretty slack work at the time. When there's slack work, that was tough times. We had to spare eight dollars a week for the board, so if you had a couple of dollars to spare, you saved it for the next time to pay the board. And then the [1925] strike comes on, and I left here and worked about a year in Quebec. When the strike was over, I got work here in the same mine—it was 1B at the time—and I worked there 'til 1947.

I worked at the coal most of the time. Then after this [other] strike when they didn't want us there [1940], I started in the deep, looking after the chain and the rollers [parts of the coal haulage apparatus]. And they were running short in the engineering, so they teach me how to run all the engines. Then they run short of rake engineer, so the company give me a certificate [after a test]. I run the rake for quite a time. The first time I lowered down that rake, well, I sweat! There was about 300 or 400 people on there. You got quite a responsibility because you are the only man that got the two hands on those controls. When I stopped the rake, I was all in a sweat.

Raffaele Gatto and Riccardo Polegato, 1980.
Courtesy of Len Stephenson.

The only time I got a little bit of a scare was the time I got burned on the wire. I got onto the end of the box [hitching a ride on the coal car]. I was sweating, and I touched these electric wires—just like electric cars, you see. A buddy of mine, he was talking to me, and I couldn't answer because the power went right through me. And then he realized and he pulled me down, and that's what saved me. I got a mark burnt right here.

Then [around 1947, when there was another long strike] I quit and went to the lumber mills [for a couple years]. I worked twenty-three years in the mine, loading coal, and then I went to the lumber mills and a lot of different things, and then I worked as a janitor, then I worked eighteen years in the town doing everything.

[My first day in the mine] it was pretty tough. You see, at the time, we had to walk about a mile and a half. Now they got what they call the "rake"—you get in this and the electric motor take you in. But at that time, you'd walk. You had a lamp—you gotta carry it like you carry the Holy Ghost in church, because as soon as you shake it, the damn thing was going off. So I was in the dark all the time, and I followed my brother. And oh, that was hard. In the dark all the time because I'd hit my head, down I goes, and the lamp goes out. 1A shaft, it's ninety feet down, right over here. My brother, he went out about six o'clock in the morning. Then you'd get out about half past five or six o'clock in the evening. So, in the winter time, you wouldn't see the sun for months. You're supposed to work eight hours, in your place and, you see, an hour to walk in, an hour to walk out, well, it's ten, ten and a half hours [altogether]. Well, I'll tell you the truth, I cried. But I didn't have any money to go back. [laughs] Half the time you don't know what's going on because you're not able to talk to anybody—in English. Many's the time I'd cry in bed. I didn't have the gall enough to say nothing to my brother, but I had no money, I didn't know what I'm going to do. I said, "He got used to it, now I gotta get used to it." So I did.

Today, I'd rather work in the mine than to work anywhere else. When you get used to it, when you're a real good miner, you're not worried about anything. You go to your work and you know what to do, and there's the same temperature, summer or winter. And me and you working together, they call you "buddies." You're like two brothers. You get along wonderful. You're a miner, and that's your job, and you get so accustomed to it that you like it.

We came with nothing, and we built ourselves up. There's no foreign people—there's not an Italian—in Dominion or anywhere around that they [don't] own their home, they got a few dollars in the bank, they're well set, every one of us. So [people] see that we didn't come up here to take the bread from their mouths; we come up here to develop the country. I'm here fifty-six years, I'm going on seventy-three, and I didn't take anything off of the country, I built up the country.

In Others' Eyes:
Pit Talk about Italians

By John deRoche

When you belong to a minority, the surrounding peoples impact deeply upon you. Cape Breton is primarily Scottish; the main cultural ways and social arrangements are un-Italian. This marked the lives of Italian immigrants and their descendants. In these pages, we will "eavesdrop" on non-Italians discussing Italians, to learn about challenges the minority group faced.

In the 1970s, I set about learning the history, culture and social doings of industrial Cape Breton, my adoptive home. I explored the everyday work-world of coal miners in long conversations with older men. With a summer grant, I hired student interviewers in 1977. We talked to more than eighty retired miners.[1] I knew that Italians had immigrated here by the hundreds, especially between the 1890s and 1920s when the burgeoning coal and steel industries drew people from Europe, the British Isles, the eastern Mediterranean, the West Indies and Newfoundland. They joined the offspring of earlier immigrant settlers, who were flocking from Acadian, Irish and Scottish Gaelic villages of rural Cape Breton. I knew I had to pay attention to this multicultural reality if I wanted to understand the daily world of "the pits" because ethnic heritage shapes who we are and what we do. It gives us identity in our own eyes and in the ideas others have about us. It draws people together while it also sets us apart, and sometimes it drives people against each other. Among the many themes of the interviews, then, we touched on ancestry, immigration, views on ethnic groups and stories about relations between groups.

As we listen to these accounts from non-Italian miners, what is especially interesting is not "*facts* about Italians." Instead, it's what others *believed* about Italians. Whether true to the "facts" or not, those impressions made up the social environment for Italians. After all, if you think I'm a demon, and you control the resources, I'll have to deal with what you think, no matter how good I "really" am.[2] Happily, though, you'll find that most of the miners show a very complimentary understanding of their Italian co-workers and neighbours!

"I Educated My Family Through a Pan Shovel"[3]

Before the mid-20th century, Cape Breton coal was mined more by muscle than machine. The corporation sent recruiters to Europe to feed the labour-hungry pits, up through the 1920s. "There wasn't enough men to work all the mines around," explains Eric Scott, "so they used to send to the old country. There was an awful lot of Italians came here in Dominion, about 200 or 300 of them." Donald Corbett remembers: "The company would pay their way over, but they'd pay the company back through the checkoff." Gordon MacGregor adds: "Some of them sent over for their relatives, and that's how it built up."

Immigrant miners gradually made their way into the full range of rank-and-file positions. But at the beginning, very few Italian newcomers landed plum jobs. Instead, immigrants were assigned to the "face" as "loaders," lifting out the blasted-down coal with large, circular, shallow "pan shovels." Wilburn McKenzie's recollection is typical: "Mostly all Italians were loading coal at that time." By law, loaders had to be certified and, as Thomas Donaldson points out, immigrants "wouldn't have no English to get them papers to load coal, you see." Pat McMahon describes the solution: "You'd have to answer some questions, but it wasn't hard. The Italians didn't have the language then, so somebody else would answer for them." Donald Corbett explains the training: "They'd put a new fella with an old foreigner that was in the pit for awhile."

Why did the heaviest, lowly work go to immigrants? "It was the easiest job to get," says Pat McMahon, "and they were tremendously strong, husky fellas." But Wilburn McKenzie comes closer to the point: "I guess the people who belonged to the place didn't care much about loading coal. You didn't get a hell of a lot for load-ing coal, and you had to work pretty damn hard, so they had to get foreign people. One Italian fella I knew was cutting coal, a couple of them, machine-runners, on the old "puncher." But mostly it was all Canadian people [on that job]. They used to make big money." John W. MacLean of Glace Bay started in the pit in 1906. He notes: "The men that were cutting, they were all big able [Scottish] men up from the country up here. Foreign men, they'd come in and load it up." Ex-manager Gordon MacGregor adds the justification that natives "were looking for those jobs long before those [immigrant] people came. And generally, your work record and the years you worked, it was making you a better miner all the time, and you understood those things, and you were given some consideration for that." The difference involved more than money. Wilburn McKenzie describes the prestige factor, around 1917 in Dominion's 1A colliery. "After I worked awhile there, I can remember the first couple of [non-immigrant Scottish] men that started to load coal. The men were saying to them, 'We got a pair of Chinamen!' Just kidding, you know."

Community: Sticking Together and Fitting In

Sketches of everyday life in the early days

Several miners remember the temporary row-housing—"the shacks"—that the coal company erected in several mining towns for new immigrant men. The most vivid stories come from Dominion. Wilburn MacKenzie recalls:

> The old Italians, when I first started in the pit [1917], all they wanted to do is make a certain amount of money and go back to Italy. And they just lived in what they called the "shacks"—small-roomed place, long buildings, just the one story. They stayed here perhaps for eight or nine years. The idea was, the faster they saved a certain amount of money, [the sooner] they'd go back to Italy. They all carried their money belt around their middle.

Donald Corbett started at Dominion's 1A in 1914. "There was three or four long shacks up there in the [mine] dump and one across the railroad. All Italians in them, and the Ukrainians lived here. We used to eat supper and go and have a beer at 'Bug Row.' It was another place over there. Italians. They sold beer. All Italians sold beer. They were all nice fellas."

Eric Scott grew up in Dominion, where he was born in 1903.

> The Italians used to live right back of our back fence. They used to call them the "shacks." They were nice houses, but they were long. There were three of them. The company built them. They had a chapel in one end of them. They used to have services on Sunday. And a co-operative store. Max Passerino was well educated, he was a smart man, and he had charge of this co-operative store, and his two brothers helped him. And he had done all the business with the Italians and the company. See, they couldn't speak English when they came here. Well, when the 1909 strike[4] came on, this Max Passerino, he was driving up through New Aberdeen [in Glace Bay] one day and a fella jumped on the back of the wagon and stabbed him. He died. See, I guess it was on account of him that all the Italians were working. He was helping them out. I remember the funeral. There must have been thousands of people there. And then the Italians had Tony Pistone, his name was. He was the consul for all the Italians. He was their boss, like. And he lived in Sydney. I used to see him often. A little short man. He used to wear one of those plug hats ... a derby. And he was going back to Italy on a trip. And he had a little donkey, with the

big ears, and a little wagon and harness. So he sent the donkey out to the Italians to look after for him when he was in Italy. I was a little fella, and I was always around with the Italians. And boy, they come over with the donkey. I used to be on his back and get drives in the wagon with him. I was only a little kid. Thought it was wonderful.

Mr. Scott enjoyed more than his donkey rides.

Italians were musical. They'd play the accordions. And they were great bicycle drivers, before the cars came in. And Sunday morning, probably there'd be about twenty or twenty-five of them, get on their bicycles, with three or four accordions, and they'd go over to Waterford or to Donkin— No. 6 then—and they'd have a dance.... And then around dark Sunday evening, they'd all come back again. The next Sunday, there'd be a bunch from Waterford or No. 6 come over here, and they'd have a dance. Then they had a game; I think it was cbee-jee" [bocce] they called it. They used to play that an awful lot. And the winner would get the big enamel pitcher of beer. They were great people for beer drinking.

Pat McMahon recalls his years in Dominion between 1906 and 1916:

...when there was only one fella could talk English, Max Passerino. He was interpreter for them. And they lived in two long shacks away up here on Mitchell Avenue where you come into the town. I suppose it was two or more years before any of the women arrived. That changed the whole situation. They started building homes. And now the nicest homes are owned by Italian families today. But the shacks, if you ever seen them eating in these shacks—it was very simple fare: salami, homemade bread. "Joe the Baker"...made the bread for them. They had a pocketknife to cut it. And they had draft beer, by the barrel. A jug—more than a quart—they paid about fifteen cents for that. And they worked. I never seen a lazy one in the pit. A lot of the natives, they'd go up there to these shacks. There was nothing but men. It was pretty rough, and it was pretty plain. They'd go up there for some of this draft beer. And of course, they were working with them in the pit. They always got along well with the Italians. Oh, the Italian really for years was the number one immigrant.

Mr. McMahon adds his colourful eyewitness version of the often-told story of the Beer Strike, sometime before the First World War:

There was an awful lot of bootleggers in them days.... They used to get draft beer by the barrel from Montreal. I don't know just how they got it, but they were never short of it. Now, this fella called Norman "Juniper" MacDonald, he was a very zealous liquor inspector. He was going to make it so dry that the whole town would be dusty. One of the first places he went was up to these shacks. And there was to be no more beer.

Next day or the day after, the natives coming to work found there was no Italians. So the manager sent an official to drive the horse and buggy up there as fast as he could and find out what the trouble was. Well, some fella that had a little more education then the rest, he had printed a sign in English: "No beer, no work." So that was a bad day for the coal company. It was also a bad day for Norman Juniper. Needless to say, as prohibition went, he wasn't a big success. Things went sour on him.

Living apart, living together

Murdock Matheson paints a strong image of his multi-ethnic community in the New Aberdeen section of Glace Bay.

> People don't understand about this place here, see. They're talking about bilingualism, biculturalism and that. I went to school with every nationality. And they all lived in these houses here and worked in the coal mine. They're still here now. They're all married into one another. I worked with every nationality that you could think of. And they all lived here in these company houses, 'til they started building for themselves on the outskirts. Pretty near all the foreign people built little places, all through the area.

At Dominion, Eric Scott tells us: "Italians, they'd stick to themselves. They were all good men. Everyone got along wonderful up here in Dominion, anyway. Wonderful." In the same town, I also asked Wilburn McKenzie: "Did you find that men from the various immigrant groups tended to stick together?" His answer includes an explanation:

> Oh yes, they stayed by themself to a man. That lasted quite a while. Well, they'd never be able to survive or get along very well if they didn't do that. That's the way with everybody in a country where a bunch of them get together. They generally try to stick together. It's about the only way they're going to survive. But now most all the old Italians are all dead. Their sons now, they're married in with Canadians. That [separateness] is all gone and done away with.

Mickey Mullins, a mine manager in New Waterford, says:

> There was no dissatisfaction. Just like today, you see how people get along: some do, some don't, but the big majority of people mind their own business and get along. Those people that came here had ambitions to build homes of their own. And kept to themselves.

New Waterford's, Angus F. MacDonald, also denies there was ever "any conflict between the Italians and the natives," except for the events of 1940.[5] He adds further details on cultural distinctiveness and eventual merging.

The Italians, of course, they had their own culture and things like that. They stayed with that closely. But then they drifted into our culture. Good citizens; church-going people. They associated well. They kept their own ways. Politically, in the beginning, they had to be careful—until they got acquainted. Of course, with the second generation coming up, or even the third now, they're here all over, Italians, they're NDP, and they're good union men. Always good union men, very best. Once they got acquainted with the people, and the kids started growing up and going to school together, they got along well together.

Negative Images and Actions

Despite the very positive tone of non-Italians' attitudes, all was not well. Next we'll see examples of mistrust, resentment and insults.

Name-calling

Prejudice and discrimination had a place in the mines and communities of Cape Breton and did their typical damage. Let's turn to some accounts from Scottish and Anglo miners, about name-calling and mimicking, to glimpse what such practices meant to *them*. The point here is only to explore the thoughts of people who did these things. The story would be quite different for persons on the receiving end.

A Glace Bay miner describes how immigrants were needled. He sees it as just another form of teasing and joking that miners practised all the time with each other. There was "very, very little [name-calling]. Of course, they'd pull off of fellas in the mines—say Polish fellas—speaking broken English and all that. You'd make fun of them. But it was only just in jest, not in earnest. They'd take it in good part. Oh, they're a good class of people."

As for name-calling, a New Waterford man says: "'Wops'—'grease ball'—that'd be an Italian. 'Squarehead,' any foreigner." A Glace Bay man notes: "They'd say, 'You big wop' or 'You big hunk.' You never knew their right name anyway because they always give you the impression that they couldn't understand English, most of them." A Dominion man says Italians were called "dagos, wops, whatnot." Like several other men who spoke to us about such talk, he doesn't think it was any problem because (he believes) "they didn't mind it."

Is such name-calling a sign that ethnic groups are at each other's throats? Sometimes. But one man from New Waterford suggests looking further. "They'd call a foreigner a 'hunk' or a 'squarehead' or something like that. Yet, if they got in trouble, they'd be the first to help them. When you were working in the mine, you got along with everybody." In other words, he believes that miners had a deeper togetherness that was untouched by such taunting.

A Glace Bay man offers another way to interpret ethnic name-calling from the viewpoint of people in his time and place. "It was through ignorance, see. Nobody meant to hurt anybody. But they'd say, 'Come here, nigger.' And 'come here, bohunk,' no matter what nationality he was. And nobody thought nothing of that. Nobody knew each other's names." He explains this language as simply a way to distinguish people's identities, just like the nicknaming of local Scottish family branches (for example, the "Satchel-Arse MacNeils"). "And," he concludes, "that's the way they'd separate them."[6]

One New Waterford man recognizes that name-calling is a way to put down and push back others. Immigrants were called "'wops' and 'hunks' or 'bohunks,'" he says. "They weren't entitled to that. They're just as good as what we are."

One man from Dominion elaborates on how Italians avoided trouble for themselves in the face of ethnic slurs.

> If they were speaking about an Italian, he was a "dago." Y'understand: if you called them something, they might keep on going. They didn't step around too much in the way or nothing. They just minded their own business. They might say something in Italian. But supposing they could speak English, they wouldn't say back, "You can go so-and-so" or something. A Canadian fella [if called a bad name] would tell the other fella to go to hell and mind his own business or something like that, or perhaps they might have a scrap over it. But Italians, if you said something to them, they just took it and didn't say nothing about it.

Note, though, that this man's whole point implies that name-calling actually was insulting.

Our interviews only once turned up blatant segregation on the job (apart from the 1940 expulsion). A Dominion man says:

> When I started here [at 1A, 1917], they had a wash house [where miners stored their street clothes and showered]. The Italians or Ukrainians or Greeks all shifted down in half of the wash house, and they wouldn't be allowed ... where the people that belonged to the place was, to wash or anything else. They were all by themselves. But after we went down to 1B [around 1924], it was all the one big wash house.

Nice people: hot tempers

Very few men criticized the personal qualities of Italian miners, but there were some exceptions. One Dominion man thought that "some Italians are pretty nice fellas, but some of them were dangerous. They were right ready for a gun or a knife, right quick. Kind of a bad-tempered bunch." A man who worked in Glace Bay had a similar mixed reading. "You couldn't trust a lot of them fellas, you know.

Italians are queer men, dangerous men, boy. They're nice people, though, if you just stay on the good side of them, but if you get out with them—the Germans were bastards too."

"Greedy" workers

For the old miners, a "greedy" worker went out of his way to get the best-paying pit jobs and took as many extra shifts as he could get. Some men admired this and even described themselves proudly as "greedy." Others resented it because they thought it spurred destructive competition among union brothers and played into the employer's hands. One Dominion man admired Italians as hard, dedicated workers but, also says that many were "greedy workers. A lot of them wanted to get enough to get out of here and spoiled conditions here. They came here just for a stake. They left and went to Ontario and bought apartment houses and like that. They were all good workers though. Helluva lot of them, nice fellas, those Italian fellas."

Two cultures at cross-purposes

The difference between bribing, on the one hand, and showing respect, on the other, will depend on people's particular cultural rules. Italian immigrants had their own understanding of the appropriate way to maintain smooth relationships with people who control resources. One non-Italian miner laughs about being a driver in 1B in the late 1920s, hauling coal from Italian loaders at the face. Loaders relied on their driver to take out the full boxes promptly and to bring a timely supply of empties.

> The Italians, they'd buy the driver tobacco. One fella'd bring out a fig [of chewing-tobacco] to me today, the next fella the next day. Then they'd invite you up for beer on Saturday, payday, you know. Got along good. You give me the boxes, and I give you the tobacco. [laughs] That's the way it was.

"The Pit Is a World of Its Own: Together in Difference"

Typically, miners everywhere will set aside their differences because of the special dangers and the need to cooperate in pit work, and that is what usually happened in Cape Breton. John Simpson of Glace Bay describes it this way: "It never seemed to make any difference in the mine. No one ever took any hate to a foreign man or a Newfoundlander. One big family."

As Patrick Power of New Waterford says:

> Pretty near every fella worked with a foreigner at one time or another....
> There's no difference: coloured, black, white or anything else. Take Italian
> fellas. There would be one or two ... working, and then there would be

another fella come along and they'd gossip in their own language. Same way with the Cheticamp French.... They'll have a conference in their own talk. The same way with us, I imagine it would be, too.

John MacKinnon, a veteran of 1B, elaborates:

[Everybody] worked with each other. A pair of men in a place, probably one Italian, the other fella'd be a foreigner, what they call an immigrant. All different nationalities in the world were underground. And they all got along very well, you know. See, there seemed to be a bond between miners, no matter where you go.

In the words of Archie Gould from Glace Bay: "The pit is a world of its own, you know."

"All Them Italians: Good Workers, B'y!"[7]

Many men (too numerous to quote here) from various communities and pits, praised highly their immigrant coworkers from all ethnic backgrounds. John W. MacLean's assessment is typical: "Oh, those foreign people worked hard loading that coal. All them foreign people were good." Men said the occasional individual loafed or bungled but never a category of people. Steve Stack, of Reserve Mines, for example, put it this way: "It's like a barrel of apples. You generally find one bad one in the whole barrel, eh?" "You know," retired manager, Big Joe MacLellan, pointed out, "the workers at all mines were good. They had to be good. At that time, you had to produce." But when we asked whether any particular group stood out above the others, Italians were most often mentioned. The following are just a few of the testimonials.

Pat McMahon holds first-generation Cape Breton Italian miners in high esteem. His own Irish family had moved to Scotland's coalfields, then he immigrated to Dominion in 1906 at age 18 and worked in No. 1A colliery 'til the early 1920s.

Italians were the best imported labour. They were strong and hardy, all great workers, for some reason. They would want to do better, produce more coal than the Polish fellows that were working, perhaps, just a short distance away. Of course, it was all contract work [paid by the ton], and they were their own boss. They didn't need anybody to push them to shovel faster. Some of those men [with] the pan shovel were like ballet dancers: the footwork, shovelling that coal into the box. And they wouldn't throw it too high; it would just glide over the side of the box. Quite interesting to watch. They were pretty expert. Two winters in the pit [around 1922], I worked with two Italians. Genio, he was a very fiery Italian, but oh, a fantastic worker. He has records in the pit that nobody would ever believe that one small man ever did. But I know the amount of coal he loaded, and the work he done on one shift. And the work to him was just a joke. He was laughing all the time. He was a fantastic worker. Work was just a pleasure. He done everything so well. Italians were the biggest [group], and they were the most important. If they stayed home, the pit would be idle. They were tremendously strong, husky fellas. Really did you ever find a lazy one? I wouldn't have any hesitation in saying that the Italians were very easy to get along with—and great workers.

Wilburn McKenzie came from rural Scottish Cape Breton to Dominion. He worked at No. 1A from 1917 to 1924, then at No. 1B for many years. I asked him, "What kind of workers did the Italians make?" To understand his answer, we need to see the differences between the two methods of paying miners: "contract" versus "day's pay." "Contract work" was piecework, where a loader was paid for each ton he shovelled into "boxes" to be hauled from the mine. A "day's pay" or "datal" man received, instead, a fixed rate for the shift, regardless of his productivity. A fit man could make more money on contract. Also, as old miners repeatedly emphasized, a contract man "was his own boss," and saw himself virtually as a self-employed entrepreneur in an individual business contract with the coal corporation. But on day's pay, you were just a hired hand. "Oh, [Italians] were good workers," says Mr. McKenzie:

> The Italians, now, loading, if they put them on day's pay, well there they were the poorest men you could get, on day's pay. Their money was coming, and they didn't see any sense in working. [laughs] So they wouldn't stretch their back too much, they wouldn't hurt themselves. But you put them into a place [on contract] and tell them they were going to get so much a ton—or if they were brushing, they were going to get so much a yard—oh, well, they'd just murder themselves then, you know.

But it wasn't only Italians who changed their work style, he added. It was a general pattern and, when the company converted many jobs to day's pay, it lowered the mines' productivity across the board.

Gordon MacGregor, of Gaelic-speaking Cape Breton parentage, was born in 1908 at Donkin, where he began work at age fourteen and started his climb toward management. Before it closed in 1925, Donkin's No. 6 attracted many Italian mining immigrants. Mr. MacGregor praises Italians as "very industrious." But it was not only the men who earned his admiration.

> I remember talking to a lady over there. She told me [that] where she lived [in Italy], they were that poor that they had a little plot of ground, and a quarter of a mile away there'd be another plot. That's what they did their farming on. She was about twenty-five when she and her husband

came over here to work. In Donkin, you've seen the company houses and the little yards around them: nothing but ashes in them. And I wish you'd see the garden that she made!

Non-Italian miners clearly shared a respect for Italian workers. In the industrial villages and small-town neighbourhoods of Cape Breton, your reputation on the job is fundamental to your image in the wider society. It is safe to say that Italian men's performance in the pits was a key to achieving acceptance and dignity in the community as a whole. To be sure, it did not prevent the dreadful rupture of 1940, when Italians—immigrant and locally-born alike—were cast as "enemy aliens" and were routed from their jobs. But that episode shamed the accusers rather than the accused, and the positive image of Italian miners lived on.

Macaroni: A Rose by Any Other Name
Edited by Sam Migliore

Humour, in its various forms, can be an important source of fun and entertainment. It can be used to make people laugh, ease tensions and, among other things, provide an important glimpse at the power relations that exist in a society. Exposing inequalities and injustices through humour may, in turn, provide a basis for change. What follows are two versions of a joke that was prominent in the past and still exists in some people's memories today.

Enzo Antonello, Dominion

My father used to tell the story about the fellow who came from Italy looking for a job in the coal mines. The company people would always tell him that they weren't hiring. He would come home feeling dejected, and he would complain. The Italians in Dominion would tease him, saying: "Listen, you'll never get a job with the coal company. You don't have the right name." So, he asked: "What do you mean?" "Well," they said, "you have to be a MacDonald, a MacLean...." Off he went, and the next Monday, when they asked him for his name, he said: "Macaroni." [laughs] The older Italian miners in Dominion ... the things they would do, eh. Here was this raw recruit from the old country, and they were going to give him his basic indoctrination. Macaroni!

Dolores (Rossetti) Moore, Sydney

Years ago, probably in the early 1940s, my brother worked in the general yard of the steel plant. He didn't have a steady job. Every morning, he and others would line up at the yard to see who would work that day. Well, he noticed that the men whose names starting with "Mac— MacDonald or MacNeil—always seemed to get the jobs, while those with Italian or foreign sounding names were often sent home. My brother used to tell the story of the Italian who, one day, told the foreman that his name was "Macaroni." And, Mr. Macaroni got work that day! Well, I thought that was cute; I got a kick out of that story.... You wouldn't get away with that kind of hiring today. [laughs]

Giacomo Tubetti:
His Life and Times

By Corrine (Tubetti) Keeling[1]

The Tubetti family resided in Nimis, a small mining town in the province of Udine, Italy. Udine is located on the northeastern strip of Italy [bordering Slovenia]. It is an area of abundant minerals and numerous mining establishments. On September 9, 1893, a boy was born to Giorgio and Rosa Tubetti; he was baptized, Giacomo. The Tubetti's had one other child who preceded Giacomo; her name was Theresa. Giacomo, like his father, followed the family tradition to become an iron miner in Udine.

Giorgio Tubetti died in 1908. It is not known whether it was due to natural causes or the conditions at the mine. Within a year-and-a-half, Rosa remarried. She was a very domineering woman, and her new husband was her complement. Giacomo and his stepfather did not get along; so in 1910, at the age of seventeen, he left Italy in search of a new life. In his travels around [the former] Czechoslovakia, Giacomo was accompanied by his sister. She later boarded a ship bound for Canada. Giacomo remained in Czechoslovakia and found a job in a brick factory. He stayed there for about three years. The sanitary conditions in the factory camps, however, kept declining during that period; the beds were crawling with bugs, and lice were to be found everywhere. With all his ill experiences in Europe, Giacomo decided to start fresh in Canada. He travelled to Hamburg, Germany, where he boarded a ship headed for Halifax, Nova Scotia. The ship, named *Amear's,* left Hamburg on May 12, 1913, and arrived in Halifax on May 31.

While in Halifax, Giacomo went to a barber shop for a haircut and, because his vocabulary and understanding of the English language were so limited, he ended up paying five dollars—which was a very dear price then. Giacomo proceeded to Glace Bay where his sister, now Theresa Micossi, lived. There, Giacomo worked in the Donkin No. 6 mine for about a year. The conditions of the mine were much the same as those in Europe—unsanitary conditions, long hours of work among the rats, and low wages that amounted to about seventy-five cents per day.

In 1919, Giacomo left Glace Bay and headed for Inverness. When he reached his destination, he met the Cuveliers, a Belgian family, and became a boarder at their home. Frank Cuvelier and his family had recently immigrated to Canada. They had two children with them: Denise, who was fourteen, and Vital, who was sixteen. Giacomo and Frank became very close friends. Frank managed to get Giacomo a job in the No. 1 mine where he worked. Here Giacomo toiled long hours for about one dollar per day.

While Giacomo lived at the Cuvelier residence, he fell in love with their daughter, Denise. They married when Denise turned sixteen. Two weeks later, while Giacomo, Frank and Angelo Varnier were in the mine a cross-beam broke. By the time the walls started to cave in, the miners had already started for the surface. When Giacomo had reached the surface, he realized that Frank was still below. The other miners, seeing that Angelo and Giacomo wanted to re-enter the mine, tried to hold them back. They were unsuccessful. Angelo and Giacomo fought like hell, escaped the miners' hold, and risked their lives by running back into the mine. They eventually found Frank pinned under one of the cross-pieces. The two men saved Frank, but Giacomo had "coal marks" on his face for the rest of his life. After this near-fatal accident, Giacomo quit the coal mine. He and Denise headed back to Glace Bay, hoping for greener pastures. Denise, however, was very unhappy there, so after three months, they returned to Inverness and its mine.

Giacomo's first experience as his own boss was operating a convenience store. He moved a one-room building from Danny Allen's Hill to Main Street. There he sold pop, candy and other goods. The only assistance Giacomo received was from Frank and his wife, Anna. A year after Giacomo and Denise were married, and she became pregnant and had a baby girl, Italia, on April 30, 1917. Two years after Italia was born, Giacomo began to make ice cream. The ice cream machinery consisted of a gasoline engine which enabled the beaters to mix the recipe in the large churns. Giacomo's ice cream was so good that many tried to copy it but never with good results.

A typical day for Giacomo Tubetti began at four o'clock in the morning, when he set out for Cape Mabou to purchase cream from the farmers. He would return home, set up the machinery, and head out for the mine at seven o'clock. While Giacomo and Frank were at work, Denise and Anna would start making the ice cream. Giacomo would return home from work around four o'clock in the afternoon, put on clean clothes, hitch up the horse to the brightly painted wagon with its Italian flag, and pack the ice into the two compartments along with the ice cream. After supper, Giacomo, sometimes accompanied by his daughter Italia, rode all over town selling his ice cream.

From the moment Giacomo arrived in Inverness, he lived with Frank and Anna in Belgium Town—Forest Street. In 1920, Giacomo and his family moved to Main Street, where they rented a small house. Three years later, in 1923, the year of the "Big Fire," their home burned down. Giacomo had always kept his money in one of the drawers in the bedroom. When the fire was nearing their home, Denise grabbed the first drawer she saw; this drawer, however, happened to contain the bills, not the money. During the fire, most of the Tubetti family records were lost.

Giacomo and Denise moved back to Belgium Town for a few years, while he went house hunting. They finally found the house he wanted, but there was one problem. It was built on Beach Hill. In 1925, Giacomo had the house taken down in four sections. The interior of the house was beautiful; it consisted all of douglas fir. Giacomo did most of the remodelling himself but did receive some help from Angus MacLellan, a carpenter, and J. J. Gillis, the contractor. The upstairs of the house accommodated his family, and the downstairs eventually became the Ice Cream Parlour. Denise had her second child, Georgina, on January 29, 1926, but at the age of eight, Georgina died from rheumatic fever.

In 1929, Giacomo started selling Sunoco and Esso gasoline. The pumps, the kind that had to be cranked, were located in front of the Ice Cream Parlour. Many customers thought that Italia was a boy because she was pumping gas. Since Giacomo was selling Esso gas, he became the Esso dealer for Inverness. Even without any assistance, Giacomo was able to build a garage next door for maintenance work on local cars. Giacomo was the first in his line of business to have electrical power. In the barn behind the house, he had a Delco generator installed. This was how he received his experience on motors.

In 1932, during Denise's third pregnancy, Giacomo was almost killed. He was working on one of the cars in the garage while it was running. He didn't realize that there were no windows open, and he collapsed because of the build-up of toxic fumes. Luckily, it was close to supper time; when Denise called him, and he didn't answer, she ran over to the garage to find him lying on the floor. Giacomo was a very large man, and Denise had to literally carry him out. As a result of the immense strain, she lost the twins; one was still-born and the other died two days later.

After Denise had returned home from the hospital, the doctor told her that because of the strain, she would probably never have more children. Two years later, on August 22, 1934, Denise had another child. The child was another girl, and her name was Frances. Giacomo was becoming very impatient because he was now forty-one years old, and he still did not have an heir to carry on the family name and business. On May 24, 1936, George Angelo Tubetti was born—George, after his grandfather Giorgio, and Angelo, after Angelo Varnier.

In June 1936, Italia returned home from Montreal with her diploma in hairdressing. Giacomo, who was very proud of his first-born, turned half of the ice cream parlour into a beauty salon. In 1939, Giacomo rented the Union Temple. Here he started the first movie theatre in Inverness. But, a year later, his lease was cancelled; he never knew why. He just went down one evening, and there was a padlock on the door. Giacomo was very angry, and said: "I'll be damned. I'll start one myself." While Giacomo and Jim MacNeil, from Southwest Margaree, were building the theatre, the Union Temple was leased to two men from Sydney who started their own theatre. Giacomo tried to obtain his licence but, because of the other theatre, this was not possible; Inverness wasn't large enough to have two theatres. Giacomo went to Halifax and had a personal interview with the Premier of Nova Scotia. Giacomo's case was put before the board, and they agreed to grant him the licence; this, in effect, forced the other two men to close their theatre. Now that Giacomo had the theatre and the garage, he put in his notice of resignation at the mine.

Giacomo Tubetti died on September 19, 1957. During his lifetime, he had become a very successful businessman. Sometimes, however, he regretted leaving the mine because being your own boss can cause a lot of troubles, and the work never ends. He became successful with the help of Frank and Anna Cuvelier. Without their help, he probably would have died a miner.

A Brief Note on Rum-Running

By Len Stephenson

Many people in Cape Breton, Italian and non-Italian, engaged in rum-running in past years. Some of my close Italian friends have left us with timely reminiscences of their involvement in the business during the prohibition years and beyond. One individual provided this account:

> [One day, in the late 1920s,] we were coming home from Westmount at about three in the morning with our last load of liquor in Joe's car when our driver noticed that we were being followed. He recognized that the car belonged to an inspector. The inspector passed us and motioned for us to pull over.

> We had fifteen, ten-gallon kegs of rum in the back seat area of the Studebaker with the back seat removed. We pulled over, stopped the car, and ran into the woods. That would be about where St. Rita's Hospital [stood] on Kings Road in Sydney. A shot was fired at us as we kept running.

> We walked through the woods and arrived at a hotel in Sydney about five in the morning. Joe and some other men were waiting for us. We explained to Joe that we had to abandon the car and the booze or be caught. He immediately went to the telephone and reported the car stolen. He was satisfied that we had made the proper moves, and he said, "To hell with the car and the booze, as long as you were not caught." A ten-gallon keg of strong rum only cost about eight dollars.

> On another occasion that year, we were hauling rum that had been landed on Dominion Beach in small row boats, ten or fifteen kegs at a time. We had about fifty, ten-gallon kegs on the beach. While we were waiting for the truck to return for the last thirteen barrels, we saw a car

approaching. We walked along the beach, away from the landing site. It was an inspector, and he called us back and asked what we were doing on the sand bar. We said we just came down for a walk.

He asked if the stuff belonged to Joe, and, if so, we should go and talk to him. Joe was waiting in a house up town to hear from us. I ran up and described the inspector to Joe. He said he knew the man, and told us to leave the last of the kegs for the inspector to take to Glace Bay. We hauled the rum in the Rio Truck to a place behind the Glace Bay post office. We kept a keg for ourselves and sold it for ten dollars.

During rum-running days, the Dominion Beach was a popular site for landing liquor and rum that came from Rum Row, a twelve-mile distance off shore. An earthquake occurred at four-thirty in the afternoon on November 18, 1929. Following the quake, a tidal wave swept completely over the Dominion Sand Bar Beach; it uncovered a large cache of kegs of rum that were quickly claimed and rolled home by the local beachcombers.

Liquor landings along the Dominion shoreline also occurred at Sampson's Cove, Park Street shore and other spots where the cliff was not too steep. Ingenious hiding places often were found for the kegs, including sewer-man-holes, vacant coal company buildings, bootleg pits and a hidden room constructed under a lawn adjoining a basement.

Another story related to me by my aforementioned friends dealt with landing rum at Baddeck and loading it into a car destined for New Waterford. A chase, however, ensued. The authorities impounded the vehicle and booze, and my friends spent a few months in jail at Baddeck.

In 1930, wages from the coal mines were sparse, and work was unsteady. My friends were fully aware that rum-running was considered illegal, but they questioned the degree of immorality involved. They decided to set up an operation along the shoreline several miles from the port of Louisbourg. Large underground tanks were hidden in the woods near the water, and rum from the barrels was emptied into the storage containers. The empty kegs were burned on the sand at low tide to conceal the evidence. It proved to be a successful, but temporary, arrangement.

One of the entrepreneurs was persuaded to invest money in the purchase of a new, larger and faster boat to haul greater quantities of rum, and thus increase profits. It proved to be a bad investment. On the first return trip, he was spotted and chased by the Coast Guard. He steered the boat near the shore, jumped overboard in the cold December water, and was forced to hide in the woods on a small island—forfeiting both boat and booze.

The risks involved in rum-running were considerable as were the profits. The product could be bought for about fifty cents a gallon and sold for at least ten times the purchase price. Prohibition in the United States ended in December 1933. In Cape Breton, the lucrative practice continued until the outbreak of war in 1939.

Bootlegging in the Past:
An Anonymous Note

Edited by Sam Migliore

During the Rum Row period, and later, a number of Cape Bretoners bought and sold liquor to supplement their income—especially during difficult periods. The Italians were no exception. When times are difficult, people sometimes turn to whatever means are available to make a living or to simply get by.

I went through 'er from one thing to another. I was always self-employed. Worked in the pits for a while, did this and that for a while, bootlegged for a little while. [laughs] It was hard to make a living. What else could you do? What the hell, I did it all. Now, I don't do anything....

Selling liquor in the Rum Row days. You could go off the beach here, three miles, and get whatever you wanted for about six or seven dollars. They would sell it to you by the barrel—maybe fifty cents a gallon. Yeah. Five-gallon barrels. Many of them I tapped, holy Christ. Used to bury them in the backyard here. Dig a trench, put them in, and then bury them. Go out at Christmas time to dig them out. You would have to dig through the frost to get at them. [laughs] Gees! The barrels would freeze but not the liquor. But the frost, trying to get through that, and me picking at twelve at night. [laughs] Oh, you would never believe what I went through.

Later, they started this permit stuff. I don't know how many times I've been on the black list. I wasn't allowed to drink my own bottle in the house. Used to carry it around, still selling. I'd carry a bottle in my pocket. Yeah, a little flask. Somebody come around looking for a drink, you'd pull out the little bottle, gees. [laughs] Couldn't keep anything in the house, had to keep it elsewhere. You'd work though.

Only a curse this booze business. Blood money. There's a lot of people that made a lot of money, barrels of money. But, the town had to bury them. My life's history [pause] if I had a book of all the trouble that I went through selling booze [pause] started with nothing and ended with nothing.

Section II

The War Years

Almonds and War[1]

By Sharon Gibson Palermo

As I was researching my first children's novel on Italian-Canadian immigrants, I came across what was to me a piece of startling history. This was the internment of over 700 Italian-Canadians during the Second World War, 500 of whom were arrested on the day Mussolini announced his alliance with Hitler, June 10, 1940. Within hours of the announcement, RCMP officers entered the homes and workplaces of people who had obviously been part of pre-existing lists of "suspicious" Italians. They were taken to Camp Petawawa in Ontario where they were kept for periods of time varying from a couple of months to five years or the end of the war.

What startled me about this information was that I had never heard of it, despite having been married to an Italian-Canadian for fourteen years. When I questioned my husband, I found that he had not heard of it, though his family had been living in Toronto since 1955. None of my immediate friends in Halifax had heard of it, though I grant that none were Italian, and almost all had been born after the war. One friend, however, had been a child in Halifax during the Second World War and had married a professor of Canadian history. She stated with considerable surprise that neither she nor her husband had heard of it. We all had heard of the Japanese internment. Why not the Italian?

I can't begin to answer this question except to make vague guesses. The Italians chose not to make a fuss. They chose to assimilate rather than create rifts with their neighbours. Yet, the Italians I knew in Toronto lived their lives primarily among Italians and continued to speak their language with gusto. They clearly saw themselves as a distinct community. Would they not want other Canadians and their own children to know about this traumatic event in their history?

I thought it important for others to know about it. The Italians have assimilated well and are no longer thought of as "foreigners." It seems inconceivable that a similar incident could happen today, yet it happened only two generations ago—worse—continues to be put upon other ethnic groups around the world. How easy it is to persecute people. How easy to judge without evidence. How easy to kill out of prejudice.

Kenneth Bagnell researched the Italian internment in detail and published it in his comprehensive book, *Canadese: Portrait of the Italian-Canadians (1989).*

I write for children, hoping that they will be drawn into the drama of my characters' lives. I read Bagnell's chapter on the Second World War with an eye to his detail. What an excellent subject for a children's book—one that can inform their hearts and minds while it entertains.

The Lie That Had To Be tries to do this with the story of a young girl, Rennie Trani, whose summer holiday is grossly disturbed by the internment of her father. Rennie knows little about the war. It is far across the sea. It disturbs dinner conversations and radio shows. It creates tension with her best friend whose brother is a soldier while her's is not, but Rennie's life continues as it has before—until that afternoon in June when her Papa is arrested.

The chapter which you are about to read tells the story of his arrest in Whitney Pier. While the specific event and characters are fictional, the way the arrest is made is in keeping with the stories I found, mostly in Bagnell's *Canadese,* of arrests made across the country on that historic day.

An Excerpt from *The Lie That Had To Be*

The nutty smell of baking almonds greeted Rennie as she followed the officers into the bakery. *Mmmm.*

Papa was behind the counter closing a sale with Mrs. Hobinsky. The policemen moved off to one side and stood tall in their dark blue uniforms. Rennie watched everyone from the middle of the room. Papa gave her a wink and everything seemed fine. She wrinkled her nose at him, then he bent behind the counter in that secret way he had and came up with some amaretti, his wonderful almond cookies. He reached one to Rennie and tucked the others into Mrs. Hobinsky's bag next to her rolls. "Those—special for Alberto," he said. Mrs. Hobinsky took them out, laughing, "No, no! There is no need!" Even when she laughed, Mrs. Hobinsky looked and sounded serious....

Papa's hand sprang up. "*Va bene!*" he said, which everyone knew meant "think nothing of it." He was in a playful mood. Rennie would ruin that if she told on Robbie, but still, Robbie wasn't allowed to ride his bike like a wild monkey. She started to munch her cookie. What did the police want?

Papa had leaned his hands on the counter top to smile at the officers. "What I may do for you?"

Rennie stopped chewing. A deep silence fell between the policemen. Rennie thought she heard Sgt. MacPhee clear his throat. "Mr. Trani," he said, "this is Officer Harnish."

"It pleases me to meet you." Papa held out his hand.

Officer Harnish kept his hand at his side. His shoulders seemed rounded though he stood straight. "Are you Cosimo Trani?"

"Why, you know I am." Papa smiled at Sgt. MacPhee, a slight question in his voice.

"Were you born in Italy in 1896?" continued Harnish.

Slowly, Papa, his eyebrows knitting together, stood up straight and stepped back from the counter. "That is correct." He used his clearest English accent. Rennie's own eyes began to squint into a frown. She finished her chew and swallowed.

Officer Harnish darted his eyes around the bakery, then walked to a bright white wall where a map of Italy, the British flag, and a picture of the Pope were tacked all in a row like colourful stamps of identity. He ripped down the map and the picture, crumpled them in his hand and tossed them to the floor. "Come with us," he ordered.

Papa's eyes widened and his jaw tightened, but he stood frozen, staring at the officers and shaking his head. Mrs. Hobinsky had been silent too long. She stepped to the counter and faced the officers.

"What's this man done?" she demanded.

Sgt. MacPhee wiped a troubled frown from his face and looked at her. "Mussolini has joined up with Hitler. We are at war with Italy."

What had that to do with Papa? Sgt. MacPhee spoke as if everyone would know, and it seemed that Mrs. Hobinsky did. She darted her eyes from the police to Papa and back again.

"But Cose is a Canadian now! He's a good, well-liked man in this town! For twenty years he's baked our bread. You know he's done nothing wrong, Angus!" She scolded like an angry mother. Rennie was standing by herself near the end of the counter. Her arms tightened at her sides.

Sgt. MacPhee's lips were grim and his knuckles seemed white around the policeman's cap he clutched in front of him. He pushed himself taller. Rennie shivered. He planted a steady gaze on Papa and said in a quiet but serious voice, "You must come with us."

Papa's playfulness had vanished, not in anger at Robbie, but in something that made his lips quiver and his eyes seem to melt. He came from behind the counter. For some reason, Rennie noticed how clean the bakery was: how the glass of the counters was completely spotless; how every cake platter and cookie tray was lined with a crisp paper doily; how the red, black and white floor tiles were perfectly square and held together with pure white lines of grout. She watched Papa remove his apron. It, too, shone white. He reached his arm around her shoulder and drew her to him. She threw her arms around his waist and looked up at him. "Papa, what are they going to do?"

"It's all right," he assured her.

"But what's wrong?"

"Not one little thing." For a second time that day he pressed her head to his chest. "There's some mistake." He lifted up her chin and looked at her with the same eyes as the tyrant king's, except they were softer. He told her he loved her, "*Ti amo.*" She held on to him to keep him safe.

Sgt. MacPhee interrupted them. "Your wife can send clothes to the police station."

Rennie had never seen such a look on Papa's face. "There is a mistake," he repeated, pulling gently away from her and fumbling in his pants pocket. He took out his key and gave it to Rennie. He took her hand in his large and cushiony one and squeezed it until it tingled. "Lock up," he told her, and he left with the officers. They walked on either side of him, reaching the sky in their smart clothes. He was between them, short and plain, but with his silvery hair glistening and his head up. Rennie could barely turn to lock the door.

When she did, her hands shook. Somehow, she steered the key into the keyhole. Mrs. Hobinsky double checked the lock for her, then Rennie dropped the key in her pocket. It made an unsettling clink that she didn't expect. She stood for a moment, not knowing what to do.

"I'll come home with you, Rennie." Mrs. Hobinsky tucked the strap of her purse into her elbow and held the bag of rolls close to her. She gave the other hand to Rennie....

There was Papa's frightened face. There he was going out the door between the two policemen.

She tightened her grip on Mrs Hobinsky. "Rotten stuff! Rotten stuff!" Mrs. Hobinsky exclaimed now and then. The dust covered buildings of Whitney Pier seemed to pass them by trance like.

She threw her arms around Papa from behind and he became invisible. The policemen kept going.

She hadn't kept Papa safe.

At home, they went straight to the kitchen. Mama stood by the stove in the ruffled green apron Loretta and Rennie had made her for Christmas. Loretta, at the table, leaned over a comic book, but she jumped right up and pulled out a chair for Mrs. Hobinsky.

Mama was always ready to welcome a guest. "Helen, sit. I make you a coffee?" She pushed a strand of dark hair from her plump cheek and gave the sauce one more stir.

Mrs. Hobinsky refused the coffee and kept standing. She explained all that had happened.

"No." Mama didn't believe it at first, but, seeing the truth in Mrs. Hobinsky's eyes, she groped for a chair and sat down. The spoon sank in her lap. It left a dark spot that would spoil the apron forever. Rennie wanted to run to her, but her legs wouldn't move. Loretta did instead.

"But why?" asked Mama when she could speak again. "Cosimo love Canada. And I need to send clothes? Where will they take him?" But there was nothing more that Mrs. Hobinsky could tell her. She jumped up and began making decisions. "*Mie figlie,*" she order her daughters in Italian, "*il pranzo.*" Have supper ready for Sergio. *E dove Roberto*? His papa will smash him! He never tells me where he goes!" She ran upstairs to collect Papa's clothes. When she came down again, she spoke to Loretta. "When Riccardo comes in, you send him to the station. He can explain to the police." Before she left, she turned to Helen Hobinsky. "Thank you, thank you," she said in English.

Mrs. Hobinsky grabbed her hands. "I've done nothing, Caterina, but I'll stay here with the girls. When Robbie comes in, I'll send him for Albert. We'll sit with you."

Mama was gone. Rennie's hands were cold. Loretta was crying—fourteen years old and weeping like a baby. Rennie grabbed the dishes and cutlery for the table. She counted enough for the entire family, including Papa and Mr. and Mrs. Hobinsky, and placed them around loudly, ordering Loretta to move her elbows. Loretta snapped at her, "Leave me alone! You don't even feel bad! Don't you love Papa?" Rennie bit her lip and ran upstairs. She would not cry. She *would* not cry. Everything was going to be fine. Hadn't Mama said Papa would be home?

Notes from the Internment Camp

Michele LaPenna[1] P/W No. 204, Petawawa, Ontario
Selected by Sam Migliore and A. Evo DiPierro

Michele LaPenna was born in Roseto, Italy. He arrived in Canada in 1911 and began work at the steel plant in Whitney Pier. Mr. LaPenna was very involved in, and committed to, his church parish. He sang in the choir, helped with the collection, and did odd jobs at St. Nicholas Church. He was the type of person that many in the community regarded in high esteem. In the 1940s, he was arrested and interned at Petawawa, Ontario. He, and others, often suspected that someone at the steel plant had reported him to the authorities, claiming he was an Italian spy, in order to take his job. After his release from the internment camp, Mr. LaPenna returned to Whitney Pier to resume his work at the steel plant. He passed away in August of 1977, at eighty-one years of age.

Although Mr. LaPenna passed away a number of years ago, he has left behind a notebook from his stay in Petawawa. The notebook contains brief entries concerning some of his work duties (and the pay he received) while at the camp, plus more detailed notes for constructing letters to several people. We have not been able to track down any of the actual letters. A selection of excerpts from the notebook[2] appears here courtesy of Dolores (Rossetti) Moore. A number of entries were directed either to her or one of her family members.

A sketch of Michele LaPenna from the internment camp. February 18, 1941. Sketch by G. Casini. Photo courtesy of Dolores (Rossetti) Moore.

From Petawawa, Ontario

January 21, 1941:   ...here in the camp [faith] is a great help for the people, and I am strong as ever. I have the most confidence in the Blessed Virgin that with her intercession some day everything will turn out fine....

January 25, 1941:   It was a pleasure for me on new years day when I received your letter.... Imagine how I felt Christmas eve when I remember St. Nicholas Church.... I may be far from you but you are constantly in my mind and ... my pray[ers].... His Excellency Apostolic Delegate visited the camp and gave us the blessing on behalf of the Holy Father Pope. His words of devotion ... are yet in our ear and in our heart, they will be for us not only spiritual comfort but also to strengthen our faith as well....

January 29, 1941:   ...best regard ... hope that soon the light will be Shine over my innocent and when I come back we have everything like the previous year....

February 10, 1941:   The weather up here is very fine so far, I didn't expect it; the thermometer has shown sometime 36 below zero but I didn't mind a bit, no wind at all ... (no rain for 3 months, about 18 inches of snow) ... I can say this is really a place for the winter.... Best regards to all, kiss to Geordie, I think he began forget me....

1941 (no specific date)   I have ... planned for some time to answer your letters but you know how it is, cannot write any time you wish ... but going by ... the regulation of the camp, however I do my best to write to everybody.... We are all well thank God ... glad also that your father is well again.

March 23, 1941:   ...very glad to hear that you are all in the best of health ... I am feeling fine, also all the Sydney people. Frank M. is better again, he walk around....

May 13, 1941:   ...very glad to hear that you are all in the best of health I feel fine thank the Blessed Virgin Mary and hope you will offer some pray[ers] during this month, especially on Sunday when the procession will take place at Holy Redeemer Church....

July 28, 1941:   May the good St. Anna give us the grace for release [to] come back as some ... have, because we are innocent....

All They Ever Wanted Was a New Life and an Apology: One Italian Family's Experience

Told by Anna Martinello
and prepared by Margaret Marshall and Paul Diekelmann[1]

Michael Martinello was one of six brothers and three sisters born in the province of Avellino, near Naples, Italy. All of the children were well educated. The family owned a large farm, which supported them very well. However, Michael's father worried about what would happen when he died. He felt that the farm would not sustain his family if it were divided among the children as an inheritance. So Mr. Martiniello,[2] in consultation with the family, decided that only one of the sons, the youngest, would inherit the property. Consequently, some of the brothers left Italy to seek their fortunes elsewhere.

At the turn of the 20th century, two Martinello brothers (Alex and Michael) emigrated from Italy to Boston, Massachusetts. While working in Boston, they heard about an economic boom in Sydney, Nova Scotia—a boom resulting from the growth of the steel industry there. So four of the brothers—Alex (Alessandro), Michael (Michele), John (Gennaro) and Frank (Nunziante)—decided to relocate to Sydney. While Alex and Michael worked for the Dominion Steel Company, Johnny opened a grocery store on Tupper Street at the Pier (and later moved the business to George Street).

As time passed, the brothers went into various family businesses together, including the grocery and bakery shop on Tupper Street. They also established "Martinello Hall" (what today might be called a "convention centre" or "banquet hall") above the store. Each of them became financially secure as the businesses prospered. Michael and Frank, for example, participated in their brother Johnny's

Italian foods import business—G. Martinello and Co. Importers and Wholesale Groceries. Johnny Martinello was doing very well at the time in the sale and distribution of imported olive oil, pasta, salami and other Pastini Italian food products from Montreal.

"Pa [Michael]," Anna said lovingly, "was the type of guy that ... loved his Italy. That was his mother country.... I think that all of the Italians around here really felt very strong for Italy, but they knew that they could not go back there to live because that part of their life was gone ... that was finished." Having established a new life in Cape Breton, their lifestyle had completely changed. Michael and his brothers had become active members of the Cape Breton community in various fields of endeavour.

After the formal declaration of war against Italy, the morale of the Italians in Cape Breton was low. On June 10, 1940, the RCMP arrested Michael without any explanation to the family. Before the evening was over, the family discovered that Frank Martinello and a cousin, Felix (Felice) Martinello, along with a number of other Cape Breton Italian men, had been taken to the city overnight lockup. "[The police] put some hoodlums in with them," Anna said, "and during the night ... the Italian men were beaten very, very badly."

In the morning, the men were put on a train to be interned at Camp Petawawa without having a chance to see their families. "They were taken away," Anna continued, searching for the proper words to describe the situation, "as prisoners of war." Alex and other family members tried to look into the situation but, as soon as the authorities discovered that they were Martinellos, no one would give out any information. "These men were taken away as prisoners of war, but there was never a charge laid against them—they stayed in the prison camp for nearly three years," Anna said incredulously.

The internment years were very hard on Michael's wife. She became ill during this time, probably because of the stress, and at one point needed her son, Eddy, to be with her. The irony is that Eddy Martinello was serving in the Canadian Army at the same time that his father was in a Canadian internment camp. Eddy came home for a weekend pass and decided to stay home with his sick mother for a few extra days. He didn't realize that this would be a problem, that he would be considered AWOL from the Army. Once people made him aware of the problem, and the trouble it might cause him, he reported back to the Army. Eddy ended up in military court. For help, Eddy called on Nick Melnick, Anna Martinello's brother. Nick was a Petty Officer in the Navy; he had a boxing background, and served as a Navy physical instructor. Nick told Eddy not to worry because he would go with him to explain the situation to the court.

At the trial, things were not going well; the Judge was preparing to "throw the book" at Eddy. Anna laughingly recalled the incident in this way: "Nick spoke up and said 'Sir, you shouldn't do that. His mother is pretty sick, and his father is at the concentration camp." The members of the court were stunned as Nick proceeded to reveal Eddy's story. At one point during the defence, the judge jumped up irate at Nick and, according to Anna, said: "You get out of this court room right this minute. We don't need any Philadelphia lawyers around here." Apparently, it was difficult for the court members to hear that a Canadian citizen serving in the Canadian Army had a parent being held as a Canadian "prisoner of war." All came out well, nevertheless, and the Judge allowed Eddy to go back on duty that day.

Eddy was not the only son of an interned Canadian of Italian descent who served in the Canadian military forces. Frank Martinello, who also was imprisoned at Camp Petawawa, had two sons and a daughter serving in the Canadian Armed Forces during the Second World War. One of Frank's sons, Harry, even served with the Canadian Forces in Italy, near Naples—the very area that the Martinello family farm was located. In addition, Anna's husband, Louis (Michael Martinello's son), participated in the war effort by working in the Sydney Steel Plant.

Life was difficult for the interned men and their families. Not only was there the economic hardship of having the wage earner away for almost three years, but there were difficulties in dealing with some of the local attitudes of the day against Italians. Family members suffered with feelings of inferiority and shame as a result of having gone through such a devastating experience. Extended family, however, rallied together to offer their help. Andrew Martinello, Michael's son, provided clothes for family members from his Charlotte Street store, the Oak Hall. Michael's brother, Johnny, helped provide food to the families through his food wholesale business while Alex helped with monetary gifts.

Having lived a comfortable life in Cape Breton prior to the war, the Italian men were not used to concentration camp conditions. Anna said, very seriously, "The food was scarce and not very good ... they were not being fed very well. When the Italian community near Petawawa heard about the poor living conditions, they helped by sending meat from hunting and fishing catches and other food and supplies. Michael was elected as a camp cook, a job which he enjoyed." In their long absence from family and home, the men were taught several craft skills at the internment camp. Although some written communication and packages were permitted, the most atrocious treatment was that visits from family members were not allowed.

After their release, Michael and Frank returned to Cape Breton. Felix and his family settled in Hamilton, Ontario, because they felt that this would be best for their young children. Michael started another business by purchasing a car and operating a taxi service in Sydney. Not much was mentioned about the war years, as the people affected tried to put the past behind them and start anew. Family members who experienced the internment tragedy looked upon those times as ones of sadness, hardship and disgrace. Even after fifty years, some family members still wonder how such a thing could happen to Canadian citizens.

"Psychologically, it affected them," Anna recalls sadly. "You know what? [The Government] never charged the men with anything. How could they keep them like that? They never did get a formal, public apology from the Canadian government. That's the only thing that they ever wanted from this experience."

My Friends, The Italians of Dominion

By Len Stephenson[1]

Shortly after 1900, the Dominion Coal Company began to recruit young men from the north of Italy to work in the coal mines of Cape Breton. For many years, the Town of Dominion had the largest concentration of Italians in Nova Scotia. Over the years, the Italians have made a remarkable contribution to the growth and development of our community. Their greatest influence has been in the coal industry. Strong, powerful men, they sought the most strenuous and hazardous jobs in the colliery. They loaded coal, removed stone and worked at any job that paid the highest wages based on performance or production. They seldom were involved in work that paid a daily minimum wage. Their influence in the early years was so great, that if they all decided to remain off work on a given day, the mine would have to be shut down.

From the beginning, our Italian citizens have been a self-reliant group, maintaining gardens and keeping livestock. Many had been farmers in the country of their birth. In 1936, they formed the Italian Community Club and the following year they constructed a community hall. This hall was the first Italian community hall in Nova Scotia and has proven to be a very valuable asset for all citizens of the community.

A great many examples could be provided to substantiate the remarkable and harmonious relationship that has existed for the past ninety-some years between the several generations of Italians and our Canadian-born citizens. Harmonious relations, excepting events that occurred during the Second World War. These events should and will be addressed here. Much of this paper deals with the "alien question" and, in particular, the period during the war when Italian miners were not allowed to work in the coal mines.

Background

My earliest association with the Italians began in 1928 when I was seven years old. Two young boys arrived in town from Italy and were enrolled in the old Central School on Mitchell Avenue. They could not speak or understand English, and my sister, who was on the teaching staff, agreed to tutor them at our home in the evenings. Their names were Etalo Casagrande and John "Macaroni" De Sero. They left our community during the 1947 coal miner's strike. Etalo still resides in Ontario, while John died in Niagara Falls, Ontario, in December 1996.

Like most immigrants, the early Italians of Dominion formed their own small colony within the community. Language and custom differences made their arrangement practical and convenient. Their settlement was located near the railroad in the Mitchell Avenue area. That territory encompassed a rough baseball field known as the "slack pile." The surface was covered with slack or fine coal that had its origin with the General Mining Association of London, England, which began operating here in 1829. Along with our young Italian friends, we learned to play baseball on that field. Apparently, we had a very good foundation to build on. In 1940 and 1941, under the management of the late Sam Melanson, we brought the first ever Maritime Baseball Championship to Cape Breton.

Included in the roster of those winning teams were our Italian friends: Egidio Costa, Sandro Cirotto and Londo Scattolon. Egidio joined the Canadian Army and was seriously wounded in the war. He resides in Ontario where he settled after the war. Sandro also lives in Ontario. His father, Giovanni Cirotto, was killed in No. 1-B Colliery on February 2, 1940. Londo served in the army also, but he returned to Dominion where he is retired. His father was interned in June 1940, along with his friend and neighbour, Mario "Baker" Furini.

We do not have mail delivery in Dominion. It is necessary for our citizens to go to the post office to pick up their mail. Having served the community as postmaster for thirty-five years, I have had an excellent and enjoyable opportunity to get to know the Italian families very well. Meeting the people, listening to their stories, led me to the interesting hobby of researching, recording and writing the history of our coal mining community.

The "Alien Question"

The community of Dominion has been very much a coal mining centre since 1829. Few, if any issues, caused more hard feelings and hardships for so many of our citizens than the refusal of the native-born men to work in the mines with men of Italian origin, and the internment of two of our well-respected citizens, when Italy declared war on France and Britain on June 10, 1940.

The Italian miners of Dominion worked almost exclusively in No. 1-B Colliery, and they were members of that Local of the United Mine Workers. The refusal of Canadian-born miners to work with men of Italian origin represented an extremely traumatic experience for the Italian families. In the interest of community history, it is important that the tactics used to deprive Italian miners of their right to continue working to feed their families be revisited. A satisfactory method to accomplish that is to return to the daily reports in the *Sydney Post-Record* for that period. A news release dated June 11, 1940, for example, reported that:

> Three collieries of the Dominion Coal Company were tied up and one was forced to work at half capacity through the refusal of Canadian-born miners to work with Italian-born men after Italy's declaration of war on the Allies. About 1200 men were affected. Operations were halted at the company's No. 1-B [in Glace Bay] and No. 10 [in Reserve Mines] pits ... and at No. 16 in nearby New Waterford. The No. 12 pit at New Waterford was hoisting coal at half its normal capacity. There were no disturbances around the pits.[2]

On June 11, a special meeting of the Local was held, and it was decided that "enemy aliens" would not be "permitted to work at No. 1-B colliery."[3] Reverend Ronald McLean, pastor of St. Nicholas parish in Whitney Pier, attended the meeting to speak on behalf of the Italian workers. "Father McLean explained that he [had] been associated with the Italian residents of Cape Breton for the last fourteen years," and that "he had found [them] to be good citizens."[4] He then made a suggestion that was to be echoed may times later by politicians and community-minded citizens—"to permit the proper authorities to deal with the situation and not to attempt to handle the trouble themselves."[5]

Dan W. Morrison, district president of the union, was also in attendance. He too told the miners that they were making things worse by trying to deal with the matter on their own. He reported that he had attended a union meeting in New Waterford earlier in the day and that the men had agreed to return to work pending settlement of the problem by the authorities. Mr. Morrison then reported that "he had conferred with the Hon. L. D. Currie," and that the "decision had been reached to keep all enemy aliens out of the collieries pending a thorough investigation by government officials."[6] An Italian miner addressed the members later in the meeting. According to the newspaper report, he stated that: "He was certain that no Italian would work until permission had been granted as they had no desire to see any trouble among the men."[7] By the end of the meeting, the Canadian-born miners had agreed to return to work as long as the Italians did not enter the mines.

At a meeting on June 27, members of the No. 1-B Local of the U.M.W. were notified of the results of an investigation into the alien question by Assistant Commissioner F. T. Meade of the RCMP. His report recommended that "aliens" be allowed to return to work whether they were naturalized or not. Robert R. Stewart, sub-district Board Member, "explained ... the ... details of the investigation. All men whom charges had been preferred against were picked up by the police and all but one are now on the way to internment camps."[8] Due to his wife's illness, the other individual was to be picked up later. The Local, however, did not take up any action on the recommendation at this meeting.

On Sunday, June 30, members of No. 1-B Local held a special meeting. At the meeting, Dan W. Morrison reported that: "every local union in the sub-district ... had accepted the findings of [the] assistant commissioner ... with the exception of No. 1-B."[9] He then urged the Local to accept the recommendation of the district office to allow foreigners, naturalized or not, to return to work.[10] In a very close vote, the membership decided to adopt the recommendation. On July 2, however, "five collieries and 3,750 men were idle" due to the "refusal of native-born miners to enter the pits and work with foreign-born colliers."[11] The pits affected included Nos. 1-B, 2, 4, 10, and 20; the New Waterford collieries were not affected.[12] When work resumed, Italian miners were not allowed to work in 1-B and some of the other collieries.

By July 12, the situation had led to two (among other) results: a number of Italian families in Dominion were in need of financial assistance; and, a shortage of labour resulted in a loss of production for the Dominion Coal Company.[13] A week later, the situation had not improved for Italian miners in Dominion. Although union members at No. 10 colliery in Reserve voted in favour of allowing six "aliens" residing in Reserve to return to work,[14] the same did not happen at No. 1-B. On July 18, after some discussion, the local endorsed a resolution prepared by the Glace Bay branch of the Army and Navy Veterans in Canada. The resolution called for "the immediate internment of all enemy aliens, whether naturalized or not."[15] Then, in a plebiscite held at the No. 1-B pithead on July 23, 603 union members voted against allowing "aliens" to return to work, while 124 voted in favour of the proposal.[16]

A news item dated July 29 reported that John Ellsworth, President of the 1-B Local, together with the mine committee of the Local and Alex Burden, the mine manager, had agreed to allow eleven Canadian-born workers of Italian and Polish background to resume work at the mine.[17] At the site, however, the other miners refused to work with these eleven individuals, and the mine remained idle until the eleven had withdrawn.[18] A plebiscite was held on August 6 to determine the fate of the eleven Canadian-born miners of "foreign extraction." The proposal to allow these individuals to return to work was rejected by a majority of 223 votes.[19]

On August 20, the *Sydney Post-Record* published a series of excerpts from a lead editorial in an August issue of the *Financial Post*. The editorial was critical of the union, which it described as "impotent" to handle the Pit Head Trouble, "although Union rules permit NO discrimination on account of race."[20] The editorial, as quoted in the *Post-Record*, states:

Since war's outbreak, a small trouble-making minority ... have been objecting to working alongside several hundred men with "foreign" names. Of these, more than 200 are specially skilled in coal face work and important to production. All these men have been "approved" by the Mounties. They are either Canadian-born with foreign names, those who were naturalized before 1929, or those found dependable by the police.

Since the war began there have been two dozen stoppages because a minority of the workers, in defiance of their union, have refused to work if these men are allowed down the mines. The "foreigners" have had to fall back on relief.... Coal production, badly needed for the war effort, has been reduced by about 50,000 tons on this account alone.[21]

Led by the above mentioned minority, the miners at No. 1-B Colliery in Glace Bay maintained their refusal to allow the Italians to return to work, and the company did not interfere with that decision. As a result, the Italians were out of work for approximately nine months.

Managing with a Difficult Situation

Condo Baggio, in a taped interview, described an illegal activity that he and a few other Italians were involved in, in an attempt to raise money to feed their families while denied work in 1940. Condo owned a small lot of land behind the Italian Hall. They dug a shaft thirty-eight feet deep to a coal seam and began mining and selling coal in a bootleg fashion.

One day, they had about fifteen tons of coal on the surface when two coal company security officers arrived on the scene. The security officers descended into the mine and stated that the Italians had been reported for digging coal under the nearby railroad line. Condo and friends were able to show the constables that that was not the case. They were mining in a different direction. The Italians were ordered to report to the company office in Glace Bay the following day. They appeared as ordered and had a favourable hearing. The official in charge understood their plight and, in at least one show of compassion, suggested that they dig only at night.

Bootleg coal mining was only one method used by the displaced miners to provide for their families. A son of one of the men affected, for example, recalls that when the Italian miners were forced to surrender their guns, his father was fortunate to obtain a replacement gun; it enabled him to hunt deer and rabbits to provide food for the table. The kill was hidden in the woods until after dark and then brought home through the thick woods to avoid detection.

Concluding Remarks

The 1940 "alien question" served as a divisive force within Dominion. Italian miners were denied access to the mines, and this meant hardship for them and their families. The situation should not have happened. Recently, I spoke with a former Dominion resident living in Boston. The conversation focused on the refusal of miners from 1-B Colliery to work with the Italians. He stated that he was one of the miners who was opposed to allowing Italians to work. He is now eighty-nine years of age, and he acknowledges that the action was unnecessary and wrong. He stated that the Italians were not a threat to the war effort, and realizes that they were at that time simply proud of their country, and not in favour of Mussolini's action. He acknowledges that they were great citizens and regrets the work action he and others took at that time.

Remembering the Pain of 1940

Compiled by John deRoche

Wars always breed fear, suspicion and anger. The combat may be far away, but these feelings can find a ready target in your very neighbours whose roots were once planted in enemy soil. That is just what happened here in Cape Breton. After Mussolini allied his Fascist regime with Hitler's Nazi Germany, Canada and Italy went to war in June of 1940. Most of Cape Breton's Italian miners and steelworkers had arrived here before Mussolini even came to power. Many were Canadian citizens and parents of second-generation Canadians. Often they had married people of non-Italian origin. They were homeowners and well established in the workplaces, churches and daily life of their communities. Yet, in the eyes of some members of the longer-settled ethnic groups, local "Italians" became the "enemy alien within."

In the 1970s, I was studying the social history of Cape Breton coal mining. The conversations on these pages are from tape-recordings that my student assistants and I did in 1975-1978, where we encountered the topic of the wartime troubles. I've inserted very few comments of my own, but I want each person to speak for herself/himself, here. People's experiences differ and, of course, so do their recollections of "facts," which is why I haven't smoothed over the inconsistencies in the various accounts.

The Nemis Families, New Waterford

Soon after 1900, a young couple named Joe and Enrica Nemis left their home in the town of Nimis, Udine Province, northeastern Italy. They settled in Glace Bay where son Dominic was born in 1908. After they had moved to New Waterford, James was born in 1914. Margaret Finlayson, daughter of Presbyterian immigrants from Scotland, married Dominic in 1938. Catherine MacDonald's parents were Catholic Scots from Judique/Port Hood; she wed James in 1934.

In 1977 we spoke with both brothers and their wives.[1] They describe their shocked frustration, and the struggle to set matters straight when fellow-workers in the United Mine Workers union went on strike in 1940 to have Italians expelled from their jobs.

Catherine MacDonald Nemis

He was always a good worker; he always worked extra shifts and on Sundays. But the time the war broke out, he came home one day from work; he said they chased all the Italians out of the pit. And he went into the manager and tried to explain that he was born in New Waterford and lived here all his life. But I think it was the people ... discrimination ... you know, the people he was working with. Oh, there was quite a few Italians, all working in the mines. And I don't know if it was the fact that they were all such good workers, they didn't want them. But he was only off work a couple of months. They fought it through the union and they had to leave them go back to work again. But while they were off, they gave them a bit of relief or something like that.

[Was it the other miners that complained?] Yeah. I guess it must have been the people that were working with them because I guess Italy was at war. [Was there a conflict between the miners and...?] No, not really, not before that. They were getting along good ... the best of friends and everything. But some of them had the impression that they would send them back to Italy and take their homes.... Because I can remember a family that lived not too far from us ... thought they were going to take our homes from us. But they couldn't do it, no. It was just hearsay.

[So after your husband went back to work, did relations?] Oh yes, it was just forgotten about after they went back to work, they didn't have any trouble with the fellows they were working with. I guess it was just something that came up when the war started.

James (Cookie) Nemis

[Catherine Nemis asks: What year was that strike you fellas lost your jobs? Remember, they put all the Italians out of the mines?] It was the time the War was on they done that. That was the silliest thing I ever heard. I was born in New Waterford, and it was a hell of a good man I was, and I lost my job because I might have "done something" to the war. I forgive but I can't forget, you know. Really, the fellas that I worked with said that to me! And I worked right in Waterford, worked all my life in the coal mine, and I lost my job. And me with five children.

We went to work one day, and they refused to work with us, eh. The government people had a big meeting with all the clergymen, all in Waterford, all the big mayors and stuff. The fellas that was tying the coal mines up, he called them in too. "Now," he says, "tomorrow morning, 16 colliery and 12 colliery is going to work. And if you fellas interfere," he said, "there's a camp for you fellas and you're going to go. We'll take yez right away in the evening, right in the camp. *Yous* are going to go; *they're* going to work. Now remember," he said, "I'm telling yez." The next day, boy, we had to all go to work and they never opened their mouths no more. 'Cause he *told* them: "I'm telling yous, we need the coal. They're good workers. They don't hurt nobody. They were born here. And we'll investigate every one of the families. And," he says, "maybe we'll have to investigate some of you fellas. Yous might be worse than they are." They called those the "dictators" tie her up ... dictate and run the coal mine, you see. They wanted this and that. They wanted our job. They took my good job. But I got it back after. And the [UMW of A headquarters], when they heard that, they were very, very mad. They said, "Every fella that works in the coal mine, if I'm Italian or coloured person or Chinese, got just as much rights as a fella born in Waterford or in Canada or anything else. And another thing, we're lucky they didn't sue you people, sue the union." Oh, they come in from Halifax, the big investigators from Halifax ... he *told* them. He said, "I'm going to blame yous if the mine don't work, so you go around and tell them to come to work." I heard that after, but it's true. It must be because all of a sudden everything was from day to night.

And myself, there's five children home with no money coming in. This is only a small house. I built this with my hard work. Nobody gave me nothing. I worked for what I got, all my life with the pan shovel. Nobody gave me anything. I wasn't off too long. A couple of weeks. But still, two or three weeks with no pay means a lot. It took me three months to get back [on track financially]. We were pretty careful with our dollar. We weren't squandering.

Margaret Finlayson Nemis

[Did your husband, Dominic, talk about any conflict?] Oh yeah. [During the War] there, they were trying to get men put in a concentration camp, you know. And him born here. See, it's just a bunch of ignorant people. Maybe they didn't have enough education to know the difference. When it comes to it, they were more foreign than he was 'cause he was born here. But I know there was a lot of friction at that time. And they took away a lot ... lots were put away that shouldn't have been put away either. That's the way she blows. They were going around taking away guns and everything. And my husband loves hunting, and he had a gun and bullets. And when I heard about that, I took the gun and I buried it outside—or I hid it, but I buried the bullets. [laughs] And here, when it was time for him to go hunting, he said, "Maggie, where is my gun?" So I told him where the gun was. "Well, where is the bullets?" Well, was he ever mad because I didn't know where to go find them afterwards. When he was digging the garden, he found some bullets. All the crazy things!

Dominic Nemis

And then the War broke out. So, I had a job. I was making $75 a week, brushing. I always had the best of jobs. But I done me work. I didn't get it for nothing, I worked all the time. So they started talking about the Italians, you know, "stabbing them in the back" and this and that. I never seen the place [Italy]. *This* is where I was born. This is my country. I'm not interested in Italy. So anyway, they took everybody's place in the union. We'd have meetings at the [union] hall, and there'd be 500 there. And I'd be the only one wasn't satisfied. I'd say, "You know, this is the rottenest thing that was ever done to anybody, taking a fella's job in the pit. This is against the [UMW union] constitution...." So we got the District officer over. So we told him what happened, it's awful. So Mr. Morrison was president of District 26 at that time. So, my brother's a little short fella, he's saucy as hell. So he asked the president of the District, he said, "Look, Mr. Morrison, do you mean to tell me that I'm a foreigner? I was born in this town here."

He says, "I'm sorry, Mr. Nemis, you're a foreigner."

[My brother said,] "I could show you the [UMW] International constitution, and it don't say that. The only thing we bar is Communists. Colour, creed or nationality don't mean a thing."

See, even the District president went against the constitution. So you couldn't do anything about it. So I lost my job. They even tried to keep me out of the mine. So I took one of the fellas on the [union local's] committee down to the Mounted Police. And we had a discussion. I says, "Now, this is a committee man. I wanna know where I stand in this country." So, [the RCMP officer said,] "I'll just tell you where you stand. You're just as good as that fella there, no difference at all. Now, you go to work tomorrow and that's it. Do you hear that, Mr. Mac[X]? You're supposed to be an official of the union. I'm telling you."

[I heard later that the committee man] called up Douglas MacDonald, [who] was the board member [representing District 26 on the UMW of A International Board]. He says, "You know, Douglas, I was down at the Mounted Police with the big dago. And he thinks he's gonna work tomorrow, but we'll god damn well stop him." So anyway, I went to work [the next day]. There was about a couple of hundred people get on the rake [for transport down the mine slope]. I get in the rake, they jump out. They jump in, I jump in, they jump out. So, the mine was tied up.

Then they had an investigation down the town hall. They sent some people from Ottawa. They had a meeting with Douglas MacDonald. But I wasn't told about that 'til after I heard about it. So the fella who was in charge, he says, "I wanna tell you, Mr. MacDonald, that those people gotta work in the mines. You can't tie up the mines any more. I'll tell you what we're gonna do, we're gonna get a thousand people that's in the internment camp and put them in the coal mines here, and you people are gonna be responsible for them. That's what's gonna happen here. And if there's another case around here about this discrimination...." Oh, they pulled in their horns. They started joining the army and they took off ... you know, some of the fellas that was the leaders [of the anti-Italian effort]. I went to join the army too; they wouldn't take me. [The recruitment officer] says, "You go back in the coal mines. We need the coal miners."

And one of the buggers come back [after the War], that fella that said those things [against the Italians]. One day I went to the beer parlour, and I knew he was there. I was dying for him to say something. I wanted to tell him how rotten he is. There was another foreigner [there], a friend of mine, he says [to that man], "How do you like the little ["foreigner" grandchildren] you got now?" His daughter was married to a foreigner, see. "How do you like them?"

"Oh," he says, "I forgot all that stuff." Water under the bridge, see. So that's the way it is.

Accounts by Non-Italian Miners

In 1976-1977, my student co-workers and I interviewed scores of other retired coal miners in New Waterford, Dominion, Glace Bay and Port Morien. Some of the non-Italian men discussed the 1940 panic.[2] I've left out their names because these are sensitive issues. The Nemis's (above) and the three Italian men of Dominion (see below) all spoke "for the record," but the comments in this particular section were not necessarily given for publication.

New Waterford

Let's hear first from a democratic socialist and union activist who was at No. 16 colliery in New Waterford during the War. He blames the government not only for arrests of "foreigners" but also for their expulsion from their jobs.

[What happened when the Second World War broke out?] Oh, that! Oh, well, of course, that wasn't the wish of the miners. I know that here [the Italians] were all laid off. The company had orders to lay them off and send them to camps. The government had ordered [it]. And our local union protested like hell about it. Some of those foreigners, their parents were born in the old country [but] they were born here. The Nemis family, them boys were born in Glace Bay. And there were four [Italians], when they were laid off, they enlisted in the Canadian army and went overseas and fought over there and came back. They were laid off because they were foreigners.

[I've heard that the reason the Italians were thrown out of the pit was because the miners refused to work with them.] That's not right. We didn't have it here. One fella refused absolutely to go. And they made up their minds, "Well, it's either him or us." So he left. And that fella came back and became president of the local union. I enjoyed that fella. He had guts. Dominic Nemis. He came back and was president of the local union for years and years. Well liked. So that shows you there was no foreign animosity there. I think that they done that to Dominic for devilment, more than anything else! He went and he sat on the rakes all by himself. [laughs] "Come on and get me!" So they left him there. The next day he didn't go out.

Dominion

Here is an account from a man who left the mine at Dominion, years before the war, but maintained lifelong friendships with several Italian miners.

At the time of the War, the Italians went with the Germans. Well, everything got so hot that all the foreigners were kicked out of the pit that year, every Italian. The company didn't want to kick them out. The company needed them. The other men refused to work with them. In spite of all the talk of "brotherhood" and "democracy" and everything else, those men were out of work. Well, of course then, the union wouldn't work. The company had an awful job. The pit was almost at a standstill. Of course, the disgraceful thing about it was that they were all belonging to the same union, and brothers, and all this crap. [How did the local men generally get along with the Italians?] Oh, they used to get along with them good, until that squabble. Oh, it was a shameful thing. There was men there that knew no other life.

Glace Bay

In 1940 at No. 1B, this Glace Bay man had just become underground colliery manager.

Now, in 26 [formerly No. 1B] here, there was a lot of Italian people. But they're nearly all gone now. [At the time of the War], the original men here—like Scotch and Irish—they wouldn't work with the Italian people, so a lot of them left. We were at war with Italy. And a lot of these people, they had sons that were in the [Canadian] army. It didn't make any difference; they wouldn't go back [into the mines] with them. When they wouldn't work with them in the collieries, a lot of them went to Toronto. They're still up there.

This next man was mining at Glace Bay's No. 24 when the War began. He joined the Canadian army as a guard transporting prisoners of war to a camp in Northern Ontario. Elsewhere in his interview, he heaps praise on the "foreign" miners that he worked with and knew well, yet here he also vents the kind of suspicion that fuelled the general reaction against the purported "enemies within" during 1940.

There were a lot of Germans put in the detention camp. Weren't allowed to work there when the war was on. They sent them home. The Italians too. All foreigners wasn't allowed in the pit. That's the time they were talking about blowing her up, and they found some kind of bullets or something over in the big pump in No. 2. And they were scared to trust them, and they sacked them all. Laid them all off, yeah. No, you couldn't trust a lot of them fellas, you know.

From Dominion: An Italian Account

In 1978 I spent a wonderful summer evening at the Italian Hall on Mitchell Avenue in Dominion, with three men who immigrated in the 1920s for work in the mines. Condo Baggio, Raffaele Gatto and Riccardo Polegato talked of many things. Leaving Italy, learning English, settling in. Their jobs in the pit, their pay, the danger. The hard times and the fun times. They especially told of their pride in a job well done in the mine, but even more in the way they built a life for themselves and their families in the community. They made their dreams come true. But the nightmare of the Second World War was also part of the memories. In the next few pages, they tell their side of that story.[3]

[R. Gatto]: When the war started away, there was all different nationality in this country, but all the rest was working because they figured they were allied with the British Empire. But the Italian was the enemy. So we were out of work for seven months. And for the first four, we never received a cent from anybody, no assistance. In fact, they cut even the power off, the light. So, after four months, we got ... $2.40 a week, between me and the wife and the [two] children. From the government, I think it was. And the town tried to compel us to go to work. I don't know how they expected us to live.... The company would've hired us back the next day, but it was the people that keep us out.

[J. deRoche]: It was the non-Italian miners that wouldn't work with you? [R. Gatto]: Yeah, that's right. We were "enemies." So then they decided to give us work on the back shift, from 11 p.m. to 7 a.m., so [that] we don't mix with them. That went on for about six or seven months. Then the thing cooled off and everybody went back to their same place. But we had a pretty hard time. But the poor people, you can't put them down: if they get a chance, they're gonna come up and be on the top. In the end of it, we got the place just as good as anybody, or better. We got along wonderful. And then, with the young generation coming up, it was changing. When I come over here,[4] I wasn't even allowed to go to a dance with anybody, to go into any dance in a hall. You see, the older people was against us. But when the children grows up, the things mix, and the intermarriage. The last twenty-five to thirty years, we were well treated here and everything turned out alright. But we went through a hard ... hard time for quite a number of years, and now we get along wonderful, all over.

[J. deRoche]: Did the UMW, the union, officially decide to keep you out of the mines? [R. Gatto]: No, it wasn't the union that decided. You see, the committee of the union in the different local, in different mine, you see, *they* stop us. Not the high officials, not the District, [but] the local.[5] They tied up every different mine; 1B, I think, was the longer that we stayed out.

[C. Baggio]: [In Waterford] they only stayed out a couple of days. All the rest of the mines was still working. Just our mine, 1B mine.... [R. Gatto]: It depends on what kind of people [you find in each community]. Here [in Dominion], I'd say, there was about a dozen ... the people that hate the foreign people ... organized [it]. But most of the people, maybe some people, was willing to work with us because I know I worked with an English fella myself and he was willing to go back to work the next day. But he was compelled by the rest to keep us out, so they kept us out for seven months. But as far as the company and the head of the union ... I mean the District ... there was no one against us. But the people, the miners that we worked with.... [R. Polegato]: Especially here in Dominion, they were against us, everyone.... They would say they were going to get our homes.

[R. Gatto]: Some people'd say, "We're gonna get your home, we're gonna send you here, we're gonna starve you to death." That's a handful of people, you know, you can't blame everybody. But the idea was, between the union and the government, they'd make a plebiscite, a vote. Everyone you talked to was in favour of us, to go back to work. But when it come to a vote, out of 1,400 miners, there was only about seventy-five that voted in favour, and the rest of them was against us. But good job we had protection from the policemen, from the Mountie. Only for that, they would have burned us out. But as far as the law, the law wasn't against us. And I'll tell you another thing. This part of the country was more or less developed by the foreign people ... all nationality, of course. Not to be proud, but a hard-working people. We tried to excel ourselves. You see, when we did a job, we *worked*. We went through a hard time, but now, thank God, we live comfortable. Everybody's well respected. And all the Italian children over here, there's maybe about two or three that work in the mine. Every damn Italian children in Dominion, they're all educated. I told them people, "Now, at one time, you wanted to put us out, you wanted the work." I said, "We give [you it] all, the whole mine ... you can take it over and do whatever you want with it!" [laughs] That's the truth, it's no lie. We show ourselves capable to be just as good as anybody, I won't say any better. They realize today that the Italian people in Dominion, we're just as good as them. That's the reason why we're respected, because ... most of our children [are] married to a Canadian girl, and they're all.... [C. Baggio]: All mixed now, you know.

[R. Gatto]: But the whole trouble, one time, it was the older people. They'd instigate their own children. Do you understand? Because, you see, they wouldn't even stop to talk to the foreigner. "You're a foreigner," you know. You don't hear that anymore. [J. deRoche]: Okay. But when you *first* came, what kinds of discrimination were there? [C. Baggio]: It used to be not so bad, in the day we come over. [R. Gatto]: No, no. What started [it] was the War. You see, when Mussolini declared war, oh!, that was the end of the whole thing.... [R. Polegato]: Everybody upset. They blamed the poor people. [R. Gatto]: That's right. People that didn't even know Mussolini ... or even the King of Italy, who the hell knows. But that's the way it is, propaganda war. But today we're well respected, right? There's no question about it.

An hour and a half into the conversation, I was still greedy to learn. We had just been talking about Italian community organizations in Dominion. In the back of my mind was what a non-Italian man of the town told me, three years earlier, about "Black Shirts" supporting Mussolini's Fascist movement before the war. I wanted to hear an Italian side of the story. So I took the chance of pushing my hosts' generosity too far, by saying: "I don't know if you want to talk about it, but there was a political club in the Thirties."

[C. Baggio]: No, no political ... [club?] here. Never. At the time of the war, they used to say there was "*fascisti,*" this and that. There was not such a thing. Oh yeah, a fella come maybe seven, eight months before the war. He started [a club]. A few fella join up, but.... [R. Gatto]: Yeah, Risarghi[?]. [The name is hard to hear on the tape. This is my best guess.] And then [started something in Sydney]. Oh, he was a *crazy man.* Because he was dressed all in black, like a fascist.... I went to a couple of meetings myself, but then I realized he was going too far. [C. Baggio]: I love my country where I come from, where my parents, where I born, but I respect the Canadian country too. That's where I make my life and my living.

[J. deRoche]: Some fellas here got hauled away, during the war. [R. Polegato]: Innocent. Innocent people. [R. Gatto]: Listen, I'll tell you something. I think there was some of our *own people* that did more damage than English people did by taking those people away. There was jealousy.... See, there was three ... fellas ... bootlegging. They had a control of the whole thing ... if you want to get a drink of beer, that's the only place you can get [it]. Nobody else was allowed, right? It was like a small mafia, more or less, on a small scale, but they had the control. They were in with the inspector.... You see, there was the jealousy, and they did a lot of damage.... They informed the Mounties that So-and-So [was a fascist].... Some of the Italian they took away ... like he say, [were] innocent.... And well then, I guess the Mountie got a hold of that because they took away a couple of men in Dominion, quite a few in Waterford. And there was nothing wrong with them; they wasn't no fascists. But you see, I think there was jealousy, because, see, those fellas here, they was ahead, and they make money and the other fella was jealous of them.

I was condemned myself. The Mountie was telling me. I didn't know anything about it. At the time [a couple of men] and Risarghi[?], [the fascist organizer] started fighting in the hall. So me and Joe [name unclear], we put the run to them, out. And that's the only thing saving me from going to the concentration camp. The Mountie know that because they told me.

[C. Baggio]: They keep [those interned], what, two years? And then find innocent. [R. Gatto]: There was nothing there. They had no trial. They had nothing. They couldn't find *anything.* There was no fascists. There was never such.

Three Women from Dominion

Edited by Sam Migliore

The circumstances surrounding the war years (1940-1945) made life particularly difficult for many Italians throughout Cape Breton. This piece addresses some of the difficulties people encountered from the point of view of three elderly Italian women—Mrs. Amalia Zorzi, Mrs. Ida Corona Ravanello and Mrs. Anna Nicoletti. I interviewed these women separately at their homes in Dominion in April of 1997. Livio Nicoletti (Anna's son) was present for all three interviews, while Mrs. Ravanello's daughter, Luigia Demeyere, was present for her mother's interview. Although the piece focuses on the war years, I have edited the material to include statements that help to frame and contextualize their wartime experiences and memories.

Mrs. Amalia Zorzi

I came to Canada in February of 1935. I was twenty-one. In Italy we had a *campagna* (farm) with cows ... pigs [laughs], everything. We lived in Riesi, Pio X, in the province of Treviso. From there we travelled to England, caught the boat to Halifax, and then the train to come here. [Sam: Why did you come here?] I don't know. I found a man, and he came here. [laughs] My husband, Agusto, worked in the mines for forty-five years.

[Sam: What was the trip like coming to Canada?] On the boat, I was sick all the time. [laughs] Agusto and I left on January 23, and we arrived here on the second of February. Two weeks. I was pregnant. Vomit, vomit, vomit. [laughs] After the second day, I stayed in bed all the time. From Halifax, we took the train to Sydney. Twelve hours. In Sydney, we caught another train for Dominion. It was a long, long trip.

When we first arrived here, it was cold, lots of snow. The snow was [several feet] high. I didn't even have boots. [laughs] We rented a place for the first little while.

There were five men as boarders, three children, and we stayed there too for a few months. There were bugs in the bed. I helped with the work and, after a while, we built this house. In the winter time, we had no water, no light. It was hard the first years. But, there were lots of Italians ... lots of families. Then, in the 1940s, everybody moved away to Ontario for work.

[Sam: Do you have any special memories of the early years?] Oh yes; I've got lots of memories. In 1940, you know, Italy went to war. A bunch of English fellas were drinking; they used to come up to the end of the street here with their cases of beer. When they heard that Italy had gone to war, they came over and let all my chickens go. Then, they came into the house. They wanted something to eat; they wanted bread and salami. We were scared that time, you know. A few men were taken to the internment camp: Romano Scattolon, Mario Furini, a few from New Waterford, Nardocchio and others from Sydney. They were taken away for nothing! And we were scared too. The Italian miners were off work for six months. And, when they went back, some of the English people would throw rocks at the train taking them into work.

Back then, we were getting nothing. [No relief was provided during the initial period.] Not even a dollar. No! Then, after a while, I guess they felt some shame and gave us something like seventy-five cents for a child, and a $1.50 per woman and man. Per week. Welfare.... [Sam: How would you manage?] Well, we had the chickens, a pig, we made bread and we had the garden. We made it anyhow. But, if it had gone longer.... When the men went back to work, they were put on back shift. They were away all night, and we were scared. [Livio: This is when some people used to come harass them—in the night, when their men were at work.] Hard, hard, hard.

Mrs. Ida Corona Ravanello

I was born in Ciano del Montello, province of Treviso, Italy. I came to Canada in 1928. My father, Secondo Polegato, was here many, many years before I came over. He came here first, and then the rest of my family. I was married in Italy. My father made the papers for me, and I came here with my husband, Mario. [Luigia: My father was here in 1927 for six months, and then went back to Italy. Dad and Mom married, and then the two of them came here to stay.] My father was thirty-three years in the mines, and my husband worked in the mines too....

[Sam: What was it like to be married to a miner?] I got used to it; I had to, you know. Sometimes he worked at night, sometimes in the day. I didn't like it when he worked back shift. But he worked, anyway. We were lucky; he had a job. I had boarders at my place, and I looked after a pig or a cow, a goose, a rabbit, a garden, and I had three little ones, you know. I worked. I milked the cow and delivered the milk. After, when my daughters grew up, they helped deliver the milk to the people who bought from us. I worked when I was young, yes.

[Sam: Do you remember the trip to Canada?] The name of the boat was the *Roma*. We sailed from Venice to Halifax, and took the train to Sydney. My mother and two sisters were waiting for me there. My parents were boarding with relatives in Dominion, and that's where we came to stay. I didn't know anyone. I didn't speak the language. But, I had my husband, my father, my family. So, I came here in 1928, and I went back to see my place in Italy maybe twelve to thirteen years ago. That was all. In sixty-eight years, I just went back once. I have relatives there, and they want me to go, but I can't; I'm too old now.... [Mrs. Ravanello celebrated her 90th birthday a short time prior to our interview.]

[Sam: What about during the war period?] Well, I remember they threw out all the Italians from the mines during the Second World War. Yes. The town gave us a little bit of money for food. But, they didn't want the Italians to work in the mines. The men were out for maybe nine to ten months. My husband went into bootleg coal. He made a hole, went down the pit, and sold the coal. [He did this] so we wouldn't suffer. We had something to eat. But, we were scared. We didn't know when they were going to go back to work. [Luigia: Is that when they put Mr. Scattolon in the camp?] Yes; your father's brother, Angelo, was also interned. [Luigia: My uncle lived in Windsor, Ontario. I didn't know that he was interned too.]

When they threw the Italians out of the mines, they used to beat them. Nothing happened to my husband, but a lot of people were scared to be out at night because the English people might beat them. It was hard. But, at that time, me and Mario went away to Ontario. When they didn't want the Italian people in the pit, Mario couldn't find any work here. So, we went to Ontario. We were there two years. [Luigia: My sister, Laura, was born in Windsor.] Yes. We worked on a farm near Windsor.

[Sam: Was it hard in Ontario too?] No, no. It was alright. We lived with my sister-in-law, Angelo's wife. I just knew a few people; they came to see us, but we didn't go out. We didn't have any money to go out, anyway. We went to work, that's all. At first, Mario couldn't find anything else, so he worked for a circus. He fed the elephants, the animals. He wasn't lazy! He worked. Then, later, his brother found him work on the farm. He planted things, weeded, and other things like that. Angelo had returned from the camp by that time. After the war, we returned here to Dominion, and Mario worked in the mines again.

After my husband retired, he would go out to collect wood and coal. [Luigia: They never bought a lump of coal from the day they moved here, 'til the day Dad died. He would collect every lump of coal by hand.] Every morning! I never bought coal. Then, one day, he almost drowned by the dump. [Livio: They used to dig big trenches, dump the garbage in, and then cover them over. Well, it rained....] There was a clear coat of ice over the hole, and Mario thought it was strong enough to hold him. [Livio: He walked across, and down he went. And he was in his seventies.] [Luigia: The only thing that saved him was that he always carried a cane. He hooked the cane around a bush and hung on until somebody heard him cry out.] [Livio: If they hadn't come by, he was dead. The trench was full of water; it was over his head.] [Luigia: He would have drowned; it was cold. But, he was tough.] He never stayed still for a minute, especially in the summer.

Two of my daughters went to Ontario to work when they were sixteen and seventeen years old. They had to go. Their father told them to go because there was nothing for them to do here. They have families there, and they come here once a year. One lives in Guelph, and the other is in Niagara Falls. My oldest daughter lives in Sydney. [Sam: It must have been hard for you when they left.] Oh my God, yes. It is still hard. At least they come once a year, and I have this one here. My daughter in Sydney also comes over once in a while, and she calls me every night.

I always worked. All the time. I took care of the kids, the garden, the animals, delivered milk, cooked.... [Luigia: She didn't have an easy life, that's for sure. But, she's still here.]

Mrs. Anna Nicoletti

[Livio: My mother was a Ravanello.] Ida Ravanello was married to my uncle. I was born here in Dominion. My father worked in the mine for quite a few years. [Livio: And Nonna (Giconda Ravanello), my grandmother, operated a club—"Bug Row."] Every Saturday there was a dance there. [Livio: So many people have said to me: 'I remember the "Bug Row," and the times we used to have there.' It was a place where they had entertainment, an accordion player. It was a dance hall, and liquor was sold there.] My parents were born in Italy. [Livio: Ciano del Montello.] They came here a long time ago, but I went back to Italy with my mother and sister when I was five or six years old. I had my first communion in Italy. We went there, because my mother wasn't feeling well. One time, people believed in going back to Italy if they needed an operation, or they felt that a change in air would do them good. [Livio: You must have gone back to Italy in 1922, and Nonno and Nonna must have come here in the early 1900s.] From Italy, I also remember going to Belgium. My mother had a sister there. Then we all came back here.

[Livio: My grandparents moved from Dominion to Trout Brook on the Mira River.] He wasn't fussy about the mines, my poor father. So, he started in Trout Brook. He did everything by pick and shovel—there was no such thing as machines. They built a home down there. [Livio: I remember my grandfather, Nonno, leaving with the horse to walk to Mira. Now, that's thirty miles! He'd walk down with the horse, clear land for the house, and walk back. I don't know how many times he did that. Nonno built a little house and moved down there. My uncle (my mother's brother) was overseas with the Canadian Forces during the war, and when he got back he built a two-storey house on the same property. My grandparents have passed away, but, at the time, there might have been a couple of Italian families living down there. They were there before my grandparents. They went down from Dominion around the time when the Italians weren't allowed in the mines. They said, "the hell with this," and they moved out to Mira and started farming. So, my grandparents went down there too. My uncle and his family are still there.] We are the only two left, my brother and I; the rest are all gone—mother, father, husband, sisters....

[Sam: Do you have any memories of the war period?] Italians were not allowed to work in the mines. They were looked at as enemies. Well, my husband, Giuseppi (Pino) Nicoletti, worked in the mine for thirty-nine years. He started when he was fourteen years old by lying about his age. He worked in Waterford with Riccardo Polegato in 26 colliery. But, during the war, they weren't allowed to go down, because they were Italian. He had to quit. He didn't want to; he had a family to raise. All the Italians had to register with the RCMP. My husband's parents had been in Germany for a while.... [Livio: My grandfather worked in the coal mines in Germany.] ...and my husband was born there. So, he was German. Anyhow, he lost all his rights. But, he was a naturalized Canadian. And, I was not counted to be a Canadian. I was born here. If I wanted to go to Italy, I had to get a passport. I lost my rights, which I couldn't see [why]. That, I remember. And the Italians had to give all their guns and things to the RCMP. All the people who went to the camp, that wasn't necessary. They didn't do anything. All the Italians were hated.

[Livio: Dad loved hunting and fishing. There was always meat in the freezer. I learned to like deer meat better than beef.] We always had a bite to eat, that's for sure. He used to clean, skin and split it into four pieces. Then, I had to chop it up. I learned to be a butcher without even knowing it. [Livio: And I learned it from helping her as a kid. If I get a deer, I'll cut it up myself. But, my father, he loved the woods. And, my grandmother, at Trout Brook, she loved going on weekend trips fishing and hunting with my father and uncles.] Runs in the family. [Livio: Oh yes, I go find myself in the woods. I enjoy it so much.... We ate a lot of wild game. There were six kids in the family, and my father was sick a lot. Dad had heart problems; he had rheumatic fever when he was young, and that left a scar on his heart. But then he got over that. He also had bad athletes' foot. But, the only time I ever saw him miss work was in hunting season. And that wasn't too often! Maybe a Saturday, or something like that, eh. He worked....] My poor husband said, "I would like to go back to Italy before I die," but he didn't make it. He would have loved to go....

From Internment to Military Service:
An Historical Paradox

Edited by Sam Migliore[1]

As Canadians, we often pride ourselves on living in a country free of the ethnic and racial tensions that exist in other parts of the world. These feelings, however, often mask problems that have existed, and in some cases continue to exist, in Canada itself. A number of ethnic and racial groups have experienced some form of discrimination at one point or another in Canadian history, while others (such as the various First Nations) have had to deal with this phenomenon over an extended period of time. For Italian Canadians, the prejudice and discrimination directed towards them reached its peak during the Second World War.

When Mussolini declared war on Britain and France on June 10, 1940, Italians residing in Canada suddenly became "the enemy within" (or "Fifth Column") in the minds of both government officials and the general public. The Federal Government made use of the War Measures Act *to force thousands of Italians to report their whereabouts to the RCMP on a regular basis, to arrest approximately 6,000 people, and eventually intern some 800 individuals.[2] This was not the first, or last, time the* War Measures Act *was used in this way. During the First World War, for example, more than 80,000 people were registered as "enemy aliens," and some 5,000 Ukrainian Canadians were interned.[3] Later, after Japan entered the Second World War, virtually the entire Japanese Canadian population, including women and children, was removed from Canada's Pacific coast and isolated in various camps (mostly in the Interior of British Columbia), while their property and assets were confiscated.[4]*

My aim is to move beyond the issue of discrimination and internment to address an important paradox. While some Italian Canadians were being verbally abused, deprived of employment, or interned, others entered the Canadian Armed Services and risked their lives to protect Canadian interests. In some cases, sons and daughters served overseas at the very moment that their parents (and siblings) were being treated as "enemy aliens." What follows is a look at some of the memories and experiences of both those who encountered (or witnessed) the effects of discrimination and those who fought bravely for the land they loved.

Establishing a Context

On Sunday, November 10, 1918, a crowd of about 800 Italians paraded through the streets of Whitney Pier and made their way to Sydney's Lyceum for a major celebration. The festivity was organized to celebrate the defeat of the Austrian forces in the First World War. The Sydney Daily Post *described the event in this way:*

Gaily decorated horses, carriages, automobiles, and men themselves took part in the parade.... At the head of the parade was Police Sargeant Rannie MacDonald ... as marshall and his two assistants T. Bruno and Louis DiPenta. Following the mounted marshalls were the Sydney Mines C.M.B.A. band ... and veterans of the army and navy. Then came the Italians of the county, followed by a float on which were tiers of girls representing Italy and her allies. Another float represented freed Poland. Officially representing the Italian nation was Consul Tony D. Pistoni (*sic*)....[5]

Excerpt from "An Address to the People of Canada Concerning Italy's Entry into the War"[7]

Broadcast by
The Right Hon. W. L. MacKenzie King, M.P.
Prime Minister of Canada
Monday, June 10, 1940

Fellow Canadians

The news reached Ottawa a few minutes after one o'clock to-day that Signor Mussolini ... had announced that Italy was entering the war on the side of Germany.... I immediately introduced a resolution which placed Canada at the side of Britain and France....

Measures Taken to Maintain Internal Security

The Minister of Justice has authorized the Royal Canadian Mounted Police to take steps to intern all residents of Italian origin whose activities have ground for the belief or reasonable suspicion that they might, in time of war, endanger the safety of the State, or engage in activities prejudicial to the prosecution of the war.... Preparation for these and other necessary steps had been made well in advance of the declaration of war....

As part of the festivities, a number of individuals spoke in praise of the Italians and their role in the war effort. W. F. Carroll, a former MP referred to the Italians as "a strong, upright people," and then went on to say: "We have welcomed Italians in the past as they make good citizens, and we will continue to welcome them with open arms in the future."[6] Twenty-two years later, Carroll's words were all but forgotten. "Good citizens," many of whom had marched in the 1918 parade, were now labelled as "enemy aliens" and subjected to various forms of discrimination. For the Italian population of Canada, having disparaging remarks and unequal treatment directed toward them was not a new phenomenon; it was something they had experienced at various times throughout their history in Canada. What was new was: the level and intensity of public hostility; and, the nature of the institutionalized discrimination of Canadian Government policy and action. As a result, the Italian communities of Cape Breton (and elsewhere) experienced a major disruption that would take many years to repair.

The Round-Up

Once Canada and Italy were officially at war, the RCMP, under orders from Ottawa, began to arrest a number of Italians across the country. Dolores (Rossetti) Moore of Whitney Pier was only a young girl at the time. She, like the character in Sharon Gibson Palermo's The Lie That Had To Be, *has retained certain vivid memories of what transpired.*[8]

Mr. Michele (Mike) LaPenna, my Dad's friend, never married. He lived with us and was like family. He walked the floor with every one of us. Mr. LaPenna was taken to the concentration camp in Petawawa. I think we heard the announcement that Italy had entered the war at three o'clock [June 10, 1940], and the police arrived by 3:30 p.m. They went right upstairs into Mr. LaPenna's room, but he wasn't home. Mike was at St. Nicholas Church, where he did a lot of work taking care of the books, the collection ... he always seemed to be there. Mike came home close to supper time. They took him away, and he didn't come back until, I guess, nearly three years later when he was released.

Mr. LaPenna belonged to the *Dopo Lavoro* (After Work) club. I don't think there was any harm in it. My Dad didn't belong to it because he was too busy working. He worked a lot of extra shifts to help pay for my brother's university education in Antigonish. The amount my brother paid for board may not seem like much today, but in those days it was a lot of money. So Dad more or less worked at every opportunity. He really didn't have time for the club; if he had, maybe he'd have been taken to the camp too. We don't know.

I was very little, but I remember what happened. The next day, the Mounted Police came here. When my sister (who was about five years older than me) and I saw the Mountie, we started to cry. We were sure he was coming back for Dad. But, no, they wanted to know if we had any firearms in the house. My mother said: "No; feel free to search." They said: "No, no; we were just checking." Then they said, "if anyone gives you any trouble, let us know; don't take any abuse." We didn't get a lot of abuse, but people would say things sometimes. "You won't be here long." "Won't be long before your father is locked up." Different things. In the steel plant, they would take cartoons from the paper, and pin them in places where my father could see them. People are strange. Two of my brothers, Frank and Alphonse, served with the Canadian forces. Frank went overseas with the first contingent.

The day after Mr. LaPenna was arrested, my uncle Carmen went over to the city lockup to see what was going on. They were all black and blue. A couple of them had black eyes, blood on them.... Somebody said that the police had put some drunks in with them and that they had beat them. Nobody knows what really went on, except the police I guess. It was the way it went.

Mr. LaPenna was such a good person. He helped a lot of people. If they needed money, he would give them a loan. I guess a lot of it he never got back. And then, of course, when he was released and went back to work, it was another situation. He worked in one of the mills at the steel plant. Some of the other workers refused to work with him. He had a hard time, but he persevered. He wouldn't leave.

Mike never said very much about life in the camp. But, I think, there were a lot of people, from all walks of life there. It didn't matter your profession. I was just saying the other night, I have a membership with the Italian association today, if anything were to happen ... I mean ... you could be so innocent and....

Londo Scattolon also recalls the day the RCMP arrived at the family home, in Dominion, to arrest his father (Romano Scattolon). He described the event to me in this way.

I was home when they came to pick up my Dad. It was around 4:30 p.m., when the Hobo [train] was transporting the workers from the coal mines to Dominion. Dad walked home from the station, and the Mounties were there waiting for him. I just stayed outside. And, after it was all over, I found out that they had taken him. He didn't even have time to have his supper. Ma always had his supper waiting for him. Nothing at all! Just washed, changed clothes as quick as he could, and they took him. For days after, I didn't even know that they had taken him to the Sydney jail. There was no explanation as to why they had taken him. They just said, "You are a member of the Italian Hall, the treasurer, we have orders to arrest you."

They were happy times if we had been left alone. But, the fact that Mussolini sided with the Germans killed the whole thing. Bang, we were hit. It had nothing to do with people here. My father came to Canada as a young fella. What I think is that the Canadian Government panicked. They grabbed everybody, and made it look like there was, what did they call it, a "Fifth Column" within Canada. It was unreal. They rounded them up like a bunch of cattle. Look at what happened to the Japanese people too. They took their properties, confiscated their money and shipped entire families inland.

The authorities didn't care about the families of the men in the camp. Who was going to feed me, and my mother, and my two brothers? We were also in constant fear. People were throwing rocks at our house; it was hell! When you come to look at it, by gees, it was terrible, wasn't it? I mean, my Dad loved Canada.

In 1944, after his father had been released from the internment camp, Londo Scattolon was called up for military service. He served four months of basic training, and then was stationed at Saint John, New Brunswick. In 1945, he began to train with his father for work in the coal pits. Londo, however, was not the only son or daughter of someone held in the internment camps to serve with the Canadian Forces. Frank (Nunziante) Martinello of Sydney had two sons and a daughter in military service during the war, yet he was arrested on June 10, 1940, and interned at Petawawa on August 12 even though he was suffering from health problems (see "All They Ever Wanted Was a New Life and an Apology" in this volume).

The Internment

Dominic Nardocchio[9]

Dominic Nardocchio was born October 15, 1904, in Miranda, Italy. In 1916, he, along with his mother (Carolina) and brother (John), travelled to Boston to join his father (Egidio). From Boston, they made their way to Whitney Pier where Egidio Nardocchio was employed as a steelworker. Dominic grew up in the Pier, got involved in music, and eventually opened a shoemaker's shop in Sydney. By the outbreak of the Second World War, he and his wife (Anna) had eight children—ranging from only ten weeks to nine years of age.

Well on June the 10th ... about two o'clock in the afternoon ... the RCMP came into my shop and said: "Are you Dominic Nardocchio?" I said: "Yes, sir." [pause] And he said to me: "You are under arrest." I said: "What have I done?" "Well," he said, "you know Italy declared war on England." "What's that got to do with me?" "Well," he said, "the orders come from Ottawa that I have you arrested [pause]...." He was a man ... doing his duty. There was nothing you could do, so I ... went with him ... [to] the city lockup.... [pause] By the evening we were about thirteen.... And then, about eight o'clock or later, they brought in four or five local people [who] acted as if they were drunk.... We didn't have supper. We were just working people; we didn't know what they were going to do with us.... [pause] One of the [local men] picked up one of the [Italian] fellas from New Waterford, and started to call him names— "You're a blackshirt, and you're a bastard...." [He] start[ed] to beat him up ... to smash with fists, and they started to kick him.... This [Italian] fellow started to defend himself, and then they started into a brawl. [*Several of the Italians were injured.*] But [pause] ... the Italians themselves ... wouldn't ... touch them, because they were scared, you see. These were four, five of them, we were thirteen, and those Italians were all pretty strong men, still working as a miner, they could have twisted their necks in no time. But, then we were told, that if that had happened ... the RCMP would have come in and shot us all....

The next morning, they ... took us away by car. Well, four or five of [the Italians] had black eyes.... They took us to Truro, and from Truro they put us on the train ... [for] Petawawa....

A month later, they had an investigation [of the men interned] ... [and] my name came from Ottawa to be an interpreter for those Italians who couldn't speak the language. I was with the RCMP eight months, every day, and at the end ... he says: "Look ... I'm going to recommend the Department of Justice to discontinue this investigation, because you people shouldn't be here. None of you! If it's up to me, I'd send you all home tomorrow...." [He said this] in February of 1941 ... but they kept me another thirteen months.... I was released in March of 1942.... I wrote all what [we] went through, and I had to hide it in my shoes—because they wouldn't let you go through with it. That's how I got a lot of stuff out of [the camp].... *Dominic Nardocchio passed away in Halifax, Nova Scotia on Thursday, February 5, 1998. He was ninety-three years old.*

Romano Scattolon's Experience[10]

Romano Scattolon was born in Salvaroso, Treviso, Italy. He came to Canada in 1921, and settled in Dominion. He worked initially at No. 6 colliery in Donkin, and later at No. 1B in Glace Bay. He was one of the founding members of the Italian Community Club in Dominion, and its treasurer at the outbreak of war.

Romano Scattolon, ca. 1964. Courtesy of Anna Scattolon.

On June 10, 1940, I came home from work ... around five o'clock in the afternoon. There were two RCMP officers waiting for me.... They asked me if I wanted to eat and change my clothes. I had no idea what was going on. I bid my wife goodbye and then I was taken to a jail in Glace Bay. There I met another gentleman from Dominion. Early the next morning we were taken to RCMP headquarters in Sydney where I met approximately seventeen other Italians from the local area. From what I could gather no one knew what was going on and no one was allowed to notify their families as to where they were. We stayed in Sydney for three hours then we were taken in three cars to Moncton, New Brunswick. We arrived late in the afternoon. There we were immediately put on a train with several RCMP officers acting as guards and taken to Montreal. We arrived late at night and the next day we were taken to Petawawa, Ontario by truck. During the trip we were not treated brutally and we were given something to eat.

The camp at Petawawa was just like a prison with high walls and barbed wire, soldiers and guns. There were interns from all over Canada, of different nationalities, most were German and Italian. Life here was not too bad. The food was good, there was no violence or beatings and of course we had to work. Each day I was taken to the bush, under guard, and I cut wood for two years and three months. I still had no correspondence with my family.

I was then taken by train to another camp at Fredericton, New Brunswick. Following three months I was put on trial and I had to answer questions concerning my life's activities and ambitions. One month later I was given my freedom. The authorities paid my train fare home. I was happy to be with my family but I did not have a job. A coal company official explained to me that if I were rehired there could very possibly be an outbreak of hostilities among the non-Italian citizens. There was a strong resentment against people like myself, in fact, people stopped buying at the small store I operated at the time of my imprisonment. Also, my wife and family were discriminated against during my internment and after my release.

I eventually managed to get a job at Sydney airport with a construction company which was carrying out an expansion program there. I worked there for several months and then went to the steel plant in Sydney. I worked at the plant for six or seven months and then I was rehired in the mines. I went back and I worked there, with little trouble, until my retirement in 1964.

Bert and Gordon Gatto[11]

[Bert Gatto]: I was born 1895, the 19th of May, in Riese, Treviso. Pope Pius X was born in the same town. I was confirmed by him in 1902, when he was Patriarch of Venice. Now, he's a Saint. In all, I think, we were fourteen brothers and sisters, but some died young. In 1912 on the 12th of December, my father and I arrived in Halifax. The Dominion Coal Company was recruiting labour to work in No. 14 mine [New Waterford], so they paid our trip [to Canada]. From Halifax [we travelled] to Sydney by train, and then took the street car to Dominion. Father and I walked from Dominion to the sandbar and near froze to death. It was a cold night. We landed in No. 14 Yard (where we had relatives). Father and I got jobs in No. 14 pit right away.

Bert Gatto worked in No. 14 colliery for a short time. In Italy, he had trained to be a tailor. Throughout much of 1913, Bert worked in tailor shops in New Waterford and Glace Bay as a coat maker. Business, however, was slow, and he returned to work in the mine—this time in No. 9 colliery, Glace Bay. With the help of friends, however, he was able to secure employment at a tailor shop in North Sydney. He worked there for four years, 1914-1918. While in North Sydney, Bert took the opportunity to work on his English language skills, and to take a correspondence course on tailoring from a company in New York.

[Bert Gatto]: All this time my father was in New Waterford. I left North Sydney in 1918 and, after a few months, I started a tailor shop on Plummer Avenue, in New Waterford. By 1921-1922, I had twenty-three people working for me. I was the only tailor left in town, and every Italian miner was getting a tailor-made suit by then. I was working day and night. *The 1923 and 1925 mine strikes, and later competition from Tip Top Tailors, brought the boom to an end.* [Bert Gatto]: I kept up the tailor shop until 1932, then I quit altogether. Then, I had a beverage room, the Citizen's Club, going here until 1940.

Bert's brother, Gordon, was born in Italy in 1899. He served with the Italian forces during the First World War, and emigrated to Cape Breton in 1921. Gordon spent ten years working in No. 12 colliery, ten years as a baker (from 1930 to 1940), and then another eighteen years in No. 16 colliery before retiring.

[Bert Gatto]: In 1940, my brother Gordon and I were picked up to go to the camp. I was there for 33 months. There were nine of us from Waterford. When I came out of the camp, in February of 1943, we moved to Montreal. I had a tailor shop there from 1943 to 1962, then we came back. *From 1962 until he retired in 1975, Bert Gatto operated both a tavern and a tailor shop in New Waterford.*

A pre-Second Word War trip to Italy. Centre: Felice Martinello and Bert Gatto. Courtesy of Francis X. Martinello.

[Len Stephenson (interviewer): Why did they put the Italians in the camps?] [Bert Gatto]: The main reason was that they put them in the camp in England. When Canada got into the war, they did the same thing. Since I was in Italy in 1937.... [Len Stephenson: They thought you could be involved.] [Bert Gatto]: Yeah. *Bert Gatto visited Italy in 1937, along with Felice Martinello (of Whitney Pier) and Peter Favretto (of New Waterford) to attend his sister's 60th Anniversary as a nun. His parents were living in Italy at that time.12 Bert was interned even though he had lived in Canada since 1912, and he was married to Margaret MacLean (who, although born in Bangor, Maine, was of Cape Breton background on both sides of her family).*

[Len Stephenson: How were conditions in the camp? Was it bad?] [Bert Gatto]: Oh no, the worst part was leaving the family. I had seven children—three boys, four girls. See, I was in the last lot to go to the camp. But, in the first lot, some of the Italians from New Waterford were beaten over in Sydney. Some guys got arrested for an excuse, and they put them together with the Italians. Peter Favretto was one of the guys who was all beat up.

[Gordon Gatto]: I was in the camp for twenty-two months. [Len Stephenson: What did you do to pass time?] [Gordon Gatto]: Well, you could work cutting wood for the stove, because there was no coal there. Sometimes we loaded gravel at the gravel pit, then worked on the road. They paid us 20 cents a day. We made one big bridge there, the Petawawa River. There was an old bridge, but she was all gone to hell. We made a new one. There were about 700 of us in the camp—[including] two from Dominion, eight from Waterford, and another ten from Sydney.

[Len Stephenson: What was the idea of putting them in camps; why did they do that?] [Gordon Gatto]: How the hell do we know. They kept all the people in the camp for nothing. I came here in 1921. During the First World War, I was in the Italian forces, but we were on the same side as the Canadians. In 1930, I got my citizenship papers. I was Canadian. Then, in 1940, they put me in the camp. I don't know. We had a little club, Dopo Lavoro (After Work club), a place to go after work. And here, they say, "Dopo Lavoro is bad." [Len Stephenson: Did they think somebody was supporting Mussolini?] [Gordon Gatto]: Yeah. What the hell do we know about Mussolini.... We didn't know who Mussolini was when we came over here....

The Experiences of Those Who Were Not Interned

Although only a select number of Cape Breton Italians were interned, everyone was affected to some extent or another. The fact that Canada and Italy were at war was sufficient to disrupt the lives of various Italian Canadians, and to create new hardships for people who were determined to make a better life for themselves and their children in this country. They struggled, each in her or his own way, to arrangiarsi (to manage, to be inventive). And, at least in certain cases, when things seemed bleak, they received help from some unexpected sources.

Childhood Memories

[Gloria (DiCesare) MacDougall]: As a child, it was difficult sometimes being brought up in an English-speaking country and being of Italian parentage. You were Canadian, but you were also Italian and, once in a while, it caused some difference of opinion. However, as an adult, of course, you realize that you have the best of both worlds ... two cultures to be a part of.

I was nine years old when the war started. After watching *Barbed Wire and Mandolins* on television and reading about the war period in Ken Bagnell, I started to remember a lot of things.[14] When I was a little girl, my mother wouldn't let me have my ears pierced. She said it would make me look "Italian." Being the only Italian girl without pierced ears bothered me a little, but I understood her reason behind it. "That's for Italian girls," she would say. "You are Canadian." Now I have my ears pierced. She would also say: "When the other girls ask what you had for lunch, don't say spaghetti or pasta" That, of course, would give away my Italian culture. But now, my Canadian-born sons are proud of our Italian heritage and of my Italian cooking.

[Ron DiPenta]:[13] In 1941, my happy childhood was interrupted. I think part of the reason why my father left the Pier was that my family found it hard being suspected of sympathizing with Mussolini simply because we were Italian. I remember how I suddenly became self-conscious about being Italian. Canada became involved in fighting Mussolini. Then if you were considered Italian, even if you were born in Whitney Pier, it went rough for you. I was called a Fascist, a Mussolini, but I didn't understand anything about what all of that meant. The kids who were being cruel didn't understand what it meant either. Eventually that all passed after the war, but it left scars in people's minds.

I can remember a good neighbour of ours, Mr. Felice Martinello, was interned, and mother doing whatever she could to help his family. Mrs. Martinello and my mother were good friends, and my mother would give them some ration coupons because they had a big family. As a school girl, the war didn't affect me too much. I played with other Italian girls and I wasn't aware of any negative feelings that other ethnic groups may have harboured against us. However, I do remember, very vividly, my father (Donato DiCesare), who was not interned, being so afraid of what was happening around us, that he removed everything from our home that denoted being Italian.... Everything! Any pictures (even one of the Pope), ornaments, or mementos from the homeland were gone. And his homemade wine! I remember my mother pleading with him not to pour it out. She insisted that the police would not arrest him just because he made some wine, but he poured it all out anyway. That wine was a lot of work and money. My mother put her foot down when it came to the *presepio* (Christmas nativity scene). My father kept saying, "but that's Italian, that's Italian." Finally, he got his way. My mother replaced it with an "English" *presepio*. That's how afraid they were. The most important thing on the wall in our house was a large poster of the Royal Family. That was predominant. I can still see it in my mind's eye. If anyone walked in, that was what they would see.

While we were afraid of the internment, I have to say that my father was the most loyal Canadian you could ever find. It's strange, you know, but a common thread through the whole story, despite all that happened to them, was that no one turned against Canada. They didn't want to go back to Italy. I used to ask my father if he ever wanted to go back, but he would say: "No! This country gave me my bread." My parents never went back to Italy.

Barbed Wire and Mandolins was an excellent program ... very sad, very revealing.... It brought me back to the war years. When I read ... *Canadese*, I realized that what happened to the Italians here was not uncommon; it didn't just happen to us.[15]

[Enzo Antonello]: My Dad was the first President of the Italian Hall in Dominion. He was a quiet man, the type of person that never caused problems. He always kept things to himself, even the hard times they had during the war. I remember the Mounted Police ... searching the house, because somebody told them that Pa was the first President of the Hall, and that he had a short wave radio to Rome. I was only eleven or twelve years old at the time. I also remember my Dad going down every Monday morning to the Town Hall, to report like a criminal. The only crime they committed was that they were Italians. I had first cousins from Donkin that were with the Canadian Army fighting over in Italy and Germany. But, Pa would never talk about what happened to us. Never!

I remember the Town cutting off our electricity ... turning the water off. Our neighbour, Newton Mitchell gave us vegetables from his farm and water from his well. And, Mrs. Sarah Lynk thought it was terrible how we were treated, and she used an extension cord from her house to give us lights. I also remember three

---

"The War Years"
To My Father
(He Will Never Be Forgotten)

As I sit here thinking about my Dad
The memories started up the tears
When I think of what he went through
Way back in those war years

He came to Canada from Italy
Married a girl from over here
They raised a family of twelve
Then the war came with its fear

My father never forgot his roots
Although Italy went to the other side
It was Canada he called his home
He gave a son to the army that died

Two mounties came to our house one day
And told him as they stood by the door
He would have to report to them each month
As long as Italy was in the war

They even took away our radio
As a kid I couldn't understand why
There even were people on our street
Thought my father may be a spy

I knew his heart felt broken
And the war years made him sad
But when Italy came back with us
Was the first time in years he felt glad

He gave all of us kids his love
Never, never let any of us down
And when he talked about Italy
Part of his heart was in his old home town

His son—Roy Plichie (Pagliccia)

---

guys coming into our house when war broke out. They insulted Mom and Dad, cursed at them, called them *wops* and *dagos*, and told them that they were going to be sent back to the old country. One of them looked at our home, and said: "This is my house; I'm taking it when you people are gone." As you get older, you forget things that happened last week, but you never forget anything that happened when you were a kid.

Dominion: Loss of Employment and the Italian Hall[16]

Italian miners working at various collieries in Industrial Cape Breton were not allowed to work for a period of time. The situation was particularly serious in Dominion, where Italian miners were off work for about nine months. Initially, they received no assistance for their families. Then, in later months, they received a small amount per week per person. When the Italian miners were allowed to return to work, they were placed on back shift (night shift) for an extended period of time. After the war, a number of Italian families left Dominion—some to settle on farms in Mira, but most to places like Guelph, Hamilton and Niagara Falls, Ontario.

[Enzo Antonello]: I remember there wasn't any income. The Italian miners were out of work for maybe ten months. They were having it tough. Then, in the last few months, they were getting something like $1.50 or $1.75 a week for adults, and 50 cents for children. I was an altar boy, and I remember that Father Charlie MacDonald used to give them hell from the pulpit, telling them it was a shame, an injustice, what they were doing to the Italian people.

The Italian community of Dominion experienced another loss in the 1940s when some of the Second World War veterans began to return from action overseas. The veterans confiscated the Italian Hall and began to use it as Legion. Eventually, however, the Italian association was able to regain control of the hall (see "La Sala Italiana in Dominion" in this volume).

Guns, Survival and Humour

Out of work, with little or no assistance, Italian miners were driven to the point where they had to find some way to help themselves and their families.

[Livio Nicoletti]: All the Italians had their guns taken from them.... And they bought guns from different people and hid them. They would go up pretending they were picking berries, and they would shoot a deer. Then, at night, they'd come back with the [meat]. That's how they survived. [Tony Basso]: I remember Sgt. Neilson came and said he had to take our guns. We had a 16-gauge and an 8 mm. My father said: "Yeah, but I want them in the same condition that you are getting them." Sgt. Neilson said, "that's a promise." And I know, when the war was over, my father went hunting with him. Oh, the guns were all greased and everything. I also remember, during the war, when the Italians were out of work and there was no money coming in, that Sgt. Neilson came back to the house. My father said: "What do you want?" And Sgt. Neilson said, "I've come for your daughter." Well, my father was in a mild fit! [laughter] But, he got my sister a job down at the Mountie barracks. She worked there in order to supplement our income. I forget what she was getting, but he did us a favour. It was great.

[Anonymous]: After the Mounties took away all the guns, when all this agony was going on, someone sold my father a 12-gauge for two dollars. This English fellow used to come around selling things, and my father asked him: "Could you get me a shotgun?" "Yeah, but it'll take a while," he said. So, we waited a couple of weeks, and then, one Sunday morning, this fellow came back. He was wearing a suit, vest full of gravy. Like the fellow says: "The coat and pants do all the work, and the vest gets all the gravy." Anyway, he was coming up the road, and boy did he have an awful limp. He comes into the house, and that's where he hauled it out. He had the barrel of the gun up his pant leg, the stock on his arm. Two dollars. He sold it to us. Yeah. We had to go out at night to hide it. When we shot a deer, we'd have to go back in the afternoon to skin it and, if it was blueberry season, we'd get a bucket for the deer meat, pick some blueberries, and put them on top. We would come home with a bucket of blueberries, leaves and everything else. But, those blueberries were sure heavy, boy. [laughs]

John and Geneva Nardocchio: Losing One's Rights[18]

The Nardocchio Family, with John (sitting). August 1916. Photo by Dodge Studio, Whitney Pier. Courtesy of John Nardocchio.

John Nardocchio was only six years old when he arrived in Boston in 1916. A short time later, the family moved to Whitney Pier. At age twenty-two, he married Geneva, and they raised a family of eight children. Over the years, John worked as a steelworker, a shoe repairer, and a salesperson. Then, in 1969, he entered municipal politics. He served as a councillor for the City of Sydney for many years, and deputy mayor for two years. The war years, however, had a negative effect on the entire Nardocchio family, including John's non-Italian spouse.

[John Nardocchio]: When war broke out on June 10, 1940, I was repairing shoes on Townsend Street. My brother was on Charlotte Street.... Two Mounties arrested him ... and took him to the jail on Bentinck Street. By the next day, twelve more were in there with him. And ah, my poor mother.... She was sitting in the car when the Mounties walked out with him by the arms, as if he was a convict. She took a turn; damn near died on account of it.

A month after that, I noticed that my trade was slipping. There were twenty-six shoe repair shops in Sydney at that time, but I noticed my business slipping because I was Italian. They were taking their shoes [somewhere else].... *For the Nardocchio family, the war years were characterized by both emotional trauma and financial hardship.*

After the war, John obtained his Canadian naturalization papers. To his surprise, he found out that his Canadian wife had to go through the same procedure. I said to myself, "I better be naturalized." I thought I was for the simple fact that my father was naturalized and I was six years of age when I came to this country.

So I went to the court house, the documents for naturalization were filled out, and I was sworn in by a magistrate. But a month later I was called by the office, and a gentleman said to me: "Mr. Nardocchio, this may sound kind of out of place, but although your wife was born in Guysborough County and she's a Canadian, when she married you, she lost her Canadian rights. Right now she's gotta get naturalized as a Canadian. Would you kindly bring her up?" And I made an appointment with him to get her naturalized.

[My wife] didn't know what to say. She said, "What do you mean I lost my Canadian rights?" I said, "well you married me, you lost your Canadian rights." She felt out of place, really.

Italians Serving in the Canadian Forces

While some Italians were interned and others, due to loss of employment, found it difficult to make ends meet for their families, a number of young Italian men and women volunteered to fight for the Canadian forces.

Romeo Sylvester[20]

Romeo Sylvester has a family history of military service that extends through at least three generations and three separate wars. Although Italian, he and his brother, father, and maternal grandfather all served with the Canadian or British Forces.

My mother's father was 6'4" tall. He and one of his sons were connected with the British forces in South Africa, during the Boer War. I was told that my grandfather was a colonel.

Pordena Smith Asks Fair Deal[19]

Pordena (Spinazzola) Smith experienced a temporary set-back in his boxing career as a direct result of action taken against Italians during the war. He wrote the following letter to the Sports Editor of the *Sydney Post-Record* as an appeal for justice. The letter was published on Tuesday, August 27, 1940.

Sir—I am writing ... to have my case placed before the sporting public.

...A few weeks ago I was matched with Dempsey MacPhail and shortly before ... the fight I was dropped and Charlie Phillips put on in my place. As no reason for this was given at the time I would like to tell the fight fans that it was no run out on my part but that the Boxing Commission decided that I was not to go on because of my parents' nationality (Italian).

... I am a native born Cape Bretoner, I have served with the Canadian militia and have a brother at present in the C.A.S.F. My family were never Fascists and had no sympathy with Fascism. In view of this I believe that I have received very shabby treatment, hardly to be expected in the field of sport.

I like boxing. I have been at it since I was fifteen years old, seven years. I have had over forty fights and have only one unavenged defeat.... I have beaten both fighters who defeated Dempsey MacPhail.... I believe that I can take Dempsey too.... I hope the fans and promoter ... will give me a chance in the near future to see just how good he is....

Yours Truly,
Pordena Smith

My father (Joseph "Pippino" Sylvester) came to Sydney with his father [around] 1910. He was about ten years old. My father joined the Canadian Army in 1915, and served in the First World War with the 185th Battalion and went into action with the Royal Canadian Regiment. He was wounded badly at Vimy Ridge. Five or six bullets caught him from a machine gun, and he was exposed to poison gases. *Although Joseph Sylvester survived, he continued to experience the negative effects of his wounds for many years. He passed away in 1960.*

After the First World War, Dad went back to Italy and married my mother. *Mrs. Aurora Laura Sylvester remained in Italy, while Joseph returned to Cape Breton to work in the steel plant. Both Romeo and his brother, Frank Dominic, were born in Italy. The family finally joined Mr. Sylvester in Sydney in 1931.*

Although my father served with the Canadian forces in the First World War, surprising as it may seem, he didn't become a Canadian citizen until 1924. My brother and I, and my mother, didn't become Canadian citizens until 1947. After the war! Even though he and I had the uniforms on for the Canadian forces. Frank was in the Navy, and I was in the army. When they asked me if I would volunteer for general service, I said: "Yes. Anywhere, but Italy." There was no hassle; they understood, didn't even question it. My grandmother was still alive in Italy, and my uncles were still over there. I was with the Canadian Airborne Regiment attached to a British unit. After the war, I was awarded the Canadian Decoration and Bar for military service.

Upon completion of his service overseas, Romeo Sylvester returned to Sydney and his work at the steel plant. He was with the steel plant, in various capacities, for more than forty-five years. At the same time, however, he continued to maintain an affiliation with the military, and eventually became involved in the teaching of First Aid.

I was chief instructor for Cape Breton Island for First Aid, St. John's Ambulance. That was something I picked up in the military. In 1955, I joined the Medical Corps. I stayed in, and became Sergeant Major in the 6th Field Company. I got my trade as medical assistant, group three, from the Military. I would go in the evenings and weekends. I then transferred to the 2nd Nova Scotia Highlanders Regiment, where I stayed until I was fifty-five years old. In 1965, I was awarded the Order of St. John for medical and military service, and the Serving Brother of the Order of St. John for medical services in 1974. Both medals were issued by Queen Elizabeth II. [Sam Migliore: So you have a long standing relationship with the Military.] Oh, yes. Over twenty-five years! I found that it disciplined; Dad brought us up that way, and my mother came from a military background also. Discipline. And, we have tried to bring up our kids the same way. Although, today, it is a different world.

Frank Legatto[21]
Vincenzo and Carmella (Carpenteri) Legatto—of Bolino, in Calabria, Italy—emigrated to Canada sometime around 1912. Vincenzo worked in the lumber camps of Quebec, before settling in Sydney Mines to work first in the steel plant and later at the Florence Colliery. He and his brother also operated a small grocery store on Ocean Street. Frank Legatto, Vincenzo and Carmella's son, was born and raised

in Sydney Mines. He is married to Jennie Barbara Aubrecht, and they have seven children. Frank served in the Canadian Forces during the war.

Everybody was wondering what was going on. I said, "my God, this is going to be grim now." In a sense, the Italian people were like the enemy to the country, you know. But I thought about joining the army. Before then, Daddy was a miner in the pit so everything was alright.... But ... if we stayed out of it.... They were rounding them up ... Italians. Putting them in a camp, you know. So I joined the army, and all went well.

I went to Amherst and we were stationed there for a year. On account of my having a grade 10 education, they wanted me to take a short course on office work. I also took a short course in Intelligence, being I understood a bit of Italian. I understand a little, but I can't speak it. So I took a short course in that and I did alright. When I was in England, I started working in the office ... handling records.... So I joined in 1940 and landed in England 1941. And we were in England ... until 1944, then the invasion came on.

At the time of the D-Day invasion, Frank Legatto was a lantz corporal in "C" Company, North Nova Scotia Highlanders, Ninth Brigade, Third Division. The Ninth Brigade was a reserve force that remained in the English Channel, while the other units of the Third Division landed at Juno Beach, Normandy, on June 6, 1944.

The Ninth Brigade consisted of three battalions: the North Nova Scotia Highlanders, the Highland Light Infantry, and the Stormont Glengarry Dundas Highlanders. We were lucky ... the Ninth Brigade

Frank Legatto, in Glasgow, Scotland, Feb. 10, 1945. Courtesy of Frank Legatto.

was really blessed, because our part was to stay in the channel for that morning.... We could see the French coast: fires burning, smoke.... So we waited there for an hour ... two hours ... then time for us to go in. It's a sandy beach. The boat rammed right into the sand. We got out and into the water. Our planes flew overhead. [We were] up to our waist in water but it was alright because it was June. And yet, you know, that's the part I find a blessing. I never even heard a shot fired, and there was like a stillness. I never heard a bombing plane. Not a thing. And we never lost a man going on the beach. Along the beach, I saw a few civilians walking around. Get this now—civilians walking around, and I said, "Lord gee, this war isn't too bad...." I never heard a shot fired. But all the other outfits had it really bad.

So the tanks came along, and we ... were taken up [to] the front.... That's where we heard the first part of the war. I guess that was about three miles up from the beach now. Then German planes came that night, going at our boats, and our boats [fired back] with tracer bullets—yellow, red, blue. The whole sky looked like Halloween night....

Then, coming on the next two-and-a-half [miles] to the front, my God they were taking a beating.... A lot of people were killed, taken prisoners of war.... Now you've heard of our fellas getting executed. The Twelfth Panzer Division ... this SS division ... [executed] twenty of our guys from "C" Company. Germans were taken prisoner of war too, but they were scared then because they heard of what their fellow soldiers done, you know.

"C" Company had around 126 people altogether—the major, the captain, three officers, three sergeants, nine corporals, and my name on there too, and the privates.... Thirty-some men were taken prisoner of war. The captain was killed. Two officers were taken prisoner or killed, along with the sergeants, corporals and the other lantz corporals. I was the only lantz corporal left. Before the next push, Sergeant MacKillop said, "Look Frank, there is only one officer and a sergeant; you're the lantz corporal. Now there is ammunition to be buried up in front line right there. Take eight men and go bury that tonight as soon as it gets dark." The company clerk doing that kind of work! That was meant for a sergeant-major or somebody, but there were none left.

Sergeant MacKillop was also killed during the next push forward. His death subsequently left "C" Company with just one officer and lantz corporal Legatto, until reinforcements arrived two weeks later. Within a month, the Third Division advanced along the coast towards Belgium. The German forces were in retreat after taking heavy troop losses. From Belgium, the Canadian and Allied troops continued their advance toward Holland and Germany.

Although the war ended in May, 1945, Frank Legatto and his unit remained in Europe for several months. Then, in December, they left Liverpool aboard the passenger ship Duchess of Bedford for Newfoundland. After a rough sea voyage, the ship entered St. John's Harbour just after Christmas. From there, they proceeded to Halifax and then by train to Sydney Mines.

When we landed in the Sydney Mines station, a big crowd was there. It was a welcome home party (and that was the night before New Year's, 1946). My wife was there with our son. I was married before I went over. He was about one year old [when I left] and four or five years old when I returned. We got in the car, got home, to my mother's place. My mother had chicken noodle soup.... Within the month I went back to Halifax and got my discharge—February 14th, Valentine's Day, 1946. And, ah, then came home and that was it.

In recognition of his service in the war effort, Frank Legatto received: the Entry Service Medal (1939-1945 Star), the Voluntary Service Medal (1939-1945), the France and Germany Star, the Gold Juno Sword Overlord Medal, the Defence Medal and the L. Montgomery Award.

After the war, Frank resumed his life in Sydney Mines where he operated the Veteran's Barber Shop, and later a confectionery store for thirty years. He officially retired at age sixty-five but returned to the workforce a short time later to work for the George Francis Funeral Home. In 1998, at over seventy-five, he spends his time with his grandchildren and helping his wife. Towards the end of the interview, he shared these thoughts with us:

> That time ... in France, we didn't know if we were going to live through the day or not.... But I went all through it, from D-Day, France, right through the war, and stayed six months after it ended. Boy, if I wasn't blessed ... it was pretty fantastic. Yeah, so my life was interesting. I'm an altar server at present, for funeral masses only. My gosh, I'm the oldest altar server on Cape Breton Island. Christ made some kind of remark ... that 'I will give you life and I will give it to you more abundantly.' I feel I'm living on the abundantly part now. I lived a good life.

John Giovannetti[22]
In May of 1996, the Giovannetti family travelled to Europe to visit their ancestral home in Italy; and, some of the places John Giovannetti had travelled through, as a member of the Canadian forces, during the Second World War. John Giovannetti provides this account.

I've been trying to find the place in Holland where I lost my arm. I have been over now three times, I guess. I still can't find the place. [Sam Migliore: You aren't sure of the name of the place?] No, no. No names! I don't have any idea where I went after Falaise, France. I was in that Falaise battle where they captured all the Germans. In fact, a sniper was firing at the boys from the church, and I put a shot in the belfry and set it afire. I went back this time and had a look. The church is still there with the bullet holes in the cement around the side of the building.

I enlisted in 1943, and I spent a couple of years in Fredericton, No. 6 depot in Halifax, and advanced training in Camp Borden, Ontario. From there, we went to England, overseas, but I wasn't there very long. I was there from D-Day until October the 4th, when I got hit and lost my arm. I landed with the Fort Gary Horse Armoured Regiment, and then was transferred to the Sherbrooke Fusiliers, 27th Armoured Regiment. We were there to support the infantry.

We left Southampton sometime in the night, and arrived at Juno Beach shortly after daybreak. The steamer went in toward the beach until she went aground, and then we drove our tank off the bow into the water. That's how we went ashore. [pause] I would imagine that the people who were going in on them little dinghies had it a hell of a lot harder than we did. They were the first to go in there. From the tank, you can't see anything. The group commander has his head out the top, and you are talking to him through the radio. That's how you get your orders, because there is too much noise in that thing. The big motor screeching, dragging in a pile of air and dirt, it wasn't a nice place to be.

[Sam Migliore: Was your tank hit?] Yeah, the tank was hit the last skirmish we had over there. I can remember going across the bridge, and down into a field. We stuck our nose out around this big hedge, and they were waiting for us. Now, the crew commander and the fellow looking after the ammunition went zip, out just like a shot. I sat there and waited until the machine gun bullets stopped hitting her. I figured that they would think everybody was gone, and that's when I made my move. Over the side like an eel. The crew commander and the other fellow were lying on the ground. Their faces looked white like the colour of that paper. I stayed there for a little while, but they blasted shells into the tank. One landed along the side of me. That's when it happened to my arm—three compound fractures. I got up and ran across the field, which was another mistake, because I got hit then. I had three pieces of steel in my back. They took two out, but another piece was left inside. Twenty-five years after, it started to get sore, and they had to cut it out of there. I also had a dozen scalp wounds; you can still feel the ridges in the bone. That leg there, I had a piece of steel go through the knee. I can hardly walk on that now.

I don't know how, but I got through a three-strand barbed wire fence. I remember just going through on the fly, and landing in a ditch full of water. And that's where I stayed from about eleven in the morning until probably four or five o'clock that afternoon. There was an English infantry fellow just a short distance from me, but he wouldn't come over to pull me out of the water, keep me from drowning. He said, "shh, they'll hear you." [laughs] Then I said, "if I had my six shooter ... you would be history." [laughs] To think, I went all the way over there to help those people, and he wouldn't crawl out from behind that bush to give me a hand. If it hadn't been for the driver.... I didn't know, but he had got out of the tank. He came hollering, got me by the scruff of the neck, and hauled me up to where the Red Cross fellows could help me. His name was Coombs, an English fellow from Montreal. I lost contact with him; I don't know if he is alive today or not. All this happened to me just a few days after my birthday.

Now, the sailor's prayer book you were looking at, I had that in my shirt pocket. It was just saturated with blood. I have had it all these years. Well, I ended up at the 22nd Canadian Hospital. I think it was somewhere in Belgium. That's where they cut the arm off. In 1945, March, I got back to Canada. I got a job and worked for thirty years.

I was back to Holland three times. I was there for the big 50th anniversary, but I didn't get into the parade. A little misunderstanding, I couldn't find my medals. But I was there on the side of the road. A family there took us in for our stay, and then we went down to Italy. They will be coming here soon. Hopefully, the Lord will keep me feeling as good so I can take them around Cape Breton, do the best I can for them.

Paradox Unresolved: A Concluding Remark

During the war years, Italian Canadians were treated as both "enemy aliens" and "friends of the nation." Certain individuals were arrested and interned, while others were allowed to represent Canada in the armed struggle overseas. Had those interned been charged with some crime, had there been any evidence of wrong doing or disloyalty, the actions of the Canadian authorities would be more understandable and acceptable. This, however, was not the case. None of the individuals interned were ever charged with any type of crime or offence against the nation. Innocent men and women were confined and isolated from their families simply because they were "Italian" at a time when Italy and Canada were at war.

The National Congress of Italian Canadians (NCIC) attempted to correct this paradox by asking the Federal Government to publicly acknowledge and apologize for the treatment members of Canada's Italian population received in the 1940s. In response to this appeal, then Prime Minister Brian Mulroney cited the "brutal injustice" inflicted on Italian Canadian internees and made a formal apology to them. Unfortunately, the apology was made as part of a luncheon speech to the NCIC and the Canadian Italian Business Professional Association on November 4, 1990, in Toronto. It was never made in the House of Commons. As a result, it did not constitute an official apology (with implications for compensation) from the Federal Government. The paradox, and the "brutal injustice" Mulroney mentioned in his speech was not resolved.

The redress issue, however, would not disappear. Finally, on November 12, 2005, Prime Minister Paul Martin signed an Agreement-in-Principle with various Italian Canadian associations (including the NCIC). The premise behind the agreement was that in lieu of compensation and an apology, the Federal Government would set aside an initial $2.5 million for educational purposes to acknowledge and commemorate the wartime experience of Italians in Canada.[24] There was some indication that the final figure could

---

Excerpts from "Notes for an Address" by Prime Minister Brian Mulroney to the National Congress of Italian Canadians and the Canadian Italian Business Professional Association

Toronto, November, 4, 1990[23]

In the 1940s, more that 100,000 people of Italian origin called Canada home. These people ... were proud Canadians whose contributions to our country were enormous. Nevertheless ... when Canada went to war with Italy, many ... were declared to be enemy aliens and were subjected to house searches, surveillance by the police, mandatory registration, employment discrimination and the denial of social services. About 700 were interned in camps....

What happened to many Italian Canadians is deeply offensive to the simple notion of respect for human dignity and the presumption of innocence. The brutal injustice was inflicted arbitrarily, not only on individuals suspected of being security risks but also on individuals whose only crime was to being of Italian origin. In fact, many of the arrests were based on membership in Italian Canadian organizations—much like the ones represented here today. None of the 700 internees was ever charged with an offence and no judicial proceedings were launched. It was often, in the simplest terms, an act of prejudice—organized and carried out under law, but prejudice nevertheless....

Forty-five years of silence about these wrongs is a shameful part of our history.... On behalf of the government and the people of Canada, I offer a full and unqualified apology for the wrongs done to our fellow Canadians of Italian origin during World War II.

I am pleased to announce today that, during this session of Parliament, I will rise in the House of Commons and extend a formal apology to all Members of the Italian Community for this unspeakable act, and to other Canadians who have suffered similar grievances....

reach as much as $12 million by the end of the program. The announcement was made in an Italian neighborhood of Montreal a couple of months before the Federal election of January 23, 2006. The new Conservative Government raised the total for the agreement to $5 million, but insisted that the $12 million the Liberals had proposed was merely a campaign promise.[25]

In 2009, Massimo Pacetti (the Liberal MP for St-Leonard/St-Michel) introduced Bill C-302 to Parliament, a private member's bill, with the aim of addressing the injustices that occurred during the Second World War. A year later, the Government of Canada passed the bill as the Italian-Canadian Recognition and Restitution Act. All parties, except the Conservatives, supported the Bill. The Act clearly stated:

> The Parliament of Canada hereby acknowledges the unjust treatment received by persons of Italian origins as a result of their designation as "enemy aliens", their registration and internment and other infringements of their rights during the Second World War, and apologizes on behalf of Parliament, the Government of Canada and the Canadian people of earlier times and of today for the suffering that this treatment caused.[26]

In terms of restitution, Bill C-302 indicated that funding would be channelled toward the "production of educational materials that will provide information on Italian-Canadian history and promote ethnic and racial harmony, and the distribution of those materials...."

Unfortunately, the Bill did not become law. The passing of C-302 was delayed in the Conservative-dominated Senate, and quietly disappeared after the Conservative victory in the Federal election of May 2011. The Harper Government, however, has provided some funding for educational purposes to address the issues surrounding the internment of Italians. No arrangements have been put in place to provide for any direct compensation for the internees and their families.

To my knowledge there are no longer any living Italian Canadians who experienced internment first-hand. Former Prime Minister Brian Mulroney's apology was an important first step toward exonerating the internees (and their families), and moving toward correction of the institutional discrimination they endured. Although subsequent governments have made some significant steps to correct the problem, no further action has been taken toward a formal apology. This type of apology would go a long way in helping to restore the dignity and pride of the many Italians who, directly or indirectly, faced various forms of injustice during the Second World War.

Family Disruption, Hard Work, and Success: A Talk with Frank and Marty Martinello

Edited by Sam Migliore

In December 1996, I met with Frank (Francis X.) and E. M. "Marty" Martinello in Hamilton, Ontario. Our conversation focused on their early years in Cape Breton; the pain and disruption the family experienced when their father, Felice Martinello, was interned in 1940; and, how the family was able to cope with these problems, and eventually achieve a measure of success. I have organized what appears below to fit into these broad themes.

The Early Years: Growing up in the Pier

Felice Martinello and Rosina DiPasquale were born in small communities outside of Avellino, near Naples. In the 1920s, a few years after they had married, Felice came to Canada in search of work. He and Rosina, along with their young daughter, Florence, were reunited in Nova Scotia several years later.

[Frank]: Our father worked in the steel plant in Sydney. He came to Canada in 1924 or 1925. A rail fell on his back, and he had to spend some time in the hospital. To help him recuperate, one of our uncles, Frank or Alex (we called them Uncle, but they were actually my father's cousins) sent him to Monastery, just outside of Antigonish, to work as a caretaker. He looked after the property after the monks returned to Germany. While there, he saved enough money to call my mother over.

My mother came to Canada with my sister Florence (Filomena). They travelled from Italy to Ellis Island. On board ship, Florence was infected with lice. When they arrived at Ellis Island and the lice were discovered, they were not allowed to leave. I think they were there for about a month—partly because of the lice, and partly because my mother was not able to read or write in English. They were supposed to travel from Ellis Island to Halifax, and then to Sydney to join my father. The authorities would not allow her to leave until they found someone who was going to the same area. Eventually, they put her on a train, and she got to Sydney. From Sydney, my father brought her to Monastery. Low and behold, about a year-and-a-half later, I was born. [laughs]

When I was about to be born, they didn't have facilities in the Monastery area. My parents had to go to Sydney by horse and wagon. [laughs] I can remember my mother recounting the story of how they were going along, the horse galloping when they came to a railway track. A train went flying by, my father hauled in the horses, and my mother (with me) went flying onto the back of the horse. I was born in St. Rita's Hospital in Sydney, and two weeks later we returned to the monastery. In the winter, my mother would chop a hole in the ice to get water. I was born in 1928, and Ralph was born in August of 1929. That was the year we moved back to Sydney [to Whitney Pier]. [Marty]: Yeah, and we were seven kids in Nova Scotia. Originally, there were nine, but two passed away—one in Italy and one in Sydney.

[Frank]: We lived in one of our father's cousin's houses on Williams Street. There was a clothesline from the outside pole to the veranda. The veranda was closed in, and there was just enough room for hanging the clothes and sending out the line. In the winter, when the sparrows landed on the clothes line, my father would pull the line in very quietly, and swat the sparrows into the house. They would fly all over the house. We had sparrow soup! [laughs] From there we moved to Tupper Street, and we went to Villa Nova School. We used to meet the kids just around the corner, at Norman Della Vella's store, and walk to school. Then, when we went to Holy Redeemer School, there would be maybe fifteen or twenty in a group, and they would take off, the big guys walking fast and the little guys running behind them.

There on Tupper Street, we had a cow. My father used to take it up to the fields. The cow was so calm that my father would sit me on its back as we walked home. We also used to kill our own pigs to make sausages. And, Pa went on a trip to Italy. But, I don't remember too much more until we moved to Henry Street. [Marty]: When we moved to Henry Street, I was a little bit older; we were going to Holy Redeemer School. All the friends we had—from Mount Pleasant, Lingan Road, Tupper Street, Williams Street—we were all together.... And the interesting part of going to school was always that we went to school as a group.

[Frank]: I was one of the senior altar boys at St. Nicholas Parish. I used to get up early to ring the church bells at seven o'clock, serve Mass and then go home for breakfast. I did this every third week. For funeral Masses, we used to have to climb right up to the top of the steeple to watch for the people. When they left the house, we would ring the bell once a minute. Ding, ding, as the procession came up to the church. Ding, ding, until they came into the church. A lot of times I would get heck for ringing the bell too long. Sometimes I would miss school to help serve the Mass in Glace Bay, Dominion, Reserve; I guess they didn't have an Italian priest there.

I remember another experience from Nova Scotia. There used to be a lot of vacant land not far from Ashby Corners. The houses in the area emptied into a cesspool. My father [and other Italians] had a garden there, and we used the stuff from the cesspool for fertilizer. My brother Ralph and I were there one day when the edge of the bank gave way and Ralph slipped into it. [laughs] In the process of trying to get him out, I was into it too. We got out, but my father, who was out in the field, saw us walking, you know, all full. He said, "*vatin ni la casa*" (go home). [laughs] We went home, but we wouldn't walk on the street. We walked through parts of the Steel Company, what we called the tar pits. We used a bridge going over the "black tar water," and we took the side roads the rest of the way home. When we got in the house, boy did we get a licking from my mother. [laughs]

Great things. Yeah. We used to have a great big tree in our backyard. Tarzan, you know, we used to swing by a rope. My sister Florence loved to make Jello in the winter time. And, I used to love drinking the liquid before it jelled. No refrigerator. She would put it in the snow under the tree. But I would go along the path, jump on the fence, walk along the railing, get up into the tree and shimmy down the rope, so I wouldn't make any footprints in the snow. I would hang there and drink the juice. One time, though, I got tangled up in the rope; I couldn't get up, and I started swinging and hollering. Florence came and said, "so that's why my Jello always seems to be diminished." [laughs] She was great. Florence was the oldest and, with so many kids in the family, she was like our mother. We went, actually, to her for advice because my mother was busy with the younger kids. Even here in Hamilton, I would go to her to ask about different things. Yeah. My older sister. Too bad! She died when she was only fifty-two.[1]

The War Years: The Pain of Dislocation

[Marty]: Things were all good. But then, when the *War Measures Act* came in, and our father was taken, along with many other Italians, to the Internment Camp, things became a little different. At that time, the government didn't allow any welfare or any food to be given to [the families of internees]. I think that's the way it was until the last year, when they offered so much potatoes or something. [Frank]: No, I don't remember them offering anything. The potatoes were given to us by Antonio and Carolina Matergio. They were my sisters' (Annie and Margaret) and brother's (Felice, Jr.) Godparents. The only way the government would give us anything was if we sold the house, used up the money, and then, when we became destitute, they would give us relief. My mother, being a fighter, said "no way!" We used to deliver newspapers, Marty delivered the *Liberty Magazines*, and from the newspapers we graduated to shining shoes—at Joe Renzi's Shoe Repair on Charlotte Street, and at MacMullin's Tobacco Store.

I remember that school used to finish at three o'clock. I would rush home from Holy Redeemer, read my books, and then go from Henry Street all the way up-town. Shine shoes until seven o'clock. That was during the week. On Friday nights I worked 'til nine, and Saturday, all day from nine o'clock in the morning, or from eight 'til eleven at night. I did that all the time, and Marty did the same thing. [Marty]: And my brother Ralph helped too.

[Frank]: When the American boats came in, I would shine the sailors' shoes. I used to make those tips, and my mother used to love me. I can remember making $35 in tips one time. I started at eight o'clock in the morning, and went steady; I didn't stop to eat because there were two ships. The sailors had money; they would come in, you know, ten cents a shine, and flip you a quarter. My pockets were bulging. [laughs]

Besides that, we had the garden. We used to dig it by hand and plant every square inch. Before my father went to the camp, he had built a wheel barrel—a steel wheel with a great big box on it. It must have been at least three-foot square, with about 14-inch sides. He had it rigged up with a harness. The one in the front would help pull the "steel wheel," and the other would pick things up. And we would alternate. We used to collect cow flops from the fields behind our house, and then dump them in the garden. That was our manure, [laughs] it would enrich the garden. We would dig the garden, and my mother would plant it and look after it. The day they picked up my father for the camp, he was putting in an irrigation system, with pipes, so he could use a hose to send water throughout the garden.

When we left Nova Scotia back in 1943, Mrs. Del Vecchio gave my mother some eggs in a brown paper bag. She turned them over to my sister Margaret (Margurite), who hung on to them from Sydney all the way to Montreal. We landed in one train station, and we had to walk to another to catch the train to Toronto. There was Marty, myself, two sisters, and mother carrying Junior, the youngest. We lugged the suitcases, and Margaret continued to hold the eggs. When we got to the other station, we had to wait at the gate before boarding. The gate area was crowded, and there was a little pushing and shoving. Low and behold, the brown paper bag broke. The eggs broke. The lady in front of Margaret had a fur coat, and the eggs were running down the fur. My mother, being sharp, whisked us all over to an-other gate. [laughs]

When we got to Hamilton there was a bit of confusion: we didn't know where to go; and, we weren't sure who was going to meet us? My father [however] was up top with Mr. Romanelli. Mr. Romanelli had a great big limousine, and he had come to the train station with my father to pick us up. After some persuasion, the station staff let my father come down to the train area. And that's the first we had seen of him since they picked him up in 1940. From June 10, 1940, to June 1943, so we hadn't seen him in over three years.

[Marty]: I think we have to say that prior to my father going to the camp, we were a good family. We were well involved with the community, and we had a lot of friends. There was a lot of community activity, and it was a very happy situation. It didn't have to be Christmas; it was always a festive occasion. A lot of things changed when the war broke out. It created a lot of mistrust between people. Even at school, kids would say: "you got guns in your cellar," and "you guys are this and that." It was quite a concern. But what you got from that is that the group you belonged to became closer and closer. The problem though was that now you had to survive. And, survival meant you had to work. We had to sell newspapers, shine shoes; no matter what it was, we had to do it. Whether it was legal or illegal was besides the point. The point was that you had to survive. The government gave you nothing. You had to live; you had to live on your wits no matter what it was. Still, we all succeeded. We went to school. We never lost school.

We were no different than any of the other kids. We played sports, skating, hockey.... It was the changes forced on us when Dad and the others were Interned that required us to move out—to leave our friends, our surroundings, everything—and to go to a place [Hamilton, Ontario] that was completely foreign to all of us. But, coming to Ontario gave us a whole new life. And, we are happy to say, we feel that we've done well, and our children and grandchildren have done well.

The More Recent Years: Success in Hamilton

[Marty]: In Hamilton, my father worked in a meat-packing house. To support the family, he worked from six o'clock in the morning 'til seven o'clock at night, every day. And, he worked overtime on Saturdays and Sundays. Always! We were fortunate; between his hard work, and the money from the house we sold in Nova Scotia, we were able to buy a house in Hamilton. His idea was to always try to improve. We were the first working class people, the first Italians, to live in that neighbourhood. If you check the deeds from that period, you'll see that they read: "no Jews, no Italians, and no Coloureds." [Frank]: Yeah, it was kind of a prestige neighbourhood in those days. I think the whole neighbourhood was in shock when we moved in.

[Marty]: The house, at that time, was $5,500. But that was my father. He just wanted to improve. And that's something he taught us all the way through life—get ahead, get ahead, get ahead. Work hard! And, that's why I think our families are in the position they are in today. [Frank]: We came up here, kept working hard, educated ourselves, and branched off into different fields. Marty played football; he's in the Nova Scotia Sports Hall of Fame. He's done well in sports, and I got into manufacturing. My sister, Margaret, became an RN (Registered Nurse), and she is married to Judge Joseph C. L. Scime of the General Division Court of Ontario here in Hamilton. They have five children (Lillian, Deborah, Margaret Rose, Joseph Jr., and Charlene) and fifteen grandchildren. My sister Annie went to work at Westinghouse and married an electrical technician (David Dolson) who worked at Stelco [one of the steel plants in Hamilton]. They have two children (Arthur and Kathleen) and four grandchildren. My brother Ralph worked at various places and ended up at Dofasco [another steel plant in Hamilton]. He is retired and enjoying himself right now. [Marty]: And we have a younger brother, Felice Jr., who worked as a teacher for the last twenty-five years or more. [Frank]: He was born on January 28, 1939—my father's birthday. [Marty]: He's a bachelor, and as happy as hell. [laughs]

[Frank]: Myself, I have four kids. The oldest, a girl, became an RN, and she's now married. Her husband is in steel sales. They live in the States, but it is only a couple of hours from here. [Marty]: Frank also has a son, Felice, that's a university professor. [Frank]: And my son, Luigi, is a master electrician. My youngest son, Vincent, who just got married about three months ago, is a systems support manager for a company in Guelph, Ontario.

[Marty]: My brother Ralph has two children. One, Rosanne, is an RN, and his son, Ralph Jr., has a very good job at the steel plant. They are both married, and they have children. The reason I didn't want to talk too much about my youth is because I had a misspent youth. I had to do something about that. So, I did something that I thought I could do, and that was play football. I played [professional] football for fourteen years [in the Canadian Football League].[2] I went to night school extension classes for eleven years, and the last degree I got was an MBA (Master of Business Administration) certificate from McMaster University. Now, I am semi-retired, Vice-President, General Manager of a metals recycling company. My son, Michael, went to a technical college, and he is a general manager of an automotive parts manufacturing company. My daughter, Lynn, became an RN; she is married and has a family. And, I have a son who is doing very well working for a casting company. [Frank]: Our sister Florence was the oldest. She passed away in 1975. She was married and had two kids.

A Further Reflection on the War Years

Later in the interview, I returned the conversation to the War Years, by asking Frank and Marty if they recalled any stories their father may have told about life in the "internment camp."

[Frank]: Stories of the camp, no. [Marty]: He wouldn't tell any. [Frank]: In the First World War, my father was in the Italian army. A *Bersaglieri* (an elite military corps in Italy). He was wounded three times while fighting on the same side as the British Forces. He carried a piece of shrapnel in his foot for the rest of his life.

Internment camp photo (From left: Mario Furini, Bert Gatto, unknown, Felice Martinello, Michele Rannie). Courtesy of Francis X. Martinello.

Actually, my father found out, just a few years before he died, that he could have collected an Italian army pension for being wounded in action. He applied, it was approved, and the first cheque came the day he was buried. But my mother benefitted, she received the pension.

Anyway, when my father came to Hamilton, he used to play cards with a group of First veterans. Sometimes they would talk and, if I happened to come in the room, I might hear some stories about the war or about the internment camp. It would be little anecdotes. When my father was first in the camp, he was with his cousins Michele and Frank. There was a group of them. I remember one story about how they were given food, and they had to fend for themselves. My father always liked to cook, so he started cooking for himself, my Uncle Frank (who was sick at the time), a few of the others from Sydney and, eventually, other people. He organized the hut they were in. He did the cooking, while the others: washed dishes, peeled potatoes, all the way down. But, that's about the only story; not too much more.

I also know that they made a lot of things in the camp. Mike LaPenna was the scribe; his job was to write the letters for many of the other men. There were people who did sketches; I have a pencil sketch of my father and a watercolour of myself.

They also used to do a lot of carving from wood. When my father came home, he had a whole suitcase full of different toys that they had made for the kids. One man would build steamers and sailboats. We used to have them as kids, but they dried up. We never realized their value. But, I do have a gin bottle with a boat inside; the boat is flying a little Italian flag. [laughs] I also have a belt. It's made from cigarette package covers—all different colours. Yeah, it's really unique. Those are the only two things I have left. When I pass on, they're going to my son Felice who was named after my father.

[Marty]: Oh, they made a lot of things out of wood. Cooking utensils. And, when my father came out of the camp, he came out with wooden suitcases that they had made themselves. People often ask, "what happened at the camp?" Well, nobody really knows, because they referred to it as "college." Okay, and they would not talk about it in front of strangers. That's the way it was. [Frank]: A lot of times we'd be talking and say, "he went to school with my father," or "they went to college together," or "university;" they were in the camp together. [Marty]: But you know, when the *War Measures Act* came in, the moment Italy went to war, the Mounted Police were at our place. It didn't take long. [Frank]: Yeah, I can remember it just as if it was yesterday. There was a Mounted Policeman, and the City Detective. [Marty]: Yeah. They were there at the house, and we didn't know what was happening. The kids went out and hid in the fields. They went through the house like you can't believe. Breaking walls, and looking for literature, guns, whatever. Then they took him away, and we were signalled to come back to the house. No one knew what was going on. They searched every house. Twenty-four hours later, we were notified to send his clothes. One month later, we got a letter stating: "prisoner of war." [Frank]: All the mail we received was censored too; there were marks all through it. We didn't know what was going on.

[Marty]: You can understand the type of situation that we were living in, with Italy going into the war. The War itself. *The War Measures Act*. Italian people taken away, and the kids, wives, mothers left behind. What they faced. And then, all the assets confiscated or, I think, it was just held. [*Frank*]: No, there was a lot confiscated. There was that fella from Toronto, the shipbuilder; they confiscated all his equipment, and eventually sold it. I don't think he got a dime for it. But, from us, all they did was seize our father's double barrel shotgun, a revolver, and a picture of Mussolini. The shotgun and the picture of Mussolini, they gave back [after the war]. The revolver they kept; I guess they considered it a concealed weapon. My mother kept the picture of Mussolini right up 'til about a year before she died. Then she tore it up.

[Marty]: I look at it this way, prior to my Dad going into the camp, life was really good. We didn't know too much about the outside, Ontario, or anything else, but, it was "community." Then when my Dad was gone, life was tough. We came to Ontario, and life was tough here at the start. But then again, learning from my father, we got ahead and life was very good. I'm not saying that we are rich or anything; what I'm saying is that my father would be proud of us.

[Frank]: The thing is, too, that when my father was picked up, the Italians were afraid of us, because they might get implicated. And the non-Italians didn't want to bother with us. They would call us "spies" or "saboteurs." We were kind of between the devil and the deep blue sea for a while. And then, I guess, time heals all wounds. Some of them came back to us. Once we got up here [to Hamilton], we worked hard, we went to school, and we educated ourselves. Thanks to our parents pushing us, we succeeded. I worked my way up to plant superintendent and eventually established a partnership with another person to set up a business. Now, I'm leisure living. I don't want to call it "retired." [laughs]

Filling-in the Gaps

After Marty had left for a meeting, I asked Frank to elaborate on several topics we had touched on earlier. One of the things I asked him to do was to talk further about his father's experiences both before and after "internment."

I think my father was taken because he was the secretary of the fascist club in Nova Scotia. I had a black shirt, and I went to an Italian school. Well, it was natural, today you have the Sons of Italy, but back then they had this "homeland" club. You had Scottish clubs, Irish clubs, English clubs, the British Imperials.... It was the same thing. When Mussolini went to war, he became the enemy. If Italy had gone in with the British, we would have been hailed as heroes. It would have been the same as when Italy fought on the side of the British in the First World War.

[Dominic Nardocchio, on CBC Radio and in newspaper articles, has talked about how the Italian men were attacked by "drunks" in the Sydney jail. I asked Frank if he had heard anything about that.] The stories I heard were that the "drunks" were put in the same area [as the Italian men]. The cell gate was left open. My father and somebody else was fighting, trying to keep the "drunks" out. I don't know if they were drunks or agitators. But, somebody saw my father the next day, and he had two good shiners.

In the internment camp, the men had to wear clothes with a "bull's eye" on the back. Marty found out about that one day when he met someone who had been a guard at Petawawa. The man knew my father. He remembered my father cooking for him sometimes. He told Marty that he couldn't figure out why the heck those men were in the camp. And he said it was too bad that they had to wear that "bull's eye" on the back of their uniform. I found out that it wasn't an actual bull's eye but a great big red circle.

My father was interned in [Petawawa], but I think he finished his time in Saint John, New Brunswick. They allowed one member of the family to visit him. The priest at our church got a few people together who had family in the camp, and my sister (Florence) visited him. I think she saw him for about one hour one day, and then another hour the next day. That was the only contact. People use the word "internment," or they call them "prisoner camps." It's incarceration!

[You mentioned earlier that your father after he was released, didn't have much of a choice about where he could live.] As I know the story, when he was to be released, it was either here in Ontario or British Columbia. He had made so many friends from Ontario in the camp, that he decided to come here. And, he kept in close contact with the ones in Hamilton and St. Catharine's. There were also a couple of women from Niagara Falls and Thorold, who had been interned. Not many women were interned, but there were a few. There were a couple of doctors interned from the Ottawa area and quite a few people from Montreal. They used to come to visit us. There was Zaffiro, Lanza, and many others from the Hamilton area. My father picked Hamilton because he had friends here and because there was a steel plant where he could work at his old job—hoist engineer at the Blast Furnace.

[So, your father was released in 1943?] Yeah, 1943, I'm not sure which month, but I know that he was one of the last ones to be released. Every six months or so, some of [the internees] were interviewed. Depending on their attitude and what they said, they might be released. I guess they didn't like my father's answers. I also heard stories of young fellas who were released and then called up for the army, the Canadian Army.

[Can you say a little more about what your father did after he was released?] Marty mentioned earlier that my father worked in a meat-packing plant. When he was released from the camp, there was talk about unions and dissension at the steel company, talk about foreigners and Italians coming in. They were trying to unionize. So, the Mounties advised my father not to go there. They had promised him a job in the steel company [in Hamilton]—the same type of job he had been doing in Nova Scotia. But, to bring somebody from the concentration camp into the plant was like throwing a bomb in there. So they got him a job at the meat packing plant. Then, after about three months, the Mounties contacted him to say that, if he wanted it, he could have the job at the steel company. I think, at that time, he was making more money at the meat packing plant, and he had made a lot of friends there, so he stayed.

He worked there until he was sixty-five. But there was no pension; you were just out. And that was a real shock. He thought he could work past sixty-five, and it broke his heart. He lasted two years. Actually, his birthday was on January 28, and he died on the thirtieth. He was sixty-seven. I remember when I was turning sixty-seven, I said gee I hope I keep going. [laughs] So, now I am sixty-eight, and I'm still going. I passed the crunch. My mother lived to be ninety, so there is still hope for me.[3]

[What did your father do in the plant?] He was a butcher. And then, for extra money, he would stay back two or three hours every evening to clean up. I worked there one summer, too.... And I shined shoes.... Back then, there were so many of us [in the family]. Although my father was making money, with seven kids you had to go to work. We had the house to pay for. When I finished grade 10, I told my father I was going to go to work full-time. He started to cry. But, he didn't stop me. The next Christmas, he bought me a watch in appreciation for my going to work. I ended up with a job, actually, where I was making more money than my father. I had taken a welding course, and I ended up with a job as an acetylene electric welder. In two years I was a young foreman. And, as I mentioned before, I eventually started my own business, and now I'm "leisure living." I always said I would never "retire." I looked up the word in the dictionary—"to withdraw from society;" to be, more or less, isolated. I said: "No, that's not me." So, I'm leisure living. I have a 1970 Dodge Challenger, Special Edition that my son fixed up, and I take to Auto Shows. I have six trophies and about four plaques. I enjoy it very much. My wife goes with me.

[You mentioned that your family has annual "get togethers."] We used to have those in Nova Scotia before the war. We would get together with Uncle Frank and Uncle Mike, my father's cousins, at Point Edward. I guess that's where it started. My father was a great swimmer, and I would hold his neck and hang on. He would swim way out, and then come back to let me off. That's the way I learned to swim. He would go out and float with a drink of rum on his chest, every so often taking a sip. In salt water it was easy to float. We also used to dig our own clams, and steam them. Everybody brought food. But, when the war came, we didn't do it anymore.

After my father passed away, somebody got the bright idea that we should have a Martinello picnic. We would pick a spot and meet on a certain Sunday. We had prizes, and games for the kids to compete in. We take a couple of portable barbecues, and everybody brings their own food. But, the best part is having the grandchildren compete in the different games, and having the parents get involved with them. Everybody gets a prize. That's been going on for quite a while now. And, we haven't been rained out yet. [laughs]

[Have you been back to Nova Scotia?] I went back with Joe Renzi in 1947. I got there and wandered through the neighbourhood. The news that I used to live on Tupper Street spread like wildfire. I could hear people say: "that's Felix's son." I went back in 1947, 1948 and 1949. In 1949, I drove down with my father, Marty, my two sisters, and Junior. We went down in our brand new 1949 Mercury. Then, in 1967, we went down to *Man and his World*, and from there to Nova Scotia. The last time I was there was in the late 1970s or early 1980s. I flew down with Marty; he was on business, and I went along. Hopefully, before I pass on [laughs], I will go there again.

[At the end of the interview, I asked Frank if there was anything that he wanted to add.] Actually, is that [tape recorder] still going? [laughs] Back in 1959 or 1960, at Christmas time, three of us got together, three boys, and we filled up a gallon bottle with whiskey. We presented to my father. I have movies of Marty walking in and giving it to him. But, he said:

> I'm not gonna open it; if I die, I want you to open the bottle and drink.
> If my youngest son gets married, we are going to open it at the wedding.
> And, if your son, Felice, graduates from university, we'll open it. Which ever of the three things happens first, we'll do it.

My father died. So, my mother opened it, and we drank about half of it at the wake. My mother said, "your father had two more wishes," so she filled the bottle up again and sealed it. [For one reason or another though] it never did get opened. After my mother died, Junior gave the bottle to me. I put a label on it, and I told my son, Felice, that the bottle was his.

Yeah, we presented it to my father in 1959, and he died in 1964.

Section III

The More
Recent Years:
Personal and Family
Experiences

Secondina DiPersio:
A Son's Tribute to His Mother

Edited by Sam Migliore

Hector DiPersio is a prominent political and community figure in Cape Breton. He served as Mayor of Sydney Mines for two terms (beginning in 1985), and he has been involved successfully at various levels of political, business and community activity, both on and off the island, for many years. This article, however, is not about Hector's accomplishments in these areas of endeavour. Instead, the article concentrates on some of his thoughts and reflections on family life in Sydney Mines; and, in particular, his mother, Secondina DiPersio (1897-1989). For many Italians, la famiglia *(the family) plays a significant role in a person's life. Within this context, the mother/son relationship has special significance. It involves a powerful emotional bond that spans both time and space and often permeates various aspects of one's life. Although the details presented below may be specific to the DiPersio family, the notion that a son would pay special tribute to his mother is something most Italians can easily relate to.*

In the early days, when my parents came over from Italy, there were a large number of Italian families in Sydney Mines. The reason the Italians came here was to work in either the steel plant or the coal mines. Sydney Mines was the most prosperous place around here.

My father [Rosario DiPersio] was born in a small village called Brittoli. My mother was from Pratola Peligna, near Pescara. [Both communities are located in the Abruzzi region of Italy.] My father left Italy sometime around 1913. He came to Sydney Mines to work in the steel plant. My mother came to Cape Breton in 1916. She had very little money at that time, and she used to tell us how she was a little hungry during the boat trip. My mother didn't want to spend any of her valuable money on [laughs] food, eh [laughs], and she wouldn't accept anything from someone else. So she went a little hungry. When she got to Cape Breton, she lived with a relative in Whitney Pier. At that time, the Italians of the area associated with each other, and a large number of them dated and married Italian men or women. (This is what happened with my parents; they met and married here in Cape Breton.)

While my father worked at the Plant, my mother helped by doing things out of our home. She made her own sausage, pasta and tomato paste. She used to do all of her own sewing and knitting, and she would make bedspreads and pillows.... The only things that she used to buy were salt, tea and sugar. My mother was pretty well self-sufficient. Since she had an education, a lot of the Italian families would have her write letters to their families in Italy, and she would read the letters they received. She also acted as a banker; many of them would give her a dollar a week to save, so they could send the money back to Italy. She would keep a separate file on each person. My mother also took in boarders and washed their clothes for extra money.

When the steel plant closed in Sydney Mines, many Italian families moved to Ontario or the United States, and to other parts of Cape Breton. My father went to work in the coal mine in Florence, Cape Breton. He worked in "the deeps" as a brusher. He would help prepare new sections of the mine, so the other miners could start mining the coal. My father was buried under rock and coal a few times, but he kept going back to work. Finally, he was buried under a rock fall, and his back was broken. This was the last time my father entered a coal mine. He went on permanent Workman's Compensation at $75 a month, and later this increased to $111 a month. There was no company pension available for him at that time.

Since my father wasn't able to work anymore, my mother opened a grocery store next to our home. It was one of four grocery stores on Pond Street. Two of the stores were owned by Italians, and the other two by people of Scottish background. Later, one of these Scottish stores was closed, and the other sold to an Italian family. They call these stores "convenience stores" now, but at the time, there were no supermarkets in town, so these small stores handled all types of meats, groceries, and confectionary. My mother was meat cutter, cashier and operator of the business. The hours of business were from 7:00 am to 11:00 pm, seven days a week. The store had no employees other than family members. We would help out with the delivery of orders in a small homemade cart that I owned. Later, as we were growing up, we took our turns "minding" the store after school, and on weekends. There would never be two of us in the store at the same time. We had to learn the trade of cutting the meat, and [providing] service to people.

We had over a hundred families that purchased their groceries on a credit basis. The majority worked in the coal mines, and could only afford to pay when they received their money each week at the pay office. When the mines fell on harder times, or there were strikes, the miners had no money, and couldn't afford to pay their bill. My mother carried them over the hard times, giving them groceries without pay until the mines got back to work. The families really appreciated this gesture and, when they got back to work, the majority paid their bills in full.

During the time my mother operated the grocery store, she began to purchase some property for rental purposes. This was done on a very small scale, but over the years, it began to add up. My mother purchased some land and decided to build a trailer park. She took on the job as a contractor and began to subcontract some of the workout. My mother got the work done as she was able to afford, and she financed the whole project herself. This proved to be quite a feat for her because it was the first trailer park on the northside and the second one in the industrial area of Cape Breton. She also made arrangements to affiliate her store with other grocery stores in the Industrial area. They became the F.N.S. (Friendly Neighbourhood Stores) chain of privately owned stores. My mother was the only female owner that belonged to this chain, and she attended every monthly meeting. My mother lived by her own wit and hard work to support a family of eleven. Besides my mother and father, there were five boys and four girls in our family.

After fifty years of operating the store, my mother decided to take a trip to Florida to visit my brother who was living there at the time. Before leaving, my mother deeded the business to my sister, so she could continue to operate the store. While mom was away, my sister closed the store down permanently, and sold everything, saying that she would never be able to devote the same time commitment to the store as my mother had done. When mom returned from the trip, she, in good humour, said to my sister, "Joe Clark lasted longer in his job as Prime Minister than you did as store owner; at least he lasted six months." [laughs]

Italians in Sydney Mines and the Industrial Area

I was born in Sydney Mines, on February 24, 1936. So I was growing up at a time after the steel plant had closed in Sydney Mines, and there were fewer Italian families living in the Town. We used to visit quite often some of my parent's friends in Dominion, Sydney, Whitney Pier, and Glace Bay.

The Italian families were closely knit at that time. My mother had all of her children at home. The other Italian women would serve as midwives, and my mother, in turn, would do the same for other families. All of my father's friends were Italian. They would play Italian card games. One of these games was played for drinks. If your team won, you controlled the drinks for that game. You could give a drink to your opponent, keep him dry, or put a little amount in a bottle cap for the loser. Someone could be held dry for the whole evening. There was always close contact between my father and his Italian friends, and my mother and her Italian friends in Sydney Mines. My age group intermingled with various people in town. But, right up to the time my mother died, the few Italian families that were still in Sydney Mines used to make contact with her, and she with them. They always maintained that type of friendship.

What I Learned From My Parents

My early education was in Sydney Mines, and all of my teachers were Nuns—the Sisters of Notre Dame. Religion played a big part in my early life. Everything was pretty strict in school, and outside of school. I had a lot of chores to do at home. We had acres and acres of gardens, cows, pigs and chickens. Before I went to school, I would milk the cows and pick and wash the eggs. When I got home, I would work in the garden, do yard work and then take a turn in our grocery store. We didn't have very much money, so everyone had to do their share of work. What I learned as a youngster was to work hard, be wise, and know the value of money. The last point was the lesson my mother taught me. My father never placed that much importance on money; he would give it away if he thought someone needed it more than himself. He liked everyone, and everyone liked him. My mother wouldn't let him stay in the store too long; she was afraid he would give everything away. As long as he had a few dollars in his pocket, he was happy. So, I learned the value of hard work from both my parents and the value of money from my mother. She would always say, "if you ever want to help someone, you have to be strong yourself; that way, you will have the capability to help whether it is financial or otherwise."

My parents were excellent to all of us. Since I was the youngest, I was probably spoiled more than the rest. We received everything we wanted within reason and affordability. When I wanted to go to university, the money was there for me, because that's what they saved up for, to help their family. When I attended St. Francis Xavier University in Antigonish, my mother used to send me $2 each week in the mail. This would be my spending money, and, without fail, it was there every Monday morning. Even after I got married, anytime I needed help, it was there for me. One thing my parents did not believe in was borrowing for any reason. So, all of their lives, they never had anything on credit. It is hard to do that in today's environment, but I try to stick by those same values. All of my children are the same way. They have their own homes and don't owe any mortgages on them. I helped them out to give them a good start in life.

A Life in Politics

I started learning about politics when I was a young lad. My father was a grass-roots worker for the Liberal Party, and he worked in all of the elections, federal or provincial. He was a ward captain and his job was to organize workers in his ward and get out the vote. I was brought up in that atmosphere. I used to go to annual meetings of the Liberal Party with my father when I was fourteen. During that time, I got a taste of what politics was all about. A little spark was instilled in me then and, later in life, this would turn into a fire.

When I decided to run for Mayor, there were various undertones from certain sources that I had to contend with. First of all was my ancestry, then my religion and also the fact that I was a well-known Liberal. These factors were emphasized by some of the people working for my opponents. I ran against a former mayor and three incumbent councillors. I was a newcomer to municipal politics but knew the inner workings of running a campaign. It was a very bitter and hard fought campaign. One of the rumours that came out was that if I won the election, my mother would call the shots and run the town. I took this as a compliment for her. My mother, who was very much alive at that time, was proud that her son was running for mayor. She contacted all of her friends and reminded them to make sure they got out to vote. We put on a great campaign, and the people of Sydney Mines elected me as their Mayor. I was the first person of Italian ancestry ever to be elected in the town. My mother was really proud of the whole process. I ran for a second term and at that time my mother's health started to go downhill. Although she was bedridden during the campaign, she wanted the blow-by-blow details of the campaign and provided her advice. When I was re-elected, she was once again overjoyed.

I have always felt I was a part of the Italian community in Cape Breton. When I became Mayor, my wife, Rebecca ("Bunnie"), and I attended a big supper hosted by the Italian Association at Cape Breton University. They were very proud that someone from within their ranks had become Mayor. I managed to attend only a couple of their meetings, however, because I was involved in so many different things. If there was time, I would have really enjoyed it. I have always been proud of my heritage, and never tried to shun or hide it at any time. And the older I get, the prouder I get, and my children feel the same way.

After I retired from politics, Father Greg MacLeod introduced me to some of the projects he was working on. Among them, he was trying to create a local bank and provide jobs for the area. Because of my background in finance and social and economic development, he asked me to volunteer some of my time to set up this bank and assist in creating some economic activity in Cape Breton. I liked what he was trying to accomplish, so I agreed to work with him. During much of my life, I have volunteered in various organizations, and now, donating my time to BCA Holdings Ltd., and several other organizations, I consider myself a professional volunteer.

A 90th Birthday Celebration

My mother died when she was ninety-one. Shortly before that, on her ninetieth birthday, we had a big celebration for her. I wrote a little speech to acknowledge and toast our mother.

The speech was a tribute to her strength and all that she did for us over the years. Yeah, she was a self-motivated woman, a hard worker. She was the only business woman in town. When the F.N.S. store owners got together for their monthly meeting, my mother would be the only woman there. She was also a lifelong member of the credit union movement, and she was the first woman to be on the credit union board in the province of Nova Scotia. I dealt with the credit union all of my life, all of our family has, because of my mother's experience with them.

Talk about politics, I remember going to various credit union board elections. In Sydney Mines everyone runs. You don't have too many positions available on acclamation. My mother would always get family, friends, and supporters out for the annual meetings. [laughs] You couldn't miss it; you had to support your mother. [laughs] After she had served on the Board for a number of years, my two brothers were elected to the Board and, after they served for a number of years, I got involved. I have been president of the Board for the last few years. While

> **"With Love and Affection"**
> Today we are here to celebrate our mother's 90th birthday.
> A mother who has had great ambition for herself and for all her family.
> A mother who has taught us to be our own person,
> and reach for greater heights.
> All of us in our own way have accomplished this.
>
> We are grateful to her for all the patience and love she has shown us through the many difficult times in her life.
>
> We wish her a very happy 90th birthday,
> and ask that God keep her in his care.
>
> As some people say, and as we all know—"You are a star."

in Halifax, I did some research on the credit union movement. I found out that my mother was the first female director of a credit union in the province of Nova Scotia—the Princess Credit Union, here in Sydney Mines. That was quite something in those days, men dominated everything. But, she was a business person, and she could hold her own with any of the men. She even has a street named after her in Sydney Mines—DiPersio Street.[1]

That was the type of background I grew up in. My parents worked hard, and I learned that work ethic from them. I also learned the value of money. All my parents ever worked for was their family. My mother wouldn't take a taxi to go uptown when she was ninety. If we weren't around to drive her, she would walk there and back. She would never spend any money on herself. My mother looked after her own children, and that was it. And, you know, that is another thing that she instilled in us. We are more family conscious with our own children. They are down here every day of the week. I was the same way with my mother. No matter how busy, I would always find time to visit. And, when my mother was sick at home, all of the grandchildren took the time to stay with her at night. They would talk with her right into the middle of the night, and she would tell them stories. They learned a little bit about their heritage that way.

Remembrance Day for a Silver Cross Mother[2]

The Legion in Sydney Mines submitted my mother's name as their representative for Canadian "Silver Cross Mother" of 1987. Every Legion in the country was trying to promote their person for the position—including some powerful Legions with members on the provincial or national executive. We are only a small Legion branch here in Sydney Mines; we don't have very much muscle to influence anyone. So, when my mother was elected, it was a pretty big deal.

My mother was invited to go to Ottawa for Remembrance Day, and she was allowed to take someone to accompany her. She was ninety years old at the time, and we didn't know how her health would be for the trip. So she went to Ottawa with my sister, Sister Ann, who has a nursing background. The Legion took care of the details. They stayed at a big hotel overlooking the cenotaph. I travelled to Ottawa for the event as well. My mother and sister got to go to supper with the Governor General, Madame Jeanne Sauvé. They had a long conversation, and the Governor General gave my mother a set of prayer beads (which she cherished afterward). All of the military chiefs of staff were there for that supper.

My mother was also interviewed on national television at that time. They did the interview right in the hotel suite. It was something else. I was sitting in the next room. Here I was, Mayor of Sydney Mines, involved in various organizations, but I wouldn't have been as calm as she was for an interview on national television. [laughs] But she was as cool as a cucumber. She was a Silver Cross Mother, and we were all proud of her.

They were great to the Silver Cross Mothers. They took care of all the arrangements. Limousines picked them up and took them to the cenotaph. My mother was right up front with Madame Sauvé and Brian Mulroney. Then someone on the national executive of the Legion escorted her for the "laying of the wreath." That was important to her. She was a Silver Cross Mother in the Town of Sydney Mines for years and years because my brother [Merino] was killed in the war at an early age. His plane was shot down over [Malta in July of 1942]. That's a hard thing for a mother to accept. She never missed going to the cenotaph on November 11th ever since I can remember. And, I still go there each Remembrance Day; I never miss the service. No matter where I am, I always go to the cenotaph and to the Legion afterward. They always treated my mother well at the Legion in Sydney Mines.

If she hadn't gone to Ottawa that year, at her age, she would never have had another chance. Over the years, she had made many highlights in her own life. This was one of them. During the service in Ottawa, at the laying of the wreath, the book with all the names of those killed in the war was opened at my brother's page.

We always had feelings for the military. I had three brothers in the military during the Second World War. [Hank served with the Cape Breton Highlanders while

Pat and Merino were with the Canadian Air Force.[3] Hank was in Italy, and he was wounded three times. He had a lot of stories about being over there but, funny; he never went back to Italy for a visit. Merino, who was shot down and killed in 1942, was the oldest in the family. I remember, as a small child, when they delivered the telegram. Merino was newly married, and his wife had just had a baby. It was such a big, big disaster. Everybody on our street came over just after the telegram was delivered. In a small town, word goes out fast. It was just as if the wake was happening at that particular moment. At that time, they didn't send the bodies home. Merino was buried in Egypt. Now, the government wanted my mother to go to Egypt on a couple of occasions to see the grave, but she didn't want to. She still carried that hurt, I guess; she carried it all of her life.... [As Hector related this story, he showed Evo DiPierro and me a photo of his mother laying the Silver Wreath at the Cenotaph in Ottawa.] Yeah, so that's her picture there as the Silver Cross Mother.

Secondina and Hector DiPersio (front row, second and third from left). Sydney Mines, 1987. Courtesy of the Cape Breton Post, *Sydney, Nova Scotia.*

Florindo Byron[1]

By A. Evo DiPierro

Florindo Biron was born in Possagno, near Venice, Italy, in 1900. Sometime around 1922, he emigrated, with his cousin, Antonio Zan, to Glace Bay, Nova Scotia. There, Florindo changed the spelling of his name to Byron. He met and married Columbina Forlivesi in 1923. They had come to Canada on separate steamers just weeks apart. Miss Forlivesi came here, from Modena, Italy, at the urging of her two sisters—Maria Furini and Quirina Passerini—who were already living in Cape Breton (Dominion and Sydney, respectively); their parents remained in Italy.

Florindo Byron, ca. 1965.
Courtesy of Afra McVicar.

Byron's principal occupation was that of a builder. Before settling in Cape Breton, he and Columbina travelled to California where, from 1924 to 1925, Florindo worked in construction. When they returned to Cape Breton, the Byrons began to raise a family in Donkin. They had two daughters, Bianca (born in 1926) and Afra (in 1928). A son, their first born, died in infancy in 1925. In 1930, the family went back to Italy for a five-year period. They then returned to Cape Breton, and permanently settled in Sydney. Byron entered the hospitality industry by opening a hotel, the Minto, on Charlotte Street. He also operated a restaurant. Later, he bought the Sydney Hotel (located next to the present-day Royal Cape Breton Yacht Club).

In 1948, Byron began construction of the Venetian Gardens. He designed the structure and was active in every stage of its construction. He accomplished the work with the assistance of only a few men. The massive structure, located on Sydney's waterfront, was four-storeys high at the rear (facing the water) and one-and-a-half storeys at the front. The roof was round in shape, and the building's construction was unique in that its walls were of double thickness. The Byrons lived in an apartment located on a lower level of the building. The Gardens accommodated boxing cards, dances and concerts, bingo, and a restaurant. Bands such as the Emilio Pace Orchestra and the Gib Whitney Orchestra entertained there, and one night a week was devoted to square dancing with Joe Murphy. The dance hall ceiling featured star-shaped lights that flickered to create a romantic effect. A huge painting of Venice, complete with scenes of gondolas and canals, was also on display in the dance hall. In his book, *The Italians in Canada*, A. V. Spada wrote of the Venetian Gardens as: "One of the finest recreational halls in eastern Canada...."[2]

"Happy New Year" ball at the Venetian Gardens, ca. 1951. Photographer: Ray Doucette of Raytel Photography. 88-607-18117. Beaton Institute, Cape Breton University.

Tragically, in 1964, the Venetian Gardens was destroyed by fire. Florindo, however, was able to rebuild his famed Gardens (although on a smaller scale). In late Fall, 1966, at the age of sixty-six, before a boxing bout scheduled for the Gardens, he suffered a fatal heart attack. Florindo Byron died that evening (his wife had passed away five years earlier). Afra's husband, Art McVicar, continued to operate the Gardens for several more years until the property was sold to other interests.

Byron was a man of many talents. According to Afra McVicar, he was involved in the construction and design of a number of projects in Sydney—including the partitions for her husband's pharmacy. The partitions were made at the Gardens, transported to the site, and then assembled to construct the building. Byron also sang operatic arias; he actually performed on local radio programs, and at the Strand Theatre in Sydney. Florindo Byron and the Venetian Gardens are fondly remembered by people throughout Cape Breton.

Angelo Cechetto (1909-1999):
A Master Shoe Repairer from Dominion

Edited by Sam Migliore[1]

Angelo Cechetto operated a shoe repair business in Dominion for more than sixty years. His establishment, New York Shoe Repairing, was a well-known landmark in the community, and he earned the reputation of being a highly-skilled tradesperson. Angelo not only repaired shoes but prepared and adjusted orthopaedic equipment, sharpened skates and always prepared to try his hand at something new. His story begins in a small community in northern Italy.

I was born in 1909 in Albaredo, about 20 kilometres from Treviso. My father came to Canada three times. He was in Cape Breton in 1902 and worked in No. 1A colliery. When the pit caught fire, he went back to Italy.[2] The second time my father went to Ontario to work in a limestone factory. While there, he called his brother over from Italy. My uncle went to New Waterford and then to Sydney to start a shoe repair business. Meanwhile, my father returned to Italy.

In Italy, we were six brothers, and we had no land. We had to work for somebody else. My oldest brother worked on a farm from five in the morning to nine or ten at night; he worked for almost nothing. So he caught a boat from Genoa and landed in New York. They damn near sent him home. My brother was supposed to land in Canada, not the States. And, besides, he forgot my uncle's address. In his mind, though, he had "Sydney, Nova Scotia." He wrote to my uncle, and my uncle called a lawyer, and they straightened things out so he could come here.

I came to Canada in 1927. There was no way I was going to work on someone's farm. I was figuring to go to Belgium, but my father said: "No. You wait, and go to Canada." Then, in January of 1927, he went to Venice to get my papers. I left

Italy [from Genoa] when I was seventeen years old. Two days later, the military came looking for me to serve in the Italian army. By that time, I was on my way to Belgium. Four days later, I was on the boat for Canada. But, I had a problem getting on the boat. They called all the names in alphabetical order. A-B-C; I was supposed to be one of the first ones called. There were more than 500 people waiting. I missed my name, and they called no more. I was the last one to get on. Someone I knew said: "you were called a long time ago; we thought you had gone home." I damn near got sent back.

I landed in Canada in late February. I remember the ship, the *Maloc*.[3] It was an old freighter. [laughs] We went through the English Channel, and on from there. When we got two, three miles out, we had a good supper, but I got sick as a dog. [laughs] I was sick the whole time. I didn't eat for four or five days.

We landed at Saint John, New Brunswick. Of the more than 500 people on the boat, there were about 200 Italians. Only four of us came to Cape Breton, the rest went to Ontario. I was only a young fella, Carlo Zorzi was looking out for me. The other two were Peppi Polegato and Matteo Bortolon. I remember being so hungry in Saint John that I could eat a bear. Everybody was hungry. We had nothing all day, just standing in a big warehouse. I'll never forget that. Anyway, they put us up at the hotel. Four men, two beds. We tried to tell the man that we wanted something to eat, but he couldn't understand us. Finally, he started backing up and then ran down the stairs. We followed him. We went through some swinging doors, and there were four men with big, long knives. [laughs] When they found out we wanted something to eat, oh God, they put the food on the table. Well, I never ate so much. And, I'll never forget, we paid fifty cents each for the meal—bacon and eggs, oh, a beautiful meal. Imagine, a meal for fifty cents; today, you would have to pay twenty dollars for the same food. You can't get a cup of tea for fifty cents.

The next morning, they marched us down to the railroad station. They put tags on us to let the conductor know where to let us off. We couldn't speak English. But, we had no trouble. The train took us from Saint John to Truro, and then to Sydney. I ate two loaves of bread and six cans of sardines. [laughs] And I was still hungry. On the train, one fella charged me fifty cents for an orange. It should have cost five, ten cents. But, you pay. At that time, you put your money out in your hand and let them take what they wanted. I'll never forget that. We arrived the next morning, and I finally got to meet my brother and uncle. All I had was my paper suitcase. [laughs] That's all we could afford, paper suitcase [laughs] and a few rags. It cost me $200 to travel to Canada. That included the ticket for the ship and the train to Sydney. I also brought twenty-five dollars spending money.

A Brief Stay in the Coal Mines

My brother and uncle had businesses in Sydney, but they didn't have enough work for me. I went to work in the coal mine; first in No. 12 pit, and then in No. 14. I didn't work there very long, maybe two months. One day I worked with a fella putting a boom across to replace one that had cracked. He told me to wait there while he went somewhere. I heard this sound. I thought it was thunder and lightning. When he came back, he said: "like hell you heard thunder and lightning, you heard the stone cracking." When you're working, you don't hear anything, but when I sat down I could hear the stone cracking above me. "Oh my God," I said, "no way I'm going to work here." I went home. Then I worked at the other pit for a while, but it was dangerous work too. So, I never worked in the pit no more.

The Shoe Repair Business

After I left the mine, my uncle took me to Sydney. I worked in his shoe repair shop on Charlotte Street for $5 a week—from nine in the morning 'til nine at night—shining shoes, stringing the machine.... I had to make more money than that! "Well," my uncle said, "you got to learn how to fix shoes good." Six months later, I was making $21 dollars a week. I always had $20, $25 in my pocket. I couldn't spend it. In them days, boy, a pack of cigarettes, 15 cents, go to the show, 10 cents, a dozen eggs 25 cents. People would give me 25 cents to shine their shoes; 10 cents for the till and 15 cents for me.

Angelo in Shoe Repair shop, 1996. Courtesy of Angelo Cechetto.

After my uncle sold the shop, I went to work for somebody else. But, I wasn't making any money. I started my own business in 1929. I rented a shop for $100 a month and ordered the machines from Montreal. They cost $1100. By the time the machines arrived, I had not a dime in my pocket. I had to borrow some money, but I've fixed shoes ever since. My father came back to Cape Breton in 1930. We needed my father here so my other brothers could come over. He worked in No. 16 colliery for a while, and then, in 1940, he returned to Italy. He died there.

During the Depression, work was slow in Sydney and the rent was high. I came to Dominion on May 8, 1935. Oh, my God, she was a rough country then, boy. I jumped on an electric car in Sydney and got stuck twice in Reserve. We had a big snow storm that week; there was four feet of snow. [laughs] I couldn't get through. Finally, the third time, I made it as far as the big trestle. I met a fellow at the rink, and he helped me find a place to rent. I rented a store for $10 a month. [laughs] Later, I bought a piece of land, built myself a new building, and I'm still here. The mayor gave me a plaque for fifty years of business in Dominion,[4] and then, last year, I received another plaque for sixty years. I'm the only businessman in town that's been around for that long. Yeah. [long pause] Lucky enough that I never got sick.

I got married in 1936 to an Italian woman from Donkin, Italia Regina (Loli), and raised a family. I've got five girls; six, but one died. Three school teachers, a physiotherapist and a dietician. One of my daughters was up in Edmonton for sixteen years and now has a job in Winnipeg.

Working in the Steel Plant

In 1949, another fella started a business here. There wasn't enough work for both of us, so I went to the steel plant. I worked there for twenty-four years and got pensioned off in 1974. [laughs] I started in the General Yard, and later worked in mechanical at the Open Hearth. The job I had was maintaining the furnace. All the time I worked there, I fixed shoes. I never quit; I never closed the store. Sometimes I would go to the plant, do a job, and then fall asleep when it was time to sit down. They couldn't wake me up. [laughs] When I worked back shift, I used to come home in the morning, eight o'clock, lay down until twelve, and then go to the shop. After working there, I'd come home, lay down for a while, and then go to work at the plant for the night. On day shift, I used to work at the shop in the evenings and, on the four o'clock shift, I worked there in the morning.

Dominion ...1997

Oh, she was hard going at first. I couldn't speak the language. But, I got along pretty well. I kept going, kept going, and I'm still here. I go to the shop every day. This past winter, it was real bad for business, but I got by. I've got the old age pension, Canada Pension, a little bit from the steel plant and, with the shop, it keeps me going. I spend the money. People wearing sneakers, though, have ruined the shoe repair business. There's no more work. Some days I never make a cent. I can't fix sneakers. But, on Easter Sunday, in 1930, in Sydney, I made $30 in one day. Just fixing and shining shoes. I'll never forget that. Right now, I could quit, but I don't want to quit.

Helping People with Braces and Orthopaedic Shoes

Angelo Cechetto has assisted a number of people in the Dominion area, by preparing and fixing their braces and orthopaedic shoes. In appreciation for his help, Ann Marie McKinnon wrote a short article about Angelo for the Globe and Mail. In the article, she states:

> When I am asked how cerebral palsy affects my life, I don't tend to focus on anything negative or that the dragging of my feet causes me to scuff out the toes of at least two pairs of sneakers per week.... My thoughts focus on what I have achieved and the people who have helped me overcome tremendous obstacles.... One person who has helped me is ...

Angelo Cechetto ... Angelo used to replace the front section of my brace boots on a weekly basis. In exchange for his skill and precision work, my mother would give him the brace when I had outgrown it so another child could use it.... "Thank you for all your help Angelo. I am extremely grateful."[5]

[During one interview, Angelo showed me a photo of one of the people he has helped over the years. As I looked at the photo, he stated:] See the shoe with the brace? That was her brace. I started fixing her shoes when she was six years old. Every year she had to go to Boston [for treatment]. Finally, she is alright now. She's married and has two children. [From the look on his face, I could see that Angelo took great pride in being able to help others.]

Angelo Cechetto passed away, at age eighty-nine, on Tuesday, March 9, 1999.

New York Shoerepairing

[Why do you call your shop "New York Shoerepairing?"] Years ago, when I started my shop in Sydney, there were fifteen or sixteen shoe repair shops in town. Everybody had a different name. My brother had John Cechetto's Shoerepairing, my uncle had Sydney Shoerepair, there was a Boston Shoerepairing, so I said, "alright, I'll put something big, New York Shoerepairing." A name for the shop. It's pretty well faded now, look [motioning to the name on the window].

Bill Gentile:
Living Under Moxham Castle

Edited by Sam Migliore

During the 1890s, Arthur J. Moxham constructed a huge residence in Lorain, Ohio. The structure stood three-storeys high and boasted 30 rooms and 14 fireplaces. In 1898, "after Moxham had acquired an interest in the Dominion Iron and Steel Co., Ltd ... the mansion was dismantled and moved to Sydney, Nova Scotia."[1] From its new location, Moxham Castle dominated the Sydney harbour skyline for more than sixty years. Then, on April 25, 1966, the proud structure fell victim to the pressures of age, repeated vandalism, and fire.[2] Today, all that remains is the little "gatehouse" on Kings Road.

Bill Gentile and his family lived on the castle grounds for many years while his father served as its caretaker. Later, he purchased and used the "gatehouse" as a residence. Moxham Castle no longer exists, but it remains a powerful symbol of past experience in Bill's memories.[3]

My mother was born in St. Pierre and Miquelon, while Dad was born in a village in Italy about forty miles from Rome. He left Italy to come to the States when he was thirteen. Not sure how long he stayed there, but he came down to Cape Breton to work. He was a baker in Whitney Pier, and after he left the bakery, he started a shoemaker shop. He ran his own business for about eight years. In 1922, he moved up to Moxham's Castle to become the caretaker. Dad also did odd jobs of landscaping for the city; he planted a lot of the trees that are down in Wentworth Park. Besides that, he had a large garden on the castle grounds and sold vegetables. Then, in his later years, he worked at the steel plant in the electrical department. [My family] moved from the castle in 1942 to a residence on Kings Road. Dad passed away when he was 73, and Mother passed away in 1975. There were originally nine

Gentile family, ca 1939. Top from left: Victor, Bill, Humbert, Frank, Lovell. Bottom from left: Lucy, Frank (father), Adele (mother), Rusty (baby), Norman. Photo by Dodge Studio, Whitney Pier. Courtesy of Rusty and Betty Gentile.

in the family; [my parents, plus] six boys and one girl, but one died at the age of two. I married in 1947 and had two sons. My wife passed away in 1967, and I have been a bachelor ever since.

I used to sell vegetables and flowers when I was fifteen or sixteen. That was when we were living in the castle. We used to pick fresh carrots, beets and lettuce and I would sell them on Union and Park Streets every Saturday morning. I also had the Isle Royale booked for flowers every weekend—thirty-five bunches of sweet peas. After I left school, I worked as a driver-salesman with the sausage factory. I worked there up until 1941, then I went overseas for two-and-a-half years in the army. When I got back, I formed a partnership to start the Dacre Brand Sausage Company. The partnership lasted for about five years. The two partners dropped out, and I ran it for about twenty-five years. I sold out and retired in 1977. At that stage, I got into horses and roamed the horse shows for about six or seven years.

I lived in the little gatehouse [of the castle] for about seventeen years. I sold it when they started building the high-rise, and I have been here at this home ever since.

The Castle

The castle property ran from the little gatehouse up across Kings Road to Newlands Avenue, across to the old exhibition grounds (the site of what later became St. Rita's Hospital) and then down to the harbour. There was a full-size wharf and a boathouse down on the water's edge—Moxham had two yachts. Behind the gatehouse, there was a stable or barn. It had a big door, panelled walls, a big room for the wagons, four stalls and marble-like drinking troughs for the horses. I remember the panels were a dark, mahogany colour. There was also a loft upstairs where the horse feed was stored. [The area] behind the building was all landscaped; there were black and red currants, plum trees and blackberries. Between the barn and the railroad tracks, there was a road that ran right down to the back of the castle. There was an orchard there with about four pear trees and fifteen apple trees. From the orchard, there was a bridge going across the brook, the little pond, that brought you into the big area of the castle where the conservatory was located. The conservatory had all kinds of flowers and bushes.

On Kings Road, there were three gates. One was located by the little gatehouse. They tell me that the horses and carriages used to go out that gate to the road and then around to the castle. The second gate was right on the castle grounds, and the third gate was by the road that went down to the area near the conservatory. Each gate was built exactly the same. They were eight inches thick, about ten feet wide, and each one had a wooden gooseneck on it. In order to get the gate to open and close at the little gatehouse, you had to pull on a great big iron lever. The brick wall ran right from the gatehouse to the end of Churchill Drive. Next to the castle there was also a big pool with trout. At the end of the big pool, on the harbour side, the falls started and it dropped about thirty-five to forty feet. I remember they put little boards going down [to the water]. There was also a huge stone wall to reinforce the bank.

The front door [of the castle] faced the harbour. So you actually didn't come out of your carriage or vehicle at the front door. You would come out underneath the archway around back, go into a hallway with coat rooms, and then take the stairway to the second floor. From the front of the castle, you came out onto a big landing, and there was a balcony on the second floor.

There was also the conservatory with flowers, a big fountain right in the centre and a fish pool with three or four water sprays. Between the conservatory and the front door, there was a small bird sanctuary. There she is [as Bill pointed to a photo of the castle]; she had fourteen fireplaces, forty-five foot-high ceilings in the main hall, and it cost $350,000. It was destroyed by fire.

Life on the Castle Grounds

When the Moxhams moved, they took the furniture they wanted and sold the rest by auction. A big yacht was sold to an American. The Americans came up and bought a lot of the finer stuff. During the First World War, the castle was used as a spital (the Moxham Military Convalescent Home). When we came up in 1922, there wasn't anyone living there. The castle was owned by M. R. Chappell Building; they ran a building supplies and lumberyard. Dad and mother were great friends of the Chappells. I think dad was just renting at the time, and the Chappells asked if he would remodel the place. If dad did a lot of the work himself, it would be rent free. All he had to do was look after the castle. So we stayed there until 1942. From the time we arrived to the time we left, the castle was empty. Then, the MacDonald family took it over. When they left, it was passed over to the city. The city owned the castle when it burned down.

The house we lived in was a laundry, eh. It was a full two stories, the size of a three bedroom house. I think the maids or the groundsmen lived there. But dad remodelled it so that we could live there as a family.

We had three goats, some hens and a milking cow. I used to milk the goats and look after them. One goat would always come up behind me while I was milking, and give it to me with the horns; right in the back, eh. [laughs] I swore that within a week I'd have her dead. [laughs] We also had a pig for slaughter every fall. There was also a beautiful orchard down back of the castle—pear trees, some real good apple trees and a few little crab apple trees. Dad taught me how to take a branch off one apple tree and graft it onto another tree. That worked out pretty good. We actually got two kinds of apples on the same tree.

After school, when the sun was about to set, I would sit up on the second floor of the castle. I used to watch the sun stream through the big plated windows, the coloured glass. All the colours would reflect along the oak walls. Did that for years. And, of course, there was a tunnel that led from the outside to the inside; we would be playing hide-and-go-seek in there all the time.

Reminiscing

On more than one occasion, I had the opportunity to sit and talk with Bill, his broth-er Rusty and sometimes other family members. Each time we talked, I heard a new story about the castle. I have chosen the following as examples of some of their tales.

Run! The Pirates are Coming

[Bill]: Remember the time the Mounties raided the place, twice, looking for a cargo of rum? We were down at the old Moxham wharf fishing. All of sudden here were two fellas landing a motorboat. They came up over the side of the wharf with knives in their mouths, screeching and hollering, and, good Lord, we hollered "Pirates!" and away we went, going 100 miles an hour for home. [laughs] It took a little while for all this to come out, but the Mounties raided the castle. They were looking for a cargo of rum; that's what they told Dad.

Later, the Mounties came down for another raid and, sure enough, this time they found 'er. There was a hill that didn't seem to belong there. It was banged up, fresh earth. They started digging and ran into 'er. Oh, there was a number of kegs down in there. This was where these pirates used to land at the wharf, see, and take it up [laughs] to bury 'er. [Rusty]: Hearing the older people talk, Sydney harbour was quite a rum-running area. The schooners would come in from Newfoundland and St. Pierre. That would be in the 1930s and early 1940s, I believe.

Schooners, Hobos and Darning Needles

[Rusty]: I can remember the French schooners sailing into the harbour and coming right below the castle to anchor. The sailors used to wash their clothes in the brook. My mom was French, so they'd come up with some food or wine to eat and talk. I can still remember the guys washing the clothes in the brook on the rocks, with a scrubbing brush, and then hanging them out. Yeah, the harbour was a lot cleaner then, I'll tell you. There were no sewers in it at that time.

[Bill]: There used to be some hobos too. They would come down at summer time and dig in there between the tracks and the harbour—where Nelga Beach used to be, eh. We'd always go down to ask them to tell us stories. [One time we were eating biscuits.] These three guys said: "Hi boys! Those are beautiful looking biscuits; suppose you can get some for us?" [Then one added]: "If you get us some cookies, I'll do a few tricks for you." So I dashed home, eh, and told mother about the guys being awful hungry down there, you know, and she gave us some biscuits and one thing or another to take down to them. It was a beautiful morning, eh, and I said to one of them: "Well, where's your tricks at." The fellow started rubbing his hand and then stuck it out to let some sun shine on it for a while. He then reached over to a bag and comes out with a big darn needle. [He put it] right clean through; it came out the other side. Not a drop of blood flowing or anything. He held it up and said, "what do you think fellas." Gees, next day we'd be down with more cookies. [laughs] I'll never ever forget that. [Rusty]: Yeah, there used to be quite a few hobos get off the train there. My mom used to feed them. Quite a few trains going by in those days; the old steam engines, eh.

The Doctors' Convention

They used to rent the castle to the public every once in a while. The Jewish society had a great big dance there five or six times. We would cut the hardwood from in around the castle grounds, get all the fire-places ready and keep them stoked while the dances were going on.

One year, the castle was hired for a doctors' convention. Doctors came in from all over the place. They brought a refrigerated boxcar full of snow for a snowball fight. This was in August! They had a whopping time down there. They had a piper to liven things up but, about eight hours after the party, they discovered the piper was missing. We were fooling around in the castle in one of the big rooms on the second floor, and I thought I heard a noise. We went over, and here curled up in the big closet was the piper, drunker than a skunk, sleeping 'er off.

The Fire

I rang in the alarm between twelve and one o'clock. I lived in the little gatehouse then, and my bedroom window faced the castle. Sometimes cars would go by, and the headlights would flicker on the windows of the castle. I was going to bed, and I noticed this little flash. I just assumed it was [from the cars], but it kept bothering

<aside>

The Tidal Wave of 1929

[Bill]: A bunch of us were out on the wharf fishing. I remember Allister was there; he was about six-and-a-half feet tall, and weighed pretty near a ton. He was dancing at the head of the wharf, watching, as we were fishing and fooling around. We heard this rattling from the wire fence near Moxham's yard. At first, we thought that rattle was from his jumping up and down; nobody paid much attention. Then, it really started rattling. We knew something was wrong; the wharf started to quiver, a big wave was coming down the harbour and, boy, we ducked home as fast as we could go. Mother was at the back door trying to save some of her dishes; they were falling off the shelves, eh. [Rusty]: That was the earthquake they had off New-foundland, and one of the highest tides ever. The water came right up on the Esplanade.

</aside>

me, so I decided to get up and have a look. I saw just a tiny flame flickering in the window.

The chandelier was gas-electric at one time. There were tunnels running through the top floor and the attic so that you could get in to bring up the chandelier. There was a pulley hung up in the rafters, and you would hook on the chandelier and bring it up for repair. There were two tunnels. That's where the fires were. But, [the fire department] couldn't find the fire until the next day. By that time she was pretty well under way. It was too late to save the castle.

"Moxham Castle" Original art by Marie Moore, 1998.

The Rossetti Legacy:
A Talk with Dolores (Rossetti) Moore

Edited by Sam Migliore[1]

I was born in this house here in Whitney Pier. I had three brothers and three sisters. I was the youngest. I went to school at Holy Redeemer Convent. My Dad, Philip Rossetti, came to Canada around 1901, from Foggia, Italy. He was born in 1884, so he must have been only seventeen or eighteen when he left his family to come here. He didn't have a soul here, not a relative; he was the first one in the family to make the move to Canada. In the beginning, he worked in the mines in Glace Bay. Once the steel plant opened in Sydney, he began to work there. He worked there for many years. Times were not very easy for him, though. He lived through the Depression and had seven children. It was quite a struggle. My mother was a seamstress, and I guess that helped a little bit. Her maiden name was Nicoline Rossi.

My mother was born in Naples and came to Canada with her family. Her parents were Alphonse and Rose Rossi. My grandfather was a bricklayer. He travelled around; he worked on the Panama Canal, and I know he did some work in Mexico. My grandmother kept boarders, and my dad was one of the people boarding with them. This is how my parents met. And, eventually, they were married at Holy Redeemer Church. They moved to this house in 1916. I was born upstairs, and I have always lived here.

In the steel plant, my father worked in the Bloom Mill. He retired when he was seventy-four years old. But, he didn't really want to retire. He was on vacation during the summer, visiting my sisters in New Jersey and Ontario. When he returned to work, they retired him. I was ironing in the kitchen when he came home. I could hear him in the backyard crying. He couldn't tell me right away. He was saying: "I am finished! I am finished! They told me I am pensioned." He thought it was the end of the world. He was heart broken.

My brothers, Frank and Alphonse, were in the service during the war. Frank went overseas with the first contingent. Bruce was the youngest of the boys; he was in university during the war. After the war, Alphonse worked at the dry dock, while Frank worked for the steel company. He was a superintendent in charge of diesels, a diesel mechanic. Two of my sisters, Rose and Nicolina (we called her Collie), moved to Ontario. Collie died very young; she was only forty seven. My sister Mary became a nurse and lived in New Jersey with her husband. My father was always so happy that none of the boys were ever in trouble. They never drank or anything like that. He was right proud. None of us were ever in trouble.

Anthony Bruce Rossetti

My parents always called him Tony; never called him Bruce. But, all the kids around here knew him as Bruce. I don't know how that got started; it just seemed to stick. Bruce was a very good student. He graduated from Sydney Academy, and then he went to work at Eaton's for a couple of years to save some money. Mary was working in New York as a nurse, she wasn't married at the time, so she was able to help. Bruce went to university at St. Francis Xavier in Antigonish. He received a number of scholarships while there, and he was on the boxing team. Then he went to the Nova Scotia Technical College. He graduated in 1942. He became a professional engineer. Bruce worked in Montreal for a few years with Canadian Industries (CIL), Dupont, and then he came back to Sydney. He worked here at Dominion Steel, and later as the engineer in charge of the Seaboard Power Plant in Glace Bay. In 1953, he joined Sydney Engineering and Dry Dock. He was there until he died in 1978.

Bruce was married to Dorothy Clark.[2] Her father originally owned the Dry Dock, and Bruce managed it. [He became president and managing director of the company.] It was quite a lucrative business. Today, it has been reduced to nothing. I'm sure my brother would turn over in his grave if he could see what it looks like now.

Bruce and Dorothy didn't have any children. [In his will, Anthony Bruce Rossetti left some money or property to various churches and organizations. He also made specific bequests to a number of educational institutions.] A lot of universities were left money from his estate. The Nova Scotia Technical College, St. Francis Xavier University, Dalhousie Medical School and the College of Cape Breton (now Cape Breton University). He also left money for the MacConnell Memorial Library in Sydney, the Cape Bretonia Museum (now the Beaton Institute) and the School Board of the City of Sydney (now the Cape Breton-Victoria Regional School Board). A lot of people benefited from the estate. It was wonderful. And, a lot of students are enjoying the scholarships at the universities now. I hope it will continue.

Father Joseph Emilio Marinelli

Born in Sydney Mines, N.S., on March 10, 1915
Died April 12, 1997

Edited by Sam Migliore

In Memorian
Father, you called your servant Joseph
to share in the priesthood of your Son.
Show him your mercy and your love,
and welcome him into the company of your saints for ever,
where Jesus is Lord for ever and ever. AMEN.[1]

My dad [Carlo Marinelli] was born in Carpineto della Nora in the Abruzzo region of central Italy. He and his brother, Vincent, came to the United States. They worked on railway construction. Later, his brother died on a construction site.

Anyway, somebody told my dad about Sydney Mines. He came to Sydney Mines, worked for a while and then went back to Italy. He married my mother [Maria Rosini]. Sometime later, he returned to Sydney Mines. He told her that when he had money to build a house, he would call for her. That took a while. When my father's brother went to Italy for a trip, my father asked him to escort my mother and her four-and-a-half-year old son to Canada. It took that long to bring them over here. In Sydney Mines, they were taken to a big boarding house. When they opened the door, my mother looked inside and saw the most exciting thing in her life—*running water.*

I was the first born in Sydney Mines. I was two years old when my father finished building our house. He worked at the steel plant. The original plant was in Sydney Mines, and it was moved to Sydney. When the [Sydney Mines] plant was broken down, he worked the furnace making electricity for the town and surrounding area. Then that was closed down. So he worked in the mine, on the surface of No. 1, Princess. He took cancer and died at age sixty-seven. Very sad.

My mother had a very good sense of humour but no schooling. Couldn't read or write. I'm sure she regretted that all her life. Her brother went to school and was supposed to teach his three sisters to read and write, but he didn't. If he had been living, I think I would have bawled him out. [laughs] But anyway, she had a great sense of humour. A loving person.

And, we grew up. Three boys (Vince, myself and Louie) and two girls (Angela and Toni). We all got along together. I went right through school, through Grade 12, and did pretty well. Then I stayed out a year because I was expecting to get a job in the mine. I didn't. At the beginning of the second year, the boss told me that he would get me a job on the next vacancy. But, Father D'Intino came to my house on a Sunday afternoon. He said: "Are you Joe Marinelli?" I said, "Yes." "Joe," he said, "did you ever think of going to college?" And I said, "No! I studied enough." [laughs] Then he said, "Joe, look at it this way. Go to college for one year, one year, if you like it, go the second year and the third year. If you don't like it come back home. Get that job in the pit, and pay your Dad back what you owe him." And pay my brother Vince back too, he was working. I thought that was a good idea. Funny, eh. He worked me around. Psychology.

So I went to see Father MacLean. He called up the college president and gave him my marks from Grade 12. The president said, "tell him to come." We had a car; so we drove up. On the way, we had a little accident—left the road. [laughs] I was driving. Little Vince had been driving; he should have driven the whole way. [laughs] But, we got it back on the road, got to [St. Francis Xavier University], and I loved it. Three years and pretty good marks. Ah, should I brag? *Summa cum laude* [with highest distinctions].

Then there was the summer in Halifax. Holy Heart! [the seminary]. Yeah, but, I have to go back a little. I took one year of Italian at Saint Francis Xavier with Father Sears. Three of us would sit in his room and share the book for the course. I learned some, but that's all because I became interested in French. Our French professor would ask somebody to read every day. It would be murder in the French. He didn't ask me, but it was murder. But, someone had the courage to ask him, "will you read a page." He read a page, and that's when I fell in love with French. I really did.

There was also a student who became my best friend—Father Girroir in West Arichat. He is seventy-nine years old, and he is still running a parish, [laughs] seventy-nine. My best friend. He was French; so, I used to meet with him and read a paragraph. He would correct me when I made mistakes. And then the seminary; that's where I learned French. The custom there was for an English speaking person, me, to contact a French person. They were all from New Brunswick. One-third of the seminarians were French. And ah, I contacted, a Frenchman that knew … a good bit of English. And he knew that I knew a little, a good bit of French. So it was fun. We'd talk French one day and English the next. After dinner, I would speak with another Frenchman. I did that for four years. By the end of the first year, I could speak French without thinking about it.

When I was ordained [on June 7, 1941, by Archbishop John Thomas McNally], I was sent to [St. Joseph's] Parish in New Victoria. I was there for six years. And then, I was sent to Mount Carmel Parish in New Waterford for two-and-a-half years. I was there with Father Johnson.

My second summer in New Waterford, Father Johnson said, "Joe" (he knew I hadn't gone on vacation the previous summer) "go on vacation." I said, "No! I got no money." Which was literally true, salaries were horrendous. Sixteen dollars a month, and the fact that we got $2 a day for Mass saved us to a great extent. He didn't say a word but, a couple of days later, he called me over and put his hand out, $100. That's a lot of money. So, a few days later, I went on vacation. [Father Joe also recalled a seven-week trip to New York City to study church music. In addition to attending to his studies, he took the opportunity to attend a number of plays and some Italian opera. He later was able to use this musical training effectively, while serving, for a time, as musical director at St. Francis Xavier University.]

I spent ten years at St. Joseph Du Moine, near Cheticamp. It was interesting learning French [in school]; and, when they sent me to St. Joseph Du Moine, I had no problem. I just got up there Sunday and preached the sermon. Gradually, I learned their kind of French, which is different. And, in some cases, I used it when I thought it wouldn't make any difference. But, if I thought they would be insulted, you know, I wouldn't say it. I didn't want to hurt anybody.

I was there with a saintly priest, who was dying of heart trouble. He was in and out of the hospital. Hospital a couple of weeks, home a couple of weeks. And ah, he could play the piano. He taught high school ... at his house. There was no high school in Cheticamp. Some of them became great men. One became an Inspector of Schools in Antigonish, and there were more. [The priest] died in January. I went there in March, and the following January he died.

St. Joseph Du Moine was a beautiful parish. Beautiful people–honest, hard working. One thing they did, when I went down to the store to buy a shirt or a pair of shoes, whatever, if they were three dollars, they charged me three dollars. No breaks. See, I like that. I wouldn't want them to [charge me less]. And, if I went to get fish, same thing. Once I went down, in the late fall, to get ten pounds of lobster meat for use in the winter. They charged me ten dollars. I didn't think much of it at the time, but when I got home I said, "They should have charged me three or four times that much." Of course things were cheaper then, but ten dollars was very, very cheap. So, I think they did give me a break that time. [laughs] Just for once.

There was a man there who had eight or nine children, and they lived in a shack. I felt terrible about that. I was talking to somebody, and this fella said that there was a house for sale; they wanted $1,500, which was cheap. So, the store manager and I split the cost, $750 each. And, that's the way it was; they had a house.

Later, I was moved to another French parish. I was in French parishes for twenty years. Life was interesting. I love the French, the Acadiens. They were all nice people. Then I came back to New Waterford, Mount Carmel; I was there for the rest of my life. Seventeen-and-a-half years. The reason they sent me to Mount Carmel was that my health wasn't the best. I was hospitalized for nerve trouble three or four times. They figured that was enough. Of course I was getting old then; I stayed there until I was 75. Then I came to the Xavier Apartments for priests. I was there for a year, and then I came here to [MacGillivray Guest Home]. And, I'm still here; six years.

Father Joseph Marinelli, 1981. St. Joseph's Church, Lingan. Courtesy of Len Stephenson.

A while back I attended a "roast" for my friend Father Girroir. Now, you know what a roast is, and I know what a roast is, but other people didn't. Most speakers just praised him. But I didn't know that was going to happen. I told a story about something funny that happened to him at St. Francis Xavier. There was a French hockey player from New Brunswick. One day, poor Conrad [Father Girroir] was sitting down, and [this hockey player] came over and started doing this and that to him. [laugh] Conrad got impatient. He just shot out like that. [The hockey player] got it right here; a place called *the button*. When you get hit on the button, you go down. He was unconscious for a while. And then, poor Father Girroir ran away. I mean, that fella was an athlete, he was tough. He could beat the heck out of Father Girroir. Then someone came to Conrad and said: "Bob [the hockey player] says he is sorry; it was his fault, it's alright." [laughs] Well, that was partly a fictitious story, but it was a roast. I talked about a lot of good stuff too—how he taught me quite a bit of French, and that I appreciated it very much. Then I told them another story:

One time, I went to see Conrad. He had a white motorboat. He took me for a ride, and after ten minutes he said, "Are you seasick?" I said, "No." After another ten minutes, he said, "Are you seasick?" He kept that up the whole time; I thought, "poor fella, he doesn't want me to get sick," eh. But then, I began thinking, "we both took psychology." [laughs] Psychology tells you that if you tell somebody something often enough, he will end up doing it. He wasn't trying to help me at all; he wanted to make me seasick. [laughs] I thought that was terrible!

So, I said, "Father Girroir and I have been friends, but there is one thing I won't forgive him, the fact that he tried to get me seasick." That's how I ended [the roast], eh.

Great, great man. But, when [Father Girroir's] anniversary came up a few months later, I couldn't go. I wasn't feeling well. I called him at home. We talked and talked and talked. Gosh, it cost me about $8 for the phone call. We must have talked for an hour. Anyway, it was well spent.

When my mother was eighty-three years old, I took her on a trip to Italy along with my sister Toni, who was a nurse. They lived together at the time. Toni was as good for me as ten doctors. She really helped me; without her I don't know what would have happened to me. She pulled me through my medical problems. Anyway, I took my mother to Italy, and she saw her two sisters. In the evening, they sang the songs they used to sing when they were children. Beautiful! My mother always had terrible headaches and stomach aches. Her stomach went as a result of the tons of aspirins she had to take for the headaches. But when she went [to Italy], no trouble, nothing at all. Healthy as a cricket. It was a beautiful trip. My mother hung in there with her headaches, stomach aches ... until she was almost ninety; she died two months short of ninety.

I think that's about it. Now you know everything that I know about my family. Yeah.

Father Joseph Emilio Marinelli passed away on April 12, 1997. A few days later, a Celebration of Christian Farewell was held at St. Anthony Daniel Church, in Sydney. Reverend Conrad Girroir served as one of the concelebrants. The church was full of people. Father Joe touched many lives during his eighty-two years here on earth.

Benny DeLorenzo:
Work in the Steel Plant

Edited by Sam Migliore[1]

I was born in Sydney. My parents (Vincenzo and Assunta DeLorenzo) were from the Abruzzi area of Italy. My father immigrated in 1909. [The company sent representatives] to Europe to recruit people for work in the steel plant. My father came here and worked at the plant as a foreman. By the time he saved enough money to send for Mama, the 1914-1918 war broke out. My mother didn't arrive here 'til 1919. The first in our immediate family was born in 1922, and then I was born in 1926. I was brought up in the Pier, which was very immigrant oriented. The larger groups at the time were the Italians, Polish and Ukrainian. There were also Slovaks, Hungarians and some Scandinavian people. There was also a large Black population. They were immigrants from the West Indies. That was the environment we grew up, in Ward Five. All came to work at the steel plant; that was the attraction, I suppose, from 1901 'til the 1930s.

I went to school in Whitney Pier during the 1930s. In those days our family was very well off. My father had businesses going. He had the first modernized meat market in this area; it had electric equipment to cut the meats. He also had a big grocery store that was very successful. Then we ran into some difficulties. We were in the midst of a Depression. By 1937-1938, he had lost everything. Of course, as kids, we had fun; we made our own fun, running around with hoops and beating old rubber tires around. I guess we didn't realize the difference. But, when I think back now, you really had to scrape to pick up any sort of job. We went through rough years at home at that time; there was no such thing as welfare. Just people helping people, eh. The Italian community was close. I completed grade eleven, and from there I went right into the plant. I went into the plant at sixteen years old, that was 1943, and I retired in 1989. I worked there all those years.

The General Yard

I started in the general yard. Well, that is where everybody started in those days. You reported with a large pool of workers to the large open area by the yard office. You walked in, gave your number at the window and then sat down to wait. There were over a thousand people employed in the yard at that time. The foremen would take groups of men, and go around doing the work. But you got to remember, at that time we didn't have payloaders or any digging apparatus—all that was done by hand. So, if you had to dig up a pipe line or a ditch, you would have a gang of fellows do it with pick and shovels. [laughs] It was tough.

They had a group of construction foremen too. A fellow that came with Cozzolino was old Mr. Bruno. Pasquale Bruno was the construction foreman, and he had four sub-gangs working under him. They did all the new construction. As a matter of fact, I worked with him on his last job—the bridge on Victoria Road crossing the tar brook. That used to be a wooden bridge, and every couple of years there used to be trouble with it. And that was the main road! The overpass wasn't there. So they got old Mr. Bruno's gang to make it concrete. And it's been there ever since. Now that was either 1950 or 1951. I was in good shape because I was in training [as a boxer], and I'd be going with the wheelbarrow. [laughs] He'd say, "good boy Benny, champion wheelbarrow driver." And then he'd get the other guys all going. [laughs] He was a great old guy. Everyone liked him, and he got his work done. That was Mr. Bruno's last year; he retired after that. Course, then, the construction got a little different. The technology changed, you didn't mix cement by hand anymore, and it was cheaper to hire trucks and contractors to do it. So, it kind of fizzled out, although they kept a small construction crew up until the mid-seventies.

The Coke Ovens

From the yard you went all over the plant. That was the beauty of the yard. You worked wherever they were short, and sometimes, if you hit a job you liked, you'd stay a week or two. Some guys stayed and made their careers [in one place]. But I roamed the plant for the first ten or twelve years. I didn't know every job, but I knew every department. And, of course, it was a fully-integrated plant. We had the wire and nail mill, rod and bar mill, the rail mill, the billet mill and the bloom mill; they were all working full capacity. So it was an interesting time. A lot of people worked close to fifty years in the open hearth, or the coke ovens ... and they didn't even know what the other departments looked like. I was lucky; my group roamed around quite a bit.

I spent some time in the coke ovens when I was in the yard. I worked there one whole summer, probably five or six months. I'd be nineteen or twenty then. Most times when you got sent to the coke ovens, it'd be on the coal trestle, which was a horrible job. You'd be about fifty feet up, and they didn't have any safety equipment for you. You'd just go up, knock the bottom doors open to empty the cars, and then go in the cars and straddle the saddle back. [laughs] I was short, and I used to find it difficult. It was a good reach. If you ever slipped, you were going straight down. You could very well get killed there. One of the troubles was that you had to go in to scrape down what was left [in the car], especially if it was sticky coal. And there would be an up-draft there. Your eyes, ears and nose [would be full of coal dust]. And, of course, they didn't have any safety regulations whatsoever then. You just took your chances.

I was there for a while, and then I worked in the yard group with the late Tony Sollazzo. I worked in around the battery. There were always gangs cleaning up the coke spillage on the track from the hot cars. You'd fill up the wheelbarrow and go dump it in the wharf. It wasn't that bad a job. You were outside, and it would be day shift. [laughs] See, in those days, the foreign guys were generally sent to the most menial, dangerous and dirty jobs. The Union wasn't very strong. The foreman would put you where he liked and take who he liked. [If you were not taken,] you would go home, even if you were senior. They didn't have such a thing as seniority. That happened to me many times.

The Departments

They had Protestant and Catholic departments. [laughs] The open hearth was called the Vatican. Catholics were prominent down there. And the mechanical and electrical department were the Masons' department. If you were Catholic and you were a foreigner, you didn't have much chance of getting in there. And they'd take advantage of people. Of course, our generation changed that. Not just the foreign guys but the other fellows. I have to give full credit to the guys we grew up with. They knew it was wrong. I mean, take a guy on his ability, not on that.

The brick department was very bad for prejudices. The brick Union was the worse offender. They wouldn't let anybody that wasn't a Newfoundlander or of white English descent become a bricklayer. The result, they had lots of people that worked there for forty-five years and never got above being a helper. And the young fellows would go in there and get the trade right away. In those days you learned your apprenticeship right on the job. One time, a Polish chap changed his name. He got in, they were all working, and somebody found out he was Polish. They all laid down their tools and walked off the job. Went on strike. They had to take him off the job. They wouldn't work with him; for no reason, except that he was Polish. It was just ridiculous, but we lived with that.

I worked in the electrical department for almost two years. There were about four of us who were, I don't like to use the word ["foreigners"], I was born here. I'm a Canadian citizen. But, they had a regulation. If you were thirty days in a department, they automatically transferred you to that department. What they would do was let us work twenty-nine days and then send us back to the yard for one day.

We'd have to start the thirty days over. They did that to [a couple of fellows] for about eight or nine years. I was there about two years, and then I said, "Ah, the hell with this!" I just went. I had a chance to work in the lab, and I went. And there would be younger fellows just coming on in the plant who'd get [into the electrical department] right away, even before they had completed their thirty days. It hurt me when that happened. That was the way it was then. But we survived it. And went on.

I started working in the lab in the early 1950s. I'd be filling in for vacations the first few years. They would always call me back. And, eventually, I got in. In them days, it was wet chemistry. You would have to take the test from each heat in the open hearth and each cast at the blast furnace. Drill out the blocks, record what furnace they came from and send them up to the chemist for analysis. You'd have to screen the coke finish product and pulverize a sample for analysis. And, you'd also do a hardness test. That was a good group in there. Really good fellows. They helped you with any kind of problem you had. That was probably the best years that I had.

The Union

Back in the early 1950s, I got involved in the union movement because of [the way jobs and transfers were being handled in some departments]. That irked me. I said, "we have to do something about that." Winston Ruck and I joined together. He became the district director of the steelworkers and did a good job. I ran for President the first year and got beat out by a handful of votes. Winston ran the second year, and I was happy as hell; he was elected President and I became Vice President. [Rose DeLorenzo (Benny's wife): "They had a Black President and an Italian Vice President."] We cracked that [barrier]. [Rose: "Winston Ruck is dead now. He was an exceptional guy. My kids loved that man."] He was a very intelligent man and courageous.

Working with the Safety Department

Okay, here is how I got started in Safety. I was with [Union local] 1064. I was chairman of the safety committee for the local and also working in the coke ovens at the lab section. In 1967, DEVCO (Cape Breton Development Corporation) bought the coke ovens from SYSCO (Sydney Steel Corporation). Although I was in the coke ovens at the time, I wasn't a coke oven department employee. I was a lab department employee. So, when the change came, we had a choice to go back to SYSCO or stay there with DEVCO. Jim Collier called me and said: "we don't have anybody here that can do the lab job. We'd like you to stay." And I stayed there. About a year later, he asked me to join their new Safety Department. It paid a considerable amount more than I was earning. But, I was strong in the Union then. I was, or had been, on the executive. He said: "I don't know what your union ambitions are, but we'll have to put you on salary; you'll be out of the Union." I talked to my friends, and they advised me. They said: "well, you're working for money. You might as well go where your chances are to get bigger pay." And I agreed. I had six children at the time. They were all small, and I had built a house; it all helped.

I started ... and then they sent me away for training to Ottawa. We were there eight weeks, and I got a tremendous amount out of it. How to investigate accidents, preventive measures and how to do safety inspections. It was really an intensive course. They also gave us fire prevention courses. We reduced accidents by about 75-80 per cent the first year. It was just a tremendous improvement. And I had a good rapport with the guys. They all helped me, backed me up, and they were all interested in it too. That would be the 1969-1971 period.

Then, [around 1973,] SYSCO took the coke ovens back. I had a choice to stay with DEVCO or return to SYSCO. I had all my seniority with SYSCO, so I decided to go back, and that is how I became head of safety for the whole plant. Then, in 1981 or 1982, they combined the safety, security and fire sections. They made that the plant protection department. I was head of that section. It was an interesting time. I enjoyed the challenges at the plant protection department from 1968 until I left in 1989. [laughs] I worked almost forty-eight years. That was enough. I did a good job, and they were pleased.

Country Living: DiVito and Marinelli Family Memories[1]

Edited by Sam Migliore

Frank DiVito, the son of Philomena (Marinelli) and Sabatino DiVito, is a St. Francis Xavier University graduate employed as a sales supervisor. His work involves travel to places throughout Cape Breton. As a child, however, Frank lived and worked on the family farm on Barren Road (what is now Keltic Drive, Sydney). This article focuses primarily on Frank's memories of "family" and "country living." Aunt Nora (Marinelli) Buchanan and Uncle Louie Marinelli contribute to the discussion.

[Frank]: I was born in Sydney Mines, 1935, and we moved to Barren Road in 1942. Not very many people there at that time. My parents felt that we should go to school in Sydney. I went to Sacred Heart School, along with one of my brothers, while my sisters went to Holy Angels Convent. I had to do various chores along with all my school work. We all helped with the family farm. I then went to Riverview High School, Junior College and finally St. Frances Xavier University. I graduated in 1958. I've done a lot of things since then, been in business most of the time, and my present position is sales manager at Canada Life.

I have two brothers and four sisters. My parents have both passed away, and I lost my sister, Theresa, in January of 1993. Anna and Mary are in Toronto, and Eleanor is in Antigonish. Carman lives on the family homestead, and Tony is in Prime Brook. I married Pat about fifteen years ago, and I have four step children.

Marinelli Family Background

[Aunt Nora]: My mother (Teresa) was born in 1880, so my father (Giovanni) was born in 1879. He was a year older than Mamma. Pappa came over to Sydney before he got married. [Uncle Louie]: He and his brother were both here. They worked

Marinelli family. Top, from left: Mary, Philomena, Patsy, Tony. Front, from left: Nora, Teresa (mother), Katherine, Giovanni (father), Louie. Courtesy of Frank DiVito.

at the steel plant for a while, and then both went back to Italy. [Aunt Nora]: My parents married in Italy and then came together to live in Sydney Mines. [Uncle Louie]: That would be maybe ninety years ago, 1907. [Aunt Nora]: They were both from the area around Pescara—Carpineto della Nora, near Brittoli. My brothers, sisters and I, all seven of us, were born in Sydney Mines. [Uncle Louie]: I was born in 1916; I'm two years older than Nora. We are the only two left. [Frank]: My mother was their sister.

[Aunt Nora]: For me, growing up in Sydney Mines was wonderful. There was a lot of discrimination, of course. People used to call the Italians "wops" or "garlics." But, we always had enough to eat, enough to wear. [Uncle Louie]: Even in the Depression years, when there was no money, there was always lots to eat. We had horses, cows, chickens and an awful lot of pigs. We also had a back field of about two acres; every inch was planted. [Frank]: Many, many Italians in Sydney Mines had gardens. That's how people survived, providing for themselves....

[Aunt Nora]: We planted all kinds of vegetables, enough to do us for the winter. We had potatoes ... cucumbers ... and green, yellow and horse beans (broad beans). And, peppers, tomatoes and corn. Practically every night, there would be a pot of fresh corn on the stove—picked and cooked right out of the garden. Beautiful. [Frank]: The animals would get the cob. [laughter] [Aunt Nora]: Yes, and they would feed the animals the small potatoes.... [Frank]: And the turnips.

[Uncle Louie]: All the work was done by hand. Twelve years old, and I was holding a plow behind a horse out there. A lot of work. Raised pigs. We had four or five sows, and in the spring of the year, they would have young ones. By fall, the piglets would be 150-200 pounds. A fellow from St. Pierre used to buy them. He would crate them here, two to a crate, and take them to the wharf in North Sydney. Get enough money to pay taxes. [laughs] They were tough times. If you had eight cents to buy a pound of sugar, you were lucky.

We also had a bakery going next door and a little shop in the front of the house. Mother did the baking, and Pappa would get out in the morning with horse and wagon to deliver. If you had the money, you got it, and if you didn't have the money, you still got it. [laughter] That's the way it was; nobody had anything anyway. A dime or a nickel was something to have in those times. You'd be looking for a nickel to go to the theatre on Saturday, and Pappa didn't have it to give you. Better than today though; there was no money, but we always had plenty to eat. Pappa passed away in 1937, and mother died in 1951. Oh, they worked hard—especially mother. She raised seven of us, fed the cattle, milked the cow and made the cheese, and had the garden going too. [Aunt Nora]: And, mother had boarders. [Uncle Louie]: No man worked like my poor mother. Later, though, they gave up the bakery and rented it to someone else.

Pappa was resourceful. We used wood or coal for heat. One time, we had about 150 cords of wood out there. You know where they came from? The Murray. There was a big mill down there, and they used to fence off the logs in the water. Well, they broke clear and drifted to the beach down here. My father hauled every last stick up to our yard. [Frank]: The Murray is in St. Ann's Bay. That's where the Mercy Paper Company was located. They were from Liverpool. [Uncle Louie]: They had a hospital, a jail.... They had a big mill going there at one time. In the Depression years, it folded up.

[Aunt Nora]: My brothers worked the crop pits, digging and hauling coal. [Uncle Louie]: The steel plant in Sydney Mines more or less folded after the First World War. Parts of it kept going, but then, little by little, we had nothing. I was too young to work there when it was going. I worked in the bootleg pits at fifteen years old. Come out of school, and go to work. Couldn't sell nothing, though. We would take it home. I'd have 100-150 loads piled up. And, because we always had a horse and wagon, we'd also haul for the other fellas. We would haul two loads and take one. That's the only way they could pay you. [laughs] The times were rough. I like to talk about it, but the young fellas don't believe it. You only know if you went through it.

In those days, if you had ten, twenty dollars, you had it made. Fellas working in the pit, very few of them made twenty dollars a week. They'd come to our store and if they had twenty dollars in their pay, you'd get something on the grocery bill; if they only had ten dollars, they'd drink it. You'd get nothing. [laughs] This one owed $300, another $400 and another maybe $500. How are you going to get it? The place would go on strike, and you would be feeding them for three weeks, a month or two months. Never get it back. You'd have to do everything you could to make a dollar. We had a lot of people on credit. My poor mother. Everybody! She couldn't turn anybody down. Then, when the war broke out, things started to pick up. There was all kinds of money. People buying bonds.... Wages started jumping.... Then, one thing and another, and there was no money to give anybody a day's work. We are in a Depression here now.

DiVito Family Background

[Frank]: My father, Sam (Sabatino) DiVito, was also from Carpineto della Nora. It was a part of Italy that was very, very poor. Sometime around 1917, he came to Sydney Mines to better his way of life. Two of his brothers came here as well. Pappa started working in the old steel plant but, when the plant was moved to Sydney, he went to work in the mines. That's where everybody went. In his fair time, however, my father was also a shoemaker and a barber. I think he picked up his shoemaking trade in Boston and his barbering in Halifax. He was resourceful that way. [Uncle Louie]: They were all handy like that; my father used to fix our shoes. [Frank]: My mother, Philomena, is a Marinelli. She and my father were married in 1926.

A Trip to Italy and the War Years

[Frank]: My mother and aunt, my father's brother's wife, went on a trip to Italy in 1938. [Uncle Louie]: We were worried to death because there was talk of war. We didn't know if they were going to get back. [Frank]: I was only three years old. [Aunt Nora]: You, Carman and Theresa stayed with us down home, your younger sister Anna stayed with the Mancinis, while your father stayed in his own place. [Uncle Louie]: I know your father was some worried. They were in Italy four or five months. He used to come to our place, every evening, to have supper. I also know they were giving him a hard time at the pit. But, he stood up to them. He said: "if you want my job, you can have it; I don't have to put up with this." That was more or less why your father left the pit. Although, of course, he always wanted to live on a farm. [Frank]: My mother and aunt came back on the *Rex*, a ship the Germans torpedoed shortly after they returned. It was a passenger ship but, once the war started, I think it was used to transport troops. [Aunt Nora]: My brother, Tony, was in the Canadian army. He signed up right at the beginning of the war. He served in Italy driving a tank. Tony was lucky; he came home, nothing happened to him.

The Farm

[Frank]: My father worked in the mines for about twenty-three years. When Mussolini sided with Hitler, there were bad, bad feelings with everyone around here. If you were Italian, you were the "enemy." There was discrimination against Italians. In our case, it was basically verbal abuse. Even going to school, it was kind of a problem. People said things to me. That's the way it was. In school, they were blowing up U-boats. Anyway, my father decided to get out of the mine and buy a farm near Sydney. It was known as Barren Road at that time, and indeed it was barren. From the top of Campbell's Hill to the church in Coxheath, there were only five homes. There was no one living along our road for roughly four or five miles. It was difficult to get started. There was nothing but forest. My father worked hard to clear the land and to build our home. We also got a lot of help from relatives and friends, and our neighbour, Peter Mancini. They, of course, had their own jobs, but they helped whenever they had some spare time. We started in 1940, and it was 1942 before our home was finished. I was seven. I helped by going to the brook for water. I was the water boy.

[Uncle Louie]: I did a lot of work over there with your father. [Frank]: We cleared the area with a Pontiac car that was converted into a small tractor. [Uncle Louie]: Jack Strickland set up a sawmill nearby. To build the new house, your father sawed the trees we cut down into lumber. Yeah, a lot of people had a hand in building that place. Cut the trees down, and dig the stumps out. Then, at the end of it, I think he got some blasting for the bigger stumps. [Frank]: It took a long time to clear all of the property. We were still working on it long after the house was built. [Uncle Louie]: No bulldozer worked like that man worked. That's all your father lived for. Work! All the Italian people were like that when it came to work.

[Frank]: We left Sydney Mines December 8, 1942. In town, we were used to having everything. On the farm, there was no electricity, no running water, no bathroom (it was outdoors) and lots of snow. But, it didn't stop us from going to school.

The Fire. [Frank]: Two months after we moved in, on a Friday afternoon in February of 1943, we lost the barn. Fire! It was a very traumatic experience to see the building go up in flames, something you remember for a long time. I recall seeing smoke coming from one of the windows, and it didn't take long before smoke was coming from all the windows. It was a two-storey barn, and within an hour, it was all over. And, at that time, insurance was something that nobody had. I can recall that we had about 500 hens, and after the fire, we were left with seven. That's a figure I will always remember. There were five hens and two roosters. But, we continued to raise some eggs and then got some young hens to build up the stock. We also had two cows. They were taken to Harry O'Neil's farm, about a mile away. He would milk the cows, and myself and my brother would walk both ways to pick up a gallon of milk every evening. I was seven, and Carman was fourteen. That's how we got along for the next three or four months. We also got a lot of help from relatives and people we knew in Sydney Mines. It didn't take long for word to spread. With their help, we had the barn up that summer.

Work and Fun on the Farm

[Frank]: We cleared and planted a large area with various vegetables, and hay and oats for the animals. We always had cows, four to ten pigs, and around 1,500 chickens to look after. There were also ducks and the small bantam roosters. At haying season, we would get help from neighbours, friends and relatives from Sydney Mines. Mr. O'Neil would come and cut the hay with his single blade mower pulled by a horse. Everything else was done manually.

At first, we grew our own vegetables. Then, gradually, other Italians started coming to our place to buy fresh fruit, vegetables and poultry. We sold chickens to some of the restaurants in Sydney, and we would take home their leftovers to feed to our pigs. There were also many large gatherings at our place on Sundays and holidays. People would come from Sydney Mines, Glace Bay, Sydney ... to visit. The biggest thing I can remember, though, is the Christmas and New Year's parties. [Aunt Nora]: We were a close family, always together.

Making Cheese. [Frank]: My mother worked very hard on the farm. The local dairy used to buy our milk. We were alright during winter but, in the summer, when the cows produced an extra supply of milk, the dairy would put us on a quota. That's when Mamma made most of her cheese. She used to make it by putting a pot of milk on the stove and adding rennet. [Aunt Nora]: The rennet came from the dried stomach of a calf ... [Frank]: ... a new born calf usually killed within two or three weeks of birth. The stomach, still full of milk, was taken out and allowed to dry. It could take three or four months. My mother would take a small amount in powder form, dissolve it in warm water, and then add it to the milk. As the pot heated, she would stir the milk until it began to form a large ball of cheese. Once the cheese was taken out, my mother would add vinegar to the pot and start stirring again. This is how she made *ricotta*. And, after the cheese and ricotta were made, whatever liquid was left in the pot was saved for the pigs.

The Milk Jar Experience.

[Frank]: One evening in early May, while on our way home from Mr. O'Neil's farm, Carman and I found a stick on the old dirt road. We put it through the knob on the jar, and began walking– each of us holding one end of the stick. This made carrying the gallon much, much easier. We thought it was great. For a seven year old, a gallon of milk was quite heavy. As we crossed the highway, all of a sudden, the stick broke. The gallon hit the pavement and smashed. When we got home, my father got another jar and said: "Ok, walk back to Mr. O'Neil's and ask for another gallon of milk." Well, I think we started out that evening at about five o'clock, and it was after nine before our [laughs] evening's work was complete. So, it was a lesson well learned. It always reminds me of the "spilt milk." [laughs] Quite an experience.

My mother would also coat the cheese with wax to prevent it from becoming too hard and dry. This way, it could keep for many, many months. We used to store the cheese in baskets we purchased from the Native people (the Mi'kmaq). I recall many people coming to the farm to buy our cheese. At any given time, there would be a half-dozen pieces of cheese (weighing at least two or three pounds each) in our pantry. We made a lot of cheese.

Preserving Food. [Frank]: The pigs were butchered very late in November, so meat wouldn't spoil. We made sausages, prosciutto and bacon for ourselves and stored it in the attic where it was very cold. We had meat for the entire winter. For vegetables, we would just try to store them the best we could. Mamma did some preserving. [Aunt Nora]: Beets, chow, pickles.... [Frank]: We would start around the middle of August, and continue right into October. [Aunt Nora]: We used to bottle the tomatoes in quart-sized beer bottles. We had tomatoes for spaghetti sauce all winter. Take the tomatoes, pour boiling water over them to get the skin off, crush them, and then, with a big funnel, push them into the bottles. We used to buy the corks to seal them. And, of course, the bottles were sterilized before and after processing the tomatoes. [Frank]: We grew just about everything—beets ... all kinds of beans—and these would all be preserved.

Gardening, Yesterday and Today

[Frank]: I still have a small garden. I grow just a few vegetables for myself—potatoes and tomatoes, rhubarb ... zucchini ... and broad beans. It's only a small plot of land, but I have a little bit of everything. My brother Carman also has a garden. It is bigger than mine, although not as big as it used to be. [Aunt Nora]: He keeps me going with tomatoes, cucumbers and zucchini.

I have a flower garden now. I love planting my flowers. [Frank]: My mother was the same; she always enjoyed flowers. We had a beautiful rock garden in front of the house. I helped her a great deal. We went to George's River to get the rainbow rock. And, of course, people would come by, stop, and want to buy some flowers. [laughs] Very nice. You wonder though, Nora, where Mamma and the other women got all the time to do these things. [Aunt Nora]: Because they were up early in the morning, got their housework done and then spent the day in the garden. They worked like dogs; they had to do it. [Frank]: But how did they manage to get it all done? My mother found time to look after nine in our family. She was cooking meals all the time; there was no microwave, no refrigerator.... [Aunt Nora]: See, your mother worked hard, because she was with the older crowd. Now, myself, and my other two sisters, we didn't work as hard. We had our own difficulties. I raised and educated three children. But, things were getting easier for us in terms of work. We didn't work half as hard as the older people.

Nothing Wasted.

[Frank]: When we butchered the pigs, nothing was wasted. [Aunt Nora]: They used to make soap from the fat. [Frank]: To render it into soap, we would boil the fat... [Aunt Nora]: ...and add a little Gillettes Lye (a bleach-like disinfectant). The soap was then used to wash clothes and scrub the floors.

[Frank]: My father did not have a job outside of the farm. It was difficult to find work. Although, occasionally, he did get some work as a carpenter's helper or doing manual labour. We would have our good times, like Christmas or Easter when everybody wanted chickens and eggs, but there were difficult times as well. We survived, not by how much we could sell, but by providing for ourselves. Anything we could sell just added to the family income.

La Mamma: Italian Canadian Mothers of Cape Breton

By Margaret Dorazio-Migliore

The following story from Canada's west coast (although the location could just have easily been Cape Breton) gives some indication of the sentiments Italians attach to *la mamma:*

> It was May 10, 1996, at an "Over 50 Club" dance in Our Lady of Sorrows Church Hall. The next day would be Mother's Day, and now the band was playing, "Mamma," with a male singer wailing out the lyrics in Italian with gusto. The song was preceded by speeches about mothers, naming the "Mother of the Year" (and surprisingly, the "Couple of the Year!"). A middle-aged woman of Sicilian ancestry leaned across the table and asked Sam: "You ever hear of any songs about the father?" Then, before he had a chance to answer, she defiantly added: "Anybody can be a father, but a *mother!*"

This little anecdote illustrates two important points about the way in which "motherhood" is perceived: *la mamma* is always praiseworthy; and, she is perceived as *achieving* the status of *la mamma* (i.e., it doesn't just come automatically through giving birth).

As part of a study of Cape Breton mothers, beginning in 1993, I have interviewed several women of Italian and non-Italian ancestry who are middle-aged or older. Each woman has raised children on Cape Breton Island, encompassed by the island's warmth as well as its harshness. I have been interested in learning how mothers view themselves and their work.

In this chapter, I focus on a small sample of mothers of Italian ancestry. These are mothers whose Italian families came to North American shores bringing with them ideas about what it means to be *la mamma*, a good mother, and to work hard. Italians probably brought similar ideas and perceptions to each place in which they settled.

In addition, however, I'd like to stress that women engage in lots of *non-mothering* work that is *equally* laudable and which also requires hard work and special skills. This non-mothering work, which contributes greatly to families and the larger society, should also be given equal appreciation. In this chapter, therefore, I suggest that women's non-mothering work deserves more visibility.

I approach the topic from a particular positioning. Although there are important differences between myself and each of the women I interviewed, I am also a woman, mother, part-Italian, and I also share a commitment to hard work. I have experienced many of the same desires and dilemmas concerning work and home as have my subjects, and we thereby share certain feelings and thoughts, empathy and background knowledge.

Being the Good Mother

The Italian Canadian mothers I interviewed generally said they were proud of what they had accomplished in their lives. They said they had worked hard, made great sacrifices and did all they could for their children.

The lone professional woman I interviewed, Julia, was somewhat critical of herself because of the time she was able to spend with her child, but even Julia struggled to coordinate her mothering and her professional life to a great degree. Surprisingly, this included planning her pregnancy to coincide with a season when work demands were lowest!

This is what the women said in response to my direct or implicit question: "Do you think you were/are a good mother?"

> [Rita]: I think I was.... I certainly didn't want to do bad to them or show them bad things, and I tried to be honest with them and tell them right from wrong, you know? What's the right and the wrong, and yes, I certainly went out of my way to guide them that way. I never neglected them. I never left them alone. That is the way it was. Because I was brought up that way and this is the way I brought up my children.

> [Delia]: Well, okay, let's put it this way.... A good mother is me! I do love my kids! Y'know, and I'll do anything for them—which I did. My husband and I wanted to give them a good education, which we did, y'know, with good money and clean clothes, and I cooked and worried, but I devoted about twenty years all to them. I never went anywhere—especially several years ago—I didn't even know a babysitter.

[Maria]: I think I was a half-decent mother, you know? They always had everything they needed: their meals, and if they wanted to go anywhere, or if they wanted anything at the stores, they got it. I think love and attention are the number one things that you have to show your children—and showing that you care is the most important thing.

[Julia]: I was in a very privileged position in being able to juggle the two [family and work]. Even after Joe was weaned, and y'know, a little, little toddler, Frank and I were able to arrange our schedules so that we could take turns being at home with him.... And so in a sense, I guess I didn't have to give up one or the other in order to have some of both.... I was home less than I might have been, or should have been even, but I missed out less on work as well.

Home is Important, but not Everything

Women were obviously proud of their mothering, but also of their employment, vocations and careers. They stressed the joys and difficulties associated with non-mothering work, discussed their attempts to coordinate various jobs, and all the hard work they did. They described their non-mothering work as follows:

[Delia]: [In Italy] I had some neighbours who were dressmakers. Once I finished working with my father in the store (about 2 o'clock in the afternoon I was all done), then I would sneak over there. There were three girls, and I'd watch and help a little bit, and little by little I'd learn.

So I learned to be a dressmaker. Then when I was twenty-one, I came to this country, Canada.... And, then, when I lived here, I started to be a dressmaker right away.

When, you know, you come over here, you don't have anything. You got to do this harder other work to have your home, and if you want your car and the kids clothed. Especially when you can't speak a word of English. Especially the first couple of years. Whoa, it was really tough!

[Maria (who learned her husband's business and how to do the bookkeeping)]: At first I was really nervous because I didn't know if I was doing it right ... then it got easier and easier as time went by, and to this day, I'm still doing it, twenty-five years later. And I mean now it's nothing.... It worked out well, and it was good because at the same time I was doing the books at home, I could stay home with the children. I was there when they left for school, and I was there when they got back.

[Julia]: Most girls didn't become professionals and didn't spend as much time building their careers before they started a family. More often than not, they went a certain distance and had families, and then went back to their careers. I was rather late in getting started with family things—and that meant that I couldn't abandon those [career] things as easily.

The loss of the domestic role and the loss in career progress, there were losses in both. Ah, but I had to give up neither one, and I could minimize those losses, and in a way that women in other jobs would never have been able to do.

Although I don't have a quotation from Rita, I also want to make visible some of the non-mothering work she (like multitudes of other women) performed: taking care of her elderly parents, especially her mother who lived into her nineties. It is no less important than paid employment outside the home. It is arduous work, the more so because, like mothering itself, it requires huge expenditures of emotion and physical labour, it is generally invisible and is unpaid.

Conclusions

My research left me with an overall impression of these Cape Breton mothers of Italian ancestry as being highly devoted to "mothering." *La mamma* is an important identification for them, and mothering is talked about very positively. Mothering seems to have brought them, and continues to bring them, rewards in terms of status, love and fulfillment. Stories about mothering emphasize devotion, sacrifice and hard work.

In addition, however, the women remembered other work which falls outside of mothering proper: Delia's specialized seamstress work; Maria's office and book-keeping know-how; Julia's professional career; and last, but not least, Rita's elder-care. These work experiences are accomplishments and achievements. This is also work, like mothering, in which they found pleasure and pain, and which inevitably helped forge their current identities. It is work, like mothering, which contributes to both personal and social well-being.

Whenever I hear the term, *la mamma*, now, I think not only of all the billions of small and large domestic "labours of love" Italian Canadian mothers engage in, but also all of the heavy, skilled and intellectual non-mothering work *le mamme* perform. No wonder people sing the praises of *la mamma*, she does it all!

The Call of the Sea:
Italian Women in the Fisheries

Edited by Sam Migliore

Rose (Sollazzo) DeLorenzo and Lynn (Giovannetti) Billard have had distinct life experiences. What they share, however, is a profound love for the sea. Both women have participated successfully in an industry traditionally dominated by men. Rose was the first "woman on Cape Breton Island to possess a Master's Certificate in seamanship."[1] During the 1960s, she and her husband, Benny, took tourists on sports fishing expeditions on both the local coastal waters and the Bras d'Or Lake. Lynn is currently a social worker with the Children's Aid Society. Prior to obtaining a degree in social work, however, she spent nine years lobster fishing with her husband, Terry.

Rose DeLorenzo

My grandfather, Francesco Sollazzo, immigrated from Reggio Calabria, Italy to Boston. The company he worked for [in Boston] had a contract for part of the construction of the steel plant in Sydney, so they sent him here to work. He was instrumental in laying all the pipelines for the Sydney Steel Plant. And, I understand, he laid the majority of pipelines in Glace Bay in the mid-1920s. He couldn't write his name, but his initials, F. S., were on all the blueprints.

There were three children in my father's family—my father (Dominic), and his brothers Joseph (Peppi) and Tony Sollazzo. Their mother died when my father was four years old, and my grandfather married again to a non-Italian. My grandfather also had a sister (Rose). She married Joe DiSano here in Whitney Pier. That was the first marriage performed in Holy Redeemer Church. My parents, Dominic and Rose Louise (LeDue) Sollazzo were married on May 12, 1934. I was one of five children. Benny and I were married on October 23, 1953; we have six children and eight grandchildren.

I've been working since I was nineteen, and I retired last year (1996). By chance, because I lived upstairs, the lady who owned the Sydney Ship Supply Company asked me to help out with some office work. She gave me an old typewriter and a book, *Learn to Type*. I worked there for more than twenty years. They wanted me to take over the company when they retired. I knew what made it operate. You were working twenty-four hours a day. If a ship came in at 10 o'clock in the morning and left at midnight, you had to supply them with whatever they wanted. You had to be at their disposal. At that time, we had six kids. The owners, Newman and Esther Dubinsky, were very good to me; I worked very hard, and then I moved on from there. It really would have been too much to take on at that time.

I went to H. B. Nickersons, the big fish plant in North Sydney. I was traffic supervisor for ships moving in and out. When the company was sold to National Sea, I was offered a job with them in Halifax, but that wasn't feasible for me. [I worked at a couple of other jobs,] and then, the last eight years or so, I was in accounts receivable with Highland Fisheries, a division of Clearwater Fine Foods (Glace Bay). Thirty-seven years I worked.

Sports Fishing

In the early 1960s, Ben and I, having been boating enthusiasts for a long time, [contacted] the tourism branch here in Sydney. They were trying to encourage tourists to come here, and there was a need for people, for boats, to take these tourists sports fishing. We decided that we would like to do that. We bought a forty-two foot Cape Island boat, the typical fishing boat down in this area, and we both took a course in seamanship. We got our Master's Certificates, and we started the Sydney Boat Charter to take people deep-sea fishing. We did that for about four to five years. It was successful, but we were both working, and then there were the kids, we were building a house, and that's when we decided we couldn't do it anymore. But, it was an exciting time.

[Sam: Do you have any special memories?] Well, the special memories would be the enjoyment that we got out of doing it, and seeing the people we went out with contented when they came back with a load of fish. We were out in some rough weather, and had to scoot back, but nothing that really bothered us. At the time, I think I was the only [woman] in the Atlantic Provinces that had a master's licence. It encouraged other women to get into sports fishing. It was quite nice. I was written up in the paper and interviewed by the late Ann Terry on CJCB Radio. A lot of

Dominic and Louise Sollazzo, May 12, 1934. Courtesy of Rose DeLorenzo. Photo by The Kelly Studio.

people referred to me as "Captain Rosie." [laughs] [Sam: Did you have any problems?] Most people coming aboard were surprised, but it didn't seem to bother them that it was a woman. As long as they got out and caught some fish, that was the important thing to most of them. But, we had some pleasant, very pleasant times with people from away places.

[Sam: And, all that time, you still had your other job?] Yes, I still worked, yeah. [Sam: What was it like trying to manage between the two?] It wasn't easy. Having five children at the time, it was difficult. When I started to work, I think it was in 1959, there weren't a lot of women in the workforce. My boss, Newman Dubinsky, used to tell me that I was the first of the "women lib'ers." [laughs] Well, you did it out of necessity too. At that time, Benny was working at the steel plant; wages at the plant weren't that great. My income was a supplement for us. It was from there that we started to build our house.

Charting the waters off Cape Breton Island. Rose (right) and Benny (centre) DeLorenzo. Courtesy of DeLorenzo family.

Lynn Billard

Lynn Billard is the great-granddaughter of Lorenzo Giovannetti, one of the first Italians to settle in Cape Breton. She grew up and has lived much of her life in Port Morien. Her family has had a long-standing relationship with the sea.

I have three older sisters, three younger sisters and four older brothers. When my oldest sister, Sherry, started at St. Joseph's School of Nursing in Glace Bay, I was in grade primary. Glace Bay was like going to Halifax, I suppose, so she stayed there. I never knew her at all. And, my older brothers were gone [from home]. It was like two families for us.

In high school I took the secretarial program. I did that for a short time and then married my husband who is a lobster fisherman. I decided to go lobster fishing with him. We fished together for nine years. It was quite interesting; the two of us fished alone in the boat for all those years. By 1990, things were starting to go down hill with the fisheries. So, one day, I said to Terry: "boy, what are we going to do; if we are both depending on this industry, if it's gone, we are both going to be out of work. Somebody is going to have to go to school." He said, "I can't do it." He went fishing with his father after grade eleven. So that's when I went back to school full-time at UCCB (now Cape Breton University). We have three children. I timed it so that my youngest was starting grade primary. I took five courses, a full load. Looking back, I must have been nuts. [laughs] But, anyway, I went into the Bachelor of Arts in Community Studies program. I came first in my class the first year, and I graduated with the Governor General's Medal. So I did really well in university, and I loved it. I had been worried because I didn't take academic in high school, and I had been out of school for fourteen years. But, I did well, and then I applied to a master's degree program. I went to Ottawa for a year-and-a-half. My husband stayed here with the kids, [laughs] and I lived with my oldest sister. I got to know her for the first time in my life, and I realized what I was missing all those years. They were really supportive of me. They were about fifty kilometres outside of Ottawa, and I travelled back and forth every day.

The education was wonderful. I enjoyed it; for me, it was a relatively stress-free time in my life. I just loved it. And, my sister enjoyed having me there. I don't know what was better, getting to know her or the educa-tion, but they both worked out well for me. It was a two-year program, but I finished it in a year-and-a-half. I wanted to finish as quickly as I could. I went up in the Fall of 1993, and I did the course work for a year. My thesis proposal was accepted by the committee; so when I came back here in the summer, I did one of my work terms and all of my interviews for the thesis. I did it on women in the fishery, displaced workers. I went back to Ottawa in September, transcribed the interviews, wrote my thesis and actually worked full-time at another placement while I was there. I finished by Christmas and came home.

Lynn Billard. Graduation photo from Carleton University, Ottawa, January, 1995. Courtesy of Lynn Billard.

[Sam: What was your degree in?] I did a Master's of Social Work at Carleton University.... I looked at the structural implications of occupational displacement and retraining of women in the fishery.[2] I'm working at Children's Aid now, as a child protection worker. So, it paid off, and just in time, because this past year has been a really bad season for my husband. Things have been economically and financially bad, but I have a decent job.

[Sam: Do you have any stories ... about working in the fisheries?] Actually, my mother's father and all the older brothers were fishermen. Glace Bay was a mining town, and Port Morien is certainly a fishing town. It is quite common that women fish now; but, when I started, I was the only woman who fished aboard a boat. I guess I was the one who started all of this. My mother-in-law started fishing with my father-in-law the year afterwards, and she still fishes. She is sixty-six. Well, anyway, the older fishermen said it was bad luck for a woman to be in the boat, eh.

So people would kind of ignore me, wouldn't even let on that I was there. I think that after a while they gained at least some respect for me because Terry and I were fishing alone in the boat. I was the only help he had. We'd be fishing alongside these boats with three or four men in them, you know, and they'd say, "what are they doing?" And we would be in at ten, eleven o'clock after hauling 275 traps. They were doing the same amount of traps, but they would be in at supper time. I always thought that was weird. It was difficult I think because that was such a male environment to be in, for sure. But, they were some of the best, most prosperous years that we had in the fishery.

I was never sea sick. All those years, it would be mind over matter. I just kept busy. We didn't even stop to eat lunch. We'd be steaming up the other end and eating a sandwich. We worked eight, nine hours straight, get up at three in the morning, and then have three kids to look after. We used to bake bread for the sandwiches, and we would be up 'til ten o'clock at night trying to get the bread made. Get to bed, and get up in the morning. But, the good side of it was that I was home for the kids for the rest of the year. It was two months work, and then I was home, which was really nice. I'd like to be doing it still, to be honest with you. If I could afford to do it, I would. I enjoyed it.

I would like to think that I helped to make some changes. Traditionally, fishermen were really bad about throwing things over. They would cut the boxes and they would go over, everything would go over. Plastic. I refused to do that; my husband didn't like it at first, but I would take a garbage bag, fill it up, and take it up out of the boat at the end of the day. Terry continued to do that after I left, and other people started to do it.

We used to have some traps right in the cove down there and, one day, there was talk of some really bad weather. Terry said: "we'd better pick up those traps, or we're going to lose them." So, he and I, and his mother and father, the four of us went out to get those traps. And, of course, it was pretty bad at that point; even the waves were pretty high, and with the breakers and the swell, it was one of the hairiest times I've been aboard a boat. We got side waves, and they were just coming right over into the boat. Terry had a trap up when the wave hit, and it was gone. There was nothing there. His mother was terrified that someone was going to go over, but, I mean, I had faith in them, if anybody could get us out of there, they could. I was on the floor on the back, coiling the ropes as they were coming in, and the wave hit me. It just flattened me out on the deck, and the traps were destroyed. But, it was exciting. [laughs] It was hard work, physical work; you would come home every night and you would feel exhausted. I could hit the pillow, and I couldn't count to five minutes, I would be gone. With the work I do now, you don't come home every night and feel that way. You dream it; you can't get it out of your mind.

I always thought of my grandfather, my mother's father, because we were very close to him growing up. I could imagine him sitting on a crate, down by the wharf. When I first started, I would be by the boat trying to keep warm, sitting on a crate with all my gear on, and I'd think: "God, if he knew," he died in 1973, "if he could see me now, he'd think it would be terrible having a woman aboard the boat." You can imagine, eh. Now they will probably blame the catastrophe in the fishery on me, I'm sure. But, I loved it. [pause] It's hard to explain. Sometimes you'd say "the best part of the day is before seven o'clock in the morning," and most people aren't up; they have missed the best part of the day. I just loved it. Now, I have a hard time getting up at seven o'clock in the morning. [laughs] I've done some interesting things with my life too.

The Mancini Family of St. Peter's

Edited by Sam Migliore

Talacano, a small community in central Italy, is a long way from Cape Breton. This town, however, has made an important contribution to the business, political and social life of the island. Sometime in the early part of this century, Dominic Mancini left Talacano and made his way to Cape Breton, eventually settling in North Sydney. Within a short period of time, he became the catalyst behind the process of chain-migration that brought a number of family members to the area—including nephew Joe "Pop" Mancini. Joe joined Dominic in North Sydney, established himself there, and then moved his family to St. Peter's. In St. Peter's, he began a new business career as the proud owner of the Cosy Corner Restaurant. Success with the restaurant allowed Joe to sponsor his brothers (Zelindo and Elio), his father (Carlo) and other family members in their efforts to immigrate to Canada. This article is based on two interviews. One in North Sydney with Tula Gouthro (Joe's daughter), and the other in St. Peter's with Elio and Evelina Mancini, Gemma Mancini (Zelindo's wife), Carlo Mancini (Joe's son), Viola Sampson (Joe's daughter) and Colin MacDougall (Joe's grandson).

Family Background

[Tula]: My father's name was Joseph Sisto Mancini, and he was married to Mary Catherine (Cassie) MacNeil from Iona. Dad came to Canada when he was about eighteen years old. He was the son of Carlo and Theresa (Petrocchi) Mancini, and he had three brothers—Tony, Zelindo and Elio—[who also came to Canada]. Dad's uncles were Dominic and Peter Mancini. My mother's family were the MacNeils from Red Point, MacKinnon's Harbour.

[Gemma]: The Mancini family comes from Talacano, province of Ascoli-Piceno, in the region called the Marche. It is not very far from Rome. [Elio]: My uncle

Dominic was the first to come to Canada. He came here to work when he was very young. Later, he called over his brother, Peter, and then my brothers Tony and Joe. [Tula]: At the time, they were very poor in that part of Italy. So my grandfather asked Dominic to bring his sons to Canada. [Elio]: Tony was thirteen years old when he [arrived]. He came first, then Joe. [Viola]: Dad came to Canada in 1927.

[Tula]: When dad arrived from Italy, he lived with uncle Dominic in North Sydney, and worked for him at the Havelock Home Bottling Company. Dad and mom got married in 1931. We lived on Brooks Street in North Sydney, and my sister, Bette, and I went to school at St. Joseph's. We all moved to St. Peter's when dad bought the Cosy Corner Restaurant in 1942.

Mancini family. Top, from left: Elio, Tony, Zelindo, and Joseph Mancini. Seated, from left: Dominic V. Mancini, Maria Adoranti, Carlo, Lena, and Peter Mancini. Courtesy of Tula (Mancini) Gouthro.

From North Sydney to St. Peter's

[Tula]: Dominic Mancini and John Coady started Havelock. The company bottled and distributed "pop." [Viola]: While working for them, my father distributed the pop throughout Cape Breton Island. He used to come through Inverness with a truckload of pop, then up to Port Hood, and along old highway No. 4 through Port Hawkesbury and Cleveland. [Tula]: Dad was well known in Cape Breton because he made deliveries to all the little stores along the way. They called him Joe "Pop" because he delivered the pop. [laughs] I remember liking Coca-Cola, but I wasn't allowed to drink it. We had to drink 7-Up or Orange Crush. Dad worked for Havelock, and those were the brands the company distributed at that time.

[Viola]: The story is that dad loved the horse races. [Tula]: A group of them went to the races in Truro and on the way back stopped at a small restaurant in St. Peter's. [Viola]: A Mrs. Dugon operated the Tea Room, and she mentioned that she would like to sell it. [Tula]: This is a true story. She wanted $500, and dad had just won $500 at the races. So, he bought the restaurant. [Viola]: He went back to North Sydney and told my mother we were moving to St. Peter's. That was in 1942. [Tula]: Dad started with a small convenience store and gradually made it into a dining room. He borrowed $10,000 and enlarged it into the Cosy Corner Restaurant. The restaurant did so well that he was able to pay off the loan in a year-and-a-half. [Viola]: Dad operated the restaurant from 1942 to 1970, twenty-eight years before he retired.

**Dominic Mancini
of North Sydney
Edited by A. Evo DiPierro
and Sam Migliore**

In 1997, Peter Mancini won the riding of Sydney-Victoria for the New Democratic Party to become the first person of Italian descent elected as a Member of Parliament from Cape Breton. He shares here some information about his grandfather, Dominic Mancini.

My grandfather came to Cape Breton in 1904, at the age of fifteen. He was married twice: first to Ellen Bonini, who died around 1919, and then to Mary Ann Gouthro of Bras d'Or. My grandfather was the owner of the Havelock Home Bottling Company, and he was also the Italian Consul for Cape Breton Island sometime before the Second World War. From his twenties until death, in 1980, he lived in Centreville, North Sydney, and raised his family there.

From both marriages, my grandfather had many children; eight or nine of them survived into adulthood. My father was born in Centreville in 1917. My parents [Dominic Benito Mancini and Isabel (Morrison) Mancini] eventually moved to Westmount, where my sisters (Vivian and Benita) and I were born.

Regarding my ethnicity, I have to say that my grandfather had the greatest influence on my life in terms of what it meant to be Italian. His home was the focal point for holy days and other occasions for which we all gathered. He was the keeper of the Italian culture, in terms of food, language and customs. Some of that spilled into my own home.

[Tula]: So that's how dad got started. He was just driving the pop truck for his uncle when he met my Mom in Iona. They eventually married, and we all came from that union. I have one brother (Carlo) and three sisters (Bette MacDougall, Viola Sampson, and Claire Richard).[1] It was different growing up with an Italian dad and a Scottish mom, but it was fun. They were a loving family, the best of parents. For such different cultures, they really got along well.

After high school, I came to North Sydney for training at St. Elizabeth's Hospital. That's where I met my husband. We married, and I stayed here. My parents started in North Sydney, but I ended up being the one to come back here to live.

Chain-Migration and Prosperity in St. Peter's

[Sam]: Were there many Italians in St. Peter's when you were growing up? [Tula]: No! It was mostly Mancinis. Dad brought over his brothers, Zelindo and Elio, and then they brought over their wives and other family members. [Elio]: Zelindo came to Canada in February of 1949, and I came in July of the same year. I remember that Carlo (Joe's son) was born just three days after I arrived here. [Carlo]: I was born July 21, 1949. [Gemma]: Elio was supposed to come here with Zelindo, but his older brother died so he stayed in Italy for a few months to help his father. [Elio]: My father came here in September or October of 1949.

Zelindo and Gemma Mancini

[Gemma]: My husband, Zelindo, settled here and worked for his brother Joe. Later, he operated his own business—a taxi service. [Tula]: Zelindo drove taxi for a number of years and then drove a school bus. [Gemma]: He started by driving the children to school in his own car and then bought a bus. He used to drive both the bus and the taxi. Even after the county bought the buses, Zelindo continued to drive the bus for them. We also owned a retail store from 1962 to 1973. So, for a while, we had the store, students renting the upstairs, the taxi and the bus. Zelindo retired after we sold the store, and he passed away in 1990.

I came to Canada in 1958. Zelindo and I were married here in St. Peter's, and we have three children. The youngest finished college in Sydney and is looking for a job. The other two work in Halifax. My son works at Oland's Brewery and has two children. My daughter is a nurse, and she has two sons. That's my life. [laughs]

Elio and Evelina Mancini

[Sam]: Can you tell me something about your life? [Elio]: My life. I could start with the war. In 1939, I was stationed in Albania. We were in the mountains, six feet of snow, and we stayed all winter. People were freezing every day. Then, in 1943, the Italian forces started fighting with the Greek army. We kept moving back and forth, all winter. We suffered too much. When the alliance between Italy and Germany broke down, I was taken prisoner by the Germans and brought to Yugoslavia. After the Russians had taken over in December of 1945, I was taken to Russia. I was sick all the time.... I spent seven months in a Russian hospital. When I got back to Italy, I was still sick. I can't stand the cold; I have asthma and chronic bronchitis.

I worked twenty years at the Cosy Corner Restaurant for my brother Joe. [Evelina]: I came to Canada in 1950. [Elio]: We worked hard. Elio, Evelina and Gemma did the cooking for the restaurant. [Tula]: They made good pasta and Italian dishes, but they also learned to make a lot of Cape Breton dishes. They provided home cooked meals and a really good place to eat. A lot of people from Sydney went there every Sunday for dinner. [Gemma]: We used to make fifty-sixty pies a week. [Evelina]: At that time, the restaurant was so busy! [Elio]: During the first ten years, before the construction of the Trans-Canada Highway, everyone passed through here. There were also thousands of people working at Sterling Mines and the plant. The Cosy Corner was full. In the morning, I used to make a hundred breakfasts. People had to wait. [Evelina]: All the buses went by here. Acadia Lines had so many buses going through in the summertime. [Elio]: There were fifteen-sixteen buses every day. Now, only two buses pass by here. [Evelina]: In the summers, we would just finish cleaning up, and two buses would arrive, and then two more buses....

[Elio]: I worked very hard and, after twenty years, in 1969, I bought the Richmond Motel and started working for myself. [Viola]: It was located in False Bay, just on the outskirts of River Bourgeois. [Elio]: Burl Ives and his wife came to the motel for an Easter Sunday meal. [Evelina]: We passed him the menu, and he said: "Oh no, what do you eat? Whatever you eat, we will eat." We had lasagna, roast pig, pie.... [Elio]: Italian minestrone. [Evelina]: He was so nice a person. Tony, my son, was so young; Burl Ives put him on his lap and sang for him. When they were leaving, he came back two times to say good-bye. He gave me a hug and said, "I never thought I would find such good food here." [Elio]: He said the Richmond Motel was the best place to eat. It was on the radio and in both the Sydney and the Halifax papers.

[Evelina]: We had a lot of people at the motel—John Allen Cameron, Tommy Hunter, all kinds of musicians. [Elio]: I remember Johnny Cash had a show in North Sydney, and they came here to eat. [Viola]: He ate eighteen fried eggs, and another man ate twenty-four. Someone else that was in the restaurant here one day was Satchmo, Louis Armstrong. [Evelina]: We had a wonderful time there. We received letters from everywhere, people saying they would never forget us. They said that it didn't seem like a motel. It felt more like a home, a big family. The motel was not fancy, but it had a brook running along the side. It was pretty, made of logs. Our motel was listed in [Anne Hardy's] *Where to Eat in Canada*.

[Tula]: Elio is a beautiful cook and so is Evelina. They make their own pasta, and she can cook beautiful lemon pies too. One of her pies made it to London, England. The *Scotia Sun* reported on this event in April of 1979. It stated:

> during the March break, one of [Evelina's] 4-inch thick pies travelled Air Canada to England. A former Isle Madame teacher studying in that country was being visited by friends from Richmond County who wanted to bring him a gift that would bring back memories of home, and what could be better than his favourite dessert? The pie withstood the plane trip like a trooper ... but it did cause a lot of comments from customs officials and fellow travellers who kept demanding when they could sample the delicacy.[2]

[Elio]: We bought the motel in 1969, and it burned down in 1979. We had good customers. Everybody talked about the motel, and how we made such good meals. My wife made dinner two times for the Governor General and his family.

Carlo Mancini, Senior

[Tula]: My grandfather came to Canada when he was eighty-two years old. He couldn't speak a word of English, and my mother couldn't speak a word of Italian, but they understood each other. He was a really nice man. [Evelina]: He was a wonderful person. Everybody in St. Peter's called him Nonno (grandpa); they must have thought it was his name.

[Tula]: I remember that my grandfather got some kind of medal from the British Embassy for helping soldiers escape from behind enemy lines. [Gemma]: Nonno would hide them overnight and then help them escape. My father also helped a lot of people. But, if the Germans had found out, we would be dead. In 1950, the *Post-Record*[3] reported on the citations Carlo Mancini received for his wartime activities:

> During the recent war, he played a vital part in the underground movement, and despite his years and the danger of having his home raided many times by the enemy, he was instrumental in hiding many Allied servicemen, and with the aid of his son, eventually guiding them to the safety of Allied zone.... For outstanding service ... Mr. Mancini has been awarded two certificates, one from the Allied Screening Commission, and the other quoted below which was signed by the present Governor General, Field Marshal Alexander: "This certificate is awarded to Carlo Mancini as a token of gratitude for and appreciation of the help given

to the sailors, soldiers and airmen of the British Commonwealth of Nations...."[4]

[Viola]: One time Nonno got lost in the woods while hunting deer. Dad stopped the car by a marshy area near Glendale. He told Nonno to stay in the car, while he and the others went looking for deer. When they came back, Nonno was gone. I'll never forget that night. It rained and rained. They hollered, and they fired shots, but they couldn't find him. A search was organized. [Elio]: The police, a doctor and about thirty people went looking for him. I went too! My father was in the field. He had a gun, and he had killed a deer. [laughs] [Viola]: He stayed right where he was. It was really rainy, but it wasn't cold. As soon as we found him, they gave him a shot of rum and took him home. [Gemma]: When Cassie took off his boots, they were full of water. But, the next day, he said: "I feel better than before." [Elio]: He was ninety years old, and he had eight more years of life after that.

[Tula]: He was a very religious man. He was always saying the rosary. [Viola]: He went to Mass every morning. [Elio]: Then, after church, he would go to the Cosy Corner and read the paper. At dinner time, he would come into the kitchen, and I would make him something to eat. After dinner, he would play golf. Three months before he died, we played golf together; my father won two games, and I won one. [laughs] Three months before he died! (October 9, 1967)

[Gemma]: He never complained. The day he died, I helped put him to bed. There was a big tear in one of his eyes. I used to hear the older people say, "when you see a big tear like that, the person is going to die." Then I heard him say: "Look Theresa (his wife), I am coming to see you." Nonno just finished saying those words, and he died.

The process of chain-migration did not stop with the arrival Zelindo, Gemma, Elio, Evelina and Carlo Mancini. In time, the Mancinis helped other family members, including members of both Gemma's and Evelina's families, immigrate to Canada.

The Joe "Pop" Mancini (1909-1992) Legacy

[Viola]: It was a culture shock to the Scottish village [when we arrived here in St. Peter's]. [laughs] This was a heavy United Church area, and then my father became active as the chairman of the School Board. He tried to get the [Roman Catholic] nuns in here to teach in the school system. There were problems like that, but they all worked out. W. D. Morrison ran the general store. He and dad were of different politics and different religions, but they were really close businessmen. They worked together for the betterment of the community.

[Tula, reading from her father's "death notice"]: Dad was "a councillor in District 8 in St. Peter's from 1961 to 1979. His involvements and positions included: chairman of St. Peter's Village Commission; vice-president and campaign manager of the

Red Cross Society for Inverness and Richmond counties (1974-1975); Richmond County school board member...." It's all here in the obituary. He was instrumental in the construction of the Richmond Villa, a member of the Knights of Columbus and very active in both the church and the community.

[Colin]: Grandpa was responsible for putting the sewer and water in town. He really set a precedent by going door to door in the early 1960s to sell water bonds. It hadn't been done before. I'm a commissioner here in the village now, and the last bond we paid out was my grandfather's. It came out to about $22,000 for, I believe, a $10,000 bond. He invested a lot of his own money into the village for the betterment of us all.

Grandpa was heavy into politics. One story was about the time he went to Halifax to collect $10,000 they had promised him, probably for the Richmond Villa. [Viola]: There is a seventy-five-bed nursing home here that employs eighty-five people. When dad was councillor, he lobbied hard to get this facility. [Colin]: When he opened the cheque, it was for $5,000. Grandpa ripped it up, and said: "No, it's for $10,000." [Viola]: Dad was a noted Liberal all his life, and he supported the party. When the Liberals were in power, he would go to Halifax and say: "Look, we need this for St. Peter's." He would sit there until he got what he was there for. Can't do that today! I don't think he missed a federal convention from 1940 to the late 1960s, and he always went to the leaderships in Halifax. [Colin]: At the end, he was an honourary member, an honourary delegate.

As family members discussed Joe's political days, they also recalled a humorous twist of fate. [Colin]: Grandpa was quite the politician; you had to get up pretty early to pull one over on him. One day, he had his Cadillac in the garage, probably getting it all shined up because Allan J. [MacEachen (a prominent Federal Liberal)] was in town. Now, one of the guys at the garage was Frankie Mombourquette, a big Tory. Frankie knew Grandpa would just go to the driver's door and drive off. So, they stuck Tory stickers all along the passenger's side of the car. Here was Grandpa driving through town with a big smile on and all these Tory stickers on his car.

Reviving the Legacy

[Colin]: I moved home from Ontario in 1989; I had worked there for ten years as a professional photographer. In St. Peter's, I ran the local Stubbert's convenience store. A few years later, I bought the store. Grandpa died in May of 1992, and I bought the store in December. [Grandpa's death] was still fresh in our memory. So, I called it Joe Pops General Store. A lot of people thought I was crazy at the time, but I came up with a nice logo design and gave it a good image. Raymond Landry thought it was such an honour that I named the store after Grandpa. [Viola]: He and dad were in the grocery business; Raymond had a small store on the outskirts of Grand Greve. [Colin]: Mr. Landry brought me an unopened bottle of Havelock pop as a present.

The store is a salute to Grandpa, and what he has done for our community. We still look to him for inspiration; he inspires us all the time. We are not going to let him be forgotten. My sister Fonda and her husband, Parker [Stone], bought and renovated the restaurant. [After some twenty years,] they brought the Cosy Corner back into the family.[5] It's called Parker's Restaurant. They have a lot of pictures up of what it used to look like. It's nice to have it back in the family again. It means so much.

My grandfather left us quite a legacy. I would do anything to keep it alive. There is a bursary in Joe and Cassie's name [to help kids go to university]. I run a hockey tournament every year to keep the bursary going. We call it the "Joe Pops Cup." [Elio]: Joe was very good for St. Peter's. [Tula]: They never had a mayor in St. Peter's, but people used to call dad the mayor. He was always trying to get something for the town.

Memories of Papa Jimmy: The Tubetti Family of Inverness

Edited by Sam Migliore

The western shores of Cape Breton are not noted as a centre of Italian immigration and settlement. The Tubetti family, however, was able to carve a special place for itself in Inverness thanks to the efforts of Papa Jimmy (Giacomo Tubetti, 1893-1957). Presented here are some of the memories and experiences of three of Papa Jimmy's grandchildren—Maureen Cameron; Daryl MacDonald; and, Frances Penney.[1]

Too Young to be a Grandfather

[Maureen]: Papa Jimmy. I used to ask my mother why we had to call him Papa. I said: "he's a grandpa." "Oh," she says: "don't ever call him grandpa; he doesn't like that word. He said it's got to be Papa 'cause he's too young to be a grandpa." That was why it was always Papa Jimmy and Grandma Neese. We never said Denise; it was always Grandma Neese. Yeah, and then with Daddy's people it was Grandma Donald and Grandpa Donald. They were MacDonalds.

Grease Monkeys, Movies and Ice Cream

Giacomo Tubetti was known as a shrewd and energetic businessman. During his lifetime, he operated a gas station and garage, the Victoria Theatre and an ice cream parlour. These business ventures were the source of many fond memories for Giacomo's grandchildren.

The Garage. [Daryl]: A high point for me was sneaking down to the garage and asking Papa Jimmy, "Can I get into the grease?" He would walk over with me, and we would get into the grease they used to lubricate the cars. I would get some on my hand, work it around. I just loved the feel of it, but my mother was always afraid I was going to turn out to be a grease monkey. She didn't want that for me. [pause] After Papa Jimmy died, I kept really interested in mechanics. Uncle George [Tubetti] was really good when he ran the garage. He would let me pump gas in the summer. I'd meet lots of tourists. In fact, Lorne Greene. I shook his hand one time.

The Victoria Theatre. [Maureen]: Papa Jimmy rented a hall to show penny movies. They'd only cost one or two cents to see. He'd have a little projector and someone to play piano. They had silent movies, eh. Then, during the war, Papa Jimmy built the theatre; but, there was not enough money at the time to complete it. So he used to have dances and bingo, that's how he got going. Then he got enough equipment, and he started up the theatre. It took him awhile, but he always got his cut. Whatever plans he had, they came true.

Tubetti and Mancini family members in front of a Havelock Home Bottling Co. truck. Joe "Pop" Mancini front row, first from left, followed by Giacomo Tubetti. Dominic Mancini front row, fifth from left. Courtesy of Mancini family.

John Dan MacDonald used to help Papa Jimmy around the property, and he operated the projection room. My brother Ron and I were always together. We would watch John Dan thread the machine. If the two of us were homesick, we would be at the old throttle machine, sewing machine eh, and we'd be pretending we were operating the theatre. We'd have thread just in and out everywhere, and of course, we'd connect it to the table and chairs too. Mom would come in and say, "What's going on? I'm going to break my neck." "No, no, just don't go in that direction," I'd say, "because we're operating a movie theatre." We used to have lots and lots of fun.

After Papa Jimmy died, it was left to my mother and Uncle George. We'd go down there at Christmas time to clean up and decorate. Ron and I were the older ones, George's family was young at that time, so it was our place to help. Then, of course, there was a big stage there, and they used to have western singers come in sometimes. After the shows, we'd pretend. I'd have the mop or a broom, from sweeping up on the stage, and I'd have Mario Lanza singing while I bellowed a blue streak. Oh yeah, I thought this was great, there was nobody watching me anyways, so I was having a ball. Yeah, lots of good times down there.

[Daryl]: Oh yes. I just loved to be up in the projection room. There were times I'd ask Uncle George, on a Sunday afternoon when there'd be nothing going on,

"wouldn't mind if I went over and ran the show?" [laughs] "No, go ahead," he'd say. Might be two of my friends down in the theatre watching, and I would be upstairs running the show. [laughter]

[Frances]: Every one of us worked there. We sold the tickets. I mean, you thought you were in heaven. You had a show to go to. We had two different features: one on Friday and Saturday and then a Sunday afternoon matinee. We were always there. It was the thing to do in Inverness. And, once the theatre closed down, it was like there was nothing to do. We had a theatre in Inverness! There was no theatre in Mabou, none in Margaree and I don't even know if there was one in Port Hawkesbury. You had to go quite a distance to go to the theatre, but we had one. Oh, yeah, many fond memories of the theatre ... yeah.... Actually, one of the little theatres here in the Empire Eight [in Sydney] is named the Victoria Theatre. Each theatre is dedicated and named after one of the original theatres from Cape Breton.

Maureen Cameron and family (husband John, daughter Italia—named after Maureen's mother—and son Cailean) live in New Westminster, British Columbia. Maureen and John have lived in British Columbia for about twenty-six years.

[Maureen]: I like it up here, but my heart's still down there. It's a long time since we've been down, ten years. [Italia]: Cape Breton is always down home. Even though I was born here, that's down home. Yeah, Gramma's house. [Sam]: You've seen a lot of changes in Inverness over the years? [Maureen]: Oh yeah. Every time I go home, there's something new. It's going to be different when we go down this time too. [Italia]: No more show hall. [Maureen]: That's gonna be terrible. [Italia]: I can't imagine going down Main Street without it there.

The Ice Cream Parlour. [Maureen]: When he first started out, Papa Jimmy and mom used to go up to the MacKay farm to get a supply of cream to make the ice cream. He'd fall asleep on the way home, and the horse would just take him right to the door. He'd wake up as soon as the sleigh stopped. After they got the cream ready, Papa Jimmy would have breakfast and go to work in the coal mine. Mom was always up with him; she'd always go for the ride. She loved wagons and horses.

After he got a head start on that, he set up an ice cream parlour. It was really nice too; they had round tables. After everything would close up, they'd have to clean up for the next day. Papa Jimmy would clear the whole floor, put the tables aside and put on his favourite music. And, he'd dance. He loved to dance, but he wouldn't go to dances. So, he says: "Okay Italia, come on, we're gonna dance." [laughs] She loved dancing herself, so they'd dance for about an hour, and the music would be just blaring. Yeah, he was fun to be around when he was well.

Ponies, Dogs and Watches. [Maureen]: Papa Jimmy always had farm animals. He had a pony once for George and, ah, I loved that pony. I'd always go down to the barn, and I'd be there brushing her down, just so happy that I was able to be near him. At every chance, I'd sneak down there. I thought I was in seven heaven, yeah, and then he got rid of her. She was full of energy. He made a sleigh one winter, and we were all gonna go for a nice ride. Papa Jimmy said, "I'm gonna test it out first before I take the kids." God, he comes home ... all full of blood. His hands were all cut. The horse went wild, and she just upset everything. She took off with the sleigh and left him in the ditch somewhere. So that was the end of the horse. I never did have one after that. I was probably eight or nine years old at the time. I was just crazy for the animals.

[Daryl]: He always had a well-trained, disciplined German Shepherd. The dogs would practically talk to him. He had one dog that all he had to do was tell him "go find my keys," and it didn't matter where they were, he would always come back with them. Fido, the older dog, was always by Papa Jimmy's side. No matter where he went, the dog was always there with him.

I also remember that, in the old building, downstairs, Papa Jimmy had a little office where he kept his account books. He was either doing book work there or repairing watches (one of his many pastimes). I used to love getting down there. He would give me the little screwdrivers and wrenches, an old watch, and I would take it apart. It didn't matter to him; he just enjoyed seeing me doing it, I guess.

Memories of Tragedy

Georgina Tubetti. [Maureen]: My Aunt Georgina died when she was eight years old. Papa Jimmy always thought he was the cause of her dying. Her legs were so sore. "Daddy," she'd say, "rub my legs," and he'd rub them to try to ease the pain. She had a blood clot, and it moved, eh. But she was going to go anyway, she had a bad case of rheumatic fever. [pause] She was really a clever little girl. My great grandmother, Anna, thought the world of her, and she had bought her a doll. After Georgina passed away, she kept the doll right 'til the end. We had my great grandmother up at our place for about six months when she was real sick. She said: "Maureen when I die you make sure that doll goes in the coffin with me." She got her wish.

Frances (Tubetti) Taylor. [Daryl]: There is one memory that I can never shake. The night the accident happened. [Frances]: Aunt Frances and Uncle Hughie were going to a dance in Mabou.... [Daryl]: I woke up, and I heard Mom really upset and crying. When I found out what it was, I just couldn't believe it. There were four of them killed in the car. They were on their way to Mabou to a dance, and they picked up another couple. It happened out in Strathlorne. They came over the brow of a hill and went head on with a pulp truck. Clare, their daughter, was only ten or eleven months old. It would have been in June or July of 1954.

[Frances]: Grandma Neese and Papa Jimmy started to bring Clare up. She lived with them until she was five. After Mom and Dad were married, and I think they had Rose Anne, Clare came to live with them. She was brought up as one of our sisters.

[Maureen]: When she and her husband were killed, Aunty Frances was only twenty-one. That was the downfall of Grandma Neese and Papa Jimmy; they started declining in health. They had six children, and Mom and George were the only ones left up until, well, he was the last to go in 1987.

Italia (1917-1983) and George (1936-1987) Tubetti

[Maureen]: Papa Jimmy wanted to teach me Italian songs ... but I was only eight or nine at that time. I didn't want to learn them; the songs he knew were from Italy. Everything reminded him of Italy. I remember hearing the story of how he once said to my grandmother: "my first born will be called Italia if she's a girl, and the boy ... we'll call him Giorgio [after my father]."

Papa Jimmy's daughter, Italia, married Ronald (Boss) MacDonald, and they had five children: Mary Georgina, Maureen, Ronald, Frank and Daryl. In addition to working at the various family businesses, Italia operated a hairdressing salon for many years.

[Daryl]: Papa Jimmy demanded a lot. I don't know if it was her decision to go to Montreal to get her hairdressing course or he encouraged her, but I know that she went at a very early age. Yeah, young girl, in her early teens, and travelling up to Montreal by train. Once back home, she was doing hairdressing, she was looking after the home, she was looking after the ice cream parlour—a lot to do. [Frances]: And then ... Papa Jimmy made part of the ice cream parlour into a beauty salon for her.

George Angelo Tubetti and his wife, Cecile Corinne Dionne, raised six daughters. They are: Rose Anne, Frances, Jacqueline, Angela, Corinne and Clare (his sister Frances' daughter). In addition to working at the various family businesses, George Tubetti served as: Fire Chief for the Inverness Volunteer Fire Department, 1966 to 1982; a long-standing member of the Knights of Columbus; and, the last Mayor of the Town of Inverness (1967-1968).

[Frances]: I know that dad, all his life, tried to live up to the expectations of his father. They were always very, very high expectations. To come from a small town, to have dad go to university and aunt Tala (Italia) go to Montreal for a hairdressing course, I mean, that was a major education. That was really important to them. Papa Jimmy put together various businesses, and there was no way dad was going to fail his father by letting any part of it go. Those were very, very important family values that were just passed on from one generation to the next. Dad took over the family business in 1957. He was only twenty. He and aunt Tala looked after the theatre together, and there were the oil business and the garage. Dad was Fire Chief for many years. He was the last mayor of Inverness. A very soft hearted person, very well respected and liked by everybody in the community. I don't think anybody would ever have harsh things to say about dad. Now, they might say that Jimmy Tubetti was a crank, but I don't think they could ever say that about dad. [laughs]

"Grandpa Cozzolino"

By A. Evo DiPierro

Thomas Cozzolino had many people in his personal life. Two of them, his grand-children, are profiled here: Dr. John Burke of Sydney and Mrs. Dorothy (Cozzolino) Brennan of Halifax. They share with us some memories of growing up and living with "Grandpa Cozzolino." For Dr. Burke, the impact of his grandfather's personality and virtue affected his decisions in public life. As a child, Mrs. Brennan was fortunate to have lived with the Cozzolinos and later the Burkes. They provided her with the security and guidance that prepared her for all sorts of challenges.

Dr. John Burke

John "Jack" Anthony Burke, a dentist from Newfoundland, married Mary Teresa Cozzolino, the oldest of Thomas Cozzolino's daughters. After having three of their own daughters in Newfoundland, the Burkes moved to Sydney in 1922 at Mr. Cozzolino's urging. A year later, they gave birth to John Francis Burke. Young John went through the school system in Sydney and then attended St. Francis Xavier University in Antigonish. After graduating from St. FX, he attended Dalhousie University in Halifax to become a dentist in 1947. Throughout this period, John worked at the Sydney Steel Plant during summer vacations.

John Burke has lived and worked in Sydney for most of his life. In addition, he served as a member of the Nova Scotia Legislative Assembly in the early 1970s. He and his wife, Carmelita, have three children. John first became exposed to his grandfather's influence at age seventeen. The Cozzolinos, along with grand-daughter Dorothy, returned to Sydney from Montreal in 1938 and settled with the Burkes. It was the beginning of a unique learning experience for young John.

I have vivid memories of my mother's parents, who lived with us for ten years. They weren't here very long when it was obvious to me that my grandfather was right in control. He was a man who knew what he was, where he was going, and he was extremely positive at all times. He was a Catholic, and he went to Mass every morning. One time I asked my grandmother why Grandpa was so religious. She said that a number of years ago, he had an illness. This was prior to antibiotics when you went through a critical period of three or four days. If you passed that time, then you were ok. When Thomas Cozzolino got one of these illnesses, he made a pledge that if God spared him, he would go to Mass everyday of his life, and he was cured.

Cozzolino Family, ca. 1910. Courtesy of Dr. John Burke.

Being a deeply religious man, Cozzolino built a chapel as part of his home in Sydney. Priests, Bishops and other Catholic clergy visited the Cozzolinos and made use of the chapel.

In his business dealings throughout North America, Thomas Cozzolino earned many lasting and important friendships. One of them was with former prime minister Louis St. Laurent. Cozzolino met St. Laurent when he was practicing law in Quebec during the early 1920s. Perhaps it was Dr. Burke's exposure to such people that guided him into public service. During the 1960s, he served as President of the Progressive Conservative Association for the riding of Cape Breton South, which covers the City of Sydney. Then, in 1970, he ran and was elected a Member of the Legislative Assembly for the riding and served in that capacity until 1974.

One interesting story Dr. Burke recalls is the "ghost of Broughton." Actually, the "ghost" was a hotel—the Broughton Arms. The hotel was a grand, extravagant complex built by Cozzolino in Broughton, near Birch Grove, Cape Breton, in 1905. At that time, geologists believed that Broughton would be the next major coal mining site on the island. As a result, a full-fledged town was built, complete with a school, church and library. Cozzolino saw an opportunity to make money from a hotel built in what was anticipated to be the new heart of Cape Breton's coal industry. Alvise Casagrande, staff writer for the *Cape Breton Post*, described the hotel as: "the finest east of Montreal. The hotel had installed the first revolving doors in North America. The structure had a spacious basement and attic, round towers with conical roofs and was encircled with a verandah."[1] It was a place that held the promise of longevity and fame. However, the geologists overestimated the prospects for coal at Broughton's seams. In 1907, coal mining at the site ceased; the town closed up, and the splendid Broughton Arms Hotel was cast into neglect. The building rotted, fell apart and was eventually destroyed by fire. Today, the only haunting reminder of Cozzolino's palatial retreat is a portion of the foundation protruding from the ground.

On a more personal level, Dr. Burke has many special memories of his grandfather. Young John, for example, often marvelled at his grandfather's amazing appetite:

> One of grandpa's physical problems was gout, and he was pretty heavy. I am convinced that metabolism is the determining factor of whether or not you are thin ... not anything else.... Anyway he always looked to me as being a little too heavy, but he was active ... going and going. As the years went by, he had trouble with his ankles, and the doctor told him to lay off certain foods, but he wouldn't. I remember my grandfather getting a large cereal bowl and filling it with different coloured onions and peppers—things that would burn the mouth off of me. He would pour olive oil all over it, and you could just see the glint in his eye when he was eating. He also had a voracious appetite for spaghetti and meatballs. He enjoyed life, and eating, and he paid for it.

Cozzolino enjoyed being with people, young and old, from any ethnic background. They fed his craving for conversation and friendship. He also took an interest in helping others.

> He belonged to the Yacht Club; he liked to play cards and talk to people. There is one part of his lifestyle that he never spoke of frequently at all— his generosity and his value of education. Through the years, he assisted a great number of students by paying for their education. He financed several young men into the priesthood and financed the general education of quite a number of students.

Tom Cozzolino enjoyed life on his own terms, and John Burke was fortunate to have been a part of that experience.

Mrs. Dorothy (Cozzolino) Brennan

Dorothy Cecilia Josephine Cozzolino was just a new-born baby in 1924, when her grandparents, the Cozzolinos, took her into their arms and raised her as their own daughter. Growing up with her grandparents in Montreal, and then with the Burkes in Sydney in the late 1930s and 1940s, young Dorothy found herself amidst a large extended family. She has no regrets, however, as she looks back on her life:

My father [James Cozzolino] was the only boy in the family and he was the second youngest. He used to work for a construction company too—it was in his blood. He learned from my grandfather, who learned a lot from his father [in Italy]. My grandfather came up the hard way ... I think everything was a challenge to him. I think his faith led him on. He always had faith.... At a church in Montreal, if the altar boys didn't show up, he'd be up on the altar ... with the priest. Strong character. I still have his prayer book at home. I just treasure it.

I was very fortunate that my grandparents brought up a second family. My grandmother took in three of us: me, my brother, Tommy, and my cousin, Mary MacAdam. Mary's mother died when she was eight months old, so my grandmother took her because [Mary's] mother was her sister. Then my mother died at twenty-four when I was just three weeks old, so they took us too. I really look back now, after having a family myself, on how wonderful they were to do this at their age. They lived to be in their eighties, and it didn't hurt them that much, but I suppose we did bring a couple of little heartaches to them. I was a real tomboy. My brother taught me all the tricks—how to wrestle if somebody came up. You just grab their arm, twist it behind their back, keep pulling it up and they'll leave you alone. He always said that he was going to look after his little baby sister. We lived in Montreal for a few years, then my grandparents and I moved to Sydney in 1938 and lived with the Burkes.[2] So that was a chance to meet all my first cousins and grow up with them. That was my family.

Tommy Cozzolino joined the army when he was only seventeen; he lied about his age in order to enlist. During the Second World War, he served in the Allied Forces' Italian campaign. In January of 1943, during a battle in Italy, his tank was damaged by enemy fire, and Tommy was killed. He was twenty-one years old.

My grandfather was very upset when he lost his grandson overseas. I did get a chance to go to Italy and see my brother's grave at Bari. I was very moved. These graves are maintained by the Commonwealth, and they are beautiful. Weeping willows all over the place, tulips and daffodils growing in front of each grave. Breathtaking it was. Marble headstones, and a big arch that we had to go under. When I arrived at my brother's grave, I re-lived the whole episode of the day it happened, and I started to cry all of a sudden. Somebody beside me was sobbing ... it was ... the taxi driver. It opened up everything for him when he saw the Italian name, the age of my brother.... He told me: "The next time I come to this graveyard, I will put flowers on your brother's grave." I said, "How did you learn English?" "From the Canadian soldiers during the war," he replied. "We were only kids, and we were starving. They were so good to give us their chocolate bars. Whatever packages they got from home, they would share with us." That was so nice to hear.

As a teen, Dorothy displayed a stubborn, independent streak. She placed a priority on being her own person, with her own opinions, despite the imposition of others in her life.

> Grandpa more or less ruled Tommy and grandmother took a hold of me. She would open the door and there I'd be, beating up a little boy in the street because he pulled off my hat and she'd be mortified, "Get in here Dorothy, this minute!"

> Dr. ["Jack"] Burke was a good man. He had a big influence on me. I was always sort of the "leader of the pack." Nothing to do? Let's do something…. We went on more hikes and played more tricks in the woods and things like that. Anyway, when he didn't want me to do anything, or go somewhere, he would say, "I'd rather you didn't do this, but I'll leave it up to you and your good judgment." I hated it when he said that…. When I was in grade eight, I told him that I was quitting school, and he just said, "Fine, if that's what you want." I didn't get an argument out of him at all! He just said, "Get yourself a job." So all summer long I boasted that I was allowed to quit school. But then when September rolled along, everybody else talked about going back to school, and I thought well, gee, I should go back too.

When she finished school, Dorothy went to Antigonish to take business courses at Mount St. Bernard College. She returned to Montreal and worked there for three years. She then moved back to Cape Breton, worked for a while longer and eventually married. After her children had grown and moved on, Dorothy Brennan took a refresher course in shorthand and typing, and then returned to the workforce. She moved to Halifax and worked at National Sea Products, and later I.G.A. Grocers. "That was a challenge for me—to go back after twenty-five years. When I was in Montreal, everything was manual, even the adding machines. Then suddenly everything became computerized … the world is advancing so fast, isn't it?"

Spiritual and Physical Healing:
A Family History in Medicine

Edited by Sam Migliore

Members of the D'Intino family have administered to the spiritual and physical needs of people in Sydney, and Cape Breton in general, for two generations. Reverend Emidio D'Intino (1910-1986) served for many years as the pastor of St. Nicholas Parish, in Whitney Pier, while his brother, Carmen (1921-1993) served as a medical doctor. More recently, Carmen D'Intino's daughters have followed in his footsteps to pursue careers in medicine—Yolanda as a specialist in dermatology, and Ann Frances in general practice.[1] What follows is an account of certain family experiences and memories based on a conversation I had with Yolanda, Ann Frances and their aunt, Angelina D'Intino, in March of 1997.

Family Background

Giuseppe (Joe) D'Intino (1881-1968), Yolanda and Ann Frances' grandfather, was born in Castiglione a Casauria, in the Abruzzi region of Italy. In 1898, at the age of seventeen, he travelled to Dresden, Germany, "to work in a china factory."[2] [Ann Frances]: Poppy worked in Dresden for some time. A lot of Italians went to Dresden because of the industrialization there at the turn of the century. He went back to Italy; then he came here, to Halifax. [Angelina]: In 1901.

"Giuseppe had a job in Halifax working with the railroad constructing the line between Halifax and Chester Basin."[3] When the project was completed, he moved to Cape Breton. [Angelina]: My father went to work at [the quarry] at Marble Mountain. [Yolanda]: He worked there until the steel plant was built in Sydney, and then he came here. [Giuseppe worked at the steel plant for fifty-six years.]

[Yolanda]: My grandfather was married three times. [His first wife, Angela Jacobita,] was Italian. They had three children—Dominic, Emidio (the priest) and Mary—but she died in childbirth. He had to put the children in St. Anthony's orphanage because he had no relatives here. He then married a French lady, Albertine Henri, who died in the swine flu epidemic of 1916. She had two daughters. So, all the children had to go to the orphanage again. [Angelina]: And then Mama [Christina Varasso] came over [from Italy] in 1920. They got married, and Mama took all the children back from the orphanage. Emidio was only two when his mother died; Mama brought him up. [Yolanda]: My grandparents had Angelina, Eustace and my father. [Angelina]: And my sister Angelina. She died four months before she was three.

[Yolanda]: It must have been very hard for my grandfather in those days. Imagine finding yourself with all those children, no family, nobody, and having to put them in an orphanage. What a horrible thing to have to do. It's kind of ironic; when my father became a physician, he took care of [everyone] at St. Anthony's Home gratis because his brothers and sisters had been there.

[Angelina]: Papa never worried though. He had troubles, but he never worried. [Yolanda]: He always used to say, "what's going to be is going to be." My grandfather had a pretty important job at the plant actually. He had to check the pressure in all the fire hydrants. He would walk from the coke ovens all the way out to the pump house in Sydney River. He would have to walk that a couple of times a day, that's probably why he lived so long. Some people used to call him Joe Bucket because he carried a bucket to check the spill-off from the fire hydrants. [Angelina]: And Mr. Disano was called Joe Wrench because he always carried a wrench. [Ann Frances]: Someone told me that Poppy could be burdened down and still walk faster than anyone. But, when I went to Castiglione in 1982, I could understand why. Castiglione is straight up a cliff. They used to walk that to get to the olive groves. They walked for miles! No wonder they were so healthy.

[Yolanda]: In 1967, the Centennial year, I won first prize in an essay contest for Grade sevens. They put the essay in a box that they are going to open in the year 2067. It was about my grandfather coming over from Italy. I called it A Dream Come True.

> On a brisk wintry November day in the year 1901, an anxious group
> of Italians aboard the ship, *The Good Hope*, were very much thrilled
> for news had been heard that land was sighted. Especially thrilled was
> a young Italian named Giuseppe, who had made the long tiresome
> journey alone.... As Giuseppe lay in bed that night, the first night in that
> strange country which was to become his own, he thanked God.... For
> Giuseppe and many other immigrants to Canada, this country was truly
> A DREAM COME TRUE.[4]

Father Emidio J. D'Intino

Emidio D'Intino "received his early education at Sydney Academy and obtained his Bachelor of Arts from St. Francis Xavier University in 1932."[5] [Angelina]: He worked in the [steel] plant for two or three years, [saved enough] money, and then went to Holy Heart Seminary in Halifax. He was ordained in June of 1936. [Yolanda]: He is still remembered quite fondly in Glace Bay. He was a curate at St. Anthony's Parish in Passchendaele. [Angelina]: Then he went to New Victoria.... [Yolanda]: To St. Agnes, and then to St. Nicholas where he followed Monsignor MacLean.

[Yolanda]: My uncle helped dad as much as he could when my father was in university. [Angelina]: Because papa was bringing home $12.50 a week from the plant. Every Friday mama would call it the curse Friday because she had so many bills to pay and before you knew it the $12.50 was gone.

[Ann Frances]: There are a lot of people who believed my uncle, the priest, had a cure. [Yolanda]: I had a [patient] who told me how his father had had a severe

Father E. J. D'Intino's ordination celebration, in St. Theresa's Hall, Ashby area of Sydney, ca. 1935. Courtesy of Theresa Della Vella.

skin disease that nobody could do anything with. He heard about Father D'Intino, and he went down to see him. [My uncle] blessed him with Holy Water, and it was cured. [Ann Frances]: There were lots of stories that he had the power in his hands. [Angelina]: There was this little girl that couldn't walk. [People say] the priest cured her. [Yolanda]: She was going down the stairs on her knees, and when he said "get up, you can get up," she walked. [Angelina]: And she did; she walked.

Father D'Intino became pastor of St. Nicholas Parish in 1943. As a native of Whitney Pier, "the first person baptized in the ... church in 1911," and "the first Italian priest ordained in the Diocese of Antigonish," it must have been a special honour for Emidio to be given charge of this Italian parish.[6] He served as pastor of the parish from 1943 to 1970. One of Emidio's most painful moments came in 1971 when the church burned to the ground. Through his efforts, and the efforts of parishioners and friends of St. Nicholas Parish, however, a new church hall, St. Nicholas Hall, was constructed in Whitney Pier for the Italian community.

[Yolanda]: The Diocese of Antigonish wanted to retire my uncle to the MacGillivary home [in Sydney]. He had taken two strokes and a heart attack, but he recovered. He just refused to retire. [In 1975,] he moved to California where he worked out of

From the left: Anne Frances D'Intino, Frances D'Intino (mother), Carmen A. D'Intino (father), Carmen Joseph D'Intino, Yolanda D'Intino. Courtesy of Dr. Yolanda D'Intino.

a parish [St. Emydius] that had a lot of Hispanics. My uncle enjoyed it. [Although] he came back every year [to Cape Breton] in the summers, he worked basically until he died. [My uncle celebrated] his 50th anniversary as a priest in 1986. [Angelina]: And he died on October 8th of the same year. He was seventy-six.

Father D'Intino was interred at All Souls Cemetery in Long Beach, California.[7] A special Memorial Mass was celebrated for him, however, at Holy Redeemer Church in Whitney Pier.[8]

Dr. Carmen D'Intino

[Yolanda]: My father got pneumonia when he was in grade five. [Angelina]: He was only nine years old. [Yolanda]: He missed school for about three months, but when he got back to school they advanced him another grade. Apparently my grandmother was quite bright. She was one of the few people [in the Italian community] who could write in English. [Angelina]: Well, she only had grade three in Italy, and Papa had grade two, but they could read and write. [Yolanda]: And then, when my father graduated from Sydney Academy…. [Angelina]: he was the youngest; he was sixteen when he graduated.

In 1938, Carmen D'Intino won a trip to Italy for his performance in an Italian language contest for children of Italian immigrants. He was seventeen years old at the time. Carmen took a coal boat from the Pier to Boston and a steamer from Boston to Italy. The trip gave him the opportunity to visit relatives in the Abruzzi region. Once back in Cape Breton, he set his sights on higher education.

[Yolanda]: My father had to take a year off and work at the [steel] plant because in those days there were no student loans. There was really no money in those days. And then he went to St. FX University. He earned money by demonstrating the [science] lab, and he actually taught an Italian class there. [Angelina]: And he waited on tables. [Yolanda]: He didn't get his degree. He did just two years and then went to [Dalhousie] Medical School. Because of the war, they were accelerating [the medical school program]. My father did medical school in three years. I think he was only twenty-one when he graduated. [Angelina]: He was the youngest doctor in Canada.

[Yolanda]: My mother and father met [through] Father D'Intino. My mother's family was at St. Agnes ... [Angelina]: in Waterford ... [Yolanda]: Mom and dad met at Sangaree at a parish camp [while dad was on leave from Medical School]. [Ann Frances]: Mom was of Irish background. They got married in 1950.

After the war, Carmen D'Intino accompanied a few of the trains transporting "war brides" from Halifax to various parts of the country. He also took post-graduate training in anesthesia at Cook County, in Chicago, before returning to practice medicine in Cape Breton—first, for a short period, in Louisbourg, and later in Whitney Pier.

[Yolanda]: Dad practiced in the Pier basically. Those were the times when doctors did everything. He would do anesthetics all morning and then do his office in the afternoon. He did the first exchange transfusion for Rh negative babies in Nova Scotia. [Ann Frances]: Yeah, here at St. Rita's [Hospital in Sydney]. [Yolanda]: Dad had a very good reputation as a diagnostician too. Patients were referred to him from the Northside, from Inverness, when no one else knew what to do. [Ann Frances]: He had a very strong work ethic. It was just second nature to him.

[Yolanda]: He was a whiz at all kinds of things—geography, baseball, economics.... [Ann Frances]: He loved to sing. He had a wonderful collection of Italian opera. And when he was in the OR [Operating Room], they would always have music playing. [Angelina]: At Christmas time, at the midnight Mass, the choir would sing *Tu Sciendi delle Stelle*. Carmen loved to sing that, and you knew he was singing in the choir. How he loved it. [Yolanda]: Even in medicine, dad [would] always go for refresher courses. [Ann Frances]: He was one of the few people who really kept up; he worked right up to the end, and he knew all the new drugs.

Carmen D'Intino passed away on October 9, 1993. [Yolanda]: People were lined up for the wake; it was unbelievable. I never would go to wakes, but after that I realized how important they are for the family. He touched a lot of people. There were people who came up to us to say, "your father paid off an oil bill for us when my husband was out of work." That was the side of him that we as his family didn't really know. [Ann Frances]: And you still hear about it today. An elderly woman told me the other day that in 1953 her little daughter was dying of leukemia. It was Christmas Day, and she needed medicine. My father said to her, "I don't have any kids yet, so you stay here and I'll get the medicine." He went to the hospital and brought back the medicine. He knew it would be her last Christmas. Isn't that something? And this woman remembers that very, very clearly. He did a lot for people before Medicare. If finances were his only motivation, he would have never come back here.... But, I can remember people coming to the door every Christmas with great big baskets of all kinds of things. They appreciated him.

Yolanda and Ann Frances D'Intino

[Sam]: How did you get into medicine? [Yolanda]: I think because my dad was a doctor. Honestly, if he had been an engineer, I might have been an engineer. We grew up with it. People often would come to our house; I remember dad stitching people up in the hall. He always took us to the rounds at the hospital on Sundays. It just becomes a part of you, you know. [Ann Frances]: It had to be that, especially when you went through; there weren't many women [in medicine at that time]. You were the first one from Holy Angels, and I was the second. [Yolanda]: I remember when I said I wanted to go into medicine. Dad said, "make sure you do it because you want to do it, not because of me." But, I know secretly he was very, very proud.

It's funny how you end up back in the same place where you started. [After I graduated from high school, I went to Dalhousie University for two years and then to Dalhousie Medical School.] When I got into medical school, dad sent me a little note. [Ann Frances]: On a prescription pad. [Yolanda]: "This is a prescription for your happiness." [Ann Frances]: "XXOO, Dad." [Yolanda]: After medical school, I did a rotating internship and then five years as a GP [general practitioner] in New Brunswick. I then went into dermatology, [and eventually came home to Sydney]. My sister came behind me. She went to St. Mary's University, graduated with the gold medal in science, and then went into medicine.

It must have been hard for dad trying to blend two views—wanting your daughters to do what they could do, but at the same time wanting the family life the way that his family life had been. 'Cause, really, mom took care of the house and Dad worked. [Ann Frances]: But he always told you that you could do anything you wanted to do. Never any question. If you worked hard you could do whatever you wanted. But my, he loved his grandchildren. Not a day went by he didn't see them.... Dad could have gone anywhere [to work], but he had strong family ties. Family was very important. That's probably why we all ended up coming back.

Bruno Marcocchio:
Family, Environmental Activism,
and the Cape Breton Experience

Edited by Sam Migliore

Bruno Marcocchio is a well-known, but controversial, figure in Cape Breton society. His role as an outspoken environmental activist has brought him both praise and abuse. He has earned the respect of people who see him as a "voice of reason" in the struggle against powerful individuals and agencies that want to draw attention away from environmental hazards. At the same time, he has felt the wrath and contempt of those who regard his work as a roadblock in their efforts to proceed with projects they maintain will benefit the community at large. My aim here is not to address this controversy, but rather to provide Bruno with a forum through which he can speak about some aspects of both his public and his private life.

Family Background

I come from a northern Italian family from the Friuli region in the Po Valley, in what is now the province of Porde Pordonone none. My parents were from rural peasant families. They came from villages about three kilometres from one another. My father emigrated to Canada in early 1949, and my mother followed four or five months later. She arrived in Toronto about two months prior to my birth. In a way, I straddled both the old and the new world—conceived in the old world and born in the new. We settled in a working-class neighbourhood in downtown Toronto. It was a lovely place for children to grow. Toronto in the 1950s was a much different place. It was a city of trees; there were parks, single family homes and nice neighbourhoods.

My grandfather, my father's father, had originally come to Canada on two occasions between 1900 and 1920 to work. He worked in Niagara Falls, and several other places, and then returned to northern Italy, a little town called Castione de Zoppola. My father's brother emigrated to Canada when he was a young man, and he paved the way for my father. My father was in the construction industry. He was a bricklayer by trade, and through the 1950s and early 1960s, he had a small contracting company with his brother. My father worked as a bricklayer all of his life, worked hard, and my mother was very much the centre of family life. She took care of all things domestic, and particularly disciplining unruly children like myself. [laughs]

Tensions Between Family Constraints and Individual Expression

I went to a public school in downtown Toronto that stressed a Victorian education. It was very militaristic and disciplined. We moved from our downtown neighbourhood to the suburbs in 1967, when I was in the eleventh grade. I continued to go to the high school in downtown Toronto, while my brother and sister transferred to a school [in North York]. At that time, North York was the most enlightened school board in the country. They were experimenting with new forms of education. For instance, in my brother's public school there were no walls in the classroom, and they were free to move around; they didn't have any exams until well into high school, I think. It was a dramatically different school environment from the one I grew up in. [My school] very much focused on corporal punishment and strict demand to adherence. This kind of mirrored the ethic of my family life. My mother ruled with a very strong and forceful hand.

So, growing up in downtown Toronto was pleasant and interesting, but increasingly, I wanted to express myself in my individuality. I began to have some reservations about who I was. I very much felt like a Canadian first and an Italian second, while my parents, who, as new immigrants, didn't understand Canada and the cultural context that I grew up in, wanted me to fulfill their expectations, to move in their cultural directions. I knew that I had to be honest to myself, be who I was in this new nation, and express myself as a Canadian. That led to a considerable amount of tension. I had a troubled adolescence, and increasingly [my views] became more and more in conflict with my family. As the oldest of a large extended family (all of my cousins were younger than me), I was expected to set a pattern and to be a model Italian Canadian. Although I couldn't articulate it at that point, I categorically rejected the notion.

I kept an even keel through my adolescent years by throwing my energies into athletics. I played football and basketball, both as a way of measuring myself in my own personally defined ways, and roles and as an escape from what seemed to me to be an oppressive mother. When I was very young, [my mother] would have to chase me back into the house at the end of the day. I saw the unbridled play of children as my escape, and playing games as a way of holding onto the freedom of childhood. It became my survival strategy. We won a Toronto city championship [in football] one year, and lost in the final game in the next. I was fairly successful and played in city all-star games the last couple of years of my high school education. I wasn't interested in having it develop into a professional career, although that probably could have been an option if I could believe the professional football coaches who told me I had a rosy future. At the end of high school, it was a chapter in my life that I sadly left behind.

I went to the University of Waterloo, sixty miles west of Toronto. I had by conscious choice escaped my mother's web. I was free to define myself in my own terms, as an Italian Canadian with the emphasis on Canadian. But, that increasingly brought me into conflict with family; they felt that I had abandoned them. They took all vestiges of my existence out of their lives. All the photographs were taken off the wall, and they spent the next twenty years basically having two children, not three, in their lives. It was a very painful and difficult part of my life, but one that I had chosen consciously. I think that most immigrant children have those pulls between the parent's culture and [the desire] to break free. In my context, it was particularly difficult and painful…. The choice [however], was made relatively easy because my mother rejected my experiences in my cultural context as much as I had hers. Really, she only understood the world that she knew, and the world that she wanted me to grow up in. Not only was she not supportive of my athletic endeavours, she was down right hostile towards them. This, of course, only hardened me more into deciding that I was going to be who I wanted to be, and [thinking that] I could never expect any familial support for the things that were important to me. And, for twenty years or so, that seemed entirely true and consistent with my life. But, I'm glad to say that in the end there was a dramatic resolution of those conflicts with my mother.

We began to understand each other as human beings, through the pain that I went through with my wife's illness and eventual demise, and my mother's wonderful support—emotional, physical and financial—during that period. And, more recently, through my mother's own battle with cancer. I began to understand her as a human being who did what she did for very good reasons. And, I think, in the end, she finally began to accept me for having done what I did in my own context. We resolved many of those things. I guess having a family sensitized me to the kind of pressures that she was under. Although I will do my best not to be oppressive and overbearing, and to be supportive [with my children], I have learned to be genuinely grateful for the kind of upbringing that I had. And, of course, all of those tests and trials through my adolescent years, now that I've survived them and come out the other side of all of that pain, have made me what I am today. It has made me better able to cope, and to be independent, resourceful, self-motivated and directed—which has been the theme of my activist life the last ten years here in Cape Breton.

Environmental Activism

The community here saw environmentalism and environmental protection as a non-issue, even at a time when it was becoming politically popular in other parts of the country. I spoke out very much as a "voice in the wilderness" about the dangers of the tar ponds, the sheer folly of our energy policy vis-à-vis the construction of the now failed, and completely unnecessary, Point Aconi power plant, and a number of other issues. Being a "voice in the wilderness," being unafraid to say things that are both unpopular and bring scorn and derision from one's peers, or extended family if you will, were lessons that I had to work through relatively early in my life as survival skills. It seemed much easier, actually, to put up with the personal attacks, the vilification, both in the media and the general perception. My painful experiences with family made me realize that the key and secret to life, in fact, is turning apparent disadvantages into your biggest advantage.

There has been a dramatic shift and change of consciousness among Cape Bretoners. Ten years ago, the view was "no smoke, no baloney;" as long as there were jobs to be had, the smoke and the tar ponds would be put up with. Today, people are sensitized to the seriousness of the environmental problems that we face here, [to the fact that we are] living in the midst of Canada's worst hazardous waste site. We know now that 60 per cent or more of coke oven workers died prematurely of cancer, and that diseases like cancer, emphysema, reproductive disorders, auto-immune diseases and skin disorders are all elevated in our populations as a result of this close proximity to these hazardous wastes. Unfortunately, the political will to do [something about the problem], to overcome the political patronage which has driven the wasting of 52 million dollars, with absolutely no results, [does not exist]. If the horribly designed low-temperature incinerator had ever worked, it would have poisoned everyone here in Sydney. You can't safely burn PCB contaminated materials at those temperatures without spewing not only PCBs into the air, but also their more dangerous by-products of incomplete combustion—dioxins and furans.

For ten years I kept saying, and I wasn't the only one [that there were PCBs in the tar ponds]. We had first-hand accounts of steelworkers who said: "I dumped PCBs into the pond as an electrical worker. You'll find them at the end of that storm sewer, that's ... the hot spot of PCBs." [Yet, they initially denied that PCBs existed at the site, and later] built this low-temperature incinerator that clearly wouldn't safely burn the PCBs. So, I kept talking about the PCBs and, in due course, yes, the PCBs were discovered. Now the tally sits at 50 thousand tons of high level PCB contaminants and counting because when they got to 50 thousand tons they stopped the testing yet again. The Provincial Government wanted the Federal Government to pick up the rest of the cost, but the Federal Government was unwilling to do so. We now know that mixed in that 700 thousand tons of sludge there are at least 50 thousand tons of high level PCB waste, and that they are intermingled to a point where it is impractical to consider any of it not PCB waste. We need to find a technology that can deal with the whole problem, and that can do it safely, so that we don't subject this community to more environmental insults in the name of a clean up. That's all that would have happened with that failed incinerator project. We would have passed the horrors of the past generations onto the next several generations, by poisoning everyone here.

In no civilized community do we allow hazardous wastes to be burned in an incinerator in the middle of a town, never mind: a low-temperature incinerator ... with a permit that is substandard to national minimum standards set just six months [earlier] ... somewhere where they wouldn't measure dioxin and furans in real time, and wouldn't even monitor the Hydrogen Chloride (HCL) going up the stack. Every municipal garbage incinerator measures HCL; it is a standard part of the monitoring package. And here, in this toxic waste incinerator in our midst, they were planning on not even monitoring the HCL. So, we continue to live with a government that sees our community as second-class citizens that can and will be subjected to environmental standards that no one else in this country would dream about.

The long, lonely battle [of environmental activism] is not one that intimidates me. If I feel secure that what I am doing is factually correct, socially just and morally upright, I'll gladly continue to stand [the abuse], to be vilified. Although, I think, things have turned around. People have begun to respond. I'm continuously inundated with people thanking me for the work that I do, and encouraging me to carry on. Maybe that belated approval from one's own peers and family is another recurring theme in my life. [laughs]

Environmental Activism vs. Familial Responsibilities

Now, ironically, it is my family responsibilities that are the fly in the ointment. There is a real pull between the primary needs and interests of my children (young, left without a mother at the age of four and six), and my responsibilities to my community. I need to develop the skills and sensitivities that normally are completely anathema to a male Italian child—one who is supposed to be strong, suffering and not concerned with day-to-day family matters. Although challenging, it is a role that I am not shrinking away from. I now see myself, my role and responsibilities in life, not as an environmental activist, but as a single parent that has an awesome responsibility to see for both [my children's] material and, more importantly, emotional and spiritual needs. For the next ten years, that has to be my role.

[I have begun the process of] stepping back, one step at a time, from my societal commitments, and to focus more and more on being close to the very hearth that

I fled so eagerly when I was a child. So, in a way, it is part of the healing, part of that circle of life, and I'm glad to say that I was not only at peace with my mother through her illness, but that we both went through a genuine forgiveness and healing with one another. And, I felt very privileged that she wanted me there holding her hand when she moved into that next world. That was a profoundly moving and momentous occasion in my life; it symbolized a lot of things: the healing, the forgiveness, the closure of the circle and the eternal link and bond of connection to family that I think has to guide me here now.

To a large measure, it is my mother, through her support, who has given me the ability to mother my children and continues to do so even from the grave. Those kinds of things bring you back to your roots, to the importance and primacy of family and to my Italian background and upbringing. It's still very much work in progress from completely rejecting my Italianness and my family in late adolescence, to realizing in my mid-forties that it really is who I am and what I am.

More and more, then, I am withdrawing from social activism. Stepping away from the tar pond stuff, that has been so much a part of my life, has been more difficult because I feel I have the skills, and I have either the stupidity or the fortitude, depending on your position, to keep at it despite [the fact] that it is a long, lonely and unfulfilling battle. It is supported now; people are telling me: "keep up the good work, don't ever quit." I understand and appreciate their sentiment, but at my weaker moments, realizing the terrible personal price that I am having to pay to do that, it also makes me angry. In the next few years, I am going to step aside and slowly, despite my phobia about computers and machines, come to terms with the technology. I will develop other skills to be able to continue my campaigning in terms of the community interests, without having to be on the front line, so to speak, and without having to take the time away from my family.

Concluding Remarks

[One thing you haven't talked about is ... how you ended up in Cape Breton.] When my university career ended, I lived in a rural area in southern Ontario. I began to experiment with rural living, gardening and being self-reliant. I wanted to live in a rural environment and abandon the urban life that I had known and grown up with. And, somehow, I knew from my heart, from the moment the thought formed, that I was going to live in Cape Breton. I wanted to be close to the sea; I wanted to live some place that was physically beautiful.

[A few years later, several friends and I] came out here. The very first place I set foot in Cape Breton was the place I eventually settled. We received an offer of a 40-acre parcel of land. The place was unique, and had virtually everything I was looking for—fertile soil, shelter from the ocean, but within sight of the sea. We took them up on the offer, and several of us started carving out a little niche out of this wilderness. [Later, my friends] went scattered in different directions. Despite my obvious limitations both in terms of my skills and my financial resources, I persisted; I planted orchards, cleared land and slowly built a house out of hand-made materials at virtually no cost—a mortgage-free home. And, more and more, Cape Breton became part of my heart and part of who I am. And, I have certainly never regretted it. It was really my fate that drew me here, and the rest of it was just meant to be. So, it was around 1975 when I first arrived, and I have been living full-time here since 1977. I feel like I very much bonded to this place.

I started working for Greenpeace in 1991 as a fisheries campaigner. Trying to sell Greenpeace to Eastern Canadians, in the ten years after this whole explosion about the seal hunt, was a role that no one else in their right mind would have anything to do with. That work [however] made me travel and gain an appreciation of the unique nature of many of the Maritime cultures around the region. I am very happy that my children are growing up here in Cape Breton, and the only sadness that I have is that with the disruptions in my life we haven't been able to explore this island. But that is something that I'm going to resolve, I'm going to spend as much time as I can, over the next several years, with them on this side of the causeway exploring, understanding and getting to know this island so they can love it as much as I certainly do.

What Is It Like To
Marry Into An Italian Family?
A reflection by Don Fraser

Edited by A. Evo DiPierro

My name is Don Fraser. I was born March 22, 1957. My Dad's name is Sam. My Mom's name is Margie. I have a sister, Shirley, and brothers Gary and Kenny. We're a very close family and always have been. We were always there for each other—good times and bad times. Since I am the oldest, I always made sure I helped Mom in any way I could. Same with my Dad. Dad used to hold two, sometimes three, jobs. It wasn't easy on him, but he always looked after us.

When I finished school, I ended up working at a health club, and there I first met Pina DiPierro. I was twenty-seven at the time. Pina was in Halifax at the Nova Scotia Institute of Technology. While home for a training course at the City Hospital, she came to our gym. Pina and her friends went upstairs to check out the weight room. Being one of the instructors, I went over to get them familiar with the equipment and the weights. And it was Pina's big brown eyes, or big black eyes, I should say, that attracted me, and her wavy black hair (she says it's not black but I think it was). Anyway, she was very nice, very friendly and easy to talk to. We became friends at the time.

When she settled back home after graduating, she started training regularly at our school. A bunch of us used to chum around together ... go to a movie ... a walk in the park. We used to go to the Bonnie on Saturday nights; watch the [hockey] game for awhile, have a few beers.... And, like I said, we became real good buddies. After a time, Pina and I started to drift off on our own, going to movies together, going to restaurants. Just sitting down with a bottle of wine and ... a photo album actually. I remember that night when she brought her photo album to the gym. We sat down together, had cheese, crackers, wine and pickles. And she laughed and told me all about her childhood from the photo album. It was very nice, and I sat there and listened and enjoyed her conversation. She is very intelligent, very smart. There is no nonsense about her. She's got a drive about her. She gets things done. Myself? Now, I'll say I'm going to do it, but to get around to it is another thing.

I remember the first Christmas when I met her family. I rang the doorbell, but I didn't want to be there. Her father answered the door. He was in real good shape—a young looking fellow. He invited me in and went to get Pina. I watched him walk down the hallway; he was real broad across the shoulders and narrow at the hip—one of those Italian bricklayers you don't want to mess with. Anyway, I finally got to introduce myself to her father. I met her brother Evo, and I met brother Nicholas outside. So that was over with. And now the biggest one was her Mom, and I was terrified. When I sat down for the Christmas meal, nobody told me that it was one portion at a time. I'm a very big pasta lover. Her mother had meatball soup. Then she came out with the ravioli. I had a plate full of that, and another, not knowing how much more food was involved. Then came the meat and salad—chicken and meatballs and ham, lamb ... my God! There was an awful lot of food, and fresh homemade bread and wine—there was that much wine. I'll tell ya, I was some full. Then the dessert came, and the fruit, then after that it was the Italian cookies, and I was just overwhelmed. And of course Pina watching and laughing at me. Nobody gave me any indication of what I was up against when I walked through that door, but her mother was a sweetheart that day. I became very close to the family. Her father is a very hard worker. He always has been and always will be. That's what makes him happy. I see a bit of that in myself sometimes. I like to work a lot, like to keep going.

In 1990, Pina and I built our home in Sydney. We had lots of help from our father, laying the brick and some carpenter work. I had my family pitch in, and they gave me a great deal of help. In September 1990, we got married (one of the happiest days of my life). I finally have a family that I can love as much as my own. They're there for each other. They're a strong family, a hard-working family, a very smart family. My Mom, well she was there for the wedding, but on June 30, 1991, she passed away. Was a pretty sad thing. Pina's family hurt as much as my own. A year later, my little girl, Genaya, was born, which brought joy into all of our lives. Now she's the best thing that ever happened to me. Work wise, I was with DEVCO for several years, and we were let go because the railroad was closing down. I really didn't know where to turn, and Pina pretty well sent me back to school. I took a plumber's trade and got work in the field. If it wasn't for Pina and her family, I don't know where I'd be today. Her mother has become a mother to me, since mine passed away. Her brother Evo is like a brother of my own. Anything I asked him for, he was there for me. Her little brother, Nicholas, was like a little brother to myself, one that I could take with me, watch him grow. I would take him out and teach him how to drive. He and I would go to a movie now and then. He'd come over and mow the lawn for me and I'd slip him a few dollars. He became a little brother that I could grow up with and help out in my own way.

Being married to an Italian family is a very warm, comfortable feeling. For the past five years, I've been involved in the Italian Association. I met many Italian families and I've been invited to many of their homes for meals, parties.... They're a very happy, loving bunch of people. We have socials at the Italian Hall, where friends and families get together to put little things on for the children as well as the adults. Once a month they have meetings, and you get to talk with them, see how they're doing. It all makes me very close to the Italian family and the Italian Association. I'm glad to be married to an Italian family.

Section IV

Food
and
Drink

Growing Tomatoes from Seed: A Family Tradition

By Jennifer Pino

My father's family came from Scotland and settled at MacAdams Lake in Cape Breton over a hundred years ago. From MacAdams Lake they moved to St. Peter's. Life in St. Peter's, however, did not provide many opportunities for a young man. So, my grandfather moved to New York, found a job, an Irish wife and had a son named John. John grew up in New York, and eventually married a beautiful young Italian woman, Josephine Marra. John and Josephine Currie are my parents.

My mother's family came from a small town near Naples. Her father, Alessandro Marra, travelled across the Atlantic in search of work. He eventually settled in Long Island, New York—in a community of mixed nationalities, including Italians. Once Alessandro had found a job, he called for his wife and family to join him in America. My grandmother, Anna Maria, prepared the children and packed up her most prized possessions for the trip. She passed on some of these possessions to her daughter, my mother (who later passed some on to me).

In time, my father moved the family back to Cape Breton, and we settled in Sydney. My mother brought her prized possessions with her. Like many Cape Bretoners, we plant vegetables in our garden each spring. By late summer, we anxiously await the ripening of our tomatoes. They are special! They come from Italy. Every year our family saves the seeds from these tomatoes so that we can replant them the following spring. Our family treasures these tomato seeds for two reasons: they were brought to North America, and handed down to us, by my grandparents; and, they are a symbol of our Italian heritage.

One's Weed, Another's Salad:
The Cultural Perils of Dandelions

Edited by John deRoche

If you want to see cultures in action, start with food. People like to explore each other's cuisine, but sometimes they can't get their minds—let alone mouths—around another culture's delicacies. "De gustibus non disputandum," said the Roman ancestors of Italy: there's no arguing with tastes. In these two tales from Dominion, we can savour the funny side of intercultural misunderstanding.

Condo Baggio: Charity Goes Two Ways

I'll tell you one story now. In 1925, around in April, them days the spring used to be early. Me and another Italian fella, we have two Italian bikes from the old country, the Bianchi. We paid $75 them days. And we go for dandelions, over at St. Joseph's Hospital [Glace Bay]. They had a barn there. They used to have their own cow for the milk for the hospital. And here around the barn, the dandelions used to be that big! *Cicoria* [dandelions]. And we had a big knife. We fill up a bag—used to be a bag in the [coal] pit, can hold twenty-five pounds of stone dust.

And jeez, we see a nurse—around quarter to seven in the morning, we see a woman in a white cap coming there. I said to my buddy, "Now we're going to get hell, boy!"

"Look," she said, "the Sister want to see ya. Come in."

Holy jeez. We go in ... and the one dressed in white, the Mother [Superior] ... said, "C'mon in.... What you do to that?"

"Eat it," I said.

"Oh. You boil?"

"No, no," I said, "we clean it, put it in olive oil, vinegar, onion," I said, "pepper and salt."

"My God! You must be hungry!" [laughter] We no hungry. She said, "C'mon in the kitchen." She give us one egg, couple pieces of bacon and two pieces of toast. [laughter]

She thought we were starving. Jeez ... oh, we had lots to eat. We used to be so happy, boy.

The good Mother never did learn what a treat lies in tender young cicoria *greens, for Condo and his friend charitably refrained from spoiling her moment of Christian generosity.*

Raffaele Gatto: Moral Panic on the Highway

Beneath this next vignette floats the more sinister potential of cultural misinterpretation. But, as in an episode of Keystone Kops, that only improves the knee-slapping quality in the end.

This is the truth. The man is dead now [an Italian from Dominion]. He wanted the dandelions. From Dominion to Sydney, alongside the highway, there's all kinds of chicory, you know—dandelions or radicchio. So, there's a couple of women in a car, and they saw this man with a long knife. So they went over to Sydney, and they got the Mountie [RCMP]. They said, "There's a crazy man with a big long knife." [laughter] That's the truth. So the Mountie from Sydney, they call the Glace Bay department. So there were two cars on this side, and two cars on that, coming in. And this fella keep on doing his work; he wasn't worried about them. So there was eight Mounties walking slow towards him, you see. So they asked the man what he was doing.... They started to laugh. They realized what he was doing. [The Mountie] said, "Now, we got a report, there's a crazy man with a long knife that started chasing everybody." So he had his bag full, and they give him a drive home. Yeah. They thought the poor Italians were starving to death. [Laughs] Just unbelievable.

Memories of Mushroom Picking

By Livio Nicoletti

It looked like an orange carpet spreading through the forest. Galiti (better known as Chanterelles). They were everywhere. This is a memory I have recalled many times. Memories of me, as a young boy, picking mushrooms with my parents. It was in the 1950s, and it was an annual event that started in August and finished in October.

I have many fond memories of these outings with family, friends and relatives. Most of the time, they ended up as a picnic that included picking all sorts of mushrooms and even fishing. Once the word was out that the prized porcini (*bresi*) had been found, the annual harvest started. Each family travelling to their mostly secret spot and returning with their harvest. Then the chore began of cleaning, boiling, bottling, canning, freezing, etc.—which usually kept my mother up most of the night.

As a young boy, I remember listening to many stories from the older Italians; stories of their episodes of mushroom picking, and not too often, they would disclose their favourite locations. When they were plentiful, many Italians would dry them and use them over the winter. I recall my grandmother sending dried mushrooms to her niece in New York and receiving around $5.00 a pound for them and that was in the 1950s. Mushrooms in the 1950s and 1960s were plentiful, but in the 1970s and 1980s, they were scarce. Many attributed this to changes in habitat and acid rain.

Last year, 1996, they seemed to be plentiful. Regardless, however, when August arrives after a heavy rain followed by a few warm days, my cousin (Louie Mazzocca), my friend, Tony Basso, and I are gone (mushroom picking) every chance we can get. It's in our blood.

Two of Carole Nicoletti's Mushroom Recipes

Pollo con Fungi (Chicken with Mushrooms)

1 onion	2 tablespoons butter
¼ cup oil	2-3 tablespoons tomato paste
Italian parsley	2 pounds chicken pieces

mushrooms (chanterelles or porcini), cut in pieces
spices (garlic, oregano, rosemary, salt and pepper)

Method

Melt butter and add onion and oil in large pot. Add chicken pieces and spices. Once chicken starts cooking, add water and tomato paste to cover chicken. Simmer chicken for one hour, then add mushrooms and parsley. Continue simmering for another thirty minutes. Serve with polenta.

Risotto con Fungi e Durei di Pollo

(Rice with Mushrooms and Chicken Giblets)

1 onion	¼ cup oil
2 tablespoons butter	1½ cups of rice
Italian parsley	Parmesan cheese
salt and pepper	spices (garlic, basil, pickling spice)

½ pound chicken giblets, cut into small pieces
6 cups chicken stock (bouillon cubes, can broth or homemade)

Method

In sauce pan, combine oil, butter and chopped onion. Add giblets (with spices), and a dash of salt and pepper. Simmer, adding broth so giblets are constantly covered. Do not let contents boil over. When giblets are tender, add rice and mushrooms. Keep adding broth during cooking process. Cook until rice is tender. This dish is best served with Parmesan cheese; add a couple of sprinkles of cheese at end of cooking.

Memories of an Annual Ritual in Dominion

Edited by Sam Migliore

[Livio Nicoletti]: A lot of the Italians made their own salami and wine. Everybody had pigs. [Angelo Cechetto]: And chickens and a garden. [Livio]: That was a way of life here, growing up as kids. [Angelo]: There's a lot of land around, and it doesn't take much to make a little garden. [Tony Basso]: The younger generation still carried that on. Land always had to be productive. [Livio]: I don't think you are allowed to raise a pig in town now. [Tony]: No. There's the by-laws. Years ago, everybody, everybody had one.

[Sam]: Last time I was here you were telling me the story about the slaughtering of the pigs. [Livio]: It was quite a ritual for two or three weeks. You could hear the pigs squealing all over Dominion, and they had it in sequence—this Saturday it was one family, and then the next week it would be another family ... and so on for about a month.

[Val Scattolon]: There was something about the full moon. [Tony]: I remember, you had to kill the pig when the full moon was waning, going down. [Val]: Yeah ... or the salami wouldn't cure right. [Tony]: It was in November or December. We used to make the regular salami with salt and some with *aglio* (garlic). And then, I remember hanging the salamis down in the basement. The ones with the *aglio* always had the longer string. When you went down to get the *aglio*, you'd know, you would pick the one with the *spago lungo*. [laughter]

But it was a real production. The table had to be spotlessly clean. The killing of the pig was early in the morning. [Angelo]: The first thing was to save the blood. [Tony]: Then they would scrape the hair off by pouring hot water on it. When that was done, they hung them up and cut them open. Well, the liver was still quivering. "Bring that in to your mother." They took it immediately, and we had liver and polenta [a corn meal dish] for dinner. The next morning, they would put half the pig on the table and cut it up. The bloody meat went on one side, that was for

261

sausages and the rest for salami. The salami was hung up in the basement. When all the *muffa* (mold) came on it, well then they were satisfied; [it was ready]. And then we used to eat the bones. They would take every bit of meat off the bones and then put them in the oven. You were supposed to eat off of that. If you found a piece of meat, it was like winning the lottery. [everyone laughs] But you wouldn't throw much away. [The only things that went were] the ears and the tip of the nose. [everyone laughs] [Livio]: And the tail.

[Tony]: Well, then with the skin you'd make what they called *cotechini*. You'd use a little bit of meat and grind it up. [Livio]: They'd boil it. It's right sticky, like glue. But it has a distinct taste to it. [Tony]: They put spices in it, and they'd have to boil forever. Then we used to have bean soup with it. But they didn't throw anything away at all. No. My mother used to render all the fat and then put it in big [empty] cans for shortening and lard to make pies and that. And you ate that, bye, that was gorgeous stuff.

We used to have two pigs. About half of one pig went to my mother. She used to pickle it in the wooden barrel. I can remember saying, "How much salt do you use, Ma?" "Oh," she said, "I'll show you. Put so much water in and then add a potato." She kept adding salt, and salt, until the potato would float, then she would put the meat in and cover it.

When furnaces came, well, that ruined everything. [Livio]: Once the hot air furnaces came in, all the Italians around here couldn't cure their salami. [Tony]: There was no place where you could keep it. But, the old homes, they were perfect [you could maintain the right temperature and other conditions].

"Nella Cucina"
Some of the Best of Italian Cooking

By A. Evo DiPierro
in collaboration with Delia DiRito

One sunny day over the Atlantic Ocean in October 1994, I sat in an airplane watching tiny supertankers on the water below. I was heading home after spending three memorable and revealing weeks with my relatives in Italy. During that trip, I immersed myself in the grand culinary experiences of my people's country dining rooms. Dish after dish of soup, pasta, fish and roast (prepared and served with attentiveness to pleasure) is what I vividly remember from that vacation. However, I was both reassured and flabbergasted by the ways in which my fellow Italians dine nowadays. That trip was the push I needed to begin this paper.

The tradition of multi-course meals, consisting of plenty of pasta, fish and roast pork, all adorned with olives and grapes, and rinsed with an endless flow of red wine and happy chatter around a long table, is unchanged and secure. However, as I reported to my parents at home, most Italians, even in the small villages, no longer make their own pasta. People now buy their pasta, bread, cured meats, chows and sweets. They still make their own pasta sauce, however, as well as wine and some chows (actually, the elderly make these and their grown children take them home). My concern, as I contemplated in the plane, was not the quantity of food that my hosts treated me to, but rather the quality of the food. If, in Italy, they have forgone the virtue of making food in the spirit of homemade freshness, then where does real Italian food go from here?

The time had come for me to revive the old cooking that my mother used to do, as well as document every recipe. And when I began sharing our food with my non-Italian friends in Cape Breton, I renewed my own enjoyment of the food as they conveyed their positive sentiments about the meals. Another factor emerged in the whole process—the need to promote healthy eating by cutting fat and calories. To accomplish this, my mother and I modified many dishes to make them leaner, while ensuring that we did not lose sight of the main purpose: to maintain and, in some cases, even enhance the rich flavour of our food.

In this section of the book, I will introduce many old and some new Italian dishes that originate from Abruzzo, a region in central Italy where my parents were born and my relatives still live. Unlike many Italian recipe books that provide recipes which are time consuming to make and require ingredients that are difficult to acquire, this collection acknowledges your need for good food without much fuss and concern for calories. You will experience dining that Italians have been used to for more than 150 years. This paper bridges old and new concepts to present recipes that are healthy, wholesome and simple. Now there are a few things which will take more time and effort, but consider these as "projects" that you can undertake when the time is right—such as holidays and vacations. This chapter is what you need if the time has come to change the way you eat or if you desire an alternative perspective on Italian cooking.

The recipes in this section come from my mother, Delia DiRito. She learned most of them from her mother, although there are a few that she learned, as a young girl, from watching other women in her hometown prepare meals. For me, these recipes are the centrepiece of real Italian cuisine. I grew up with pasta, fish, beans and eggplant. All through my youth, my metabolism demanded complete meals that covered all the food groups. I was cultured to expect fresh food cooked with tomatoes and seasonings; I always had a balanced diet. My mother never undercooked her food nor cut corners in the preparation. For me, mealtime at home evokes feelings of old country living; I feel immersed in a completely Italian atmosphere of food, language, etc. while the real world temporarily detaches from my mind. Perhaps this is how a perfect ethnic dining experience is achieved.

While doing my research for this book, I looked to other Italian cookbooks for tips on organization and content. They were helpful yet, as friends pointed out, a critical factor to the applicability of such recipes to the kitchens of Cape Breton and Eastern Canada is the availability of the ingredients. Many cookbooks seem rather uncompromising with their ingredients; they insist on fresh tomatoes for sauce, exotic cheeses and mushrooms, fresh seasonings and spices. These things often are hard to find, or they can be expensive for average meals—the last thing you need is a guilt trip for compromising on that special dinner. My mother understood the availability factor early in her new life in Canada, and she adapted her cooking in the new environment to produce the same great dishes, with variations that made them even better. More recently, I have modified or varied some of our traditional dishes by adding certain East Indian spices and flavours, and by incorporating certain elements of French cuisine that my friend, Mr. Bernard Lalanne, has kindly shared with me.

Some Notes on Ingredients

The recipes in this section are easy to prepare, and most ingredients can be obtained at any supermarket. Pasta is normally cooked al dente or "to the tooth"—the noodles are boiled to a point short of softness, so that they retain some of their firm texture. However, my mother never liked her pasta al dente; she cooked it completely but made sure it did not become too soft. There really is no right or wrong way, but al dente is the norm. Our experience has been that when pasta is cooked all the way to softness, it absorbs sauce better, has a tender texture, and you may eat less pasta, which would benefit your diet.

Italians love herbs and seasonings—especially basil, parsley and oregano—but our food is not too spicy. Basil is stronger than parsley, so as a rule, we use a teaspoon of basil (dried or fresh) for every tablespoon of parsley. Garlic is very important to Italian cooking, so we always have it handy. Don't be afraid to use plenty of fresh garlic; once cooked with other ingredients for a prolonged period, the smell and taste will blend with the other ingredients. We also like dried, hot red peppers sprinkled as flakes on pasta. Bay leaves are great in roasts and stuffing, and Italian seasoning, a blend of spices, delivers a mellow yet well-rounded aroma to meat. Italians also eat all kinds of fish; practically none of the creatures from the murky depths is too ugly for us. Fish is one of the cornerstones of our Italian cuisine.

Nothing beats fresh chicken or beef in tomato sauce or lamb in a cacciatora. But to support our diet, we slightly alter the method of preparation. For example: we remove the skin and fat from chicken and par cook it by either frying or oven-grilling to shed additional grease. At this point, it is ready to include in the primary cooking process. For lean beef or pork steaks, cut off as much fat as possible. The point is health, obviously, but pasta sauce has a richer, more uniform texture, and a cleaner, sweeter taste when meat fat is cut.

Generally, Italians cook vegetables in large pieces. When making gnocchi (potato noodles), your potatoes need to be aged and a little soft. Canned tomatoes are just as good as fresh ones for sauce. Olive oil is synonymous with Italian cooking, and extra virgin olive oil is tastier and more nutritious. Extra virgin means that the oil is derived from the first pressing of the finest olives; it has a clean, greenish colour and tastes wonderful. I use it for fish, salads and sauce. Regular olive oil, which has been through additional pressings, is good for cooking that requires more oil, but a light, unsaturated vegetable oil will also do. Three cheeses my family enjoys are mozzarella, Parmesan and provolone. A slice of provolone is good with antipasto or in sandwiches of roast eggplant slices, prosciutto and bread with olive oil.

Read each recipe completely before starting, and check that you have the required ingredients. For the few long recipes, ensure that you have enough time available. In cooking, nothing is written in stone so feel free to experiment. Above all, whether it is breakfast, lunch or dinner, enjoy the food by allowing yourself plenty of time to eat slowly and to savour every morsel, like we Italians do.

Antipasto, Salads & Soups

Antipasto

Antipasto means "before the pasta." It is the appetizer to the main course of an Italian dinner. We usually have it when special guests visit. Traditionally, however, another reason for serving antipasto was to show off the particular specialties that the hosts had made and acquired. A typical plate of antipasto would have:

2 very thin strips of prosciutto
2 slices of salami or mortadella
1 slice of ham or pastrami
1 piece of provolone cheese with either mozzarella or
    parmigiano reggiano beside it
1 slice of honeydew or cantaloupe
4 olives, green or black
1 piece of dill pickle or some pickled green tomatoes, a couple of marinated
    artichoke hearts in olive oil and some fresh homemade bread on the side.

Pickled Green Tomatoes

When I visited relatives in Italy two years ago, my aunt served these tomatoes with antipasto during evening meals. I fell in love with them. Once home, I explained what I had discovered to my mother, and she immediately understood. Pickled tomatoes had drifted out of thought at our home, because no one had requested them. Today, they are a resident of our fridge, and I am so pleased that it has been reintroduced to our household.

Pickled tomatoes are a chow eaten, like an antipasto, with cheese, cured meats, fresh bread and other pickled items. These tomatoes, however, can also be enjoyed with a roast or fried meat. The following recipe makes plenty to cover the months ahead. To begin, have ready:

10 lbs. green tomatoes (washed and sliced thinly into small pieces)
½ cup salt   10 cloves garlic, chopped
4 cups vinegar   2 tablespoon parsley, chopped
4 cups water   2 cups vegetable oil
1 tablespoon oregano

Method

The sliced tomatoes should be in a large bin with salt sprinkled all over them. Cover and let stand for 24 hours, then wash the tomatoes with cold water and drain. Soak them in vinegar and water for another 24 hours. Drain well, place tomatoes on a table, and dry them with a cloth. Next, place tomatoes in a large bowl. In a smaller bowl, combine the oregano, garlic and parsley with the oil, and pour this all over the tomatoes. Mix well.

Sterilize eight ½ litre mason jars, and fill each one with pickled tomatoes. Press down, add another tablespoon of oil to the jar and seal for two weeks before serving. Store in a cool place.

Ricotta Cheese

Ricotta is a soft, white, almost bland tasting cheese. It reminds me of brie or Camembert, but the texture is very different. This Italian cheese is used often as a filling for pasta, but can be enjoyed alone mixed with some seasonings or eaten with fruit.

4 litres homogenized milk	3 eggs
½ litre coffee cream	½ cup white vinegar

Method
In a large, non-stick pot, pour the milk (less 2 cups) and add the coffee cream. In a bowl, beat the eggs with the rest of the milk and then add to the pot. On maximum heat, while stirring to prevent sticking, bring the pot to near boiling, and then reduce heat to medium. This should take about 15 minutes. When the milk mixture is very hot, almost boiling, add the vinegar and mix very well. Over the next five minutes, the milk should form curds. At this point, immediately remove from heat and leave to cool. Next, place a strainer in a small bowl. With a smaller, hand-held strainer, collect some of the cooled cheese and place in the strainer/bowl. Allow all to drain completely before moving the cheese to a dry bowl for storage. To prepare ricotta as a filling for ravioli, combine the cheese with one cup of grated parmesan, finely chopped parsley and four large eggs.

Vegetable Minestrone

This all vegetable potpourri makes a superb lunch or first course that is both wholesome and nutritious. It is also highly adaptable to any variance of taste.

2 celery stocks, chopped	½ large can of tomatoes, diced
¼ medium cabbage, chopped	5 cloves garlic
1 small turnip, chopped	3 tablespoons olive oil
2 carrots, chopped	1 tablespoon salt (more or less)
1 - 2 large onions, chopped	½ teaspoon black pepper

Add as optional: peas, broccoli or cauliflower (at the end of cooking).

Method
Dump vegetables into a large soup pot. Add water to a level of one inch above the vegetables. Bring to a boil, then reduce to medium heat and cook for two hours.

All vegetables must be tender. During the last ten minutes, add any extras—such as peas or cauliflower. Serve with crackers or slices of whole wheat bread.

Other options include: adding cooked beans; or, for an extra "hot" and "spicy" taste, adding half a teaspoon of hot curry paste midway through the cooking process.

Lentil Soup

Lentils are rich in nutrients, and they make a very tasty dish with this old recipe.

1 lb. lentils	1 teaspoon salt
1 onion, coarsely diced	½ teaspoon black pepper
2 celery sticks, chopped	¼ cup olive oil
2 cloves garlic	1 bay leaf
3 tomatoes from a can, finely chopped	1 carrot, chopped into 2 or 3 pieces

Method

Soak lentils in water overnight (the level of the water should be ½ higher than the lentils). Next day, add all other ingredients and bring to a boil, then cook over medium heat for one hour. Add more water if necessary. Serve with fresh bread or crackers.

Chicken Soup

This soup dish is good for just about everything: your hunger; your desire for a hot, soothing alternative to other meals; your cold; your date; or, your kids. I have it for my hunger and my cold (my date—pretty soon!). My mother likes to use celery when she cooks; perhaps it is this ingredient that makes her chicken soup distinct. The simple recipe below serves four.

First, the broth:

3 chicken quarters (fat removed)	2 good sized carrots
1 chicken breast (fat removed)	2 celery stocks, plus a few leaves
2½ litres water	salt
1 large onion, quartered	2 full tomatoes, canned or fresh (peeled)

Method

Place chicken, water and salt in a soup pot and bring to a boil. As it boils, remove the foam that accumulates. Add vegetables and continue boiling until the meat becomes flaky and loose. Remove the meat and set aside in a bowl.

You can prepare this soup in two ways, with either noodles or vegetables:

(1) Boil ½ lb of star, tempestine, elbow or egg noodles in water. Drain and dump into the boiling broth to cook for another ten minutes.

(2) Add one cup cubed potatoes, one cup peas, extra carrots and some cabbage to the broth. Cook for another 20 minutes, or until the vegetables are soft.

Note. The broth is a fine stock for future cooking and can be frozen in small containers. Turkey can be substituted for chicken, using the same amounts. To remove even more fat from the soup, let the pot of broth cool, then refrigerate overnight. Next day, remove the fat that has risen to the top and boil again to complete your soup. And, finally, if you use egg noodles in the soup, sprinkle some grated parmesan cheese into the bowl and enjoy the extra flavour.

Pasta Dishes

Homemade Spaghetti

On some Sundays, my mother likes to treat us to pasta made from scratch—in the form of spaghetti, matalotti, ravioli.... She makes pasta based on a simple Italian recipe that goes back two or three centuries. I easily can devour two plates of her spaghetti, drenched in meat sauce, followed by meat and salad, and my father's red wine. While enjoying this homemade meal, I can feel my "reality" changing. My whole world view is transformed during those special moments of immersion into an "old country" consciousness.

For four to five plates of spaghetti:

4 eggs	1 teaspoon salt
4 cups flour	½ cup warm water

Method

Mix ingredients together, and knead on a floured surface to form a smooth and somewhat shiny dough. Put the dough inside a plastic bag and leave for an hour. Next, return dough back to the floured surface. Slice into ½ inch thick sections. Flatten slightly each section with a wooden roller to prepare the dough for the noodle maker.

The pasta maker: roll the flattened dough through the machine starting at maximum thickness. Redo, decreasing by a notch each time (on some makers, this means starting the knob at no. 7, and working your way down). What is important here is to gradually flatten the dough, in stages, until it is left to a thickness of just two millimetres. Allow the broad, flat dough to dry on the table for another hour.

Finally, flour the pieces and roll each one through the spaghetti cutter of the noodle maker. Collect the noodles as they exit. Start cooking when all spaghetti is cut. To freeze for another day, simply lay the noodles on a floured cookie sheet, place inside a large bag, and store in the freezer.

To make fettucini: the exact same ingredients and procedures are required. The only difference is that when flattening the dough through the noodle maker, fettucini noodles need to be a little thinner, about 1½ millimetres. And, of course, you use the wide noodle cutter.

Matalotti

Matalotti are flat, triangular shaped noodles that require the same ingredients as the spaghetti discussed previously. The procedure used to make them is different, but simpler. Slice your dough into ½ inch sections and roll briefly with a wooden roller. Flatten in the noodle maker, at successive levels on the machine, until you reach a thickness of 1½ millimetres. Allow the wide bands to dry on the table for 1½ hours. Finally, slice the pasta bands, from end to end, into two inch strips. Cut each strip into triangular pieces. Drop them into boiling water after all are cut. To freeze matalotti for later use, lay them on a floured cookie sheet and freeze. When frozen, dump into a plastic bag and return to freezer for storage.

Note: You can make lasagna too! Those wide bands of dough that you flattened in the noodle maker are the lasagna noodles themselves! They should also be 1½ millimetres in thickness. Only spaghetti noodles need to be thicker for texture and resiliency while boiling.

Gnocchi al patate

Gnocchi are pasta noodles that contain potato.

1 kg. aged potatoes, peeled and boiled	2 eggs
3 cups flour	1 teaspoon salt

Method

Mash the potatoes. In a large bowl, form a well with the flour and dump the mashed potato into the well. Add eggs and salt, and mix well into a dough. Knead gently on a floured surface for about 20 minutes to form a solid, smooth ball. Flour as necessary to avoid stickiness. Take a portion and, on a floured surface, flatten with a wooden roller to ½ inch thickness. Slice into 1½ inch wide strips. Cut each strip into one centimetre long piece. Gently press, with two fingers, into the middle of the noodle and toward you to form a sickle shape. Leave aside on a floured surface until all the gnocchi pieces are ready.

Water must be boiling before noodles can be dropped in. When ready, add one tablespoon of salt and place gnocchi in pot. A minute after they have risen to the surface, collect them with a small strainer and place in the serving bowl. Add sauce to each batch and serve.

Pasta & Peas (or Chic Peas)

Talk about delicious! Have you ever had pasta with peas? This recipe is excellent in terms of nutrition; all four food groups are represented here. Legumes are often neglected for meals, but in this recipe they are given prominence. This recipe makes enough for a family of four.

1 large onion, diced	1½ cans tomatoes, mashed
2 cloves garlic, chopped	½ teaspoon salt

¾ cup minced bacon	1 tablespoon parsley
¼ cup olive oil	1 teaspoon basil
1 teaspoon diced celery leaves	3 cups green peas or 2 cups chic peas
½ teaspoon black pepper	1 (500g) package elbow pasta

Method

Fast fry the onion, garlic and bacon until browned. Add other ingredients, except the pasta and peas. Simmer for 1½ hours, then add peas. For green peas, there is an additional cooking time of ¾ hour (or until they are tender). Chic peas must be washed before cooking; once added to the pot, they will require only 15 to 20 minutes of additional cooking time. While the legumes are cooking, boil the elbow pasta, drain and dump into a serving bowl (the time at which you begin cooking the pasta depends on which peas you choose). Finally, pour the cooked sauce over the pasta and mix together. This is a marvellous dish to have alone or with garlic bread on the side.

Delia's Tomato and Meat Sauce

We use this sauce on our pasta every Sunday for lunch. This dish is followed by a second course of meat (which has been prepared in the sauce), salad and bread. It is an Italian tradition to eat a large lunch on Sundays.

1 onion, chopped	2-3 cloves of garlic, chopped well
¼ green bell pepper, chopped	1½ tablespoon parsley
1 tablespoon basil	1 tablespoon celery leaves, chopped

Pinch of Italian seasoning and/or oregano
½ cup olive oil, plus 3 teaspoons more for later
salt & ½ teaspoon black pepper
½ of a 13 ounce can of tomato paste (or up to a whole can, depending
    on desired thickness)
2 large cans tomatoes, crushed
meat, almost cooked
1 small peeled carrot (optional for sweetness)

Method

Grind onion to oregano in a blender or food processor. Midway, add oil and continue grinding until the mixture is fine. Cook on medium heat, adding more oil (about three teaspoons), salt and black pepper until it turns a bit sticky and golden in colour. Add tomato paste; stir and reduce to simmer. Finely grind tomatoes in blender or food processor and add to the simmering mixture. Drop in the peeled carrot, add one teaspoon salt and cook on medium. Then reduce to simmer for one to one-and-a-half hours. Afterwards, drop the meat into the sauce and simmer for another hour.

The meat. Meatballs—no problem, leave in sauce for as long as you like. Chicken and turkey—don't overcook, poultry tends to break apart. Beef, lamb and pork—

cooking depends on the age of the meat, however avoid overcooking. When cooking meat, we like to bake it in the oven over a sprayed grill to reduce its fat content.

Fish & Other Non-Mean Dishes

Pesce al sugo (Fish and Tomato Sauce)

This is the other sauce recipe that my family and I enjoy often. For fish, there is nothing better; the sauce tenderizes the fish and enriches its flavour. I have it with fresh Italian bread and red wine. The recipe below makes enough for two people. There is plenty of sauce here for a ½ pound of spaghetti as a separate dish, leaving enough sauce for the fish on each plate. Virtually any fish can be used in this recipe. Some suggestions are: salmon, halibut, swordfish, turbot, shrimp, haddock, lobster, crab, shark or cod.

1½ can tomatoes, crushed	green pepper, chopped
7 cloves garlic	½ teaspoon salt
2 heaping tablespoons parsley	¼ cup oil
2 teaspoons basil or 3-4 leaves of fresh basil, diced	

Method

Mix ingredients and bring to a boil in a large saucepan. Reduce heat to simmer for 20 minutes. Add fish filets or steaks, and cook for another 10 to 20 minutes (or until the fish is completely cooked). Fish should be flaky when done. To maximize the flavour of your meal, especially when it involves lobster, leave fish in the pan, covered, for another 20 to 30 minutes at the lowest heat setting. Serve with anything you desire.

For spaghetti, simply boil the pasta, drain, place some in each plate, and then add the sauce. For a two-course meal, have the spaghetti first. Leave fish with some sauce in the pan, covered and warmed, then, when ready, serve fish with a tossed salad and rolls.

Italian Salmon Roast

While in Italy three years ago, I had roast salmon at my uncle's home. All he and my aunt did was lay the fish in a roast pot and surround it with yellow potatoes, herbs, spices and plenty of the purest virgin olive oil. It was so delicious that I had fish almost every day thereafter! Back in Canada, I wanted to experience this roast often and with some slight variations. Since I also like mixed vegetables and curry, I sometimes include an East Indian twist to the recipe to give it extra flavour. Although my recipe is mainly for salmon, I sometimes use trout or mackerel.

A roast for three	½ lb mushrooms
½ kg fresh Atlantic salmon	¼ cup extra virgin olive oil

three large potatoes, quartered
one sweet potato, quartered
some carrots
some broccoli
salt, pepper
1 tablespoon curry powder or medium curry paste (optional)

1 tablespoon parsley
1 teaspoon basil
2 cloves garlic, chopped
1 large onion, sliced
half a lemon, sliced

Method

Clean scales from salmon by immersing it in water and scraping them off with a knife. Place fish in a roasting pan and slice deep cuts into the flesh at one inch intervals. Surround fish with the vegetables. Sprinkle some parsley and basil inside the fish, along with some of the curry. Sprinkle the rest of these spices all over the roast, followed by salt and pepper. Pour olive oil all over as well and, finally, insert a slice of lemon into each of the deep cuts in the fish. Bake, covered, in the oven at 400°F for 40 minutes or until the potatoes are soft.

Pizza Sauce

Italian pizzas are usually rectangular in shape and contain few toppings—sauce, green peppers and maybe pepperoni and cheese. The sauce, made simply from tomatoes and basic seasonings, provides a rich, flavourful texture for the pizza, while the crust is hard and crunchy. On Saturdays, my mother makes this pizza for lunch so all of us can eat the same thing together.

1 can tomatoes
½ teaspoon oregano
½ teaspoon black pepper, salt
½ cup vegetable oil

garlic, fresh, finely chopped
½ teaspoon basil
¼ teaspoon sugar

Method

Drain tomatoes completely, place in a bowl, and remove the dark portion at the top of each piece. Mash tomatoes well and move them to another bowl. Add remaining ingredients, mixing thoroughly. It is now ready to be spread on the pizza. Just put the uncooked sauce aside until the dough is ready. Refrigerate any excess tomato sauce for the next time.

Pizza Dough

For one pizza:
1 cup water
1 tablespoon sugar
1 yeast packet
8 cups flour

1 tablespoon salt
½ cup vegetable oil
2 cups water

Method

In a bowl, combine water and sugar, and add yeast. Leave to rise for 10 minutes, then combine yeast mixture with flour, salt, oil and water until the dough forms.

Let set for two hours in a warm place to allow it to rise before baking. Cover dough with a cloth to prevent excessive drying. Next, flatten dough on a pizza pan. Cover and leave to rise for another ½ hour. Spread sauce (not too much) on pizza, and add the green peppers and mushrooms (if desired). Bake at 400°F or 375°F in a slower oven. When the pizza is half cooked, after about 25 minutes, take it out of the oven and add any remaining ingredients, and resume baking for another 15 minutes. Pizza is completely done when crust is golden and hard. Remove pizza from pan, and allow it to cool on a cooling rack.

Simple Tomato & Onion Sauce

This sauce contains no meat or fish, and it is rather light and sweet tasting. My mother and I developed it, in an effort to produce a low-fat, low calorie recipe for some of our meals. Since tomatoes are central to a great Italian pasta sauce, I figured that a sauce without meat would be just fine. In terms of taste, it has become a winner for me. There are no edges to the taste, nor are there any special ingredients to make up for the missing meat. Everything you need is probably in your kitchen now.

For two bowls of pasta (such as rotini, penne or shells):

1 onion, diced	1 teaspoon basil
4 cloves of garlic, chopped	1 tablespoon parsley
½ tsp. salt	½ teaspoon black pepper
1 can tomatoes	2 celery leaves, chopped
¼ cup extra virgin olive oil or basic olive oil	

Method
Fry onion, garlic and oil in a sauce pan. Add the remaining ingredients, and simmer for one hour. Boil pasta and drain. Serve with sauce. Enjoy!

Cheese Balls

Cheese balls are tasty round pieces of cheese mixed with bread crumbs and spices. They are served, at my home, with fresh bread (and sometimes a vegetable dish on the side).

The cheese mixture:

1 cup bread crumbs (fine)	some parsley and black pepper
1 cup grated Parmesan cheese	3 eggs
salt (optional, since the cheese has enough salt anyway)	
Mix well. Cover and set aside.	

The tomato sauce:

2 onions, sliced	1 can tomatoes, crushed
¼ cup oil	1 teaspoon basil
2 cloves garlic, chopped	1 teaspoon parsley

½ green pepper, chopped   salt and pepper

Method

Briefly fry onions, oil, garlic and green pepper. Add tomatoes and seasonings. Cook for ½ hour. During this time, form small oval-shaped balls from the cheese mixture. Add these to the sauce and cook for another 20 minutes.

Pasta alla rabbia

Pasta alla rabbia is another simple meat-free dish. We usually use penne or rotini for this meal, but shell pasta can be used as well. It is a rich and spicy Italian dish that comes straight from the rural regions of southern and central Italy. This recipe will produce enough sauce for three or four servings, depending on how much sauce you like on your pasta.

1 can tomatoes or 6 to 7 very ripe fresh tomatoes, crushed
¼ cup oil   1 cup fresh parsley
½ teaspoon salt   5 cloves garlic, chopped
red or chili pepper, plus some black pepper
pasta of your choice

Method

Mix and cook (except pasta and parsley) in a sauce pan for ¾ of an hour. Boil pasta. One minute before draining, dump parsley into pot and reduce heat. Cover to lock in the aroma. Drain pasta and place in a serving bowl. Pour sauce over pasta, mix, and serve with garlic bread.

Roast Peppers

For three people:

5 bell peppers, of various colours, or all red (Red peppers are sweetest, but green, red, yellow and orange make a colourful dish)
1 clove garlic, chopped   2 tablespoons extra virgin olive oil
some parsley   salt

Method

On a baking sheet, covered with foil and sprayed with a non-stick spray, roast peppers for 30 minutes at 450°F or until they are shrivelled and turning brown. Take out and leave to cool in a bowl, covered with a tea towel, so that the steam inside will loosen the skins. Next, slice each pepper in half. Flatten them on a board and peel skins. Slice peppers into thin strips and place in a serving dish. Add garlic, oil, parsley and salt; mix well. Peppers should be lukewarm by now and ready to serve.

I enjoy these peppers on a slice of crusty Italian or French baguette bread with cheese or prosciutto on the side, and a glass of red wine. But you decide how best to savour them.

Stuffed Eggplant

Eggplant is a popular vegetable in Italy, where it is widely grown and inexpensive to obtain. This meat-free recipe is sure to appeal to practically everyone's tastes; it scores top grades for nutrition and dining pleasure.

Gently beat eight medium-size eggplants to soften them. Hollow out each one. Finely chop the insides and rinse with water in a pasta strainer; wring with your hands to mash, and then dump into a mixing bowl. Add and mix:

2 fresh tomatoes, chopped	½ teaspoon black pepper
2 eggs	1 teaspoon salt
½ cup grated Parmesan cheese	1 teaspoon basil
½ green pepper, diced	1 teaspoon parsley
2 cloves garlic, diced	1 tablespoon extra virgin olive oil

Method

Stuff each eggplant with this mixture, place them in a roasting pan, and set aside. Blend any remaining stuffing with the sauce. To make the sauce, mix together in a bowl:

1 can tomatoes, crushed	some garlic
some basil	½ teaspoon salt
½ teaspoon black pepper	¼ cup olive oil

Method

Pour this sauce over the eggplants. Bake at 375°F for one hour. Check for tenderness; fork should pierce the eggplant effortlessly when done. Serve with potatoes, bread or rice.

Grilled Eggplant Slices

1 large eggplant, sliced into ½ inch slices
1 teaspoon salt
Some olive oil, parsley, oregano and 1 clove of garlic, finely diced

Method

Soak slices in water, mixed with the salt, for one hour. Drain and dry. Grill over a flame until browned, then lay on a wide serving dish. Dress them with the seasonings and serve. Excellent with roasts and other meat dishes, in hamburgers, and in sandwiches.

Frittata

Frittata is simply an Italian variation of scrambled eggs. All you need are six eggs (beaten), olive oil, and whatever extra items you wish to add. In a large frying pan, heat two tablespoons of oil, and then add the egg. When half-cooked, cut into four sections and flip over each piece to complete the frying. To give your frittata extra flavour, fry some diced onions and/or mushrooms first, then pour in the egg. However, I am certain that anything you might prefer to add will work with this recipe.

Polenta

Polenta is cornmeal cooked the Italian way. There are variations, however, in the method of preparing polenta from region to region in Italy. The recipe below comes from my mother's region of Abruzzo, in central Italy. This recipe makes a creamy meal in a gorgeous tomato and pork sauce for six people. Simply cut in half for a smaller group.

The sauce:

1 lb. pork, chopped or ground
1 onion, chopped
2 cans tomatoes, crushed
2 cloves garlic, chopped
1 tablespoon ground basil

1 tablespoon chopped parsley
¼ cup olive oil
1 teaspoon salt
½ teaspoon black pepper

Method

In a large sauce pan, fry meat, adding onion halfway through. Add the rest of the ingredients and slowly cook, or simmer, for 1½ hours.

The cornmeal:

1 (500g) package cornmeal
10 cups water
1 tablespoon salt

Method

Bring water to a full boil in a large pot. Move pot to a cool stove top, then add the cornmeal, a little at a time, stirring continuously. Turn on stove to medium heat and, for 20 minutes, stir steadily to maintain a creamy texture. (It is a good idea to do this with someone else, so you can take turns stirring). In the last five minutes, add two scoops of the tomato sauce and mix with the cornmeal. To serve, scoop some sauce onto each plate, followed by the polenta, and topped with more sauce.

For leftover polenta: place it in a bread baking pan and level. Refrigerate. For the next meal, cut the polenta into thick slices and remove each piece from the bread pan. Fry in olive oil, and top with garlic powder and paprika. Serve with cabbage and beans on the side.

Meats and Marinades

Meat Balls

These are the true Italian meat balls that complement our pasta dishes.

1 teaspoon parsley
1 cup bread or cracker crumbs
2 eggs
¼ cup milk
2 lbs lean ground beef

½ teaspoon black pepper
1 teaspoon garlic powder
¼ + cup Parmesan cheese
½ teaspoon salt

Method

Grease your palms, mash ingredients together with your hands, and then roll them into a ball. Place on a baking sheet. Bake meat balls at 400°F for 20 minutes. Then allow to cool.

Fettine

Fettine are a tasty main part of any meal that requires no special occasion. They are breaded veal cutlets that are served (at my home) with mashed potatoes, greens, rice, etc.

3 individual packages of 25 soda crackers, ground
½ cup Parmesan cheese, grated
some salt, black pepper and parsley
3 eggs, scrambled raw
2½ lbs. veal cutlets or similar meat, finely sliced

Method

Prepare a non-stick skillet with oil for frying. In a dish, mix the crackers, salt, pepper and parsley together. Pound meat to tenderize. Dip each cutlet in the egg to soak, then roll into the cracker mixture. Fry until golden-brown. Place on paper towels to dry.

Marinade for Pork Roast

This marinade dresses your roast with a tangy and stimulating flavour. Suitable for a two pound section, sliced either horizontally to roll or into vertical sections.

Combine:
½ cup Italian dressing
2 cloves garlic, crushed

2 tbsp. soya sauce
some parsley

Method

Pour the mixture over meat and refrigerate for several hours before roasting. If the meat is rolled, use string to fasten and lock in the juices.

Stuffed Green Peppers

This dish is both delicious and colourful. A stuffed pepper, sliced in half and surrounded by sweet tomato sauce, with fresh rolls and a glass of red wine, makes for a picture perfect meal.

For six whole peppers:

The filling:
¾ cup rice, cooked   1½ lbs. lean ground beef, fried & drained
½ teaspoon of salt & pepper   ½ cup grated Parmesan cheese
2 eggs

Method
Mix rice and meat; add salt and pepper, followed by the cheese and eggs. Wash and hollow peppers, then stuff with filling. Set aside.

The sauce:

1 can tomatoes, mashed   ¼ cup vegetable or olive oil
2 cloves garlic, chopped   some basil, parsley, salt, pepper and oregano

Method
Combine sauce ingredients, and simmer for at least ½ hour. Lay peppers in a roasting pot and pour sauce over them. Bake, covered, at 400°F, then reduce to 375° when boiling. Continue roasting until peppers are tender, about one hour before serving.

Poultry Stuffing

This stuffing, for an average-size chicken or small turkey, can serve as your Italian alternative to the North American bread crumb stuffing. It is very easy to make and, with the almonds, so tasty.

1 lb. lean or extra lean ground beef   2 eggs
pinch black pepper, salt   1 cup Italian or French bread crumbs
½ cup grated Parmesan cheese   ¼ cup almonds or walnuts, chopped

Method
Fry meat, drain grease, and then add remaining ingredients. Cook for several minutes, until the eggs are done. Mixture is now ready for stuffing. However, I recommend that you place a couple of bay leaves inside the chicken or turkey before stuffing to add a nice aroma to the roast.

Chicken alla cacciatora

My mother learned this recipe as a child in her hometown of San Salvo, Chieti province. It involves baked chicken with sauce and dressings. She sometimes makes it with chili pepper; but, with or without the hot stuff, it makes a wonderful meal for family or guests.

1 whole chicken, sectioned	1 tablespoon parsley
1 can tomatoes	1 teaspoon basil
½ cup olive oil	1 teaspoon chili pepper (optional)
2 cloves garlic	2 onions, thinly sliced
couple of bay leaves	1 green bell pepper, chopped or sliced
some fresh celery leaves, chopped	

Method

Remove much of the skin and fat from the chicken pieces, and bake halfway for ½ hour at 425°F. Drain the fat, and transfer pieces to a roasting pot. Combine and cook the remaining ingredients (except the onions and bell pepper) in a saucepan for ½ hour so that it is half-cooked. Spread the onion over the chicken, followed by the green pepper. Now pour sauce on chicken and bake, covered, for one hour at 400°F, then reduce to 375°F when boiling. Serve with rice, mashed potato or garlic bread on the side. Note: You can easily substitute lamb, or any wild meat (such as deer or rabbit), for the chicken.

Lamb & Swiss Chard

Every fall, we pick Swiss chard from our garden and cook it with lamb in a tasty tomato sauce. For a family meal, we use approximately four cups of Swiss chard. Boil in ½ cup of water, in a covered pan, at medium heat. Next, use a large skillet to fry (at medium heat) two pounds of lamb cutlets (fat removed) in three tablespoons of olive oil with salt, pepper and 5-6 cloves of garlic. The cutlets should be just browned and half-cooked. At this point, add the following ingredients to make the sauce:

1 can tomatoes, mashed	2 tablespoons chopped bell pepper
1 teaspoon basil	½ teaspoon black pepper
1 tablespoon parsley	salt

Method

Mix well and resume cooking for another hour at medium heat. Finally, add the Swiss chard to the skillet and cook for another 20 minutes, so that the greens take on the flavour of the lamb and tomato sauce. Serve with rice or potato, plus fresh, crusty Italian or French bread.

The Sweeter Side of Italian Cooking

In the past, dinner at many Italian households rarely concluded with dessert (except on holidays or very special occasions). People tended to serve fruit at the end of a meal, and in Italy this tradition has changed little. Following the fruit was often a cup of espresso with liqueur flavouring. My parents explained to me that, during the Second World War, sweets were hard to come by, because supplies were limited and bakeries were often targeted in bombing raids. My grandfather's bakery was destroyed in this way. Sugar, cocoa and other ingredients were almost impossible to acquire, and prohibitively expensive for average citizens, at that time. As a result, my parents grew up to neither know well nor care for confections.

Over the last decade, Italian baking, certainly in our region, evolved to include more sugar, chocolate and cream; however, ingredients such as almonds, cocoa, vanilla and lemon still form the foundation of the "sweeter side of Italian cooking." Mom makes "sweets" more often now, because I enjoy them and, socially, they complement many occasions. My favourite is the Pasta Rigina. The following recipes are neither complicated to make, nor junky; they involve simple processes that my Mom learned from her mother (and so on, into the past). What I present here are some of Mom's best recipes, and I am certain that you, too, will like them with your coffee or tea.

Biscotti Cioccolate con Mandorle
(Chocolate Biscuits with Almonds)

This recipe is as old as the hills of Abruzzo. Traditionally made at Easter, Christmas and other special occasions, these biscuits are now enjoyed at any time.

6 eggs	7 cups flour
1½ cups sugar	2 cups almonds, roasted and crushed
16 oz. honey	5 teaspoons baking powder
1 cup of oil	4 tablespoons cocoa
grated lemon peel of one lemon	

Method

In a large bowl, beat the eggs and sugar, add honey and oil, and finally the lemon peel. In another bowl, mix the remaining ingredients together and add to the egg and sugar mixture. Knead a little, then cover with plastic wrap and leave for 4-5 hours.

On an oiled board, place a small piece of dough and flatten to ¼ inch thickness. Cut into diamond shapes (or any shape you wish) and place on a greased cookie baking sheet. Fill the sheet with these shapes and bake at 400°F for 15-20 minutes or until slightly golden. When done, remove from the oven and leave to cool. Cookies must not be over-baked or they will burn!

Glaze: Mix 4 cups icing sugar with ¾ cup cocoa and some milk (added gradually as you mix) until a creamy texture forms. Spread the glaze with your finger on each cookie. Allow to dry and harden before serving.

Pizzelle

These are Italian waffle cookies made on a special pizzelle iron, from a traditional Abruzzese recipe.

12 eggs	4 cups flour
1¼ cups sugar	1 teaspoon vanilla or anise flavouring
1¼ cups oil	

Method

Beat eggs well. Then beat in sugar and oil, followed by flour and flavourings. Place a teaspoon of batter on the hot pizzelle iron. Close cover for a few minutes. Remove pizzelle from iron when it is lightly browned. Let each pizzelle cool slightly before stacking. No refrigeration is required, just store in an air-tight container.

Almond Cookies

4 eggs	4 oz. butter, melted
16 oz. sugar	1 teaspoon baking powder
1 teaspoon vanilla	3 teaspoons cinnamon
2 tablespoons rum	3 cups flour
2 cups icing sugar	
2 lbs. almonds, first roasted then chopped into three pieces	

Method

Mix eggs and sugar, then add vanilla and rum; mix well. Lastly, mix remaining ingredients (except the icing sugar) into a mass of dough. Place parchment or wax paper on a cookie sheet. Put icing sugar in a clean bowl. Take a teaspoon of dough, drop it into the icing sugar, and roll to form a finger-length piece. Place on cookie sheet, and repeat the process until finished. Bake at 350°F for 15 to 20 minutes or until firm to touch. Check carefully while baking.

Pasta Rigina

Irresistibly delicious, yet surprisingly simple, these melt-in-your-mouth cookies never fail to please the most particular of tastes. Pasta rigina is made from only three ingredients. Almonds, a main element in Italian confectionery baking, however, are the key to this recipe.

3 egg whites
1 cup sugar
1 cup almonds (sliced fine)

Method

Beat egg whites and sugar together (eight to ten minutes) until stiff; gently fold in the almonds. Drop either a teaspoon or tablespoon sized portion onto a cookie sheet covered with wax paper. Bake at 200°F for ½ hour, until firm. Turn off oven and leave for another ½ hour.

Italian Tea Biscuits

4 eggs	2 teaspoons baking powder
½ cup sugar	1 teaspoon grated lemon peel
½ cup oil	1 teaspoon vanilla

2 cups flour (maybe more until dough is easy to handle)

Method

Beat eggs and sugar, then add remaining ingredients. Mix until dough is smooth. Place a piece of dough on a board and flatten to a band of one inch thickness by 2½ inches in width. Cut into strips and place on a greased cookie baking sheet. Bake at 400°F or until golden (approximately 20 minutes).

The glaze: Blend two cups icing sugar with two tablespoons of milk until creamy. Add more milk if necessary. Spread with your finger and leave to harden for a few minutes.

Jam Cookies

These jam-filled biscuits are popular with our friends, and Dad likes to eat them with coffee in the evening.

The cookie:

4 eggs	½ cup sugar
3 cups flour	2 teaspoon baking powder
pinch of salt	½ cup oil
1 teaspoon vanilla	

The filling:

1 (500 ml) jar grape jam
1 cup or less crushed almonds
1½ cup bread crumbs, finely ground & toasted
1 tablespoon grated orange peel, roasted
1 teaspoon cinnamon
1 teaspoon grated lemon peel

Method

Briefly beat eggs and sugar; combine flour, baking powder and salt together then add to the egg and sugar mixture. Finally, add the rest and mix well with a wooden spoon. Knead gently for a couple of minutes.

To make the filling, cook the jam in a saucepan, on low heat, to melt to a watery texture. Add the rest of the filling ingredients and stir to blend. Cook for another five minutes on low heat. Leave to cool in a container.

Flatten a portion of dough to ¼ inch thickness. Slice into strips (three inches wide by five inches long). Line some jam, finger width, along the centre of the band and then fold one side over to the other, sealing in the jam. Fasten edges with your fingers and remove any excess to form a smooth shape all around. Collect excess pieces of dough to make another cookie. Bend these tube-shaped cookies to form a sickle shape. Bake jam cookies at 400°F until they have risen. Reduce temperature a little and bake for another 15 minutes or until golden.

The glaze: Blend two cups icing sugar with two tablespoons milk until creamy. Add more milk if necessary. Spread with finger and leave to harden for a few minutes.

La pizza dolce con rum

As far as my mother can remember, this large sponge cake with rum and cream is both a holiday and a birthday treat that has remained popular among Italians today. It is easy to make, and the rum gives it a splendid aroma. You can divide everything in half for a smaller cake.

12 eggs, separated
12 heaping tablespoons sugar
12 heaping tablespoons flour
1 teaspoon baking powder

Method
Beat egg whites until stiff peaks form; in a separate bowl beat the yolks and sugar until creamy (about 20 minutes), then mix together by hand. Combine flour and baking powder, and gradually fold this into the egg mixture followed by the egg white. Line a 12¾ inch (32.5 cm) cake pan with wax paper. Pour the batter into the pan and bake at 350°F for 15 minutes, then reduce to 300° for another 25 minutes. Cake is done when golden on the top, and the sides have contracted. Do not insert anything into the cake. When cool, remove cake from pan and form two layers by slicing it in half, horizontally, with a long knife. Leave aside.

Topping:
8 egg yolks   1 cup flour
2 cups sugar   4 cups milk
½ cup rum (more or less as desired)

Method
Whip egg yolks and sugar together until creamy. Gradually add flour, and finally the milk. Slowly cook to thicken, then let cool. Divide into one-third and two-third portions. First, pour rum over both cake layers. Next, spread the one-third portion

of cream over the lower cake layer. Place the second layer on top and spread on the rest of the cream. Note: to make chocolate cream, just add one cup cocoa to the cooled mixture.

Conclusion

These recipes are the very core of what my family and I enjoy, and I shall carry them on for decades to come. My mother is a master of Italian cuisine; she knows the special touches that allow a meal to reach its full potential of taste and texture. I am still learning these intricacies, but this is nothing for you to worry about. Recipes are abstract forms that guide our aspirations to create the perfect meal. My mother has spent fifty years perfecting and modifying her recipes, and still she and I discuss new possibilities as we encounter new spices, herbs and methods. What remains unchanged in this process are the basic ingredients and the style of preparation that constitute an Italian recipe. As long as you follow those basics, you will not fail: each recipe in this chapter has been prepared a million times and, necessary at every one of those occasions, was enough time, the right ingredients and a genuine pleasure in making the meal.

Finally, do not hesitate to add variations to the recipes to make them richer or leaner, or more or less spicy. Dividing a recipe in half to make a smaller meal is no problem either. Remember: tomatoes, olive oil, parsley and basil never let us down. Keep in mind, when you cook, that this is the real Italian way with no shortcuts—these are the dishes that Italians the world over know and love. We hope that you use this book often; by trying the recipes, you are helping to preserve the essence of traditional Italian cooking. *Buon appetito!*

A Rich and Varied Tradition

Compiled by A. Evo DiPierro
and Sam Migliore

Recipes for Any Occasion (Constance deRoche)

Italian cuisine represents a rich and varied tradition. Butter and white sauces are characteristic of cooking in the north, while southerners favour olive oil and red (or tomato-based) sauces. Within these areas, cooking varies regionally. And beyond the recipes passed along informally in the kitchen by home cooks, there are those that have been developed (such as Alfredo Sauce) by professional chefs for commercial kitchens. Some dishes have been elaborated in new settings to which Italians have immigrated. Pizza, for example, has changed since it became popular in North America, where new ingredients and combinations have been added.

In short, there's "no end" to what Italian cuisine has to offer. Personally, I think the best cooks know what they like and are willing to be innovative. They know recipes but never follow them slavishly. They draw inspiration from traditions. They come to know what taste combinations are pleasing and develop a sense of the flavours that characterize an ethnic tradition. That is, recipes are an important starting point, but each cook should feel free to leave her (or his) mark on the dishes prepared.

Rice Salad (Constance deRoche)

Rice is to northern Italians what pasta is to southerners. I was served this dish in a "trattoria" (a modest, small, family-run restaurant) in Florence. However, I've never seen it in cookbooks or at any other of the few Northern Italian restaurants I've been lucky enough to visit. Before leaving the trattoria, I asked about the recipe. The proprietor was perplexed—maybe by my hopelessly broken Italian—but managed to explain that there was no recipe; the dish was made as it appeared when served. So, I had to resort to reconstructing it at home, from a recollection of its taste and ingredients. In Florence, it was served as a first course, as are other starches and soups in Italian meals. But it can be used as a side dish in meals presented in North American style. Since it's cold, it's good for summer dining or picnics. It's strong tasting, and I think it goes well with Italian sausage.

2 cups cold cooked rice
1 cup of mixed marinated vegetables (see below)
1 tablespoon capers (These small plant buds can be bought in jars.)
2 hard-boiled eggs

Method
Using the following recipe, marinate halved small mushrooms, quartered (canned) artichoke hearts, (unpickled) olives, thinly sliced onion, and/or sliced sweet peppers.

½ cup olive oil
¼ cup wine vinegar (or lemon juice)
¼ cup brine in which vegetables were canned (optional)
1 minced or crushed garlic clove
(or ¼ teaspoon of garlic powder—not garlic salt!)
½ teaspoon dried basil and/or ¼ teaspoon dried oregano
¼ teaspoon fresh ground black pepper
½ teaspoon salt (omit if using brine)

Method
Shake the liquids and seasonings together in a jar that has a tightly fitting cover and is large enough to fit the vegetables. Add the vegetables and shake again to coat them well. Set aside for a few hours, shaking or stirring them periodically so that they'll be evenly flavoured.

Put the rice into a bowl. Mix in the vegetables, along with their marinate and (drained) capers. Chop the eggs into bite-sized pieces, and gently toss them in. Serve.

Veal Scaloppine (Constance deRoche)

I've seen veal recipes that derive from southern Italy. I grew up in a Neapolitan household where breaded veal cutlets were served baked in a tomato sauce. But I believe that veal figures more prominently in northern cooking, possibly because the meat of young animals is more expensive and northerners are more well-to-do. The following recipe, which is "white" and uses butter, is northern in style.

1 ½ lbs. thinly sliced veal, cut into 1½ x 3 inch strips
flour, for dredging
butter, as needed to saute other ingredients
2 cloves of roughly chopped garlic
1 finely chopped medium onion
½ lb. fresh, thickly sliced mushroom
1 teaspoon lemon juice
1 cup Marsala or other sweet white wine
¼ lb. paper-thin slices of prosciutto, cut into narrow strips
½ teaspoon dried parsley
½ teaspoon dried basil
salt and pepper, to taste

Method

Hammer the veal, under wax paper, until it's less than a ¼ inch thick. Cut it into strips (above). Lightly flour and lightly brown them in butter. Don't overcook them or they'll dry out. Drain them on paper towel. Set aside and keep warm.

In a tablespoon of butter, saute the garlic until golden, not brown. Remove garlic and discard it. Put onions into the pan and saute them until tender, adding just enough more butter to keep them from sticking. Remove them to a small bowl. Then saute the mushrooms with a teaspoon of lemon juice, adding more butter as needed. When soft, not brown, remove and set them aside.

Sprinkle a teaspoon of flour into the butter that remains in the skillet (or add another tablespoon, if needed) to form a thin paste. Slowly add the wine and stir, being careful not to let the sauce lump. Add the sauteed onions and mushrooms, herbs and seasonings. Simmer for 5-10 minutes over low heat, adding a bit of water if needed. Toss in the prosciutto in the last two minutes. Pour over the veal and serve. Garnish with black pepper and fresh parsley.

Two Tasty Dishes (Theresa Della Vella)

Green Bean Salad, "Insalata di Fagiolini"

1 lb. fresh green beans
garlic dressing (recipe below)
salt and pepper to taste

lettuce leaves
1 tablespoon Parsley, chopped

Method

Cook beans, uncut, in boiling salted water for five minutes. Drain. Toss in the garlic dressing; season to taste. Serve on lettuce leaves and garnish with parsley. Serves four to six.

Garlic Dressing: ½ cup olive oil; juice of one lemon; salt, pepper and one clove of garlic, crushed. Combine all ingredients in a jar; shake well.

Roast Lamb, "Agnello al Forno"

4 lb. leg of lamb	½ cup olive oil
2 cloves garlic	4 onions
fresh rosemary	2 lbs. new potatoes
salt, pepper to taste	

Method

Make small cuts in lamb. Insert slices of garlic and bits of rosemary. Rub meat with salt and pepper and then the oil. Roast in 400°F oven for 1½ hours. Add the onions and potatoes. Baste occasionally. Serves six to eight.

Two Polenta Recipes (Mario Hogan)

My mother, Beglia Hogan, was born in Sterling, Glace Bay. Her parents, Antonio and Rose DeGiobbi, emigrated there around 1902 from Rigoletto, a small rural community in the northern region of Lombardi in Italy. Both my grandfather and my father, Michael Hogan, worked as coal miners while their wives looked after the home. The recipes below were passed down from my Mom's family. They were in her family as far back as she can remember.

Polenta and Cheese (Serves four)

1 cup of cornmeal	4 cups of water
salt	Cheddar cheese, shredded, about 2 cups
Mozzarella cheese, shredded, about 2 cups	

Method

Boil water and add salt before adding the cornmeal. Stir and cook until it is thick and creamy. In a small lasagna pan, make a layer with half of the cornmeal, then form a layer of red cheese. Follow with more cornmeal, then the mozzarella. Bake at 300°F, until the cheese melts and the cornmeal has thickened to the desired hardness. Similar to a cake, but do not dry cornmeal entirely.

Polenta with Chicken or Veal, in Tomato Sauce
(Serves four)

In a skillet, have 2 pounds of stewing chicken or veal, sliced into 3-5 inch strips. Add some salt, pepper and garlic to taste, and cook the meat for 5-10 minutes or until slightly browned. To make the sauce, add the following to the skillet:

half of a 5½ oz. can tomato paste
1 medium onion, diced
2 cups boiling water

Method

Bring to a boil, then simmer until the meat is tender. Finally, cook the cornmeal (one cup to four cups of water) and add some salt to taste. Bring to a boil, then reduce to medium heat and stir constantly for about ten minutes. Cornmeal is cooked when it is thick and creamy, like a porridge. To serve, place some cornmeal on a plate and add some sauce on top.

Italian Green Beans (Joseph Rizzetto)

There are a multitude of different types of green beans available; however, this recipe is for the preparation of Italian style broad beans only. Other beans cannot be prepared using this recipe because they are stringy, they do not mash well. The beans I am referring to for this recipe are the large, flat green beans, which grow on high stalks and are commonly called "pole beans" here in Canada. They are at their very best when freshly picked, just as they develop little seeds in the pod, and are about six inches long and about half an inch wide. If left to seed, they develop large beans which are excellent for drying and stewing. My grandmother tells the story of how my grandfather, Fiorvante, upon arriving from Italy, went about trying to obtain some beans for seed to start his garden. He only wanted this variety, but there was only one other Italian in the No. 14 Yard area of New Waterford who had these. This other gentleman refused to share his beans, so my grandfather would go for evening walks during the summer, reach between the fence, and "borrow" a few stalks each trip. Needless to say, his beans were in full force the next year and for many thereafter. Here is the recipe for Fiorvante's favourite vegetable dish.

3 lbs of fresh, cleaned pole beans, ends removed
2 medium potatoes (preferably new potatoes)
5 large fresh garlic cloves flattened, but not minced
about 1/3 cup of good quality olive oil (add more if necessary)
a handful of fresh sage leaves
salt and pepper

Method

Boil the beans and the potatoes until both are soft (about half an hour). While potatoes are boiling, lightly fry the garlic and the sage leaves in the oil over low heat. Take care not to burn either one because it will leave a bitter taste, and do not make this recipe unless you have fresh sage leaves. Sage is a perennial which grows about 1½ feet high if well taken care of. It is my favourite herb. It can be purchased at the supermarket, but it is somewhat expensive. For about $2, you can buy and plant some sage in the summer, and it will come back year after year, or of course you can find someone who has it growing in their yard and "borrow" a few.

When potatoes and beans are done, mash them together well. You can use a food processor, but I find it makes the mixture too smooth for my liking; I prefer to do it by hand. Remove garlic from oil and discard it. Then pour the oil and sage into the bean/potato mixture, and mix well with salt and pepper to taste. This can be served hot or at room temperature. It is an excellent accompaniment to grilled meat, particularly lamb, or a roasted chicken.

Rabbit, Stewed with Tomatoes and Wine (Joseph Rizzetto)

Cape Breton has an abundance of wild rabbits. I can remember my grandfather buying a pair of snared rabbits for $1 and cleaning them in the backyard. It is not common to see domestic, cultivated rabbits sold here, although I have seen them at supermarkets, imported from Ontario. Wild rabbits have a definite gamey taste, while the farm raised ones have a whiter flesh and more of a chicken taste. It is all simply a matter of preference. This is my grandmother Rina (Nemis) Rizzetto's recipe for preparing rabbit stew.

2 skinned and cleaned wild rabbits, or one large domestic rabbit, cut up
    into about 8 pieces
3 tablespoons butter
¼ cup of extra virgin olive oil
2 cloves of fresh garlic, finely minced
1 cup of white or red wine
½ cup each of finely diced onion, carrot, celery and fresh parsley
a small handful of fresh sage leaves
2 sprigs of fresh rosemary
1 small can of Italian plum tomatoes mashed with your fingers (plus, one teaspoon
    of cinnamon),
1 cup of clear beef or chicken broth

Method
If using wild rabbits, soak in cold water in the refrigerator overnight. Farm raised rabbits do not need to be soaked. Rinse rabbits well and pat very dry. Melt butter and oil; brown rabbits well on all sides and remove from pan. Add all vegetables to pan and cook until wilted (about 10 minutes). Return rabbit to pan, along with the wine, and cook rapidly, uncovered until liquid evaporates a small amount. Use red wine if you want a richer, darker stew, and white wine if you like a slightly sweeter, lighter stew. Add all remaining ingredients, plus salt and pepper to taste, and reduce to a simmer with the cover ajar. After about one hour, the rabbit should be starting to soften. Remove cover and let simmer, until sauce has thickened into a rich consistency and rabbit is tender. Make sure that you use low

heat and stir the bottom to prevent sticking. This dish is best served hot over fresh polenta with a chilled light red wine.

Bean Soup (Yolanda Cechetto)

4 litres water
1 lb. beans (soaked overnight)
1 small onion, finely chopped
1 small carrot, finely chopped
1 small celery stock, finely chopped

1 8-ounce can stewed tomatoes, mashed
1 pork hock, or 1¼ cup olive oil
salt and pepper to taste
small sea shell pasta noodles

Method

In a sauce pan of water, add all of the ingredients (expect the noodles) and bring to a boil. Lower heat and simmer for three hours. Remove the pork hock. Finally, add the pasta noodles, and cook for another ten minutes. Serves six.

Haddock & Potatoes (Yolanda Cechetto)

1½ lbs. frozen haddock fillets
3 med. potatoes, peeled & sliced in halves
1 tablespoon butter

1 teaspoon garlic
1 teaspoon parsley
salt, pepper to taste

Method

Arrange fish and potatoes in a casserole dish, with the fish (seasoned) in the middle; add dots of butter on top. Microwave on high for five minutes. Remove and baste fish with butter; mix the potatoes, and then return the dish to the microwave to resume cooking on high for another five minutes (or until completely done). Fish should be flaky and potatoes soft. Serves three.

Cannoli al Forno, Baked Cannoli (Elisa Fasciani)[1]

These are tube-shaped pastries that you fill with lemon cream, whipped cream or ricotta cheese. They are simple to make and quite attractive when filled.

5 eggs
½ cup oil
1½ tablespoon baking powder

¾ cup of sugar
½ cup milk
4 cups flour

Method

Beat eggs and sugar; then, as you add first oil and then milk, continue beating until mixture turns creamy and consistent. Finally, combine baking powder and flour, and add to mixture to form a dough. Turn dough onto a floured surface and knead until smooth and elastic.

Divide the dough into halves. Roll each piece into a fairly thin sheet and cut into 3 x 5 inch square shapes. Roll squares around greased metal tubes, from one corner of the square to its opposite corner, then seal edges by pressing together.

Bake rolls at 375°F until golden. When done, let cool. Finally, slip them off their tubes and fill before serving.

Crostoli (Amalia Zorzi)

2 tablespoons sugar

4 ounces dark rum

4 cups flour

2 ounces of butter (melted)

1 teaspoon salt

¼ cup milk

4 eggs

Method

Mix all ingredients into a ball of dough. Cut into small pieces, about half the size of a golf ball. Run each piece through a pasta machine twice. Strips should be paper thin, approximately three inches wide by twelve inches long. Place on cotton cloth. Cut diagonally into pieces and make a slit in each piece. Deep fry in hot oil until golden brown. Remove from oil, place on paper towels and immediately sprinkle with white sugar.

Lemon Granita (Sam Migliore)

For roughly two hundred years (from the 9th to the 11th centuries) the Arabs ruled Sicily. During this time period, they introduced a variety of beliefs, customs and material items—including a number of food items—that eventually became an integral part of the Sicilian tradition. With respect to this recipe, it was the Arabs that introduced both the lemon tree and the custom of making granita to the island. Granita is an ice dish served as a refreshing treat on a hot day. It can be made using various flavourings, although lemon is the most popular.

4 lemons

1 to 2 cups sugar

4 cups water

Method

Take the juice from four lemons. Add water and sugar (one to two cups, to taste). Stir until sugar is completely blended into the liquid. Grate and add lemon peel (from about half a lemon or less) to the liquid. Pour contents into a plastic container and place in the freezer. It should be ready in a few hours. The sugar content gives the granita its texture and helps prevent it from forming a simple block of ice. Use a spoon to scrape out as much as you would like to eat at any one time. This recipe should produce enough granita for a serving of four.

Hint: You can use a fork to break up the ice during the first half hour of freezing. This will ensure that the granita remains flaky and easier to scrape out of the container when ready to serve.

Winemaking as a Source of Well-Being[1]

By Sam Migliore

One glass of wine makes you strong like a lion,
Two glasses makes you happy like a monkey,
While three glasses can change you into a pig.

One evening, while having a glass of wine with friends in Whitney Pier, the late Alberico DiSano told a humorous story that ended with the above statement. The statement is significant because it reveals a central feature of the Italian philosophy concerning wine: consumed in moderation, wine can be a source of both "physical power" and "health." Its importance for an Italian family, however, extends well beyond health; wine can represent, for instance, a source of pride, a symbol of ethnic identity, a religious symbol (i.e., wine as a component of the Roman Catholic sacrament of communion) as well as an essential aspect of hospitality and sociability.

Among Italians wine tends to serve many purposes. My goal is to address this issue by giving "voice" to some of the thoughts and experiences of three Italian Canadians from Sydney, Nova Scotia—Gabriele, Anna and their son, Gian Carlo, DiMichele.[2]

Truth in Wine: Sharing a Family Tradition

Both Anna and Gabriele DiMichele were born in the Abruzzi region of Italy—Anna in Brittoli, province of Pescara, and Gabriele in Isola Del Gran Sasso, province of Teramo. Anna emigrated to Canada with her family in 1956 and settled in Whitney Pier. Gabriele, in contrast, arrived in Halifax on May 8, 1961, travelled to Toronto to join his brother and migrated to Cape Breton a few years later for work purposes. They first met, and later married, in Sydney. They have three children: Luisa, Gian Carlo and Paolo.

[Gabriele]: When I was four or five years old, I remember my parents making wine every year in the fall. Wine was ... a big part of the family. Without wine on the table, it was like having food with almost nothing. You have to have that glass of wine in the old country ... for everybody to be happy. Without wine, there was something missing. So, when I came over to Canada, and I started making this wine, I was very [concerned] to continue the culture.... I can't wait for the month of October when these grapes arrive from California to Halifax, and I can't wait to get the grapes from Halifax to Sydney. For me it's a very special day when I make this wine....

> [Gabriele]: We make a good vinegar out of the wine.... We don't buy vinegar. My sister came from Toronto with my niece, and they took my vinegar back because there is nothing that compares to homemade vinegar from the wine.

[Gian Carlo]: We start off with grapes imported from California.... We opened the cases and dumped [the grapes] into a crusher.... We crushed them by hand, all the juices came out into a big tub, approximately six feet long. Then from there it fell into a bucket, and as the bucket was getting full we would empty it into a demijohn [a 12 gallon container].

Once a demijohn is filled, it is stored for a period of time to allow the juice to ferment. It is this fermentation process that eventually transforms the juice into wine. [Gabriele]: In a range of about forty-five days to fifty days, we start testing the wine. But, it doesn't mean the wine is already mature to drink. It's good, it tastes as wine, but it's not ... old enough. To have a good result, a good taste, the wine ... has to be anywhere from six months to a year [old].

The mature wine becomes a central component in family meals. It represents not only a tasty beverage but also an ingredient for cooking and something that can be transformed into vinegar to add flavour to salads and other dishes. [Anna]: In our family, same as a lot of Italian families, when you set the table, wine is one of the first things that go on ... we enjoy having it with the food, and you can also cook with wine. I do a lot of cooking with wine. Just about every meal there's a little bit of wine that goes into it somewhere along the line ... it's just a very important part of an Italian family.

The DiMichele family produces both red and white wine. As someone who has sampled this wine, I can say that it adds a special quality to the enjoyment of a meal.

Wine, Tradition and Well-Being

Wine is a nutritious drink that can have positive effects on one's health. According to Anna, "it seems that it gives you more strength and ... it's very healthy for you." From an Italian point of view, however, well-being is linked to conceptions of equilibrium or balance. The interrelationship between wine and health is based precisely on this principle. Moderation is the key to wine consumption. This is the point Anna and Gabriele stressed repeatedly, and it is the message Mr. DiSano

Gabriele DiMichele, Salute! Photo by Sam Migliore.

conveyed through his humorous tale. Alcohol is not something to be abused. Excessive wine consumption can have a negative effect on one's health, as well as disrupt family relations.

[Gabriele]: I like to put this wine on the table and show my family, my kids, the tradition in our family ... from grandparents making wine, my parents making wine, I'm making wine, and I would like to see my children make wine in the future. It is very important to have [wine] on the table. Only, I recommend with a meal. Not abusing and getting drunk. That's what I teach my kids about drinking wine. And drinking a glass of wine with meals is more like health. It's like a prescription. Helps the blood circulate better. And, all this makes me happy to make wine.

Gabriele then elaborated on the potential role of wine in promoting health. This discussion focused on two issues: the link between wine consumption and blood circulation and the power of wine to reduce the level of cholesterol in one's system. I really believe this wine helps the health by drinking moderately.... It gives you ... strength ... because it has a certain amount of alcohol and sugar. The sugar produces power in the body, and the alcohol, the wine alcohol, which is different [than other alcohol] helps the cholesterol level ... and it makes your blood go faster and by the blood circulating faster you will have more power....

[Gian Carlo]: A big thing we have to take into consideration is the ... difference between homemade wine and the wine you would buy in the store. In homemade wine, there are no preservatives ... no added chemicals.... And I think the wines that you buy today in the stores, quite a few of them, have these added chemicals and, well, things that are not really good for you....

[Gabriele]: The wine ... gives you appetite ... [and] it is very good for helping in digesting the meal—providing [you] drink one glass and two, because, if you abuse [it, the] acid in the wine will stop your digestion. See, we need a certain amount of acid in the body ... which you have in wine, but if you put in too much it wouldn't be any good.... [It] will make you sick....

The discussion may shift from the interrelationship between wine and strength, or cholesterol or digestion, but the central theme remains the same, moderation is at the heart of Gabriele's philosophy concerning wine and its consumption.

Wine, Hospitality and Sociability

Well-being extends beyond physical and mental health. Family, friendship and other social relationships can have a significant effect on a person's quality of life. Wine plays a vital role in this process. [Gabriele]: In our tradition, I remember since I was

... a little young fellow, the first thing [my parents] put on the table when they had a friend in the house was the bottle of wine. And, I keep this tradition going.... Today, I realize that when an Italian family comes to visit, if you don't offer them a glass of wine, they are not very well welcomed. They think about it that way, and I feel the same way too.... Other people, when they have guests, present a bottle of beer or liquor, rum, but in the Italian tradition, we've got to have wine on the table.... Without wine, I don't think it would be the same evening to be happy, as much as the wine makes you happy. [Anna]: It seems that if you don't have wine, you don't have anything. [Gabriele]: So the wine serves a purpose for a lot of different reasons.

Anna DiMichele. Photo by Sam Migliore.

A Concluding Remark

Members of the Italian Canadian community do not necessarily share precisely the same conception of "wine." The ideas Gabriele, Anna and Gian Carlo DiMichele express are their own. Their statements, however, do provide an insight into the Italian culture of winemaking and the position of wine in their family tradition. Wine is intimately linked to notions of health; what constitutes a well prepared and desirable meal; the etiquette of hospitality and sociability, ethnic identity as well as what it means to be a part of an Italian family. For the DiMicheles, and many other Italian families, wine is something special; it can, because of its significance at both the individual and the cultural level, add substance to a person's and a family's quality of life. The key, however, is balance and moderation. It is important to allow the wine to serve your needs and interests, not to let it control your life.

Section V

Performance as
Art and Folklore

A House Full of Memories:
Art as Legacy

By A. Evo DiPierro

When Alfred Goduto passed away several years ago, everyone I knew felt a profound loss. He was a master at everything he liked to do, but what he enjoyed most was painting, storytelling and his occupation as a mason. Sam Migliore and I interviewed Mrs. Goduto and her son, Dominic, in late winter, 1997. I had not been to the house in a long time. The experience rekindled many memories of the friendship I had shared with Alfred. I was also fascinated by the many stories they told of his life—stories as varied in subject and mood as the range of colours Alfred used to paint nearly 250 portraits and scenes during his life in Cape Breton.

In March 1952, Mr. and Mrs. Goduto, along with infant sons, Dominic and Blaise, arrived in Halifax after a long and tiring sea voyage from Italy. Their hometown, Roseto, was being deserted by waves of Italian emigrants seeking a better life in North America. For the Godutos, one impetus for leaving Italy was the fact that Mrs. Goduto's parents and brother had already emigrated to Canada. When in Nova Scotia, the family's initial experience was bittersweet. According to Mrs. Goduto:

> When we reached Halifax, my husband was taking care of the suitcase. I sat with my two children in another part of the station. Two nuns came to me and wanted the children. I said, "No, you can't have them." They spoke English and I thought they wanted to take them away. My husband came over after they left, and said it was too late in the evening to go to Sydney. Later I told him about the nuns and he said, "Why didn't you give the kids to them?" I replied, "Are you crazy? I don't know them." He said, "If they come back, you go with them." So after awhile they returned and took me and my kids to a beautiful room. They thought the kids wanted to rest but they didn't rest ... they were dancing on the bed.... The nuns gave us milk and things to eat, plus the room for the night....

Alfred Goduto's occupation in Cape Breton was chiefly as a brick-layer. While plenty of construction work was available at sites such as St. Rita and City Hospitals, he was refused work because he was not a union member. To join the union, he had to be in Canada for at least a year. "It was Catch-22," explained Dominic, "they wouldn't allow him in the union unless he proved his abilities, and he couldn't prove his abilities because he wasn't in the union, so he was really in a bind." Mr. Goduto, however, was a craftsman; he was a professional at plastering and painting. Before moving to Canada, Alfred was part of his own construction company in Italy. When the plastering was finished in a home, he would handle the stylish and decorative painting on the walls, corners and ceilings. When the Godutos bought their first home in Whitney Pier, Alfred began to paint more frequently and produce different types of art work.

Alfredo Goduto, a self-portrait. Photo by A. Evo DiPierro.

[Mrs. Goduto]: At night, or on Saturdays or Sundays, he passed time by painting the two pictures which are in my bedroom. [Dominic Goduto]: He actually made those on the back of old shades ... old green pull-down shades. He mounted them himself on a little frame and then painted on these shades. He couldn't find canvases like we have now. As a young child, I had never seen my father paint. As I was growing up, I didn't believe my mother when she told me that Dad did the paintings and murals, because I was only aware of his ability as a bricklayer.... Until one Christmas, he decided to paint a nativity scene to put outside, and that was the first time I saw him with a paint brush. I might have been thirteen or fourteen at the time. He later painted all the scrolls and scenes that appear in our dining room. This is what they did in Italy. Years later, he painted the Madonna and child on our living room ceiling.

Alfred's public recognition as a painter was perhaps born when his daughter, Vincenza, wrote to the Cape Breton Artists Association to inform them about her father's work. When they met Alfred, they were so impressed that they wanted him to be their president, but he declined the offer because his skills in reading and writing in English were limited. Then they asked Alfred to teach them to paint in his style, but his sincere and common-sense response was, quite simply, "I'd love to teach you, but I can't explain, in English, the way I do it." As Alfred Goduto started selling his paintings, he painted more frequently—portraits, still-life, as well as his famous wall and ceiling work. During the last fifteen years of his life, while officially retired from the workforce, he painted almost exclusively for his pleasure.

Alfred Goduto's experience with art began in Italy at a very young age. During the Second World War, his artistic ability carried him through some unique situations.

[Mrs. Goduto]: I remember when we got married, he did a beautiful room. It was a double wedding ... him and his brother. So when he painted his bedroom, his brother saw it and said, "Why don't you paint mine too?" "Because," Alfred replied, "this is my room and that one's yours." When he was in school—grade five—he drew pictures and his teacher used to save them for years. When he got back from the war, she showed them to him because her daughter was getting married, and she wanted him to paint her home.

[Dominic Goduto]: My father served in the Italian army during World War Two. He was nineteen when he joined. He served in North Africa for six or seven months, where he was captured, and he spent the next six years or so in a prisoner-of-war camp, first in India, then in Australia and finally in Tasmania. And while he was in Australia and Tasmania, he painted a lot.

This is a story that he told me often. In Australia, they paid rations of five cigarettes a day to the working prisoners, and what Dad would do was trade them to get art lessons. There was a renowned artist in the community where he was placed. This professor actually helped my father with his artistic ability. My father excelled at painting portraits. Someone would come along and ask him to paint ... his girlfriend, for example, and they would pay him with cigarettes. So he ended up with thousands of them.

In Australia, someone noticed his painting and wanted him to paint a full-sized portrait of King George V to hang in a community hall. It took Dad months to paint this life size portrait. The Australians treated him like a king at that point...they gave him anything he wanted because he was working very hard on this important project. When he notified the official that he was finished, he was told that an art expert wished to see it. Not expecting this, he panicked. He was really worried about someone coming to critique his work, and he told them that he was not a real artist. But the expert came and spent a couple of hours examining the portrait of the king. The expert was truly impressed with the work and could only find one problem. He pointed to the king's hands. "You made his hands too feminine; they should show his veins." Dad quickly touched up the King's hands. The expert offered Dad a job in Australia after the war, but Dad never did go back. Much of his artistic ability was nurtured during that period because he had a lot of leisure time at his disposal.

Alfred Goduto was no typical prisoner-of-war. In fact, one can easily forget that he was a prisoner, given the admiration and affection he won in Australia, and the rather humorous circumstances under which he sometimes found himself.

[Dominic Goduto]: He used to tell us about his time in Australia and how tough it was in the camps. He was told that if he could get work on an Australian farm, it would be good because there would be lots to eat. Fortunately he was placed on a farm owned by the Gibbs family. Dad remembered sitting down to dinner with the Gibbs family. It was very formal; they all dressed for dinner. Now, Italians love bread but the Australians didn't at the time. They felt it was bad for you. Mr. Gibbs, the master of the household, kept a loaf of bread on a bread board beside him at mealtime. After work, my father, being very hungry, would ask: "Bread, please." "Very well," replied Mr. Gibbs, and he would slice it so thin...*so thin*...you could fold it like paper. After slicing it, he folded it over his knife, then handed it to my father who rolled and quickly swallowed it. Minutes later, my father would again ask, "Bread, please," and the same thing would happen. Eventually he told the gentleman, "I like bread!" and Mr. Gibbs just handed the whole loaf to him.

One of the reasons Dad got on the farm was because he said he was good with the farm tractor. He really didn't know the first thing about driving a tractor. So when he got on the farm, Mr. Gibbs directed him to the tractor and said: "Here's the tractor, now do the fields." But Dad practically ruined all the crops.

As a painter, Alfred Goduto strove continuously to improve the quality of his work. His philosophy was that each new painting should be better than the one before. In 1976, at age fifty-six, he was forced into retirement from the workforce due to illness. Rather than dwell on problems, he used the lengthy recuperative period as an opportunity to devote more time to his painting. Mr. Goduto began slowly but, by 1978, he was completing an average of one painting per week. His art was on exhibit at a number of Italia Day celebrations in Sydney, during the 1980s. Today, some of these works can be found in the Marconi Museum, the Nova Scotia Art Gallery, as well as many homes throughout Cape Breton (and elsewhere). In the early 1980s, he also did two paintings that appear on the alcoves of Holy Redeemer Church in Whitney Pier—one is of Jesus Christ, while the other depicts the Baptism of John. Once the public learned of his mastery at producing portraits, Goduto frequently was asked to do portraits for special occasions (such as graduations and weddings). During the peak of his creativity, his work appeared in certain art and heritage publications, in Canada and Italy.

Portraits were Goduto's main strength. Next came the still-life works of mainly nature scenes, table settings and Cape Breton landscapes. However, he particularly enjoyed devoting his time and effort in the creation of religious portraits. Goduto's keen understanding of colour and tone, combined with a knack for mixing various base colours to produce his own paints, allowed him to produce works that are both unique and strikingly vivid. Although he learned to develop these skills during his lengthy stay in Australia, he was inspired by the Renaissance masterpieces of his native Italy. As a result, the vast majority of his paintings have a Mediterranean flavour.

All of Goduto's paintings are pleasing to the senses. His portraits have the effect of drawing one's gaze to the subject's contented facial expressions, while his still-life scenes leave you with the impression that you are seeing something very familiar. Goduto's main goal seems to be to move beyond surface appearances to capture the essence of the subject's inner beauty or meaning. For Alfred Goduto, a "bowl of fruit" is not simply a bowl with fruit; it is a vehicle through which he can convey notions of "goodness" and "tradition."

The paintings also reflect the appealing and friendly nature of his personality. Dominic Goduto remembers his father in this way:

> My father was always a worker; that memory is fresh in my mind. He was like most Italian men who didn't play much with their children. But I remember my brother and me helping my father with his work. We used to help him mix the compound to plaster the walls. That's how we spent quality time together.

> My Dad and I used to have many heated arguments, usually during meal time. I was always sure that if I said black he would say white just to keep us arguing. And I think that's one of the reasons I got into law. Although my Dad didn't have a complete formal education, he was a very smart man, common-sense wise.

> Dad also challenged us in other ways. He always smoked, and when my brother and I got into physical fitness, we'd pick on Dad. He'd say, "Ah, I can still put you fellas down." I remember once, when I was fourteen years old, my Dad saying that since he played soccer when he was in Italy, he could beat me in a foot race. "Dad," I answered, "not in a million years." He used to smoke two packs of cigarettes a day. "But there's one condition," he shrewdly stipulated, "it has to be a short race because I'm built for speed, not fitness." So out on the street we drew a start line and a finish line. As we got ready I thought, 'I'm gonna leave this fella in the dirt!' But, sure enough, he did beat me. It was only fifty or seventy-five feet, but he actually won, and he never let me live that down.

> He also told lots of war stories. There are people who came out of the war and refused to talk about it, but my father could've written a book with the stories he had. I remember Sunday afternoons, after dinner, we'd sit down and drink wine, and he'd tell me these stories over and over again. I remember them all and I often tell my kids these stories.

The storytelling and light-hearted arguing also predominate in my memories of the man. As a child, it was always a pleasure to visit Alfred's summer cottage near Barachois Harbour with my family. I spent many Sunday afternoons trekking through the woods and following the railroad tracks. Alfred would show us the progress he was making on a painting that he was working on at the time. And, while on Alfred's motorboat, heading towards the Campbell Cove sandbar, he got a kick out of initiating arguments with me about such things as how deep the water was, what sorts of fish were in it and how much erosion affected

Ceiling painting. Photo by A. Evo DiPierro.

the sandbar. He would challenge my approximation of when the next train would come barrelling through the cove. My time at his bungalow helped me to forget about how long and boring summer vacation was.

I also remember Alfred telling my Dad about how much he longed to return to Italy. He finally did visit Italy in 1988. Unfortunately, he became ill during the trip. It was the beginning of a prolonged deterioration of his health. Over the next two years, he struggled to retain those aspects of his life which were most important to him: his ability to paint and to tell wonderful stories. He died peacefully in 1990, at age seventy. His paintings are scattered throughout this province for all to admire. Alfred Goduto's artistic legacy is two-fold: he reminded everyone in the field that no limit exists in the concept of colour, and that the artist can move beyond simple reproduction to achieve a deeper level of expression. The fact that he nurtured his special gift while remaining a hard-working provider, loving father and a good friend is perhaps the best example he could have set for us all.

A Funny Side of the
Immigration Experience

By A. Evo DiPierro

Learning to deal with a new language can be a frustrating, yet humorous, challenge. This is especially true when the urgent need arises to express oneself with a limited vocabulary. Practically every Italian who has immigrated to Cape Breton can tell a story or two about such an experience. This article focuses on two humorous tales that Mrs. Gloria MacDougall related to Sam Migliore and me, from her experience as a youth.

Mrs. MacDougall was born Gloria DiCesare—the daughter of Italian parents, Donato DiCesare and Concetta DiNino. They were from Pratola Peligna, in the region of l'Aquila, Italy. Donato emigrated to Cape Breton in 1923 and settled in Whitney Pier to work in the steel plant. Concetta joined him six years later. Gloria was born by the end of her parents' first year together in Canada. She received her early education at Holy Redeemer Convent in the Pier. At home, her parents emphasized education, family togetherness and religion as cornerstones of their existence.

Mrs. MacDougall has many fond memories of growing up in Whitney Pier. Today, living in Sydney, she misses the contact she once had with people in the vicinity of her childhood home.

> I still consider [the Pier] my home. There were all these different cultures, and I miss that. We tasted each other's food ... and everybody learned each other's recipes. You knew what nationality they were by the language they spoke, but you didn't know what they were talking about.... We felt related to each other, despite the fact that we spoke different languages. We were sort of at one with [each other]. Now, I know I can't

generalize about everything, but I know that the Pier produced good, responsible people.... And, as for English, I have to say that we learned to speak English better than [non-immigrant children]. Our grammar was better; our marks were higher. In a way, I think that's what saved us from much of the prejudice.

Along the road to mastering the English language, however, young Gloria and her mother had to overcome certain real-life tests and hurdles:

My mother told me this story. For a time, my father was a barber. He learned the trade but didn't stay too long in it. Anyway, I remember the time when my father left the keys to the house at the barber shop, so my mother was to go there and get them. He coached her on this, because she had just arrived here. "Give me the key," she was supposed to say. When she got there, she said to the barber, "Geev me keess ... geev me keess," and they were all looking at her. She was embarrassed because the barber didn't know [what she was saying], and everyone there said: "She wants a kiss; give her a kiss." Anyway, I remember her telling me that and how embarrassed she was about it. I don't know if she ever did get the keys.

I can also remember another story about the Pier. There was a store just down the road from our house that my father used to deal with. He sent me down one day to get cigarette papers. My English wasn't good at the time, and [I spoke] the broken Italian. I could still remember crying because I wanted a package of car-tines, and the woman at the counter didn't know what [in the world] cartines were. It was neither English nor Italian. I went home to my father, crying that the girl wouldn't give me the cartines. [Well], I know how to say it now in either English or Italian.

Humorous Tales from Dominion
Tony Basso

"A Leg of Celery"
When I went to school, I could speak a little bit of English because of the kids I hung around with, but I spoke Italian. My mother sent me down to the Co-op to buy "na gamba di saeno." So I'm walking down the street, and I'm saying, "how do I say that in English." And I said, "gamba is leg, a leg of celery." I translated literally. So I went in the Co-op. "Yes?" [said the store attendant]. "I want a leg of celery." "Just a minute." Well, this one went and got the other clerk. "What do you want?" "A leg of celery." I must have said it ten times. [laughter] "What do you want?" "A leg of celery." And they'd be laughing. I felt like a nut. Oh, didn't I hate her. [laughter] Never translate literally from one language to another. "A leg of celery." Honest to God....

The Poacher
This man was out hunting illegally, you know, and the game warden came upon him. Of course the man started to run, and so did the game warden. The warden was chasing him yelling, "Stop!" And the man turned around and said: 'You stop! There's nobody chasing you.' [laughter] I always got a kick out of that one.

Although the details may change, immigrants of various ethnic backgrounds could tell similar stories of their personal difficulties with the English language. These difficulties are often an important part of the immigration experience. In some cases, however, the frustrations of the past have a way of becoming the funny and entertaining tales of the present.

Alvise Casagrande: A "Scoop" for the *Cape Breton Post*

Edited by Sam Migliore

I was born in 1932. My mother died when I was two years of age, so my grandparents, Teresa and Carlo, brought me up. They came here from the Treviso area of Italy, in 1927. We lived right near the Italian Hall [in Dominion]. My grandfather worked in the coal mine, No. 1B Colliery. He died in 1944, after a bout of cancer. Back in 1937, my grandmother opened a store; she operated that store until 1975, the year before she died. She died in 1976, at the age of ninety-one.

I went to school in Dominion and also at St. Anne's in Glace Bay. But, I gave up school in 1949. My grandmother needed help, so I went to work in the store. Some time later, I got interested in newspaper work—*reporting*. I started at the *Post* in July 1955, was taken on full-time in 1959 and retired this past February [1997]. I wrote a little bit about everything from social events to court cases.

Most of my time was spent with the Glace Bay office. I started carrying a camera in 1974, and I took pictures right up until the time I retired. During my years with the paper, I worked under different publishers. The paper was owned by Mr. Duchemin. He later sold the paper to the Thompson group, and just recently it was taken over by Southam News. I worked out of the Sydney office this past year, and on February the 7th, that was the end. But, I still have a column on Wednesdays—the *Bay Report*. I made an awful lot of friends through the newspaper.

I got quite a few happy send-offs when I retired. A lot of people didn't want to see me go, but I guess when you reach the age of sixty-five it's time for that old pension. The police in the East Division had a do for me at the station in Glace Bay. The union members at the *Cape Breton Post* had a dinner for me at the Casino. And, of course, the day before I retired it was my sixty-fifth birthday; so, the staff at the *Post* had a cake with candles. On Friday, my last day, they had another celebration for me. And then, on February 22, there was an open house at the Italian Hall in Dominion. It was held in honour of myself and two co-workers, Greg Hines and Dolores Marsh. In the evening, there was also a supper at the Italian Hall.

[Any memories you want to share about growing up in Dominion?] Even when I was going to school, I helped out with the neighbourhood store and deliveries. Sometimes I would even get the orders delivered during my lunch hour and then go back to school. I did take a few mandolin lessons from one of the Sisters of Charity in Reserve [Mines], but that didn't last too long. I gave that up. I think in the end they gave the mandolin to one of my cousins in Ontario. [laughs] But, no, I think I spent more time working than anything else. I was a working fella.

Later, when I got tired of working in the store, I started thinking about newspaper work. [How did that interest start?] Well, I happened to go to Sydney one day [in 1955]. I saw a second-hand typewriter for 50 bucks at Merritt Business Machines, on Townsend Street. So, I went to Ma (I called my grandmother "Ma" because she brought me up) and asked for fifty dollars. She said, "What do you want a typewriter for?" I said, "Well, it may come in handy." So she gave me the fifty bucks. I went to Sydney, bought the typewriter [laughs], and took it home. Ma asked, "Can you type?" I said, "No, but they have books for $1.95." So, I went back and got a typewriter book. I started out with the book, but I couldn't make heads or tails of it. I opened and closed it; it's still at home somewhere. I learned on my own. [laughs]

So then, I went down to Glace Bay and spoke to Mr. Joseph G. Hines. He was the manager of the Glace Bay bureau of the *Sydney Post-Record*. Mr. Hines asked me what I was interested in—news, advertising, circulation. "News," I said. He said, "We have had correspondents in Dominion before; if you want to give her a try, go ahead." I was on part-time for four years or so. Besides covering Dominion, he would send me out to public speaking engagements at school auditoriums, debates, and other events.

The first major assignment Mr. Hines gave me was to cover the police beat. I remember going to the station (I guess it was the first time I was ever inside a police station), it was in the basement of the old Town Hall on McKeen Street in Glace Bay. I didn't know what to do; I was green at it. This man came out of the office and scratched his head. He wasn't wearing a uniform. It was a Sunday afternoon. He said to me, "What the hell do you want here?" I don't know if he knew me; I didn't know him. So, I told him I was with the newspaper, and that I was sent to cover the police beat. "There's the books, help yourself," that's what he said. No trouble. I found out later that I had been talking to the Chief of Police. In the 1950s, the Glace Bay Police started to call me "Scoop." It became my handle. Even today, some people run into me on the street and say: "Hi Scoop, what's new today." It must refer to my work; it couldn't be a scoop of ice-cream. [laughs] Over the years I received a great deal of cooperation from the Police, in both Glace Bay and Dominion, and the RCMP.

I covered the court cases in Glace Bay. I would go to court in the daytime and then work in the office at night. It was mostly night work because, at one time, the *Post* didn't publish until the afternoon. Since they started the morning paper, well, most of my work has been on the day shift. There were a lot of interesting cases over the years.

[Alvise also has covered various community, religious and social organizations, and their activities, in the greater Dominion - Glace Bay area.] There isn't too much that we didn't cover. [Is there any story that sticks out in your mind, that was special?] No; they were all special. I would take notes and then start writing. They would often say, "keep your story short; the shorter the better, so we have more space for other stories." But, when I started writing, I'd end up with a story that was a mile too long. The poor editor would say, "you have to chop it to size." I used to find the court cases and the council meetings interesting. For years, the former Town of Dominion had council meetings on Saturday night. Well, that was great! Because there was no paper the next day, it gave me all day Sunday to write up the story. And, police work. I used to cover the police beat twice a day. I would call at the police station during the day, and then again at night before going home. We also had news sources—people that would phone and give us tips. "Don't say where you got it," they'd say. I would double check before using the information, though. [laughs] Yeah, police, council meetings, and taking pictures were my favourites. I always looked forward to that. Everywhere I went I would take the camera with me.

[Alvise also talked about the Italian community in Dominion at various points in our interview.] I covered quite a number of events and services for the Italian community. I covered the installation of officers at the Italian Hall in Dominion for years. The hall was built in 1936. In 1986, they had their 50th anniversary celebration. I remember covering that too.[1] Dominion has Seaside Daze each summer. The Italian community holds an open house at the hall. There are Italian cultural displays, food samples, wine and other things. They attract a lot of people.

At one time, Dominion was quite a big place. Now, like every other place, everything is dwindling, dwindling and people are moving away. Many Italians have left the area. I have an uncle in Ontario, his name is Italo. He worked in the coal mine here, until he moved in the 1940s to Niagara Falls. He still visits down this area quite frequently. And, I had another uncle, Flavio—they used to call him "Flip" or "Flipper." He served overseas with the Armed Forces, and when he came home he operated a taxi in Dominion. He later moved to Hamilton, Ontario, where he worked with the Canada Post Corporation. He died a few years ago.

A lot of Italian people went to college. One was Dr. Etalo Secco. He lives in Antigonish. Etalo was connected with the chemistry department at St. Francis Xavier University for a number of years. His parents used to live on Henry Street, but when they retired they joined him in Antigonish. They were best of friends with my people. I know, after they moved, I'd always take Ma to Antigonish on Sundays to visit them. Etalo's father was Silvio (or Sylvester) and his mother's name was Agnes. Then there was Father Edo Gatto. His parents, Ralph and Maria are dead now, but they used to live right by the Italian Hall. Edo went to school in Dominion, then to college, and was ordained as a priest. He died a few years ago in a car accident. And, of course, there was Lino Polegato. He was a professor with the Engineering Department at the University College of Cape Breton (now Cape Breton University). He passed away recently too, but he was a Dominion fella.

Dominion could also boast to having an Italian as the oldest businessman out there—Angelo Cechetto. He was a shoemaker. I did a feature story on his business some time ago.[2] Angelo passed away recently. The name of his shop was the New York Shoe Repair. Over the years an awful lot of Italians have run businesses. If you want information about the Italian community in Dominion, though, you should contact Lenny Stephenson. He's got more information in his head than I could write down in a book. Lenny's retired now, but he was the postmaster in Dominion for years. He's known as the local historian. A lot of the Italian people are indebted to him; he would go out of his way to help you—fill out documents and papers, and other things.

I do remember, though, an Italian priest, Reverend Emidio D'Intino, who used to come to Dominion to visit Italian families. He was from St. Nicholas Church, in Whitney Pier. I think he came out to give my grandfather the "last rites." One day, he gave me a bundle of newspapers to deliver—*The Crusader*, or *Il Crociato* in Italian. It was a four-page newspaper; three pages were in Italian, while the last page was in English. I delivered about 25 copies per week to Italians in Dominion, and two or three copies to people in Reserve and Glace Bay. That's what I was doing in my spare time. The paper cost a nickel or ten cents, and I sent the money to New York every six months. I did that for a number of years. [Was it before you got into journalism?] I think it was. I don't know, was it that Italian paper that got me going into journalism? [laughs] I think it was, yeah. Father D'Intino. I remember going to his funeral Mass. They had the Mass at Holy Redeemer, in Whitney Pier.[3]

[Alvise also has written a number of stories in recent years that are directly or indirectly related to the Italian community—including coverage of Italian language classes in both Dominion and Sydney, and material on the Marconi home and museum.[4] Although he is officially retired, Alvise still writes for the *Cape Breton Post*.] So, now I'm retired, and all I'm doing is one column, the *Bay Report*. And people are looking forward to that; they'd be used to it. See how long I'll be able to continue it.

The *Bay Report* covers various events and announcements for the general Glace Bay area. I also include my opinion. One of the situations in Glace Bay now is the dire need for doctors. People are crying for doctors. Sometimes people have to wait at "out-patients" with a broken arm or bleeding, because the doctor is busy; the "out-patients" department is jammed sometimes. Council members are hollering, complaining and begging the government to open up more beds in the hospital. For a time, there were two hospitals in Glace Bay. Now there is only one. The other hospital will be replaced with a nursing home. Anyway, people are crying for hospital beds. So, we worked on that for quite a while. I guess it's bad everywhere. They tell me hospitals are closing in Ontario too. One of the problems in the Glace Bay area is that some of the doctors have been moving away, while others have retired. So, the *Bay Report* covers things in Glace Bay and surrounding area, including: Dominion, Gardiner, Reserve, Donkin and Port Morien.

[Did you have training ... or just learned from experience?] Well, they gave us courses; but, you'd go for a course today, and next week there would be a different course. I just picked it up. I didn't go to journalism school; I just picked it up as I went along.

Expressions of Thought and Sentiment: The Poetry of Roy Plichie

Presented by Sam Migliore

On April 8, 1893, Rosetta (DeSanto) and Franco Pagliccia celebrated the birth of their son, Giuseppe, in Brittoli, Italy. Giuseppe, however, was not destined to remain in his land of birth. At the young age of twelve, he and an uncle joined the mass exodus of Italian labourers setting sail for America. They landed at Ellis Island, New York, in 1906, and made their way to Montreal. A few years later the uncle was on his way back to Italy. Giuseppe did not return with him; instead, he travelled to Sydney Mines, Cape Breton, where he began work in the steel plant. For a while, times were good. Then, in the early 1920s, the steel plant closed its doors, and Giuseppe was forced to seek employment elsewhere. His experience in the steel plant enabled him to acquire work as a moulder at the old Dominion Coal Company foundry in Glace Bay. Giuseppe's original plan was to work in Canada "for ten years then go back to Italy, but he married and had a family in Glace Bay."[1] He continued to work at the foundry until he retired in 1964. Giuseppe Plichie (in America Pagliccia was transformed into Plichie) died in Glace Bay on August 30, 1979. He was eighty-six years of age.

Roy "Sonny" Plichie is one of Giuseppe's twelve children. He was born in 1933. Roy too has spent much of his life working at the Glace Bay foundry.[2] In his spare time, however, he enjoys both gardening and writing poetry. Roy does not make a living from his writing, but writing is an important part of his life. He uses poetry as a vehicle to express thoughts and feelings about a variety of topics. When I asked him how he got started in writing poetry, he replied:

In 1969, I wrote one about the Coalminer, and they printed it in *The Coastal Courier* in Glace Bay. I got a few phone calls on it; some people liked it eh. I kept writing, on and off, twenty odd years. Now I have over

100 poems. Some of them are good and some of them ... funny you know, [laughs] a lot of people call me, the ones that I think are terrible, they love them. The ones that I'm proud of, some of those guys call me and say "throw the pen away Roy, forget about it." So you're not pleasing everybody ... but someone is reading it.

Over the years Roy has covered a number of themes in his poetry, and the poems themselves range from short humorous pieces to the sad and serious. One theme that consistently appears and reappears in his work is the memory of his father, Giuseppe Pagliccia. He has written poems, for example, titled *Fatherly Advice*, *Poppa's Garden*, *Parents* and *Poppa (My Dad)*.

Poppa (My Dad)

I passed by the old home today
Then my memories started to stray
Thoughts of Poppa came to my mind
A Dad that was always gentle and kind
He never had much, didn't even own a car
But to me he was always a star
Had twelve children, and he loved them all
He told me stories that I recall
Back in Italy when he was young
With his family and having fun
Just twelve years old when he left home
With his uncle they started to roam
Landed in Canada, the promised land
Holding his uncle by the hand
Married a girl from over here
Always worked hard, year after year
Was contented to stay at home
He never left us kids alone
There were secrets he never told
Even when he grew old
Always kept everything inside
Up to the day that he died
When that happened it made me cry
I never thought Poppa would ever die
Don't think I'm strange, don't ask me why
But now there's a new star up in the sky
He will never be forgotten

Roy has also written poems about a number of other family members. His mother, Florence MacKinnion, was born in Bay St. Lawrence, Cape Breton, in 1901. She and Giuseppe Pagliccia met in Sydney Mines and were married around 1917 at the old St. Mary's Catholic Church by Father Viola. She too is often the focus of Roy's poetry.

My Mother (an excerpt)

It's too late to tell her,
How much I loved her so.
She's buried up on top of a hill,
Where only roses and flowers grow
....
As you get older you think a lot,
There's times I wish she were here.
Just to sit and talk to her,
To hold her hand and have her near.

I know there's things we cannot have,
Or change things about our past.
But when I think about my mother,
I know her memory will always last.

The family, and its importance in one's life, is a central theme in Roy's work. The following excerpt from a poem about his grandson further illustrates this sentiment.

Christian

Christian loves hockey and ball
And when he scores a goal
You can see it on his face
He loves it with all his soul.
....
And when he makes the NHL
I know that day will come
And I'll be there hollering
For Christian, my grandson.

Although Roy is a proud Cape Bretoner, he has maintained a strong attachment to his Italian heritage. For Roy, family and ethnicity are phenomena that cannot easily be separated. The following piece expresses this sentiment explicitly.

Italians

I came into this world Italian
It made me proud from the start
When I see what they gave to this world
I must say they were really smart

We always had the best Popes
Valentino with his good looks
There's no one around can deny
Italians were always good cooks
Now when it comes to singing
Dino and Caruso had the best style

And don't forget John Cabot
The Italian who first came to our Isle

Was Capone really that bad
We know he gave us great beer
They say Italians are great lovers
All the girls still call me dear

DeMaggio was the best in baseball
Marciano the greatest fighter around
Even Ireland's St. Patrick was Italian
And Livio with his great sound

But the greatest Italian born
That this world ever had
When God made him he broke the mold
He was the Man I called Dad

I am proud of my heritage.

Given the importance of family in many of Roy's poems, I asked him what family members thought of his writing. He laughed and replied:

> Well, my two sons think I'm crazy, [laughs] they laugh at most of them, eh. But my daughter, Carol, she likes them. She believes in me. But they get a kick out of them.... [My son] has two boys, one is eight, one is six. The paper comes every week, and they want their father to read my poetry.

> It's funny now how things come out. Anthony [grandson] is eight; he wrote a poem last year. A good poem. My grandson. Tyrone's son. And he wrote one this week. See. The one he wrote last year, it's kinda cute. But he's got the attitude, it must be in the blood or something.[3]

The following is an excerpt from a poem that Anthony Plichie prepared, at age seven, while attending St. Anne's School. The poem was published in one of the 1996 issues of *The Coastal Courier* in Glace Bay.

8 - Ball

Pool is a game for everyone to play
You play it continuously every single day
At the start it is hard and requires some thought
But once you get better, a pastime it is not....

The family portraits, memories and vignettes Roy creates through his poetry give us an insight into his inner thoughts, feelings and experiences. In some respects, they also provide a glimpse into his family history. His writing in the present helps situate him firmly within both the family's past and his hopes for the future. The grandchildren's interest in his writing, and their Italian background are for Roy a source of pride and pleasure.

"The Best I Got"
The Story of Emilio Pace

By A. Evo DiPierro

The name Emilio Pace is widely known throughout Cape Breton. During the first half of this century, he entertained a whole generation of dance music lovers both on and off the island. "I'm gonna give you the best I got," was his assurance that everyone was in for a class performance. To many music lovers, Pace reigned as "the king" of the Cape Breton music scene. From his vaudeville days of the 1920s to the Second World War, Pace, along with family and friends, performed music that catered to practically every occasion. He was a versatile musician who could both play various instruments and write his own music. His dashing partnership with Dominic Nardocchio in The Harmony Duo, and later his own Emilio Pace Orchestra, were the primary foundations upon which he built a strong relationship with the public. He both understood, and performed well, the different genres of music of the time—whether popular, classical or ethnic. But these are just some of the things that made Emilio Pace a special figure in Cape Breton society. He loved people, especially children, and he delighted in teaching others to make music. If anyone could be called "sunny" in nature, it was Emilio Pace.

In February 1996, I had the opportunity to sit and chat with Mrs. Elsie Pace, and daughters Mary Mitchell and Linda Strickey, about Emilio's life and times. They provided me with a profile of the great man and his music. Below are some of the highlights of our revealing stroll down memory lane.

> [Mrs. Pace]: I was born on February 7, 1911, and met Emilio when he was boarding next door to where we lived. He was thirteen years older than me, but I guess he fell for me, and I fell for him and married him when I was sixteen. We had five children: one boy and four girls. Emilio's parents wanted him to be a tailor when he was in Italy. But ... all he wanted

to do was play; he used to sneak up to the attic and play the violin. He was working as an apprentice in a tailor shop. The boss went out one day and when he came back, he caught Emilio playing the mandolin, and the whole shop was dancing.... The boss said, "I didn't get you here to play. You don't want to work, and you don't want anybody else to work...." so he kicked him out. Well that was the end of his apprenticeship. Then he just spent his time with the music; that's all he cared about. Then he was in the army at seventeen. I think he did something with the mail, but I am not quite sure.

[Mrs. Mitchell]: And he never missed playing the "Last Post," every Armistice Day. He never missed it. Once we were playing 'til four o'clock in the morning, and he would get up and play that "Last Post." I can remember before Daddy died, Armistice Day was that November and he wasn't well, but he got up and paraded, and played the "Last Post." Nobody played it like he did.

[Mrs. Pace]: He didn't care about anything else. He played any kind of instrument ... he got the orchestra and used to write the music for it. Never had a teacher in his life. If he couldn't buy an orchestration at the bookstore, he would get a record of the number he wanted, then take it home to play, and he would keep on playing it until he finished writing the part of each member of the orchestra.

Emilio Pace was born, the oldest of six children, on January 9, 1898, in the village of Pratola Peligna in the central region of Abruzzo, Italy. He came to Cape Breton at age twenty-four and later arranged for his two younger brothers to join him. They settled in Glace Bay at first, then Emilio moved to Sydney. While boarding with some friends from the same Italian village, he found a job playing trumpet for the orchestra that accompanied the showing of silent movies at the Strand Theatre. According to Mrs. Pace, her husband became seriously involved in music, as an occupation, when he came to Cape Breton. Several years after playing at the Strand, he joined the orchestra of Lucio Agastini in Montreal. Emilio, however, cared little for the larger centres, so he moved back to Sydney and returned to the Strand. It was at that time that he met and married Elsie Adore and developed his profession as a musician.

[Mrs. Pace]: At the Strand Theatre, they had an orchestra downstairs and the picture upstairs. Seventy-five years ago, that is where he started. He got the job there because he was really good at the trumpet, and that's what he played there.

[What instruments did he play?]

[Mrs. Pace]: He played the guitar, the mandolin, the violin, the trumpet ... anything, really, and he could teach—such as the piano. He taught Rudy [his son] the saxophone. Right before he died, I think he was trying to learn the bagpipes.

[Mrs. Mitchell]: And he also taught guitar at Holy Angels. Then came along this Mr. Brown [from the Hawaiian School of Music] and gave Daddy this job ... to teach the Hawaiian guitar. That is really what put us on our feet. So he did that for a few years, and that is how a lot of people would remember him—as their teacher. And then of course, they would remember him from the dances too. Oh, and the guitar. He was a classical guitarist ... that was his favourite.

[Mrs. Pace]: Andre Segovia, the guitarist, was his favourite ... his mentor and idol. He sounded like a whole orchestra when he played the guitar.

[What about the Harmony Duo?]

[Mrs. Pace]: Well, they [Emilio Pace and Dominic Nardocchio] played all those instruments ... the guitar, mandolin and the trumpet. That went on for a couple of years. They were good friends. The Harmony Duo travelled and played east of Montreal and including that city.

> **[What kind of a person was he?]**
> Mrs. Pace]: Full of the old nick. A real tease ... oh, he would be going down Charlotte Street singing. The storekeepers used wait for him to walk by because he could cheer them up. He liked to take the kids up and down Charlotte Street, along with anybody else. Yes, he always had a lot of people around. Up on the veranda playing, everybody stopping and listening to him ... he loved that. Or he would be on the back veranda, where we lived on Charlotte Street, and everybody going through the alley way would hear him.

Eventually, Pace formed the Emilio Pace Orchestra. Elsie Pace sang, while their son, Rudy, played the saxophone, and daughter Mary, the piano. The orchestra played at dance halls throughout Cape Breton, in Antigonish and on CJCB radio. When radio listeners began calling to ask about the vocalist, Mrs. Pace's popularity was launched. Local papers dubbed her the Kate Smith of Sydney.

[Mrs. Pace]: I sang on the radio but would hide behind the piano at the dances because I didn't want anybody to see me ... I was so fat. But they called me Sydney's Kate Smith. He said, "I will buy you a new dress if you will come and sing on the radio." I said, "Ok, but don't tell them who I am." He was on the radio every Sunday with the request program, Mandolin Melodies. People used to listen for it every Sunday. Oh, he made lots of records, but God knows where they are ... they are all gone. He made records playing the mandolin, the guitar.... He composed music too. He didn't sell any records; they were just for our own use.

[Mrs. Strickey]: People used to request them on Mandolin Melodies ... his show on CJCB. Our sister, Evelyne, handled the requests and sang on the program, while our other sister, Anne Lee, played the piano. The Sicilian

Tarantella was one record that he loved, and they used to always request it at the dances.

[Mrs. Mitchell]: He composed that piece and used to play it all the time at the dances, and they loved it.

[Mrs. Strickey]: He used to play at the bar mitzvahs. [Mrs. Mitchell]: The Jewish people loved him. We played for all their dances, and they had to have special music. Daddy made sure they had everything they wanted. They really liked my father. They were good to play for, and they were good to us. Yes, we would play at the synagogue, Daddy and I.

[Mrs. Pace]: He learned the classical violin by himself and said that was the hardest instrument to play.

[Mrs. Mitchell]: Well, there was nobody who could play "Ave Maria" on the violin like my father. When he played "Ave Maria," you would cry. He played it with such emotion.

[Mrs. Strickey]: What he always used to say, "If you play, you have to have sympatico. If you don't have sympatico, then there is nothing."

[Mrs. Pace]: And he didn't want anybody to make a noise when he was playing. If he heard anybody talking, he would say, "If you don't stop, I will stop playing." And they would be quiet.

Mrs. Mitchell recalled an important highlight in her father's life. It occurred when he was chosen as a contestant to perform, with his guitar, on the television show, *Pick The Stars*, in Toronto. Although Emilio came second in the contest, he felt honoured to have been chosen to perform on national television. He was thrilled, and everyone was proud of him. Emilio used his talents to make records, fill the dance halls and provide suitably for his family. He was a perfectionist and, as Mrs. Pace recalled, he would spend all hours of the night practising on his guitar, conditioning his fingers, in order to play at his best at concerts. Pace was also a popular entertainer among the many sailors who stopped in Cape Breton during the Second World War.

[Mrs. Strickey]: Well, the Second World War affected him in that he got lots of business. I mean, they played lots of dances and his orchestra thrived. He made lots of money then.

[And Mary, what are your strongest memories of your father?]

[Mrs. Mitchell]: He was such a good father ... he was so affectionate.

[Mrs. Strickey]: He used to call her Maryuch.

[Mrs. Mitchell]: I was proud to walk down the street with him because he was so well known and everybody liked him. And of course, I played in the orchestra, and probably I was with my father more than anybody

Emilio Pace, ca. 1954. Photo possibly by The Kelly Studio, Sydney. Courtesy of Linda Strickey.

because I was with him all day and evening. He took me out of school because he wanted me to play in the orchestra, and I really didn't mind. I was glad to quit school anyway. I started playing in the orchestra when I was thirteen years old. When the war was on, he used to have two or three bands playing, and Rudy, my brother and I played together at these different dances. That's really how I got started playing in the orchestra. I had very little of a social life because I played so much. But you would see a lot of people there, and I got to know a lot of people. I liked that part about it.

[What was he like to work for?]

[Mrs. Mitchell]: Oh, he would get cranky at times, you know, and get after me, but he was pretty good. He was a good leader; everybody liked him ... he would carry on and he would get mad, you know, the Italian in him.... [Call you] "stupido," if you make a mistake.... That was just his way, but he would never hurt you, you know. I can still hear him now. He was good because the musicians who played in our band played there for years unless they either moved away or died, so I guess they liked him.

Another thing that I remember about my father was that he loved Christmas. He just lived for Christmas. We didn't have a big home, but we always had lots to eat and lots of people, especially at Christmas time, and lots of music. Everybody crammed into our little house for Christmas dinner. He played "Silent Night" and the Italian hymns, and that's all we had. Christmas Day was all Italian hymns, Christmas music and singing. We just loved it.

[Mrs. Strickly]: We had a little upright piano in the living room. Everybody stood around it, and we would sing different parts. Mary played the piano and Daddy would play.... Well, I was eleven when he died so I don't remember the orchestra part of it, but I remember in the evenings he and I would be home alone. He would be there playing his guitar, his favourite instrument. Then he would ask me to listen to him. He would say, "Come in Linduch, come in and listen." He would play it again and ask me to listen to different aspects. I never played any instruments, but I took singing lessons. I used to go to the festivals, and Daddy would say to me, "you come ... you sing for me like you are going to sing in the festival," so I would have to stand there in the living room and sing my piece in front of him. I didn't have any expression, but my father had all kinds of it. I was so nervous and shy, and he used to try to coach me. He would say ... "put expression, put expression," because I would be like, you know, a dead person. I could sing the notes but didn't have any expression, so he would sort of coach me ... try to encourage me ... but never got very far. But anyway, I do remember him, like my sister said, at Christmas, and all of us together.

For Emilio Pace, music not only pleased the senses but also brought people and families closer together. He was the type of person that liked to entertain socially. His home was always open to friends and family.

[Mrs. Strickey]: I remember when we used to have spaghetti on Thursdays, and he always had visitors. Thursdays were always kind of special, and the priests would come. We used to have them over all the time. Daddy used to invite the priest from Sacred Heart parish to our house on Thursdays (everybody was welcome, you know), and then he would play and entertain them while we sat around the table. On Sundays, his brothers, who lived in Glace Bay, would come in with their families, and my mother would make polenta.

[Mrs. Mitchell]: Daddy used to pour [the polenta] on the centre of the table and then the sauce all over it. He would also hide a dime in the polenta (ten cents then was like a dollar today) and whoever found it kept the money. It was delicious ... oh my, if anybody walked in and saw us eating off the table!

Toward the end of his life, Emilio developed serious heart problems. He suffered a heart attack at age fifty-seven and was urged by his doctor to cease playing the trumpet. Emilio, however, ignored the doctor's warning. Music was his life! His family, in fact, did not discover that he had a history of heart trouble until after his death. Emilio Pace passed away on December 2, 1955. The orchestra disbanded about a year later. Recordings of his music still exist; some can be found in the archives, while others have been retained by the family. Occasionally, the Paces receive calls from people still interested in hearing Emilio's music.

There was a time in Cape Breton when well-dressed women and men, including sharply groomed sailors, danced the night away to the sound of a live orchestra playing their favourite tunes of the 1930s and 1940s. Emilio Pace and his orchestra made this possible and, because of that, they hold a special place in the history of music in Cape Breton. But, that is only one side of the story. For Emilio Pace, any-time was the right time for making music. He enjoyed performing, whether it was in a concert hall on a Saturday night, or a street corner with a group of children in the early morning. It is this image of the man that survives in the minds and hearts of many Cape Bretoners.

Mario Pino (1919-1997): A Life in Music

Edited by Sam Migliore

Mario Pino. Photo by Raytel Photography. Courtesy of the Pino family.

On April 6, 1997, Cape Breton lost a friend, an entertainer, and a musical legend as Mario Angelo Pino passed away at the age of seventy-eight. He will be remembered by many as the man who could "liven up any group right quick!" with a simple touch of his accordion keys. He knew thousands of songs by heart, and he could play in a number of musical styles. During his lifetime, however, Mario Pino was involved in much more than musical performance. He loved sports, and he actively took part in various ventures and organizations. What follows is a glimpse into Mario's life based on: written material he himself prepared; two interviews with him and his wife, Alma Gladys French; and, informal talks with family members.[1]

[Mario]: My parents came here together in 1914 from a small town near Cagliari, in Sardinia. Salvatore Pino and Anna Maria Josephine Congia. My father came as an electrician to work in the coal mine in Glace Bay. After years, he got rheumatism; that's when he came to Sydney to work at the steel plant, and we took up residence on Laurier Street. I was brought up mostly in Whitney Pier and went to school there. In the plant, Dad drove a locomotive. He used to say, "this is a dangerous place [compared to the coal mine], there is no roof over your head."

My parents had six children when my mother died of tuberculosis. She was thirty-three years old. I was nine. [Alma]: They didn't know what the disease was, and it ate the lungs out of her. It started with pneumonia and kept going. And she was a hard worker.... [Mario]: Yeah, I think she worked to death. Had boarders then, one fellow from Italy. [Alma]: Cows and hens.... [Mario]: and a garden. Well, that was good during the Depression. We had our own food.

Then Dad remarried Mary Camus, and they had eight more children.

Childhood Memories

[Mario]: I had to mind the cows after school and on weekends. Look after the hens.... I had lots to do. Too much! I wasn't allowed to play ball or anything, [but] I used to sneak away....

Dad bought an old pump organ for my sister. She took lessons but, apparently, I used to end up playing the organ. [pause] From there, Johnny Nemis used to come to the house with the accordion. I was only a kid. I used to watch him, and when he'd go to bed, I used to pick it up and play until I got caught in the morning. [Alma]: His father played button accordion. [Mario]: He played at dances and everything. Dad got the button accordions from France. He could sing too with the Italian fellas. They always sang together. [Sam: You just picked it up?] [Mario]: Yeah. I liked playing see, and I liked to follow. I was good; if somebody was singing, I could pick up the key they were doing. [Alma]: He was far advanced by ear. [Mario]: Listen, and I play it.

Military Service

Although Mario played on CJCB radio (in Sydney, NS) as part of a trio with brother Tony (guitar) and Mike DiPenta (sticks) in 1933, he did not own an accordion until he entered military service in 1941. During his stay in the service, he was stationed in New Glasgow for basic training and then placed in Halifax. Mario was transferred to the Royal Canadian Army Service Corps in Sydney in 1945.

[Mario]: In the army, I used to drive the ambulance and the colonel's car. But I mostly entertained and played sports. [I played] hockey, baseball and softball. And that's all I ever did in the army. Entertain. I played for army and navy shows and at the Salvation army. When stationed in Halifax, I also played on the CHNS radio station every Saturday. There was the *Uncle Mel* show; he used to have bands play for the Services, and I used to play for them.

And then I came home on leave, [pause] and I stood home overtime. They call it AWOL. So I went back, and the colonel said: "How come you didn't come back?" I said: "Well, I wasn't feeling good." They had me locked up. Then Johnny Nemis come down and brought his accordion to practice. I said: "I'm a prisoner; I'm not supposed to practice...." So they took me before the colonel, and he told me: "Well you better be there tonight to entertain." So that's about all I had to do in the Service, entertain. [pause] Of course that was enough.

Then, at the time I was supposed to go overseas, I got diphtheria. And here I didn't go over, but my platoon [pause] they were all killed that time. So I probably wasn't supposed to go. They were all ambushed. [pause]

I came home, and I was in the hospital here [in Sydney] for a while. [When I was released, the army] kept me here. I played ball and hockey. That was enough. Four and a half years in the army.... Drive the ambulance, deliver supplies to the old folks, and then you still have to entertain at night. It wasn't an eight-hour job at all.

[Sam: Was it a band that you were playing with?] [Mario]: I was by myself. At that time, you couldn't get no one to play with you. I've always played alone, for years. Well, the accordion is a band in itself. The only thing I couldn't do was sing, but somebody else sang. That's what I did in the Service, entertain them—stage work, outposts, clubs—and all for morale builders. Like the Colonel said: "You're doing more than a lot of fellows that went overseas, because you're keeping the morale, keeping them all entertained." It served a purpose, I guess. Kept us entertained, kept them happy, so everybody was happy.

Experiences and Accomplishments in Later Life

Mario began work at the coke ovens in Sydney in 1941, just prior to entering military service. Once he had completed his stay in the army, he returned to work in the steel plant. He worked there until he retired in 1968. Full-time employment at the plant, however, did not prevent Mario from continuing his interests in both music and sports.

[Mario]: I worked in New Waterford delivering wholesale stuff to three stores. But on Saturday night, we had to deliver groceries. Everybody used to wait for me; time went good. Yeah, fifteen dollars a week. Then I went [to work at the steel plant]. I got eighteen dollars a week for seven shifts. At the time, rent was six dollars a month, so that wasn't bad see.

[Jennifer Pino (Mario's grandson's wife)]: What did you do [in the steel plant]? [Mario]: I done everything. [everyone laughs] I worked. [Alma]: When he left, the plant folded up. [Mario]: I worked with the combustion engineers, I worked in the machine shop, I drove cranes ... all that. You had to do it. I worked on the coal bank down Sydney there. When they dropped the coal, we shovelled it to the side so they could move the [railway] cars. I also shovelled coal at the boiler house to make steam. That was hard work.

[Sam: Do you have any stories about working in the steel plant?] [Mario]: Oh yeah. There was the time that Clem Hansen was the manager of the steel plant. Every time they brought in [potential] buyers from the other side, I was called in to entertain. Clem Hansen would say: "I want you to go to the Cove ... take Buddy Best" (who played harmonica). Everything was fixed so we would get paid for our time. We used to get a lot of calls [to entertain]. And that was it, [pause] otherwise [pause] I played ball, and I played hockey for the steel plant. I retired in 1968.

Participation in Sports

For many years, Mario played baseball in summer and hockey in winter. [Mario]: I started playing baseball in the early 1930s on the ball field of St. Nicholas Parish, Hankard Street. At that time there was no Little League. Later, I played junior and then senior baseball as a catcher. In the winter of 1939, I played in the nets for the Bombers in Whitney Pier. The team was a top contender in the league; it was coached by Maynard MacEwan of the Sydney Millionaires and managed by Rocky DiPenta [at first], and later by Larry Dobranski. On the first game of the Junior Loop opening, the team came through with a 1-0 upset win over Sydney Mines. Kennie Braithwaite scored the lone goal on a pass from Oscar Seale and Stephenson. I received the first shutout of opening night. The only loss I had [that year] was against the Sydney Mines team, 2-1. The Bombers were suspended [however] because of a player two days over the junior age, and we were not allowed in the playoffs. This was my last year in junior hockey.

In 1941 I enlisted in the army. I played baseball, softball and hockey [during my years in the Service]. After I was discharged in 1946, I went back to work in the coke ovens and played softball for them in the Colliery League.

Mario continued to play for various teams throughout the 1940s and 1950s. [Alma]: He was a goaltender in Suburban Hockey. [Mario]: I was secretary-treasurer of the Suburban Hockey League. See, I was an all round man. [pause] I earned my keep. [Mario played for the Sydney Forks team in 1956 and earned the league's first shutout with his team's 3-0 win over South Bar.] And no equipment, and no mask in the nets. [laughs] I got the [Mario pointed to the scars on his face].

In addition to playing ball and hockey, Mario also served as a coach for a while. He was as competitive as a coach as he was as a player. Bubba (Silvio Pino), Mario's son, recalls:

> Unlike other coaches, Dad did not necessarily play his sons simply
> because they were his sons. On one occasion, he benched my brother
> Gino. Gino didn't like it, but Dad's only reply was: "I have to play my best
> players." Gino didn't play; Dad was a competitive coach. Gino went out
> and bought a trophy that said "Coach of the Year," and gave it to Dad.

Mario was also an active bowler. He served as President of the St. Augustine Mixed Bowling League in 1966, and he played on the Ashby Legion Bowling Team when they won the Nova Scotia Bowling Tournament in 1979.

Music

[Mario]: [When I got out of the army], I did a lot of volunteer work entertaining at Point Edward Annex [and other TB Annexes], the C.N.I.B. (Canadian National Institute for the Blind), St. Anthony Home (now the MacGillivray Guest Home) and [other places]. I played for the C.N.I.B. for thirty years. There was no money, but you were happy to supply the entertainment.

[Alma]: He played when the tall ships came [to SydPort], and he played on the *Bluenose* when it came to Louisbourg. [Mario]: Then [Maria DeLorenzo and I performed] for the Queen Mother in Wentworth Park, in Sydney, for Canada Day. Well, she wanted to meet us. The [Queen Mother] asked me, "Where were you born?" I said, "New Aberdeen." She said, "Scotland." I says: "No, Glace Bay." [everyone laughs] [We had a conversation, and spoke a little Italian together.] [Alma]: He played for Pierre Trudeau. [Mario]: That was at old Louisbourg.

> ### "I'll Go On Alone" — An Embarrassing Moment
>
> [Jennifer]: Tell Sam about your most embarrassing moment. [Alma]: I'll go on alone. [Mario]: Oh yeah. Me and my brother, Joe, used to do stage work. He sang, and [I played the accordion]. I always asked him, "What are you going to [sing] now." So [this time] he says, I'll go on alone. So, [pause] I let him go. And he's looking back and looking back. [I just watched.] When he comes back, he says, "What happened to you?" I said, "I asked what you were gonna do, and you said, I'll go on alone." He said, "That's the name of the tune." [everyone laughs] That was comical. [Alma]: Everyone in the theatre took to laughing; they roared.

Mario Pino entertained people at numerous functions and locations throughout Cape Breton. Most often, he performed alone using various techniques to produce a full, pleasing sound with his accordion. At the same time, however, Mario entertained with others; over the years, for example, he performed with: the Italian choirs of both Sydney and Dominion; Joe Pino (brother) and the Haylofters; Jim Wyle's Aces; the Kings Trio, with the late Gino Pino (1946-1969), Mario's son, as vocalist; the Eddy Borgeau Trio; and, St. Augustine's Church Choir. Mario also was known to pick up the accordion and play, just for fun, as he walked up and down Charlotte Street in Sydney.

In recognition of both his volunteer work and his achievements in music, Mario received a number of awards. These awards range from a certificate of merit for entertainment from the Northside Guest Home to recognition of dedicated service from the Cape Breton Musicians Association. Alma also has received awards for her work with the St. John's Ambulance Corps.

[Alma]: We went up to the St. John's Ambulance investitures. Mario played there, and I received a Serving Sister award. He got an award too—for driving the ambulance for us when we didn't have a driver. [Mario]: Well, she has been with them for thirty-five years. [Alma]: I got four medals [over the years] and other awards. In 1966, I was the winner of the St. John's Ambulance's Sir George Burns Trophy. [Mario]: I taught her all of that [laughs]. Between the two of us, we got a lot of awards. I got three life memberships: with the Legion of Musicians, the Royal Canadian Legion and the Corps of Signals (Veterans). And I got a fifty-year medal from the Legion and a medal for entertainment from them. A thank you. Don't mind that.

During our interview, Mario mentioned only one regret; the fact that none of his children had taken up the accordion. [Mario]: None of my boys bothered with it. See, I wanted somebody, even the girls, to play the accordion. I said, "Everybody should have music in the family." You know, that keeps the family together. Entertainment. Like our place down on the Pier, every Saturday night there was something going on. All the time. And everybody came there, cause we had a big room in the back—about twenty-five feet square. We used to call it the "Hall." There was always lots to eat and lots to drink. And that was a lot of fun.

Concluding Remarks

Mario Pino's funeral took place at St. Theresa's Church on April 10, 1997. It was a touching service attended by a large number of people. You could feel the emotion as Livio Nicoletti sang in Italian. Livio and Mario were well acquainted; they performed together, along with other members of the Italian Choir of Dominion, on many occasions. You could tell from Livio's voice—a voice that spoke for us all—that he and everyone present was going to miss Mario greatly. Later, at the Forest Haven Memorial Gardens, members of the Legion gave Mario their final salute and stood at attention for the playing of the "Last Post." It was a touching tribute to a man who had served five years in military service and had spent a lifetime entertaining members of various legions throughout the Maritimes.

"Magnolias and Other Sweet Things"
The Story of Angelo Spinazzola

By A. Evo DiPierro

When I began this project, the last things I expected to encounter, if I could name them, were kayaks, schooners and Dr. Seuss. I had in mind certain assumptions of what constitutes a "typical" Italian in Cape Breton. This was a big mistake! Using the word "typical" to describe anyone on an ethnic basis is an ethnocentric preconception. I think we all get caught in that trap from time to time, unfortunately. To understand a community is to study all of its various aspects and segments. In the process, the researcher often becomes pleasantly surprised by the different and refreshing realities of that community. Meeting someone like Angelo Spinazzola reminded me of that important point.

Angelo Spinazzola, November 1997. Photo by Vaughan Merchant. Courtesy of Angelo Spinazzola.

Angelo is a musician, singer, songwriter and businessman. He attributes his business sense to his father, Patsy Smith (who established such popular nightspots as the Capri in Sydney), and his singing ability to his mother, Marilyn (who worked as a professional singer). In addition to being a member of the popular band, Green Eggs And Jam, and its predecessor, Father John's Medicine Train, Angelo has produced two solo efforts, From Roots to Wings and Home from the Tides. These works show clear evidence of an evolving musical style that is both complex and innovative. During the summer, when he is not performing at various venues, he operates North River Kayak Tours. He takes people kayaking in the St. Anne's area of Victoria County, Cape Breton. Spinazzola seems to thrive on individualism and adventure; he also seems to have a knack for transforming the excitement this generates into a creative musical energy.

I believe it was 1994.... I sailed from Sydney to the Azores, which is part of Portugal and 2,000 nautical miles (one way) from Sydney. We went over and back in a period of a month-and-a-half.... Although I wasn't a sailor, I wanted to become inspired to come up with an album. I needed to travel and to experience ... another culture. I ended up writing the title track to the second album, *Home From The Tides*. I was half-way across the Atlantic when we didn't have a breath of wind for 24 hours. It was my shift at the helm, we weren't moving, so I just played music. *Home From The Tides* came out of that.

[How did you end up on a schooner?]

It was a 55-foot schooner called the *Sorca*, and the skipper was Dr. Martin Brennan.... Terry Kelly told me that there was this man going across the Atlantic ... and back, and might need a crew. I only sailed occasionally ... I wasn't really a sailor, but ... I needed some inspiration, and a trip like that wouldn't cost a lot because you wouldn't spend too much money crossing the ocean. I approached the skipper and asked if I could ... be a crew member. He didn't know who I was; he said, definitively, "We have our crew." I came back a week later and asked again. Again he refused, but I told him that I do electrical work.... I also told him I was a musician, which was nice because it could break the monotony of the long trip.... In the end, he decided to give me a chance.... I gladly did any work that was required—such as cleaning, varnishing, etc. I wanted to learn all about the boat before I went across the ocean.

I worked for it, and I'm glad I went.... It was ... just an incredible experience. I figured it would be more of a physical experience, you know, manning the sails and stuff, but it was the mental experience that really had an impact [on me]. I know that, at one point, I was very sea sick ... and I honestly wanted to end it all.... It was only a couple of days. Some people are sick for weeks, but I wasn't that bad. But I remember talking to myself—psyching myself—at one point saying, "You've got to do this; it's important." I also remember telling myself and writing in my journal that I would not come back across the ocean this way. Turns out that when I arrived in the Azores, I had a great time there. I met a lot of people around the islands. While the crew was preparing for the return trip, I really didn't want to be a coward, so I did it—I went back, and that was a rather big decision for me. I actually wasn't sick; I was healthy throughout the entire trip back and a lot of interesting things ... incredible things ... happened on the trip.

August 13th—*Friday the 13th*—we lost our main sail; it ripped in two ... that sure was interesting.... Next we had trouble with our motor.... Then we hit a whale.... I was down in the galley; the cook was up at the helm. We felt these two quick bumps and jerks on the boat, and it's a twenty-four-ton boat, twenty-eight tons loaded, so to feel that we must've hit something. We went up to look out, and there was this whale opening its mouth and spewing something ... it could've been blood.... We believed we knocked him out or killed him. A lot of other little things happened along the way too. We saw more whales, dolphins, Portuguese Man o' War.... The album, *Home from the Tides*, sums up the trip—back from an incredible oceanic voyage.

"Home from the Tides," "Magnolia" and other songs from the CD conjure up for me impressions of encounters with the strange and the beautiful. What true artist could return from a sailing adventure without being affected by the height of inspiration? Astoundingly, still not settled from his ocean voyage, Angelo embarked on yet another interesting trip.

> When I came back, I spent ... eight months in Cape Breton and then I travelled to eleven countries in Europe. I flew over with a backpack and instruments.... I didn't have a schedule so I would just jump on a train and go somewhere.... I would [go to a pub] play [my instruments] and then get my room and board taken care of. I was sort of sponsoring myself by playing music on the trip. I didn't have a lot of money, and I planned to travel for about two-and-a-half months on my own. That trip opened my eyes to other music and places, such as Italy and Greece, and to see the cultures and the people, how they play and how other people react to the playing. That was really neat, and it helped for this new album, *From Roots To Wings*. There are tunes on the album that came out of my head a year ... two years later ... from that trip.

When Angelo returned to Cape Breton, the time had come to settle down, somewhat, and put some structure in his life.

> When I was in Ireland, I went on a bicycle tour ... and it was incredible. I was really envious of the tour guide. He was great ... and it made me think, "What could I do to incorporate my music, be outside, and do something that would keep me healthy?" I came back and realized that I had been kayaking for twelve years so a kayak tour would be neat. There are other ones all over the world. So I started one up, did the research and the business plan.... I wanted to be my own boss, and in the kayak tours, I am. I set my own hours and ... the way things turn out is my responsibility. I like to have a little bit of pressure on me in that sense. It's just the way I'm developed. Well, my father had the Italian Club, the Capri Club and the Benedette Club. He was an entrepreneur. So I guess I'm ... genetically following his road. He didn't tell me to start a kayak tour or a music business. I just did it! And, I'm sure, I got my business sense from him.

Angelo developed a solid musical reputation long before his schooner trip and the recording of his first solo album. In 1992, after finishing with *Father John's Medicine Train*, Angelo, along with brother Carlo, and other musicians, formed a group called *Green Eggs and Jam*. In addition to singing, Angelo played flute, harmonica, guitar and the mandolin.

> That was an excellent experience, really. *Green Eggs & Ham* is Dr. Seuss, and the motto was, "try it and you might like it," so we put together "Green Eggs" and "Jam,"—which is a jam session where people get together and play. Our first gig was the University College of Cape Breton (now Cape Breton University). They went bananas; they really enjoyed the music. We were playing with, well: Gordie Sampson ... he's a very incredible musician; Stuart Cameron; my brother, Carlo; and, David Mahalik. So it was a bunch of artistic folks just getting together and having fun, and the College liked it, so we started booking more gigs. The band was extremely popular, and we came out with an album called *No-Thing* which did really, really well.

Angelo also does both freelance and studio work—including backing other musicians for their recordings. With Green Eggs and Jam, Angelo's musical expertise began to develop at a rapid pace. The popularity of the band placed him in a circle with other well-known and established artists in Cape Breton. In our discussion, Angelo remembered the special times when he played at his father's former club, the Capri:

> The Capri [brought] in top bands from all over the place. It was nice to be affiliated with a place that did that. When we played there, on the same stage as let's say, Colin James or the Barra MacNeils, it was a nice feeling. When Green Eggs and Jam played ... musicians, from all walks of life, would come up and play with us. It was a loose jam. The Barra MacNeils would come up. It was just great because we got to know all these people.... I remember one time the Barra MacNeils asked me to come up and sing with them. That made me feel so good [to have] people you respect so much ask you to come up and sing with them. Mind you, there were other people that they asked to come up, but they asked me too, and it made me feel like this *is really happening*.

I also was curious to know what music did for Angelo in a deeper, more personal way.

> I've been listening to music since I was fourteen. It boosted my self-confidence.... [Later,] I started catching on, playing, and getting better.... When I started writing, I found I could express my feelings totally. I play every single day, but I don't see the growth because I'm playing so much. But when I look back at the records and studio sessions ... then I hear it and say, "Wow, I played that, like, six years ago and now ... now listen to what I'm doing...." Now I am confident enough with my instruments that I don't have to focus so much on my playing. I focus more on writing tunes.... Every song I've written has been about a personal experience or something that had an impact on my life.

At the time of this interview, Angelo was putting the finishing touches on a new CD, *From Roots to Wings*. When he played the tape for me, I immediately took to the song: "Wonder Where The Days Go." Taken together, this and the other songs on the album, indicated to me that Angelo Spinazzola had soared to new heights in his musical life.[1]

> It's a real diverse album. It has jazz, a contemporary tune.... "Wonder Where the Days Go" was written about ... me and my brother: *Happiness runs solo; he's laughing at his name while brother's in the backyard acting out his fame....* Carlo was the athlete; he was always acting out his fame in the backyard, and ... happiness runs solo ... I guess that would be me laughing at the name: Angelo Pasquale Spinazzola.

But, Spinazzola was not always Angelo Pasquale's last name. At eighteen, he made a serious decision that reflected the fundamentals of who he was and what he wanted to be. He decided to make the change from "Smith" to "Spinazzola."

> I was kind of young then, and I thought "Spinazzola" was a funny sounding name. I wondered how people would react to it, after calling me Smith all these years. Would they think I just pulled this name out to play music or something, like a pseudonym? But I did it anyway, and it's a good move. I think it boils down to this is what I am, and I am not Smith. I want to be real. [Smith] didn't make sense, you know what I mean?

It all made sense to the immigration officials when Angelo's grandfather arrived in Halifax, at the turn of the century. They decided that the name should be Anglicized to make it easier for them to identify him, and more convenient for Mr. Spinazzola to integrate into the new society. But for Angelo, the name "Smith" did not fit. The name change was not a marketing tool. It had to do with identity, ethnicity and self-satisfaction. With an expression of sincere pride, Angelo calls himself Italian. His father's father was from Bari, in southern Italy, while his grandmother came from Ozzano in the north. He loves Italian food, prefers home-made Italian wine, has been to Italy and studied the language. According to Angelo, making wine and being able to speak the language are important aspects of being Italian:

> Ever since I was thirteen or fourteen, we've been [making wine]. We have a certain ... way of doing it, and, when I'm having a glass of wine, I feel the Italian in me ... I can't explain it.... I just took a course in Italian ... put on by the Italian Cultural Association, so, um, *parlo Italiano, poco e molto male* ... that would sum it up. [chuckles] It's a beautiful language, and I'm going to learn it, but it will take some time. I can't learn it by getting a teacher to teach me. I'm going to go to Italy and stick myself somewhere where no one speaks English.

Maybe on his next schooner voyage, he'll head to Italy for that immersion training.

Sports Memories from Dominion

By Len Stephenson

Tug O'War. Prior to the Declaration of War in 1940, the Italians of Dominion were engaged in a sport that provided them an opportunity to demonstrate their great strength and stamina, while entertaining large crowds of spectators. The sport was Tug O'War. The late Eric Scott, renowned strong man and weightlifter, was extremely proud to have been invited to join the Italian team. Eric also had a keen interest in community history and wrote many fine articles on the subject. Included in his reports were some of the activities of the team.

The team was organized in 1938 and was made up of ten men and some spares. Their first match was against the Sydney Police Club at the North Sydney Race Track. Charlie Ballard donated a prize of $50 for the winner. The match took place between heats of the last race of the season. The Sydney Police team weighed 2,400 pounds, the Italians, 1,900. The match was best two out of three. The teams split the first two pulls, and the Italians won the third. The Italians celebrated that night at the home of coach, Pino Piva.

A match was arranged with the Caledonia Club in 1939 to be held at the Glace Bay Miners Forum. The Italians voted for a two out of three contest, but Caledonia wanted a single pull. The Italians won easily. The next challenge was by a team from the swordfishing fleet at the Glace Bay harbour. This match also was held at the Forum. The Italians won easily on the first pull. The fishermen were then allowed to add two additional men to their team, but they still lost.

The team then was invited to pull against a team from Antigonish, at their Fall Fair. The Antigonish team weighed 1,600 pounds while the Italian team weighed in at 1,900. The Italians agreed to remove two of their heaviest pullers and replace them with two of the lightest. The match proved to be very difficult, but the Italians were the winners. They were then persuaded to pull against a second team. Quite exhausted, they finally lost a match.

Cycling. The Italian miners very much enjoyed the sport of cycling. In 1980, the late Condo Baggio described one of their most memorable cycling episodes. He was one of twenty-eight Italians that left the Red Onion Hotel in Dominion, on bicycles, at about nine o'clock on a sunny Sunday morning in 1927 or 1928. They were from Dominion and New Waterford and were destined for North Sydney and Sydney Mines to visit relatives of Mrs. Zaniol.

Members of the Italian team included coach Pino Piva, Sisto Piva, Joe, "The Baker," Frank Peori, Tavio Zaniol, Big "Mario," Fred Canova, Patsy "Pop" Peori, Dominico Dezagiacoma, "Big Gus," Canadian-born Sandy MacPherson and Eric Scott.

The roads were all gravelled at that time, no pavement. They arrived in North Sydney shortly after noon, and they decided to have lunch at a Chinese restaurant. As the men entered the restaurant, the owner became considerably excited and agitated. Apparently, the sight and sound of twenty-eight burly men speaking a foreign language was a bit unnerving for the fellow. The chief of police appeared on the scene and requested an explanation. A Mr. Manelli, a cyclist from New Waterford, had a better command of the English language than the others, and he assured the chief they were harmless. The men were only there to visit relatives.

The next person to interrupt their lunch proved to be a fine friend and a finer host. He was Dominic Mancini, operator of a pop factory. Mr. Mancini invited them to a party for which he bought a 24-gallon keg of beer, salami and Italian bread among other treats. Condo recalled, "We had a great party, but we also had a big problem. How do we get twenty-eight staggering Italians and their bicycles back to Dominion?" The problem was solved by their host. Mr. Mancini arranged to have the owner of a large fishing boat sail the men and their bikes to the harbour at Lingan. They were then able to unsteadily pedal their bikes across the beach back to the Red Onion Hotel.

Back at the hotel, music makers were recruited, and the party continued. It continued until four o'clock in the morning when another chief of police appeared in the person, 350 pound Victor Gouthro of Dominion. The chief broke up the party. Fortunately for the revellers, that day was a holiday.

Halls of Fun and Fame:
The Amadios of Cape Breton

By A. Evo DiPierro

When sixteen-year-old Giuseppe Amadio emigrated to Cape Breton from Mussano, Italy, in 1914, he settled in Donkin and worked in the coal mines like many other Italian immigrants at the time. He was a hardworking man who earned a decent living and provided well for his large family. Mr. Amadio (or Joe Beppi as he was called for short) found his own special place in the sun and, from there, marked out an unusual career path for three of his eight children. That path was in the realm of sports. It began with Beppi's love of bicycle racing and, through sons Neil, Dave and Leo, carried on to professional hockey in the 1950s and 1960s. The Amadio family's moral strength was based on a philosophy comprising togetherness and self-determination. Through athletic competition, they earned even greater respect and admiration from the community, at a time when prejudice against immigrants still laid too close to the surface. The family history, as told to us by Neil Amadio, is one of sensation, discipline and fun. Neil is the last surviving member of the hockey threesome. In March 1997, Sam Migliore and I visited Neil at his home in Port Morien for an afternoon of memory hashing.

My first impression of the Amadios was really one of surprise. I hardly expected Neil to introduce his family's legacy in sport by way of his father's experiences as a bicycle racer:

> My father worked at No. 6 coal mine for two or three years then married my mother [Cecilia Campbell] when she was sixteen. Then he worked in No. 1B and then went back to Caledonia after the 1925 strike. We had a big family: six boys and two girls. The older boys never played hockey but the three younger ones ... well they were kind of famous in hockey. My two younger brothers played hockey all over Newfoundland and Canada.

They made a living out of it ... fished lobsters, did carpenter work, but never went into the coal mines. My father was the last to [work] there.

My father was a diehard bicycle racer. He started racing in Canada, and he used to race from Glace Bay to Sydney. He wore size fourteen slippers (they'd cut the back of them so he could wear them). He was into all kinds of sports. Couldn't play that well but he loved them, and he was always there trying to help others out.

From his photo, it is obvious that Beppi was a large, strong man, with superb legs for cycling. As a father, he laid down the rules clearly to his sons from the very beginning. When he summoned them, all it took was a whistle:

Giuseppe Amadio, ca. 1935. Courtesy of Neil Amadio.

He had us trained—all of us. When he came home from work, we'd all be at the shore swimming. He'd blow his whistle, and when we heard that whistle, every Amadio headed for home.... It meant he was looking for us. He was a kind man too. Nobody was hungry. I remember my father snaring rabbits, killing a chicken ... as long as we had something to eat, he was happy. He always had a garden....

Joe Beppi became fluent in English soon after his arrival in Cape Breton. Neil suggested that he learned the language through his involvement in sports. As a result, he earned extra money working as an interpreter. His wife was of Scottish decent. He cooked his favourite Italian food, such as polenta and chicken, while Cecilia contributed her Scottish and English dishes. At home, Beppi spoke no Italian, so the children were never directly exposed to the language. However, they were still quite conscious of their ethnic background. Neil's uncles, Tony and Angelo Amadio, were two of the original founders of the Italian Hall in Dominion. But there are other colourful stories of the Amadios' experience in Cape Breton:

When he came here to work for the coal company, he boarded with an Italian woman ... he'd give the pay to her, and she'd give him back two dollars—for a week's work. And I guess they worked ten to twelve hours in those days. She also owned the store so, if you wanted anything, you had to buy it from her. Then his uncle Louie took him out of there and put him in the shacks. They both lived there at first ... paid five dollars a week, cooked their own meals, etc. Quite an experience—coming to this country and not speaking a word of English and picking it up so fast. You'd never know he could speak Italian.... We had a great family ... and a rough family. We fought everybody in the school. Nobody called us "dagos," because they'd get the piss pounded out of them. Other

Italians had a rough time when the Second World War broke out, but they never bothered us too much because we'd get right back at them. I had a brother overseas, in the Cape Breton Highlanders, so I figured I'm Canadian; we're all Canadians.

Following in his father's footsteps in sports, Neil started playing midget hockey in Donkin. In time, he (along with brothers Leo and Dave) was destined to play alongside some of those individuals who now stand as legends of the sport.

In the hockey wars, I played with the great Jean Béliveau against Dickey Moore, "Boom Boom" Geoffrion and Donnie Marshall. Leo played with the "Pocket Rocket" [Henri Richard] in Montreal. My brother Dave had three years in the NHL. In 1950, I played junior hockey with Béliveau and the Québec Citadels. Before that, I played with the Glace Bay Miners. After Québec City, I played in the Maritime Major League. That was semi-pro. I coached for ten years in Newfoundland and sent Leo to Québec where he played in the Junior Major League in Québec and Ontario. Dave played in Hamilton for the Red Wings. At nineteen, they turned him pro for Edmonton in the Western Hockey League. My father, who had never seen him play in the NHL, went to Ontario with my sister and brothers. Dave was playing in Toronto on the eighth of January. So Leo and I got Dad all shined up and sent him away. He spent Christmas there with my sister, but on New Year's—that night—he took a stroke. He didn't get to see Dave playing in the NHL ... he came that close.... Leo retired from pro hockey to play for the New Glasgow Rangers, then he ended up back in Glace Bay.

Dave "Butch" Amadio's hockey career really began at age fourteen, when he played for the Glace Bay Miners. With Leo, he then went to Québec and played first in the Junior Major League, then the Ontario League with the Burlington Junior B Team and the Hamilton Red Wings.[1] At eighteen, he played for a short time with the Detroit Red Wings. Later, he was to spend the greatest part of his hockey life with Springfield before moving to Los Angeles and the Kings; he finally concluded his career in the Western Hockey League before settling down with his family in Calgary. He died in 1983 at the young age of forty-two. His impressive statistics are listed in the Hockey Hall of Fame at Sydney's Centre 200, as well as in Halifax. They indicate that his two best seasons were in 1959-1960 and 1966-1967, when, for example, he scored thirteen goals and seventeen assists for Sudbury, and eleven goals and twenty-nine assists for Springfield.

Leo Amadio's life in hockey developed in two stages: as a player (a defenceman); and, as a coach. Like brother Dave, he played for the Glace Bay Junior Miners while in his midteens. Then, in Québec, he played first for the Frontenacs and later, in 1955, with the Montréal Royals of the former Québec Hockey League. Leo's next stint was in the Western Hockey League, where he played with Spokane and Victoria until 1962.[2] At that point, he returned to Nova Scotia and worked as a playing coach in the Nova Scotia Senior League. His last serious period in hockey was as a star defenceman with the Glace Bay Miners from 1963 to 1965.

Had the three Amadio brothers been born a few years later, it would have been possible to see them all playing in the NHL. In 1955, only six teams existed in the NHL, and the future of the regional professional leagues was just beginning to be debated. Those individuals equipped to play in the highest of leagues possessed not only the expert knowledge of hockey but also the strengths of solid character and mature adaptability. Although the Amadios possessed these qualities, the room at the top was small. By the time the NHL had expanded, it was too late for the Amadios. In their prime, they, along with the vast majority of players, found themselves moved about the continent like chess pieces. Furthermore, they could hardly envision the freedom and exorbitant salaries attained by today's professional athletes. But, because they loved hockey in its true form, and desired nothing more than to play to the best of their ability for a fair reward, these predecessors to today's NHL endured the many difficulties along their way to success. Neil Amadio summed up that notion in this way:

> Hockey was my living. When I was with the Citadels, I played in the Maple Leaf Gardens and the Montréal Forum against the Junior Canadiens. It was the Eastern Memorial Cup Finals. Seventeen … sixteen thousand people there and I was a little fella from Cape Breton, but it was a great thrill … a great thrill. My brothers went through that too, in Montréal. First you play in Glace Bay, then you walk into this coliseum in Québec City, and there would be 16,000 people there, no matter who was playing—every game. I said to Copper Leyte, "Bud, they're not coming here to see us; they're here to see Jean Béliveau." But he was a prince of a man … still is.

Neil also recalls that period in the sport when principle and honour were of paramount importance:

> There's too much contact in the corners; too much fighting and slamming against the boards. Used to be you could do a nice, clean body check in the centre of the rink. The coaches want their stars on the ice to score, but the other team will try … to put them out of commission. That's all they want to do. In my day, you never dropped your head for anybody … not for a pass or if you see the puck behind you. If you showed that kind of disrespect, especially in the big leagues, they'd carry you out on a stretcher.

After playing with the Citadels, Neil entered the Glace Bay Major Hockey League and then the Nova Scotia Senior Hockey League. After a short season in the American Hockey League, he went to Newfoundland, where he worked as a player-coach for ten years. Some of his friends there included Howie Meeker and Bob Cole (who used to broadcast their games). "At the Memorial Stadium in Newfoundland, [Bob Cole] used a coat hanger to hold up his microphone. He knew all the numbers and the names of all the numbers, and he knew where you were going. Oh, you met all kinds of people. I was right there in the golden years. The wife didn't like it that much, but I said to hell with it; I liked it." During the off season, Neil, along with his brothers, fished lobster and did carpenter work to garnish a comfortable living.

Although the Amadios' played a lot of serious hockey during the 1950s and 1960s, they also encountered some humorous experiences:

> I remember my father and mother were at a hockey game in Verdun. Leo got into a fight and my mother started swingin' her purse. They were trying to beat up on Leo. She was pretty well over the boards. My poor sister Vera ... she'd shame me to death at the hockey games. She wouldn't let anybody touch "Neily" or Leo or anybody ... she'd be screechin' and hollerin' and ready to fight anybody in the stands. She embarrassed ya. Poor Vera ... she's dead and gone now but took it all straight to heart. My father did too because he would be hollerin,' "C'mon Buck! C'mon Buck!" I'd look up and give him a nod. It was quite a thing ... memories I'll never forget.

> I had no money starting out, just a suitcase. When they heard I was going to Québec, all the neighbours in Donkin took a collection ... a hundred-and-something dollars for spending money. Not too bad, eh? You can't forget those people. And Leo—I gave him a suit, clothes ... all that I had coming back. I dressed him up to go to Québec. We just shared.... It was a lot of fun. We really enjoyed doing it.

Neil did not get a chance to play with Dave and Leo. Dave passed away before that opportunity could be realized. However, they spent many moments together off the ice, often in preparation for their challenges on it. Toward the end of our conversation, Neil reflected further on his special moments in hockey. As many people still recall, he was known for his speed and grace on the ice, whereas Dave and Leo are remembered for their physical strength.

> [I was primarily a defenceman, but] I also played left wing.... When I was a player-coach, who ever was with me, I'd say, "Ok, what side are you the best?" and I'd just play the other side ... didn't matter to me because I was a terrific skater. I could skate backwards faster than the other fellas could skate forwards. I could go at top speed. One night, I was in Sydney

playing for Glace Bay against the Sydney Millionaires in the Maritime Major League. A shot was fired, I went down to block it and went ahead ... and kept going as fast as I could ... I could hear that ice crunching behind me ... they couldn't catch me ... and I scored.

We had a big reunion in Barrie two years ago. All the guys who played in the Maritime Major League were there. It was a great thing. They were all my own age, retired, with businesses. I was involved in business too. I remember in the fall, my father would have the traps ready for me to go fishing. I haven't stopped, and I still won't. I go to Port Hawkesbury to work while I still can. The guys down there are all great. They say they can't believe how fit I am ... I say, "you should've seen me when I was in shape!"

Neil Amadio, ca. 1951. Courtesy of Neil Amadio.

Perhaps Neil's love of traditional Italian food maintains him in good health. Every spring, he picks dandelion greens for his popular lobster salad. "The neighbours love it. They always say, 'Make your lobster salad.' They can't make it, and I won't tell them how to." Well, we were lucky to be able to wrestle that puck from him and here it is: Chop up the dandelions real fine. Add a little garlic, olive oil, vinegar (more vinegar than oil) and mix it up. Then enjoy it. Another tradition in the Amadio family is the preparation of risotto on Christmas Eve:

On Christmas Eve, we all go to Mass. Then Theresa has a big pot of risotto made up and all the kids come over and are right into it. They call it "Italian rice." Christmas dinner, [the next day], they all come over. Before the turkey, you gotta have a little bowl of risotto. It's a tradition we have and we're not going to lose it. My father taught her how to make it ... it's all in the sauce, eh ... it's all in the sauce....

Dave Amadio, ca. 1967. Courtesy of Neil Amadio.

To conclude, I asked Neil to summarize his views on hockey today:

Hockey nowadays is watered-down. They're taking kids at age eighteen or so from the drafts. They're perfect skaters, but they lack the experience and discipline. They're recruiting these kids just to fill all the teams in the NHL. And the new teams are in the USA. You won't see any in Canada because the U.S. is where the bucks are ... it's become a big money racket. On the other hand, equipment is lighter today than it was in my time. If we had lighter padding then, I'd have skated even faster! The players also got better protection. But like I said before, there's too much violence—in the corners, at the boards—it's all about winning no matter what, because if you lose, then you're boo'ed off the rink. The fans are only interested in seeing their team win. I still watch the games on TV, but it's not a thrill like it used to be, and most people won't bother watching unless it's a good game, you know.

Many of us do know and likely agree. Yet, whatever the future of hockey may be, it was the contribution of players like the Amadios that helped secure the sport's long-term success and popularity. The Amadio family has made an important contribution to the evolution of sports in Nova Scotia.

Leo Amadio, ca. 1955. Courtesy of Neil Amadio.

A Split Decision:
Italian Boxers of Cape Breton

Edited by Sam Migliore

Cape Breton has contributed many good, tough fighters to the competitive ranks of both amateur and professional boxing. Names such as Tyrone Gardiner, Blair Richardson, Tommy "Gun" Spencer, and many others come easily to mind. The Italian presence in the sport, however, cannot be underestimated. A reading of various materials, including the "membership list" of the Canadian Boxing Hall of Fame, reveals that the Italian communities of Cape Breton have produced a number of outstanding boxing personalities. This article focuses on the lives and accomplishments of several of these individuals.

Joe "The Hammer" Nemis[1]

Boxing in the Nemis family started with my brother Johnny. His first fight was in 1922 with a chap called Norman Elcock. Johnny KO'ed him in three or four rounds.

My parents were from the province of Udine, Italy—the same area as Primo Carnera [the 1933-34 World Heavyweight Boxing Champion]. They came to Canada [in 1905] when Johnny was only four or five months old. Dominic and Louie were born in Glace Bay in 1907 and 1908, and my brother Jimmy and I were born in New Waterford. I also have three sisters. I'm the baby; I was born in 1923. All of the boys boxed. Johnny, Louie and me fought professional.[2]

Johnny and Louie Nemis[3]

Johnny started boxing with Joe Uvanni. Uvanni ran a boxing school in Whitney Pier. Johnny was only young and right small, but he got built up. He had over 200 fights, and he was never knocked out. I think Johnny lost possibly thirteen decisions. He boxed in Massachusetts for a short while and then returned to Canada. I think he retired around 1934 and made a comeback in 1936. I remember Johnny KO'ing David Smith in Sydney Mines and stopping another fighter at the Fireman's Hall, Glace Bay, in 1937. Then he fought Earl Kinsman on New Year's Day, 1938, at the St. Agnus gym in New Waterford. That was his last fight; his eyes were failing.

Louie fought out of Maine. He fought Andy Callaghan [the New England Lightweight Champion]. Callaghan beat Lou Brouillard before Brouillard became Welterweight Champion of the World; and, Battling Battalino, before Battalino became the Featherweight Champion of the World. Well, my brother Louie fought a draw with Andy Callaghan in 1932. Then he beat Al MacCoy from Winslow, Maine. Twice! Louie stopped him in one or two rounds in 1932, and repeated a year later. They fought again in 1934 to a draw. Al MacCoy fought Joe Louis in the Boston Gardens in 1940.

Louie retired roughly in 1934 [because of health problems and a stormy relationship with trainer Frankie Burns]. He was on the threshold of getting a shot at the world championship. He fought all big men, all good men. Louie could punch like Rocky Graziano [World Middleweight Champion, 1947-

> **Johnny Nemis, New Waterford, Wins Ten Round Bout From Nedder Healey**
> *The Sydney Post*
> Friday, March 12, 1926
> Quoting from the *Evening News* in New Glasgow
>
> [The] New Glasgow Firemen ... staged ... last night one of the best professional boxing tournaments of the season ... a big crowd filled the theatre and were greatly pleased with ... Johnny Nemis of New Waterford and Nedder Healey of Halifax.... Nemis got the decision ... at the end of ten hard rounds. The decision was a popular one as Nemis has acquired quite a reputation in New Glasgow.... Probably no boxer who has visited New Glasgow is in better shape physically than the nineteen-year-old Italian boy known as ...[the] "pride of New Waterford." He is hard as nails ... a picture of good health and perfect training. He is careful with his diet, trains daily, does not smoke or hit the hops, and looks like a boy who will go far in the fight game. He works in the mine in Cape Breton, and is his own trainer, which speaks well for his mental fitness also....

48]. He used to break bones! Johnny was more of a boxer, but Louie would hit guys and didn't need a referee. He was too strong. His manager would say, "We are fighting Tuesday, Louie," and Louie never asked who he was going to fight, or how heavy he was. He was a born champion. What a fighter. They tell me that one time he trained with a heavyweight. Louie was only a lightweight, but he would lift the fella right off his feet with upper cuts.

A Jab as Quick as a Serpent's Tongue

Louie and Johnny used to work out in the field right by the house. They'd start boxing, and it would turn to war. One time, I was told, my mother went out crying, telling them to "stop," and they had to stop. She didn't want to see the brothers fighting. Louie put Johnny down while training once; that was in the 1920s. Then, Johnny was only knocked down once more while training. I did it in 1942. I was training for a fight; I jabbed, and all of a sudden I caught him with a right. Put him right down. Oh, I went right after him; it was just like I was fighting a stranger. He shook his head, and said: "Good!" We finished the round and went down to the

Strand Gymnasium for more training. I gave him a left hook under the rib cage, and I bent him over. Right there, I said: "That is the end of the fighting." I never sparred with him again, but he still trained me for some of my fights.

Johnny was stationed in the army, but he would come home for a month to train me. He used to train me so hard that I couldn't lift my hands. I was too weak to fight. The fella rubbing me down would tell me that he could see ice-water coming out of me. Cold sweat! I was over-trained. Other times, I trained with Joe Pyle and Tommy "Gun" Spencer under Wilf Clements [in New Waterford]. The three of us never lost a fight under him. I would just train, box a few rounds, take my time, and that would be all. After training, I would feel better than when I started. That's the way you were supposed to feel. Clements knew. If I got sloppy, he would say "take a couple of days off." When I came back, I looked as sharp as a pin.

With Clements training me, I'd do nothing for two days before a fight. When fight time came, I was strong and raring to go. See, I only had a short career. I won all the fights Clements trained me for. Danny Burchell, KO'ed in two. Sgt. Vic Oliver of the Royal Air Force, KO'ed in two. Mickey MacMullen, TKO'ed in six. Jackie Bryant, left hook, KO'ed in three.

I fought Bryant in Halifax, in August of 1944. Eight of us went up in a 1938 Buick. I remember I got sixty dollars for the fight and a hotel room. Before the fight I extended my hand to Bryant, but he wouldn't shake. I guess I looked kinda young and maybe easy. I didn't hear him, but he told the navy guys: "I'll knock that kid out in one round." Anyway, it was pretty even in the second round. Clements told me to take it easy. He said: "Every time he throws a right, he leans forward; watch him now." I got set. Bryant threw his right, and I went with a left hook. Caught him! He was coming in, and vooom.... It was the only time I put a fellow right down with a left hook. Right down cold! The referee could have counted to fifteen.

Joe "The Hammer" Nemis, 1943. Courtesy of Joe Nemis.

I always looked fighters in the eye, never made a grin, and never laughed. If they stung me, I wouldn't let them know. Straight face at all times. We never goaded one another. Fighters don't do that. You shake hands. It made me sore when that Navy guy wouldn't shake my hand. I was so sore, I couldn't look at him during the instructions. Well, I put him right on the canvas, and he shook hands after the fight.... That night, a scout for Joe Vella, the manager of Light Heavyweight Champion Gus Lesnevich, told Johnny: "Your brother has a lot of potential; we'd like to take him to the United States." Later, I got an invitation, by registered mail, from Tex Sullivan of New York City (who was the manager of leading fighters at the time, including Lee Oma). They both wanted me to box under them, but I decided not to go.

In October 1944, I fought leading seaman Sailor Hawkins (of Toronto), at the Miner's Forum in Glace Bay. He was six inches taller [and twenty pounds heavier] than me. I said to Wilf Clements: "That guy is gonna kill me." "Listen kiddo," said Clements, "he might be bigger than you, but he can't fight like you." I won the fight easily in a unanimous six-round decision.

I also fought "Sailor" Art Therriault, of Windsor, Ontario, in July of 1945. It was scheduled as a ten round fight in New Glasgow, but my left was working like a serpent's tongue that night. Three left jabs and I started boxing, moving, making him miss. *Vooom, vooom*, three or four left jabs. I cut his eye. He went into his corner after the first round, and the doctor said the fight was finished. My left hand was like a serpent's tongue. I had the best left jab in the business.

One of my last fights was in 1945 against Gorden "Kid" McNeil in New Glasgow. TKO'ed him in three rounds. In October of 1945, I fought him again in the Truro skating rink. My brother Johnny was in my corner, but Clements was training me for those fights. I KO'ed him in four rounds. Then I didn't fight again until September 1946. I lost a split decision to Alvin Upshaw at the Miner's Forum. I had about four days of boxing. I was in good shape, but my timing was off. I boxed beautifully for three rounds, and then I faded. Buddy Lewis trained me for the fight. We talked in the dressing room afterwards, and I decided, for no reason, that this would be my last fight. [Joe Nemis retired from boxing at twenty-three years of age.]

Going back to 1942, I was voted the most outstanding boxer [in a forty-fight tournament]. *As his prize, Joe received the Clary Harris Trophy.* It was my first amateur fight. I turned my head to wink at someone, and all of a sudden, wham! I was boxing a fella called Walckey. I heard the referee counting, "four, five." I got up, and I stayed right in close until the round ended. I learned to stay close from watching my brother Johnny and another fighter. If the other fella doesn't have any leverage, he can't punch you. The second round was pretty even, but in the last round, I boxed rings around him. He was surprised. We had lunch together, and he congratulated me. The fight could have gone either way. [I lost on a split decision,] but I was picked the outstanding boxer of the tournament! I came off the floor. They thought I was finished, but I came back. I was strong; I was in good condition. Johnny was training me.

Sometimes, in the late 1930s, there would be professional fights in Waterford and Glace Bay. The promoters would say: "Will you fight for 50 cents?" We'd fight. One time, I think we got a high of maybe 35 cents each. I remember fighting Charlie

Pyle at the old Hub Club in Glace Bay, in 1935. It was a small building, and there was so much smoke you couldn't see yourself. Then I fought his brother, Joe Pyle, in 1937. We fought to a draw. It was a very good fight. But, like I told you before, I didn't really start boxing in earnest until '44. Wilf Clements used to say I could punch as fast as a lightweight; Joe Pyle could punch harder, but I had the fastest hands he ever saw. Some say I should be in the Hall of Fame, but I tell them: "I don't want to be in the Hall of Fame; I didn't have enough fights." See, I was only an amateur. I had one amateur fight, and just a quick eight to twelve pro fights, then I retired.

The fight game now, Sam, is just about caput. People want too much money. Muhammad Ali started that. Boxers, hockey players, baseball players are not worth the money. There is no baseball player worth ten million dollars for a season, no way, and neither am I. People tell me that we used to box better than anything you can see on television today. My wife would say: "you were born forty years too early." I used to go out and fight my heart out. Fought six rounds for 45 to 50 dollars. For ten rounds, I might get $150. One fight, I got $285—that was the highest I got paid. Fought my heart out; an honest, good fight. Whether I won or lost, I wanted to put up a good fight. I wanted to fight clean, hard, and I certainly wouldn't try to take anyone's life.

I never drank. You couldn't give me a drink. I take a 7-Up, a Coke, but nothing in it. I just don't drink, and I don't smoke. And, if you see me skating now, you'd think I played in the NHL.... I was born in April 1923, so they say. I am the last of the fighting Nemises.

Nicholas "Hawky" Del Vecchio (1909-1980)[5]

Tony Del Vecchio emigrated to Canada from Casserta, Italy around the turn of the century. In Sydney, he met and married Maria Artabano. Nicholas, one of nine children born to the couple, came into this world on May 1, 1909. The family lived in Whitney Pier where Tony Del Vecchio ran a grocery store and bakery. According to Jack Duggan, it was Mr. Del Vecchio who "advised Nicholas, as a young boy ... if you want to fight, don't do it for nothing, box in the ring."[6] Nicholas entered the ranks of amateur boxing at the age of twelve and became a professional boxer when he was only fifteen years old. As a professional boxer, Nicholas fought successfully in both Canada and the United States. He earned the title of Maritime Bantamweight Champion, and then, suddenly, while at his peak and next in line for the Canadian Bantamweight title, he gave up fighting to spend more time with his family.

[Nunzi Martinello]: "Hawky" worked at Jake Levitan's grocery store for a while. Oh boy, did they ever work—two o'clock in the morning delivering orders with horse and sleigh. Later, he worked in the steel plant here in Sydney. [Theresa Della Vella]: And, of course, he had a career in boxing when he was just a young teenager. They trained him, they though he was a good prospect, and he pursued it for a while. [Nunzi]: They practiced upstairs at Martinello's Hall, on Tupper Street. "Hawky" won quite a few fights. [Theresa]: Then he got married, raised a family and worked. [Nunzi]: And then they moved away from here and went to Ajax, Ontario. *"Hawky" passed away on January 1, 1980.*

Because of his size, and the fact that he boxed at such a young age, Nicholas became known to many as "Young" Del Vecchio. Others referred to him as either "Hawky" Del Vecchio or the "Italian Thunderbolt." Everyone agreed, however, that Nicholas boxed with speed, power and precision. In 1995, Nicholas Del Vecchio was rewarded for his achievements by being inducted into the Canadian Boxing Hall of Fame.

Benito (Benny) DeLorenzo[8]

I was light and small in stature. I used to play hockey, and I was a good baseball player. We played down at the St. Nicholas field. But, you would get a month or two of activity, and there wasn't much else to do. A group of us were too young to join the army but old enough, fifteen or sixteen, to work at the steel plant. We poured the steel for the war effort.

After the war, two brothers from the Pier, Ernie and Archie Dalton, started a boxing club for kids. I decided to join because I was always right quick and active. We trained at the old Imperial Hall. I didn't know anything about boxing, but I could hit like a mule. In a fist fight, even with bigger guys, I would always give a good account of myself. I'll never forget my first fight for the club. I was fighting Johnny Whitehouse, from New Waterford; I was scared, but he must have thought he was in there with a whirly derby. I would close my eyes and start punching and, when he caught up, I would run around. It was a good fight. The crowd went crazy. I think the fight was a draw. I remember saying: "Well, I didn't lose anyway." From there, I got going. I trained and, slowly, I started to mature as a fighter. There were boxing teams at St. Michael's in Glace Bay, Mount Carmel in New Waterford, and we had the one in the Pier [with Holy Redeemer at the Imperial Hall]. We used to have fights every week at one place or another.

In 1947, I won the Golden Glove Tournament here in Nova Scotia, and went to the Maritime box-off for the 1948 Olympics. I won there too. Then, we went to the Montreal Forum to fight. There was a crowd of

---

The Italian Thunderbolt

"Nicholas Delvecchio ... was truly a thunderbolt.... [He] was one of the gamest little fighters Cape Breton has ever produced. While boxing in the United States, Nick was able to defeat every person he was matched with. He [then] came home ... and [won] the Maritime Bantamweight title....

Nicholas "Young" Delvecchio won twenty-eight Amateur bouts in as many starts before turning professional. As a pro he boxed thirty-four bouts with thirteen knockouts ... one loss and one draw. This is a tremendous record.... Welcome to the Canadian Boxing Hall of Fame.... You are truly deserving."

Jack Duggan[7]

Nicholas "Young" Del Vecchio, ca. 1950. Courtesy of Nunzi (Del Vecchio) Martinello.

Benny DeLorenzo with painting of himself by Alfred Goduto. Photo by A. Evo DiPierro.

four or five thousand people and boxers from all over Canada. I was a featherweight, 126 pounds. There were six or seven hundred participants in the different divisions, and we must have had a couple of hundred in our division alone. Boxing was big in Canada back then. You only needed a pair of trunks, a pair of sneakers, and you were all set. They were hard times. We arrived in the morning, and I fought at two or three in the afternoon, and then again at around six o'clock, eleven o'clock, two thirty in the morning, and a fifth fight at five o'clock that morning. I fought a guy from the army. He won that last fight, and that put me out of the tournament. After the fight, he asked me if I had a brother in the service. He had trained at Camp Borden and been overseas with my brother Peppy. What a small world! But, if I had won that fight, I would have had a chance at the finals ... and the 1948 Olympics to represent Canada.

I had about a hundred or so amateur fights, won the Golden Gloves a couple of years, and won the Maritime titles. Then I went to train in Toronto for a year. I had a number of fights, but I remember one with the Welterweight Champion from New York State. I was a lightweight, but I took him on. We had a terrific fight. I was doing well, and the trainers wanted me to stay. But, I was homesick. I had nobody around that I could talk to, you know. I had a leave of absence from the steel plant in Sydney, so I decided to go home and think things over. When I got home, I met a special person. I asked myself: "Do I go back to Toronto, or stay and make a life for myself?" Anyway, I stayed, but I had a few more fights around the Maritimes.

Over the years, I had 144 fights—amateur and pro—and I did well. Professionally, I had 106 fights; I won ninety-three, lost seven, and had six draws. It wasn't a bad record. I could have done better, but here is the trouble with boxing: the better you get, the better your opponents in each fight; it doesn't get easier, it gets tougher. [Rose DeLorenzo: I only saw two of Benny's fights, and I didn't want to see any more.] You get to the stage where you are going to get a battering whether you win or lose. I made the decision to go back to my job and raise a family. I've never had any regrets. I loved to box, my record was very good, and I never got hurt. My style was very aggressive, but I was good defensively. It was a good experience. I think it is the only sport where you can look across the ring, and it's just you and him. You learned respect for people. And, I made a few dollars. In those days, coming out of the Depression and the war years, it gave us a chance to get a step ahead. I've never regretted getting into boxing, I enjoyed those years, but I have never regretted the decision to stop either. I don't know how far I could have gone in the world ranks, but a lot of people thought I could have done really well. But, Rose and I did alright; we have six kids.

After I retired from boxing, we started a boxing club here—the Whitney Pier Athletic Club. We were at the first Canada Games, 1971, in Winnipeg. Our boys won fights here, the Nova Scotia competition, and the competition in Moncton. Two, Mike Cipak and George Hennick, ended up going to Winnipeg. They were the first Cape Bretoners to participate in the Canada Games. *Although Benny is no longer involved with boxing, he continues to serve the community through his work with the Whitney Pier Community Rink.*

[Sam: What year were you inducted into the Canadian Boxing Hall of Fame?] I was inducted in September of 1987. The Cape Breton Italian Cultural Association had a celebration for me at our church hall, and they presented me with a painting done by Alfredo Goduto from a photo. On the back of the painting, we wrote: "...presented to Benny DeLorenzo ... on October 24, 1987, in commemoration of my induction into the Canadian Boxing Hall of Fame, September 6, 1987. This picture was taken when I won the Maritime Amateur Featherweight title in 1947. I was twenty years old." We hang it in our home, and I am very proud of it.

Pordena Smith (1918-1969) and the Spinazzola Family[9]

[Patsy (Spinazzola) Smith]: My father, Pasquale Spinazzola, was from Melito, Italy, in the Bari region. He was born in 1878 and died in 1937. My mother, Tresana (Theresa) Massimello, came from Mon Ferrato, near Ozzano in northern Italy. My father landed in Halifax in 1898. He came here and, in 1905, started working as an interpreter for the Dominion Coal Company. Once settled, he sent for my mother. She arrived in 1908, and they were married here. *In Canada, the name Spinazzola was changed to Smith.* At that time, we lived in Whitney Pier. Later, we moved to Charlotte Street in Sydney and then to Alexandra Street. We had a farm there years ago—probably sixty-two acres of land.

We are a family of thirteen children, five boys and six girls (two other children died in infancy). Most of us grew up on the farm. I was born in 1935, and Pordena was born in 1918. My father died when I was two years old, and my mother passed away in 1953. I was the second youngest in the family. I took a few beatings from my brothers, but we were a close knit family—just as most Italians are. My sons, Angelo and Carlo, now follow the family name of Spinazzola.

The Venetian Gardens

[Benny DeLorenzo]: The Venetian Gardens was built by Mr. Florindo Byron.... I got involved with Mr. Byron to put on a few boxing bouts there. I got a boxing ring made at the steel plant, and we set it up in the basement. We had the boxing matches downstairs, and the dances upstairs. The Venetian Gardens caught fire around 1964, and has since been torn down.

For a while, Johnny Nemis trained boxers at the Venetian Gardens. Blair Richardson won the British Empire Middleweight Championship. Later, Johnny Cechetto (1905-1978) ran a boxing club there. Johnny did a good job; some of his guys won Canadian championships. Mr. Cechetto was inducted as an Honourary Member of the Canadian Boxing Hall of Fame in 1978.

Pordena Smith. Courtesy of Patsy Smith.

[Maria DeLorenzo]: In the field of sports, we had our share of prominent people. Pordena (Spinazzola) Smith was one of the more prominent boxers. He started boxing at the age of thirteen at the old Palace and was making a name for himself knocking out men in their late twenties and thirties while they travelled the Maritimes. [Rudy Plichie]: Pordena Smith was a personal friend of mine. He was the Middleweight Champion of the Maritime provinces, and the Eastern Canadian Champion. He also campaigned in the United States for several fights.

In 1945, Eddie Welch,[10] a Boston area writer, described Pordena in this way:

The twenty-six-year-old pipefitter [at the Sydney Steel Plant] is a rugged individual, five feet seven inches tall and in his best fighting condition weighs in the neighbourhood of 155 pounds. He boasts an impressive record of fifty-nine wins and one draw in sixty starts and is classed as the best middleweight prospect to come out of the Maritime Provinces in recent years....

Pordena Smith was employed as a steelworker for about thirty-three years. He often trained between shifts and, sometimes, during work breaks. One acquaintance recalled seeing Pordena running in the plant and wearing weights around his ankles and wrists as he worked. Then, after twelve years of active boxing, and roughly eighty bouts with very few losses, he retired from the fight game. Pordena, however, was not the only family member involved in boxing.

[Rudy Plichie]: Gino was the Maritime Featherweight Champion of the Maritimes.... [Maria DeLorenzo]: He fought thirty-nine fights before losing to a Clyde Warwick of Toronto. [Rudy Plichie]: ...and Pino was a Golden Glove fighter. They were a fighting family. *Pordena also trained his younger brother, Patsy, to box. Patsy Smith got involved in boxing at age fifteen and continued to box throughout his teens. Another brother, Orlando, served in the merchant marines during the Second World War.* [Rudy Plichie]: Patsy Smith was in several fights as an amateur, but he excelled mostly as a boxing referee. He refereed a number of times at the Venetian Gardens. But, the most active boxers in the family, the best known, were Gino and Pordena. Pordena excelled in boxing, was one of the outstanding boxing referees here in Cape Breton, and a great horse trainer in the world of harness racing.

Mr. Patsy Spinazzola, Sr. raised and raced horses from the family farm near Sydney. Pordena took over the stables after his father's death and carried on the family tradition from about 1950 to 1960. At any given time, he owned about four horses. Pordena trained the horses and served as their driver in harness races. Patsy Smith also helped in the process of conditioning, training and racing the horses.[11] Pordena's best known horse was "Bob Long." In their first outing together, "Bob Long" finished dead last. Pordena, however, got the horse into good shape a short time later to win several "daily doubles."

Pordena Smith died in 1969 at the age of fifty-one.[12] During his life he excelled at various endeavours. Boxing, however, was his claim to fame. On July 19, 1986, Pordena was inducted into the Canadian Boxing Hall of Fame. The induction letter stated what fight fans already knew: "for meritorious achievement and sportsman-like conduct in the sport of champions."

Rudy Plichie: The "Angel of Mercy"[13]

Rudy Plichie, the son of Florence (MacKinnon) and Giuseppe (Pagliccia) Plichie, was born in Glace Bay, on January 25, 1934. He boxed in the amateur ranks for a period of time and then left the ring to become a respected manager, trainer and corner attendant. In fact, his work in the corner, administering to various "cuts" and "bruises," earned him the title of "Angel of Mercy." Although very active in boxing, Rudy has also had a successful career with DEVCO (the Cape Breton Development Corporation). He worked for many years as a member of the No. 26 Draeger crew, a mine rescue unit, in Glace Bay.

I started in the boxing game when I was fourteen years old. I was active in about twenty-nine amateur fights, winning twenty-eight with one draw. Then, I got very interested in the administration of boxing—how it was run, the training and corner work as a "cut man." This work brought me across Canada with some of the best boxers developed here in Cape Breton, individuals who went on to win British Empire, Canadian, Maritime, regional and local titles.

Actually, I ran a club with Johnny Cechetto at the Venetian Gardens. He developed three Canadian champions: Rocky MacDougall, Tyrone Gardiner and Ronnie Sampson. He also had an Eastern Canadian Champion by the name of Bea Arsenault, a light heavyweight. Johnny ran the gym for over twenty years, and then I worked with him in managing fighters. I was very fortunate. He took me in, and we always had a stable of good fighters. They represented Cape Breton very well. The Venetian Gardens was one of the best-known boxing clubs, the breeding ground of great fighters. When Mr. Cechetto got sick, I went on my own—acquiring and representing fighters, training fighters for their management and booking fights. I was available on a 24-hour notice to go anywhere in Canada with a fighter. It was quite interesting. I was possibly the most active corner man in North America. I worked for guys like George Gainsford, the gentleman who brought Milo Calhoun here to fight for the British Empire Middleweight title. Gainsford, in the world of boxing, is recognized because he handled one of the greatest fighters in the world—Sugar Ray Robinson. I was Gainsford's number one man in the corner for Milo Calhoun during his successful defence of the title at the Glace Bay Miner's Forum.

Rudy Plichie, ca. 1985. Photo by Raytel Photography. Courtesy of Rudy Plichie.

Now, during this time, I hooked up with Gus MacLellan, maybe one of the greatest promoters to ever come out of Cape Breton. I did a lot of travelling with Gussie, and I represented a lot of fighters that he brought in. I met people from all walks of life, possibly some of the biggest names in boxing, including Charlie Goldman. He handled Rocky Marciano, one of the greatest heavyweights that ever lived. But, the names would be too numerous to mention. I've had about twenty-five active years. The funny part is that with anyone from Cape Breton it never cost them a cent. I did it as a hobby. What I had going for me was that I knew the promoters, and they knew my work; they took me along and picked up the tab so to speak. I am not as active today because I have been appointed to the Nova Scotia Boxing Authority. Presently, though, pro-boxing in Cape Breton is not as active as it used to be, for the simple reason that we don't have the promoters. We have the talent here, but most of the kids are amateur boxers. For professional boxing, you have to go to Halifax, New Brunswick and Montreal.

An Italian gentleman, Tony Unitas of Toronto, Ontario, started the Canadian Boxing Hall of Fame and asked me to represent the Atlantic provinces. I had the opportunity to represent a number of top Canadian boxers from this area for induction into the Hall of Fame—the Nemises, Stevie "Kid" MacDonald ... Gus MacLellan, Benny DeLorenzo ... Blair Richardson, and many, many others. I would like to mention too that I was possibly the first Canadian inducted into the Canadian Boxing Hall of Fame as a "cut man," and possibly the first Canadian to represent Canadian boxing on the "Bible of Boxing" panel, *Ring Magazine Ratings U.S.A.*, in New York.

[Sam: Are there any fights that stick out in your memory?] The Milo Calhoun fight. Calhoun got a very nasty cut on the inside of his mouth, around the second round. I kept it closed for thirteen rounds. It was a fifteen round fight, and he won. That really stands out because you couldn't see the cut. It was one of the worst types of cuts you can handle in boxing because, once you start swallowing your own blood, it can be an awful handicap.

I was curious about what had happened, and I checked into things after the fight. A month earlier, he had had one of his back teeth filled. This off-set his custom mouthpiece. But, at the time, we didn't know this. It gave us a lot of work. We were very fortunate to stop the cut. It was four or five inches long, inside the mouth, and it went down through the jaw from the earlobe. That's one of the things you very rarely run into, but I had the right stuff to stop it. I used a powder mixture of thromboplastin. This was the only way the cut could be stopped. That was really an exciting bout.

I think the greatest thing that can happen to a corner man is to be part of history when it is made. A lot of fellas that I worked with won Canadian titles. The greatest thing that can happen to an athlete is to become a champion in a country one is born in. It doesn't happen to everybody. And, I was there when it was happening. I helped to make a mark in the history of Canadian boxing, and that is a big thing for me.

[Sam: How did you get involved in boxing?] Actually, boxing was in the family. My brother, Johnny, promoted some fights at the Table Head Club. He died in the Canadian Army during the war. I was brought up in boxing, in the kitchen so to speak. My mother used to make our boxing trunks and the boxing tapes for the hand wraps. My brother was active in boxing, and I took it from where he left off. I was born in a mining area, and there were good Canadian fighters nearby. World ranked Stevie "Kid" MacDonald lived two streets from me. So, I was surrounded by some great old-time athletes. The famous promoter, Gussie MacLellan, also came from my neighbourhood, the No. 2 area of Glace Bay. With all these boxing personalities in the area, I just couldn't help but get involved. [laughs] They were interesting guys who made a mark in the sport, and now it's on display at the Canadian Boxing Hall of Fame.

[Sam: How did you get involved as a "cut man?"] I saw a friend lose a Canadian title. I figured, "If I'm going to be involved with fighters, I need to pick up the trade." I was very fortunate to run into a gentleman from New York, Al Bachman, who got me started. Bachman had a special salve made by the famous boxing trainer, Charlie Goldman. Right to this day, I am the only Canadian that knows the recipe for that salve. I use it in the corner only with the permission of the doctor. After a while, several promoters would call for my services. If a visiting fighter didn't have a "cut man," they sent for me. I also travelled with different promoters. Even today, as we speak, I get calls, but my services aren't available because I am with the Nova Scotia Boxing Authority; it would be a conflict of interest. But, I had some of the best teachers in the world in Bachman and Goldman. I learned their techniques and took it from there.

[Sam: Can you say a little more about the salve?] The salve is a combination of thrombin powder and adrenalin mixed with a certain amount of wax to keep it hard and soft. Then you use a combination of gel foam; this won't damage the tissue at all. There are times, however, when you are not allowed to use this salve, depending on the jurisdiction. But, I have other techniques which are also safe and allowable. I don't use anything unless I get the okay from the doctor. And, I was very fortunate; none of the hundreds of guys I handled were ever stopped by cuts. Excuse me, what I'm saying is, as long as the fighter gets to the corner, he never leaves the corner bleeding. But, if the fight is stopped in progress, in the ring, well, I have no bearing on that. It is no fault of the corner. You see, the worst fear of the corner man is having a referee who makes decisions himself. He is the number one man, but what we feel is that the referee should call in the doctor first. If they don't, as a corner man, regardless of who you are, you have a problem. So, God bless the majority of them; 99 per cent call on the doctor first.

After the interview, Rudy went on to talk about what it takes to be a "cut man" during a boxing match. In addition to all the knowledge and materials at their disposal, "cut men" must be very clean and able to work quickly, carefully and with confidence. What follows is my reconstruction of Rudy's statement:

> The crowd is yelling, there is so much going on, and you need to think clearly and work fast. You can't be intimidated by the crowd and the noise because you could end up harming the boxer if you are not aware and careful.
>
> You have to work fast. You only have fifty seconds to work with. The clock starts ticking as soon as the bell rings to end the round. And, the boxer may take up four or five seconds just getting to the corner. You have to be ready. You can't spend several valuable seconds unscrewing bottles and opening cases, etc. You have to recognize the problem, know how to work around it and maintain your composure.
>
> You have to work quickly without giving the impression that you are hurrying or that you are anxious about something. Boxers can sense the urgency, and it may affect their performance. And, the other team may gain confidence, if they think it is a serious cut.

[Sam: Is there anything you would like to add?] I would also like to mention what I've done for a living outside boxing. I was a coal miner. I started in bootleg mines right off the Table Head shore when I was about twelve years old. At fifteen or sixteen because of a mix up in my birth certificate, I got hired on at No. 1B colliery. I worked there for three years until the mine closed. Left for Ontario in 1953, worked at Westinghouse in Hamilton, and returned here in 1957. I started in No. 20 colliery, mined coal there for seventeen years and then transferred to the foundry department for another twelve years. I finished up with DEVCO's security department.

In that period of time, for about fifteen years, I was part of a mine rescue team working out of No. 26 colliery in Glace Bay. The team was captained by Sandy White. We were quite fortunate; we won five Canadian and several Eastern titles in mine rescue work. The team competed against some of the best mining companies in the world—gold, potash, nickel and different coal mines. This was possibly the best part of my life. I like mining and, through my mine rescue work, I met some great people in the mining industry throughout Canada. In the foundry department, I worked as a mine melter. We were part of history there, when we made the cannons which are now on display at the Fortress of Louisbourg. I helped to melt the iron and pour several of the cannons. And, as I say, I ended my career with DEVCO's security department.

Back to mine rescue, we fought some of the biggest mine disasters in the country. I was in 26 Colliery, when the mine rescue teams were given credit for saving that mine in the 1970s. My brother, Louis, was also involved; he was there at the explosion that killed nine miners. Louis was the first miner to go in to try to help those people. That was the last time I was involved in mine rescue. When you're forty-five years old, your days are over in mine rescue. It is government policy. But, I was kept on an extra three years because of my condition and health.

[Sam: How did you manage between boxing and the mining company?] Well, at that time, I had an arrangement with the bosses at the colliery. I made up for lost time by working weekends or working between shifts. I also banked time when I worked as a mine rescuer and later in security. When a fight came to town, I was always available without missing any time at work. I was fortunate; it worked in my interest. I made a good living with DEVCO.

E. M. "Marty" Martinello:
A Career in the CFL[1]

By Sam Migliore

On Saturday, October 25, 1986, Marty Martinello was inducted into the Nova Scotia Sports Hall of Fame in recognition of his many achievements during a fourteen-year career in the Canadian Football League. Marty played as a middle guard on four professional teams, including the Grey Cup winning Hamilton Tiger Cats of 1965.[2]

Years earlier, when participation in professional sports was a distant dream, Marty played hockey, baseball and other games with family and friends in Whitney Pier, Cape Breton. He was one of nine children born to Felice and Rosina Martinello. Marty was born in 1931, grew up in the Pier and attended first Villa Nova and later Holy Redeemer Boys School. During a conversation with me in December of 1996, he spoke of those years in this way:

> We were no different than any other kids. We played sports, skating, hockey.... We lived on Tupper Street, [and] when we moved to Henry Street ... we were going to Holy Redeemer School. But you know all the friends we had—from Mount Pleasant, Lingan Road, Tupper Street, Williams Street—we were all together.... And the interesting part of going to school was always that we went to school as a group.

> One of the enjoyable things, when we were kids down there, was that if it snowed in the morning, there was no school in the afternoon, because when it snowed there, it really snowed.... When the cars went by, and there was snow and ice on the road, [we would] hang on to the back of the bumper and go all the way.

We were a good family. We were well involved with the community, and [we had] a lot of friends. [There was] a lot of community activity there.

In those early years, however, Marty and his family experienced both "good" and "bad" times. His father was one of the many Italian men (and some women) interned in 1940 (without ever being charged or convicted of any crime) when Mussolini declared war on Britain. This brought about a major disruption in the life of the Martinello family. In 1943, Felice Martinello moved his family to Hamilton, Ontario. It was there that Marty began his formal football training.

Marty Martinello is a modest man. When I asked him to talk about his football accomplishments, he kept his description simple and brief. He stated:

Let me make it as brief as possible. I was very fortunate in high school [at Cathedral Boys School, in Hamilton] to play one year of football, because I was too small. Ok, so I couldn't play.... But, I rowed for about four or five years at the lightweight.[3] Then I played [football] for what we called the junior teams for a couple of years, and one year in Brantford. Then [in 1953] I went to Montreal and spent five years with the Montreal [Alouettes]. BC Lions for two years [1958-59], five years with Toronto [Argonauts], the last few years with Hamilton. During that period, I was what you would call today a nose guard. In those days, they called it a middle guard. All-Star for the years 1960 and 1961. I was in Grey Cups in 1954, 1955, 1956 [with the Alouettes] and we won the Grey Cup in '65 with the Hamilton Tiger Cats. And, it was enjoyable. That's all I can say about that....

Marty Martinello, ca. 1963. Photo courtesy of Nova Scotia Sport Hall of Fame.

His All-Star nominations, his Grey Cup appearances, and his induction into the Nova Scotia Sports Hall of Fame, however, indicate that much more could be said about this gifted athlete. For now though, his accomplishments will have to speak for themselves.

Although football was an important part of Marty's life, he never lost sight of the fact that an education was essential for future success. At various speaking engagements, he has been quick to point out to children that: "Medals, plaques and cups soon tarnish; an education stays with you all of your life."[4] He himself attended night school extension classes at McMaster University for eleven years to earn certificates in Metallurgy and Business Administration. Marty later completed a Master of Business Administration

(MBA) program at the same university. He was one of seven students chosen for a special pilot course for the MBA certificate.

Marty worked as a Sales and Plant Manager for Kent Steel in Hamilton and later with Intermetco Limited. The Intermetco connection, as Russ Doyle points out, helped "keep alive his association with Sydney through dealings as a supplier to SYSCO Steel."[5] By the time Marty retired in 1996, he had worked his way up to Vice-President and General Manager of the Metals Division at Intermetco Limited. He now resides in Hamilton, Ontario, with his wife, Mary. They have been married for thirty-seven years and have three children and three grandchildren.

Section VI

*Formal
Organizations
and
Activities*

La Sala Italiana in Dominion

Edited by Sam Migliore[1]

> "To promote and foster the social, economic and cultural
> well-being of its members and the community."[2]

The Dominion Italian Community Club was one of the earliest Italian associations established in Canada. It came into existence in 1936, and it continues to hold a special place in the hearts of many second- and third- generation Italians from the former Town of Dominion. In fact, as a number of association members point out, it is the presence of a community club and hall which has helped maintain a sense of Italian ethnic identity for many people in the area. The hall is a powerful "symbol" that links people together and serves as a visible reminder of the cultural heritage they share. Through some of its activities, the association also has done a great deal to foster good will and friendship among people of different backgrounds.

Background

[Giovanni (John) Antonello]: I came to this country in 1919. The majority of Italians came here after the First World War. [Tony Basso]: The idea to build a hall started with those people who fought in the war, the *combattisti*. But, there wasn't enough of them, so they got other people involved. [Livio Nicoletti]: There were so many Italians in Dominion at that time, that they decided to get together and make something for themselves. *As other people got involved, discussion turned toward construction of a Roman Catholic church where the Mass could be celebrated in Italian.*

[Raffaele (Ralph) Gatto]: Father Ronald MacLean was the pastor at St. Nicholas Church [in Whitney Pier]. [Tony Basso]: He was also the spiritual advisor for the Italians in Dominion. [Raffaele Gatto]: The [Dominion] Coal Company gave Father MacLean about seventy feet of land, for one dollar, to build a church for the Italians. That would be before 1930. But ... the Bishop ... didn't give us permission to build the chapel.... [So] I asked Father MacLean if I could build a skating rink there. I then leased the land—from that seventy feet, right down to Mitchell Avenue—from the coal company. I built the rink, the Winter Garden, with Sisto Piva and Mario Morellato.

I owned the rink for three years, 1930 to 1933. Someone wanted to buy the land from the coal company but, because I had leased it for six or seven years, I was given the first chance to buy it. Later, I sold it to the [Dominion Italian Community Club]. We then had two or three picnics and started making money to build the hall. We became the owners of the front lot, [the original seventy feet of land], in about [1975]. Father D'Intino talked to the Bishop, and we bought the land from the Diocese of Antigonish.

[Livio Nicoletti]: The hall was built in 1936. [Leo Carrigan]: Johnny Antonello, the first president of the club, and others, went around from house to house collecting a quarter a week to build it. They built the hall by hand. [Remo Gatto]: The Italians were fantastic workers. We can be so proud of them; they were all decent people. [Tony Basso]: It would be an insult to be called "lazy"—the ultimate insult. They worked very hard in the mines, and then they worked in their gardens on Saturdays and in the evenings. They certainly took pride in working. I can remember when they dug the posts for the hall. I was only five, but that was something that impressed me. The work! Holy suffering, it seemed to me that they went at it with a vengeance.

[Leo Carrigan]: They worked hard to build the hall, and they worked very hard to preserve it—that's why we are quite proud of the hall. The Italian women also played a big role. Really, I mean, they are the backbone of the club; they have worked very hard. Their chicken suppers are quite famous. The women raised a lot of money for this organization.

The War Years

The Italians of Dominion experienced a number of hardships during the war years. Italian miners were not allowed to work in the local colliery for a period of about seven to nine months. When they finally returned to work, they were placed on "back-shift" for several years. The problems did not end there. The Italian community lost control of its hall, and the association became dormant. With the help of a number of concerned individuals, however, they were able eventually to regain control of the hall and reestablish the association.

[Livio Nicoletti]: I have heard all kinds of stories about the war, and how the Italians were treated. The war veterans took the hall at one time. [Angelo Cechetto]: The returning veterans had a tavern there for a couple of years. [Tony Basso]: I don't think they got permission; they just took it. [Angelo Cechetto]: Then they went around trying to pressure people to let them have it. I helped save the hall. They came to me and others, and said: "will you sign to let the hall go?" I told them: "if anybody lets the hall go, I need a house, I'll take my family there." I didn't sign. [Tony Basso]: The veterans wanted the hall for a Legion. The old Legion burned down during the war. [Angelo Cechetto]: That's when they came here. They could do whatever they wanted. After the war, they were going to take everything inside. Sammy Leonard, the Chief of Police of Dominion, stopped them. If it wasn't for him, God only knows what would have happened.

[Enzo Antonello] Sammy Leonard had a farm in Broughton. He had five or six Italians working for him when they were kicked out of the mines. He kept them going. [Londo Scattolon]: I don't think they got any money. They were working for their vegetables. Sammy Leonard helped a lot of Italians in Dominion. If they got into trouble, they could run to him. He was an ex-Mountie, a former boxer, and he could handle his dukes. He helped a lot of people. [Enzo Antonello]: I also remember my father telling me how Francis Stephenson, a major in the army, came home and helped the Italians get the hall back after the war. Later, when he ran for mayor, a lot of Italians voted for him. They didn't forget that.

Picnics and Other Activities

[Leo Carrigan]: The association attempts to promote the Italian culture today, but I don't think that was the original intent. The Italians were segregated in this area because of the language barrier and other factors. They wanted a place for themselves—a place where they could hold wedding receptions, bridal showers, family parties and an annual Italian picnic.

Picnic at the Meadows (outside of Sydney River on the way to East Bay). Courtesy of Maria Razzolini.

[Ida Ravanello]: I remember the picnics in front of the hall. We used to take the seats outside. There were also many dances at the hall. [Luigia, Mrs. Ravanello's daughter]: Well, I remember going to the hall with my parents. When I got tired, they would let me go upstairs to sleep. Children went everywhere with their parents. There was no such thing as a babysitter at that time. [Ida Ravanello]: I didn't know what a babysitter was.

[Enzo Antonello]: I remember going out to Grand Mira for our picnics when I was a kid. Later, they were moved to the Meadows. It was something to look forward to, especially in the 1940s. They used to have a fish pond. You would throw the rod over the side, and someone would put a prize on the hook. [Amalia Zorzi]: Oh yes, we had good picnics at the Meadows. [Livio Nicoletti]: They used to take the dance floor out for the picnic.... I was a kid. I remember sitting on the back of the truck with the tables, chairs, the stove, coal.... On the way there, we would stop in Sydney, at Ideal Ice-Cream, and we would fill the big, insulated bags with ice and little tubs of ice cream. They would disassemble the stove in Dominion, and then set it back up at the Meadows. [Amalia Zorzi]: And we made spaghetti there. [Livio Nicoletti]: The black smoke! But, they would make spaghetti, have the dance floor ... it was nice. [Amalia Zorzi]: There were a lot of people, and sometimes Louie DiGiobbi would play the accordion. [Livio Nicoletti]: There would be 200 people—playing cards, bocce and having quite a time. I remember it well. This would be the 1950s and 1960s. [Leo Carrigan]: Now, we have the picnics at the boat club in Mira.

[Len Stephenson]: I remember a picnic in Dominion, by the Italian Hall, that featured the greasy pole. There was a prize at the top as an incentive. Angelo Cechetto (one of the original founding members of the Italian Hall in Dominion) was the only one in my recollection that could conquer it. [Enzo Antonello]: The idea was to get up the pole and grab the prize, but the pole was covered with grease. [laughs]

The Greasy Pole (L'albero della cuccagna). [Angelo Cechetto]: I went up the first time, but I couldn't get it. All my muscles locked. I had to slide all the way down. I couldn't move. A couple of friends had to rub my legs before I could walk. The next Sunday, my brother started up the greasy pole, and I went right behind him. The pole was twenty-five feet high. The prize at the top was ten dollars, a chicken, a couple of salami, two bottles of wine and baccala (salt cod).... They used to get a bucket of grease from the pit and grease the pole. Just squeeze it, and you'd see the grease come out between your fingers. What a job! My brother went up half way and quit. He slid down, and I kept going. The pole was only four inches thick at the top. I went up; I got the prize. But, there was more grease on me than there was on the pole. [laughs] That was a hard day in my life. [laughter] You would never know unless you tried it. That was in 1936. I did it twice in the old country too.

> **Bocce.** [Tony Basso]: Every Sunday morning the men would play bocce (Italian lawn bowling). They would play "48" and regular bocce. In "48," they would play more balls. Well, we used to get a nickel for throwing the balls back to them. Boy, that was fantastic. [Livio Nicoletti]: I remember, as a kid, going to the Italian hall, in August, and they'd be playing bocce. White shirts, sleeves rolled up, and their winter underwear. [laughter] [Tony Basso]: Ricco had two new courts. My father always took me there. It was just like going to Italy. They'd be playing *mora* (an Italian number game), cards, bocce.... This was Italy! A lot of people used to call it "little Italy." [Len Stephenson]: Some people called it the "Bronx," and Angelo Cechetto's shoemaker shop was the "Senate." Those were two of the places people met and discussed things.

Out-migration

[Tony Basso]: My father, Angelo, was from Fossalonga in the Veneto region of Italy. He came to Canada in 1912 and started working in the coal mines. He was sixteen years old. During the strike, in the 1920s, he went out west. My father worked in Alberta for a few years, and then came back when he heard that the mines had re-opened. We had quite a migration of Italians from Dominion in the 1940s, after the war. A lot of people went to Niagara Falls, Guelph and Windsor. Just better opportunities, I guess, and the commotion during the war. One fellow went out, wrote, said how beautiful it was, the opportunities there were, and so they left. [Livio Nicoletti]: Some of them probably had relatives in Ontario—someone they could stay with until they got on their feet. Other people weren't in that position. I have an aunt in Ontario but, if my father had a brother working up there, we might have gone too.

The Reunion in Guelph, Ontario, 1977.[3] [Tony Basso]: We attended a reunion of Cape Breton Italians living in other parts of Canada and the United States. Monty (Moncie) Cirotto [who had moved to Guelph] organized the reunion. The hall was decorated beautifully. He had pit lamps and shovels scattered around the hall, and pictures of the older Italians ... the old homes, and the Italian Hall [in Dominion]. A big sign: "Welcome, Cape Breton." I think thirty of us went up for the reunion. Oh, it was beautiful. And, of course, we met all the friends we had thirty years ago. The social hour lasted three hours. Then we had a five-course meal, wine.... The accordion player playing through dinner. On the bandstand, they had an old fashioned coal stove. After dinner, the band came in and things continued until the wee hours. It was very good. Oh, nobody makes more noise than 500 Italians. These reunions should be held more often. The Facchins, I think, came all the way from California.

The 50th Anniversary

[Enzo Antonello]: In 1986, I was general program chair for the Club's 50th Anniversary. We did a survey, found all the former members who were still living, and invited them to attend the celebration. Quite a few of them came down. Father Edo Gatto (son of Raffaele and Maria Gatto) celebrated a Memorial Mass in honour of the deceased, founding members of the association. During the Mass, in the part where you pray for the dead, we read out all their names. It was very impressive; it was something that you never forget. Everyone did a good job.

From left: Romano Scattolon, Giovanni Antonello, Lino Polegato, and Sheldon Canova. Courtesy of Enzo Antonello.

The 50th Anniversary banquet and dance was held on Saturday, July 26, in the Italian Hall. Once Lino Polegato, the Master of Ceremonies, had called the proceedings to order, Tony Basso and the Italian Chorale performed the Canadian and Italian national anthems. This was followed by an introduction of all the fifty-year members in attendance, and special guests (including Rodolfo Meloni, the Vice Consul for the Italian Government). As part of the proceedings, Luigi Mazzocca (Association President,

1986) and Enzo Antonello (Chair, 50th Anniversary Committee) presented the founding members with a certificate in recognition of their efforts to establish the club in 1936. Giovanni Antonello (first President of the Association) and Mazzocca then unveiled the special plaque commemorating the anniversary celebration. The meal itself, I have been told, was a wonderful production, compliments of the women's auxiliary. The menu included: antipasto (salami, cheese, copocolo and wine), the main meal (roast beef, peas, carrots, rapa, potatoes, gravy and salad), fruit (melon, orange segments, apple slices and grapes) and dessert (strawberry tarts, with coffee or tea). The late Father Edo Gatto completed this portion of the program with a closing prayer, and the festivities continued with music and dance. It was an evening association members continue to cherish and discuss today.

The Recent Years

[Livio Nicoletti]: This hall is what kept the Italians of Dominion together. If we didn't have a meeting place—a place for Italian classes, to meet with friends—80 per cent of us would be melted into society. We may argue and fight amongst ourselves, but, as we say: "Thank God we've got a place of our own to do it in." [laughs] [Tony Basso]: If we didn't have this hall, we would have to build another one. I think it is very important.

[Stephen Polegato]: There are little things we do here that we don't recognize as promoting the Italian culture. But, in my opinion, they do promote the culture. There are five or six members that I enjoy being with, and they will purposely talk Italian, even though I don't fully understand what they are saying. I learn a little bit more every time they speak. After some meetings, members go into the kitchen, cook up traditional Italian dishes, and we have a bite to eat together. To me, that is promoting the culture. The language, the cultural days, the Italian picnics, the choir performances—for me, both the cultural events and the little things mean a lot. [Livio Nicoletti]: Oh, yes, and it is all based around this hall.

Entertaining the Zeffrio. *In 1995, the Italian Frigate* Zeffrio *and Princess Elettra Marconi Giovanelli arrived in Sydney for the Marconi Centennial Celebrations. The Italian associations of Dominion and Sydney were invited to participate in the festivities.*

[Livio Nicoletti]: The day the ship landed in Sydney, our Italian Chorale went there to perform. The next day, there was an open house aboard the ship, and then there was a celebration at the Civic Centre in Sydney. The highlight for us, though, was the festivity at our hall to entertain the ship's captain, officers and a hundred sailors. [We had dignitaries, speeches], and a fabulous meal. But, something was missing. I said to Mario Pino: "We've got to get this thing moving ... let's get that accordion going." And we had a remote mike [for singing]. Once that started, the sailors went crazy; they were rocking back and forth with their hands. They knew some of the songs, and there were a couple of lively ones—like "La Spagnola." Mario and I did a fabulous job on that, and we rocked the place down. The Dominion Italian Chorale sang about twelve to fifteen songs. Then, finally, the sailors calmed down, we had the speeches and, when that was over, we started again. We cleared the tables, and the sailors started dancing....

The Italian Consul from Montreal was so impressed; he thought that this was all arranged by the Dominion Club. Although I would have loved to take all the credit, I explained that we had done this in association with the Sydney organization. He told us that he had been to Halifax for both the Marconi celebrations and the Group of Seven economic activities, but what happened in the Hall that night, without hesitation, was unbelievable. It was so spontaneous. We were well received by the captain and crew; they spoke highly of the event. It made us feel real good to know that the effort, all the nights we spent planning, were appreciated.

Returning Something to the Community. [Livio Nicoletti]: We also try to give something back to the community. [Enzo Antonello]: We have contributed money to the scholarship fund at the local high school, the hospital, the church.... [Livio Nicoletti]: Very few requests that we turn down. We also participate in Seaside Daze—suppers, a cultural afternoon and other activities. We don't sell tickets for our cultural afternoon. We provide food and wine samples as a way of giving something back to the community of Dominion. [Enzo Antonello]: We try to be good citizens. [Stephen Polegato]: That is one day we don't want to commercialize. People have nothing but praise for it; they can't wait until the next year. It is also a way for us to show people that our culture is a little different.

Leigha (Nicoletti) Gouthro at Italia Day, Dominion, ca. 1993. Photo by Jan Gentile and Jason Skinner.

Seaside Daze. [Len Stephenson]: Seaside Daze is one week pulled out of the miner's vacation time. Late July, early August. All the facilities in the community try to promote the Daze, but the Italian Hall does a tremendous job. They put on the famous chicken suppers, and they have Italia Day (where they display the culture). They make a great contribution. We have as many as eight or nine thousand people on the beach during Seaside Daze, and a lot of them end up at the Italian Hall (and the supper, if they are lucky, because it is sold out very quickly).

[Livio Nicoletti]: We started putting on a cultural afternoon for Seaside Daze in 1995. For our 1997 cultural day: Amalia Zorzi made the *crostoli* (a dessert); Leo Carrigan had the sausages; Bunsmaster, in Sydney, had a display of Italian bread products; there was a display of Venetian Salami products from Hamilton, Ontario; we had wine, red and white, for people to sample; and, all the women made a dish for the event—ravioli, gnocchi.... We opened the doors at two o'clock, and from two to six o'clock you just couldn't move. We had so many visitors. It was spectacular. They gave us so many comments and praises. We had some donations from Nova Scotia Power and others, but it still cost us about $500 to hold the event. We didn't charge any admission. Each year our cultural day seems to get bigger and bigger. We had a 20 per cent increase in people attending over last year.

We also have other activities. A 50s and 60s night, with a DJ. At least two sit-down chicken suppers ... with our chorale sometimes performing during the meals. We can generate some money out of that. During Seaside Daze, we could hold a chicken supper every day of the week, 250 tickets, and still sell out. But, it would just be too much work for the women. Sunday, though, is the highlight, that's when we have our cultural day, the Italia Fest.

The Future

[Enzo Antonello]: We had a membership of close to 100 people at one time, maybe more. Now, our numbers are down, as people leave the area, and the founding fathers gradually pass away. [Livio Nicoletti]: We need to make an effort to get the young people to join the association. I don't think it is an immediate problem, but it may become one in ten years time. You see, the only way we get new members now is through our sons and daughters. There are no more Italians coming into the area. And, if they did come to Cape Breton, I doubt if they would come to Dominion. [Tony Basso]: We have had only one Italian come to Dominion since the war. [Livio

The Italian Hall, February, 1998. Photo by A. Evo DiPierro.

Nicoletti]: There is no reason to come here now. If they come to Canada, they are going to go to places like Toronto or Hamilton where there are opportunities. We have to start putting things in place to get people interested in the hall.

[Stephen Polegato]: I think, as time went on, the second and third generation children got absorbed by the Canadian society and culture. A lot of them have lost track of their Italian culture, their heritage. I know myself that it wasn't until I went back to Italy, saw where my grandparents came from, saw their culture first-hand, that I truly acquired an appreciation for the hall, what we do, and what we believe in. [Leo Carrigan]: I would like to see our organization set up a fund to charter a flight to Italy for our members. Steve and I are fortunate; we have relatives in Italy, and we have been able to maintain the ties, but there are people here who have lost their ties overseas. I would like to see the organization help people renew their ties with Italy. I would also like to see more recreational activities at the hall.

The Cape Breton Italian
Cultural Association

By A. Evo DiPierro

Over the years, the Cape Breton Italian Cultural Association (CBICA) has done everything possible to fulfill its constitutional mandate: "to promote and foster the Italian culture in Cape Breton ... and to take positive action in matters concerning the well-being of the Italian community." The CBICA is much more than a club, it is a centre for the Italian community in Sydney and the surrounding area. It holds special relevance for Italians in their attempt to preserve a unique heritage and identity.[1]

There have been various Italian clubs and associations in industrial Cape Breton since the turn of the century. During the 1960s and 1970s, Mr. Giorno and others attempted to organize the Italian community, and perhaps this is when the idea was first conceived for the development of the current CBICA. Mr. Giorno explained:

> In 1966, when they were getting ready for EXPO, they wanted the [Italian] community to [contribute] a float. So [a small group] at [St. Nicholas Church in Whitney Pier] got together.... To raise money for the float, we had to travel all over and solicit funds from everybody, so it was pretty hard.... We thought that down the road...we [could]...start up some sort of organization that would pull all of the Italians together.

Although officially established in 1984, the CBICA was conceived during the late 1970s, when Mr. Goduto (the Association's first President), Mr. Giorno and others began working on the idea with members of the Italian community in Dominion. Mr. Goduto provides this account:

When I returned from Halifax in 1978, after studying law at Dalhousie, [I realized] that the Italians in Sydney were not organized. So we thought it would be a good idea to form an association. We knew that there was a well-developed club in Dominion, so we approached them. We thought we'd get together to form an amalgamated association, with [a joint] executive.... After several meetings, however, we decided that it would be best to form our own association, the Cape Breton Italian Cultural Association. For the first two or three years, it was great. The Dominion group came to Sydney [St. Nicholas Parish Hall in Whitney Pier] and the Sydney group went to Dominion [the Italian Hall], alternating every month. The groups got along well together. It was almost a bit of a competition: we would go to Dominion, and they would put on a big spread for us, and they would come to Sydney and we would put one on for them. A year after the Association was formed, we decided to have an Italia Day—a joint festivity—and it was a great success.

Joint Association photo, Italian Hall, Dominion, ca. 1980. Courtesy of Anna DiMichele.

Italia Day brought together the Italians from Dominion and Sydney under one roof, to demonstrate and celebrate the particulars of a culture that makes them Italian. The first Italia Day took place around 1980, according to Mr. Goduto. The location was St. Nicholas Parish Hall in Whitney Pier. As the event grew in size and popularity, it was moved to the Cape Breton University. There, on a Saturday afternoon in early July, Italians, dressed in traditional costumes, invited the public to attend and be immersed in the Italian atmosphere. The women made homemade pasta and old-style biscuits, while showing the appliances and methods they used. On display were Italian artifacts and memorabilia from the "Old Country." There was a wine-making display, abundant food, music and art (including Alfred Goduto's paintings). The joint Association also had a chorale, comprised of singers from Dominion, Glace Bay, New Waterford and Sydney. When I was there, in my early teens, I remember boys playing soccer on the field outside, and hearing the choir sing in the College Playhouse. At that time, Italia Day was really my only opportunity to meet other Italian kids who lived far from my own community. It was an entirely Italian afternoon, and I really enjoyed it.

Mrs. DeLorenzo, another of the Association's past-presidents, has her own specific memories of the *Italia Days*:

It first started at our little hall here [in Whitney Pier]. We had a display of artifacts from Italy, Alfred Goduto's paintings, food, plus singing and dancing. We [made] homemade pasta, *pizzelles* and sausage. The men would play sports and card games. There were also games for the children. People used to come in droves. We used to sell T-shirts, pins and everything else. We always had samples of wine, and this was all free, and we would have the roasted pig [*porchetta*]...to make sandwiches [*panina*]. People would be coming and going all afternoon. Then we would have the priest over ... for Mass, followed by a big supper ... and dance. One year, we even had an Italian band down from Toronto. During the break Mario [Pino] and Meechu [Maria DeLorenzo] would go around to all the tables singing Italian songs.

Mrs. MacDougall, the Association's secretary in 1981, fondly remembers that year's Italia Day festivities:

My participation in the Cape Breton Italian Cultural Association was a rewarding experience for me, one that personally reinforced my cultural heritage. The early days of the Association were a great challenge. Bringing the Italian culture and the nature of its people to the awareness of others was of utmost importance to me.... For me, the greatest satisfaction was Italia Day of 1981 at the University College of Cape Breton campus, when my efforts as Public Relations Officer brought together the Italian community of Cape Breton and the general public in a most successful day of promoting the Italian culture. An afternoon of exhibits and demonstrations, contests, games, and a concert, was well attended by members of the public who were very impressed and delighted with our presentation. The evening consisted of Mass, followed by an Italian buffet, a dance, and a rousing sing-song. It was a day to feel proud as an Italian, a member of the CBICA, and of being able to share our rich culture with others.

For Mrs. Camilli, the importance of the Association and its activities stems from people's commitment to the principles of togetherness and family:

Personally, I have been an active member of the organization since it began. One of the main reasons for my interest in the Italian culture is the feeling of *family*. Since my own ancestry is Scottish, we are not as familiar in our dealings with each other, and I particularly like this in my husband's family. I was anxious for my children to learn as much as possible about their Italian heritage and the CBICA provided that opportunity.... On one particular occasion, I remember Prince Andrew visiting Sydney's Wentworth Park in 1985 for the city's 200th anniversary. The different cultures were asked to have five or six of their members dressed in traditional costumes in the audience at the park where the Prince had a walkabout. My oldest daughter, Maria, was in costume and my youngest, Pia, was standing next to her. It was a highlight for them when he commented on Maria's costume and admired Pia's long, dangling earrings.

Much of the fun and excitement of those Italia Days (and other annual events) began to wind down in the late 1980s, and the CBICA experienced a period of stagnation. The reasons are not much different from those of other associations. Members moved on to other interests, some had health problems, and others moved away. It is often difficult to maintain or increase the momentum of an organization from year to year. Patsy Smith, one of the first presidents of the Association, shared these thoughts about what happened in the 1980s:

> It was very strong in 1981, '82, '83. Then ... people didn't get involved as strongly as they had and ... things fade off.... The thing I miss the most is the Italia Day. That was a really big thing, especially for the people that aren't Italian, to come out and see our culture, what we do, the dance, how the food and wine is made. This was good for the children to see. There was lots of entertainment. Sometimes, there were two or three hundred people there. I think that if we all got our heads together, we could do it again.

Over the last three or four years, interest in the CBICA has re-emerged. Young people want to familiarize themselves with their heritage, and older folks simply want to rekindle the fun. The key annual events have now been revived. The Easter and Christmas celebrations, at St. Nicholas Parish Hall in Whitney Pier, are events just as meaningful and popular as the Italia Day. At the Easter party, the highlight is always the display of Gabriel DiMichele's roasted pig—the porchetta. At Christmas time, the Association puts on a party at the hall. It promotes togetherness and is enjoyed by young and old alike. Mr. DiMichele explains:

> In Italy we have a holiday called "La Befana" on the 6th of January, which is just as big as Christmas Day itself. It is a time when friends get together with their kids and present gifts. The kids hang stockings at the fireplace so that the Befana [a female version of Santa Claus] can fill your stockings with goodies. As kids we were told that if you were good to your parents, in school and good all around, the saint will treat you well. If

you were a bad boy or girl, then the stockings were filled with ashes. Here in Cape Breton, we don't want to confuse the kids with two traditions, but we still teach this tradition to our kids. At the Italian hall, we do a lot of things at Christmas time. The kids dress up in pretty Italian style costumes and the choir dresses up too. We still fill stockings for the kids and eat Italian food.

Italia Day, 1981. (Back, from left: Maria Iannetti, Giuseppina Camilli, Theresa Giorno, Gloria MacDougall, Joan Camilli; front, from left: Laura Iannetti, Pia Camilli and Gabriela Camilli). Courtesy of Cape Breton Italian Cultural Association.

The July 1997 *Italia Day*, held at Centre 200 in Sydney, was a packed event. There were displays of Italian heritage items, and Italian folk music was played on a stereo sound system. Angelo Spinazzola was also there to play some melodies with his guitar. However, what everyone who visited the event had in common was an interest in the Italian food. People had choices of *panina* sandwiches from Mr. DiMichele's *porchetta*, or servings of pasta with meatballs. One could try the sausages in tomato sauce, and observe the cooking process while waiting. Afterwards, there were Italian-style biscuits, with coffee or tea, for dessert. By the end of the afternoon affair, needless to say, all the food was gone!

The Association's key fundraising activity is the sale of spaghetti and meatball dinners. Mrs. DiMichele, the Association's treasurer from 1995 to 1997, described this event:

> We started that about four or five years ago because we are a non-profit organization and we needed funds to operate. We have one every year, and we sell about 300 spaghetti dinners. A bunch of ladies get together and we make our own meatballs and sauce.... Homemade spaghetti is very good but it is expensive to make and hard to handle. When you're doing 300 dinners, it is not easy to handle all that pasta. So we use the regular spaghetti that you buy in the store, but the sauce is the real Italian style.

In 1995, people's long-held wish to establish Italian language classes came true, thanks in large part to Leandro D'Addario, who helped facilitate the language study program in Cape Breton. It was a joint effort by the associations of Sydney and Dominion. Many other things now go on at St. Nicholas Parish Hall, including the monthly meetings, and the "bring a new member" night which takes place each fall. In short, the yearly activities of the CBICA now fill the calendar. Traditional events, like Italia Day, have been revived and new projects have been added to the agenda. The CBICA has also gone back to the summer picnic tradition. Mrs. DeLorenzo and Mrs. DiMichele offer some final reflections on the Association and its future:

[Mrs. DiMichele]: I feel very good about the Association continuing. I think it will because it is very important for our children to know about the Italian culture, their background and their family's background. This is what we try to do [at the Association], to pass it on to the younger generation. The Italian language classes are started now and we have a lot of children interested in it. They may be able to say just a few phrases but that's a very good thing ... they will be able to go to Italy and likely get along well.

Italia Day at UCCB, 1987. From left: Theresa Della Vella, Anna DiMichele, Gabriel DiMichele and Ann Bacich. Courtesy of CBICA.

[Mrs. DeLorenzo]: I've been involved in the Association from the very beginning, and I've been president several times. I know the number of Italians here is getting smaller and a lot of them are moving away. I just hope we can hold on to it as long as we can. I always say that I'm Italian but I'm Canadian first. In my heart, I'm an Italian. I don't think there is anything wrong with holding on to your culture or heritage. No matter what nationality you are, I think everybody looks back and says these are my roots.... Just enjoy being who you are and doing what you can for the community, your own and your cultural association.

The Cape Breton Italian Cultural Association has now been in existence for almost twenty years. Throughout this period, it has overcome various problems that face all volunteer-based organizations. Its mandate has remained intact, and the association continues to be an important factor in people's lives. It is important in my life, and I intend to share it with my children some day. With a steady resurgence of its membership, and the marvellous revival of its activities, the CBICA, at least for now, holds true promise for the future.

Porchetta and the Italian Tradition

Gabriele DiMichele

Edited by A. Evo DiPierro

Gabriele DiMichele emigrated to Canada from central Italy in 1960. He lived and worked in Toronto for a few years, and then settled in Cape Breton to raise a family and start a masonry business. He has been a member of the Cape Breton Italian Cultural Association for many years, and he coordinates the porchetta preparations for the Association's annual Easter celebration. Porchetta is basically roast pig with seasonings. The golden-brown, crusty skin is a crunchy delight, and the meat is out of this world. The Easter celebration at St. Nicholas Hall in Whitney Pier is a fun and festive event attended by scores of people eager to try Gabriele's porchetta (along with all of the other great food). It is also a great way to kick-off the beginning of spring in the Italian tradition.

The reason for having the Cape Breton Italian Cultural Association is so that we can gather together to show our children the Italian culture, how it was in the old country, and to maintain the tradition. We make porchetta, spaghetti and meatballs because that's what we do for a party in Italy. The Cape Breton Italian Cultural Association is not a club where you go and have "a social drink." [The aim is] to bring the activities that we had in Italy, and maintain these traditions with our children, with the hope that they will bring them to their own children.

On special days in Italy, like Easter, we used to have roast pork, *porchetta* in Italian. In Canada, roast pork is basically a leg of pork that is roasted in the oven. The Italian people take the whole pig and roast it with the head and legs intact. The pig is a normal size and has a better flavour. After you roast it, there's the juice and the crusty skin.... The porchetta looks good when you dress it and surround it with decorations. It is easy to slice the meat and make a good sandwich. You can also make a "gravy" from the pork juice. The sandwich is actually called a *panina*.

You split the bun and put inside some meat and crust (people like the crust most). An added touch is to spread some of the "gravy" on each slice of bread. Porchetta is simple to do because it doesn't require refrigeration. You just roast it and serve it throughout the day. In Italy, people used to stop on the side of the road and prepare a porchetta. When others drove by and saw that, they would stop and buy a *panina*. In those days, it was very hard to afford meat like we can today. You ate meat only two or three times a year, and this pork was a big favourite. It was always cheap to buy and many people raised pigs.

At a festival, where there could be as many as two or three thousand people, you needed five or six pigs, and all the pork would be finished. It seems that in Canada, the main choice is the turkey for special times like Thanksgiving, but the Italians have porchetta at Easter, the day of the village saint, etc. Thirty years ago, when people made the pilgrimage to Saint Gabriel, there were no hotels or restaurants. People would leave San Salvo and walk, for five days, to get to Saint Gabriel. When they got there, they were hungry, but there was no food ... nothing, so the porchetta went like a cake. Everyone bought a sandwich, so that is the tradition (porchetta, panina) which remains today. It's the same with wine, which goes so well with porchetta. You serve one porchetta sandwich with half a litre of wine—and that makes you happy for the whole day. So, fifty or so years later, the Italian people are still here, and we love wine, we love porchetta. The Cape Breton Italian Cultural Association has people to make wine and porchetta every year, and others to make meatballs and spaghetti, plus sweets like *pizza dolce* and *pizzelle*. The organization maintains the tradition and the culture.

To make porchetta, you first need a pig that's right for the size of the occasion. We kill it, then shave it to prepare the crust. There are two ways to shave. One is with a dry fire (burning the skin and hair off) or with a rag and hot, boiling water. You cover the pig with the rags and pour hot, boiling water all over it. Now, there are three layers of skin. The water burns off the first layer and, with a sharp knife, you just shave everything off to the bottom layer. Take out all of the [intestines and internal organs], and then remove all of the bones. Wash the pig well by hosing it with water. When the bones and everything are taken out, sew it back together with a string because when you cook the pig, it will swell. Before cooking, you need to add certain spices to give it flavour: garlic, rosemary, bay leaves, black pepper, paprika, chili pepper and salt. Cover the inside of the pig with these spices. Now if the pig is a hundred pounds, for example, you need a pound and a half of salt; if it is 200 pounds, then you need three pounds of salt, etc. In a pan, which is about four feet in length, and four to five inches deep, you set the pig. All the fat and juices from the pig must stay in the pan, or it will catch fire. Add three parts water and one part wine. You have to have some alcohol. But, if you don't like wine, you could use cognac. The mixture keeps the pork from getting dry and prevents burning. Sometimes, every two or three hours, you have to add a little more water. Many Italians use their homemade wine. The oven must be at 500 to 600 degrees

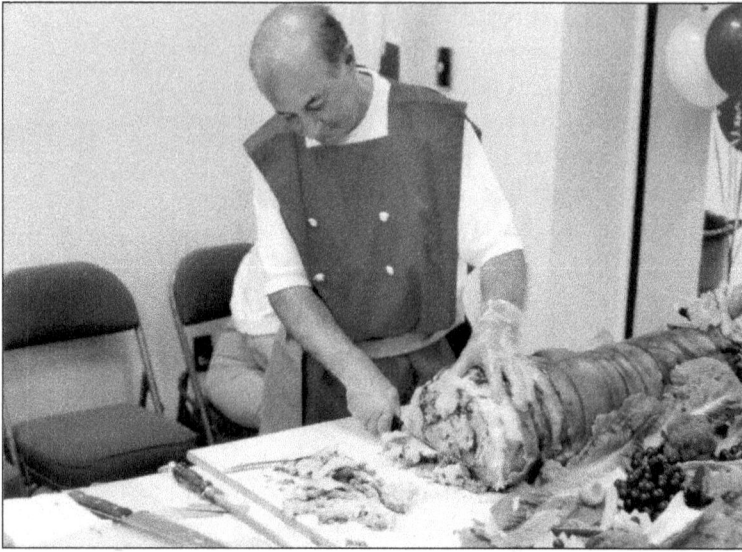

Gabriele DiMichele and porchetta, Italia Day, Sydney, 1997. Photo by A. Evo DiPierro.

Fahrenheit to cook for four hours. So you need a good commercial oven. If the oven goes only up to 400 degrees, then leave the pig in a little longer ... about six hours. It also depends on the size of the pig. If it is 200 lbs, you have to cook for eight hours, because it takes that long for the heat to go through. Keep the porchetta covered while cooking. In the last hour, remove the stuff on top of the meat and leave off the cover to slightly burn the skin and make it brown and crispy. Then take the pig out of the oven and let it cool over night; the fat will rise to the top. The next day, remove the fat and under that is the "jello"—the juice—which is all the flavour of the pork and spices. If you spread some of that on a piece of bread (like a pâté), well, it is so great. That is also a tradition. You need a couple of slices of thick, homemade bread, with that juice spread on them, and three or four slices of porchetta in between. When you eat that, you become a different person ... you will enjoy it. This tradition is still big in Italy, but Easter is a time when friends and family are together. When Easter comes in Italy, there are already flowers and warm temperatures, and it marks the beginning of summer. The people do porchetta on the week after Easter, rather than Easter Day, because that is a family day. On the week after Easter, the Italians go up the mountain and celebrate Easter; and, it is a very big, big day, with the porchetta and all.

The Voice of Music

Edited by Sam Migliore

The Italian communities of Cape Breton have made a number of contributions to the musical life of the island. They have produced a variety of celebrated individual and group performers. What this article concentrates on are the Italian Choirs of Dominion and Sydney. Both communities have produced popular and successful choirs in the past (for example the Sydney group was successful in a Nova Scotia Arts Festival competition in 1967, while the Dominion group has performed live on CBC Radio, Cape Breton), and are in the process of re-establishing their choirs at present.

The Dominion Italian Chorale

Over the years, Tony Basso and Livio Nicoletti have been two of the primary mainstays behind the Italian choir of Dominion. Tony as its director, and Livio as both a group performer and soloist. What follows is a brief history of the Chorale as presented by Livio Nicoletti.

As far as I can remember, the Chorale was formed around 1977. The TV documentary drama Roots was being aired that year. While watching the program, I realized that there were a lot of areas in our culture that the Italians of Dominion were not passing on to their children—mostly in the areas of music, singing, and language. A number of us decided to attempt to revive some of these old customs and, as a result, a group was formed to start an Italian Chorale under the direction of Tony Basso. Many old, traditional Italian songs were chosen, and practices began. Our first accompanist was Kay Gouthro, a local musician who played piano.

The group sang in church at various ceremonies. We were also asked to sing at St. Nicholas Church for the Sydney Italian Association on one of their festivities. It was shortly after that performance that many from the Dominion Chorale joined with the Sydney Choir to form one group. The combined group performed at many functions, including functions at the annual Italia Day celebrations at Cape Breton University. The first accordion player to accompany us was Mario Pino. He played his music from the heart and brought a lot of expertise to the group. Maria DeLorenzo, who directed the combined groups, became ill and recently passed away; she will be greatly missed. Tony Basso directed the combined chorales for a while, but, eventually, the Dominion group drifted back to their own hall with Tony Basso directing and Mario Pino as accompanist. Mario passed away April 6, 1997. Louie DeGiobbi of New Waterford also filled in as accordion accompanist for a few years, until he moved to Halifax where he recently passed away.

The Italian Chorale of Dominion at Sydney waterfront, June 1995. Courtesy of Livio Nicoletti.

The Dominion group, with some additions from the Sydney Association, continued to perform at functions such as the Dominion Annual Italia Fest, the Marconi Celebrations and a performance at the Savoy Theatre. Although numbers are few, and there are problems due to the unavailability of the traditional accordion, we can always rely on Kay Gouthro our pianist to help us out when needed.

It is very difficult in this day and age to keep this custom alive. At present though, a sincere effort is underway to recruit new singers and an accompanist in the hopes of keeping the Dominion Italian Chorale alive.

Livio Nicoletti prepared the statement above in the spring of 1997. By the fall of that year, the Dominion Italian Chorale showed signs of life and vitality as they began practices at the Italian Hall.

A Choir for Sydney

The Cape Breton Italian Cultural Association also initiated an attempt to revive a choir in the Sydney area recently. Rose DeLorenzo, a past-president of the Association, is one of the active participants in this process. She has provided these reflections on the history of the choir.

The Italian Choir in Sydney was formed in "Centennial Year," 1967. It was made up of young people from the Italian community, aged from five years and up. Because it was Centennial Year, a celebration of Canada's 100th birthday, we felt that it was important to participate in the many celebrations taking place all across Canada. As Italians, we were aware that many, many of our parents and grandparents had emigrated to Canada, and helped in making this wonderful country a place where we could live and raise our families in peace.

Mrs. Carmen Rossetti, Mary, with the help of other women in our community, made the first costumes—skirts, blouses, vests, aprons, etc.—for the choir. Maria DeLorenzo, an accomplished vocalist in her own right, was our director and soloist, while Mario Pino, one of a few accomplished accordion players in our area, was our accompanist. Both Maria and Mario were very dedicated to the preservation of our Italian culture through music. They spent many hours over the years teaching and practicing with the choir. We began with just the children, but the choir evolved into something where men and women also participated. Maria also formed a children's dance group to complement the choir.

One very special performance that comes to mind occurred in the summer of July 1967. The choir was asked to perform in a concert at the bandshell in Wentworth Park, Sydney, along with members of other ethnic groups. The concert was in honour of the Queen Mother's visit to Sydney for the Centennial celebrations. At the end of the concert, Maria and Mario were presented to the Queen Mother. This was very exciting for them, as well as the entire choir.

> **Maria DeLorenzo-Baggio (1941-1994)[1]**
> Maria DeLorenzo was born in Sydney in 1941. Her father, Max Brygidyr, was of Ukrainian background, while her mother, Frances Mantonio, was of Italian background. She grew up in the multi-cultural community of Whitney Pier and eventually made a career for herself in cosmetology. She owned and operated Maria's Beauty Boutique for a period of time, served as colour technician for L'Oreal Canada in Eastern and Northern Nova Scotia, and worked as an instructor in Cosmetology at the Nova Scotia Community College, Sydney Campus.
>
> Maria was one of the key people involved in the formation of the original Italian Choir in Sydney. She not only directed the group but also taught the children to dance to the Tarantella and other Italian songs. Maria also served as a vocalist and director for the Ukrainian Choir at Holy Ghost Parish in Sydney.

We also took the kids on a trip to Halifax; they performed in the Nova Scotia Arts Festival [under Maria's direction and Mario's accompaniment]. I think we came in first in the little competition. The kids used to call Maria, "Aunt Meechu." Her mother called her "Mar-i-chu" (I think it was Ukrainian for Maria), and we just called her Meechu. She was just a mainstay for us, and it was so good to see the children involved—they enjoyed it. Now, Mario was a real character. We didn't get to perform until ten that evening. In the afternoon, we had nothing to do with the kids. So, we dressed them up, fixed their hair, and asked Mario to do something. "Come on kids," he says, and he took them all the way up Citadel Hill. The children were in their Italian costumes, and Mario was playing the accordion. It reminded me of the Pied Piper. He was a riot, and he and Meechu got along very well. As a matter of fact, Mario was one of the very few people she was comfortable with accompanying her.

The choir also performed on many occasions for civic functions, festivals, Italian community functions, *Italia Days*, etc. We had a good repertoire of Italian folk and classical songs. The practice sessions were usually held at St. Nicholas Parish Church, and later at St. Nicholas Hall. Some of the numbers we sang included:

"Funiculi-Funicula," "La Belle Gigogin," "Addio Ninena," "Mamma," "O Sole Mio," "Torna a Surriento" and others.

The choir remained active until the early 1990s. Maria was not well at that time, and the choir disbanded. Maria passed away in May of 1994, and Mario in April of 1997. This was a great loss to the community at large and the Italian community in particular. Both of them are deeply missed; they gave so much of themselves to enhance our Italian culture.

Maria DeLorenzo and the Italian Choir of Sydney, ca. 1980. Courtesy of the Cape Breton Italian Cultural Association.

We have now reactivated the choir under the direction of Michael MacDonald of Sydney. We have performed recently at our Italia Day celebrations, at the 1998 Pier Scape festivities in Whitney Pier, and at Holy Redeemer Church.

When a Princess Comes to Dinner: Anna DiMichele Recalls the 1995 Marconi Celebrations

By A. Evo DiPierro

Have you ever had the opportunity of inviting royalty to your home for dinner? During the 1995 Marconi celebrations in Cape Breton, Mrs. Anna (DiSano) DiMichele was asked to host a dinner at her home, for Princess Elettra Marconi Giovanelli (Guglielmo Marconi's daughter) and her son. Mrs. DiMichele is a member of the Cape Breton Italian Cultural Association and, at the time; she was involved in organizing certain activities for the Princess' visit to Cape Breton. The Princess, her son and officials of the Italian government, as well as the captain and crew of an Italian naval warship, came to Cape Breton in the early summer of 1995 to commemorate the 100th anniversary of Marconi's invention of the wireless transmitter.[1] The Association mobilized in preparation for the arrival of Princess Giovanelli and her son to Cape Breton. While ready to help in any way, Anna hardly expected to have a direct impact on the royal visit.

> We talked about how we were going to entertain them for a few days. Then someone asked me if I would mind having them over for dinner one evening. In other words, "do you want to entertain a princess and her son?" My first reaction was, "Well gee, you don't know what they're like or anything ..." and it made me a little nervous. But we did it. We had a few ladies at our home to help. When the guests arrived we didn't know what to expect but after the initial introductions were done, everything was great. The Princess is a very nice lady and very down-to-earth; her son is wonderful. And into the evening it felt like they were old friends visiting. She was so friendly and easy to talk to.... She was very well dressed and perfectly charming. When we realized that she could speak

English it was really comforting, especially for the other ladies who couldn't speak Italian. I thoroughly enjoyed it that evening.

The dinner Mrs. DiMichele and friends prepared was simply exquisite. After the initial drinks and conversation, the Princess and her son were treated to a shrimp cocktail appetizer, following by lasagna and cannelloni, and then stuffed chicken breast and another meat dish. The table was adorned with final courses of salad, eggplant with Parmesan cheese, zucchini and other dishes. For dessert, they were treated to a beautiful Italian-style rum cake. Later in the evening, some of the DiMicheles' friends dropped by. Once again, Anna was ready for the occasion with late-evening snacks and coffee. It was a completely Italian occasion in terms of traditional meal preparation and an endless outpouring of warm hospitality. Mrs. DiMichele also recalls the afternoon tea that was arranged for the Princess at the Rocking Horse Inn in Sydney.

> That was a nice experience too, to have a cup of tea with the Princess. I have some pictures that we took and, from time to time, when I look at them; I say: "Can you imagine ... we really had dinner and tea and spent some time with the Princess." It was wonderful.

At about the same time, an Italian naval vessel, the Frigate *Zeffrio*, docked at Sydney Harbour for the Marconi celebration. Once again, Anna DiMichele and the other members of the Association joined with the Dominion Italian Club to welcome the Captain and crew.

> We were asked to put something together for the ship that had come. By this time, the Princess and her son were gone. But we had a social in Dominion for a lot of the Italian community here and the crew of the ship. We put a dinner together and afterwards had a sing-song of Italian songs. The crew members really enjoyed it and so did we. I know they had a great time. They were singing with us, standing up and singing along, dancing, clapping their hands. We made them feel good but they made us feel even better.

The crew of the *Zeffrio* returned the hospitality of the Italian community by inviting residents aboard for socials during the ship's stay. One evening, in particular, was phenomenal, according to Mrs. DiMichele. While there was no grand dining room aboard the *Zeffrio*, space apparently was no object for the kind of feast they had laid before their guests.

> When you went on that ship it was like you were in Italy. Everything... was Italian. They spoke Italian, the food was Italian ... everything. They invited a group of us from the Italian community to the ship for dinner. They had cheeses, pizzas, salamis, prosciutto, olives ... and all from Italy.

And, after that, just when we thought dinner was over, they announced dinner! It was a buffet ... about a 150 feet long. There were all these different foods: pastas, roasts, cold cuts and breads from Italy. It just didn't seem like your ordinary naval vessel. They had fruits, vegetables, main dishes of all kinds, hors d'oeuvres, various wines and sweets ... they had everything! The whole time the ship was here, everything went by so fast, but the thing that I enjoyed most was watching the *Zeffrio* come in to dock. There was a wonderful feeling knowing that an Italian ship was coming to Sydney.

The summer of 1995 was an important and memorable time for Anna DiMichele and the many Italians of Cape Breton. Special events took place which heightened their sense of pride in their culture and in the contributions of Italians to the quality of life for everyone. In a wider sense, the Marconi celebrations also served to remind Cape Bretoners of the history that was made here, and how that has bestowed upon Cape Breton a unique position of prominence in the context of Canada's heritage.

The Italian Government Connection
Lino Polegato[1]

The Italian Ambassador in Ottawa is the Italian Government's representative in Canada. The Ambassador's job is relegated normally to formal liaisons with the Canadian Government. He will take care of any treaties, state visits by Italian VIP's, and will be the Italian Government's listening post in Canada regarding international events. Now, the Ambassador will appoint a Consul General to take care of domestic problems Italians may have in Canada: pension claims, war veterans benefits, passports, etc. The Consul General has a diplomatic staff; people that come from Italy, and work for the Italian Government.

The Consul General appoints representatives, Consuls, for each area in Canada where Italians are located. These people live in that particular area. The Consul here in the Atlantic Provinces is in Halifax, and his territory is Nova Scotia, PEI, Newfoundland, and New Brunswick. Beneath the Consuls are Vice Consuls and Consular Correspondents. I'm Vice Consul for half of the province of Nova Scotia. The Consul and I agreed that he would take care of domestic problems from Antigonish west, I would take care of anything from Antigonish east.

The characteristics a representative should have include being bilingual (trilingual, if possible). Italian and English or French. The person should have some kind of status in the community. It should be someone who has proven by his lifestyle that he is accepted and at least semi-respected by Italians in the community, but, more importantly, by the non-Italians in the community. The next characteristic is that he should have some experience in community service. He should be able to speak freely with the mayors and councillors in the area. His job should be relatively secure, so he can be free of the worry of earning a living; because, if he has to worry too much about this, he won't be able to devote the time required to the job. He should be well enough educated ... to converse, read and write fluently in at least two languages.

As the representative you deal with any problems members of the Italian community of your area encounter. The most common one has to do with passports. For example, one lady who has lived in Dominion for the last 45 years wanted to go back to Italy to visit. I automatically went to the Canadian post office, got a passport application, started to fill it out. In the form, it states: "if you are not born in Canada, show your birth certificate and your naturalization papers." Only Canadian citizens can get a Canadian passport. "Oh, I don't have any naturalization papers. I got married, came over here, and I assumed I was a Canadian citizen because I came over with my husband." But, she wasn't a Canadian citizen. We discovered that, and I started the process for her to become a naturalized Canadian—45 years after she came and lived in Canada. In the meantime, she was eligible to apply for the Italian passport. So, I got her the forms to apply for an Italian passport, as an Italian citizen. That was a technical problem. Other problems include the settling of estates in Italy; and pensions—whether Italian or Canadian. Italy and Canada concluded an agreement; pensions are now portable from one country to the other. If a man is here for fifty years, gets his Canada pension, and goes to live in Italy for the rest of his days, his cheques will be mailed to him. Before, you couldn't leave the country for more than six months. Finally, the representative has a responsibility to inform people that the Italian government will try to help preserve and foster their Italian culture and, to that end, it offers some resources. My job as consul was to try to make sure that people avail themselves of those resources.

Leandro D'Addario:
Italian Consular Agent for Cape Breton

Edited by A. Evo DiPierro[1]

We have been here for five generations now. My grandfather came to Cape Breton in 1904, when the steel plant was being built; he worked as a supervisor. He would take a gang of men to the various work sites to construct or fix bridges—to do work with concrete. He stayed here until 1922; then he went back to Italy to settle down and raise his family. By the end of the Second World War, my father was married with three children. In 1950, he decided to move back to Canada for better employment opportunities. In those days there was just no work in Italy. My father came to Sydney because he was born here, and he had work waiting for him. He arrived by himself, my late brother came in 1951 and finally my mother, sister and myself joined them in 1952. We had the family right here again. So, with me, my daughter, and my grandchildren, it is five generations.

When we arrived in Sydney we lived in the Pier. Back then the Pier had mainly Italian people and, on Lingan Road, it was all Italian. I would talk to them in Italian, but they didn't understand me too much. But, I persisted, and over a few weeks, I learned the English language. Since then, I have gotten along fine. I started work with a construction company, but after about a year-and-a-half, I left construction work completely. I wanted to be self-employed. At the time, I was twenty-three years old and being an entrepreneur was a challenge. I wanted to be my own boss, to have more control over my future. My first venture was actually in Montreal, but I became established in business in Sydney around 1959.

I opened my first pizza shop on Charlotte Street. Many people came to try it. But they didn't know how to eat pizza, and they had no idea how to handle spaghetti. I had to go from table to table, to show them how to twist the spaghetti on a spoon like we Italians do. Another time, a gentleman came in and ordered pizza, "a combination," so I made him one with the works. When I put it on his table, he simply sat there and stared at it. I noticed he wasn't touching the pizza so I asked if anything was wrong. "Oh," he said, "how am I going to eat this now?!" Again, I showed him how to slice it, then use his fork and knife to cut smaller pieces. Eventually everything was fine; he started to eat pizza and other Italian food.

I figured that if I stayed in the pizza business I could do well. At the end of each night, the money I made was mine. That was satisfying. Of course, I had bills to pay and other expenses, but I managed the environment and determined my own income. I relocated to George Street in 1963 and that was even better. In three years, I made enough money to buy a piece of land on Grand Lake Road. It was my intention to erect a large building there. I thought about building a dance hall, pizza shop and dining room—a grand place. I couldn't do it all at once, but I put the foundation in and built the first section—the downstairs for a pizza shop and the upstairs as living quarters. At first, the critics told me nobody would go all the way down to Grand Lake Road—"out in the woods," as they would say. But soon some people started coming, and then more and more people came. I wanted something that I could call my own, and the Roma Pizzeria & Lounge turned into quite a popular establishment.

D'Addario family—Leandro's father, Giuseppe, and grandparents, Francesco and Lucia (Dalesandro) D'Addario, Sydney, 1922. Courtesy of Leandro D'Addario. Photo possibly by Dodge Studios, Whitney Pier.

As I grew established in my community, both as a resident and businessman, I became a member of the Cape Breton Italian Cultural Association. That was in the mid-1970s. I served as its president for a couple of years. In 1976, I was asked to join the Congress of Italian Canadians; they were looking for a representative from Cape Breton because of the considerable Italian community here. It was around that time that I came to know Lino Polegato. He was involved with the Marconi Foundation, trying to establish a museum about Marconi. Thanks to Lino, I was introduced to many other Italians throughout Cape Breton. Lino did a lot of the work for the museum, and I helped by introducing people to what he was doing. We became good friends.

In 1995, I became an official agent of the Italian Consulate in Montreal—Consular Agent for Italy in Cape Breton. I assist people with pension claims, citizenship applications and family genealogy projects. I also perform protocol functions. When the Italian Ambassador (in Ottawa) and the President of the Marconi Foundation (from Valona, Italy) visited Cape Breton for the Marconi celebrations, I escorted them to the museum and showed them around. I also was present for all of the social events that took place at that time. You don't get paid for it, but there are bigger reasons for doing these tasks. The expressions of gratitude I receive from the people I help are more than sufficient. Not too many people have the time to do this, but I like to do it, and I will continue for as long as I can.

Of special importance to me was the establishment of Italian language classes in Cape Breton, in 1996. With the help of the consulate, I located two instructors and sent them to Halifax for training. We now have four adult classes (two in Dominion and two in Sydney), plus one for children (in Sydney). One teacher handles the adult classes while our substitute teaches the kids. Both are working and enjoying it. The consulate also provided equipment, supplies and other necessities. The classes are doing well and the system will improve with time and practice. I consider the establishment of Italian classes to be my most important endeavour. They will educate young and old about their language. It means that the survival of that part of our culture now has a better chance.

I suppose, in a way, all my work paid off when I was appointed consular agent (Agente consolare onorario). It is an official recognition of the duties I performed all these years and an encouragement to continue. It's a very nice thing to have under your belt. And the work goes on.

In concluding this story, I have written a tribute for the late Lino Polegato in Italian. It sums up the valuable friendship that we had and the unforgettable impression that he left on me.

L'Omaggio per Lino Polegato

Conobbi Lino nel 1978 quando organizzava luoghi di riunioni per l'associazione Italiana per Dominion e per Sydney. A questo punto, Lino mi domandai se mi piacerebbe attendere questi riunioni. Da li sviluppo un amicizia fondamentale, che ho deciso di coinvolgermi con la fondazione museo di Marconi. L'orgoliositá e l'importanza che aveva per la cultura Italiana, consegui Lino di tenerlo sempre piú vivo e attivo nella nostra comunità e multiculturisma.

Dopo anni di dedicazione e determinazione, nel 1984, il governo Italiano concesse a Lino il titolo di Cavaliere della Repubblica Italiana. Nel passato egli era il Presidente dell'associazione Italiana di Dominion e Agente Consolare Onorario di Capo Bretone. E stato un onore di averlo conosciuto. Era una persona che voleva sempre sviluppare, creare tante cose per la nostra comunità Italiana in Capo Bretone. Ma la cosa piú importante era la sua amicizia, che purtroppo manchera per sempre specialmente da parte mia e degli altri.

Tribute to Lino Polegato

I first met Lino in 1978. He was organizing a meeting for Dominion and Sydney Italian clubs and invited me to attend. We soon became good friends. As a result of this friendship, I became involved in the Marconi Museum Foundation. Working together, I soon realized how proud Lino was of his Italian heritage. It was important to him to keep his cultural heritage alive. He supported community cultural activities and multiculturalism.

For many years, he contributed much of his time and energy to the Italian community. His determination and guidance opened many doors. In 1984, Lino was given the title "Cavaliere della Repubblica" by the Italian government. He was past president of the Italian Hall in Dominion and was the Italian consular agent for Cape Breton in 1976. It was a privilege knowing him. He was a great motivator, and he accomplished so much. Most of all, he was a close friend whose friendship is greatly missed.

A New Life in Canada

By Lina Mleczko

I was born Lina DiRito in Sydney on August 20, 1959. Both my parents are pure blood Italian. I also have a younger brother living in Italy. The first ten years of my life in Canada were not the most pleasant, nor were the ten years I spent in Italy. However, my parents had a bakery business on Grand Lake Road in Sydney; it was called the Italian Bakery, and they made bread, pizzas and pastries. They also owned a small chain of pizza shops. In 1970, my father decided to move back to Italy, and so I lived there for ten years. Italy's climate didn't agree with me. Furthermore, the water, food and other environmental conditions played havoc with my health. After finishing school, I studied business administration at a college in Rome. Then, having had enough of the country, I returned to Canada, for good, to make a life for myself.

For a time, I lived with my mother's parents, both of whom are now passed away, and I took additional courses to upgrade my English language skills. Then I started my first job as a clerk and seamstress. Two weeks after I arrived in Sydney, I met Michael Mleczko. He was the best thing to have happened to me at that time; now he is my husband, partner and best friend. We were married on August 15, 1987. He is Polish-Ukrainian; a hard-working, private individual. He never goes to bars and prefers to stay home, which is okay with me. Our relationship is based on trust, love and mutual respect. We just don't have time to fight; we do have disagreements but never fight. Life is too short to waste on such foolishness.

A lot of people tell me that Italian and Polish make a great combination, and I happen to agree. Sure, he is old-fashioned and, at times, stubborn. But the alternative was much less appealing: An Italian man is more demanding ... narrow-minded. Everything must be done perfectly, especially when it comes to their homes. Of course, much of Italy and the Italian culture has changed over the years, but in the small towns throughout the country, little of the individual Italian male has actually changed, in my opinion, and I learned that first-hand when I was living there. In Italy, I was made to believe that men must be the leaders, but I do not agree with that. Sorry. Michael and I have a great relationship. We hide nothing from each other and keep each other posted on where we are and what we're doing. For me, that is the difference between him and the Italian men I knew.

Being married to a Polish man has been a comforting release for me. Actually, (and it's a little sad to say this in regards to my own culture) it's probably the best thing I ever did. His culture is different from ours when it comes to food, rituals and other aspects, but we blend the two together. For example, they like to have turkey for Christmas dinner, and I will contribute lasagna or ravioli as additional courses. As long as we eat, that it is the main thing, but Michael and I enjoy being introduced to each other's culture. The Polish community is very helpful; they are there when you need help or advice, whether it's a special occasion or everyday-type things. The Italian community is a good one as well, but I don't miss anything because I am well looked-after by the Polish community.

My Italian heritage will always be with me, and the Italian language is an old, beautiful one. I had an opportunity to teach it when, early last year, my uncle, who is the Italian consular agent for the Cape Breton area, contacted me about teaching the language to Italian children here. The overall mission, presently, is to re-introduce the youth of Italian background to that aspect of their culture. Many of them are learning Italian for the very first time. It was an interesting challenge for me. I was interviewed by an official of the Italian Consulate and, after I accepted their offer, I went to Halifax for training while the program was set up in Cape Breton.

It's a wonderful experience, really, for both myself and the students. The kids seem to enjoy it, especially the teenagers. I have two classes: one for the little kids and another for the teens. In the teens' class, simply by virtue of their higher level of education, I try to help them learn to handle the peculiarities of the language, and to speak it in a relatively competent manner. What they must learn is the pure, correct version of Italian, without any compromise. By the sixth week, they were able to read and write Italian. Later on came the dialogue and conversations. I have nine students; they are doing great, and I love them. One needs to feel privileged to be able to speak another language; it opens many doors. It was not easy for me when I moved to Italy because I could only speak English fluently. The interest in Italian language classes in Cape Breton is definitely there, so I am confident that more classes will start next fall. In the meantime, I prepared some reading material for the teens to use during the summer. This will help keep things fresh in their minds for next year.

Nowadays, when overseas travel is a more common activity, to be able to overcome the barrier of another culture's language means unlocking the mysteries of that culture, and I feel that I am doing an important service to young people, both Italian and non-Italian, with my work. Teaching Italian classes has sort of reconnected me to the Italian community in Cape Breton. I now attend meetings of the Cape Breton Italian Cultural Association and partake in their events. I don't know if I will ever go back to Italy; I really have no desire to go back there. Could I handle even a couple of weeks there? However, if my husband is interested in a trip, then I may go one more time. One thing is for certain, whatever I do next will, as usual, be on my own terms.

Section VII

Looking Beyond
Cape Breton
(Home and Away)

Arrival in Canada: An Indirect Route

Edited by Sam Migliore

On Thursday, April 24, 1997, Evo DiPierro and I discussed various aspects of the emigration experience with Giuseppe and Antonietta (Ciccotelli) Ciocca. Their emigration experience was quite different from that of most Italian-born individuals in Cape Breton. First, they emigrated to Canada relatively late compared to the vast majority of others. They arrived in Cape Breton in 1965. Second, the Cioccas did not emigrate here directly from Italy. They lived in Argentina for a considerable time prior to reaching a decision to continue their journey. What follows is an account of their experiences and travels as related by Giuseppe, with occasional comment from Antonietta.

[Giuseppe]: We are from the province of Campobasso, in Molise, Italy. [Antonietta]: From the same town. [Giuseppe]: Ricca, a town of about 35,000 inhabitants. It is the same size as Sydney, Cape Breton. I knew Antonietta's parents and brother, but she and I didn't know each other in Italy. We met in Argentina, in Buenos Aires.

[Sam: When did you leave Italy for Argentina?] [Giuseppe]: Me, my brother, Michele, and a cousin left from Naples on November 9, 1949. It took twenty days to reach Buenos Aires. [Evo: Why Argentina?] [Giuseppe]: Well, after the war, people returned to the town, the population grew, but there were no jobs. No jobs on the farm, no jobs anywhere. There were too many people. Millions of people emigrated from Italy. I went to Argentina because my father, Giuseppe Salvatore Ciocca, was there. He was in Argentina from 1928 to 1932, and then he went back there after the war. He had some relatives in Buenos Aires, and they prepared the application for him to go back. There were a lot of people from my hometown over there. There are lots of Italians in Buenos Aires. It was a place to go. I wanted to go somewhere else, but this was the place where I had the chance to go. See, Italian people want to emigrate to what will be a better place to live. Italy was a good place, but there was no work. What can you do? [laughs]

So, my father was in Argentina first, then me and my brother, and after that my mother, Angela (Moffa) Ciocca, and the rest of the family came over. [Sam: And for you, Antonietta?] [Antonietta]: Well, my older brother, Michelino, went to Argentina first, then he called over all the family. We were eight kids; three boys and five girls. [Giuseppe]: Her parents, Giuseppe and Pasqualina (Notortomaso) Ciccotelli, and seven kids came there together. One time it was easy to go to Argentina. The Government wanted the people. They would give you the chance to go there by paying one quarter the cost. Families could go over there together. Antonietta and her family came to Argentina in 1956. She and I were married on January 19, 1959.

[Evo: How did you feel when you left Italy?] [Giuseppe]: You don't feel very good, but the situation pushes you to go. There was nothing for us to do in Italy. You say to yourself: "My father is in Argentina, and the rest of the family will join us later." [Evo: So you were saying "goodbye" to your country.] [Giuseppe]: You say "goodbye," but all the time you think about one day going back. [laughs] We all lived in Argentina for a while, then my father and mother went back to Italy. Later, my brother got a good job in Paris, France, and they joined him there. My parents died in Paris. I was back in Italy for a visit in 1978, after so many years. [laughs] I found so many changes. It was the same when I went back for a visit to Argentina in 1993.

The Voyage to Argentina

[Sam: You took the boat from Italy to Argentina. What was that like?] [Giuseppe]: Twenty days. The ship was called *Sises*. We went from Naples to Buenos Aires. The ship stopped in Spain, the island of Palma, Rio de Janeiro and Montevideo. In the Mediterranean there were a couple of rough days. But, in the Atlantic, it was perfect, beautiful. It was the same as if you were sitting in the house here. Then, near Brazil, in the channel of Santa Catarina, zoooom, zoooom [rocking motion of ship]. You had to hold on to stay on top of the bed. [laughs] One morning I went up top, and there was only one man out. I went to eat, and there were only four people in the refectory. [laughs] Nobody came up to eat.

When we arrived in Argentina, there was somebody there to meet us. My father and two cousins were living in Buenos Aires. I didn't speak any Spanish but, after a while, I caught on.

Life in Argentina

[Sam: So, how long were you in Argentina?] [Giuseppe]: Fifteen years, from 1949 to 1965. We came to Canada in April 1965. When I first got to Argentina, I worked in a factory making industrial washing machines. I worked there for three or four years. After that, I went to school to take courses in refrigeration, and I got a job in the fabrication of domestic refrigeration equipment. I got to know every little piece of those machines. A few years before I came to Canada, I was in charge of twenty people. [Antonietta]: He was a supervisor. [Giuseppe]: Because, after so many years, I knew how to do all the jobs in the factory.

I didn't leave Argentina because of the job. The work in the factory was good. Nobody pushed us, you knew what to do, and everything was completed at a normal pace. We had a big house over there, and it was all paid for. The reason I left Argentina was because the money didn't have a very high value at the time. There was devaluation of money and inflation of prices. The dollar was worth a lot more. There were seven pesos to the dollar in the United States. The country was in trouble after the revolution. Perón was president for a long time. There was construction jobs, you could work in four places if you wanted. It was easy to find a job, you had your choice of where to go. [laughs] Anywhere you asked for a job, they would say, "you can start tomorrow." Everybody could work. He was a good president. After the revolution, there were no jobs, and the money had less and less value. There was trouble; that's why we left.

Now, when I went back to Argentina for a visit in 1993, the peso was at the same level as the dollar in the United States. The Canadian dollar is lower than the peso. But, people don't make very much money. A bricklayer makes three dollars an hour. That's it! One kilo of good meat costs four pesos. If somebody from Argentina came over here, they could make a lot more money. I came here for one reason, the money problems. The weather over there was like paradise. You didn't need a furnace.

Emigration to Canada

There were some people from my hometown living in Montreal, but we had nobody here. I just made an application for immigration. We took the plane from Argentina to Halifax. In 1965, the trip cost $750 for me, Antonietta and our son, Roberto. We were in Halifax for a few days, and then someone at the immigration office said, "There is a refrigeration contractor in Sydney who needs a man like you. Do you want to go?" So we came to Cape Breton. We lived in the Pier with Alberico and Rosa Disano for the first little while and then moved to Sydney River. See, when we immigrated here, we just flew to Canada [laughs] and landed in one place. We didn't know where we were going. We were looking for better conditions. For a long time, I wanted to go to the United States, but we couldn't go there. Now, I don't want to go; I like it here.

[Evo: So, when you came to Canada in 1965, what was your first impression?] [Giuseppe]: Oh, don't talk about it. [laughs] I'll tell you just one story. In 1966, I bought a half-ton truck. One day, it wouldn't start. It was minus twenty-seven degrees Fahrenheit in Sydney River for three days. I had to walk to work. My face was frozen; it was like a rock. I couldn't open my mouth. [laughs] A real impression, twenty-seven below. I don't think we've had cold like that since.

I also spent three months in Toronto in 1965. I went there at the end of September, and I was back to Cape Breton before Christmas. In Toronto you could make a little bit more money, but the situation was bad. One fellow from my hometown worked in construction. He had to leave home at five o'clock in the morning to get to work for eight o'clock. By the time he got home from work, it was another five hours. He used to say, "ten hours driving, for eight hours work." This was no good for me. I found a job there, but I didn't know the place; it was too much trouble. Sydney was a smaller place; it was different. I worked for J. R. Mahoney, refrigeration. It was me and Mr. Mahoney. We worked together; we went to Inverness, Port Hood, Louisbourg, all around Cape Breton. But, in Toronto, you don't know where to go. I said: "Ah, this is no life. Ten hours driving, for eight hours work? [laughs] No life! No good!" [laughs] So I came back here. You make a little less, but it is different living.

Our first child was born in Argentina. Roberto was two-and-a-half years old when we came here. He spoke very good Spanish, but he forgot everything. We came to the Pier, and after a week, he lost one language and caught another. He was speaking English. Kids catch on fast. [Antonietta]: The other two boys—Tonino and Mario—were born here. They are Cape Bretoners. [laughs]

To Australia, Colombia and Cape Breton: Biagi Family Migrations

Mark Biagi
Edited by Sam Migliore

My grandfather (Attilio Biagi) came from Bologna in the northern part of Italy. He came from a very large family of nineteen brothers and sisters, so they weren't extremely well to do. As he grew older, he decided that going overseas was a way to bring back riches to help his mother and father with the upbringing of all the other siblings. [My grandfather sailed out of Venice, but] he got on the wrong boat and wound up in Barranquilla, Colombia. Apparently, he had intended to go to Australia. Since he didn't have a lot of money, [laughs] there was really no way for him to start meandering around the oceans again.

In the early 1900s, Barranquilla was just a port; there was really nothing there. So my grandfather decided that, if he was going to make his fortune, he was going to have to go to the capital, to Bogotá. The only way up there at the time was on a donkey. Now, Bogotá is 2,600 metres above sea level, and it goes up some pretty rough terrain. He had to go over two mountain chains.... The trek took weeks. He had never really been on a donkey before; so, he spent another week on his stomach because his rear end was raw from the trip. [laughs]

Once in Bogotá, my grandfather started to establish contact with other Italians. South America was pretty well colonized by Italians, and Venezuela and Colombia seem to have gotten their fair share. He and his new friends started some businesses. I know they bought a tomato farm in a place called Mesitos del Calegio, and that my grandfather started a cannery.

When war broke out, and Mussolini did his bit, Colombia threatened to start taking away Italian properties. What my grandfather did was to put the farm in the name of my father (Augusto), because my father was born in Colombia. That was one way they were able to stave off losing the land. However, the movement of Italians was restricted, and my father was only an infant, so they couldn't really travel to the farm that often. What happened, basically, was that the farm collapsed; the foreman knew they were Italian, and he took advantage of the situation. He stole all the produce and sold it.

My grandfather was travelling, meeting Italians, looking for business opportunities when he met my grandmother (Sara). He courted her for quite a while, as was the rule of the day, and eventually married her. She was a woman of both Spanish and Native extraction from Colombia. Very beautiful and, as it turned out, an extremely talented woman. She was an excellent chess player, an avid photographer, a very good artist, very strong personality. My grandfather was the force behind the various businesses he got involved in, but my grandmother was the savvy businesswoman. She was very shrewd. So, my grandparents were quite successful.

Sometime after they married, my grandfather started the business where I think he made most of his money. He followed the old family tradition of making his own wine. My grandfather started a winery. He would buy grapes and, I think, they would import some grapes from Italy. The country was starting to deal with grapes of their own, but they were not very good quality. He made wine, champagne, and then he started distilling rum. He exported those products to Ecuador and Venezuela. He did quite well until the government decided that they were going to nationalize and take control of liquor production in the country. They saw that there was revenue in liquor production, and they took it away from those that had started doing the work.

My grandfather was asked to stay on as the main producer of wines and champagnes; but, he was a very independent man, he didn't like having a boss, and so he sold the business to the government. He didn't get a helluva lot. From there, though, he got into the delicatessen market. My grandfather imported salamis and meats from Italy and later produced his own salamis and panettone bread for special Italian festivities. He also provided the money for the start of two major companies: the Italo Colombiana, a chocolate manufacturer; and, Pastas Dorio, which produced different pasta products. It was Italian friends who borrowed the money to start these businesses. He didn't charge them any interest, and he wouldn't accept any shares for the loans. It's too bad because they became extremely successful and popular companies in Colombia.

My grandfather brought two of his brothers, Dante and Ubaldo, [to Colombia]. He also took the family back to Italy for a couple of years. My father and aunt (Yolanda) were there as young children; they went to school in Italy, but I don't know very much about that period.

Childhood Memories

Some of the most vivid memories I have of my grandfather are of his relationship with me. He was an extremely loving man, who enjoyed my company and my sister's (Dyana) company. He would take me for walks, and he would buy me candy. He always bought shares for me in one of the big brewing companies [in Colombia]. And, every week, he would give me five or six pesos, which I deposited into a piggy bank. That money, and the shares he invested for me, actually paid for a couple of my years at university. So, it was a significant amount of money. His relationship with my sister was also quite interesting. He adored her; she was his little angel. My grandfather was a very easy going man, a very good heart.

The Delicatessen. My grandfather developed the delicatessen in a fairly populated area of Bogotá. The city was growing very quickly, so there was a lot of construction, a lot of men working in the area. My grandfather provided these men with a decent sandwich. A friend, a baker, baked miniature French bread loaves, maybe thirty centimetres long. The sandwiches had butter, mustard, really good salami, imported cheese, lettuce and tomato. And, he charged the same amount other people were charging for a plain sandwich. So he was very, very popular.

I can remember going to the deli to visit him. There would be people literally lined up outside to get these sandwiches. My grandfather would sit at the cash register, elevated from the floor so he would have command of the whole store. My father would put me up on his shoulders. When my grandfather saw me, he would bang his cane on the floor until everybody was quiet. He'd order that not one more sandwich be served until his grandson was sitting with him. [laughs] I would travel over these people from hand to hand until I was delivered across the counter and taken to my grandfather, then everything would resume. I can still remember the pandemonium in the store. Guys constantly slicing bread, almost like an assembly line, guys cutting salami, and others putting on the mustard. It was a very successful business.

Tasting the Wine. Meals were always very important. My grandfather was of the opinion that when you are sitting at the table, you should always have some wine in your glass. My being little had no bearing on the fact that ... I should be just like him. I sat at his right, and he had a special wine glass blown for me. It was a very small glass made exactly like his. He would always temper my eagerness to drink the wine. He would say, "No, you drink with me." So, when he'd take a drink, I would take a sip. When our glasses were empty, we would get more wine. We would sit and discuss school and other things in a very business-like manner. Almost like he was giving me that acknowledgement of being a man. I can remember that quite vividly.

My grandfather always made wine for his personal consumption. He used to take me to the wine cellar to sample and choose the wine for our meals. He would open the casks, and use a sampling spoon to taste the wine. My grandfather would role the wine around his mouth and then spit it out, but I would swallow it. By the time I got upstairs, I was half-cocked [laughs] just from sampling the wine. And, it made no difference what wine he wanted, or if he was holding a big party, I chose the wines that got served for dinner. I don't think it made much difference, because all the wine he made was good. But, it was curious that he always went with my decisions.

My grandfather died when I was twelve. He was eighty-four years old. My grand-mother died when she was ninety-nine.

The Canadian Connection

My mother (Peggie) was from Dalhousie, New Brunswick. She was a nurse. My father studied medicine in Colombia and went to Monte Fiori Hospital in New York to do his specialization. That's where they met. It was love at first sight. They started going out together and eventually married in New York and moved down to Colombia. They did that forty-four years ago, so my mother has been living there for a long time.

I was born in Colombia, and I had much the same pathway as my father. I met my wife, Susan, who was from Sydney, at the University of New Brunswick. We eventually married, and we now have three children (Daniel Augusto, Julian Attilio, Ariana Linda).

I finished my Master's [degree] in New Brunswick and then went to Montreal to do a PhD in Biological Oceanography. That went well, until my professor ran out of money. I had a young son by that time, and finances were getting tricky, so I accepted a job offer in Colombia. We moved there in 1985. I worked there for six or seven years. Two of our children were born in Cartagena, Colombia, where I was working.

One of our children had a hole in the heart. They recommended that we come to Canada, to the IWK [Isaac Walton Killam Hospital in Halifax] to have it operated on. These operations were not that common [in Colombia]. The doctors wanted the child to stay six months before and six months after the operation, so they could deal with any possible tropical diseases that might come up. I wasn't willing to spend a year away from the family, or to commute every three months. The kids were young enough that they would have really missed my company, but I think it was more of a selfish thing. I think I would have missed them more than they would have missed me. I terminated all my contracts in Colombia; we sold everything, and we moved up to Canada, to Sydney. Sydney was the logical place for us to stay because Susan's parents lived here. The family home was here.

I'm a marine biologist, and I work in aquaculture. I'm also involved with environ-mental issues. And, I build aquariums for research and for ornamentation. I've done a lot of international consulting; I've gone to Asia, South America, Central America, the Caribbean. And so, through my profession, I've had an interesting life travelling from place to place.

A Trip to Relatives in Italy

Shirley (Martinello) Grinnell[1]

Shirley Grinnell (along with husband Dale, daughter Renee and mother Anna Martinello) visited Italy several years after a devastating earthquake had rocked southern Italy. Their intent, in part, was to visit the area where her grandfather, Michele Martinello, was born and to meet relatives who reside there. Their first contact was Tommaso Luongo, Michele's sister's son.

In Sorrento, we had the desk clerk, who spoke perfect English, call Tommaso in Taurasi to let him know that we had arrived. We made contact on the first try and arranged to meet at eleven o'clock on Saturday morning (September 3, 1983), at the Benevento exit of the Naples-Bari A16 Autostrada. Tommaso assured us that he would have someone with him to translate since neither of us spoke the other's language. On the way we stopped to see the city of Avellino. The mountain scenery was very beautiful, and the highway in excellent condition. We could see some of the effects of the November 1980 earthquake, but on the whole the area looked quite prosperous. The weather was excellent—sunny and warm, not too hot like Rome.

Tommaso and his cousin, David Luongo, were waiting when we arrived. They had been there since ten o'clock in the morning hoping that we might come early. David, who had lived in England for twenty years, was in the process of relocating his family back to Avellino. He spoke perfect English. After greeting one another, we followed Tommaso's car to Taurasi to meet his lovely family.

As we entered his home, we came into a large hallway with circular marble steps running up to the second floor. From there we were taken into an ante-room; it had a marble floor, a large round wooden table with lace tablecloth and cabinets full of vintage wines, liqueurs, liquor and a large stereo system. We were so surprised at the size of the home that we thought, at first, it might be a duplex. The house had a total of twelve huge rooms, including two tiled bathrooms complete with all the modern conveniences. In the kitchen, they had a brick oven for making bread, open fireplace barbecue, electric stove, washer and refrigerator. Carmella and Tommaso's bedroom had beautiful antique furniture. All of the upstairs bedrooms were huge, and they opened onto a balcony which ran all around the house. The floors were made of either marble or ceramic tile, and an oriental rug adorned the living room floor. Dale and I slept in a large bedroom with a king-sized bed, while Mama and Renee had single beds in their own rooms.

The family was just terrific to us. [Carmella and Tommaso had five children.] Vincenzo, the oldest, worked in Naples as an accountant. Raffaele was employed as a forest ranger while Maria Grazia worked in an office. Roberto, the youngest, was the most quiet and shy of the children. All four were unmarried, lived at home and had their own car. They were very modern in their tastes and owned the latest in American records. [Another daughter lived in Florence with her husband and two young children.] Tommaso looked just like [my uncle] Eddy Martinello. Carmella's unmarried sister lived with them and helped Carmella with the various chores.

We brought gifts of liquor, cigarettes, perfume, jade pendants and candy. We left with five bottles of their homemade wine, tons of hazel nuts, figs, peppers and Renee was given a beautiful piece of porcelain. The luncheon meal was an absolute feast—melon and prosciutto, rigatoni, braciole, bread, six kinds of cheese, fresh fruit, dessert, wine, coffee, liquor and chocolates. For supper, we had chicken soup, salad, barbecue veal steaks, cheese, dessert, fruit and finished with the usual wine and liqueurs. The food was so delicious; the braciole tasted just like Pa's, and the tomato sauce just like ours.

In the cellar, they had a complete winemaking operation with about 300 bottles of homemade wine in storage. The cellar also stored all kinds of fruit, vegetables, nuts and large tins of olive oil. Outside, they had a large garden and numerous fruit trees. About one mile away from the house, they had a small farm with chickens, rabbits and two dogs. The farm had several vegetables growing (plum tomatoes, peppers and corn) and many fruit trees (primarily fig and hazelnut). The farm was also covered with an extensive grape vineyard. When we asked how they ate all the corn, we were informed that it was only fed to the animals.

We then went to the old farmhouse in neighbouring Calore. The farm now belongs to Rolando Martiniello (they spell the name a bit different). Rolando is the son of my grandfather's brother, Carmen. Rolando's wife died about ten years ago, and he was forced to bring up the eight children (five girls and three boys) by himself. Two of the children, girls aged twelve and thirteen, still live at home. The old stone farm house was still there, but Rolando recently had finished building a beautiful two story stucco home similar to Tommaso's. Both homes were well kept and very modern. When we entered the old farm house, we were surprised to see that it also had marble stairs and tile floors. [On the front entrance appeared the date "1928."] We questioned the significance of that date. They were not sure when the farm was originally constructed, but 1928 was the date when it was last remodelled. Evidently, the four [Martinello] brothers in Sydney had been sending money back, and that helped defray the cost of remodelling. The farm itself was so large that we couldn't see all of it from one location. Tobacco appeared to be the primary crop. We drank wine as we sat around Rolando's kitchen table and left with large bags of hazel nuts, which had been drying outside on the pavement. Tommaso also climbed a nearby tree to pick fresh figs for us.... Needless to say, we all enjoyed the visit immensely.

From the farm, Raffaele took us to an outside café for a drink. We drove through narrow streets that had barely enough room for two small cars to pass. He then drove us around to view the effects of the earthquake. In some cases whole buildings remained as rubble. We also went to a local church to see about fifty life-sized figures of various saints and Jesus Christ. They were quite beautiful and impressive. Later, we visited Vincenzo Luongo and his second wife. His first wife, who passed away a few years earlier, had been Pa's sister, Sabina (Seraphina) Silvia. Vincenzo, who is seventy-nine and partially blind from cataracts, actually cried when he first saw us. Again, we sat around the kitchen table drinking wine and had a most enjoyable visit with the whole group. We then went back to Tommaso's home for the lovely supper I described earlier. After dinner, we went next door to visit with Tommaso's brother, Carmen, and his family. Finally, we drove David back to Avellino and then returned to Taurasi for a good night's sleep.

In the morning, we were awakened by church bells ringing and roosters crowing. Then, at seven o'clock in the morning, the church steeple started to play the most beautiful non-religious music that seemed to echo and rebound throughout the mountains. From our balcony, we could look out at the church and the mountains in the distance—what a lovely experience. After breakfast we returned to Tommaso's farm because Renee wanted to see the little white rabbit again. The Luongo's wanted Renee to take the rabbit with her, but it was just not possible. David decided to come with us the next day to sightsee at Pompeii and Vesuvius, after we had said goodbye to the other relatives. The departure was naturally quite emotional. We all kissed each other a couple of times, and we were all so happy to know how well they had done for themselves by staying in Italy.

Funny Who You Might Meet in Italy

Enzo Antonello
Edited by Sam Migliore

I was born in San Martino di Lupari, in the province of Padua, and came to Canada with my mother in 1931. I returned to Italy for a visit in 1973 and stayed with my aunt and uncle. After meeting other relatives, I decided to visit a second cousin in the next town. My uncle gave me directions—you go this way, that way.... I got on his motorscooter, and off I went. Needless to say, I got lost! I noticed an elderly gentleman walking down the road with the aid of two canes. I asked him for instructions. He told me I had gone too far, and then added: "You're not from around here; I can tell by your accent." I was speaking the dialect. He asked: "Where are you from?" I responded by saying, "North America," and he told me that at one time he had been in Nova Scotia. I said: "That's where I'm from." And, he asked me: "What part of Nova Scotia?" I figured he wouldn't recognize Dominion, so I said, "Sydney." He replied: "That's where I was, not too far from there. I was in Dominion, No. 6." I asked him what year that was, and he said: "1913. I was working in the coal mine and boarding with a woman by the name of Roma Antonello." She was my father's sister; she came to Canada in 1912 with her husband Louis and

Enzo Antonello and family, May 1980. From left: Geraldine (wife), Giovanni (father), Cesira (mother), Lorinda (daughter), Enzo and Alisa (daughter.) Courtesy of Enzo Antonello.

lived in Dominion No. 6 (Donkin). I said: "Gees, that's my aunt." Well, didn't he get all excited. I never did see my cousin. The old fellow took me to his house and introduced me to his family.

It turned out that he was the best man at my aunt and uncle's wedding. My aunt thought he had passed away, and he thought she had passed away. He wrote her a letter which I brought back with me, and they started corresponding again. Now, isn't that something. Small place. What's the population of Italy, maybe 75 million? And we met, just like that.

A Search for One's Roots: An Interview with John Giovannetti and Lynn Billard

Edited by Sam Migliore

In "Early Settlement: The Giovannetti Family in Port Morien," I presented two versions of an account of how Lorenzo Giovannetti first came to Cape Breton in the 19th century. This article builds on this material to focus specifically on the efforts John, Lynn and other family members have made to discover their roots and visit their ancestral home.

[Lynn]: In both stories, Lorenzo landed in St. John's, Newfoundland, and then came here to Cape Breton. He and his brother, Nicodemus, came to Port Morien in the mid-1800s. They appear in the census records for the 1880s and 1890s, so it was sometime before that.[1] While researching at the Beaton Institute, I also found mention of an Anthony Giovannetti. I asked the older relatives, but nobody seemed to have heard of him. According to the census material, he was about sixteen years old in 1890. I found out later that he was Lorenzo and Nicodemus's brother, and that he went back to Italy. There were nine of them in the family, five boys and four girls. I know all of the brothers and sisters names, but I don't know who their parents were.

The Trip to Tereglio

[Lynn]: Our trip to [Europe in the spring of 1996] had a couple of objectives. Dad was in the Second World War; he landed at Juno Beach on D-Day, and he wanted to go back there for a visit. The second objective was to go to Italy. [In Europe], we rented a van and travelled about 6,500 kilometres—from Amsterdam down through Belgium, France and Italy, and then back to Holland through Switzerland and Germany. [Seven family members made the trip.] Dad had told his father that one day he would go to Tereglio. It was quite emotional.

[John]: We drove up to Luca and stayed in a motel for the night. We knew we weren't far from where we were going. The fella at the hotel says: "Well, you got two or three hours before dark, and you are not going to get supper 'til then. Go, it's only seven miles." So, up the mountain we went [to Tereglio]. [Lynn]: The road was as wide as this table [laughs], and there were hairpin turns. We were 600 metres up. [John]: You had to pull in the van mirrors so you wouldn't scrape them on the walls. [Lynn]: And two way traffic [laughs].

[John]: When we got to the top, there was a little parking lot. We had a picture of the woman we wanted to find. There were two people sitting at a table at the corner of the parking lot. We walked over, and there they were. [Sam: They were the people you were looking for?] [Lynn]: Yeah. My sister was going to show them this picture, and it was her. They had no idea we were coming [laughs]. [John]: Hard to believe, yeah.

Lorenzo Giovannetti

Lorenzo Giovannetti was born on June 28, 1834 in Sommoco-lonia, Italy. He was the oldest of nine children. The family moved from Sommocolonia to Tereglio, and Lorenzo remained there until coming to Canada in the 1850s or 1860s. He settled in Port Morien, Nova Scotia, and married Florence Turner (1856-1927) of South Head. Lorenzo and Florence raised a family of eleven children, six girls and five boys. Three children died during childhood. Lorenzo died on June 9, 1907, and is buried in Port Morien.

[Lynn]: Guglielmina Giovannetti Fiori was there with her cousin, Benedette Giovannetti, and his wife, Anna. None of them could speak English, and we couldn't speak Italian. But, they came out with all these pictures that had Dominion, Nova Scotia, on them. Benedette's father, Adolfo, had come to Dominion to barber for a short time. He was with Angelo Giovannetti in Dominion.... Anyway, he didn't stay. They showed us a letter written by the Italian Consular Agent in Sydney asking for safe passage for Adolfo, who was very young at the time. He travelled to Hull, Quebec, I believe, to board a boat for France and then to Italy. They had all kinds of documents. I wish I had a photocopier. [laughs]

Dad looked at one of the pictures, and said: "That's Lorenzo." [John]: My grandfather. First time I had ever seen him. I don't know why, but I knew it was him. [Lynn]: Because he looked just like your father. It was such a strong resemblance. Then [Claudia Lucchesi] arrived. She could speak English. [John]: She was a distant cousin. [Lynn]: She translated for us and, the next day, she spent the whole day with us. Guglielmina told her the Italian version of the story of how Lorenzo came to Canada, and she wrote it out for us in English. It was really great, but we didn't have enough time.... I would have loved to find out more, but, at least we made the connection. I have the address, and I will write to Claudia. She knows enough English to be able to pass on our hellos to the other relatives. The next trip, we will definitely go to Sommocolonia, visit the church there, and try to get more information.

[John]: I missed the best part. I couldn't go to the graveyard. [Lynn]: You see, he was in a wheelchair; his heart is very bad. [John]: I can't walk. [Lynn]: These little hill top villages are very steep, all cobble stone. Just getting Dad from the parking lot to Guglielmina's house was quite a feat. And, it was raining. So Dad stayed at the house while we went to the graveyard with Benedette. The graveyard was on the side of the mountain in a walled-in area.

There are lots of things that I would follow up on [for the next trip]. As we walked through the main street of the village, Benedette pointed out a green door. He said: "Mamma, Pappa, Casa Pappa." That was his father's home.... I didn't put much into it because we were under the impression that Guglielmina's home was the house my great-grandfather had lived in. It wasn't; this house with the green door was the original home. The letter my grandmother received from Dad's uncle, when my grandfather died, described the house. It said that the year, I think it was 1745, was on the doorway, and I remember seeing that over the green door. But, I didn't connect the two at that time.

[Sam: So, how long did you spend there?] [John]: Not long enough! No. We spent another day there with them. They treated us to a dinner that you wouldn't believe. [Lynn]: Every Giovannetti in the village was there, and we were so over-whelmed. It was so frustrating not knowing the language ... it's such a disability. We had so much we wanted to know, but there was only one person [Claudia] who could interpret, and she was quite busy. You can imagine. [John]: We were lucky, though, one girl could speak French. My oldest daughter, Sherry, and her husband speak good French, so they got along famously. She knew what was going on, and who was who.... [Lynn]: We still didn't get it all sorted out, though. Not to my satisfaction. But

John Giovannetti, ca. 1970. Courtesy of Giovannetti family.

certainly, if I go to Italy again, I will know where I'm going and where I'm going to stay. It's not all strange anymore.

I kept a journal of the trip. I was reading it to Dad the other day and found it very emotional just talking about it. You can't imagine what those days in Tereglio meant to us. You can't even put your feelings down on paper a lot of the time—the feeling of just being there, walking the same streets our ancestors had walked. The streets are the same now as they were then; nothing has changed, I'm sure. The travel diary is wonderful; I hope I never lose it because it's just a special document.

Sample Excerpts from Lynn's Diary

April 28, 1996

Passed through Genoa, the port from which Lorenzo Giovannetti (my great grandfather) and Christopher Columbus sailed. This is a land of hills, valleys, bridges and tunnels.

April 28, 1996   Tereglio, Italy

When we first met our Italian relatives Benedette and Anna Giovannetti and Guglielmina (Giovannetti) Fiori, they showed us many pictures. Some were of Lorenzo and others that were printed in Sydney and North Sydney. There were also postcards from Angelo Giovannetti from Dominion. It was so strange to see these pieces of home here in Italy.

April 29, 1996

I wish we could spend many more days in Tereglio. There are so many questions to ask. However, I feel very fortunate to have been able to visit this beautiful village of my ancestors. I have walked the same steps that my great grandfather would have walked more than 150 years ago. A trip of a lifetime and a dream come true. I would love to return to Tereglio one day. Maybe, God willing.

This Christmas's Gift to Everyone is the Joy of Having Lived to 100[1]

Paul Palango

My grandfather's name is Christmas. It was on Christmas Day in 1888 that he was born, and his mother called him Natale. It is Italian for Christmas. On this Christmas Day, he will give his family in Hamilton, a present to remember always. For Natale Palango is 100 years old tomorrow. "I've been very fortunate," he says, squinting through his thick glasses. "I've lived a good, long life. I've looked after myself, and I am very happy to have lived this long. Canada has been a good country to me and my family." Indeed it has.

Before the First World War, more than a million Italians left Italy for the new world. My grandfather was one of the first to come here. The son of shepherd Vincenzo Palanca and Rigetta Conti, he came from a hamlet of twenty stone houses called Tellacane in the rugged province of Ascoli Piceno. It is in the region known as The Marches, northeast of Rome near the Adriatic Sea. It was in 1905, and he was seventeen. He borrowed money from a cousin who had been to America and booked passage on a leaky ship called the *Irena*. "When you were a boy in Italy, everyone talked about America, nobody knew what Canada was," he says. Canada, itself, was just thirty-eight.

Landfall in America was Ellis Island, New York City. There he joined the hordes of immigrants from across Europe, who were herded into stalls, stripped, examined and processed. When he put his clothes back on, he had a new name, Pelango. (Later, it would be altered to Palango by two of his daughters who wanted to soften the way it was being pronounced.) But he didn't care about things like that. "The man at the immigration said to me, "Is this your name?" I said it was because I didn't want to cause any trouble and maybe be sent back to Italy. Once accepted, he had a choice between living with a cousin in Pennsylvania or with another on Cape Breton Island. He chose Sydney Mines, and just like that his descendants ended up Canadian.

Natale Palango, 100th birthday.
Photo by Thomas Szlukoveny, the
Globe and Mail. *Courtesy of Paul*
Palango.

The house he and his cousin, Pasquale Tortola, built for $200 still stands on Atlantic Street in Sydney Mines, across from where the old steel mill used to be. That was where he met my grandmother, Mary Sarah, the imposing five-foot, nine-inch daughter of two-fisted Scottish-born mill superintendent, Allan MacLellan, and his Nova Scotia-born wife, Mary Kennedy. Mary Sarah was eighteen. Nat made twenty-five cents an hour, could barely speak English and had had one day of schooling in Italy. "There was nothing to do that day with the sheep, so my father sent me to the school in Acquasanta to see what it was like. It wasn't for me."

He and Mary Sarah were married on November 22, 1911. "We didn't tell anyone about it and got married early in the morning. Her father saw the wedding carriage and went to work laughing," my grandfather says with a glint in his eye. "He told everyone: 'I just saw someone getting married, on a Wednesday! Imagine getting married on a Wednesday!'" Mr. MacLellan didn't realize that it was his daughter who was in the carriage. "I got fired after the wedding," Nat recalls.

Mary and Nat would have five children in Nova Scotia. The first, Elizabeth, died at eighteen months. The next year the First World War broke out, and he found himself in the Cape Breton Highlanders, thereby becoming the first and only Palango to wear a kilt. For three years he cooked for the troops in England.

In 1923, as so many Maritimers were to do, Nat headed down the road to Ontario, the land of opportunity. He got a job at the massive Hilton Works of the Steel Company of Canada (Stelco) in Hamilton. His Stelco career began in the Dickensian hell of the No. 1 open hearth shop. Thirty-five years later, in 1958, he retired. His last job was skullcracker, the skulls being the molds on ingot castings which were broken open by a heavy iron ball being dropped on them. Today, he makes more from his Stelco pension, $212 a month, than he did on the job.

In Hamilton he settled his family down right next to Stelco in a neighbourhood called Brightside. It was anything but. Built on land reclaimed from Burlington Bay, its streets were named after English mill towns. In a country where the English and the French were top dogs, Brightside was home for those newer Canadians—Panek, Camiletti ... Gallo ... Codispodi ... Giavedoni ... Murmylyk ... Procop, and the Palangos and their Cape Breton cousins, the MacDonalds.

In a succession of three homes in Brightside, my grandparents would have five more children, including my father, the quintessential Scottish-Italian-Canadian, Arnold Gordon Palango. The nine children would provide thirty-two grandchildren, forty-one great-grandchildren and one great-great grandchild, Paul Maiero.

In Brightside, my grandfather says, they started out poor and got poorer. In the Thirties they moved from 37 Sheffield to 155 Birmingham Street. They rented it cheap from a bootlegger. The Palangos still refer to that house as the air-conditioned one. My uncle Joe recalls: "I remember waking up and saying to one of my brothers, "Geez, there's a lot of snow. I wonder how much there is outside." And everyone laughs. They always laugh. "We were poor," my grandfather remembers, "but we didn't need a lot. We made do with what we had. If we needed food, we grew it, or we caught it. We used screen-door traps to catch blackbirds and starlings and then we would roast them on a spit. And we had fun. I don't think people today have fun like we did."

The nine-room house at 64 Lancaster Street, at the corner of Plymouth St., is the one I remember. The lot cost $175 and my grandfather built the house for $4,600 in 1941. Uncles, aunts, grandchildren and friends would go there almost every Sunday, and the former army cook would feed dozens of us at a time. Easily. His grandchildren called him Choo Choo Grandpa. We all remember how exciting it was to be in the house when the empty ore cars were being humped into trains in the yard across the street. A crash would shake you out of your sleep and, sometimes, out of your bed. The smoke from the old steam engines would get right up into your nose, and the soot stuck in your pores. And we didn't care. Just twenty-seven years after it was built, the house was expropriated as the steel company took over and flattened the neighbourhood. Brightside had served its purpose. It is now a parking lot.

My grandfather likes to say that he led a clean life, a careful life. He never ran a step. He walked everywhere. He didn't drink tap water for thirty-five years. Those are secrets of long life, he says. That's how he got to be one hundred. But that's not the whole story. As my father put it the other day: "He defied all the laws of good health. He lived as close to the pollution as you could get. He grew all his vegetables and much of his fruit in the shadow of the steel mill. He drank homemade wine every day. He smoked those stinky Marca Gallo stogies 'til you couldn't breathe in the house. And he ate everything that was put in front of him, except desserts. He was never really fond of dessert."

Among the many blows visited upon him—bouts with skin cancer; abdominal surgery in his mid-90s; the loss of his wife, who suffered a stroke on November 19, 1963, and died on January 26, 1964; the death of a son, and the deaths of so many friends and loved ones—none was a knockout. "All the people I used to know are dead. I've buried all my friends," he used to say. But his disposition was so sweet that over the years he attracted hundreds of new friends, many of them only a third his age.

Nat has had a strong sense of independence and believed he was too young for a senior citizens' home. Now he is spending his third Christmas in Macassa Lodge, after giving up the basement apartment downtown that he moved into when he was ninety-two. As he takes you on a tour of Macassa Lodge, he says, without irony: "There are a helluva lot of old people here."

In his century, Natale Palango has gone from being a shepherd in an isolated, virtu-ally medieval society to being a pampered senior citizen in one of the world's most progressive societies. He has been a witness to all the technological advances that most people now take for granted. The biggest change he has noticed, however, is in the people. "It began after the last war. The soldiers came home, and it wasn't very long before the young people were the bosses. When they became the boss, everything changed. Now, the young kids are the boss." He can't understand why there is so much greed, waste and pretentiousness today. "People don't know how to make do anymore," he says. "There is no humility. Everyone wants to be a show off. Everyone wants to be a big shot...."

Fifteen years ago, my grandfather bought the suit he was going to be buried in. He wore that out and bought another. He is now on his third burial suit and concedes that, yes, he might have been a little melodramatic about his demise. The greatest secret of his long life may have been in his blood. His mother lived to ninety-eight and his father to ninety-six. His brother lived to ninety-nine, two of his five sisters to ninety-six, and two others to ninety-five. (The fifth sister broke her back and died at sixty.) He had an uncle who died at one hundred and seven. At one hundred, Nat's hands are worn and blue, but his memory is stunningly sharp.

Last Sunday, his family held an open house at the Knights of Columbus Hall in east-end Hamilton to celebrate his birthday. There were citations from a host of political leaders, and even one from the Pope. Four hundred people showed up. Typically, the night before Nat had called his seventy-two-year-old daughter, Nora, and told her to get to bed early because she had a big day ahead of her. The day of the event, there he was for five hours sitting at the door in his wheelchair, occasionally standing up, greeting people he hadn't seen for years. "He's absolutely amazing," said visitor Albert Ricci. "I've met him only two or three times in my life, but he looks at me, squints and then says, 'Yeah, I know you. You're Lou Falco's grandfather.'"

That day my grandfather had on that soft, true smile of his, once again flashing the teeth he bought for $82 in 1946. His great-grandchildren, including my Lindsay and Virginia, were amazed that anyone could live to be one hundred, and even more amazed, they could be related to someone that old. They all touched and hugged and kissed the rare bird and got their pictures taken doing so.

For my grandfather, tomorrow is not just another Christmas Day. For the past three years, he has had it in his sights, not taking any chances, pacing himself to the goal. You can see in his old eyes the victory he feels. He has won the last game worth winning and says he is not afraid to die. Maybe he'll make 107 like his uncle, he says, but from now on everything will be taken day by day. It's all gravy.

"Merry Christmas...," the visitors said to him one by one as they left the Knights of Columbus Hall. It could have gone without saying. "...and a Happy New Year."

That, too.

Natale Palango passed away in 1989, a short time before what would have been his 101st birthday.

Memories of Yesterday and Today: A Talk with Theresa Della Vella and Nunzi Martinello

Edited by Sam Migliore

[Theresa]: My father, Giuseppe Serventi, landed in New York in 1906. Alone! It was from there that he sent for my mother (Maria Verdi).[1] They stayed there until their oldest child was born, and a few years later, my father heard about this boom in Halifax. Work! A lot of Italians were leaving for Halifax, so my parents went too. They stayed there for a few years, and then the talk turned to the steel plant here in Sydney. So my father made the move, and we have been here ever since. My parents raised a family of eight. Pappa worked in the steel plant for a good many years, while my mother was a homemaker. She grew us up, and everybody made their role in life. Pappa suffered a stroke, and that was the end of his working days at the plant. He was sick at home for about seven years; my mother and I cared for him until he passed away.

We have had good times and sad times. There were several tragedies. Family members have passed away. Mamma passed away when she was ninety-three. And, there were good times. The Italians would get together in each other's homes. Nobody had cars, there was no television then, maybe a phone or two, but everybody would visit and be so united, you know. We had a happy childhood. We were never in want. Our parents insisted that we go to school. Some of us reached to finish school, some of us didn't. But, we had enough to read and write and to know right from wrong. And, that pretty well sums it up.

[Nunzi]: Well, my father, Tony Del Vecchio, was from Casserta. He came to Canada around 1900. Pappa met my mother, Maria Artabano, here in Sydney. Mamma came from Naples to join her two brothers, but she lived with the Cozzolino family on Dorchester Street until she married Pappa. The Cozzolinos watched over her because she was only young when she came here. At that time, they didn't even have streets in town; it was all dirt roads. My parents married and had a family of nine. Five died when they were young; and, of the living, I was the only girl.

Now, I don't have the whole story, but my parents moved to New Brunswick for a while. They were there for a few years, and then they came back here. One of my uncles had a bakery in the Pier and the other one had a bakery in Glace Bay. My father moved to the Pier and started a grocery store and a bakery. All the Italian people used to come and shop there. It was their meeting place. The store had much more Italian products than you can buy in Sydney today. We had a wonderful life, really, because we were meeting all the people. It was really nice, compared to today. There are not that many Italians around today.

The Grocery Store and Bakery. [Nunzi]: Pappa used to give people credit. When the pay cheques came in, they would pay their bills. He used to pull out the large Italian cigars, Marca Gallo, and offer them to the men; and, to the women, he would offer a wedge of watermelon. So he would make so much from the sales, and then return a little something back to people through these gifts. [Theresa]: They also delivered bread daily by horse and buggy. Fresh bread! I remember that well. [Nunzi]: We would buy things wholesale from Johnny Martinello's Italian wholesale store. The Italian foods came from Montreal or Italy. [Theresa]: They carried the green olive oil imported from Italy, all the lines of pasta, salami ... sausages.... [Nunzi]: Pickled peppers. Oh, everything. Now, I'll tell you something else. Marconi, when he came to Glace Bay, shopped at my father's store.

Gathering Coal in Whitney Pier. [Theresa]: In those days, they would bring coal from the mines to the steel plant. [Nunzi]: The railway tracks were in the back of the houses. When the trains passed, the coal would drop off the cars. People would go with buckets to pick up the pieces. [Theresa]: It was a means of providing warmth for the house. They would either burn wood or coal. There was no such thing as furnaces back then. Besides the kitchen coal stoves, people had those little potbelly stoves in the hall, or a bedroom, to give a little extra heat. So, the kids would go gather the coal. And not just kids! I'm sure my father did too and my brothers. I remember. Some kids would fill bags of coal and sell them for a few pennies. There would be lots of coal on the tracks; sometimes it would be heaped high. It was a way of life for some people; they would fill bags, haul them home, and use the coal to heat their homes.

The Piano. [Theresa]: Nunzi's family was the only one in our area that had a piano. [Nunzi]: It was a player piano, and every Sunday night we'd have a ball. Our home was a gathering place. Theresa's niece and Gerry Giorno would sing. And, we played cards together for years. My mother loved company; she loved having people around. [Theresa]: I used to love going over and pretending that I was playing the piano. Yeah, I remember those Sunday nights.

Having Family Away

[Theresa]: My daughter and her husband were working here in Sydney for little or nothing. There was nothing here. Now, one of my daughter's friends had married a fella from up Ontario, and they had gone to live there. The factories were booming in Ontario at that time. So, sure enough, my son-in-law and my daughter made the move. They stayed with her friend until they got their own apartment. They started to work and eventually bought a home. So, that's how she is up there. It was because of the work.

[Nunzi]: But, Theresa, don't you think that they all did better by leaving here? [Theresa]: Oh, definitely! As the years have gone by, this place has gotten worse, and worse. [Nunzi]: Yes, right! They are all well established there. Good jobs. [Theresa]: Great life. Now, if they were here, where would they end up? Nothing! They had to leave for work. My daughter is in Hamilton, and my son is near Toronto. They have been out there every bit of twenty-five to thirty years. My daughter has two daughters, and they are married and have children of their own. There are grandchildren there for her and great grandchildren for me. They are getting along fine.

[Nunzi]: I have a daughter in Oakville, Ontario, and another one in New Jersey. [Theresa]: They are married, have families, and they are settled there. They come back for visits, but they wouldn't want to move here. [Nunzi]: No, the girls wouldn't move back here, but my son, Bob, is here. He worked in Montreal and Toronto for a while, but he came back. He runs the clothing business on Charlotte Street, the Oak Hall. But, most young people don't stay here. [Theresa]: No, they are going, going and still going.

A Town in the Life of Maria Razzolini

By Jan Gentile and A. Evo DiPierro

Although Maria Filomena Razzolini and her family relocated from Dominion to Dartmouth in 1968 (as a result of her husband's employment), her memories of the little town in Cape Breton remain quite vivid. Mrs. Razzolini's experiences as a young girl in Dominion were somewhat different than those of her Italian friends. Her parents exposed her to a blend of Italian and Belgian culture. Federico Sanvido, Maria's father, came to Canada in 1920, at the age of seventeen, from the province of Treviso Caselle D'Altivole, Italy. Her mother, Renelle Thomas, came from Belgium with her family in 1923; she was only eleven years old at the time. Maria was their only child. She was educated in Dominion and, up until the time of her marriage to Esperando (Buster) Razzolini of New Waterford, she worked as a bookkeeper at a bakery in Glace Bay. The Razzolinis have one daughter, Esperanza Maria (Razzolini) Crook, author of *All Our Fathers: The North Italian Community in Industrial Cape Breton*.

During their marriage of forty-five years, Mrs. Razzolini busied herself as a home-maker, while her husband worked for the federal government. Now retired, Maria and Esperando reside in Dartmouth while their daughter lives with her family in western Canada. Maria's father died in 1955, at the age of fifty-two, and her mother left Dominion in 1959 to live in Ontario. The long absence of the Sanvido-Razzolini family from Cape Breton, however, has not decreased Mrs. Razzolini's feelings of attachment to her childhood home.

In Dominion, Mr. Sanvido was one of the founding members of the Italian Community Hall. The hall was an important part of Maria's upbringing. She spent a great deal of time there during the period that her family rented the back rooms as temporary living quarters. Because the hall was such an important part of her father's life, Mrs. Razzolini explains that she still senses his presence within its walls.

The social things at the Italian Hall were a big thing back then. People got together more ... it was like a happy time.... I remember there would be at least one or two picnics each year. A couple of bus loads of people went "down to the Meadows," and everyone took their food. There was music and sometimes a place to swim.... My father ran a lot of the functions at the hall. In fact, to repay the organization, he worked in the hall. It was a big part of his life, and he enjoyed being a part of it. They would have banquets, and he did a lot of running around for that. He made a bocce lane beside the hall. Every Sunday, during summer, the men would be there; they would do a little step and a yell, and I used to laugh when I watched them—grown men running around, but they enjoyed it. When I go to the Italian Hall, even though it has changed, I can still see my father there.

From left: Mrs. Renelle (Thomas) Sanvido, Mrs. Mazzocca, Mrs. Assunta Coretta (?), Mrs. Zorzi, Mrs. Ravanello, Mrs. Antonello. Courtesy of Maria Razzolini.

Mrs. Razzolini also recalls some of the problems that went along with being the child of immigrant parents. While the Italians of Dominion were supportive of each other, some non-Italian children teased her because of her unusual name and lifestyle. For example, because Italians enjoy salad (such as lettuce and dandelion greens) with their meals, some non-Italian children made fun of their liking for "grass." But nowadays, salad is a main staple of the average Canadian diet. Over time, attitudes gradually changed as Italians and non-Italians became better acquainted. Mrs. Razzolini remembers an English Canadian friend who lived next door to her home, and who was fascinated by Maria's Italian ways. Today they are still in touch and share each other's ethnic experiences.

Then came the Second World War and, along with some other Italian men, Maria's father-in-law, Rodolfo Razzolini, was taken away by the RCMP.

They were gone for two and one-half years and were not seen [during that time]. I don't think they fully understood what went on. They were fairly well treated, and letters going in and out were censored. The families had to make do, and the community would help. My husband helped his mother in the shoe shop where she worked, and then he got a job in the coal mines, and that helped too. He also had three older sisters and two younger brothers at the time. He was called up for the military, but because his father was taken away, he couldn't go. Strange, that at the time, they would take the father away, and he would be called up to go [into the service].

Federico Sanvido (first from left, seated). Courtesy of Maria Razzolini.

The RCMP arrested Rodolfo Razzolini and seized his hunting rifles. Before leaving, they told the family that Rodolfo was being taken away "for his own protection."

Today, Maria seems to have few regrets as she reflects on her past. She feels fortunate in having two diverse ethnic backgrounds. She also is thankful for the close relationship she had with her maternal grandmother, Honorine Thomas.

My grandmother [used to say that,] in the beginning, it was hard [here in Canada] because she did not have the language. Everything was so different. In Belgium, during winter, she could wear just a shawl over her shoulders, but in this country, she had to wear winter coats. That shawl was one of the things she kept, and I have it now. I think she kept it because it was a part of the times she knew. She was a good seamstress, and my grandfather worked in the coal mines. Everyone worked in the mines at the time. She adjusted ... they all did.

Mrs. Razzolini learned to cook both Belgian dishes (with the help of her grandmother) and to prepare Italian food. Although Maria's parents taught her to appreciate her two ethnic backgrounds, they reminded her of how lucky she was to be Canadian. Her father worked hard to build a life for himself and his family here in Canada.

Mrs. Razzolini misses certain aspects of her youth, especially exposure to different languages and friendly interaction with other Italian women in Dominion. The Razzolinis, however, have been able to maintain a strong connection to Cape Breton, and they occasionally return for visits. Maria sometimes surprises herself with the amount of Italian she has retained and, understandably, feels a flood of emotions whenever she hears the language spoken. Although she notices various changes with each visit (the passing of an old friend, or the disappearance of another home), the town of Dominion will always hold fond memories for her— memories that resurface each time she revisits the town.

How I got to Arizona from Sydney, Nova Scotia

Paul Alexander Diekelmann

Alessandro (Alex) Martinello and Maria Josephine Albano of Sydney, Nova Scotia, had four children: Nicholas, Harry, Angela and Marie (Minnie). Nicholas died at age sixteen of complications from diphtheria. Harry worked as a chemist for the Ford Motor Company in Windsor, Ontario. Angela married Joseph Blaquire and moved to Los Angeles, California. While Minnie went to Chicago, Illinois, sometime around 1930, where she married an American, Paul Bernhard Diekelmann.

I was born in Chicago on October 6, 1932. Minnie returned with me (her blue-eyed, blond-haired son) to the Italian community in Sydney when I was approximately two years old. She divorced my father in 1936 because he was imprisoned for a twenty-year jail term in Joliet, Illinois. We moved into the Martinello home on Charlotte Street and lived with my grandparents. From information that I gleaned growing up, my grandfather, Alex Martinello, was not very accepting of the situation; he believed that my mother had me out of wedlock. Consequently, she was tolerated, but not entirely welcomed, at home.

Sometime around 1937, a new young immigrant from Italy, Giuseppi (Joe) Renzi, caught my mother's eye. He was working as a shoe repairer at Nardocchio's Shoe Repair Shop. They began to date and, during that period, for some unknown reason, I was placed at the Little Bras d'Or Catholic Orphanage. I think I was about three years old. I recall Joe Renzi and my mother coming to visit and taking me for Sunday drives. I remained at the orphanage for three years.

Joe and my mother were married April 13, 1939, by a United Church minister in Reserve Mines, Nova Scotia. Somehow, my mother was able to persuade her father to lend Joe Renzi about $8,000 to open his own shoe repair shop. The shop prospered from 1940 through to 1945. Thousands of U.S. sailors came through the Sydney area during that time. The ships docked in Sydney harbour heading for ports unknown. I worked as a shoe shine boy after school and on weekends, from age eight to eighteen, and learned the shoe repair business.

Three children were born to Joe and Minnie Renzi: one died at birth; my half-sister Angela was born on November 4, 1941; and, my half-brother Joseph was born on January 12, 1943. Angela is a homemaker married to Bruce Cummings, a retired Vice-President of Detroit National Bank; they live in Grosse Pointe Farms, Michigan. Joe is a Director of the Nova Scotia Gaming Control Commission Security and a retired RCMP constable. He and his wife Jean live in Halifax.

Between 1947 and 1950, I attended Sydney Academy. I dropped out of school, however, without completing the final exams for grade eleven. From 1950 through 1954, I worked at the shoe repair shop and held short-term positions at other locations. I also taught piano accordion lessons at the Hawaiian School of Music on Charlotte Street. This is where I met my wife-to-be, Mary Margaret Antonia (Toni) Dennis, in 1953. She is the daughter of Margaret and Leonard Dennis of Sydney. Mrs. Dennis passed away February 2, 1998, at age ninety-three; Leonard predeceased her in 1969.

On June 9, 1951, my grandfather, Alex Martinello, passed away from congestive heart failure.

During the Second World War and the years that followed, I expressed a desire to be a tail gunner on a bomber. Apparently, I was influenced, along with many other boys, by constant exposure to the many wartime films, radio programs and news reports. By 1954, I was ready to leave Sydney to join the Air Force. My mother, however, suggested I go to Chicago to visit my father's family and to enlist in the service there. I agreed. She gave me $35 and a train ticket. So, in December of 1954, the Renzi family escorted me to the Sydney train station where I boarded a train bound for Chicago.

In Chicago, I met the Diekelmann family—including my father, who had been released from prison in 1952 after serving sixteen years of his sentence. I didn't know him, so the meeting was more a first-time acquaintance rather than an emotional father-son reunion. On January 18, 1955, I enlisted in the U.S. Air Force. I was assigned to Lackland Air Force Base (AFB) in San Antonio, Texas, for basic training and career placement. Although I scored in the top 5 per cent of my class in radio communications, the Air Force needed weather observers, so I was assigned in May of 1955 to the Weather School at Rantoul AFB, Illinois. While there, I asked sixteen-year-old Toni to marry me. Her mother paid the plane fare, and we married on July 16, 1955, at Rantoul AFB Chapel No. 3.

On July 10, 1955, my grandmother, Maria Josephine (Albano) Martinello passed away due to loneliness and age.

I graduated at the bottom of the class in Weather School. Those who placed high in the class had their choice of bases for assignment. The final two choices were Newfoundland and Hawaii. I picked Newfoundland because it was closer to Sydney and our families. However, the other guy had higher marks, and he wanted Newfoundland. So, I was left with Hawaii by default. Toni and I spent four-and-one-half years living in Honolulu (Hickam AFB). Two of our daughters, Margaret and Pauline, were born there.

I left the Air Force in June of 1959, and we returned to Sydney. We stayed at the Dennis home while I applied for work. By September, my mother started to worry that I would be unemployed forever, so we left the children with Mrs. Dennis, and I went to Boston to re-enlist in the service. I was assigned to Tinker AFB, in Oklahoma. We had two more children, a boy and a girl, in Oklahoma. Both died from Rh complications.

On October 13, 1961, I was assigned to Howard AFB in the Panama Canal Zone. While there a daughter, Josephine Anne (Joanne), was born in 1964.

During my assignments in Hawaii, Oklahoma and Panama, I took advantage of various military education opportunities. Toni and I completed high school in Hawaii, and I began to take courses at various American universities. I was awarded a Bachelor of Arts degree with majors in History and Psychology from Florida State University in 1965.

In March of 1967, I was accepted for training as a Program Representative in the expanding Syphilis Eradication Program with the U.S. Public Health Service, Centre of Disease Control (CDC). I was honourably discharged from the Air Force, having served twelve years and three months, and began my work assignment in Charlotte, North Carolina. I received training in microscopy, contact interviewing and disease identification at the CDC, and began my career working with Public Health Officials and Physicians in western North Carolina. My job was to identify, interview and advise on treatment of persons infected with and exposed to syphilis.

My mother, Marie (Minnie) Martinello, passed away in 1968, at the age of sixty-four.

I stayed with the Syphilis Eradication Program for two years. I later transferred to the Immunization Program of the CDC. As part of my new duties, I helped set up children's rubella immunization programs in towns and cities across North Carolina. Then, in 1971, I was transferred to Albuquerque, New Mexico, to establish and promote immunization programs statewide. During this assignment, I enrolled in the University of Oklahoma Adult Graduate Program. In 1972, I received a Masters in Public Administration. I also joined the New Mexico National

Guard and was assigned as the NCO in charge of Nuclear, Chemical and Biological Warfare training.

In 1973, I accepted a position as Field Operations Manager with the New Mexico Department of Health in Santa Fe. I was one of two operations managers who travelled the State assisting in the centralization of local health departments and the training of health officers in management techniques. That October, I accepted a position as an administrator with the Arizona Department of Health, Maternal and Child Health Services. I also joined the Arizona Air National Guard.

In 1977, I became the Chief of Arizona's Sexually Transmissible Disease Program. I remained in that position until I resigned in 1983. That year I also retired from the National Guard, having completed enough points and years to receive full military retirement benefits when I reached age sixty. From 1983 to 1993, I served as the Records System Administrator with the Clerk's Office of the Superior Court of Maricopa County. During that period, I continued my studies. I now have a non-accredited PhD in Public Health Administration and Certification from both the Institute of Financial Planning and the International Institute of Records Management.

Giuseppi (Joe) Renzi passed away in November of 1986.

In March of 1993, at age sixty-one, I accepted early retirement from my position at the Clerk's Office. I then enrolled in an Associate Degree Program in Paralegal Studies at a private college and graduated in 1995. I established my own home-based business in Tempe, Arizona, as a financial planner. Toni has had a book-keeping and tax business for twenty-five years. I offer her clients financial, trust and paralegal services. I have also taught Public Health undergraduate courses for Northern Arizona University in Phoenix, and intensive graduate courses for Golden Gate University, San Francisco, for their local military base extension classes.

Sometime in 1988, my daughter, Pauline, and I purchased jointly forty-three acres of land in Upper Baddeck, Nova Scotia. Pauline resides in Arizona with us. She is a City of Tempe Police Officer, who expects to retire with twenty years of service in the year 2003. She loves Cape Breton. Since 1990, we have been renovating the 130-year-old Scottish farmhouse on the property. And, for the past three years, from June through October, Toni and I have been returning to Cape Breton to both work on the house and visit with our daughter, Margaret, and two grandchildren in Louisbourg. We then return to Arizona to continue our businesses.

The goal seems to be to move to Baddeck when the house is ready. Returning to Cape Breton had never been in my plan for retirement. But it looks like "the best laid plans of mice and men do go oft astray."

A Second Generation Italian American of Cape Breton

Constance deRoche

Edited by Margaret Dorazio-Migliore

Earlier this year, sitting across from Connie deRoche at her kitchen table, I asked this lively woman questions about her life. Maybe too many questions! Connie is a very private person, and as I left her home, Connie jokingly said something like,"now you know more about me than anyone else in the entire world!"

I wish I could have taken a photograph of her in her kitchen that day. An April storm had left the streets snowy and the air chilled. Inside her Sydney home, however, everything was aglow with a golden warmth. Connie herself seemed content, radiant with charm, wit and wisdom, and she inspired me to think more about my own Italian roots. To begin with, I told Connie that what I'd be most interested in knowing about was her life. I knew she had spent the last twenty-five years in Cape Breton, but I also wanted to know what it was like where she grew up.... I asked her, "You spent all of your early life in Boston ... what was it like growing up there?"

I grew up in the north end of Boston, which was 99.9 per cent or more, Italian. Most of the people were Southern Italians or South-Central Italians. They were from Campania, Abruzzi, Sicily, and Calabria. The community was very crowded. The homes were four and five storey walk-up flats, apartments being four to five rooms each, and the families having maybe three to four children, on the average.

The community was seen from the outside as being a slum, and in fact it didn't have all the amenities. Maybe, relative to rural Cape Breton at the time, it would have seemed plush, but relative to urban American standards it wasn't. I can still remember in the 1950s, maybe early 1960s, some people didn't have baths or showers. We had a public bathhouse. That'll give some of the flavour of the community.

It was poor, and it was known to be poor, and people who lived there thought of it as poor. But in terms of the social environment, it was just the opposite. It was very rich, because people had relatives in the vicinity; they had neighbours, and many of the neighbours were people who were from the same village. So they were surrounded by *paesani!*

One of the big themes that I think is important to second generation Italians, as well as immigrants, is the ambivalence that you're made to feel about your home culture. Italians, like southern and eastern Europeans generally, were looked down upon by North Americans. You learn those attitudes. You know that you're seen as living in a slum, that you're poor but more than that, that you're seen as being somehow culturally inferior. You don't know the manners, you're not sophisticated, or your family's not stylish. I think there's a whole array of ways in which people come to know they're seen as inferior. And so I think there's a lot of ambivalence.

There's ambivalence to begin with, because the immigrants, being largely from the south, were second-class citizens at home. They were "economic immigrants." They came to better themselves, to have a better life. They understood that their economic, their material lives, were limited at home. They were relatively un-educated—which is not to say stupid or incapable of doing things—but in formal terms they were uneducated. And they knew they were from backwater kinds of places. So basically I think what you have is a bunch of people who've already suffered prejudice, who are coming to a place where they're going to suffer preju-dice. Beyond that, in order to fit into the new society, and to achieve your material goals, you have to become more like the host society. In effect, you have to give up something of your own lifeways. So to the extent that you're successful, you're ambivalent. And you lose some of your culture. I think that's a big theme in my life—not in my life uniquely or particularly—but it's a big theme in my life, be-cause I'm second-generation Italian.

When I was growing up, what the people around me consciously wanted was to live the "American Dream:" to get a house in the suburbs, where they had a little land, could park a car and grow a garden. And to have their children free from the kind of heavy, dirty work of their parents, and move on to white-collar jobs and get a little social status. Most of the fathers, the immigrants, worked as labour-ers in construction or worked in factories. If the women worked, they worked in sweatshops, doing sewing. They didn't want that for their children.

They wanted something better for us, but that meant we became different. While I think the kinship ties remained strong—they did for me—I think you become a kind of person your parents don't quite understand. And you can't quite under-stand them. So to the extent that our parents were successful in getting what they wanted for us, they were part of a process which required some cultural loss. Like most second-generation people, I learned to understand Italian, but not speak it.

That's part of becoming Americanized or Canadianized. As I said, I wasn't alone. I'm not the only one by any means. I think that's been the general experience. You're embarrassed to speak the language and to be seen as being too Italian. You lose a tremendous opportunity in those early years to learn the language, to learn the culture, to an extent that you can't recapture.

Most of us at school were second-generation. There was the occasional immigrant. We called them "greasers," and we thought of them as inferior, in part, because in order to learn English, they were put back a grade or more. So they would always be a little bit older, and a little bit more awkward and out of place. So you have a ten year old doing grade two work. Without thinking, people see that person as being stupid, not just being impeded by language.

When the little Italian nun came to teach us Italian, nobody did their homework. Nobody paid attention, partly, because she was the housekeeping nun. She wasn't a teacher. And that gave you the impression that Italian wasn't a serious part of the curriculum. Even if she had been a regular teacher, I don't think that kids would have taken Italian seriously, because we were supposed to be becoming American. As I said, there was a big cost there.

The only kids who weren't 100 per cent Italian were 50 per cent Italian. A few men or women had married non-Italians and brought them home. There were about fifty of us in a class, and there were two classes in the school, and that was one of four schools. So, if you think of the number of children ... and I can remember just two or three families that were only half Italian.

But I had a different experience as well, which I suppose drew me away from the ethnic community more than my peers. There were three Catholic schools and a public school. Most kids went to the Catholic schools, and the nuns would choose a few of the most studious and successful students, and send them to high schools that were more academic. Oddly enough, in the case of the boys, there was an academic high school in the community. So they could stay home and still be routed into a college stream and into the middle class. The studious girls, though, were sent to schools outside the community, because the local high school, which most of the Italian girls attended, was oriented to clerical courses. This was in the late 1950s and early 1960s, and that would have been a kind of transitional time for girls. Most girls were doing clerical courses. So when the nuns wanted to give a little bit of a push to the more studious ones, they'd send them to high schools outside the community. I really didn't think of this gender difference much, until I started to think about being Italian for this interview.

I started to realize the irony of it. It's really women, I think, who keep the family "ethnic," who keep the ethnic traditions—because so many of the traditions are around household and family. They're the traditions you can keep. The other stuff has to go, or you don't ever fit into the new society. But, in this community, at that particular time, it was the girls that were being more acculturated—by being sent out of the neighbourhood. And I was one of a few who were sent to high school in the suburbs. In the suburbs, those of us from the "slum" were marked as inferior—because we were poor and had different lifeways. Being poor and being Italian got stuck together. You knew you were seen as inferior for those two things. But the two weren't really separable.

So if you were going to fulfill your parents' hopes, you were going to become middle class, get an education, a suburban home and learn how to deal with Americans. You were going to learn how to actually eat with Americans, dress like Americans and sound American. And, if you're going to do that, you pretty much feel that there's something wrong with being an Italian....

I went to university with an awareness of being Italian, but that wasn't a big part of my identity. Most of my university friends weren't Italian, but one of my very best friends was. We understood each other better. But *Italianness* wasn't really an issue for me then. It only was an issue for me when I was in graduate school. I left the north end, left Boston, and went to St. Louis. I had left the community; I had left the ethnicity. All of that was behind me. It was only in graduate school that I began to feel as if I wanted to be Italian. I felt I was different, and it was all right to be different. It wasn't a threat anymore. (This sounds weird to me. I never thought of myself as being enormously status conscious, but I guess you have to be.) Anyway, once I had made it out, and made it on my own, and proven that I could assimilate, I realized that I wanted to recapture some of what I'd lost.

I can tell you about this in two very stupid stories: The first thing I tried to do was make Italian cookies. But, I didn't have a recipe, and I had never paid attention. This is part of what you ignore when you're a kid. So I just made it up from the most casual observations I'd made of my aunt's baking. And the cookies? Well, we gave them to a friend who had a dog. That's how they came out! The second thing I did was to dye my hair black. I've never felt as though I looked like an Italian. When people look at me, they don't see Italian. That's probably good in some ways, so they don't stereotype me as being *mafioso* or something. But, at the same time, they don't see my ethnic identity. So I dyed my hair black. But the very first time I went to university registration after that, the foreign students asked me to join their society, and I think it was because they thought I was Oriental: A five foot girl (and I had brown-framed glasses at the time, so you couldn't tell my eyes were blue), with straight black hair, looks like a little Chinese girl or something. Not that it's a bad thing to look Oriental, but that wasn't the point. So both of those attempts failed. I wasn't going to become Italian that way.

When you set up a house of your own, you sort of fall back on your own role-models. You have your own kitchen, and that I think is one of the ways in which I could recapture the ethnicity. I learned to cook a little bit of Italian, talking to my mother on the phone for recipes, or just making up stuff that I remembered. I think that's basically the way that immigrants and second-generation people maintain their ethnicity, because the home is a private sphere, and you can be as different as you want there. You can't afford to be too different outside the home or you'd be misjudged and misunderstood, and you'll never fit in. In your own home, you can do the ethnic thing. I think there's a lot of stuff that's particularly Italian about the home, the culture of the home, where you can maintain some traditions. Little reminders.

[I was just wondering what kind of things you think you've lost?] Well, one is a sense of community. Again, I think that's a very general pattern. To the extent that the immigrants and their offspring attain the American dream, they lose social supports for their ethnic identity. Everybody wanted their kids to move to the suburbs. But I remember many stories of people who got to the suburbs and were grossly disappointed when they realized what it had cost them in terms of living in a familiar place, of living around (as my mother would say) "people like us," and the comfort that you feel from that. You know everybody. People come and go all the time. If anybody is around your house within an hour of mealtime, they simply can't go home. They have to eat with you or somebody's insulting someone. It's that kind of ongoing hospitality. In the suburbs, a lot of people found their neighbours to be very unfriendly. Well, obviously they had different ways of doing things. If you ask a suburban American to sit down and eat, because they happen to be passing through your house at mealtime, they're likely not going to do it. And you take offence. You think that they don't like you. Likewise, if they don't invite you.

So I think it was largely that sense of hospitality and communal feeling. I've missed endless opportunities for that. I've missed weddings and funerals, and the like, which are those special markers that happen only once in a while, but which bring you together, and say: "This is your family. This is your community. These are the people like you."

Also, I've always minded being unable to get food products to support an Italian kitchen. Again, this is a general pattern. People who moved into the Boston suburbs—they didn't have to move a thousand miles away—found the same thing. Those products are an important symbol. So I'm on an endless quest for good olive oil, and ricotta, and cured meats like *mortadella*, and all those things that you can't get here. At least in the suburbs of Boston, you're at a little bit of an advantage, because you can travel back to the old neighbourhood once a week or so.

But there's something else. This is touchy and sensitive and difficult to talk about. I don't feel culturally understood. I don't feel as if people interpret my behaviour in ways that make sense to me. There seems to be a big difference between what they see me doing and what I think I'm doing. This took me about twenty-five years— and probably a little anthropological training—to figure out. (It's not a very good track record. I should have figured this out a long time ago.) But I think that even more than in American culture, in Canadian culture (and maybe especially in the Maritimes), there's a different form of expressiveness. I grew up with Italians: lots of people in a small space making a lot of noise. Roaring and railing against each other in debates that might make a Maritimer fear violence and call the police! But to those people I grew up with, they were just having a good time.

Let me tell you another story. Not too long ago I was in the supermarket with my son Ben, here in Cape Breton. And we encountered a very good friend, somebody who's always been kind and warm, and who we've known for a long, long time. We'd gone into the store and were looking at the produce. We were laughing and joking, and I was saying, I guess with lots of noise and lots of gestures: "Take anything you want! You want that, take it! Pick what you want!" And this guy, who's a native Maritimer, came up behind us and said, "Why are you people fighting and bickering?" So I was seen as being what a southern Italian would call a *cafone*, as being not only boisterous and loud but also negative and hostile.[1] I was just unwittingly following a tradition I'd learned, about what it meant to be a mother: being generous and effusive. A misunderstanding, sure, but, in my experience, it's not an isolated incident. I mean, that only happened a few years ago. It confirmed this growing realization that cultural differences don't stop at dress, or food or other exterior things.

I think that North Americans, maybe all people, think of culture as something that's skin deep. It's like the decoration on an Easter egg, or some kind of superficial, trivial, peripheral kind of difference. They don't see the differences that go deeper.

So, I've come to feel misunderstood. When I think I'm being normal and involved and expressive, I guess I'm seen as something of a mad woman. I'm not saying my style is true of all Italians, because in any community there are going to be some people who are quieter and some people who are louder. There are going to be differences. Maybe I'm at one end of the Italian spectrum. And I'm not saying this doesn't have a personal factor. But I think there's an ethnic factor at play. I also think gender figures into the situation too. But I do think that Canadians really misinterpret some fundamental forms of expression that are Italian in origin. So I've never felt understood. And I never feel at home.

Now the Italians. I guess it's my own stupid fault that I was in Cape Breton for twenty years without realizing there really were Italians around here. I guess I accepted the public image of Nova Scotia as being Scottish. Publicly the Scottish identity is pretty strong, and there's no Italian district here, and you can't even find Italian products in the supermarkets. I was also told there's been so much intermarriage with other ethnic groups that Italian culture was lost.

When I first went to the Italian Club, I was very surprised. I saw people there who looked like ... like Italians. Some of the older women in particular, I just looked at them and said, "My God! There are Italians in Sydney. And they're real." It was like being transported in time and back to Boston. These people had counterparts in my memory. Even some of the second-generation people, I looked at them and said, "These people look and act like people I went to school with." That was a revelation to me. It was startling. It was something very special.

A year or so ago, we were at the club for a big meeting. While we were all in the hall enjoying ourselves, some local kids (presumably) slashed the tires of the cars outside. There was a lot of damage. Rose, the president of the Association, felt very bad. She's from that neighbourhood, and she felt very sorry for us. Sure, it was a terrible thing. Our car was dented and scratched, our rear-view mirror was broken, and we had two tires slashed. That wasn't pleasant. But everybody pulled together, to get help and to offer each other rides home. It made the problem much less disruptive and upsetting than it could have been. So, I saw the experience from another side, from the side of community. The incident unveiled community. It precipitated a reaction of community, of people caring for one another. I'm not saying that wouldn't happen in any Cape Breton community, whether Scottish, Acadian, or whatever. In fact, I'm quite sure that it would, but what it said to me was: "These people may live in their different places. They may not see each other everyday, and they may not all be relatives of one another. But there is an Italian basis for creating community, and that's real community."

We had a stimulating conversation that day. We discussed and laughed, and during our talk Connie deRoche did reveal a lot about herself. She also, however, said much about being a second generation Italian that all of us, Italians and non-Italians alike, can profit from.

Connie left me exquisitely curious about how my second-generation heritage has affected my own life. What "ethnicity" means? What it means to be Italian? An Italian woman? To belong to a community? What we have lost? And, what can be recaptured? On a larger scale, it made me also question how these same factors affect whole groups of people, Italians and non-Italians around the world, and the individuals within these groups. I'm thinking of people living in poverty, in slums, people who are "Othered," and people who have "gotten out," but have also forfeited much in the process.

Italian Voyages

Assunta Mascioli Mahar
Edited by Constance deRoche

In the following pages, you'll read recollections and reflections about two kinds of moves. One type is geographical movement. That is, it refers to relocating from Italy and from place to place within North America. The second is cultural movement. In our own minds and hearts, we can move away from thinking and feeling Italian, but we can also go back to being Italian in a different, but still real, way. The experiences upon which these recollections are based belong to Assunta (Mascioli) Mahar, a thoughtful, buoyant and wonderfully good-natured member of Sydney's Italian Canadian community. I enjoyed listening to her insights and covering ground with her that was familiar to me, a second-generation Italian (but one who grew up in Boston).

I'm also an anthropologist. My job (or part of it) is to learn from and about people and to share that knowledge with others. Anthropologists realize that people's stories speak for themselves. But we also find it useful to speak about them, setting individuals' stories in a broader context by using the ideas and observations we trade among ourselves. So, I feel driven, professionally, as well as personally, to comment a bit upon the themes that Assunta's story raised. It's hard, though, for anthropologists to decide just how much we should intrude or impose ourselves on other people's stories. So, you can decide. My commentaries are in italics, so you can read the transcript of the interview—or the portions of it that space allows—or you can read both Assunta's reflections and the thoughts that they provoked in me.

Migration

When we think about the enormous challenges of uprooting and moving to strange and distant places, it's natural to ask "why"? No Italian Canadian will be surprised about the motives that Assunta talks about below. Most Italians came to North America seeking better material conditions and economic opportunities. But the initial journey is only part of the story of immigration. People don't necessarily just move once and stay put. Some immigrants only intended to stay away a while. In other cases, the new country didn't fulfill its promise, and people with the courage to stray far from home also had the courage to change their minds and go home. In my youth, I was surprised to discover that my grandfather, like Assunta's, was a "circular migrant," that is, someone who makes a round trip.

Interviewer [I]: In terms of coming into Canada, were you old enough to remember why your family decided to come?

Assunta [AM]: I'd say economics was the reason. It was shortly after the War. My father's parents lived on a farm, and basically that's all there was. I guess you couldn't make a living with that. My parents had five children, and my father actually was born in Canada. His parents moved back to Italy when he was two years old. And so, I really don't know, but economics was the main reason that he decided to move here. He came over with his sister. The following year, my aunt's husband and children came, I believe in July. In that same year we came—my mother and five kids. We landed in Halifax in October.

[I]: So your aunt came without her family? Which was unusual.... [AM]: Yes, she's a very different type of person. She has a mind of her own. She'll be eighty-four on her birthday and, I think if she hadn't made the move, her family wouldn't have made the move.

We tend to think of strong women as a modern, North American phenomenon as if the recent women's liberation movement gave women a voice for the first time. Older, academic studies sometimes overlooked the role played by women, in other times and places, in shaping important family decisions, such as decisions to immigrate. Real-life stories tell us something different: "traditional" and "old-country" women weren't necessarily passive and oppressed, obedient servants of their men. Assunta recognizes this. Elsewhere—in a part of the interview that space doesn't allow me to include—she questions the truth of stereotypes about Italian men and women. Her remarks suggest that the myth of Italian male dominance is too simple. She reminds us that women had influence in the Italian family, though it was shaped and expressed in very different ways than it is in "modern" families. She led me to reflect on my own experience. My mother's father was very domineering. However, according to my mother, his mother was called "la mamma di San' Pietro," because she would have told even St. Peter what to think. She had a mind of her own and would say what she thought. Women had a clear voice in many of the families I knew when I was growing up.

[I]: Do you think she motivated your father? [AM]: I'd definitely say she motivated [him]. I've said to my father, "I don't believe you and Zia Lena are brother and sister, because you're so totally opposite." He's not the "typical" Italian male. I mean he likes his food on the table, that sort of thing, but—I don't know how you'd describe it—he's very quiet. He doesn't speak very much, but she's just the opposite. [I]: Kind of determined? [AM]: Determined—very determined.

[I]: Do you think your father chose Canada because he was born here? [AM]: I'd say so. Both he and his sister were born in Sydney, so I think that was the reason they came here, as opposed to going to Ontario or to the States. It was a familiar place to them. The reasons for coming here were never discussed. But I think it was because of economics. [I]: So was your aunt older or younger than your father? [AM]: She was older. There's about seven years difference.

[I]: Do you know why your grandfather immigrated? [AM]: No. My father was born in 1920, so it was right after the First World War, I think, when they came. But I'm assuming my grandfather didn't like it here. He was a big man, tall, six-foot-six. I have a picture. He used to work in the coal mines. I believe he came for the same reason—economics. I guess coal mining was the wrong thing for him. See, this is something I'd like to get into myself, to find out a bit about—like a family tree. You get those things in bits and pieces. Nobody talks about the reasons they moved unless you start asking questions. I really don't know how long my grandfather was here before he went back. My parents would have a better idea.

[I]: So your father arrived in Halifax? [AM]: My father and his sister arrived in 1952. They lived down the Pier. They had an apartment. He started to work, and she looked after the apartment. They lived together. He worked in construction all his life, 'til he retired about thirteen years ago. [I]: Did he work with an Italian company? [AM]: No, not here in Sydney; there weren't any. He worked with Municipal Ready Mix. And then he worked for Harris and Harris. But, now, the companies, I don't think any of them were Italian based. But there was a lot of Italian people working in them. [I]: So how long did he work here in Sydney? [AM]: We moved to Hamilton [Ontario] in 1964, so it was about twelve years. When we moved to Hamilton, I was about twenty....

In the next passage, and later again, you'll find a reference to "chain migration," that is, moves that are linked to other people's. Motivation and the need to move are rarely enough. People also need opportunity. They need, for example, knowledge about job markets or specific help in getting a job and a place to stay while they're getting settled. In making better lives for ourselves and our children, we often draw upon the care and concern of family and friends. There are, of course, government services and agencies that help people find work, but these do only part of the job, and they're generally localized. "Informal" (unofficial and personal) connections can play a big role not only in helping people make the first move to a new continent but also in helping them move within it. When people help family and friends move from places of high unemployment to those where workers are needed, they're providing a service to the wider economy. I've never heard public officials acknowledge this contribution that chain migration makes to "workforce adjustments." Maybe they should.

[I]: How did your family decide to move to Hamilton? Why leave Sydney? [AM]: Because of the work. My father had a friend in Hamilton who told them there was lots of work up there, and there was a job waiting for him. So my father went up and started working right away. He found a house for us, and I went up with the older kids. My mother stayed (to sell our house here) with the younger kids. The youngest is now thirty-three; she was an infant at the time. [In] Hamilton, I was responsible for the cleaning, cooking and getting the kids to school.

I finished school in Sydney, and I had applied to take a CNA (Certified Nursing Assistant) course in Halifax. They didn't offer it here. I lived in Hamilton for about nine months before I received the notice that I was accepted, and the course started in December. My father was very opposed to me coming back. He liked to have his family together. But I had been accepted, so I came back to Halifax. I was very stubborn. When I finished, he wanted me to go back to Hamilton. But I wouldn't. [I]: Why? [AM]: Because it was like my escape, I guess. Italian families back then were so restrictive. He was very strict, so in being the oldest of the nine ... I wanted my own bit of life, I guess.

It was a year's course. The Sisters of Charity had a home on Tobin Street for girls who were away from home, in Halifax, going to school.... They made a place for me because they were full. There's a turnover, so when one of the girls left, they assigned me to a room. There might've been four or five girls in one room. But, at first, I slept in a curtained area in a hall.

[I]: Would your father have let you come back if you hadn't had that kind of shelter? [AM]: I don't know. It never came up. But I don't know if I would have told him that. [I]: Well, would you have been intimidated, yourself, to come back? [AM]: No, no, I would have found a place. If they couldn't accommodate me for a long time, I'm sure they would've been able to recommend a place. There were different places back in those days because there were a lot of kids going there to school, taking ... hairdressing, nursing, or CNA, or just going to university. I took my training at the Halifax Infirmary. [I]: So when you finished, why come back here? [AM]: My option was to come back here because my boyfriend lived here.

[I]: Oh, how did you get a boyfriend if your father wouldn't let you out the house? [AM]: We moved to Mira Road [a community on the edge of Sydney] when I was sixteen. We belonged to the Immaculate Heart Parish, and they had a CYO (Catholic Youth Organization), and that's where I met him. So we used to have dances and parties, just on a Friday night. It was just a place we fixed up like a club-house. There was a pool table and stuff, and you could go there and play records. [I]: So you did get out of the house? [AM]: I did because I was going to the church

... it was in the basement of the church. [I]: Did your father know that there were boys there? [AM]: Well he never asked, and I never told him. I wasn't going to rock the boat.

[I]: Did your father know that you had a boyfriend? [AM]: Not until the night I came home late. And that was my own stupid fault. I was working at the Isle Royale Hotel. I worked there during the summers and the Christmas holidays. If there was a party at the hotel, you'd work late, so my hours were so irregular. But after I came home unusually late, he knew I had the boyfriend. [I]: Was that part of his reluctance to let you come back? [AM]: Probably, yes.

[I]: So your decision to come back to Sydney wasn't so much work related? [AM]: It was personal. I got a job at St. Rita's Hospital. When I came back, I lived with my father's sister, Zia Lena. Not long after that I got married. But my father wanted me to go back to Hamilton to be with the family. It wasn't that he wanted to control you. He had a lot of fears. He needed to know what you're doing, where you're going and that.

[I]: But now how many relatives did you have in Sydney? Not too many? [AM]: No, we had my aunt and her family and my father's brother and his family. [I]: Did your father call for his brother? There are immigration laws. [AM]: Yes, I think they did. They spoke for him to come over. Now, I believe, he came the year after, and actually he and his family moved to Island Park, New York. [I]: Why? [AM]: I think it was my aunt who wanted to make the move. She thought there were better opportunities there. Well, back in the 1950s, I think it might have been rough for him workwise. He worked like my father, I think, but I'm not sure if my aunt, his wife, had family there or what. But they decided one day that they were going to make the move, and they did.

[I]: It seems to be very, very difficult to get up and leave. [AM]: But, see, from here to New York isn't that big a deal compared to coming from Italy. This was almost like a transition type of move. [I]: How long was he here? [AM]: Just a few years. I can't remember exactly when they moved. It was before we moved to Hamilton in 1964.

My mother has a brother "George," but his name is really Luigi. He lived with us from the time he came to Canada. He was the second youngest in their family of seven. My mother has often said "I didn't have nine kids, I had ten," because he lived with us, up until he got married. [I]: How old was he when he came? [AM]: Twenty maybe. He's sixty-five or sixty-six. When I was nine, he would've been about twenty-one. We grew up together, as an older brother.

Actually, he moved to Ontario first, [and] lived in Toronto. When we moved to Hamilton, he came over and lived with us again. [I]: Did he have anybody in Toronto? [AM]: No, he just decided one day that Sydney wasn't the place for him.

There were more opportunities somewhere else, and he went for work. I'd say it was 1963, about a year before we went up. I guess he was working when we moved, and then he gave up his job and came to Hamilton and got a job with the city.

Then my mother's sister came, in 1970, I guess, or 1972. So my mother has a brother and a sister in Hamilton, which is kind of good for them, nice for her. But they still have a sister and a brother in Italy, and they lost two brothers who died there in Italy a few years back.

My mother's sister came to Hamilton with her family. They came with their three girls. When they came over, they lived with my mother and father, until they got settled and found a place of their own.

At another point in the interview, Assunta shows how her relatives have continued to help one another make economically beneficial moves.

[AM]: My oldest son, Scott, has been in Hamilton since he was twenty-one, back in 1988. I'm proud of what he's accomplished. He took a two-year refrigeration course at the vocational school. [It's the Community College, Sydney Campus, now.] My brother called and said there was a job for him, if he wanted it, in refrigeration and air-conditioning. So all I could do was ask him "Do you want to go?" He was gone. There was no question. He stayed with my mother and father. That was a change for him, because he went up there not knowing anybody except my parents, who he hadn't seen on a regular basis and my brothers and my sisters who he didn't know on a regular basis. But by going away, he grew up, which he wouldn't have done here in Sydney. And I'm very proud that he went up there and stuck it out, and he just bought a house.

[I]: When you first came to Sydney, tell me how you felt about being uprooted and brought to a totally different place. [AM]: I don't think I liked it. Well, you're going to the unknown for one thing. You left friends. I left my grandparents who I never saw again, both sets of grandparents. I left cousins, aunts and uncles that I never saw again. Just three years after we came here, my mother's father passed away all of a sudden. So there was never any hope of seeing him again. And you're coming to a different culture. I don't think I was very happy. I was very unhappy at school, because I couldn't speak the language, and they made you go back to a lower grade. I was in grade three when we left Italy. But I had to go back to grade one here, which was very demoralizing. Here you are, nine years old in a class with six year olds and five year olds. It was very traumatic.

[I]: And you were also used to living on a farm? [AM]: Yes, and all of a sudden you're living in an apartment. On a farm, you can go where you want. You had horses to ride, and the fields were your playground. Here, all of a sudden, it was all concrete. It's very, very traumatic. I always look back and think how my mother must have felt in a strange country. I know how I felt, but she never ever complained. She must have been thirty-two years old at her uprooting. Leaving her mother and father behind, she knew the only way she might ever see them again was if, God willing, she'd be able to go back to visit. My father never saw his parents again. He never wanted to go back. I don't know why. My mother went back to see her mother, and a couple of years later, her mother passed away. But she never saw her father again.

[I]: Did you have a sense of loss? [AM]: When my mother's father died, I had a sense of loss, yes. I might have been about eleven years old. It was like an ending for me. Before that, you kind of had a sense of hope that some day you might see him again. But he died young. When he died, that was like a part of you died. I found it hard really. It really bothered me that he was so far away. You couldn't even go back to see him.

[I]: So have you been back? [AM]: No. But that's one thing I am planning on doing in the next short while. It's always been my dream to go back. I've always wanted to go back, always, as far back as I can remember. *Assunta also mentioned that she hopes to visit the old country with her mother's brother and his wife in the near future.*

So, "economic immigrants" are going to some place where, they hope, their lives will be better materially. But every immigrant is also an "emigrant," that is, he or she is going from some place. Emigrants leave behind, not only poverty and deprivation, but loved ones, as well as the comforts of the familiar and customs that have meaning. They bring with them mementos through which memories maintain a reality. Unfortunately, these too can be lost.

On New Year's Eve, 1956, a fire started in a tavern beneath the Masciolis' apartment. It spread through the building. The family was lucky to survive, but they lost all their possessions.

[AM]: Everything was lost. All we had on was pyjamas, and we went next door. We had pictures from when we were kids in Italy. I have a few that my mother got from her sister because my uncle was a photographer. When she went back to visit, she asked for some because she had nothing left. Even if we had brought any toys with us, they were all gone, you know, things that we had back in Italy. It was very devastating because, all of a sudden, you had nothing. All the things that might have meant something as a remembrance were gone. I felt so bad for my mother because she'd brought beautiful things with her. All that biancaria was gone: beautiful blankets and embroidered sheets that she herself had worked. Yes, heritage. [She brought out a picture of her grandparents.] I could look at this picture and say, "This is my grandparents." I'm lucky to have it because the ones we had were gone.

I want to be able to show my grandchildren "this is your great grandfather and grandmother, and this is where I was born, where I came from." I have very few pictures of myself when I was a little girl back in Italy. I managed to get some that my mother got from her brother or sister back in Italy when she went over for a visit. My mother's not one to dwell on things. She felt the loss, but she said to me "with seven children you just can't sit down and cry" even if you feel like it. She just made do with what she had. The priest at the church at St. Nicholas Parish, which burnt down years ago, found us another place to live, and the Red Cross gave us blankets and stuff, but it wasn't the same. But she just kept on going.

[I]: Well, did she still have the craft skill? Did she then begin to reproduce some of that? [AM]: She did that when she was a young girl. With nine children she never had the time to do it. If she did anything, it was to make a dress for the girls or a shirt for the boys.

A Cultural Journey

Immigrants sacrifice more than objects or even the memories things hold. They and their children live with one foot in each of two worlds. They typically feel some pressures to "acculturate," that is, to modify old customs and ideas to fit those of the new place. Some degree of acculturation is inevitable. But how it happens depends on a number of factors, some of which are mentioned in the transcripts that follow.

Immigration has an impact on many relationships, including those between parents and children. Children are generally less set in the old ways; they learn the new culture faster than their parents. Italian families are relatively close-knit, but for immigrant children, in the North American context, they can be too close for comfort in some ways. When youngsters grow up and search for a little personal space, they can find themselves at odds with their parents' standards, especially when these are restrictive relative to the time and the place. Italian immigrant parents typically take their duty as protectors, especially of their daughters, very seriously. So, their watchfulness can seem very old-fashioned and excessive. That is, the younger generation doesn't see all aspects of the old culture in a positive light. Sometimes change is welcome. Assunta's observations of her experiences are not unusual. Many of us will find them familiar.

[AM]: It seemed like every time I went anywhere I had one of the kids with me. I couldn't go anywhere without one of them. I wasn't allowed to date. I mean, I couldn't even go to a movie or anything, not even with girl friends. I don't know whether my father had fears of something happening and not being able to be there for you to avoid it or he just liked to know. The boys could come and go whenever they wanted. But for the girls, it was entirely different. Well, it wasn't so much the girls. It was me because I was the oldest. The next oldest girl, Anna, is about forty. So there's a big span. So that kind of put, well, not a damper on your lifestyle but, I mean, even to go to a movie would have been nice. But that was a "no, no." Italian girls didn't do that. I think all Italian families were the same. The girls were treated different. They could get into trouble, where the boys can't. Well, they can, but they don't bring it home.

[I]: So when your next youngest sister was growing up things had changed a little bit? [AM]: Oh, definitely. Anna's very laid back and takes things as they come. Nothing seems to bother her too much. But she didn't have the restrictions I had because of the difference in our ages. [I]: So things were easier for her? [AM]: For all the girls afterwards. But that's the way it was.

[I]: But you didn't feel as if your family was different than other Italian families? [AM]: No, no, very much the same. It was the times. It was the custom. That was the way things were done back in the old country, and they kind of brought it with them. It's almost like, if you wanted to go to a show, a dance or go out with a boy, you were almost branded as loose.

Generally, the parts of culture that are expressed in material things are easier to identify and thus maintain. Other customs are less evident, because they live in feelings and in passing events. Strength of family is not unique to Italians, but it's a very real part of Italian culture. And it survives, despite all the stresses caused by jumping a generation gap that's widened by culture change. But feeling overprotected, doesn't mean that a child will reject family. Familial attachments have remained a strong positive force in Assunta's life. As it's said, home is where the heart is, and for Assunta home is family.

[I]: Well, when you went to Hamilton, did you miss Sydney? [AM]: No, actually I didn't. It was because of my boyfriend that I came back here. I didn't miss the place. I would've been content to stay in Hamilton. Actually, my heart's in Hamilton because my whole family is there. [I]: Your boy is there. [AM]: Yes, but I think it's always been like that, and it's just kind of surfacing. You keep things buried. It's there, but it's not there, not every day. But especially at certain times of the year, it's very difficult. I always hated Christmas because my whole family was away, and I used to build myself up so much. I used to do so much, like the baking and the cooking. Come Christmas day, it was just like you fell off a cliff. Christmas for me is very depressing. [I]: You haven't spent many with your family? [AM]: No, it's only in the past couple of years that I have. In my whole married life, I was never home for Christmas.

[I]: All your sisters and brothers are they in the Hamilton area? [AM]: Yes, except I have one brother in St. Catherines. But they're all around my mother, around my parents. [I]: Hamilton is much more Italian than here. [AM]: I guess, that's part of it too because you can get different things there that I'm interested in, that let you keep a little bit of your culture. In Sydney you can't get half the stuff that you'd want. But that's not the biggest draw. It's the family because, to me, without your family you don't have much of anything.

The family is a private world, but not a world onto itself. Most family members have to go out into the wider world where they face pressures to conform and thus to change. In the ideal, Canada is a "cultural mosaic," where ethnic differences remain intact and form a distinctive piece of the whole picture. But in reality, most peoples are "ethnocentric" to some degree. They're uncomfortable with unfamiliar customs that they don't quite understand. Even when reactions to newcomers aren't negative, there's pressure on them to conform, since sharing customs allows them to understand and be understood and thus accepted.

[AM]: We moved to Mira Road, probably, because my parents thought it was a better neighbourhood to bring up kids. They bought a house. I guess they were getting a little bit ahead. That was very traumatic for me because word had gotten out that an Italian family had moved in the neighbourhood. When we started school, they were all waiting outside to see what we looked like. [I]: Did they call you names or anything? [AM]: No, they just wanted to see what you looked like.

[I]: But you did experience some name calling in the Pier? [AM]: Yes, when we were younger. Oh, yes, because I think we were the new family on the block. We'd just moved from Italy, so you were very green, couldn't speak the language, so you stood out. If anybody spoke to you, you didn't know what they were saying. It's funny, that word dago, I hadn't heard that in years 'til a day at work, not long ago. I could feel the hair stand up on the back of my neck. I don't mind being called a lot of things, but I really take exception to that. The fellow who used the word asked, "Do you mind being called that?" I said "Yeah, I took exception to being called a dago. I think it is very derogatory." I think it brought back memories. Back in those days there was a lot of prejudice against immigrants. It was like you were different, like you were from another planet. I tried to learn the language as fast as I could, so they wouldn't know I was Italian. It was almost like you were embarrassed to admit you were Italian. There weren't that many Italian families in the Pier that I remember. If there were, they were older. So most of my friends at that time were the girls I met at school.

The pace of acculturation is affected by many factors. Beyond the attitudes of members of the new community is the area's ethnic make-up. The fact that Assunta had no Italian agemates at school would have speeded the pace of her Canadianization. She also had few relatives her own age when she was growing up (though later in life, when age differences become less significant, she could befriend her cousins and share Italian customs with them). Maintaining the old culture is easier if the supports and services (school, church, stores, etc.) needed for everyday life can be provided by your own kind and for your own kind. This, in turn, depends on the size of the ethnic community and the degree to which it can form a pocket within the larger population. (There's a hint of this in comments about Hamilton, above, as well as in the observations, made below, about the use of Italian in that community.)

An old area of ethnic concentration can serve as a centre for the culture, even after residents of the neighbourhood begin to move to "better" neighbourhoods where they're dispersed among other populations. I grew up in such an Italian neighbourhood. But there too, we picked up prejudices against our own. We, in the second generation, looked down upon the immigrant kids. We didn't call them dagos, but we did call them greasers, and we deprived ourselves of their company. Successful acculturation thus has a dark side. It's accompanied, too, for economic migrants, by material success that can also lead to divisions and feelings of discrimination. The last great wave of Italians to North America happened in the 1950s after many earlier arrivals had already "made it."

[AM]: Italian families are strange. I think they're very prejudiced, like if you have a beautiful home and fancy furniture you're "in," but if you don't…. We had a big family, and it's almost like you're looked down on because of it. [I]: By other Italians? [AM]: Yes, back then, not so much now. It's almost like they forgot where they came from, that everybody had the same hardship, and the reason they came to this country was to make their lives better. And it's like they didn't want you to associate with them.

We became Canadianized because four of the nine children were born in Canada. It's almost like we Canadianized ourselves so we wouldn't stick out like a sore thumb. I think the reason my mother speaks English as well as she does is because we all spoke to her in English. We didn't want to speak the Italian. My mother always spoke to us in Italian, so we always understood what she was saying, but we never answered her in Italian. Today, she still has an accent, but she speaks English fluently. She learned it from us. She reads the newspaper cover to cover, and she taught herself from what we brought to her and what she picked up on her own.

[I]: Did she ever work outside the house? [AM:] For a very short time, she worked at E. D. Smith. They packed tomatoes during tomato season. Just for a couple of summers, not for very long. [I]: Did she need English to work there? [AM]: No, most of those factories hired immigrants. I worked in a candy factory up in Hamilton, and most workers were Italian or Portuguese. When I moved to Hamilton, I had no choice because everybody there spoke Italian. All my father's friends hardly spoke any English. I think Italian was still there in my head. I'd just felt embarrassed to speak it. I guess going up there gave me back my roots. It kind of made you see that it's not bad to be other than an English-speaking person. It gave me back my sense of identity: I am an Italian, I am a born Italian.

There seems to be something cyclical in the ethnic experience, as if there has to be a phase of loss. During that time, we're busy learning to fit into the new culture and rejecting, as a consequence, the old. But once that's done, when the shame's gone, we become free to rediscover and take back some of the old ways. It's in the privacy of our own homes that we're most free to be our ethnic selves. It's not at all surprising, then, for women to become more ethnic in early adulthood, after they set up house-holds of their own.

[AM]: I never wanted to get married. I remember working as a girl. My cousin got me the job at the Isle Royale Hotel, and she was of the old school. The dining room would close at two o'clock, but you'd have to get things ready for suppertime. By the time you finished, it might be three-thirty or four o'clock. You had an hour to an hour-and-a-half of free time and with my cousin time is the devil's. She'd come to work with crochet cotton, a crochet hook, and a little book. She was going to teach me how to crochet. I said, "Lisa, I don't want to know how to crochet." "But you have to learn," she'd say. "But I don't want to learn." I wanted to go out, up to the stores or for a walk. The last thing I wanted was to be stuck inside on a nice summer afternoon, in this hotel, down in the locker room, crocheting. She's ten years older than I am, so she was married. But when you're fifteen or sixteen years old, it's the last thing you want to do.

But when I got married, I couldn't get enough knowledge. I could boil water, but that was as far as it went. When you're married, you think, "Okay, now I have to learn how to cook." So, my poor aunt, every day I'd say, "Zia Lena, I want to make this, how do I make it?" She has no recipes. They're all in her head, so it's like "well, you take a little bit of this, a little bit of that." She'd give me all the ingredients, but I'd have to sit down and try to make it the way it's supposed to be. I remember the way my mother did it, the way it used to taste. It's the same if someone asks me for a recipe, I can't give a specific recipe.

I try to keep a little of my culture, basically in the cooking. I've always tried to keep traditional Christmas and Easter dinner. My sons were never embarrassed. Actually, they were proud. Every Saturday night here used to be hockey night and pizza. I'd make the pizza. To this day, my sons' friends still talk about coming here and having pizza, ravioli and the homemade spaghetti. It's almost like somehow you created your own little culture all over again.

It was almost like there was shame in knowing you were an immigrant. But both my parents are Italian. They're still Italian. It's almost like they have two cultures, but I didn't have any culture except what was forced on me, as being the Canadian culture. But late in my teens, I came to realize that there's no shame in being an Italian that immigrated. There's no shame in coming here because things were bad in Italy or your parents were trying to make a better life for themselves and their children.

I went back to school when my oldest was ten, and I started working when I was thirty-three. That Christmas, the girls in the office were talking about Christmas dinner. They asked me, what I was going to have, and I said ravioli. They looked and said, "What, you're going to open a can?" "No," I said, "I'm going to make ravioli." "What do you mean you are going to make ravioli?" They had no concept of making pasta—which I did my whole married life—or gnocchi, or any of those things. I felt good doing something different.

Sons aren't interested in that type of thing. I regret that I won't be able to pass on some of my crafts, like the cooking. But I might have a granddaughter one day. I have some beautiful things that I'd love to leave. I still have the earrings I wore from Italy when I was nine. If I have a little granddaughter, I'd like to be able to give them to her and say "These belonged to me. These came from Italy." I'd like to be able to pass them down to my family.

I had mixed feelings about being Italian. But today it's a different story altogether. You kind of come to "This is what I am," you know. I've sort of come full circle.

Life Thoughts

By Esperanza Maria Razzolini Crook

Born
4 September 1952, New Waterford, Cape Breton, Nova Scotia.

Married to:
James Andrew Kenneth Crook (born: Pembroke Ontario, 3 August 1955),
in Aylesford, Nova Scotia, 4 September 1982.

Children:
Robyn Mara Dierdre Crook, born: 10 December 1984, Berwick, Nova Scotia,
Dayle Kacie Jessamyn Crook, born: 1 November 1986, Berwick, Nova Scotia.

Father:
Esperando Razzolini, born: 9 November 1923, New Waterford, Cape Breton, Nova Scotia.

Paternal Grandparents:
Rudolfo Razzolini, born: 15 January 1888, Asolo, Treviso, Italy.
Annabelle Marsh, born: 15 December 1900, Lingan, Cape Breton, Nova Scotia.

Mother:
Maria Filomena Sanvido, born: 31 July 1932, Dominion, Cape Breton, Nova Scotia.

Maternal Grandparents:
Frederico Sanvido, born: 14 June 1903, Altivole, Treviso, Italy.
Renelle Thomas, born: 31 October 1912, Chatelineau, Hainault, Belgium.

Education:
Primary - Grade 3 (1957-1960), Central School, Dominion. Grades 4 - 9 (1960-1967), MacDonald High School, Dominion. Grade 10 (1967-68), Ingonish Beach Consolidated School, MacDonald High School (Dominion), Prince Andrew High School (Dartmouth). Grades 11 - 12 (1967-70), Prince Andrew High School (Dartmouth). BA (Honours) History (1970-74), Dalhousie University. MA History (1974-75), University of Waterloo [degree granted 1979].

Employment:
Public Archives of Nova Scotia, casual, 1975. University of Waterloo, research assistant, 1975-76. Parks Canada:(1) Fortress of Louisbourg, NHP, researcher, 1976-77, 1978-79; and, (2) Halifax Defence Complex Restoration Project, researcher/archivist, 1977-78, 1979-84. Palliser Regional Library, Saskatchewan, Bushell Park Branch, casual, 1994 to present.

Migration:
New Waterford (1952) > Dominion (1954) > Ingonish Beach (1967) > Dominion (1967) > Dartmouth (1968) > Waterloo (1974) > Dartmouth (1975) > Sydney (1976) > Dartmouth (1977) > Louisbourg (1978) > Dartmouth (1979) > Greenwood (1984) > Bushell Park (1991); presently residing in Saskatchewan attached to 15 Wing Moose Jaw, with husband, daughters, dog, cats, and entirely too many books.

Well, here we are, the skeleton of a life—framework without fabric, fact devoid of understanding. So, what is important. How does the historian become history herself without sounding like a pompous twit? Taking into consideration that memory is not so much a sequence of facts as how a particular mind perceives that chain of events suppose we put down what seems personally significant from the viewpoint of age and experience at which I now stand. The article ("All Our Fathers: The North Italian Colony in Industrial Cape Breton") included in this collection is a condensation of a pamphlet of the same name produced in 1983 from research done in 1981. Sixteen years ago, I was engaged but not married, so the anchors of my present existence—husband and children—were not dominant. I worked for Parks Canada at the Halifax Defence Complex Project, my specialty being restoration/recreation history, an area to which I still adhere strongly. While in graduate school, my research in Canadian ethnohistory had centred on racial minorities. As I belonged to a number of ethnic minorities, however, this avenue had also been explored, albeit without associated papers. "All Our Fathers" changed that, allowing me to pursue another segment of the role of Canadian minorities in the formation of the national identity and culture, while permitting me to express my thoughts and feelings concerning the Italo-Canadian world to which I belonged.

Consequently, in 1981, my mother and I travelled back to Cape Breton to fulfill this goal. While we had maintained contact with friends and relatives remaining on the island, it was a time of renewal of ties and re-evaluation of experience. So many years later, my recall is faulty, existing in images like snapshots. Sitting in the Antonellos' kitchen listening to my mother and them reminisce while I kept the tape recorder on line and remembered childhood, visiting trips with my grandmother, eating peaches while the sound of Italian washed over my head. Talking to Mr. Stephenson in the post office and getting to sit in the area behind the boxes. (The child in me was as delighted with this treat as the adult in me was with the discovery of the wonderful oral history tapes already done by Mr. Stephenson and Mr. Vaninetti.) My project at that point became less an oral history task and more a collecting of existing data into a cohesive form—an attempt to create a solid jumping-off platform for further study. It also gave me a chance to renew elements within myself and solidify ties important to my heritage and identity at a time when my life was changing.

The fifteen-year-old girl who sorrowfully left Dominion with her parents "following the work" had been replaced with an analytical woman of almost thirty. Growing up in Dominion, I had been an Italo-Canadian whose mixed ethnic background had made total inclusion in the Italian community not quite possible. On the mainland, my Italian heritage was viewed secondary to my birth on Cape Breton Island. During this trip, I put the two together. I had been born a Cape Bretoner, and despite the fact that I had not lived there for fifteen years, and my background was not Celt (or at least not much), that distinction was one to which I had always clung, proudly and tenaciously. Like so many of my fellow islanders, I lived somewhere else, adhering to the culture I had left behind through food, friends and music. Of equal significance, I was Italo-Canadian, born to those Italian immigrant communities existing in the coal towns of industrial Cape Breton, preserving the remnants of a way-of-life belonging to the past of a country I had never seen, only felt. Bitter recollections of long-ago discrimination had fallen victim to the onslaught of the modern pizza-induced popularity of Italian culture. My Cape Breton childhood emerged as a good place and time to have grown up—freedom with security, discipline with laughter—canoeing, walking the shore, picnics, Sunday drives. My father's employment at the Fortress of Louisbourg during the early days of restoration had transformed one of my favourite places into an object of compelling fascination—a site of archeological digs, stone masons, smiths and researchers. Always interested in the past, the park created in me an obsession with history which dominated both work and play. These are the forces which had combined intrinsically to form my third generation "self."

At bones' core, these two main influences have continued to sustain the essence of my identity, affecting my views and opinions through time, even though I have lived outside in the mainland English-Canadian majority for most of my life. When, in 1991, ten years and two daughters later, I "followed the work" again when my Canadian Armed Forces husband was transferred to 15 Wing Moose Jaw, I ended up on the prairie, as reluctant an immigrant as ever there was, without even having to leave the country. Here my efforts to understand and relate to a new environment and people have resulted more in the solidifying of my past than the adjustment of my present. While as Mrs. Crook I disappeared into the mainstream with nary a ripple, my Italian roots unknown, the east-west culture shock I encountered here almost equalled that felt by my grandparents upon immigrating to Canada and went a great deal toward expanding my understanding of that phenomenon. "Maritime clubs" parallel those cultural organizations created by most minority groups in this country, making this reaction to social isolation a universal one. Sometimes the world felt definitely upside down. I came to understand clearly that I am a "minority Canadian" because that is what my sense of identity says I am—that is how I act, how I feel, how I think, how I act and react. This is not to negate the influence of the mainstream Canadian culture—rather it permits the encompassing of the general while preserving the specific. I rejoice in the complex diversity—no apologies.

My own singular response to this conclusion was, in 1993, to join the Society for Creative Anachronism, a recreational organization which utilizes the animation approach to history to which Parks Canada and I adhere. A combination of martial art, lecture circuit, banquet round and drama role-playing, the group encompasses many aspects of both my professional training and personal inclination. Through it I have explored the histories of Italy and Scotland and acted out material manifestations of these cultures, an activity which has furthered my, and my husband's, self-explorations, interested my daughters in their own heritage, as well as provided a working model of the great worth of Canada's multi-culturalism for both participant and observer alike.

"So ... what are we?"
"I beg your pardon?"
"You know—Italian, Scottish...."
"Oh, here, let me show you."
"So ... what does that make us *exactly*?"
"Canadian."
"Canadian?"
"Canadian."
"Cool."
"Yeah—I think so too."
"Cool."
"Yeah—I think so too."

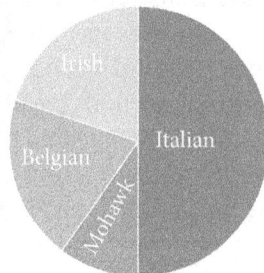

Maria

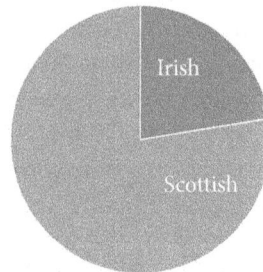

James

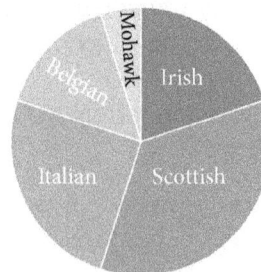

Robyn and Dayle

In Memoriam:
Lino Polegato (1936-1993)

By Sam Migliore

Lino Polegato, the son of Margarita (Andrazza) and Riccardo Polegato, was born on December 10, 1936. He grew up, and lived most of his life, in the town of Dominion. His education was in the field of engineering—first at St. Francis Xavier University, then the Nova Scotia Technical College and finally the University of Connecticut (where he received a Masters degree in 1975). Lino became a faculty member of the Xavier Junior College in Sydney in 1961 and then a faculty member of the University College of Cape Breton (now Cape Breton University) in 1975. By 1992, he had worked his way up to the position of Dean of Science, Technology and Engineering.

Over the years, Lino served and represented the Cape Breton community in various capacities. His involvements, although too numerous to list here, have included: Police Commissioner, Dominion, 1977-1980; member and secretary, Cape Breton East Richmond Federal Liberal Association; Consular Correspondent (1978-1986) and Honourary Consular Agent (1987-1993) for Italians in Cape Breton, Government of Italy; longstanding member and Chair, Dominion Italian Community Club (including participation in the organization of several Italia Day cultural festivals); Vice-President, Cape Breton Miners Museum Foundation;

Courtesy of Theresa Polegato. Photo by Shepherd Photo Ltd., Glace Bay (October 26, 1992).

member, Marconi Museum Foundation; member and Chair (1987-1988), Board of Directors, Big Brothers and Sisters of Cape Breton, and President, Big Brothers, Cape Breton, 1989-1990; President, Association of Professional Engineers of Nova Scotia, 1989-1990.

Through these involvements, Lino earned not only the respect of community members but also a number of honours and distinctions. For example: the title of Cavaliere della Repubblica, Government of Italy, 1984; the Nova Scotia Environmental Award, Professional Category, 1984; a Certificate of Merit (contributions to engineering, Centennial Year of Engineering), CBU, 1987; a Citizenship Citation, Minister of State, Multiculturalism and Citizenship, Government of Canada, 1989; the Les Carbot Award (for community cultural activities), Government of Canada, 1991; and, an award for Outstanding Cultural Contributions to the Community of Dominion, 1992 (Cultural Federation of Nova Scotia).

"Lino Polegato was a man who knew how to treat people with respect." These were the words I used to begin my eulogy for Lino at the CBU on January 20, 1993. It was a simple statement, but it touched an emotional chord with just about everyone I spoke with that day. The response was not to the "words" themselves. Words are meaningless and powerless until we breathe life into them as we think, speak and listen. The phrase touched an emotional chord because we shared an image of Lino as "a man of respect," and we were deeply affected by the tragic turn of events that took him away. Lino had died suddenly of a massive heart attack just two days earlier. His death came as a surprise and a shock to us all. We did not expect fate to work so quickly, so suddenly. It was a tragedy! Lino's death has been a great loss not only for his wife, Theresa, family and friends but to everyone at CBU the Italian community, and Cape Breton in general.

During the short time I knew him, Lino became an important figure in my life. I feel the pain of his death deeply. He was one of the people who made me feel at home in Cape Breton. I come from a closely-knit Italian family and community. It meant a great deal to me to meet Lino in the halls of CBU and to have him greet me or talk to me in my native language. I miss that. Lino was also the one who helped me establish contact with members of the Italian community in the area and to begin work on this project. For me, he was a good friend and a good colleague. This book is dedicated, in part, to his memory.

Notes

1-7 – Introduction

1 See: I. McKay, "Tartanism Triumphant: The Construction of Scottishness in Nova Scotia, 1933-1954," *Acadiensis*, 1992, 21 (2): 5-47; and, J. A. Rolls, "Culture for Sale," *The Centre of the World at the Edge of a Continent: Cultural Studies of Cape Breton Island*, C. Corbin and J. A. Rolls, eds., Sydney: University College of Cape Breton, 1996, pp. 79-82.

2 *Nova Scotia Census, 1871*, C-10569, Cape Breton and Victoria Counties Census, 1871, Cow Bay Divisions # 1 and 2, and Louisburg Division # 1. Public Archives of Canada, Ottawa: Central Microfilm Operations. The names of people and places appear here as spelled in the census records; the hand written entries, however, are not always easy to decipher.

3 See "Early Settlement: The Giovannetti Family in Port Morien" and "A Search for One's Roots."

4 *Nova Scotia Census, 1901*, Cape Breton County, Public Archives of Canada, Ottawa: Central Microfilm Operations. Note: Nova Scotia was not part of Canada in 1855. I take the reference to the date of immigration to Canada to refer to the year Lorenzo Giovannetti arrived in Nova Scotia (which, in 1901, was part of Canada).

5 Fourth Census of Canada, 1901: Volume I, Population, Ottawa: S. E. Dawson, the King's Printer, 1902, pp. 298-99. The number of Italians in Cape Breton was probably higher than these figures indicate because individuals considered to be on temporary work assignments may not have been recorded for the census.

6 Ibid, pp. 298-309, 1902; *Fifth Census of Canada, 1911: Volume II*, Ottawa: C. H. Parmelee, the King's Printer, 1913, pp. 186-203; *Sixth Census of Canada, 1921: Volume I, Population*, Ottawa: F. A. Acland, the King's Printer, 1924, pp. 386-99; *Seventh Census of Canada, 1931: Bulletin No. XXII, Population Du Canada, 1931 Par Races d'Origine*, Ottawa: F. A. Acland, the King's Printer, 1933, pp. 34-47; *Eighth Census of Canada, 1941: Volume II, Population by Local Subdivisions*, Ottawa: Edmond Cloutier, the King's Printer, 1944, pp. 324-39.

7 See: "Italian Society will have Parade," *Sydney Daily Post*, August 15, 1908; "Italian Society Big Celebration," *Sydney Daily Post*, August 17, 1908; and, "Angela Giacomantonio," "All Our Fathers," and "*La Sala Italiana* in Dominion," in this book.

8 *Ninth Census of Canada, 1951: Volume I, Population, General Characteristics*, Ottawa: Edmond Cloutier, Queen's Printer and Controller of Stationery, 1953, pp. 34 (1-4).

9 See various articles in *The War Years* section of the book.

10 See: "Country Living" and "*La Sala Italiana in Dominion*."

11 See section *Looking Beyond Cape Breton (Home and Away)* in this book.

12 See Statistics Canada, *Census of Canada, 1961. Volume 1, Population, Ethnic Groups*, Bulletin 1.2-5, Ottawa: Queen's Printer and Controller of Stationary, 1962.

13 Statistics Canada, *1991 Census, J9102: Population by Ethnic Origin Showing Single and Multiple Origins, Italian*. Custom search. 1998. The 3,850 figure quoted here is based on both single and multiple responses indicating "Italian" as people's ethnic origin.

14 See "La Mamma: Italian Canadian Mothers of Cape Breton" in this book, plus: "The Call of the Sea;" "Spiritual and Physical Healing;" "A Second Generation Italian American of Cape Breton;" "Italian Voyages;" and "Life Thoughts."

8-17 – All Our Fathers: The North Italian Colony in Industrial Cape Breton

1 This article is a condensation of the pamphlet of the same name published as Volume VIII of the Ethnic Heritage Series, Halifax: International Education Centre, St. Mary's University, 1983. The content of the article is based both on written materials and a series of interviews with community members.

2 Canada, Department of the Secretary of State, Canadian Citizenship Branch, *The Canadian Family Tree*, Ottawa: The Queen's Printer for the Centennial Commission, 1967, pp. 9-12; James S. Woodsworth, *Strangers Within Our Gates or Coming Canadians*, Toronto: Missionary Society of the Methodist Church, Canada, 1909, pp. 3-5, 161-2, 198-9, 202-8, 218-312; Robert

F. Foerster, *The Italian Emigration of Our Times*, New York: Russell and Russell, 1968 (original printing, 1919), pp. 9, 21-49, 106-24, 171-87; Edwin Fenton, *Immigrants and Unions, A Case Study: Italians and American Labour*, 1870-1920, New York: Arno Press, 1975, pp. 2-5; John M. Gibbon, *Canadian Mosaic: The Making of a Northern Nation*, Toronto: McClelland and Stewart Limited, 1938, p. 385; A. V. Spada, *The Italians in Canada*, Canadian Ethnica VI, Ottawa: Canadian Ethnic Press Federation, 1969, pp. 75, 135; Betty Boyd Caroli, *Italian Reparation From the United States, 1900-1914*, New York: Centre for Migration Studies, 1973, pp. 93-99.

3   Spada, *The Italians in Canada*, pp. 213, 223-24; Canada, Department of the Secretary of State, *The Canadian Family Tree*, p. 185; Gibbon, *Canadian Mosaic*, pp. 380-86; Robert F. Harney, *Italians in Canada*, Occasional Papers on Ethnic and Immigration Studies, Toronto: The Mutlicultural History Society of Ontario, 1978, pp. 1-21; E. J. Julian, "Brief History of the Italian Colony of Cape Breton," unpublished manuscript; Leonard Stephenson, Dominion, N.S. *1906-1981: a Brief History of the Town of Dominion and Its Early Development*, A Souvenir Publication to Commemorate the 75th Anniversary of the Incorporation of the Town, Sydney: Robertson Print-Craft for the Town of Dominion, 1981; Leonard Stephenson, "Address given to the Italian Community Club, 28 February 1981," unpublished manuscript; Woodsworth, *Strangers within Our Gate or Coming Canadians*, pp. 160-66; Foerster, *The Italian Emigration of Our Times*, pp. 11-5, 223-24, 325-26; Brian Joseph, "The Others; 'Newcomers'," in Douglas F. Campbell, ed., *Banked Fires: The Ethnics of Nova Scotia*, Port Credit: The Scribbner's Press, 1978.

4   Stephenson, "Address to the Italian Community Club;" Spada, The Italians in Canada, pp. 123, 217-19; Harney, *Italians in Canada*, pp. 8-21.

5   Spada, *The Italians in Canada*, pp. 217-19; *Sydney Daily Post*, Cape Breton Island, Nova Scotia, miscellaneous articles.

6   Julien, "Brief History of the Italian Colony in Cape Breton;" Spada, *The Italians in Canada*, pp. 217-20; Stephenson, *Dominion, N.S. 1906-1981*; Stephenson, "Address to the Italian Community Club."

7   Stephenson, *Dominion, N.S. 1906-1981*; Emilio Vaninetti, "The Italian Community in Dominion," unpublished manuscript; Julian, "Brief History of the Italian Colony in Cape Breton;" Spada, *The Italians in Canada*, pp. 217-19; Stephenson, "Address to the Italian Community Club."

8   Canada, Department of the Secretary of State, Canadian Citizenship Branch, *The Canadian Family Tree*, pp. 18-19, 185; Joseph, "The Others," pp. 204-05; Harney, Italians in Canada, pp. 25, 32; Gibbon, *Canadian Mosaic*, pp. 380-81, 386-91; The fact that all Italian born males were subject to the draft led to interesting situations. Like many others, John Antonello's son, who, while born in Italy, had lived virtually all of his life in Canada, received papers notifying him of his conscription into the Italian military at eighteen. He had to go to the Consul General in Montreal for dispensation.

9   Stephenson, "Address to the Italian Community Club;" and Interviews.

10   Spada, *The Italians in Canada*, p. 218.

11   Vaninetti, "The Italian Community in Dominion," pp. 10-12; Canada, Department of the Secretary of State, *The Canadian Family Tree*, pp. 20-21, 185-86; Stephenson, *Dominion, N.S. 1906-1981*; Stephenson, "Address to the Italian Community Club;" Joseph, "The Others," pp. 191, 205.

12   Campbell, ed., *Banked Fires: The Ethnics of Nova Scotia*, p. 224; Canada, Department of the Secretary of State, *The Canadian Family Tree*, pp. 20-21, 185-86; Stephenson, *Dominion, N.S. 1906-1981*; Stephenson, "Address to the Italian Community Club;" Joseph, "The Others," pp. 191, 200-05; Spada, *The Italians in Canada*, pp. 217-21; Harney, *Italians in Canada*, pp. 34-39; Hugh A. Millward, *Regional Patterns of Ethnicity in Nova Scotia: A Geographical Study*. Ethnic Heritage Series, Volume VI, Halifax: International Education Centre, St. Mary's University, 1981; Janet Intscher, "Little Italy," in *Canadian Heritage*, October 1981, p. 24; Warren E. Kalbach, "Growth and Distribution of Canada's Ethnic Populations, 1871-1971," in Leo Driedger, ed., *The Canadian Ethnic Mosaic: A Quest For Identity*, Canadian Ethnic Studies Association Series, Volume VI, Toronto: McClelland and Stewart Limited, 1978, pp. 82-104; Clifford J. Jansen, "The Italian Community in Toronto," in Jean L. Elliott, ed., *Immigrant Groups. Minority Canadians 2*, Scarborough: Prentice-Hall of Canada Ltd., 1971, pp. 207-15.

28-30 – Early Settlement: The Giovannetti Family in Port Morien

1 See: *Nova Scotia Census, 1871*, C-10569, Cape Breton and Victoria Counties Census, 1871, Cow Bay Division # 2, Public Archives of Canada, Ottawa: Central Microfilm Operations; and, *Nova Scotia Census, 1901*, Cape Breton County, Public Archives of Canada, Ottawa: Central Microfilm Operations. The 1901 census provides the date of Lorenzo Giovannetti's arrival in Canada.

2 This story was related to them, in a letter, by Guglielmina Giovannetti Fiori, the granddaughter of Bennedette Giovannetti—Lorenzo's brother. The letter was translated for the family by Claudia Lucchesi.

31-39 – Guglielmo Marconi and His Cape Breton Wireless Telegraphy (Radio) Station, 1901-1904

1 Keith Geddes, *Guglielmo Marconi: 1874-1937*, London, Science Museum, 1974, p. 6.

2 Ibid.

3 Ibid.

4 William Baker, *A History of the Marconi Company*, London, Methuen, 1979, p. 34.

5 Ibid, p. 35.

6 "History of the Canadian Marconi Company, 1901-1960." MS, MG 28/111/72, National Archives of Canada.

7 *Sydney Record*, December 31, 1902.

8 Quoted in the *Halifax Herald*, January 4, 1902.

9 Ibid.

10 *Halifax Herald*, December 30, 1901.

11 "History of the Canadian Marconi Company, 1901-1960."

12 Richard N. Vyvyan, *Wireless Over Thirty Years*, London, Routledge, 1933, p. 37.

13 Ibid.

14 Ibid.

15 Ibid, p. 38.

16 Ibid, p. 38.

17 Ibid, p. 38.

18 Ibid, p. 40.

19 *Guglielmo Marconi: 1874-1937*, p. 21, 1974.

20 "History of the Canadian Marconi Company, 1901-1960."

21 *Wireless Over Thirty Years*, p. 48, 1933.

40-45 – Thomas Cozzolino: An Introduction

1 John Bodner, *The Transplanted: A History of Immigrants in Urban America*. Bloomington: Indiana University Press, 1985, p. 21.

2 Robert F. Harney, "Toronto's Little Italy," in Robert F. Harney and J. Vincenza Scarpaci, eds., *Little Italies in North America*. Toronto: Multicultural History Society of Ontario, 1981, p. 48, suggests those skills were acquired on the job, or were derived from the experience of farming rocky and hilly lands at home in Italy.

3 Shirley E. Woods, *Cinders and Saltwater*. Halifax: Nimbus, 1992, p. 88. Conceived of in 1863, the ICR was completed in 1876; it ran from Riviere Du Loup and linked up with existing lines from Halifax and St. John's. For years afterward, extensions were made to the ICR, adding spur lines to coastal communities and finally reaching Sydney in 1889-90.

4 For example, the *Daily Record* on January 8, 1901: "200 construction workers laid off ... no work till spring...." Also, Bruno Ramirez, *On the Move: French-Canadian and Italian Migrants in the North Atlantic Economy, 1860-1914*. Toronto: McClelland and Stewart, 1991.

5 *Alien Labour Act* of 1897 and the 1905 amendment which made it a crime to import foreign labour without the permission of a judge.

6 Donald Avery, "Canadian Immigration Policy and the Alien Labour Question," PhD Thesis, University of Western Ontario, 1973, pp. 120, 211.

7 W. D. Scott to E. P. Nadeau, RG76, c-10, 627, vol. 539, file no. 803901. National Archives, Ottawa.

8 *Daily Record*, August 22, 1901: "Local Topics." These "agents" are sometimes identified as padroni. Although not identified as such, parts of Cozzolino's life reflect the phenomenon of padronism. See Robert Harney, "Montreal's King of Italian Labour: A Case Study of Padronism," *Labour/Le Travail*, vol. 4, no. 4 (1979); "Boarding and Belonging: Thoughts on Sojourner Institutions," *Urban History Review*, vol. 78, no. 2 (1978); "The Commerce of Migration," *Canadian Ethnic Studies*, vol. IX, no. 1 (1977); Ramirez, *On The Move*.

9 1907 Goad Fire Insurance Atlas of Sydney, Beaton Institute; National Map Collection, 0026087, Map of Sydney, dated 1910, National Archives. The *Sydney Post*, September 7, 1905, noted that "Italian shacks near the S & L road...."

10 Informal interviews with Ron DiPenta, 1990-1993. Also, *Daily Record*, April 2, 1903: "Warehouse and Shack for 50 Italians burned at George's River."

11 *Daily Record*, August 22, 1901: "Local Topics."

12 Ibid.

13 Photograph of "hotel" on Ferry Street, 1912 (ca.). United Church Archives of Canada.

14 *Daily Record*, June 25, 1901.

15 *Daily Record*, February 25, 1901.

16 *Sydney Record*, February 20, 1904.

17 *Daily Record*, February 14, 1901.

18 *Daily Record*, August 10, 1900.

19 For instance, *Daily Record*, September 24, 1900: "An Italian charged with stabbing another at one of the shacks on Friday night was arrested this morning and subsequently released on bail;" *Daily Record*, September 17, 1900: "Italian charged with stabbing a woman named Ward at the shacks." See also Ralph Ripley, "The Attraction of Immigrant Workers to Cape Breton County, 1893-1914," MA Thesis, Queen's University, 1980.

20 *Daily Record*, August 22, 1901.

21 Although the Italians were among the first immigrant workers to suffer discrimination, others, such as Blacks, were given similar treatment by the local newspapers. See, Elizabeth Beaton, "An African-American Community in Cape Breton, 1901-1905," *Acadiensis*, vol. 24, no. 2, p 19.

22 Ramirez, *On the Move*, pp. 102-104 relates that an American Congressional Inquiry interview in which an Italian worker stated that work would be taken on only if the wages were adequate to enable him to live and to send money back home. Ramirez notes that E. P. Thompson referred to this negotiation for a particular wage, as a sort of "moral economy."

23 *Daily Record*, November 7, 1900: "Strike at an End;" *Daily Record*, November 17, 1900: "A number of Italians who were employed on construction work at the steel company's plant left for Boston by the last express this morning;" *Daily Record*, August 9, 1901: "Strike at the Coke Ovens, Over 100 Out;" *Sydney Record*, March 2, 1903: "One Hundred Italians Armed with Clubs in Clash with Policemen at Coke Ovens.... Italians with Grievances on Strike try to Prevent Workmen from Entering Plant;" *Sydney Record*, March 4, 1903: "...the strikers, mainly Italians, got notice to quit their shacks."

24 Joe MacDonald, "The 1904 Strike at the Sydney Steel Plant: Unskilled Labour Faces the Establishment," unpublished paper, Carleton University, 1977; also, *Sydney Post*, July 21, 1904; July 28, 1904; August 16, 1904.

25 Ramirez, *On the Move*, pp. 105-106, indicates that this was true of Italian workers across North America. The situation changed with the formation of the Industrial Workers of the World in the first decade of the 20th century.

26 *Sydney Record*, February 17, 1902. There is a suggestion a restaurant existed at Cozzolino's home address.

27 *Sydney Record*, February 15(?), 1902.

46-66 – Memoirs of Thomas Cozzolino

1   The version of the *Memoirs* presented here has been edited for both readability and length. The original work was written by Thomas Cozzolino in 1935, while a second, edited version was prepared by his daughter, Regina (Cozzolino) Keating, sometime after his death in 1949. I have used both manuscripts to prepare the present version. The manuscripts are available as MG 7E, 2 at the Beaton Institute, Cape Breton University, Sydney, NS. A copy is also available through the Public Archives of Nova Scotia, Halifax (PANS MG 1, vol. 1191C). There is also a brief entry on Thomas Cozzolino in *Prominent People of the Maritime Provinces*, St. John: J. & A. McMillan, Printers, 1922, p.43.

2   Teresa (Quartucci) Cozzolino.

3   Andrea Cozzolino (*Prominent People of the Maritime Provinces*, p. 43).

4   At one level, Cozzolino's description probably describes fairly accurately the conditions many African Americans faced in the southern United States at the time. It also reflects his feelings of ethnic pride and superiority in being Italian. At another level, however, it may indicate that he did not understand fully the differential power relations, based on "race," that existed in the South, and how these relations often prevented African Americans from taking the type of steps he felt Italians would have taken under similar circumstances.

5   This sentence does not appear in the original manuscript. I have taken it, in modified form, from the version of the *Memoirs* edited by Cozzolino's daughter (see p. 19). Since his mother was named Teresa (see note number 2), the child may also have been named after her grandmother.

6   There is a discrepancy in the figures. In the original manuscript, Cozzolino presents a figure of $50,000 (see p. 23), while his daughter's edited version presents a figure of $5,000 (see p. 31). Other family members, however, suggest that the $50,000 figure is correct.

7   This information appears in the daughter's version of the *Memoirs*.

8   Although the original manuscript, on p. 25, makes reference to January 1901 at this point in the text, both the preceding and following statements suggest that he actually may be referring to January 1902.

9   Cozzolino's daughter, as recorded in her version of the *Memoirs* (p. 40), added that the explosion "was even felt in Sydney where glass was shattered by the blast."

67-70 –The Early Years: A Talk with Tony Bruno (1902-1979)[1]

1   Excerpts from Tape #372, Beaton Institute, Betty Lynch Collection, Cape Breton University, Sydney, N.S. The interview was conducted by Betty Lynch in 1972. It has been transcribed and edited for this volume by Sam Migliore with the assistance of Tony Bruno's wife, Mrs. Helen (Peters) Bruno.

2   Mr. Bruno's brother, Joseph, was born in New Haven, while his other brothers—Andrew, Ernest, Eddie, and one who died in infancy—were all born in Canada.

3   While working full-time as a chauffeur at the steel plant, Tony Bruno took correspondence courses from the Blackstone School of Law, in Chicago, to earn a Bachelor of Laws degree in 1962. During the 1960s, he was appointed a Commissioner of the Supreme and County Courts of Nova Scotia, and later Provincial Constable for Cape Breton County. Mrs. Bruno also recalls that Tony helped a number of people with free legal advice and services.

71-73 – Learning "English" at Barachois Mountain: A Talk with Romeo Sylvester

1   The Methodist Missionary Society "established an Italian Mission at the corner of Lingan Rd. and Laurier St." in 1912 (*Pier Times*, vol. 1, no. 2, June 15, 1986). By the time Romeo Sylvester had enrolled for English classes, the Italian Mission had merged with the Presbyterian Mission to serve the needs of various ethnic groups. This merger took place in 1925, and the new structure became known as the United Mission (Ibid.)

74-80 – Dominic and James Nemis of New Waterford

1   My thanks to Rena ("Little Rena") Nemis, daughter of the late Dominic Nemis, and to Mrs. Catherine Nemis, widow of Cookie Nemis, for permission to publish extracts from the interviews.

81-85 – Three Men of Dominion

1 For easier reading, I've patched together statements from different parts of the conversation, but I left everything in the speakers' own words. *Italic print* shows passages spoken in Italian, which Sam Migliore and I translated. Also see "Remembering the Pain of 1940," in this book, for more stories from this interview.

2 A "machine-runner" was high in pay and status. The "punching machine" or "puncher" was massively heavy and hard to run. The operator rolled it, on its low trolley, up to the coal "face" at the end of the advancing tunnel ("room"), where he made a deep, narrow cut across the bottom of the face. This weakened the solid coal before it was "shot down" with explosives. The "loaders" then used large "pan shovels" to lift the coal by hand into "boxes" (small railcars). A "driver" travelled a section of mine with his "pit pony," collecting boxes into a short train, called a "trip," to be hauled out of the mine. In the 1920s, the "puncher" was replaced by the "radial machine."

3 A "day's pay" or "datal" man got a fixed rate for his shift. On "contract" (piecework), a fit man could make much more money, and had more say over his own work.

4 When Dominion Coal Company was formed in 1893, its No. 1 (1A) colliery in the Phalen coal seam gave the present town its name. By the early 1920s, that mine's main tunnel ("deep") ran about two and a half kilometres toward the ocean's edge on the near side of Glace Bay, at Bridgeport. It was expensive to haul coal that extra distance, so a new shaft (1B) was sunk at Bridgeport into the deep of No. 1, and hoisting began around 1924. Years later, 1B shaft became the entry point for No. 26 colliery, in the shallower Harbour seam. This is why people often say "1B" and "26" interchangeably.

5 In the "longwall" system, two parallel tunnels were driven across the sloping layer or "seam" of coal. To enlarge the tunnels for coal transport and ventilation, "brushers" removed stone from the roof and/or floor. Connecting these two tunnels, which were 100 feet or more apart, another was driven up through the seam. The result was a pattern like a squared U. Then, on each shift, more coal was cut from the whole length of one "wall" of that cross-tunnel. As the cross-tunnel widened, the stone roof was allowed to sink down (in a controlled way) to the floor, on the side opposite to the working wall. In the early years of longwall, loaders manually shovelled the mined coal onto a conveyer system ("pan line" or "shaker pans") which spilled the coal into boxes at the low end of the wall, for haulage out of the mine. In later years, machines cut and loaded the coal from the wall, and conveyer belts took over most of the transportation. Before longwall, in the old "room-and-pillar" system, coal was mined from the advancing ends of many narrow parallel tunnels called "rooms." Between the rooms, smaller "crosscut" tunnels were also driven, to maximize coal recovery and to help air circulate. In the resulting crosshatch pattern, "pillars" were the large blocks of coal that remained.

6 A "bump" is a sudden shifting of the strata, underground. The infamous 1958 mine disaster in Springhill, Nova Scotia, was caused by a series of major bumps.

7 The "rake" is a train of open railcars in which miners ride from the shaft bottom or from the mouth of a slope mine, down the main tunnel to their work areas. Most of Cape Breton's coal seams lie at a considerable angle ("pitch"), and the "deeps" slope down and far out beneath the ocean. Both rakes and "trips" (trains of coal boxes) were winched up and down on a steel cable. If this "rope" broke, the obvious end result was a "smash on the deep," often with loss of life. In later years, electric trams replaced rope-haulage.

86-96 – In Others' Eyes: Pit Talk about Italians

1 Special thanks to interviewers Beverley MacLean, Connie McPherson, Ann Nicholson and Kathleen Rudderham, and to secretary Anne Whalley and office coordinator Gary Degaust. Young Canada Works funded the study. Thanks also to UCCB's Committee on Evaluation of Research Proposals for help in transcribing tapes.

2 These are memories of experiences and ideas that occurred *many decades before* these men found themselves trying to make them sensible to we eager young interviewers with our tape recorders. Some of the men entered the pits well before the First World War.

3 James "Cookie" Nemis, New Waterford, son of Italian immigrants.

4   There was a long and bitterly divisive strike in 1909-1910. Supporters of the old union, the Provincial Workmen's Association (PWA), stayed on the job. The strikers wanted recognition of the United Mine Workers of America (UMW).

5   When Italy and Canada went to war in 1940, Cape Breton miners walked off the job, demanding (with temporary success) that Italians be barred from the pits. See "Remembering the Pain of 1940," for recollections from both Italian and non-Italian miners.

6   Race was not always this insignificant. Black miners worked in many Cape Breton collieries, but were unwelcome in others. In an interview with a white non-Italian man, for example, he cheerfully reported how he and his friends threatened some visiting black carpenters and forced them out of 1A pit.

7   Dave Cathcart from Port Morien, of long-settled Cape Breton Scottish and Irish extraction.

97-100 – Giacomo Tubetti: His Life and Times

1   *Editors' Note:* Corrine Keeling is Giacomo Tubetti's granddaughter. She originally wrote the paper, as a Grade 12 thesis, on June 2, 1981. The paper has been edited for appearance in this volume.

106-110 – Almonds and War

1   Sharon Gibson Palermo's *The Lie That Had To Be* was published as a children's book by Thistledown Press Ltd., Saskatoon, in 1995. What appears here is an introduction specifically written for this book, and a chapter ("Almonds and War") from her book, appearing here courtesy of Sharon Gibson Palermo and Thistledown Press Ltd.

111-112 – Notes from the Internment Camp

1   Background information about Mr. LaPenna was obtained primarily from friends in Sydney, Nova Scotia. For more information about Mr. LaPenna, see "From Internment to Military Service: An Historical Paradox" in this volume.

2   We have made only a few changes to the grammar, so that the notebook entries do not lose their original quality. The reader, however, should note that Italian was Mr. LaPenna's first language, and that his Italian-language skills were much stronger than his English-language skills. The notebook includes entries written in Italian, but we were not able to complete a translation of this material in time for publication here.

113-116 – All They Ever Wanted Was A New Life And An Apology: One Italian Family's Experience

1   Anna Martinello (nee Melnick) was married to Louis Martinello, a son of the late Michael Martinello of Sydney, Nova Scotia. Anna lives in Sydney. Margaret Marshall, who also lives in Cape Breton, is the great-granddaughter of the late Alex Martinello, Michael's brother. Paul Diekelmann is a grandson of Alex Martinello. He resides in Tempe, Arizona.

2   The family name was originally Martiniello, but at some point changed to Martinello.

117-122 – My Friends, The Italians of Dominion

1   Additional information on the Italian community of Dominion can be found in Len Stephenson's: (a) *Dominion, N.S., 1906-1981: A Brief History of the Town of Dominion and Its Early Development. A Souvenir Publication.* Dominion, 1981; and, (b) an address to the Italian Community Club, February 28, 1981 (Record 657, Italians in Cape Breton, Beaton Institute, Cape Breton University).

2   "Anti-Italian Feeling Ties Up Collieries." *Sydney Post-Record*, Tuesday, June 11, 1940.

3   "Decision is Reached to Resume Work." *Sydney Post-Record*, Wednesday, June 12, 1940.

4   Ibid.

5   Ibid.

6   Ibid.

7   Ibid.

8   "Local Takes No Action on Alien Report." *Sydney Post-Record*, Friday, June 28, 1940.

9   "Foreign-Born Miners to be Allowed to Work," *Sydney Post-Record*, Tuesday, July 2, 1940.

10 Ibid.

11 "Five Collieries and 3750 Men Idle Last Night." *Sydney Post-Record*, Wednesday, July 3, 1940.

12 See: (1) "Five Collieries and 3750 Men Idle Last Night," *Sydney Post-Record*, Wednesday, July 3, 1940; and, (2) "Foreign Born Miners Working at Waterford," *Sydney Post-Record*, Wednesday, July 3, 1940.

13 See: (1) "Dependents of Alien Miners Require Help," *Sydney Post-Record*, Thursday, July 11, 1940; and, (2) "Labor Shortage Causes Loss of Production," *Sydney Post-Record*, Friday, July 12, 1940.

14 "Local Members Vote to Work with Aliens." *Sydney Post-Record*, Wednesday, July 17, 1940.

15 "Internment of All Enemy Aliens Asked." *Sydney Post-Record*, Friday, July 19, 1940.

16 "No. 1-B Mine Workers Turn Down Proposal." *Sydney Post-Record*, Wednesday, July 24, 1940.

17 "Men to Resume Places in No. 1-B Colliery." *Sydney Post-Record*, Tuesday, July 30, 1940.

18 "Night Shift at No. 20 Colliery Remains Idle: Alien Question Flares Anew at Two Mines; No. 1-B Operates after Men of Foreign Extraction Withdrawn." *Sydney Post-Record*, Wednesday, July 31, 1940.

19 "Proposal is Rejected by Large Majority." *Sydney Post-Record*, Wednesday, August 7, 1940.

20 "Labor Minister McLarty to Leave for Cape Breton to Investigate 'Pit Head Trouble,' is Report." *Sydney Post-Record*, Thursday, August 20, 1940.

21 Ibid.

123-131 – Remembering the Pain of 1940

1 Student research assistants did these four interviews: Connie McPherson with James; Kathleen Rudderham with Margaret; and Bev MacLean with Dominic and Catherine.

2 Of the men quoted in this section, Connie McPherson talked to the third person, in 1977. I did the other interviews, mostly in 1975.

3 My good and kind friend, Lino Polegato (son of Riccardo), arranged this gathering. Until his untimely death, he was Italian Consul, and my colleague at UCCB as Professor of Engineering. My father-in-law, Felice Pennacchio, was visiting from Boston, and joined us to meet his *paesani* and to help me with my weak Italian language. Thanks also to Sam Migliore, who helped me translate the Italian passages from the tapes. For other extracts from this meeting, see the article called "Three Men of Dominion," in this book.

4 Mr. Gatto arrived in 1922, before his 17th birthday. Mr. Baggio was 17 when he came in 1920. Mr. Polegato left Italy in 1922, after finishing his military service, but worked nearly five years in France before moving to Canada.

5 Each mine had its own union local and executive committee. All locals in Nova Scotia and New Brunswick comprised District 26, which also had an executive (for example, D. W. Morrison was District President in 1940). The districts made up the international federation, the United Mine Workers of America.

137-156 – From Internment to Military Service: An Historical Paradox

1 The material in this article, unless otherwise indicated, comes from interviews and conversations I had with various people between 1993 and 1997.

2 Colonel H. Stethem (Director of Internment Operations), in a letter to the Under-Secretary of State for External Affairs, Ottawa, indicated that there were 850 Italians (this may include some prisoners of war) interned in Canada as of February 12, 1941. The letter can be found at the National Archives of Canada, Record Group 25, vol. 2857, file 1643-40. For additional information on internment of Italians see: Kenneth Bagnell, *Canadese: A Portrait of the Italian Canadians*, Toronto, Macmillan, 1989; Mario Duliani, *The City Without Women: A Chronicle of Internment Life in Canada during World War II*, translated with an essay by Antonio Mazza, Oakville, Mosaic Press, 1994.

3 For a discussion of the internment of Ukrainians see: "Internment of Ukrainians in Canada 1914-1920," http://soma.crl.mcmaster.ca//ukes/ua-links/Ukraine8/ukraine8.html (1997); and, *Freedom Had a Price*, a film documentary by Yurij Luhovy, produced by La Maison de Montage Luhovy Inc., in association with the National Film Board of Canada (1996).

4 For information on the internment of Japanese in Canada see: Ken Adachi, *The Enemy that Never Was: A History of the Japanese Canadians*, Toronto, McClelland and Stewart Inc., 1991; Maryka Cmatsu, *Bittersweet Passage: Redress and the Japanese Canadian Experience*, Toronto, Between the Lines, 1992; Joy Kogawa, Obasan, Toronto, Penguin Books, 1981.

5 "Celebration by Sydney Italians," *Sydney Daily Post*, Monday, November 11, 1918, p. 1.

6 Ibid., pp. 1 and 8.

7 W. L. MacKenzie King. *Canada and the War: New Situations and Responsibilities: (1) Canada's War Effort Viewed in Relation to the War Effort of the Allied Powers; (2) Italy's Entry into the War.* Broadcasts...Friday, June 7 and Monday, June 10, 1940. Ottawa: King's Printer, 1940, 18 pp.

8 Sharon Gibson Palermo, *The Lie That Had To Be*, Saskatoon: Thistledown Press Ltd., 1995.

9 The complete statement can be found on: T2214, Dominic Nardocchio, "Internment of Italians," Beaton Institute, Cape Breton University, 1986. The interviewer is not identified, but it may have been done for a CBC Radio program. For more information, see: "A Talk with Dominic Nardocchio," edited and published by Ronald Caplan, *Cape Breton's Magazine*, Number 53, pp. 69-88, January, 1990.

10 A modified excerpt from Emilio Vaninetti's 1977 article: "The Italian Community in Dominion." The article is located under Reports: Ethnic: Italian, in the Beaton Institute, Cape Breton University.

11 I have transcribed and edited the material on Bert and Gordon Gatto from: T2101, Beaton Institute, Leonard Stephenson Collection, Cape Breton University, Sydney, Nova Scotia, 1981.

12 See notes to T2101, Beaton Institute, 1981.

13 Quote from: Ron DiPenta (based on an interview conducted by Mary Anne Ducharme), "Perspectives from the Pier: A View from Ward V," *From the Pier, Dear! Images of a Multicultural Community*, Sydney, the Whitney Pier Historical Society, 1993, p. 75.

14 *Barbed Wire and Mandolins*, Co-produced by the National Film Board and CBC's "Witness." Televised on CBC Witness, March 4, 1997. Bagnell, *Canadese: A Portrait of the Italian Canadians*, 1989.

15 Bagnell, *Canadese: A Portrait of the Italian Canadians*, 1989.

16 These events also are described in: "My Friends, The Italians of Dominion;" "Remembering the Pain of 1940;" "Three Women from Dominion;" and,"*La Sala Italiana* in Dominion."

17 Quote from T941, The Italian Community of Dominion, Beaton Institute, Cape Breton University. Interview taped for "Cape Breton: The Hidden Identity," CBC Radio, Sydney, Nova Scotia, September 27, 1977. Wendy O'Conner (research) and Bill Doyle (producer).

18 This section was prepared and written in collaboration with A. Evo DiPierro. Mrs. Nardocchio passed away in 1993.

19 This piece appears here courtesy of the *Cape Breton Post*, Sydney, Nova Scotia. For more information on Pordena Smith see "A Split Decision: Italian Boxers of Cape Breton" in this volume, and John Campbell's "Boxer KO'd by Prejudice," *Cape Breton Post*, Saturday, September 10, 1994.

20 Additional information on the Sylvester family can be found in "Learning 'English' at Barachois Mountain."

21 This section was prepared and written in collaboration with A. Evo DiPierro.

22 For more information on the Giovannetti family see: "Early Settlement: The Giovannetti Family in Port Morien;" and, "A Search for One's Roots."

23 The segments of the speech which appear here can be found on pp. 3-5 of the "Notes for an Address." The speech was obtained courtesy of the Department of Foreign Affairs and International Trade. Reproduced with the permission of the Minister for Public Works and Government Services Canada, 1997.

24 See Angelo Persichilli's artice, "Ottawa announces $2.5 million for internment 'fund', but offers no apologies." http://www.tandemnews.com/viewstory.php?storyid=5754. November 20, 2005. Accessed July 19, 2009.

25 Keely Grasser. "Rivals spar over redress for Italian-Canadians." http://www.yorkregion.com/printarticle/82605. October 9, 2008. Accessed July 19, 2009.

26 Government of Canada. Bill C-302, the *Italian-Canadian Recognition and Restitution Act.* Ottawa, Ontario: Publishing and Depository Services, Public Works and Government Services Canada, 2010. Also available at http://www.parl.gc.ca/HousePublications/Publication.aspx?DocId=4477133&Language=e&Mod e=1&File=24#1. Accessed July 3, 2011.

157-168 –Family Disruption, Hard Work, and Success: A Talk with Frank and Marty Martinello

1   Florence was born February 23, 1923, and died on August 24, 1975. She was married to Donato (Danny) Giuliani, a tailor. They had two children, Vincent and Rosemarie.

2   For a discussion of Marty Martinello's football career, and later achievements, see the article "E. M. 'Marty' Martinello: A Career in the CFL," in this volume.

3   [Frank]: My parents were both born in 1897. My father on January 28th and my mother on October 15th.

170-177 – Secondina DiPersio: A Son's Tribute to His Mother

1   The book issued by the Town of Sydney Mines as part of their Centennial Project—*The History of Sydney Mines: "The Little Town with the Big Heart,"* 1990—has a section on "Street Names and Their History" (pp. 125-30). The entry under *DiPersio Street* states: "This is a trailer park... named after Sydney Mines business woman, Mrs. Secondina DiPersio" (p. 127). The only other street in Sydney Mines named after an Italian is *Dominic Street*, which was "named after well known businessman, Dominic Mancini" (p. 127).

2   For additional information see Wes Stewart, "To lay wreath at service in Ottawa," *The Cape Breton Post,* Thursday, September 3, 1987.

3   Wes Stewart, 1987, ibid.

178-179 – Florindo Byron

1   I obtained information on the late Florindo Byron from his daughter, Mrs. Afra McVicar of Sydney, in February of 1998.

2   A. V. Spada, *Canada Ethnica, IV: The Italians in Canada.* Montreal: Riviera Printers and Publishers, Inc., 1969, p. 220.

180-184 – Angelo Cechetto (1909-1999): A Master Shoe Repairer from Dominion

1   This article is based primarily on five taped interviews with Mr. Cechetto: four that I conducted with him in 1996-97 (two of these in collaboration with high school students, including Angelo's granddaughter, from the MacDonald Complex in Dominion); and, a 1989 recording (T2428) by Paul Steele for the Elizabeth Beaton collection, Beaton Institute, Cape Breton University.

2   The coal mine Mr. Cechetto is referring to caught fire in 1903, and had to be flooded from the ocean. It was down for a long period of time.

3   Mr. Cechetto was not sure of the spelling of the name of the ship.

4   See also Alvise Casagrande, "Over 50 Years in Shoe Business," *Cape Breton Post,* March 28, 1985.

5   Ann Marie McKinnon's article, "A Good Sole," appears in one of the Nova Scotia Supplements (p. NS-6) to the *Globe and Mail,* in either 1993 or 1994. I have not been able to locate the full reference.

185-190 – Bill Gentile: Living Under Moxham Castle

1   Moxham Castle, Historical Note #2: Extract from the *Lorain* (Ohio) *Journal,* July 18, 1959. *Cape Breton Regional Planning Commission, Preservation of Buildings of Historical and Architectural Merit.* October, 1965. Located in the Beaton Institute, Cape Breton University, MS 12/57 (3).

2   "Castle Burns," *Cape Breton Post,* April 26, 1966; and, Michael MacKenzie, "Moxham Castle Story," *Remember the Time: True Stories, Old and New,* 1981, pp. 91-95.

3   This paper provides a composite account based on four interviews between 1993 and 1997. The first interview was conducted by my student assistants, Jan Gentile (Bill's niece) and Jason

Skinner. The other interviews are based on conversations I had with Bill either alone or with other family members.

191-192 – The Rossetti Legacy: A Talk with Dolores (Rossetti) Moore
1   This article is based primarily on an interview I did with Dolores Moore in November of 1996, and material supplied by Dr. Robert Morgan, Beaton Institute, Cape Breton University.

2   Dorothy Ward (Clark) Rossetti (1914-1970) was the daughter of Henrietta Burchell and Wilfred Ernest Clark of Sydney. She was an accomplished cellist and music teacher in the city. See: Notes to MG 12, 179, Beaton Institute, Cape Breton University.

193-197 – Father Joseph Emilio Marinelli
1   This *In Memorian Prayer* appeared on the back of the Mass card distributed at the celebration of the Christian Farewell service.

198-202 – Benny DeLorenzo: Work in the Steel Plant
1   This article is based on: (1) excerpts from Tape #2525L, Beaton Institute (Elizabeth Beaton's Steel Project Interviews, recorded in 1990), Cape Breton University; and, (2) material from conversations I had with Mr. DeLorenzo in 1996 and 1997.

203-209 – Country Living: DiVito and Marinelli Family Memories
1   This article is based on three sources. First, an interview with Frank DiVito (August 19, 1993) conducted by Jan Gentile and Jason Skinner for my project *Coal, Steel, and the Italian Immigration Experience* (Cape Breton University). Second, an informal discussion I had with Frank and his uncle, Louie Marinelli, on March 13, 1997. And, third, an informal discussion I had with Frank and his aunt, Nora (Marinelli) Buchanan, on April 21, 1997.

214-219 – The Call of the Sea:Italian Women in the Fisheries
1   Eleanor Huntington, "Glamor at Sea: 'Captain Rosie' Wins Her Braid," *Cape Breton Post*, May 17, 1963.

2   Lynn Billard, *On Women and the Fishery: An Exploratory Study into the Effects of Occupational Displacement and Retraining*, MA Thesis, Ottawa, Carleton University, 1994.

220-227 – The Mancini Family of St. Peter's
1   Two other children, Joseph and Charlotte, had passed away some time before our interview.

2   "Evelina's pie survives air flight to England," *The Scotia Sun*, Port Hawkesbury, NS, April 18, 1979, p. 14.

3   "Carlo Mancini To Make Home In Cape Breton," *The Post-Record*, Sydney, NS, January 25, 1950.

4   Field Marshal H. R. Alexander was the Supreme Allied Commander, Mediterranean area, from 1939 to 1945.

5   See "Popular landmark a family tradition," *The Reporter*, Port Hawkesbury, NS, May 14, 1996, p. 9.

228-233 – Memories of Papa Jimmy: The Tubetti Family of Inverness
1   Frank DiVito (Cape Breton Italian Cultural Association) and I interviewed Daryl and Frances in Sydney, April, 1997. My wife, Margaret, and I interviewed Maureen in New Westminster, British Columbia, in May of the same year. Maureen and Daryl are children of Giacomo's daughter Italia (Tubetti) MacDonald, while Frances is a daughter of George Tubetti. Daryl is a high school teacher, while both Frances and Maureen have worked in nursing. For more information on Papa Jimmy himself, see: "Giacomo Tubetti: His Life and Times."

234-238 – "Grandpa Cozzolino"
1   Alvise Casagrande, "Broughton Rd.: Town of Broughton once a thriving mining town," *Cape Breton Post*, Sydney, Nova Scotia, 1993, p. 34.

2   Tommy Cozzolino did not move to Sydney with his sister and grandparents; instead he joined the army. Mary MacAdam remained in Montréal.

239-244 – Spiritual and Physical Healing: A Family History in Medicine

1 In contrast, Dr. Carmen D'Intino's son, also named Carmen (Joseph), followed in his grandfather's footsteps by becoming an engineer and getting involved in building construction. He was away working in Port Hawkesbury at the time of the taped interview.

2 Joan Elman, Joan Hunt and Toby Halloran, "The D'Intino Family: Staying in Touch with Their Heritage," *Cape Breton Post*, May 2, 1985.

3 Ibid.

4 This is a brief excerpt from Yolanda D'Intino's prize paper, *A Dream Come True*, written while in grade 7 at Holy Redeemer Girls' School, Sydney, Nova Scotia.

5 "Rev. Emidio J. D'Intino, 76, California," Obituary in the *Cape Breton Post*, October 9, 1986.

6 "St. Nicholas Italian Church," *Pier Times*, volume 1, number 8, September 14, 1986.

7 "Rev. Emidio J. D'Intino, 76, California," October 9, 1986.

8 Alvise Casagrande, "In Memory of Rev. D'Intino," *Cape Breton Post*, November 15, 1986.

286-293 – A Rich and Varied Tradition

1 Mrs. Elisa Fasciani and her cousin, Loretta Chiola operated the popular *E & L Pasta Centre* in Sydney for many years.

294-298 – Winemaking as a Source of Well-Being

1 A more detailed version of this paper appeared as "Wine, Health, and Sociability: An Italian Family Experience in Cape Breton," in Carol Corbin and Judith A. Rolls, editors, *The Centre of the World at the Edge of a Continent*. Sydney: Cape Breton University Press, 1996.

2 The paper is based primarily on an interview I had with the DiMicheles in 1993. Additional material comes from interviews conducted by Gabriella Camilli (1993) and Jan Gentile (1994) as part of my *Steel, Coal, and the Italian Canadian Immigration Experience* project (Cape Breton University, Sydney, NS). Anna's statements are relatively short, and her "voice" is heard less frequently, partly because winemaking tends to be a male activity and partly because it is easier for a male ethnographer to interview male informants.

308-312 – Alvise Casagrande: A "Scoop" for the *Cape Breton Post*

1 See, Alvise Casagrande, "Memorial Mass Held in Honor of Italian Community Founders," *Cape Breton Post*, July 31, 1986.

2 See, Alvise Casagrande, "Over 50 Years in Shoe Business," *Cape Breton Post*, March 28, 1985.

3 See, Alvise Casagrande, "In Memory of Rev. D'Intino," *Cape Breton Post*, November 15, 1986.

4 The following articles, for example, have appeared in the *Cape Breton Post*: (1) "Marconi Magic on Display this Weekend," April 24, 1992; (2) "Marconi Museum Plans June Opening," April 17, 1996; (3) "Marconi Museum on Par," August 5, 1996; (4) "The House Guglielmo Built: Foundation Hopes to Make the Marconi's Home a Museum," January 4, 1997; (5) "Language Course to be Offered," January 20, 1997. "Language Classes Popular," February 4, 1997.

313-317 – Expressions of Thought and Sentiment: The Poetry of Roy Plichie

1 Christian Gallagher, "Italians," a grade 9 paper written in April, 1995. Christian is Roy Plichie's grandson.

2 Working in the foundry, in fact, became somewhat of a family tradition. Between Giuseppe, Roy, and two of Roy's brothers the family has accumulated a total of more than 116 years of foundry work.

3 Roy has published a number of poems in *The Coastal Courier* of Glace Bay. His sister Corletta, who lives in Ontario, is also a poet; she has published her work in book form. Roy's brother, Rudy, also writes poetry occasionally.

324-329 – Mario Pino (1919-1997): A Life in Music

1 I interviewed the Pinos on February 8, 1996, while my student assistants (Jan Gentile and Jason Skinner) conducted a preliminary interview with them on July 17, 1993.

330-334 – "Magnolias And Other Sweet Things" The Story of Angelo Spinazzola

1 On January 30, 1998, Angelo Spinazzola represented Cape Breton at the East Coast Music Awards in Halifax, as a showcasing artist.

337-343 – Halls of Fun and Fame: The Amadios of Cape Breton

1 *Memories Not Forgotten, 1942-92: 50th Anniversary, Cape Breton, NS,* Glace Bay, Nova Scotia: Glace Bay Minor Hockey Association, 1992, p. 35.

2 Ibid.

344-357 – A Split Decision: Italian Boxers of Cape Breton

1 The material in this section is based primarily on an interview I had with Mr. Nemis on April 22, 1997. For more information on the Nemis family, see the John deRoche article, "Dominic and James Nemis of New Waterford," in this volume.

2 Dominic Nemis held the Maritime Amateur Light Heavyweight crown in 1935. See "Louie Nemis: A great heart in a rugged chest," *Highlander,* March 18, 1981, p. 15.

3 Both Johnny and Louie Nemis have been inducted into the Canadian Boxing Hall of Fame.

4 As quoted in the article "Louie Nemis: A great heart in a rugged chest," *Highlander,* March 18, 1981, p. 15.

5 The material in this section is based on two sources: (1) an interview with Nunzi Martinello, Hawky Del Vecchio's sister, and her friend Theresa Della Vella; and, (2) a short article by Jack Duggan, "Nicholas 'Young' Delvecchio: The Italian Thunderbolt," *Boxing Newsletter,* the Canadian Boxing Hall of Fame, 1995, p. 76. For more information on the Del Vecchio family see the article, "Memories of Yesterday and Today: A Talk with Theresa Della Vella and Nunzi Martinello," in this volume.

6 Jack Duggan, "Nicholas 'Young' Delvecchio: The Italian Thunderbolt," *Boxing Newsletter,* the Canadian Boxing Hall of Fame, 1995, p. 76.

7 Ibid.

8 This section is based primarily on two interviews with Benny and Rose DeLorenzo—one in November of 1996, and the other in April of 1997—in Whitney Pier.

9 Some of the material in this section comes from an interview Jan Gentile and Jason Skinner had with Patsy Smith, in August of 1993 (for my research project, *Steel, Coal, and the Italian Canadian Immigration Experience,* Cape Breton University). Evo DiPierro obtained additional information from Patsy Smith in the spring of 1998. I have transcribed and edited Maria DeLorenzo's statements from: T-732, "Italia Day Exhibit" (an interview by Elizabeth Beaton), Beaton Institute, Cape Breton University, 1983.

10 Eddie Welch, "Pordena Smith Makes Air Trip From Sydney, NS," 1945. I have no further information on the article. My copy comes form Gino Spinazzola's Scrapbook. Gino is the late Pordena Smith's son.

11 Patsy and Pordena Smith were also business partners. They owned and operated the Benedette Club in Sydney from 1957 to 1960. In 1963, Patsy opened what was to become a very popular establishment—the Capri Club. Over the years, the Capri featured prominent musical performers from both the local area and outside the region. Patsy Smith sold the business and retired in 1985. In addition to the clubs, he developed a portion of the City of Sydney, off Alexandra Street. He constructed a number of streets in the area in the mid-1950s, including Carang Drive (named after his sons, Carlo and Angelo).

12 See "Once Boxing's 'Boy Wonder,' Pordena Smith dead at 51," *Highlander,* October 1, 1969, p. 19.

13 For more information on the Plichie family, see "Expressions of Thought and Sentiment: The Poetry of Roy Plichie." Roy and Rudy are brothers. See also: Jackie Duggan, "A Living Legend: Mr. Wonderful Rudy Plichie—The Mercy Man of Boxing," *Boxing Newsletter,* Canadian Boxing Hall of Fame, 1995, pp. 81-82; and, Greg Hines, "Bay Sports," *Cape Breton Post,* Sydney, N. S., Friday, May 2, 1975, p. 13.

358-360 – E. M. "Marty" Martinello: A Career in the CFL

1 The information for this article comes primarily from a conversation/interview I had with Marty in December of 1996, plus additional material he mailed to me in the spring of 1997.

2 Hamilton defeated the Winnipeg Blue Bombers that year to win the Grey Cup.

3 Marty failed to mention this in our conversation, but his "145 lbs and under" 4-person crew at Cathedral High School won the Canadian Rowing Championship. By 1953, he had put on a few extra pounds, and came in second in the Ontario heavyweight Wrestling Championships. (From Dr. A. J. "Sandy" Young's speech at the induction ceremonies of Nova Scotia Sports Heritage Centre, October 25, 1986).

4 From Dr. "Sandy" Young. Ibid., 1986.

5 Russ Doyle, "Nobody Asked, But ... Marty Martinello Played 14 Years in CFL," *Cape Breton Post*, September 16, 1986." The article is reprinted in "1986 Inductees," *Nova Scotia Sports Heritage Centre Magazine*, 1986.

362-369 – La Sala Italiana in Dominion

1 For this article, I have pieced together statements from interviews my assistants (Jan Gentile and Jason Skinner) and I conducted with various people between 1993 and 1997. In addition, I have transcribed and edited statements from two recordings in the Beaton Institute, Cape Breton University: (a) T2101, an interview with Raffaele Gatto, 1980, the Len Stephenson Collection; and, (b) T941, "The Italian Community in Dominion," September 27, 1977, prepared for a CBC Sydney radio program titled *Cape Breton: The Hidden Identity*—Wendy O'Conner (research) and Bill Doyle (producer).

2 From the Dominion Italian Community Club constitution.

3 See also: Emilio Vaninetti, "The Italian Community of Dominion," Beaton Institute, Cape Breton University, 1977; and, "Italian Canadians Hold Reunion," *Cape Breton Post*, September, 1977.

370-375 – The Cape Breton Italian Cultural Association

1 Sam Migliore and I interviewed Dominic Goduto and Rose DeLorenzo. I interviewed Gabriel and Anna DiMichele. We also obtained information on the early years of the CBICA from Joan Camilli, Gerry Giorno, Gloria MacDougall and Patsy (Spinazzola) Smith. Jan Gentile and Jason Skinner interviewed Mr. Giorno and Mr. Smith in 1993 (for Sam Migliore's project: *Steel, Coal, and the Italian Canadian Immigration Experience*, Cape Breton Univeristy). I informally interviewed Joan Camilli and Gloria MacDougall in 1997.

379-382 – The Voice of Music

1 The information presented here comes from two sources: (1) Obituaries: "Maria DeLorenzo-Baggio," *Cape Breton Post*, May 30, 1994; and, (2) an interview with Maria conducted by Jan Gentile and Jason Skinner—research assistants for my project, *Steel, Coal, and the Italian Canadian Immigration Experience*, Cape Breton University, Sydney, Nova Scotia.

383-385 – When a Princess Comes to Dinner: Anna DiMichele Recalls the 1995 Marconi Celebrations

1 As part of the celebration, Allan Jones and a group of students at MacLennan Junior High School in Sydney produced a CD-Rom, The Marconi Interactive CD Rom, about Marconi and his accomplishments.

386-387 – The Italian Government Connection

1 From T1916, Marilyn Baillieul interviewer, Beaton Institute, Cape Breton University, 1980—as transcribed and edited by Sam Migliore.

388-391 – Leandro D'Addario: Italian Consular Agent for Cape Breton

1 Sam Migliore and I interviewed Mr. D'Addario on February 1, 1997.

404-406 – A Trip to Relatives in Italy

1 Shirley Grinnell, the daughter of Louis and Anna Martinello of Sydney, now resides in California. The original paper was written a short time after the trip, and it has been edited for length by Sam Migliore.

409-412 – A Search for One's Roots: An interview with John Giovannetti and Lynn Billard

1 The Census of 1861 indicates that there were no individuals of Italian background resident in Cape Breton (*Censuses of Canada. 1665-1871*, Statistics Canada, Volume IV. Ottawa: I. B. Taylor, 1876). By 1871, however, three Giovannettis—Lawrence (Trader, age 26), John (Shopkeeper, age 30), and Nikodemus (Shopkeeper, age 28)—appear in the Cow Bay, Division #2 section of the Cape Breton and Victoria Counties Census (Nova Scotia Census, 1871, C-10569, Ottawa: Public Archives of Canada, Central Microfilm Operations). If the census material is reliable, the Giovannettis came to the Port Morien area sometime between 1861 and 1871.

413-416 – This Christmas's Gift to Everyone is the Joy of Having Lived to 100

1 This article first appeared in the December 24, 1988 issue of *The Globe and Mail*, pp. 1, 8. It appears here courtesy of Paul Palango.

417-419 – Memories of Yesterday and Today: A Talk with Theresa Della Vella and Nunzi Martinello

1 Mrs. Della Vella's parents were from the Abruzzi region of Italy; her father from Ortona, and her mother from Castelmare. Her husband's people were from northern Italy, the area around Como.

427 433 – A Second Generation Italian American of Cape Breton

1 *Cafone*: the original southern Italian "peasant" has become a general word for "lout," "ill-bred upstart," "vulgar person" (Cassell's *Colloquial Italian: Handbook to Idiomatic Usage*, London: MacMillan Publishing, 1993, p. 35).